METHODOLOGY OF RESEARCH IN SOCIAL SCIENCES

Dr. O. R. KRISHNASWAMI

Visiting Professor, Department of Management Studies,
Indian Institute of Science,
Bangalore.

Dr. M. RANGANATHAM

Professor and Head of the Department of Commerce,
University of Madras,
Chennai.

Himalaya Publishing House

ISO 9001 : 2015 CERTIFIED

First Edition : 1993
Edition : 1996, 1997, 1998, 2000, 2002, 2003, 2004
Second Revised Edition : 2005
Edition : 2006, 2007, 2009, 2010, 2011, 2012, 2013
Edition : 2014, 2015, 2016, 2017, 2018, 2019, 2020
Edition : 2022,
Edition : 2025

Published by : Mrs. Meena Pandey for **Himalaya Publishing House Pvt. Ltd.,**
"Ramdoot", Dr. Bhalerao Marg, Girgaon, Mumbai - 400 004.
Phone: 022-23860170, 23863863; **Fax:** 022-23877178
E-mail: himpub@bharatmail.co.in; **Website:** www.himpub.com

Branch Offices :

New Delhi : "Pooja Apartments", 4-B, Murari Lal Street, Ansari Road, Darya Ganj, New Delhi - 110 002. Phone: 011-23270392, 23278631; Fax: 011-23256286

Nagpur : Kundanlal Chandak Industrial Estate, Ghat Road, Nagpur - 440 018. Phone: 0712-2721215, 2721216

Bengaluru : Plot No. 91-33, 2nd Main Road, Seshadripuram, Behind Nataraja Theatre, Bengaluru - 560 020. Phone: 080-41138821; Mobile: 09379847017, 09379847005

Hyderabad : No. 3-4-184, Lingampally, Besides Raghavendra Swamy Matham, Kachiguda, Hyderabad - 500 027. Phone: 040-27560041, 27550139

Chennai : No. 34/44, Motilal Street, T. Nagar, Chennai - 600 017. Mobile: 09380460419

Pune : "Laksha" Apartment, First Floor, No. 527, Mehunpura, Shaniwarpeth (Near Prabhat Theatre), Pune - 411 030. Phone: 020-24496323, 24496333; Mobile: 09370579333

Cuttack : Plot No 5F-755/4, Sector-9, CDA Market Nagar, Cuttack - 753 014, Odisha. Mobile: 09338746007

Kolkata : 3, S.M. Bose Road, Near Gate No. 5, Agarpara Railway Station, North 24 Parganas, West Bengal - 700109. Mobile: 9674536325

Printed at : Geetanjali Press Pvt. Ltd., Nagpur. On behalf of HPH.

PREFACE TO THE REVISED EDITION

The second edition is a thoroughly revised version emphasizing on greater clarity and understanding of the concepts, methods and application of research techniques. The approach is broad based covering the interests and requirements of researchers in different branches of knowledge in social sciences, humanities and commerce and management. The special features of this new edition include more illustrations, greater coverage and in-depth analysis and explanation to most of the topics. All chapters are meticulously revised incorporating latest techniques and theories.

Authors hope that this new edition will be appreciated and invite from the researchers any new ideas and objective criticism of the contents of this edition to improve and enhance the value of this publication. Authors thank the publishers for their sincere efforts and care in the publication of this edition. We also than thank all those well-wishers, who have contributed to the enrichment of the contents of this edition.

We are grateful to God for this inspiration and effort, which we hope, will satisfy the inquisitiveness of young budding researchers.

AUTHORS

PREFACE TO THE FIRST EDITION

The Methodology of Research is a course of study in several Master level programs like M.A., M.B.A., M.S.W., M.Com., etc. and also for M.Phil., M.S., and Ph.D. in all social sciences in most of the universities. It is also a course of study in professional diploma courses like D.B.A., D.P.M., D.I.M. offered by universities and professional bodies.

The course in Methodology of Research is often a problem course to both the faculty and the students, because there is no single comprehensive publication that is integrated in concept, sufficient in scope and coverage and challenge to serve as the basic text for such a course. There are, of course, a few good publications on methodology of research, but they are mostly discipline specific and do not cover all aspects of methodology and statistical analysis.

The research students' ordeal is far more severe. They mostly grope in dark and struggle and waste a lot of time and effort without exactly knowing how to go about in each stage of research work — from selection of the problem through report writing. In fact, they need specific guidelines on various research techniques with illustrations drawn from actual research studies, for planning and carrying out their research projects.

The book is a response to the above perceived needs for a *cross-discipline practice-oriented comprehensive* book on research methodology. It has grown out of my long and rich experience in guiding and evaluating research projects at Master, M.Phil. and Doctoral levels, in directing sponsored projects, in teaching methodology of research to the Master and Doctoral students over three decades, and in directing workshops on methodology of research for Doctoral research scholars and teachers.

The *objective* of this book is to serve as a *textbook* for courses in Research Methodology in social sciences and also to serve as a *handbook* for research scholars.

This book has several *distinctive features.* It —

- is suitable for *all social sciences:* Economics, Commerce, Management, Sociology, Psychology, Behavioural Science, Education, Political Science, Social Work, etc.,
- adequately covers *all aspects of research methodology:* Scientific method, conceptual models, social science research, types and methods of research, *review* of literature and note-taking, selection of a research problem, hypotheses, concepts, measurement, research plan, sampling techniques and sample size, methods of collection of data, construction of questionnaire and scales/ field work, processing and tabulation of data, graphic representation, statistical analysis of data and hypothesis testing and report writing and evaluation,
- provides step-by-step *guidelines* on *all* aspects of the research process,
- *illustrates* the various research strategies and techniques with examples drawn *from* recent *research publications* in various social sciences, and
- written in *simple* and interesting style.

The book is organized into twelve chapters. In each chapter, the concepts are exactly defined, the techniques and processes are described with operational guidelines and illustrations, and suggested readings and review questions and exercises are listed.

I owe an incalculable debt to the many pioneers of research-methodology in social sciences whose contributions have enriched my knowledge of research methodology. I would like to express special thanks to the hundreds of students who, over the years, have struggled in learning methodology, and in carrying out research studies. It is their difficulties, and the methodological flaws and imperfections found in the hundreds of project reports and dissertations which I have evaluated over the years, which had prompted me to write this book.

I am also grateful to my old students Dr. M. Ranganathan, Associate Professor of Commerce, University of Madras, Dr. A. John Winfred, Professor of Cooperation, Sri Ramakrishna Mission Vidyalaya Autonomous Arts College, and. Dr. N. Narayanaswamy, Assistant Professor, Gandhigram Rural University for their assistance in collecting case illustrations from published studies.

Among my colleagues at the Indian Institute of Science, Prof. A. K. N. Reddy, Chairman, Department of Management Studies has been especially helpful and encouraging. Prof. B.G. Raghavendra critiqued the chapter on Statistical Analysis and offered valuable suggestions for improving it.

I gratefully acknowledge a lump-sum grant granted by the University Grants Commission, New Delhi, which covered some of the travel, stationery, typing and duplicating expenses.

Finally, I would like to express my thanks to my old student Dr. B.C. Sanjeevaiah and my beloved daughter, Meera, who organised typing and xeroxing work, and to Mrs. Sheela, Mr. K. Ramakrishnan and Mr. Eswarachari who typed the manuscript with skill and great patience.

Above all, I am grateful to God for His blessings and grace and I dedicate this humble publication to His Lotus Feet as an offering unto Him.

Bangalore **O. R. KRISHNASWAMI**

CONTENTS

1.1 WHAT IS RESEARCH?

Introduction

Curiosity or inquisitiveness is a distinctive feature of human beings. Curiosity to know about ourselves, our institutions, our environment, our planet, other planets, and the universe is inherent in us. Innumerable questions go on arising in our mind: What are the parameters of sound health of a person? How do problems of health arise? What are the remedies? What is the shape of the earth? How do solar and lunar eclipses arise? How is rain formed? Why are places like Ootacamund, Simla cooler than their nearby places? Is there any life in other planets? What are stars? Why day and night alternate? Why the mode of life and activities of human beings vary from place to place? Why there is no communal harmony in certain places? Why there is abject poverty in some countries like India and African countries? Why does the performance of similar organizations vary? What are the causes of various business problems like recession or industrial unrest? And so on. Whenever such questions arise we seek answers to them. Whenever we encounter problems, we try to find solutions to them. Seeking answers to questions and finding solutions to problems have been the basis of human progress. A systematic search for an answer to a question or a solution to a problem is called research.

Definition of Research

Research simply means a search for facts — answers to questions and solutions to problems. It is a purposive investigation. It is an "organized inquiry."[1] It seeks to find explanations to unexplained phenomenon, to clarify the doubtful propositions and to correct the misconceived facts. How is this search made? What are possible methods or approaches?

1. Emory, C. William, *Business Research Methods,* Homewood, Illinois: Richard D. Irwin, 1976 p. 8.

The search for facts may be made through either (a) arbitrary (or unscientific) method or (b) scientific method.

Arbitrary method: Arbitrary method of seeking answers to questions is based on imagination, opinion, blind belief or impression. For example, it was believed that the shape of the earth was flat; a big snake swallows the sun or moon causing solar or lunar eclipse. Similarly, we form our own impressions about various phenomena and issues.

The arbitrary method suffers from serious weaknesses or drawbacks. It is subjective, the finding will vary from person to person depending on his impression or imagination. It is vague and inaccurate.

Scientific method: This is a systematic rational approach to seeking facts. It eliminated the drawbacks of the arbitrary method. It is objective, precise and arrives at conclusions on the basis of verifiable evidences. (For details, see topic 1.2 Scientific method, below.)

Therefore, search for facts should be made by scientific method rather than by arbitrary method. Then only we may get verifiable and accurate facts. Hence *Research is a systematic and logical study of an issue or problem or phenomenon through scientific method.* An analysis of the definitions given by notable authorities may reveal the proper meaning and nature of the concept of research.

Kerlinger defines research as a "systematic, controlled, empirical and critical investigation of hypothetical propositions about the presumed relations among natural phenomena."[2] The term "systematic, controlled, empirical and critical" describe the characteristics of scientific method. Whether research needs to be an "investigation of hypothetical propositions about presumed relations" is debatable. Research does not always call for a hypothesis. It may also be carried out for the formulation of hypotheses. It may also be designed to gather descriptive information on a phenomenon.

Emory defines research as "any organized inquiry designed and carried out to provide information for solving a problem."[3] This definition is an inclusive one. But it emphasizes the problem – solving purpose only. Research may also aim at finding answer to questions.

The Encyclopedia of Social Sciences[4] defines research as "the manipulation of generalizing to extend, correct or verify knowledge..." This definition highlights the primary purpose of research, viz., arriving at generalization and the method of manipulation, which is an aspect of experimentation adopted for the purpose.

Best endorses the above purpose and method of research in his definition of research: "the systematic and objective analysis and recording of controlled observations that may lead to the development of generalizations, principles or theories, resulting in prediction and possibly ultimate control of events."[5]

According to Black and Champion, "Scientific research consists of obtaining information through empirical observation that can be used for the systematic development of logically related propositions attempting to establish casual relations among variables."[6]

---

2. Kerlinger, Fred W., *Foundations of Behavioural Research,* New York: Holt, Rinehart and Winston, 1973, p. 11.
3. Emory, C. William, *op. cit.,* p. 8.
4. *The Encyclopedia of Social Science,* Vol. IX, The Macmillan Company, 1930.
5. Best, John W., *Research in Education,* New Delhi: Prentice-Hall of India (P) Ltd., 1982, p. 18.
6. Black, James A., and Dean J. Champion, *Methods and Issues in Social Research,* New York: John Wiley & Sons, 1976, p. 6.

Clover and Balsley define research as "the process of systematically obtaining accurate answers to significant and pertinent questions by the use of the scientific method of gathering and interpreting information."[7] This simple definition refers to the systematic approach and scientific method to be adopted for finding answers to pertinent questions.

Young defines Research as "a scientific undertaking which, by means of logical and systematic techniques, aims to: (1)discover new facts or verify and test old facts, (2) analyse their sequences, interrelationships and causal explanations, (3) develop new scientific tools, concepts and theories which would facilitate reliable and valid study of human behaviour."[8] This exhaustive all-inclusive definition specifies all the major aims of research, viz., discovery of new facts, verification and testing of old facts, analysis of interrelationships and causal explanations and development of new tools, concepts and theories.

Characteristics of Research

The above definitions reveal the various characteristics of research:

1. Research is a *systematic and critical investigation* into a phenomenon.
2. It is not a mere compilation, but a purposive investigation; it aims at describing, interpreting and explaining a phenomenon.
3. It adopts *scientific* method
4. It is *objective* and *logical,* applying possible *tests* to validate the measuring tools and the conclusions reached.
5. It is based upon *observable experience or empirical evidence.*
6. Research is directed towards finding answers to pertinent *questions* and solutions to *problems.*
7. It emphasizes the development of *generalization, principles or theories.*
8. The purpose of research is not to arrive at an answer, which is personally pleasing to the researcher, but rather one, which will stand up the *test of criticism.*[9]

Objectives or Purposes of Research

The objectives or purposes of research are varied. They are:

1. Research *extends knowledge* of human beings, social life and environment. Scientists and researchers build up the wealth of knowledge through their research findings. They search answers for various types of questions: What, Where, When, How and Why of various phenomena, and enlighten us. The bodies of knowledge have been developed by research in general and pure or fundamental research in particular.
2. Research unravels the mysteries of nature; brings to light hidden information that might never be discovered fully during the ordinary course of life.
3. Research *establishes generalizations and general laws* and contributes to theory building in various fields of knowledge. Our knowledge of isolated events is connected together to

7. Clover, Vernon T., and Howard L. Balsley, *Business Research Methods,* Columbus, Ohio: Grid Publishing, 1979. p. 1.
8. Young, Pauline V., *Scientific Social Surveys and Research,* New Delhi: Prentice-Hall of India, 1977, p. 30.
9. Good, V. Carter, *Introduction to Educational Research,* New York: Appleton-Century Crofts, 1959, p. 3.

draw generalizations and general laws. Law of gravitation, Law of demand, and principles of organization such as unity of command and scalar principle, the theory of consumer behaviour and motivation theories are some examples for such generalizations, laws and theories.

4. Research *verifies and tests* existing facts and theory and these help improving our knowledge and ability to handle situations and events. Merton argues: " Empirical research goes far beyond the passive role of verifying and testing theory...Research plays an active role, it performs at least four major functions.... It initiates, it formulates, it deflects, and it clarifies theory."[10]

5. General laws developed through research may enable us to make reliable predictions of events yet to happen.

6. Research aims to *analyse inter-relationships* between variables and to derive *causal explanations*; and thus enables us to have a better understanding of the world in which we live.

7. Applied research aims at *finding solutions* to problems.... socio-economic problems (e.g., social unrest, unemployment, poverty) health problems, human relations problems in organizations and so on. Thanks to the fruits of research, we have better quality of life, longer life span and better control over events.

8. Research also aims at *developing new tools, concepts, and theories* for a better study of unknown phenomena.

9. Research aids planning and thus contributes to *national development.* Research – social science research in particular – aids planning in the following ways:

Research brings out factual data on prevailing situations and problems for drawing up plans and schemes on a realistic basis. Research uncovers needed facts on which sound decisions can be made before committing resources. Studies open up the possibility of testing the validity of planning assumptions or premises. For example, in the first four Five Year Plans of India it was assumed that a fast rate of the general economic growth will by itself create fuller employment and produce higher living standards for the poor through the 'trickle down' effect of such growth. Evaluation studies have shown that this assumption was not correct and the strategy of development in the Fifth and subsequent Five Year Plans was modified, providing for special and deliberate programmes for eradication of poverty in rural areas.

Research studies enable the planners to evaluate alternative strategies and choose the most appropriate strategies for development of the various sectors like agriculture, industry, education, health, social welfare etc.

The benefit-cost evaluation studies of projects like irrigation projects throw out valuable lessons for improving the formulation of similar projects subsequently.

Evaluation studies of on-going programmes like family planning schemes, lead bank schemes, Integrated Rural Development Programme etc., point out their shortcomings and implementation problems and enable the planners to revise the schemes and implementation strategies appropriately.

---

10. Merton, Robert K., *Social Theory and Social Structure,* New York: Free Press, 1957, p. 103.

The dissemination of research finding creates a general awareness of the country's current situations and problems among the public, which inspire them to participate in formulation and implementation of development schemes.

The above possibilities can be realized provided social science research is geared to planning needs and the planners are responsive and sensitive to the research findings.[11]

10. Analytical studies of internal and external environment of business and non-business organizations provide factual *data* for *rational decision making* – formulation of strategies and policies. Studies of their operational problems contribute to an improvement in their performance.

1.2 SCIENTIFIC METHOD

Meaning

Research is a scientific endeavour. It involves scientific method. "The scientific method is a systematic step-by-step procedure following the logical processes of reasoning."[12] Scientific method is a means for gaining knowledge of the universe. As Karl Pearson emphasizes "the scientific method is one and same in all branches and that method of all logically trained minds ... the unity of all sciences consists alone in their method, not in their materials; the man who classifies facts of any kind whatever, who sees their mutual relation describes their sequence is a man of science."[13] The facts may be related to any field. "It is not the facts themselves which make science"[14] but the method by which they are dealt with. "Science is not wrapped up with any particular body of facts."[15] Science is independent of any particular subject matter. "It deals with knowable universe for its subject. It deals with physical as well as psychological processes, with man as much as with nature. It has to do with everything to which its method can be applied. What makes a science is not, of course, the nature of things with which it is concerned, but the method by which it deals with these things."[16] Thus, the scientific method does not refer to a field of specific subject of matter, but rather to a procedure or mode of investigation. It is "an objective, logical and systematic method of analysis of phenomena, devised to permit the accumulation of reliable knowledge. It is a systematized form of analysis[17] ...It is characterized by an intellectual attitude. (See "Scientific attitude", last part of this section, below).

Basis of Scientific Method

The scientific method is based on certain "articles of faith" these are:

- reliance on empirical evidence
- use of relevant concepts
- commitment to objectivity
- ethical neutrality

11. Dube, S.C., "Role and Function of Social Science", in B.A.V. Sharma and others, *Research Methods in Social Sciences,* New Delhi: Sterling Publishers, 1984, p. 5.
12. Clover, Vernon T., and Howard L. Balsley, *Business Research Methods, op. cit.,* p. 13.
13. Karl Pearson, *The Grammar of Science,* Part I, London: A and C Black; 1911, pp. 10-12.
14. *Ibid.*
15. Thomson, J. Arthur, *Introduction to Science,* Oxford University Press (reprinted in India), p. 58.
16. *Ibid,* p. 25.
17. Lastrucci, *Scientific Approach,* Cambridge, 1967, p. 6.

- generalization
- verifiability
- logical reasoning process

Reliance on evidence: Truth is established on the basis of evidence. Conclusion is admitted, only when it is based on evidence. Scientific method involves a systematic process. The answer to a question is not decided by intuition or imagination. Relevant data are collected through observation or experimentation. The validity and the reliability[18] of data are checked carefully and the data are analysed thoroughly, using appropriate methods of analysis. Conclusion is reached on the basis of the result of analysis.

Use of concepts: We experience a vast number of facts through our senses. Facts are things, which actually exist. In order to deal with them, we use concepts with specific meanings. *Concepts*[19] are logical constructs or abstractions created from sense impressions, percepts and experiences. They are symbols representing the meaning that we hold. We use them in our thinking and communication. Otherwise clarity and correct understanding cannot be achieved.

Commitment to objectivity: Objectivity is the hallmark of the scientific method. It means forming a judgement upon facts unbiased by personal impressions. According to Green "Objectivity is the willingness and ability to examine evidence dispassionately." The conclusion should not vary from person to person. It should be the same for all persons. A person of science must "above all things...strive at self-elimination in his judgement and provide an argument which is as true for each individual mind as his own."[20]

Ethical neutrality: Science does not pass normative judgement on facts. It does not say that they are good or bad. As schroedniger says, "science never imposes anything, science states. Science aims at nothing but making true and adequate statements about its objects."[21]

Generalization: Scientists are not concerned with isolated events, but with the commonality of a series of event. They aim at discovering "under the surface layer of diversity the thread of uniformity. Around a discovered uniformity a logical class and its observed pattern, a descriptive generalization is formulated.[22] In formulating a generalization, we should avoid the danger of committing the *particularistic fallacy*,[23] which arises through an inclination to generalize on insufficient or incomplete and unrelated data. This can be avoided by the accumulation of a large body of data and by the employment of comparisons and control groups.

Verifiability: The conclusions arrived at by a scientist should be verifiable. He must make known to others how he arrived at his conclusions. He should thus expose his own methods and conclusions to critical scrutiny. When others test his conclusion under the same conditions, then it is accepted as correct. Such verification through replication may either confirm established conclusions or modify them or even invalidate them. For example, originally an atom was considered to be

18. See topic, 5.6 *Measurement,* below.
19. See Section 5.5 of chapter 5, below.
20. Karl Pearson, *op. cit.,* p. 6.
21. Schroedniger, *Mind and Matter,* Cambridge, 1958, p. 37.
22. Greenwood, Ernest, "Social Science and Social Work: A Theory of their interrelationships", *The Social Service Review* XXIX, 1955, p. 20.
23. Thomas, W.I *Source Book for Social Origins,* Chicago: University of Chicago press, 1909, pp. 22-26.

indivisible, but subsequent researches have proved that it is divisible and thus provided the basis for developing atomic energy.

Logical reasoning process: The scientific method involves the logical process of reasoning. This reasoning process is used for drawing inference from the finding of a study or for arriving at conclusion. For example, in a survey of the expenditure pattern on basic necessaries forms a very high proportion of the total expenditure, it is concluded that lower the household income, the higher is the proportion spent on basic necessaries. The logical reasoning process consists of induction and deduction.

Induction

Meaning: Induction is one of the methods of logical reasoning process. The inductive method consists of studying several individual cases and drawing a generalization. Therefore, induction involves two processes – observation and generalization. Conclusions from induction are tentative inferences and they are subject to further confirmation based on more evidence.

When followed: This method is followed when new facts are studied, new truths are uncovered and new generalizations are formulated from a research project. For example, in a farm management study it is proposed to test the hypothesis: "The application of recommended dosage of chemical fertilizers results in an increase in the yield per hectare." A sample of experimental farms and control farms is selected in an area. In the experimental farms, chemical fertilizer is applied and in controlled farms it is not applied, but other conditions – quality of seeds, irrigation, cultural practice, etc., - are the same. After the harvest the average yield per hectare is computed for experimental and control groups and the hypothesis is tested. The inductive method of reasoning is used in the analysis.

Essential conditions: Four conditions[24] are essential to satisfactory induction. They are:

1. ***Observation must be correctly performed and recorded, data collected should be accurate.*** Mistakes in conducting experiments or interviews and faulty recordings of the information can vitiate the value of any conclusions reached.
2. ***Observations must cover representative cases drawn from a specific universe.*** For instance, in a survey of job-satisfaction of bank executives the universe from which a sample has to be drawn should be defined exactly, say officers of public sector banks in a specific geographical area and all cadres of officers should be included in the sample and an appropriate sampling method like stratified random sampling has to be adopted.
3. ***Observations must cover an adequate number of cases.*** The size of the sample must be large enough to make it representative and to get reliable result. (See chapter 6, section-4).
4. ***Conclusion must be confined to inferences drawn from the findings.*** Conclusions reached after an analysis of data collected on a given study must be confined to the inferences drawn from the findings only. They should not be generalized to apply to types of cases not covered in the sample.

Types of induction: Theodorson and Theodorson[25] have identified two basic types of induction, viz., *enumerative* and *analytic*.

---

24. Clover, Vernon T., and Howard L., Balsley, *op.cit.*, pp. 14-15.
25. Theodorson, T., and A Theodorson, eds., *A Modern Dictionary of Sociology*, New York: T.Y. Corwell, 1969, pp. 199-200.

Enumerative induction is the most common form of induction used in social science research. In general, this type of induction involves generalization from samples and the generalizations are usually derived through the analysis of data.

Analytic induction involves case-by-case analysis of specific features. Cressy[26] outlined the step-by-step procedure of analytic induction:

1. Define the phenomenon to be explained.
2. Formulate hypothesis to explain the phenomenon.
3. Study a case to determine whether hypothesis fits in the case.
4. If the hypothesis does not fit the facts, either reformulate the hypothesis or redefine the phenomenon so that the case is excluded. (This definition must be more precise than the first one).
5. Examine a small number of cases to attain practical certainty; but whenever a negative case disproving the explanation is discovered, reformulate the hypothesis.
6. Continue this procedure of examining cases, redefining the phenomenon and reformulating the hypothesis, until a universal relationship is established.
7. For purposes of proof, examine cases outside the area circumscribed by the definition to determine whether or not the final hypothesis applies to them.

Deduction

Meaning: Deduction is reasoning process of applying a general accepted principle to a specific individual case falling under the general principle. It is regarded "as reasoning from the general to the particular."[27] This reasoning establishes a "logical relationship between a major premise, a minor premise and a conclusion."[28] A major premise is a previously established generalization or assumption; a minor premise is a particular case related to the major premise. The logical relationship of these premises lead to conclusion, e.g.,

Major premise	All men are mortal.
Minor premise	A is a man.
Conclusion	A is mortal.

Use: This deductive method of moving from the general assumption to the specific application is useful for solving problems. But it is not useful in arriving at new truths. The inductive process overcomes this limitation of deductive process.

Essential conditions: The conditions necessary for valid deduction are:

1. The general rule or assumption must be correct.
2. The general rule must be applied only to the cases, which properly fall under it.

The general rule or the major premise must be correct. If it is not correct, then the conclusion cannot be correct. For example, consider the following deduction:

26. Cressy, R. Donald, *Other Peoples Money,* New York: Free Press, 1953.
27. Clover, Vernon T., and Howard L. Balsley, *op. cit.,* p. 15.
28. Best, John W., *Research in Education,* New Delhi: Prentice-Hall of India (P) Ltd., 1982, p. 4.

Major premise: All regular employees are insincere

Minor premise: Mohan is a regular employee

Conclusion: Mohan is insincere.

The conclusion is justified only if both the premises are acceptable as true. Since the major premise is not true, the conclusion is therefore defective, even if Mohan turns out to be insincere.

Relevance of Induction and Deduction: The logical processes of both induction and deduction are useful in research studies. Both are "inseparable parts of a system of reasoning. In other words, distinct processes of inductive and deductive reasoning do not exist."[29] Both processes are often used simultaneously. There is a sequencing of induction-deduction processes, which is described by John Dewey as the "*double movement* of reflective thought."[30] When a puzzling condition occurs, one seeks inductively to explain by a hypothesis. In turn, the hypothesis is used in the deduction of further facts, which can confirm or deny the truth of the hypothesis. For example, the chief executive of an enterprise observes that profits are lower than expected (fact). He asks, "What is the cause"? His tentative conclusion (hypothesis$_1$) is "lower profits are due to fall in sales." He examines the sales records and finds that the actual sales volume is lower than the budgeted figure (fact). This fact confirms his hypothesis. Now he may raise a second question, "Why is sales volume low?" Recalling that there had been some problem of competition, he infers (hypothesis$_2$) "Competition accounts for a fall in sales." He will analyse the market reports received from regional offices and verify the truth of this hypothesis. This process of fact/question/hypothesis/deducted fact/ confirmation/question, and so on may be continued till the final explanation is arrived at.

Requisites of a Good Scientific Method

The essentials[31] of a good scientific method as summed up by the Advisory Committee on Economic and Social Research of the Council of Social Science Research are:

1. Careful logical analysis of the problem, separating its elements and whenever possible, formulating hypothesis;
2. Unequivocal definition of terms and concepts and statistical units and measures, so that others will understand exactly and be able to repeat the analysis and test the generalizations;
3. Collection of data pertinent to the problem under study;
4. Classification of data;
5. Expression of variables in quantitative terms whenever possible;
6. Rigorous and exacting experimental or statistical procedure in summarizing the data and in isolating the attributes or variables and measuring their relationship and inter-effects;
7. Sound logical reasoning as to the testing of hypothesis and drawing generalizations;
8. Statement in unassailable terms of the exact conclusion arrived at from the findings;
9. Specific and clear statement of generalizations to facilitate checking and testing by others;

---

29. Young, Pauline V., *op. cit.*, p. 111.
30. Dewey, John, *How We Think*, Boston: D.G. Health & Co., 1910. p. 79.
31. Sharma, B.A.V., and others, *Research Methods in Social Sciences*, New Delhi: Sterling Publishers (P) Ltd., 1981, p. 54.

10. Complete elimination of personal equation; and
11. Complete and careful reporting of the research process, definitions and the methods of analysis so that others can check the analysis or test the generalizations with new sets of data.

The Components of Scientific Approach

The scientific approach has two components: the procedural and the personal.

Procedural component: The procedure of scientific method involves the following major steps:

1. Define the problem.
2. Establish hypothesis as to causes/explanations/solutions of the problem.
3. Collect the data.
4. Analyse the data to test the hypothesis and draw inferences.

The researcher must have a thorough knowledge of the subject matter of the problem so as to formulate a conceptual model for its study. He must operationalise the concepts to determine the data requirements. He must select appropriate methods for collection of data and use relevant statistical techniques and tests for testing hypothesis. All these steps[32] require creative imagination, extraordinary care and patience.

The researcher's personal qualities: The researcher's qualities and attitudes are more important than the procedural steps. The researcher needs, as rightly emphasized by Eigelberner, "the scientific imagination to construct hypothesis, the resourcefulness, manipulative skill and persistence to carry through the experiment, the perspective which distinguishes the essential from the non-essential, and the reasoning which coordinated individual facts into a principle."[33] He must possess integrity, honesty, sincerity, poise and perseverance. He must also possess "the spirit of independence and the spirit of originality."[34]

In short, a true scientist must possess "the devotion of a mother, the poise of a judge, the objectivity of a philosopher, the courage of a soldier, the perseverance and patience of a beaver, the fervor of a patriot and the vision of a prophet."[35]

Scientific attitude: Above all, the scientific method calls for scientific attitude. The scientific attitude is based on a complexity of elements, viz.,

- Consistent thinking;
- Objective, dispassionate and unbiased devotion to collection and treatment of facts;
- Overcoming personal preconceptions and value judgments, because they not only have a distorting effect on the data but are also highly insidious;
- Avoiding, personal and vested interests-the scientist does not tailor his views to fit preconceived notions or preferences of men in power;

---

32. For a detailed discussion, see respective chapter, below.
33. Eigelberner, *Investigation of Business Problems,* p. 44, quoted by M.H. Gopal, *An Introduction to Research Procedures in Social Sciences,* Bombay: Asia Publishing House, 1964, p. 68.
34. Maurice Arthus, *Philosophy of Scientific Investigation,* Baltimore: John Hopkins University Press, 1943, p. 25.
35. Gopal, M. H., *op. cit.,* p. 73.

- Avoiding wishful thinking;
- Stubborn determination to analyse one's own system of thinking and taking nothing for granted without evidence, tests and proofs;
- "Faith in the universality of cause and effect."[36] Without this faith, a pursuit of scientific knowledge may be flouted whenever it interferes with special interest or prejudices;
- Ardent curiosity, fertile imagination and love of experimental inquiry;[37]
- "Compassion and understanding"[38] — without these knowledge could be dangerous;
- Patience and self-control and ability to overcome wishful thinking; and
- Keeping an open mind.

All these elements are components of the scientific attitude. "These elements tend to correct not only factual error, but also mental, emotional and volitional frailties of a research worker."[39]

1.3 RESEARCH AND THEORY

Research is closely related to theory. Theory provides a conceptual model for research. Research, in turn contributes to theory. What is theory? What are its uses to research? What does research do for theory? These questions are discussed in this section.

Meaning of Theory

In the popular usage, theory is perceived as speculative or unsubstantiated or unrealistic or ivory-tower ideas. This is a wrong notion. A theory in science is not the result of mere speculation. It is the gradual outgrowth of constructive study of the accumulated sorted facts.

Theory is more properly defined as "a set of systematically interrelated concepts, definitions, and propositions that are advanced to explain and predict phenomena (facts)."[40] Jack Gibbs defines theory as "a set of logically interrelated statements in the form of empirical assertions about properties of infinite classes of events or things."[41] A theory may not only explain or predict phenomena, but also specify causal relationships among variables. In the latter sense, a theory may be defined as " a set of systematically related propositions specifying causal relationships among variables."[42]

Strictly defined, a theory, as used in science, is a coherent "set of hypotheses", says R.B. Braithwaite, " which form a deductive system that is, which is arranged in such a way that from some of the hypotheses as premises all the other hypotheses follow."[43] Arnold Rose's view is similar to the above statement. He defines theory as " an integrated body of definitions, assumptions and general propositions covering a given subject matter from which a comprehensive and consistent set of specific and testable (principles) can be deducted logically."[44]

36. Wolfe, A.B., *Conservation Radicalism and Scientific Attitude,* New York: The Macmillan Company, 1923, p. 203.
37. Dewey, John, *How We Think, op. cit.,* p. iii.
38. Bacon, Sir Francis, *The Advancement of Learning,* Oxford University Press, London: 1986, p. 100.
39. Young, Pauline V., *op. cit.,* p. 129.
40. Kerlinger, Fred N., *Foundations of Behavioural Research,* New York: Holt, Rinehart and Winston, 1965, p. 11.
41. Gibbs, Jack, *Sociological Theory Construction,* Hindsdale, III, Dryden Press, 1972, p. 5.
42. Black; James A., and Champion, Dean, J., *Methods and Issues in Social Research,* New York: John Wiley & Sons, 1976, p. 56.
43. Quoted in Pauline V. Young, *op. cit.,* p. 113.
44. Rose, Arnold, "Generalizations in the Social Sciences", *American Journal of Sociology,* July 1953, p. 52.

A few examples may clarify the meaning of theory.

- A frustrated person, who is unable or afraid to express his aggression directly toward the perceived source of his frustration, may divert his aggression into another channel.

This theory explains why a frustrated manager takes it out on a subordinate instead of his boss.

- The standard of living of a family is the function of its income, size and life style.

This theory provides a basis for studying consumer behaviour and formulating appropriate marketing strategies.

Criteria of Theory

Theories start out as ideas. It is the extent to which ideas conform to basic demands of proposition formulation that determines whether or not they will assume the stature of theory. The criteria to be met by the set of ideas are:

1. They must be logically consistent. There must be no internal contradictions.
2. They must be interrelated.
3. The statements must be exhaustive as to cover the full range of variations concerning the nature of the phenomena in question.
4. The propositions should be mutually exclusive.
5. They must be capable of being tested through research.

The set of ideas in social sciences generally fail to meet the above basic demands of theories. They are broadly grouped into general configurations referred to as *"frames of reference," "perspectives" or "approaches."*

Components of Theoretical Ideas

The major components of theoretical ideas in social science include:

1. ***Assumptions and ideas:*** They consist of untestable premises about the nature of selected aspects of social life.
2. ***Frames of reference:*** They identify the major dimensions of social life that will be subjected to empirical scrutiny.
3. ***Concepts*** are abstractions; e.g., group, motivations, democracy.
4. ***Variables*** are relational units of analysis that can assume designated sets of values, e.g., age, educational level, and income.
5. ***Propositions*** are statements between or among variables.
6. ***Theory:*** The end-product of the above components is a theory.

Theory vs. Fact

Theory and facts are interrelated. While a fact is an "empirically verifiable observation,"[45] a theory specifies the relationships between facts or order them in a meaningful way. Facts gathered at random like counting the grains of sand in sand pile, counting the number of vehicles plying on a

45. Good William J., and Paul K. Hatt, *Methods in Social Research,* New York: McGraw-Hill Book Co., 1952, p. 8.

road, etc., cannot produce a body of knowledge. Only when related facts are gathered and studied, the development of science can take place.

Theory indicates the kinds of data to be gathered; it offers a conceptual scheme for systematizing a phenomenon; it summaries facts into empirical generalizations; and it predicts facts.

Facts, in turn, help to initiate theories, they lead to the reformulation of an existing theory, they cause the rejection of theories, which do not conform, to facts; and they clarify and modify theories.[46]

Theory and Fact belong to two different worlds – conceptual and empirical worlds respectively. Can there be a bridge between the two? The researchers use some techniques to bridge the gulf between theory and fact. One of them is conceptualization. Theory uses concepts for explaining a phenomenon. When new facts invalidate a theory; new concepts are developed to reformulate the theory. For example, when inflation cannot be explained in terms of the concept of demand-pull inflation, another concept of cost-push inflation is used for the purpose.

Another technique used for bridging theory and fact is the process of *classification or typology.* Classification is an attempt to impose some sort of order on an amorphous mass of facts. It is an attempt to trace interrelationships through the process of grouping. Scientists in various disciplines have made effective use of classification as a tool of analysis.

Adam smith, a classical economist, for example, classified society into different kinds of producers, in his *Wealth of nations,* to show that exchange is beneficial to everybody. Karl Marx classified the society into 'haves' and 'have nots' and showed that exchange benefits only the former. Colin Clarke classified the economy into the primary, secondary and tertiary sectors in his study of the empirical laws of economic growth. (Conditions of Economic Progress, London, Macmillan, 1951).

Theory vs. Hypothesis

A hypothesis[47] is formulated before empirical evidences or facts are gathered. It deals with a narrow range of ideas. It is a preliminary assumption adopted for the explanation of phenomenon. A theory, on the other hand, is a generalization arrived at after verification and it deals with a broader range of facts. It is one of the sources of hypotheses.

The assembled facts are transformed by a researcher into constructs. The constructs are then assembled into a provisional hypothesis. When it is tested and verified and found to be true, it is designated as a scientific theory. When the theory is tested and accepted by scientists as correct under the same conditions, it is regarded as a law.

Role of Theory in Research

Theory serves research in many useful ways.

1. ***Delimitation of Study:*** Theory narrows the range of facts to be studied. It helps to select a few relevant aspects of a phenomenon. Any phenomenon may be studied from different angles. A co-operative society, for example, can be studied as an economic enterprise, or as a social organisation or as an instrument for the promotion of the welfare of weaker sections, or as a democratic institution or a member-unit of a federal structure. Each science/ discipline deals with a specific aspect of a phenomenon. Only then can the work of a

---

46. For a detailed discussion of the rules of theory and fact, see *Ibid.*, pp. 9-16.
47. For a detailed discussion, See, Section 5.4 in Chapter 5.

discipline be reduced to manageability. Thus theory relating to a discipline delimits/ narrows the range of things, which come within its purview.

2. ***Conceptual model:*** Theory provides a conceptual framework for a study. Every science/ discipline is an organized body of facts — a structure of interrelated concepts with precise definitions. A researcher selects a *priori* a few facts from the theory and develops conceptual structure of their interrelationships — conceptual schemata — for the proper formulation of the selected problem.

3. ***Summarization:*** Another function of theory is to summarize concisely what is already known about the object of study. Theorizing integrates the major empirical generalizations of an era. From time to time in any science there will be changes in the structure of relationships between propositions. In each era, scientists move from older systems of theory towards a more acceptable new system. For example, in the discipline of management, by stressing social needs, the human relations movement improved on the classical approach, which treated productivity as a mere engineering problem.

   It is through systems of propositions that many of our common statements must be interpreted. Facts are seen as parts of a framework rather than as isolated observations. Take a few examples: "the whole is greater than the sum of its parts"; "The management is culture-found"; "Indian society is caste-ridden and hierarchical." These statements are apparently simple ones; but if we study them in depth we may find that behind each of them is a complex series of observations, a set of assumptions and a systems of propositions. "These are an implicit or explicit fact chain or theory which gives such 'simple' statements their full meaning."[48]

4. ***Uniformity:*** Theory states a general uniformity beyond the immediate observations. A person sitting under a mango tree may observe ripe mangoes falling on the ground. But beyond this observation, there is the general law of gravitation.

5. ***Prediction:*** Theoretical generalizations can be used to predict further facts. The most obvious is the extrapolation from the known to the unknown. For example, we may observe that in a modern civilized community there is a low birth rate. From this, we may predict that if modern way of life is introduced into a traditional rural or tribal community, its birth rate would decline.

6. ***Gaps in knowledge:*** Theory also points to areas, which have not been explored. If a theory states that professionalisation of management contributes to enterprises success, we can see where further facts might be sought. What are the variables of professional management? How can we explain the success of family-managed undertakings? Such gaps in knowledge are brought to light through the questions arising out of theory.

Contribution of Research to Theory

Since the relationship between theory and research is interactional, Research in turn, contributes to development of theory.

1. Research initiates theory: The findings of research may lead to the formulation of theories. Scientific experiments have led to the development of various theories in physics, chemistry etc.

48. Goode, William J., Hatt, Paul K., Methods in Social Research, *op.cit.*, p. 11.

similarly research in social sciences have contributed to the development of several theories, e.g., organizational theories, Herzberg Theory of Motivation.

In the course of conducting a research, the researcher may accidentally stumble upon unanticipated, anomalous and striking fact, which may lead to new theories. Some examples of such accidental findings are: the penicillium fungus inhibits bacterial growth; a pendulum of given length, in free motion, will swing back and forth in equal time.

2. Research tests an existing theory: One major function of empirical research is to test hypotheses deduced from existing theories. If a hypothesis is not confirmed by research, the theory from which the hypothesis is deduced, is re-examined and tested.

3. Reformulation of an existing theory: When a theory does not fit into new findings of research, it is rejected and reformulated to encompass the new findings.

For example, Elton Mayo's experiments in Hawthorne plant of Western Electric from 1927 to 1932 have led to the replacement of the old theory – 'A person is motivated by personal economic needs, to a new theory – 'A person is motivated by social needs, wanting rewarding on-the-job relationships, and more responsive to work group pressures.'

4. Research refocuses theory: Empirical research may give a new focus to the existing theory. When we find that the ineffectiveness of co-operative democracy in India cannot be understood in terms of political administration but rather in terms of socio-economic and cultural dimensions, we explore these latter dimensions by further study. It gives a new focus to the theory of co-operative democracy.[49]

5. Research clarifies theory: Concepts are drawn from theory. But research cannot proceed on the basis of their theoretical meanings. For research purposes the concepts have to be operationalised, i.e., defined specially with concrete empirical indicators. For example, such concepts as 'intelligence', 'morale', 'democratic participation', 'operational efficiency', small farmer' have been clarified by researchers by constructing indices or scales for their measurement. Such clarifications and redefinitions lead to the discovery of new hypotheses. Then we have to sharpen our theories to test those hypotheses.

In short, theory and research may be separate distinct operating, but they are inseparable complementary components of scientific endeavour. To quote Blumer Herbert, "theory exercises compelling influence on research setting problems, staking out objects and leading enquiry into asserted relations. In turn, findings of fact test theories and in suggesting new problems invite the formulation of new proposals. Theory, inquiry and empirical fact are interwoven in a texture of operation with theory guiding inquiry, inquiry seeking and isolating facts and facts affecting theory. The fruitfulness of their interplay is the means by which an empirical science develops."[50]

Use of Theory in Research

Theory may enter into a research study in different ways by:

- suggesting a problem for study,
- giving a hypothesis to be tested,
- providing a conceptual model for delimiting the scope of the study,

---

49. See Krishnaswami O.R., *Co-operative Democracy in Action,* Bombay: Somaiya Publications, 1976.
50. Herbert, Blumer, "What is Wrong with Social Theory", *American Sociological Review,* xix, 4.

- helping selection of variables or identification of classes of data to be collected,
- making research findings intelligible.

One may also use the research findings to formulate new theoretical propositions or testing an existing theory. Thus, there is no fixed way of bringing theory into research process.

However, there are some general principles[51] regarding the use of theory in research. There are:

1. A knowledge of the existing theory in one's area of research is essential for conducting research. One should become familiar with relevant theory without, of course, becoming lost in it.
2. Concepts are the crucial components of theory and so their clear definitions and operationalisations are essential to the designing of the study.
3. One should view theory as hypothetical proposition and not as conclusive fact. In this way one will be more alert to observations, which challenge the theory and thus be better prepared to revise it so as to fit the empirical observations.
4. One should pay close attention to all odd and puzzling unexpected observations as they are a source for new theoretical approaches.

To sum up, a researcher should use theory to plan and direct his lines of study, but use empirical observations to test and refine his theoretical propositions.

1.4 CONCEPTUAL OR THEORETICAL MODELS

Introduction

The body of knowledge relating to any subject is vast. When one reviews it for the study of a selected problem, one may get lost in it, unless one knows what is relevant and what is not relevant. How can this be determined? To aid in this difficult process, a conceptual model is developed, "Model building is a universal method of scientific research, in the same way that quantifying knowledge is a self-evident aim of research."[52]

Definition of Model

Conceptual or theoretical model is a simplified *systematic conceptual structure of interrelated elements in some schematic form*[53] such as narrative statement or mathematical equation. It describes relationships between and among concepts and variables.

A model possesses five different characteristics: namely, level of analysis, boundaries, specificity, construct relationship statement, and assumptions.

Process of Model Building

The process of model building involves several steps, viz.,

1. identify the phenomenon to be represented by a model;
2. determine the nature and purpose of analysis for which the model is constructed;

51. Statement prepared by Herbert Blumer for *Scientific Social Surveys and Research* by Pauline V. Young, *op. cit.*, pp. 118-119.
52. Myrdal, Gunnar M., *The Challenge of World Poverty,* Harmondsworth: Penguin Books Ltd., 1970, p. 40.
53. Black, James A., and Dean, J. Champion, *Methods and Issues in Social Research*, New York: John Wiley & Sons, 1976, p. 68.

3. gain a thorough understanding of the phenomenon through observation or survey of available literature relating to it;
4. conceptualize its meaning and nature;
5. identity the important variables and attributes;
6. examine the nature of inter-relationships among them;
7. formulate the structure of the inter-relationships; and
8. present the structure in the form of a precise statement or mathematical equation, defining the concepts, stating the assumptions and using the rules of logic.

Thus, model building calls for high levels of logical skill and mathematical competence.

Conditions

A model must *satisfy* certain *conditions.*

First, a model should be (a) *explicit* in terms of construct definition and critical relationship among them, (b) *clear* about the operationalization of each construct and (c) *empirically* testable.[54]

Second, there must be *one-to-one correspondence between the elements of the phenomenon* under study and the *elements of the model* representing it.

Third, the model must *preserve the important relationships* noticed in the phenomenon.

Fourth, the *causative factors* in the model must be well defined, for example, can we be able to explain inflation as resulting from an increase in the quantity of money without causal connection? The Keynesian theory gave the causal connection between inflation and investment and thus provided a rational base for explaining inflation.

Lastly, the model must *satisfy the principle of internal consistency.* One cannot assume that production equipment undergoes technical progress and still remains the same as was done in the neo-classical analysis of growth.

Typology of Models

Models may be broadly classified into (a) *abstract* models and (b) *real* models.

Abstract models represent high-level abstraction for making a simplified conceptual framework. They are divorced from application to real problems. *Real models,* on the other hand, represent a blueprint of real problems and are applicable to given situations.

The real models may be classified into (a) *Heuristic model and* (b) *Extensor model.* The former makes an exploratory suggestion and the latter extends it into detailed form nearer to reality, amplifying it.

Models, which depict the causal relationships between the variables, may be described as causal models.

Choice of Models

There are some principles or guidelines governing the selection of models relevant to the problems under study.

---

54. Argyris C., and D.A. Schon, *Theory in Practice,* San Francisco: Jossey-Bass, 1974.

The first principle is to choose initially a simple model, i.e., Heuristic one in order to explore the area of analysis under simplified assumptions. The socio-economic situations are extremely complex in the real world. Therefore, it is desirable to select a few important variables and make simplified assumptions and then build up the model, covering those important variables only, because the analysis is likely to be complicated even with a few variables.

The second principle is to have an in built procedure for enhancing the scope so as to take it and enlarging the model for coming closer to the reality. Then the model becomes Extensory one, as it extends the scope of the initial model. If the simplified assumptions cannot be removed without breaking down the whole model, then the original model must be discarded and a new model developed.

The most obvious example is the use of the Cobb Douglas Function[55] in Production Economics. It relates output in manufacturing industries to labour and capital inputs, and it is expressed as $P = bL^aC^{l-a}$ where P= total output; L = Index of labour input C= Index of fixed capital; the exponents 'a' and "l-a' are the elasticity of production, i.e., the percentage response of output to percentage changes in labour and capital respectively.

This model is based on the assumptions of malleability of capital and constancy of the share of wages in income. These assumptions are highly restrictive for analyzing production. When these are removed, the whole system breaks down.

Illustration: In order to illustrate research models, a model developed by Subrata Pandey[56] is given below.

The organisational effectiveness in a R & D organisation is determined by five sets of variables, viz., macroclimate (organizational climate), microclimate (job climate), personality of scientists, and their attitudinal and performance variables.

The organizational effectiveness is indicated by the scientists' rated performances. The interrelationships between and among the determinant variables are depicted in a schematic diagram. (See Exh. 1.1). All the variables were operationalised and measured by appropriate measuring tools.

Advantages

Models may be of great help in research.

A model is a guiding tool for the entire process of research from the conceptualization to analysis through the testing of hypotheses.

A model enables the researcher to identify and concentrate on important and relevant variables and attributes, instead of getting lost in irrelevant and unimportant details.

A model helps considerably in ensuring that the reasoning is sound, as the model builder has to define his concepts, state his premises and use the rules of logic in his exercise.

A model represents pictures of theories. As such, it enables the researcher to grasp more quickly and comprehensively the sorts of relations among variables postulated by theories.

A model enables us to comprehend precisely the direction of the relations among variables. Whether a given factor has positive or negative impact on another can be readily ascertained.

55. Varshney R.L., and K.L. Maheshwari, *Managerial Economics,* New Delhi: Sultan Chand & Sons, 1979, pp. 130-131.

56. Subrata Pandey, *A Study of Organisational and Individual Characteristics in R&D Organisations,* (Unpublished Ph.D. Thesis), Bangalore: Indian Institute of Science, 1986.

A model shows more clearly the boundaries or conceptual limits of theories. It tells us where a theory ends. We can concentrate on the phenomena to which it is applicable.

A model reminds us the need for abstraction in any systematic investigation.

In social sciences it is impossible to conduct strictly controlled experiments. A series of models can serve as a reasonable substitute for controlled experiments by acting as a mental laboratory for identifying new relationships and clarifying thought.

A model suggests the techniques of analysis, ways to interpretation of data and ways to draw conclusions.[57]

Limitations of Models

Models are not unmixed blessings. They have some drawbacks and limitations.

A model building calls for high levels of logical skills and mathematical competence, persons who do not have these skills, cannot build useful models.

There is also the opposite danger. Those who have expertise in constructing models may go too far. They may be tempted to create abstract models unrelated to any real understanding of problems. Rigour is necessary for any analysis, but rigour is no substitute for relevance.

Another danger in the indiscriminate use of models is that abstract models have a tendency to pose themselves as reality. Models, which are analytical tools, then tend to become objects of worship.

Another problem associated with the use of model is that model builders who are usually craftsmen, and not theorists take too much for granted regarding meanings of concepts, which they use. "Concepts are intrinsically relational; they are not like the bricks that anyone can use in any construction."[58] Concepts used in each model must be defined afresh in terms of the relationships of that model. "To construct models in the air, out of uncritically conceived concepts that are inadequate to reality and not logically consistent" ...... as rightly stressed by Gunnar Myrdal, "does not represent scientific progress, it come nearer to being an intellectual fraud."[59]

Models may suffer from the problem of inadequacy of the functional forms of mathematics. In mathematical analysis, there are two basic functional forms: additive and multiplicative. There are situations in which either one is appropriate. For example, neither the existence of a strong union nor that of good profit would by itself be sufficient to explain wage increase obtained by workers.

Models constitute rather severe simplifications. In social sciences, for example, there is a tendency to present extremes or polar ends as dichotomies, e.g., good/bad; objective/subjective; formal/informal. Variables like these are, in fact, no discrete entities but continuous dimensions.

Models narrow the full implications of theories so much that fruitful avenues of exploration not portrayed explicitly may be ignored.

Models tend to convey the impression that all the logically consistent dimensions have been included. This, however, is not always the case.

Therefore, one should not rely on models mechanically, one should keep in mind the limitations of models.

---

57. Hausser, D.L., "Comparison of Different Models for Organisational Analysis", in E.E. Lawlee, *et al.*, (eds.), *Organizational Assessment*, New York: John Wiley & Sons, 1980, pp. 133-134.
58. Kurien, C.T., *A Guide to Research in Economics, op. cit.*, p. 14.
59. Myrdal, Gunnar M., *op. cit.*, p. 41.

SUGGESTED READINGS

1. Black, Max, *Critical Thinking,* Englewood Cliffs N.J: Prentice-Hall, 1952.
2. Blalock, Hubert M., *Theory of Construction: From Verbal to Mathematical Formulations,* Englewood Cliffs N.J: Prentice Hall, 1969.
3. Braithwaite, Richard B., *Scientific Explanation,* New York: Harper & Brothers, 1960.
4. Cohen, Morris R., and Ernest Nagel, *An Introduction to Logic and Scientific Method,* New York: Harcourt, Brace, 1934.
5. Dubin, Robert, *Theory Building,* New York: Free Press, 1969.
6. Lave, Charles A., and March, James G., An Introduction to Models in the Social Sciences, New York: Harper & Row, 1975.
7. Phillips Bernard S., *Social Research,* New York: The Macmillan Co., 1971.
8. Rigby, Paul H., *Conceptual Foundations of Business Research,* New York: John Wiley & Sons, 1965.
9. Wilson, E. Bright, Jr., *An Introduction to Scientific Research,* New York: McGraw-Hill, 1952.

QUESTIONS

1. Define research and examine its characteristics.
2. "Search for facts should be made by scientific method rather than by arbitrary method." Substantiate.
3. Discuss the purpose of research.
4. How does research aid planning?
5. What is scientific method? What are its bases?
6. Does the term " scientific method" refer to a set of procedures or to 'science' as a subject? Discuss.
7. Can the scientific method involve reasoning process? Justify your answer.
8. Does the scientific method involve reasoning process? Discuss.
9. What is induction? When is it followed?
10. Describe the four conditions necessary to satisfactory induction.
11. Describe the process of analytic induction.
12. What is deduction? What are its essential conditions?
13. Compare and contrast induction and deduction, giving examples of each.
14. What are the essentials of a good scientific method?
15. Analyse the procedural and personal components of the scientific approach.
16. What is scientific attitude? What are its elements?
17. Distinguish between:
    (a) arbitrary and scientific methods
    (b) concept and construct
    (c) theory and fact
    (d) theory and hypothesis.
18. Define theory and discuss its criteria.
19. What are the uses of theory to research?

20. What does research do for theory?
21. What is a conceptual model? What are its requirements?
22. Describe the process of model building.
23. How should a model relevant to the problem under study be selected?
24. How do models aid research?
25. What are the limitations of models?

❑ ❑ ❑

2 SOCIAL SCIENCE RESEARCH

2.1 SOCIAL SCIENCE RESEARCH

Social Sciences

Sciences are broadly divided into natural (or physical) sciences and social sciences. Social sciences include various disciplines dealing with human life, human behaviour, social groups and social institutions. They consist of Anthropology, Behaviour Science, Commerce, Demography, Economics, Education, Geography, History, Law, Linguistics, Management, Political Science, Psychology, Public Administration, Sociology and Social Work. Though these sciences are treated as separate branches of knowledge for the purpose of study, they are interdependent studies of the different aspects of the same object, viz., man. By applying scientific method of study, the social sciences have grown and advanced man's knowledge of himself.

Social sciences are not exact science like physical sciences, as they, unlike the latter, deal with human beings. Human nature and man's environment are so complex that it is more difficult to comprehend and predict human behaviour than the physical phenomena. No two persons are alike in feelings, drives or emotions. No one is consistent from one moment to another. The behaviour of human beings is influenced by biological, psychological, socio-cultural, temporal and environmental factors. It is difficult to see the underlying uniformities in the diversity of complex human behaviour. A controlled experiment, which is *sine qua non* of an empirical science, in general well nigh impossible in social sciences.

Social Science Research

Social science research is a systematic method of exploring, analyzing and conceptualizing human life in order to extend, correct or verify knowledge of human behaviour and social life. In other words, Social science research "seek to find explanations to unexplained social phenomena, to clarify the doubtful, and correct the misconceived facts of social life."[1]

Objectives of Social Science Research

The aim of social science research, like research in physical sciences, is to *discover new facts* or *verify* and *test* old facts.

It tries to understand the *human behaviour* and its *interaction* with the environment and the social institutions.

It tries to find out the *causal connection* between human activities and natural laws governing them.

Another purpose of social science research is to develop *new scientific tools*, concepts and theories, which would facilitate reliable and valid study of human behaviour and social life.

Functions or Uses of Social Science Research

The functions of Social Science Research are varied. They are:

1. ***Discovery of Facts and their Interpretation:*** Research provides answer to questions of what, where, when, how and why of man, social life and institutions. They are half-truths, pseudo-truths and superstitions. Discovery of facts and their interpretation help us discard such distortions and thus enlighten us and contribute to our understanding of social reality. Research strengthens our desire for truth and opens up before our eyes, hidden social mysteries.
2. ***Diagnosis of Problems and their Analysis:*** The developing countries have innumerable problems such as poverty, unemployment, economic imbalance, economic inequality, social tension, low productivity, technological backwardness, etc. The nature and dimensions of such problems have to be diagnosed and analysed; social science research plays a significant role in this respect. An analysis of problems leads to an identification of appropriate remedial actions.
3. ***Systematization of Knowledge:*** The facts discovered through research are systematized and the body of knowledge is developed. Thus, research contributes to the growth of various social sciences and theory building.
4. ***Control over Social Phenomena:*** Research in social science areas equips us with first-hand knowledge about the organizing and working of the society and its institutions. This knowledge gives us a greater power of control over the social phenomena.
5. ***Prediction:*** Research aims at finding an order among social facts and their causal relation. This affords a sound basis for prediction in several cases. Although the predictions cannot be perfect because of the inherent limitations of social sciences, they will be fairly useful for better social planning and control.
6. ***Development Planning:*** Planning for socio-economic development calls for baseline data on the various aspects of our society and economy, resource endowment, peoples needs and aspirations, etc., Systematic Research can give us the required data base for planning and designing developmental schemes and programmes. Analytical studies can illuminate critical

1. Young, Pauline V., *op. cit.*, p. 30.

areas of policy and testing the validity of planning assumptions. Evaluation studies point out the impact of plan, policies and programmes and throw out suggestions for their proper reformulation.

7. *Social Welfare:* Social research can unfold and identify the causes of social evils and problems. It can thus help in taking appropriate remedial actions. It can also give us sound guidelines for appropriate positive measures of reform and social welfare.

Scope of Social Science Research

The fields of social science research are virtually unlimited, and the materials of research endless. Every group of social phenomena, every phase of human life, and every stage of past and present development are materials for the social scientists.[2] The areas of research in various social sciences listed in the Annexure would give an idea of the vast scope for research in social sciences.

Inter-disciplinary Approach

Social Science research calls for inter-disciplinary approach, for human life cannot be compartmentalized into psychological, social, economic or political aspects. "Man lives in a socio-economic and political world and thrives on its varied relationships. It is inconceivable that the study of bare and isolated events on any one aspect of man's life would yield any meaningful results."[3] A discipline-specific study of a social problem from an angle of, say economics or sociology or political science only cannot give a correct and total view of the problem. As Gunnar Myrdal points out, " In reality there are no economic, sociological or psychological problems, but simply problems, and they are complex."[4] Myrdal's most enduring contribution of "*circular cumulative causation*" stresses that no social science by itself is sufficiently self-contained to deal with any social problem. It is affected cumulatively by economic, sociological, psychological, legal, historical forces and factors. For example, the problem of poverty cannot be just studied as a mere economic problem or a social problem or a political issue. The approaches and theories of all these disciplines must be blended to provide a meaningful and valid approach to the problem. This inter-disciplinary approach facilitates better understanding of the complex level of social-psychological-economic-political forces, intricately interwoven in modern life.

2.2 OBJECTIVITY

Meaning

Objectivity is *sine qua non* of the scientific method. It means the willingness and ability to examine evidence dispassionately. It is the first condition of research. *Objectivity means basing conclusion on facts without any bias and value judgement.* The conclusion should be independent of one's personal beliefs, likes, dislikes and hopes. Both the data and the inference drawn from their analysis must be free from *bias* and *prejudices.*

Research, as stressed by Myrdal, has an inbuilt, self-cleaning, or self-healing capacity. Facts kick, and do so even-though with some delay when data are first assembled under categories that correspond to the biased approach applied but are inadequate to reality.[5]

2. Pearson, Karl, *The Grammar of Science,* London: J. M. Dent and Sons, 1937, p. 16.
3. Yong, Pauline V., *op. cit.,* p. 31.
4. Myrdal, Gunnar M., *Objectivity in Social Research,* London: Gerald Duckworth Co., Ltd., 1969, p. 10.
5. *Ibid.,* Sec. 8.

Factors Affecting Objectivity

It is very difficult to achieve objectivity in social science research. This difficulty arises out of the adverse influences of (1) personal prejudices and bias, (2) value judgement, (3) ethical dilemma and (4) complexity of social phenomena.

Personal prejudices and biases emanate from habits of thought, temperamental weaknesses, skeptical attitude, wishful thinking, vested interest etc. " Prejudice and biases are like fantasies- to believe what is comforting to believe."[6] These make on to believe something without considering evidence.

Value related problem arises from the social context within which research occurs. A researcher's attitudes towards socio-economic issues are influenced by his values. His judgement is coloured by the 'ism'— capitalism or communism or socialism, etc., to which he belongs and the writer/philosopher who inspired him. Even great social scientists project their values and views in their theories. The proletarian interpretation of Karl Marx, Bertrand Russel's power interpretation of social order, Freud's sex interpretation of society, Fabian socialism of George Bernard Shaw and Gandhiji's philosophy of limiting wants and trusteeship are illustrations. To quote Gunnar Myrdal, "value premises are needed even in the theoretical stage of establishing knowledge about facts and factual relations. A view is impossible except from a viewpoint. A disinterested social science has never existed and can never come to exist — for logical reasons, valuations are always implied in our search for truth."[7]

Personal preconceptions may not only have a distorting effect on the data but are also highly insidious, because they are so " subtle, so implicit, so deeply noted that it is difficult for us to discern them in ourselves, or when they are called to our attention, to avoid rationalizing them, instead of examining them objectively."[8]

Ethical dilemmas arises out of the researcher's relations with other participants in the research process. There are four types of interpersonal relations that pose potential ethical dilemmas: (1) relations with those sponsoring the research, (2) relations with those permitting access to sources of data, (3) relations with the investigators connected with the project, and (4) relations with research subjects themselves (See Section 2.4, below).

Social phenomena are too complex for easy comprehension, and too vast to provide precise verifiable knowledge. A physical scientist is confined to the four walls of a laboratory, and he can conduct controlled experimentation. On the other hand, laboratory of social scientists is as vast as the entire society and it is not amenable for controllers' experimentation.

Although strict objectivity is next to impossibility, it is possible for a reflective researcher of social life to attain a *reasonable level* of *objectivity* consistent with logical and systematic thinking.

Achieving Reasonable Objectivity in Social Science Research

The following approaches and measures may contribute to some degree of objectivity.

1. ***Patience and Self-control:*** A researcher must have utmost patience and self-control. He should not be overwhelmed by personal likes and undisciplined imagination and wishful thinking. He must discipline himself to avoid prejudging the phenomenon under study.

6. Guentin Gibson, *The Logic of Social Enquiry,* London: Poutledge and Degan Paul, 1953, p. 78.
7. Myrdal, Gunnar M., *The Challenge of World Poverty,* Harmondsworth: Penguin Books Ltd., 1970, p. 42.
8. Hant, Clyde. W., "Some Factors Affecting the Organisation and Prosecution of given Research Projects," *American Sociological Review,* xii, 516.

2. ***Open mind:*** A researcher often succumbs to the habit of thinking and personal notions that leads him to presuppose that certain facts are "truths." He must have an open mind to subject his research process and interpretations to the critical review of other scientists. Only by such interaction, can corrections be made.
3. ***Use of standardized concepts:*** The concepts should be precisely defined and used consistently so as to avoid misconceptions and confusion.
4. ***Use of quantitative method:*** Appropriate statistical and mathematical techniques of analysis may be used, as they are free from subjective bias.
5. ***Co-operative research:*** Group research will be more objective than an individual research. Group interaction will reduce the influence of personal bias.
6. ***Use of random sampling:*** In drawing a sample of units of study, random sampling technique may be used, as it is free from personal prejudices.

2.3 LIMITATIONS OF SOCIAL SCIENCE RESEARCH

Research in social sciences has certain limitations and problems when compared with research in physical sciences. They are discussed below:

Scientist – A Part of What is Studied

The fact that social scientist is part of the human society which he studies gives rise to certain limitations.

Man must have to be his own guinea pig, as pointed out by Julian Huxley. This has a number of methodological consequences. For example, it restricts the scope for controlled experiments. It limits the scope for objectivity in social science research, as explained earlier. (See Section 2.2 above).

Complexity of the Subject Matter

The subject matter of research in social science, viz., human society and human behaviour is too complex, varied and changing to yield to the scientific categorization, measurement, analysis and prediction. The multiplicity and complexity of causation make it difficult to apply the technique of experimentation.

Human behaviour can be studied only by other human beings, and this always distorts fundamentally the facts being studied so that there can be no objective procedure for achieving the truth.[9]

Human Problems

A social scientist faces certain human problems, which the natural scientist is spared.[10] These problems are varied and include refusal of respondents, improper understanding of questions by them, their loss of memory, their reluctance to furnish certain information, etc. All these problems cause biases and invalidate the research findings and conclusions.

---

9. Goode and Hatt, *op. cit.*, p. 2.
10. Festinger, Leon and Daniel Kartz, *Research Methods in the Behavioural Sciences,* New York: Holt, Rinehart and Winston, 1966, p. 2.

Personal Values

Subjects and clients, as well as investigators, have personal values, which are apt to become involved in the research process.[11] One should not assume that these are freely exploitable. The investigator must have respect for the client's values.

Anthropomorphization

Another hazard of social science research is the danger of "the temptation to anthropomorphize about humans."[12] It results in using observations obtained by sheer intuition or empathy in conceptualizing in anthropomorphic manner.

Wrong Decisions

The quality of research findings depends upon the soundness of decisions made by the social scientist on such crucial stages of his research process as definition of the unit of study, operationalization of concepts, selection of sampling techniques and statistical techniques. Any mistake in any of these decisions will vitiate the validity of his findings.

2.4 ETHICS IN SOCIAL SCIENCE RESEARCH

Introduction

Research in social science often involves use of unethical practices. Issues of ethics arise primarily out of researcher's relations with (a) sponsors of research, (b) those who permit access to sources of data, and (c) research participants/respondents.

Ethical Issues of Research Sponsorship

Research may be funded by either research promotional bodies like research foundation, Indian Council of Social Science Research and similar Councils and University Grants Commission or research-users like Planning Commission, Government Departments and business undertakings and financial institutions. In the former case, the funding takes the form of research grant and the researcher himself takes initiative. He forwards his research proposal to the promotional body for research grant. The granting agency does not prohibit the publication of the results for consumption by the scientific community.

A contracted research undertaken for a sponsoring user organization specifies the nature of the work to be done, the time period for its completion and the conditions relating to the use of results. Given the highly structured and restricted nature of contract research and the explicitly stated intention of the sponsor, the primary ethical questions posed are: whether the researcher wants to operate within the confines of such restrictions and whether he is willing to accept the restrictions regarding the publication of the research findings. The researcher must decide these issues before accepting the assignment.

Approval of Access to Data

A social science research may require collection of data from the document and records of an institution or from its employees. The permission from the head of the institution has to be sought. The ethical issues that arise in this context are:

- Should the nature of the research project and its objective be indicated to the permission granting authority?

- What should be the degree of anonymity to be accorded to the institution concerned?
- Should the procedure for handling data in ways assuring the degree of anonymity guaranteed be stated?
- Should the findings of the study be made available to the institution concerned? If so, in what form they should be made available?

There is no hard and fast rule for deciding these questions. They have to be settled mutually by the researcher and the head of the institution concerned.

Ethical Issues Relating to the Respondents/Subjects

Of all the ethical issues, the issues concerned with the respondents are far more important. The respondents constitute the research subjects. They are individuals from whom data are obtained. The major categories of ethical issues relating to the research subjects are:

1. Sometimes people are made to participate in a research project *without their knowledge or consent.* For example, in social-anthropological studies of rural or tribal communities, the researcher may conduct his research without the knowledge of the people concerned, fearing that their awareness of the research may affect the naturalness of their responses or behaviour. The researcher who involves the research subject in research thus infringes upon their right to make their own decision to participate or not to participate.

   Ideally speaking, the research subjects' consent should be obtained after giving them enough information about the proposed research. But often, the consent may be wholly or partially forced. For instance, the employer may direct his employees to 'cooperate' with a research project, or strong incentives may be offered to tempt the participants to give consent. Such coercions restrict the research subjects' freedom to decide whether or not to participate in a research.
2. In some researches, the consent of respondents is obtained without informing them of the purpose of the research. Such concealment naturally curtails the free choice of the respondents.
3. In some researches, the researcher may find it necessary to give *incorrect information* about the proposed research to potential subjects in order to manipulate their perceptions and behaviour. Such *deceptions* are regarded as questionable practices.
4. In studies relating to human values, the social scientists may create opportunities for research subjects to lie, steal or cheat. Is it appropriate to expose research subjects to such moral hazards? Opinions differ.
5. Another questionable/non-ethical practice is to *expose participants to physical or mental stress* with a view to studying their reactions. For example, in a mock-hijacking of an aircraft or a mock-panic situation in a crowd without a fore-warning, people are subject to physical or mental stress.
6. A behavioural scientist may dig out information from respondents on private or personal matters such as marital life or religious faith or personal opinions by employing techniques of participant observation, indepth interviews or disguised projective test. Such practices amount to *invasion of privacy.*

7. Finally, there is the ethical issue relating to the obligation of maintaining the anonymity of the research respondents and keeping research data in confidence. Anonymity might be violated through reports and publications. Despite the practice of using pseudonyms, the identity of the community or institutions becomes known indirectly.

Although a respondent's name remains anonymous, his data contribute to the averages/percentages reported for the group to which he belongs. Should the respondents be told before hand of the uses to which their data will be put?

Ethical Dilemmas or Benefits of Research

The above categories of ethical difficulties arise in social science research. The crucial question that arises is: "Should a social scientist adopt some unethical practices out of necessity or abandon his proposed research? It is not easy to decide this question. One of the alternatives — ethics or research — has to be sacrificed. However, in the larger interest of developing useful knowledge, it is desirable to strike a balance between the moral cost of unethical practices and the potential benefits of research. No doubt that researchers have an obligation to the research subjects. But they have a greater social responsibility to find facts relevant to the solution of pressing human problems and thus to promote social welfare. An evaluation of such potential benefits of research and the moral cost of unethical practices will provide the clue to the choice. When the benefits far exceed the moral cost, it is desirable to go ahead with the research, even it calls for some unethical practice like concealing facts, invasion of privacy of respondents, etc. however, participants should not be exposed to physical or mental stress. Professional association must devise codes of ethics to be followed while obtaining information from individuals.

SUGGESTED READINGS

1. Abrams, M.A., *Social Surveys and Social Action,* London: Heinemann, 1951.
2. American Psychological Association, *Ethical Principles in the Conduct of Research with Human Participants,* Washington, D.C.: APA, 1973.
3. Arthur, Maurice, *Philosophy of Scientific Investigation,* Baltimore: John Hopkins University Press, 1943.
4. Bernal, J.D., *The Social Function of Science,* London: George Routledge and Sons, 1939.
5. Chase, Stuart, *The Proper Study of Mankind: An inquiry into the Science of Human Relations,* New York: Harper and Row Publishers, 1958.
6. Cook, Stuart, "Ethical Implications", in Kidder, Lousie H., and Judd, Charles, M., *Research Methods in Social Relations,* New York: CBS Publishing Japan Ltd., 1986, pp. 425-510.
7. Denzin, Norman K., "On the Ethics of Disguised Observation", *Social Problems,* 15, 1968, pp. 502-506.
8. ICSSR, *A Report on Social Sciences in India: Retrospective and Prospective,* Vol. I, New Delhi: ICSSR Review Committee, 1973.
9. Katz, J., *Experimentation with Human Beings,* New York: Russell Sage Foundation, 1972.
10. Lambert, R.D., *Workers, Factories and Social Change in India,* Mumbai: Asia Publishing House, 1965.
11. Murdal, G., *Asian Drama: An Enquiry into the Poverty of Nations,* Vol. I, New York, Penguin Books, 1968.
12. Political and Economic Planning, *Sample Surveys,* Part One, Part Two, *Planning*, London: 16 (Nos. 314 & 315).

13. Sjoberg, Gideon, (ed.) *Ethics, Politics and Social Research,* Cambridge, Mass: Schenkman Publishing, 1967.

14. Warwick, Donald P., "The Politics and Ethics of Field Research", in Bulmer, Martin and Warwick, Donald P., (Eds.) *Social Research in Developing Countries,* New York: John Wiley & Sons, 1983, pp. 315-331.

15. Wolfe, A.B., *Conservatism, Radicalism and Scientific Attitude,* The Macmillan Co., 1923.

QUESTIONS

1. What is social science research? What are its objectives?
2. Discuss the uses of Social Science Research.
3. Is inter-disciplinary approach necessary in social science research?
4. What are the limitations of Social Science Research?
5. What is 'Objectivity'? Is it possible to achieve objectivity in social science research?
6. Distinguish between ethics and objectivity in Social Science Research. Why is such a distinction important?
7. Discuss the types of interpersonal relations that pose potential ethical dilemmas.
8. How can reasonable objectivity in social science research be achieved?
9. What are the major issues relating to the research subjects?
10. Should a Social Scientist adopt some ethical practices out of necessity or abandon his research?

❑ ❑ ❑

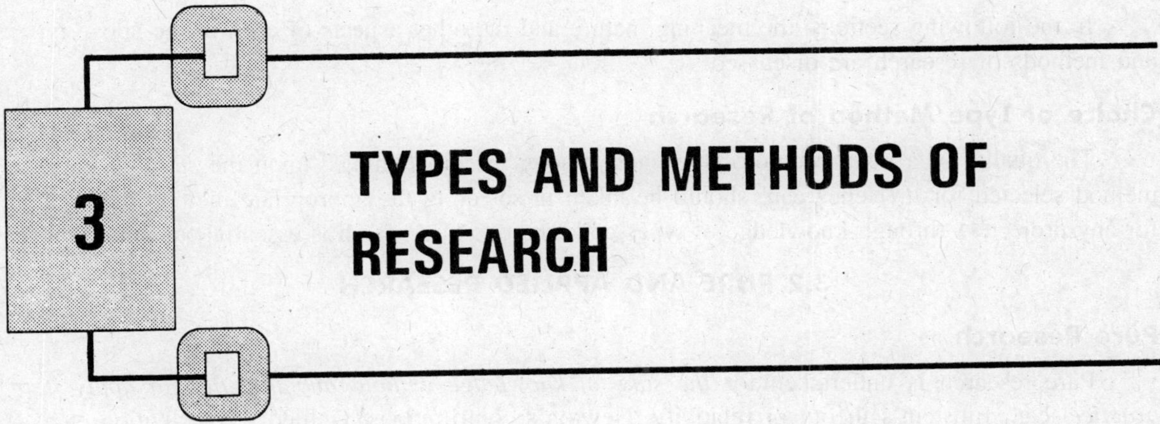

3 TYPES AND METHODS OF RESEARCH

3.1 CLASSIFICATION OF RESEARCH

Introduction

Although any typology of research is inevitably arbitrary, Research may be classified crudely according to its major intent or the methods. According to the *intent*, research may be classified as:

- Pure Research
- Applied Research
- Exploratory Research
- Descriptive Study
- Diagnostic Study
- Evaluation Studies
- Action Research

According to the *methods of study*, research may be classified as:

- Experimental Research
- Analytical Study
- Historical Research
- Survey

The Nature of Classification

The above classification is not a watertight demarcation. It is just an *approach* to differentiate the distinctive approaches to research for the purpose of better understanding. The different types of research are, of course, not sharply distinguishable from one another. There may be overlapping between one type/method and another. For example, pure research may involve experimentation or case study or analytical study; Evaluation studies may apply experimental or survey methods; Experimental Research is necessarily an analytical study; Survey Research may involve quasi-experimental approach or analytical approach; and so on.

In the following sections, the meaning, nature and the other aspects of each of the above types and methods of research are discussed.

Choice of Type/Method of Research

The quality of a research project depends, among the other things, upon the *suitability* of the method selected for it. Hence care should be taken in selecting the appropriate method of research for any project. A through knowledge of types and methods of research is essential for this purpose.

3.2 PURE AND APPLIED RESEARCH

Pure Research

Pure research is undertaken for *the sake of knowledge without any intention to apply it in practice,* e.g., Einstein's theory of relativity, Newton's contributions, Galileo's contribution etc.

Pure research is also known as *basic* or *fundamental* research. It is undertaken out of *intellectual curiosity* or inquisitiveness. It is not necessarily problem-oriented. It aims at extension of knowledge. It may lead to either discovery of a new theory or refinement of an existing theory. The development of various sciences owes much to pure research. The findings of pure research enrich the storehouse of knowledge that can be drawn upon in the future to formulate significant practical researches. In the words of Dixey, "natural knowledge pursued for its own sake without any direct view to future utility will often lead to results of most unexpected kind and of very highest practical importance."[1] Thus, pure research lays the foundation for applied research. The findings of pure research formed the basis for innumerable scientific and technological inventions like steam engine, machines, automobiles, electronic gadgets, electronic data processing, telecommunication, etc., which have revolutionized and enriched our human life.

Applied Research

Applied research is carried on to find solution to a real-life problem requiring an action or policy decision. It is thus problem-oriented and action-directed. It seeks an immediate and practical result, e.g., marketing research carried on for developing a new market or for studying the post-purchase experience of customers.

There is vast scope for applied research in the fields of technology, management, commerce, economics and other social sciences. Innumerable problems are faced in these areas. They need empirical study for finding solutions.

Though the immediate purpose of an applied research is to find solutions to a practical problem, it may incidentally contribute to the development of theoretical knowledge by leading to the discovery of new facts or testing of a theory or to conceptual clarity.

---

1. Thomson, J.A., *Introduction to Science,* Oxford University Press, p. 181.

The Interplay between Pure and Applied Research

The distinction between pure and applied research is *not absolute,* but at best only *relative,* for pure research may have significant potential for its application to the solution of a practical problem now or later (e.g., application of Newton's Law of Gravity in space research); and applied research may end up making a scientific contribution to the development of the theoretical knowledge (e.g., Elton Mayo's Hawthorne Study's contribution to Behavioural science).

The terms, 'pure' and 'applied' just represent the *polar ends* of a *continuum.* "Research studies have differing degrees of 'purity' and 'applicability', depending on whether their purpose is solely to advance knowledge in a field or to solve some functional problem."[2]

Goode and Hatt have highlighted the mutual contribution between pure and applied research.[3]

Contribution of Pure Research

1. By developing principle, pure research *offers solutions* to many *practical problems.* For example, Maslow's theory of motivation serves as a guideline for formulating incentive schemes and approaches to motivating employees in organizations. Generalizations have many practical applications. In fact, nothing is so practical for the goals of diagnosis or treatment as good theoretical research.
2. Pure research helps to *find the critical factors* in a practical problem. For example, a common-sense approach to problems like communal disharmony or ethnic conflict fail to abstract the key factors. On the other hand, by deeper study such social maladies can be better understood and it may be possible to find a solution to such problems.
3. Pure research develops many *alternative solutions* and thus enables us to choose the *best solution.* By applying scientific knowledge developed by pure researches, various appliances like radio, television, refrigerator, computer etc. have been invented. Continuous basic research in these fields has contributed to the manufacture of more effective and useful models at the least cost.

Contribution of Applied Research

1. Applied research can *contribute new facts.* A practical study designed to improve productivity in agricultural farms may stimulate theoretical analysis of extension technology, land tenure system, price parity between agricultural inputs and outputs, etc. Applied research uncovers new facts, which enrich the concerned body of knowledge.
2. Applied research can *put theory to the test.* Applied research is also a scientific endeavour. The researcher has to design it scientifically. From his knowledge of theory, he has to develop a conceptual framework for his study and formulate hypothesis. Thus, his study offers an opportunity to test the validity of existing theory.
3. Applied research may *aid in conceptual clarification.* Many concepts like 'small farmer', 'agricultural labourer', 'social responsibility', 'social structure', etc. are not precise. Different people define them differently leading to confusion and lack of clarity. The vagueness of

---

2. Emory, C. William, *op. cit,* p. 21.
3. Goode, William J., Hatt, Paul K., *op. cit.,* p. 34-38.

a concept surfaces most sharply when we attempt to operationalise it for dealing with it in research. Thus, research aids conceptual clarity.

4. Applied research may *integrate previously existing theories.* A practical problem has many facts. It cannot be solved by the application of abstract principles from a single science. Township development, for example, may draw upon such disciplines as town planning, geology, demography, sociology, economics, etc. Thus, the solution of a practical problem may require some integration of the theories and principles of various disciplines.

3.3 EXPLORATORY OR FORMULATIVE RESEARCH

Meaning

Exploratory research is preliminary study of an unfamiliar problem about which the researcher has little or no knowledge. It is similar to a doctor's initial investigation of a patient suffering from an unfamiliar malady for getting some clues for identifying it. "It is ill-structured and much less focused on pre-determined objectives."[4] It usually takes the form of a pilot study.[5]

Though it is a separate type of research, it is appropriate to consider it as the first stage of a three-stage process of exploration, description and experimentation.

Purposes

The purpose of an exploratory study may be:

- to generate new ideas or
- to increase the researcher's familiarity with the problem or
- to make a precise formulation of the problem or
- to gather information for clarifying concepts or
- to determine whether it is feasible to attempt the study.

Sometimes, a scientist may find, after spending a tremendous amount of energy and time on a research project, that it is not possible to secure the required data. A preliminary exploration could help avoiding such dismay. For example, a research student of the author wanted to study the pattern of marketing strategies of large manufacturing enterprises. A critical pre-requisite to this study was to know whether marketing executives would divulge adequate information about their marketing strategies. An exploration determined that they would not.

An exploratory study does not aim at testing hypothesis. According to Daniel Katz, it just attempts "to see what is there rather than to predict the relationships that will be founded."[6] But it should be so designed as to provide as definite information as possible for a set of research objectives.

Levels of Exploratory Studies

Katz conceptualizes two levels of exploratory studies. "At the *first level* is the *discovery* of the significant *variables* in the situation; at the *second,* the *discovery of relationship* between variables."[7]

4. Emory, C. William, *op. cit,* p. 79.
5. See Section 8.4, *Pilot Studies and Pre-tests,* below.
6. Festinger, Leon and Daniel Katz, (eds.), *Research Methods in the Behavioural Sciences,* New York: Holt, Rinehart and Winston, 1966, p. 74.
7. *Ibid.,* p. 75.

It is necessary to delimit the area to be studied even at the first level. Katz warns that it is a mistake to believe that one study is going to be able to account for all the variance in complex social phenomena. He advises that "it is much more effective to take one central set of variables and investigate them as thoroughly as possible than to try to study the universe in one piece of research."[8]

The Need for Exploratory Studies

Social sciences are relatively young. Researches in them are scarce. Many of them inevitably have to be exploratory ones. Few well-trodden paths exist to follow for the investigators of social life. Most existing theories in social sciences are either too general or too specific to provide clear guidance for empirical research. Hence, exploratory research is necessary to get initial insight into the problems for the purpose of formulating them for more precise investigation. Hence, it is also known as formulative research.

The Steps in Exploration

Selltiz and others[9] have suggested the following three steps/methods for the exploratory study:

(a) A review of pertinent literature

(b) An experience survey

(c) An analysis of 'insight stimulating' cases.

Literature survey: A study of related and pertinent books, articles and reports turns up a number of leads and clues for further investigation that will advance the research. A workable hypothesis may be formulated; important variables may be identified.

Experience survey: Informal interviews with persons experience in the area of study will help the researcher in securing insight into the subject and its various facts. In selecting the person for this survey, representation to different facts of experience should be given. For example, in an exploratory study of the problem of rural development, it is profitable to interview researchers familiar with rural studies, rural development administrators, social workers, rural financial institutions and village leaders.

The researcher should prepare an interview guide so as to have an idea of issues and aspects of the problem on which questions may be posed. Of course, this interview guide should be flexible enough to explore various avenues that emerge during the interviews.

This survey may yield a new hypothesis and information on the various dimensions of the study, facilities and cooperation available for the study, and the factors to be controlled.

Analysis of insight-stimulating cases: In an unexplored area of study, an intensive study of some selected cases can yield stimulating insight. For example, the extraordinary theoretical insights of Sigmund Freud on human psyche were the result of his intensive study of patients. Profound insights into the relationship between the individual and society have been brought out by anthropological case studies of primitive cultures.

The types of people[10] who provide 'insight-stimulating' information could include the following:

---

8. *Ibid.*, p. 77.

9. Selltiz, Claira, Marie Jahoda, Morton Deutsch and Stuart W. Cook, *Research Methods in Social Relations*, New York: Holt, Rinehart and Winston, 1959, pp. 32-47.

10. *Ibid.*, pp. 61-64.

1. New comers to the scene.
2. Marginal or peripheral individuals who are placed on the margin between contending groups. For example, in an organizational hierarchy, foremen are neither managers nor workers but something in between.
3. Individuals in transition, e.g., recently promoted or transferred employees.
4. Deviants and isolates in a group who hold a different view from the majority.
5. 'Pure' cases or cases that should be extreme examples of the conditions under study, e.g., the most dissatisfied beneficiary of a rural development scheme.
6. Those who fit well and those who do not.
7. Those who represent different categories in the system.

The end of an exploratory study comes when the researcher finds that further research is not presently possible on the problem or succeeds in identifying the major dimensions of the problem. In the latter case, he has to plan the formal research design.

3.4 DESCRIPTIVE RESEARCH

Meaning

Descriptive study is a *fact-finding* investigation with adequate interpretation. It is the simplest type of research. It is more specific than an exploratory study, as it has focus on particular aspects or dimensions of the problem studied. It is designed to gather descriptive information and provides information for formulating more sophisticated studies. Data are collected by using one or more appropriate methods: observation, interviewing and mail questionnaire.

Criteria

All problems do not lend themselves to descriptive study. This method is applicable to problems, which satisfy certain criteria. First, the problem must be describable and not arguable. For instance, philosophical and controversial issues are not suitable for descriptive study. Second, the data should be *amenable* to an accurate, *objective*, and, if possible, quantitative *assemblage* for reliability and significance. Third, it should be possible to develop *valid* standards of *comparison.* Last, it should lend itself to *verifiable procedure* of collection and analysis of data.

Objective

A descriptive study aims at identifying the various characteristics of a community or institution or problem under study, but it does not deal with the testing of proposition or hypothesis. However, it "can reveal potential relationships between variables thus setting the stage for more elaborate investigation later."[11]

A descriptive study also aims at a classification of the range of elements comprising the subject matter of study. The classification must satisfy two criteria, viz., (1) exhaustiveness and (2) mutual exclusiveness. Exhaustiveness is achieved when all the important elements are identified. Mutual exclusiveness occurs when each item can be unambiguously placed in only one category in the system. Descriptive information should also be useful for explanation, prediction and awareness.

11. Black, James A., and Dean J. Champion, *op. cit.,* p. 80.

Descriptive Study vs. Analytical Study

A descriptive study identifies relevant variables but does not aim at testing hypothesis. On the other hand, an analytical study is primarily concerned with testing hypothesis and specifying and interpreting relationships.

A descriptive study is relatively less limited by the rigorous requirements of measurement and analysis than an analytical study. An analytical study's design approximates to the model of an experimental design.

A descriptive study employs simple statistical techniques like averages and percentages, but an analytical study employs advanced statistical techniques like correlation and multivariate analysis.

Usefulness

The descriptive studies are useful in their own way.

1. They have much to contribute to the development of a young science, as descriptive information can focus directly on a *theoretical* point. It may be useful in verifying focal concepts through empirical observation. "The more adequate the description, the greater is the likelihood that the units derived from the description will be useful in subsequent theory building."[12]
2. Descriptive information can highlight important *methodological* aspects of data collection and interpretation. The collection of factual data increases our awareness of the relative accuracy of our measuring devices. Thus, our ability to accumulate further knowledge is significantly broadened.
3. Descriptive information obtained in a research may be useful for *prediction* about areas of social life outside the boundaries of the research.
4. Descriptive studies are valuable in providing facts needed for planning social action programmes.

Limitations

The descriptive method of study has certain limitations:

1. It is not applicable to problems, which cannot satisfy the required criteria mentioned earlier.
2. The researcher may make description an end in itself. Research must lead to discovery of facts.
3. Although social science problems are continuous and have a past and a future, the researcher may lose himself in current conditions only.
4. The researcher may tend to over-use statistics. In making statistical analysis, its limitations should be recognized.

---

12. Dubin, Robert, *Theory Building,* New York: Macmillan Publishing Co., Quoted in W. Emory, *Business Research Methods, op. cit.,* pp. 7-8.

3.5 DIAGNOSTIC STUDY

Meaning

This is similar to descriptive study but with a different *focus.* It is directed towards *discovering what* is happening, *why* is it happening and *what can be done* about. It aims at identifying the *causes* of a problem and the *possible solutions* for it.

Purpose

A diagnostic study may also be concerned with discovering and testing whether certain variables are associated, e.g., are persons hailing from rural areas more suitable for manning the rural branches of banks? Do more villagers than city-voters vote for a particular party?

Requirements

Both descriptive and diagnostic studies share common requirements, viz., prior knowledge of the problem, its thorough formulation, clear-cut definition of the given population, adequate methods for collecting accurate information, precise measurement of variables, statistical analysis and test of significance. As the aim is to obtain complete and accurate information about a given situation/ phenomenon, the research design must make much more provision for protection against bias than is required in an exploratory study. Moreover, the amount of work involved is considerable and so concern with economy of research effort is extremely important.

Diagnostic Study vs. Descriptive Study

Though these two types of studies have in common emphasis on the specific characteristics of given phenomenon, they differ from each other in some respects.

First, a diagnostic study is more directly concerned with *causal* relationships and with implications for action than is a descriptive study.

Second, while a descriptive study is oriented towards finding out *what* is occurring, a diagnostic study is directed towards discovering not only what is occurring but *why* it is occurring and *what can be done* about it.

Third, a diagnostic study is more actively guided by hypothesis than is a descriptive study.

Last, a diagnostic study is not possible in areas where knowledge is not advanced enough to make possible adequate diagnosis. In such cases, the social scientist limits his effort to descriptive studies.

3.6 EVALUATION STUDIES

Meaning

Evaluation study is one type of applied research. It is made for *assessing the effectiveness* of social or economic *programmes* implemented (e.g., family planning scheme) or for assessing the impact of developmentai projects (e.g., irrigation project) on the development of the project area.

Suchman defines evaluation as " determination of the results attained by some activity (whether a programme, a drug or a therapy or an approach) designed to accomplish some valued goal or objective."[13]

---

13. Suchman, Edward A., *Evaluative Research,* New York: Russell Sage Foundation, 1967, pp. 31-32.

Purpose

Evaluative research is thus, directed to assess or appraise the quality and quantity of an activity and its performance, and to specify its attributes and conditions required for it success. It is also concerned with *change* over time. As suchman puts it, "evaluative research asks about the kind of change the program views as desirable, the *means* by which the change is to be brought about, and the *signs* according to which such change can be recognized."

Types of Evaluation

Evaluation are of *three* types:

1. ***Concurrent evaluation:*** This is a continuous process and partakes the nature of an inspection or social audit of an *on-going* programme. It aims at the evaluation of the *quality* implementation and services as a feed back for improving the performance.
2. ***Periodic evaluation:*** This is made after each distinct phase or state of a project has been completed. In the case of a medium period time-bound programme like 5- year plan, this evaluation may be done in the middle of the period and it may be called *mid-term/interim* evaluation.
3. ***Terminal evaluation:*** This is done after the completion of a programme or project (e.g., an irrigation project). This is designed to assess the extent of the achievement of its goals or objectives. It may also involve a benefit-cost analysis. In the case of a project with long-gestation period (e.g., an irrigation project), the appropriate methodology for terminal evaluation will consist of a survey-cum experimental design.

See section 3.8 *Experimental Research,* below:

Criteria of Evaluation Research

Weiss[14] and Coleman[15] list a number of specific criteria, which distinguish evaluative research from other types of research.

First, evaluation research is usually *conducted for a* client who intends to use the finding as a basis for decision – making. This is quite different from basic research, which aims at knowledge for its own sake.

Second, the evaluation researcher deals with his *client's* questions relating to the latter's programme, while the basic researcher formulates his own research questions.

Third, the evaluation researcher *measures* whether the *programme goals* are being *reached.* Other scientific researchers concern themselves with 'what is' rather than with comparisons of 'what is' with 'what ought to be'.

Fourth, unlike basic researcher who normally has control over research work, the evaluation researcher works in a setting where priority goes to the programme as opposed to the evaluation. This means that the evaluation researcher must fit time schedule to the programme/project's built-in time schedule. The programme staff tend to see data-collection work as hindrance to their work.

---

14. Wiss, Carol, *Evaluation Research: Methods of Assessing Program Effectiveness,* Englewood Cliffs, N.J. Prentice Hall, 1972, pp. 6-8.
15. Coleman, James, *Policy Research in Social Sciences,* Morristown N.J. General Learning Press, 1972, pp. 3-4.

Fifth, researcher-programme personnel conflicts are inherent in evaluation study. While the researcher is interested in objective evaluation and public dissemination of results, the project personnel expect that the evaluation results should be meant for in-house use only.

Nevertheless, evaluation research does not differ from other types of research in methodology. The problems of reliability, validity and operationalization and research method, techniques and principles are common to evaluation and other types of research.

Design and Measurement

An evaluation researcher must plan his design as to probe deeper into the following questions:

1. What is the nature of content of the objectives of the programme to be evaluated?
2. Are the objectives *unitary or multiple*?
3. *How* are the objectives to be achieved?
4. *Who* is the target of the programme?
5. *When* is the desired change to take place?
6. What is the desired *magnitude* of effect?
7. Do the benefits *really reach* the target group?
8. What are the *unintentional effects* or side effects of the programme?

The evaluation researcher's *operationalization* is concerned with one or more of the following indicators:

1. Effort or activity (i.e., input) variables.
2. *Performance* or programme output in terms of the policy objectives.
3. *Adequacy* of performance (one common index of adequacy is "the rate of effectiveness x the number of people exposed to the programme")[16]
4. *Efficiency* — a measure of benefit-cost.
5. *Process* — measures *why* the programme is successful or unsuccessful.

A few types of special designs suitable for evaluation research are:

1. ***Social audits:*** These are a useful means of getting at process and efficiency. They aim at examining: How much of resource inputs actually reaches the intended recipients in some form (i.e., cash subsidy, food and clothing for flood victims)? Of that portion which does not reach them, where does this loss of input go? Does the intended change take place? Etc.
2. ***Benefit-cost analysis:*** This is made in order to measure the programme efficiency and to measure its effectiveness by comparison with alternative programmes. This analysis depends on availability of reliable and valid data. Monetary costs can be easily estimated, but many social costs are purely speculative. For example, how could one financially measure the anguishes of rape, the emotional costs of assault or murder? Some social costs can be rationally dealt with, e.g., the social costs of total disability of an industrial employer arising out of injury could be measured in terms of society's loss of the disabled person's work power and the loss of his potential tax amount.

---

16. Suchman, Edward, *op. cit.*, p. 63.

3.7 ACTION RESEARCH

Meaning

Action research is a type of evaluation study. It is a *concurrent evaluation* study of an *action programme* launched for solving a problem/for improving an existing situation.

In the quest for development, advancement, excellence and promotion of welfare of people, government, institutions and voluntary agencies undertake action programmes for achieving specific goals or objectives. Land reform programmes, agricultural extension programmes, social welfare programmes, human resource development programmes, managerial improvement programmes, rural development programmes, programmes for improving the quality of life in factories and offices, etc., are some examples of action programmes. This plethora of development programme has given impetus to action research. With the pressing need to assess the relative effectiveness of different approaches to the same goal or the worthwhileness of one goal as against another, research has been called upon to play a closer and relevant role for action. The criterion of relevance for action is of critical importance in action research.

Typologies of Action Research

Prospero R. Covar[17] categorizes action research into five types.

Type I: Classical design: Research and action are separate and independent. The connection between research and action is not purposely sought. It may occur by chance. Action programme agency may not know/use the research finding. The researcher may not deliberately gear his work toward contributing to the effectiveness of an action programme.

Type II: Interdependence of action and research: Action is carried out by an agency not connected with a research institution. Research on action may be entrusted to an independent research body. For example, government may launch a development programme and a university social scientist may be welcomed to study the on-going programme. The researcher may include in his report a section on implications for action, and give a copy of the report to the implementing agency, but he had no further obligation to the action programme.

Type III: Evaluate research built into an action programme: In this case, research is dependent upon action, and the action people define the scope of the research.

Type IV: Action for research: Here the activities of the action programme are designed and modified to carry out tests of hypothesis of research. For example, a researcher may wish to test the relative effectiveness of three different methods of introducing family planning information: personal contact with the wife, personal contact with both husband and wife, and impersonal contact through the mass media alone. For this research purpose, a family planning programme applying each approach to different groups of couples with similar characteristics and under similar circumstances has to be launched. Thus, the research requirements dictate how the action will be carried out.

Type V: Research-cum-action: Action and research go together as a joint endeavour. Researcher and decision makers jointly design and launch the action programme and research on it. Once the operational design is completed and action launched, they record what happens under specified conditions. They may vary the conditions if they want.

17. See Castillo, R*esearch and the Action Program,* Singapore: The Agricultural Development Council, 1972, pp. 1-5.

Evaluation in Action Research

Action research always has an evaluative component. As an action programme is designed to bring about some change, an action research usually studies the following questions as proposed by Hinkle:[18]

1. What is it that has changed?
2. How much has it changed (extent)?
3. How quickly has it changed (rate)?
4. What were the conditions before and after the change?
5. What were the stimuli that induced change?
6. What occurred during the transition?
7. Through what mechanisms did change occur?
8. What brought stabilization at a particular point in change?
9. Can directionality be observed in the change?

These questions indicate the problem areas, which can be the focus of evaluation. They are:

(a) Impact of the programme on intended recipients.

(b) Extent of the programmes effect on the intended recipients.

(c) Time involved in bringing about the impact of effects.

(d) Before-after measures of the variables, which are supposed to undergo change.

(e) Identification of the events and processes that took place between the before-and-after measures.

(f) Analysis of the subject matter or content of the programme.

(g) Organizational, structural and operational aspects of the programme.

(h) Factors in the change introduced.

(i) Direction of the changes observed relative to the objectives of the programme.

The Phases in the Action Research

The different phases in the action research are:

(1) a baseline survey of the pre-action situation;

(2) a feasibility study of the proposed action programme;

(3) planning and launching the programme;

(4) concurrent evaluation of the programme;

(5) making modifications and changes in the programme and its method of implementation in the light of the research findings; and

(6) final evaluation, if the programme is time-bound.

18. Hinkle, Roscoe C., "Howard Beer's Approach to Social Change", *The Sociological Quarterly,* Vol. 2, No. 3, July 1961, pp. 155-180.

The success of the action research depends on the cooperation of action implementing people and the beneficiaries of the action programme.

The Action Research Model developed and adopted by Akhilesh and Ganguly[19] in their study on Organizational Development through participation and communication programme (1980) provides a good illustration for action research. This model embodies six major steps:

(1) Diagnosis, (2) sharing of diagnostic information, (3) planning: developing change programme, (4) initiation of organizational change, (5) implementation of participation and communication process, and (6) post-experimental evaluation. This action research attempted to solve the actual problems in the work situation in a large public sector organisation at Bangalore through participation and communication programme. This research was mostly successful in bridging the perceived gap between the system practiced and the system desired and demonstrated the efficacy of the action research as an effective approach to organization development.

3.8 EXPERIMENTAL RESEARCH

Introduction

There are various phenomena such as motivation, productivity, development and operational efficiency, which are influenced by various variables. It may become necessary to assess the effect of one particular variable or one set of variables on a phenomenon. This need has given rise to experimental research.

Meaning

Experimental research is designed to assess the effects of particular variables on a phenomenon by keeping the other variables constant or controlled. It aims at determining *whether* and in *what manner* variables are related to each other. The factor, which is influenced, by other factors is called a *dependent variable*, and the other factors, which influence it, are known as *independent variables*. For example, agricultural productivity, i.e., crop yield per hectare is a dependent variable and the factors such as soil fertility, irrigation, quality of seed, manuring and cultural practices which influence the yield are independent variables.

The nature of relationship between independent variables and dependent variables is perceived and stated in the form of causal hypothesis. A closely controlled procedure is adopted to test them. The testing of the hypothesis is described in detail in Section 5.4 *Hypothesis* of Chapter 5, below.

Procedure

Two identical groups are selected. These should be 'identical' in terms of the Characteristics of the phenomenon under study. For example, in a farm productivity experiment, two plots of farmland with same soil composition, soil fertility, same size, same climate and same irrigation facility should be selected for the study.

One of the groups is used as *experimental* group, and the other as *control* group. Experimental group is exposed to an experimental variable or stimatulus. Control group is not exposed to the experimental variable. The difference between the experimental and control groups' outcome is attributed to the effect of the experimental variable.

---

19. Akhilesh K.B., and T. Ganguly, "Organization Development Through Participation & Communication Programme – A case study", *Indian Journal of Industrial Relations,* Vol. 17, No.4, 1982, pp. 549-561.

Illustration: An agricultural scientist desires to study the impact of application of a particular chemical fertilizer (say urea) on the yield of a crop.

He selects two identical plots of land in a farm. All conditions — soil fertility, climate, irrigation, seed, cultural practice — are the same. Thus, all variables are kept constant.

In the experimental plot alone, he applied chemical fertilizer. This is the only variation between the two plots. Hence the difference in yield is attributable to the application of the chemical fertilizer.

In some cases, a single group may be used as both control and experimental group. For example, a cooperative extension worker wants to know the effect of a member-education programme on the cooperative knowledge of the members of a cooperative. He selects a cross section of members of a society at random. He measures the type and extent of cooperative knowledge of the group. He then exposes them to a member-education programme. He again measures their knowledge. The difference in knowledge can be attributed to the programme.

Conditions

From an analysis of the above procedure, the conditions required for an experimental study may be identified. They are:

1. It should be possible for selecting exactly *identical* groups. This possibility exists in physical and natural sciences, but not so in social sciences, which deal with human life. It is difficult to find exactly identical groups of persons. We may get approximately similar groups only.
2. The target groups should be amenable for experimentation. This is ensured in physical sciences. But human beings may not always be willing to be subject to experimentation.
3. It should be possible to *identify* all the *independent variables* that affect the dependent variables under study. This again is ensured in physical sciences, but not in social phenomena, as our knowledge of human mind and behaviour is limited.
4. It should be possible to *keep non-experimental variables* constant so as to study the effect of experimental variables on the phenomenon. Such close controls over the subject variables are possible in laboratory experimentation. But they are almost impossible in human life situations, which are dynamic and complex. Thus, strictly controlled experimentation is rarely feasible with human beings.

Nevertheless, useful and fairly valid experimental research is possible in several areas of social sciences such as economic development, welfare programmes, social education, teaching technology, political administration, industrial and agricultural finance, management of enterprises and institutions and so on. It is possible to achieve reasonable degree of validity by adopting appropriate techniques as explained in Section 5.6: *Measurement* of Chapter 5, below.

Types of Experimental Designs

The major types of experimental designs are:

1. After-only design
2. One group Before-after design
3. Before-after design with control group.

1. After-only design: This is the simplest type of experimental design. The effect on a dependent variable (Y) is assessed by measuring it in both experimental (E) and control (C) groups after E has been exposed to an independent variable (X). In a fertilizer application experiment cited above the crop yield (Y) is measured in both E and C plots, after the experiment is over. The difference is attributed to the application of chemical fertilizer (X).

	Measurement after Experimentation
E	Ye
C	Yc

Difference = Ye − Yc

2. One group before-after design: In this design the same group is used as E and C, measuring Y before and after, the group has been exposed to X. Suppose a researcher wants to evaluate the effectiveness of a film in changing attitudes towards drinking and driving. He may employ this second type of design. The change in score on an attitude test given on the target group before and after seeing the film measures the film's effect.

	Before	*After*
Target Group	Y_1	Y_2

Difference = $Y_2 - Y_1$

3. Before-after design with control group: In this design, both the E and C groups are measured before and after E is exposed to X. This is a better design than the previous ones. This eliminates the impact of extraneous factors occurring during time period.

	Before	*After*
E	Ye_1	Ye_2
C	Yc_1	Yc_2

Difference in E = $Y_{e_2} - Ye_1 = D_e$

Difference in C = $Y_{c_2} - Y_{c_1} = D_c$

Net Difference $D_e - D_c$

Evaluation of Experimental Research

The use of experimental designs in social science research is complicated. It is difficult to establish comparable experimental and control groups. There are limits to experimentation among human beings. Experiment is often difficult to design; it is expensive and time consuming. It can be used to study the present only, and cannot be used for studies of the past or the future.

Nevertheless, experimentation has certain unique *advantages*. No other method can equal experimentation in objectivity and in studying causal relationships between variables. The effect of extraneous variables can be controlled more effectively in experimental design than in other designs. Above all, an experimental design offers a means for testing social values.

Quasi-Experimental Designs

The relationships studied by scientists, according to Rosenberg[20], may be classified into following kinds:

1. Stimulus-response relationship: It is characterized by an independent specific external variable with a dependent variable being a particular response to it, e.g., relationships between reward and satisfaction; between advertisement and consumption patterns.*

2. One- shot case study: This involves an observation of a single group at one point in time, usually subsequent to an event supposed to have produced change, e.g., a study of a rural community after a rural development programme; study of a political system after a general election.

This is a study of only what exists at the time of study; therefore, it has no control over extrinsic and intrinsic factors. Besides, it does not allow for manipulation of the independent variable or for before-after or control-experimental group comparison. Further, a case study analyses a single unsampled system, it is weak on generalization as well. It has also no checks on internal validity and thus is of little use in testing causal relations. However, this study is useful in exploratory research.

3. Cross-section study (or correlation design): This is the most predominant design employed in survey research. It is an attempt to approximate the after-only control group design by using cross tabulations and statistical techniques like correlation and multi-variate analysis.(see Chapter 11, *Statistical Analysis*, below)

A sample of individuals is drawn and data relating to their background characteristics and dependent variables under study are collected from them. For example, to test a hypothesis: "the birth rates vary inversely with socio-economic status." Data may be collected from a sample of families belonging to various socio-economic levels; the relations between variables may be studied by using correlation technique. The important limitation of this analysis is that the time order of direction of causation cannot be easily determined.

4. Ex-post-facto-design: This is a variation of the correlational design. It provides a partial solution to the time order problem. This is *retrospective* or *after-the-event* study. It looks from the past to the present.

It requires information about the past by asking retrospective questions regarding an earlier period. For example, an investigator desiring to assess the effect of a family planning publicity programme on the attitude of women could ask them about their present views as well as about their views before their exposure to the publicity programme. The drawback of this approach is the bias arising out of respondent's memory distortions. A partial solution is to introduce checks for detecting gross inaccuracies in the memory of respondents.

---

20. Rosengberg, Morris, *The Logic of Survey Analysis,* New York: Basic Books, 1968.

* For a more detailed discussion of experimental research, see (1) Donald T. Campbell and Julian C. Stanely, *Experimental and Quasi-Experimental Designs for Research*, Chicago: Rand McNally & Co., 1963; (2) E. Aronson and J.M. Carlsmith, "Experimentation is Social Psychology", in G. Lindzey and E. Aronson (eds.) *The Handbook of Social Psychology*, Reading, Mass: Addison Wesley Publishing Co., 1968, (3) F. Stuart Chapin, *Experimental Design in Social Research*, New York: Harper & Row Publishers, 1955.

3.9 ANALYTICAL STUDY OR STATISTICAL METHOD

Meaning

Analytical study is a system of procedures and techniques of analysis applied to quantitative data. It may consist of a system of mathematical models or statistical techniques applicable to numerical data. Hence, it is also known as the *Statistical Method.* (For detailed discussion see chapter 11: *Statistical Analysis*).

Aim

This study aims at testing hypothesis and specifying and interpreting relationships. It concentrates on analyzing data in depth and examining relationships from various angles by bringing in as many relevant variables as possible in the analysis plan.

Uses

This method is extensively used in business and other fields in which quantitative numerical data are generated. It is used for measuring variables, comparing groups and examining association between factors.

Data may be collected from either primary sources or secondary sources.

There is vast scope for making analytical studies by using data published by various Departments of Government and institutions like the Reserve Bank of India, Bureau of Public Enterprise, NABARD, and Central Statistical Organization.

Analytical Study Vs. Experimental Research

One way to distinguish Analytical studies from experimental research is that the former rely heavily on the post-facto-analysis of data generally collected in a natural or real-life setting or from records. Unlike descriptive studies, analytical studies are characterized by rigorous requirements of measurement and analysis, and design approximated to the model of an experimental design.

3.10 HISTORICAL RESEARCH

Meaning

Historical study is a study of past records and other information sources with a view to reconstructing the origin and development of an institution or a movement or a system and discovering the trends in the past.

It is descriptive in nature. It is a difficult task; it must often depend upon inference and logical analysis of recorded data and indirect evidences rather than upon direct observation. Hence, it is aptly described as "the induction of principles through research into the past and social forces which have shaped the present."

Objective

Its objective is to draw explanations and generalizations from the past trends in order to understand the present and to anticipate the future. It enables us to grasp our relationship with the past and to plan more intelligently for the future. The past contains the key to the present and the past and the present influences the future. Historical study helps us in visualizing the society as a dynamic organism and its structures and functions as evolving, steadily growing and undergoing change and transformation.

Sources of Data

The sources of data for historical research consists of (1) eyewitness accounts narrated by an actual observer or participant in an event, (2) oral testimony by elders, (3) records and other documentary materials and (4) relics. The data available from the above sources may be scattered and discontinuous and fragmented. Personal accounts are mostly subjective and so should be studied with great caution and corroborated with documentary evidences. The origin and genuineness of the sources and the validity of facts contained in them should be critically tested and examined. Their authenticity should be tested. Only authentic sources should be depended upon for collection of data. It is essential to check and cross-check the data from as many sources as possible.

Steps in Historical Method

First, the *feasibility* of the study should be examined. The researcher should see whether the selected problem lends itself to historical analysis. It should be one of tracing and describing the past or relating to the recent past to draw out its significance for the present and the future. It should also be feasible in terms of his research ability, time and cost.

Second, the selected problem should be *formulated* and the *plan* of *study* should be designed.

Third, the *sources of data* should be located.

Fourth, the *genuineness* of the sources and the *validity* of the *facts* contained in them should be tested.

Fifth, relevant *facts* should be *collected* from the authentic sources and they should be checked and cross-checked.

Sixth, the facts should be *arranged* into a logical sequence and this synthesis of facts is the basis for rebuilding of the past situation.

Last, by adopting *induction* process meaningful *interpretations* and generalizations should be made.

The quality of a historical study depends on the relevance, adequacy and completeness of facts collected, their reliability, and the ingenuity of the researcher in classifying and integrating them and in drawing inferences.

Limitations and Difficulties

As the historical study is concerned with the past, reliable and adequate data *may not be available*. The remoter is the past, the greater is the difficulty in obtaining relevant facts.

It is also *difficult* to test the *genuineness* and authenticity of sources and the data available from them. Personal biases and private interpretations often enter unconsciously.

It is *difficult* to *establish* the time order of events.

The records available are not kept in the order and with the precision that a researcher expects. Hence, his *inferences may not be* full or *accurate*.

The *dispersal* of documents is another limitation. The researcher may not succeed in locating all documents.

It is *difficult* to *perceive* the real *significance* of the data because of their remote time period.

Further, in historical research, *precise measurements,* verifications and replication are *not possible*.

Nevertheless, a thorough and systematic historical study is of immense use in understanding the past and drawing inferences for the present and future.

3.11 SURVEYS

Meaning

Survey is a 'fact finding' study. It is a method of research involving collection of data directly from a population or a sample thereof at particular time. It must not be confused with the mere clerical routine of gathering and tabulating figures. It requires expert and imaginative planning, careful analysis and rational interpretation of the findings.

Data may be collected by observation, or interviewing or mailing questionnaires.

The analysis of data may be made by using simple or complex statistical techniques depending upon the objectives of the study.

The Characteristics of Survey Method

The survey method has certain characteristics:

1. It is always conducted in a *natural setting*: it is a field study.
2. It seeks *responses directly* from the respondents.
3. It can cover a very *large population*, thanks to sampling techniques.
4. A survey may involve an *extensive* study or an *intensive* study. An extensive study covers a wider sample. An intensive one covers a few samples and tends to 'dig deeper'. These two approaches serve different ends; where generalization or estimation is necessary, the extensive approach is useful, but where one wants to make an indepth study of some aspects of a subject-matter, the intensive approach is preferable.
5. A survey covers a definite *geographical* area: a city, or a district, or a state.

The quality of a survey depends upon the thoroughness of the planning, the soundness of sampling, the adequacy and reliability of data, the quality of analysis and the interpretation of the findings.

Steps Involved in a Survey

The sequence of the tasks involved in carrying out a survey from the first of planning to the final stage of preparing the report is presented below:

1. Selection of a problem and its formulation,
2. Preparation of the research design,
3. Operationalisation of concepts and construction of measuring indexes and scales,
4. Sampling,
5. Construction of tools for collection of data and their pre-test,
6. Field work and collection of data,
7. Processing of data and tabulation,

8. Analysis of data, and
9. Reporting.

All these steps are discussed in detail in the relevant chapters.

The Purposes of Surveys

Survey serves several purposes:

1. The purpose of many surveys such as population census, socio-economic surveys, expenditure surveys, marketing surveys etc., is simple to *provide information* to government or planners or business enterprises. These surveys have a *descriptive* purpose. In short, all fact-finding surveys have this purpose.
2. Many enquiries aim to *explain* certain phenomena. Their function is to test hypotheses, to explain the causal relationships between variables and to assess the influences or various factors on a given phenomenon like job-satisfaction, labour productivity and consumer behaviour. Surveys aiming at explanation involve indepth analysis and complex interpretations.
3. Surveys may be designed to make *comparisons* of demographic groups (e.g., comparison of low income groups with high income groups) or real groups, e.g., work groups in factories or offices. Comparison of behavioural or attitudinal groups can also be made. For example, in a factory, the attitudes of high-production workers toward the company may be compared with the attitudes of low-production workers.
4. Surveys concerned with *cause and effect relationships* can be useful for making *predictions*. For example, if relationships between income increases and purchase of durable goods are established in a consumer behaviour survey, a prediction about future demand for durable goods with reference to anticipated income increases can be made. A survey of people's future plans and intentions is another approach to make predictions. This is one of the methods adopted for demand forecasts.

The Subject-matter of Surveys

All aspects of human behaviour, social institutions, economic system, and business undertakings lend themselves to surveys. The subject matter of surveys may be broadly categorized into:

A: Social Surveys

1. Demographic characteristics of a group of people
2. Social environment of people
3. People's opinions and attitudes
4. People's behaviour and activities.

B: Economic Surveys

1. Economic conditions of people
2. Working of economic units
3. Operations of an economic system.

Demographic characteristics include family composition, marital status, fertility age and so on. Population census is primarily on the demographic aspects of people. All social surveys include some demographic aspects.

Social environment covers all social factors, housing conditions and social amenities and social institutions.

Surveys of opinions and attitudes deal with various issues (e.g., direct Vs. indirect election of the head of government), systems (e.g., democracy) and schemes and programmes (e.g., family planning).

People's activities refer to 'what people do', e.g., use of leisure time, newspaper reading, and recreation etc. people's behaviour is concerned with their consumption pattern, life-style, organizational behaviour, group dynamics etc.

Economic conditions include occupation, income, saving, investment, assets, etc.,

Economic units refer to shops, business firms, financial institutions, etc. Economic system may refer to capitalism, cooperative system, socialism and mixed economy.

Fields of Application

From the above discussion of the subject-matter of surveys, it is apparent that the survey method is applicable to various fields and disciplines such as sociology, economics, behavioural sciences, political science, public health, commerce and management. Surveys may be considered to be belonging to a particular discipline like sociology or economics or political science. Surveys of group belonging, leader-follower relations, of family life etc., belong to sociology; studies of income, expenditure, and savings may be classified as economic surveys; studies of voting, of participation in political movements and of political attitudes of people belong to political science. And so on.

Such classification, however, are somewhat arbitrary. All surveys are essentially *interdisciplinary* and contribute to the integration of separate disciplines. For example, economic or political surveys have something to do with people's sociological or psychological aspects.

Survey research has no specific disciplinary anchor point. Specialists in all fields of social and behavioural sciences use it. It broadens the empirical base of various fields. It also provides data for interdisciplinary analysis.

Surveys can be used as a *tool* for *both* basic and *applied research*. They are extensively used by planning bodies and by policy-makers in government both for formulating plans and programmes and for evaluating them. The survey method is also widely used by business enterprises in their research on markets, consumer preferences and buying habits, environment, training needs, effectiveness of advertisement and the like.

Above all, the survey method makes a very significant contribution to the growth of knowledge in social sciences.

Many outstanding researches in social sciences would have been impossible without the modern survey method.

Coverage of Surveys: Census Vs. Sample

A survey may cover all the units of a given universe. Then it is called a census survey. If the survey covers a fraction of the universe, then it is called *sample survey*. ((See chapter 6: *Sampling*).

A survey may cover a small, highly selected universe as well as a broad segment of the population depending on the nature of the problems studied. For example, such specialized studies as a study of political leadership, a study of managerial style of top business executives, a study of factors affecting industrial location etc., cover only a specific selected small universe. On the other hand, general surveys like poverty studies, survey of expenditure pattern, consumer behaviour studies, credit surveys, etc., cover broad segments of population and are usually designed as sample surveys. The development of large-scale sampling methods has made fact-collecting along methodologically sound lines much easier.

Advantages/Merits of Survey Research

The major advantages of a survey method are:

1. The *versatility* of the survey method is its greatest strength. It is the *only practical* way to collect *many types* of information from individuals, such as personal characteristics, socio-economic data, attitudes, opinions, experiences and expectations.
2. The survey method facilitates drawing *generalizations* about large populations on the basis of studies of representative sample.
3. The survey method is flexible to permit the use of *various methods* of *collection of data*: observation interviewing and mailing.
4. Surveys *sensitize* the researcher to *unanticipated* or unknown problems. The collection of data from respondents through interviewing or mailing often uncovers facts previously unknown to the researcher.
5. Surveys are useful instruments for *verifying theories*.

Limitations

Although survey method is a research instrument of great versatility and extensive application, it has certain limitations:

1. Survey method is primarily meant for collection of data from primary sources: individuals, households and institutions; hence its *feasibility* depends upon the *willingness* and *cooperation* of the respondents.
2. A sample survey is subject to *sampling error*. (See Section 6.5 of Chapter 6). Its findings must be interpreted in the light of this error.
3. The survey method depends primarily on verbal behaviour. The respondent can give untrue or misleading answers. Hence, a survey is subject to response errors. (See Sections 7.8 and 7.10 of Chapter 7).
4. A survey is also subject to the *errors of measurement* implicit in quantifying attitudes, abilities, behaviour and other personal traits. (See Section 6.5 of Chapter 6).
5. There is a limit of the *number of items* of *information* that can be collected in a single survey. There is an optimal length of time for an interview. Beyond that point, interview weariness sets in. Hence the extent of data requirement should be delimited to the tolerance level of respondents.

6. A sample survey designed to represent a population over a wider geographical area may *not give adequate representation* to any population characteristic, which is highly localized. This means that the influences of specific local social groups cannot be assessed through a national survey.
7. The survey method alone is *inadequate* to analyse adequately the *complex* fabric of social organisation. It is also not well *suited* to studies of *historical development.*
8. Survey is very *expensive* in terms of time and cost. Hence, an individual cannot afford to carry out an extensive survey out of his resources.

3.12 CASE STUDY

Meaning

A case study is an *in-depth* comprehensive study of a person, a social group, an episode, a process, a situation, a programme, a community , an institution or any other social unit.

It is one of the most popular types of research methods. Its purpose may be to understand the *life cycle* of the unit under study or the *interaction* between factors that explain the present status or the development over a period of time. Some examples of a case study are: a social-anthropological study of a rural or tribal community; a causative study of a successful cooperative society; a study of the financial health of a business undertaking; a study of labour participation in management in a particular enterprise; a study of juvenile delinquency; a study of life-style of working women; a study of slum dwellers; a study of urban poor; a study of economic offenses; a study of refugees from another country.

Functions

The case study method describes a case in terms of its *peculiarities.* It gives us an insight into the *typical* or *extreme cases* whose unique features are not reflected by the usual statistical method.

A case study helps to secure a wealth of information about the unit of study, which may provide clues and ideas for further research. It provides an opportunity for the *intensive analysis* of many specific details that are overlooked in other methods.

It examines *complex* factors involved in a given situation so as to identify *causal* factors operating in it.

A case study aims at studying *everything* about something rather than something about everything as in the case of a statistical method.

While in a statistical approach the 'individual' disappears from the analysis, in a case study the '*individual*' representing the 'wholeness' is *preserved*, as it is an approach which views any social unit as a whole. Thus, a case study gives us a *total view* of a unit or a *clear insight* into a situation or process in its total setting. Thus, the perspective of a case study is both qualitative and organic. It gives an overall generic picture of a problem.

The case study, as a research method, often employs more techniques than one. Thus, for tracing a developmental process, it uses historical method, it employs descriptive method where a factual picture is needed, it employs interviewing, mail questionnaire, check lists, rating scales, etc., to gather data, it looks to statistics for testing hypotheses.

The aim of a case study is to ascertain the *generic* development of a social unit under study, revealing the factors that moulded its life within its cultural setting. Because of its aid in studying behaviour in specific, precise detail, Burgess termed the case study method as "*the social microscope.*"[21]

It is most *valuable* for diagnostic, administrative and therapeutic purposes.

It develops ideas, sometimes *leading to conclusion* and sometimes to *hypotheses* to be tested. It may also be useful for developing new concepts or testing existing concepts.

Case Study Vs. Survey

Case study may be conducted as an independent study or a supplementary investigation to a survey. The primary distinctions between a case study and a survey lie in the intensity and *depth* of investigation and its *coverage.*

1. While a survey is a *broad based* investigation of a phenomenon, a case study is an *intensive* investigation.
2. A survey covers a *large* number of units — all units of a universe or a sample of them; but a case study is a study of a single unit/group.
3. The findings of a study can be generalized when it is based on a representative sample; whereas the findings of a case study *cannot be generalized.*
4. While a survey is useful for *testing hypotheses* about large social *aggregates*, a case study is useful for testing hypotheses about the *structural* and *procedural* characteristics (e.g., status relation, interpersonal behaviour, managerial style) of a specific social unit (e.g., an organisation, a small group or a community).

Disadvantages/Limitations

The major disadvantages/limitation of case study are:

1. The most prominent disadvantage of case studies is their *limited generalizability*. As case studies of stray cases, they are not sufficient for making meaningful generalizations to larger social aggregates.
2. Case studies are generally more *time-consuming* than surveys.
3. Case study method is *inadequate* for an analysis of macro-problems.
4. The *danger* of investigator's *over-confidence* is more in a case study. This leads to various biases such as errors of perception, judgement and over-emphasis of unusual events, unwarranted extrapolation, and *ad hoc* theorizing and sweeping generalizations.

Merits

The merits of a case study method far exceeds its limitations.

1. Case studies are flexible with respect to data collection methods. All methods of data collection are useful to case studies.
2. A case study can extend virtually to *any dimension* of the topic studied. All aspects may be studied or specific aspects may be emphasized.

---

21. "Research Methods in Sociology", in Georges Gurvitch and W.S. Moore, (eds.), *Twentieth Century Sociology*, The Philosophical Library, 1949, pp. 25-26.

3. Case studies may be conducted in practically *any kind* of social setting.
4. Case studies offer *specific instances* of tests of theories.
5. Case study is a highly fruitful approach for the purpose of group or process analysis as against the analysis of individual traits alone.
6. Case studies give to the researcher a *wider range of insights* into human life, which cannot be gained through a general survey.

3.13 FIELD STUDIES

Meaning

Field studies are scientific enquiries aimed at discovering the *relations and interactions* among sociological, psychological and educational variables in social institutions and actual life situations like communities, schools, factories, organizations and institutions. A social or institutional situation is selected and the relations among the attitudes, values, perceptions and behaviours of individuals and groups in the selected situation are studied. Some examples of field studies are: Dollard's study of *caste and class in a southern town,*[22] Malinowski's *investigations of the Trobriand Islanders*[23]; Lynd's study of *Middletown*[24], Jone's study of *the socio-economic basis of class in Aknon, Ohio*[25]; Mann-Kanitkau's study of *land and labour in a Deccan village*[26]; Aiyyappan's study of *social revolution in a Kerala village.*[27]

Field Study Vs. Surveys

Although it is not easy to draw a fine logical distinction between survey and field study, there are *practical differences* between them. First, a survey attempts to be *representative* of the universe under study and thus calls for an *adequate and representative sample.* This emphasis on sampling may or may not be found in a field study, because it is more concerned with a *thorough account* of the processes under study than with their typicality in a large universe.

Second, while a field study aims at *directly studying* the interrelations of the parts of social structure of a single community or a single group, a survey aims at covering a larger universe, and it may indirectly deal with social and psychological processes, through inference from the statistical analysis rather than through direct observation, thus, field study will provide a more detailed *natural picture* of social interrelations of the group than does a survey.

Types of Field Studies

Katz[28] has classified field studies into (1) anthropological studies and (2) quantitative field studies. In an *anthropological study*, the researcher lives in the selected community, observes its people, talks with them at great length, and thus gains a thorough insight into the social structure of

22. Dollard, J., *Caste and Class in a Southern Town,* New Haven: Yale University Press, 1937.
23. Malinowski, B., *Crime and Custom in Savage Society,* New York: Harcourt, 1926.
24. Lynd, R.S. and H.M. Lynd, *Middletown*, New York: Harcourt, 1929.
25. Jones, A. W., *Life, Liberty and Property,* New York: Lippincott, 1941.
26. Mann, H.H., and N.V. Kanitkau, *Land and Labour in a Deccan Village,* New Delhi: Oxford University Press.
27. Aiyyappan, A., *Social Revolution in a Kerala Village* — A Study in Cultural Change, Madras: Asia Publishing House, 1965.
28. Katz, Daniel, "Field Studies" in Seon Festinger and Daniel Katz, *Research Methods in the Behavioural Sciences,* New York: Holt, Rinehart and Winston, 1966, pp. 56-97.

the community and the people's life, culture and ideologies. But the *anthropological approach* does not aim at precise measurement of specific variables and relations.

On the other hand, a *social-psychological field study* employs quantitative approach and measures variables and their interrelationships. Newcomb's research on *Bennington College, a self-contained college community*[29] is an example for this type of study. The conclusions of a quantitative study can be readily confirmed by other investigators.

The conflict between the two approached can be resolved by utilizing anthropological approach as the initial stage in a field study. In this stage, the situation as a whole can be studied and the fundamental relationship s grasped. These insights can yield hypotheses which can be tested by a detailed quantitative study. In the Festinger-Schachter-Back[30] study of a processing community this procedure was employed. In the combined approach, the initial anthropological study serves as an exploratory stage and the subsequent quantitative study tests hypotheses derived from the exploratory stage.

Steps in Field Study

Katz suggests a general model consisting of the following phases[31] in the conduct of a field study: (1) preliminary planning, (2) the scouting expedition or the anthropological study, (3) the formulation of the research design, (4) the pretesting of research instruments and procedures, (5) the full-scale field operations, and (6) the analysis of materials.

Preliminary planning: It is better to start a field study with a tentative plan covering the scope of the study, its broad objectives and time schedule. The plan will be finalized after the results of the scouting expedition are available.

The Scouting expedition: This phase of study involves an *informal* and *free investigation* in which the field workers try to get a thorough understanding of the important forces in the situation. The objective of this exploratory work is to identify the significant variables in the situation and group behaviour. Informal procedures can be adopted for gathering information. They may include: consulting informal leaders; contacting informants like newspaper reporters, local teachers etc., using discrepancies in the accounts of informants as a basis for further exploration; living in the community and participating in its activities; observing specific situations; studying available records and secondary sources. Field workers should keep daily full records of their work and observations.

Formulation of the research design: On the basis of the results of the scouting exploration, the design of the final study can be formulated. It is important to delimit the scope of the study and to introduce controls into the data-collection process through standardization of tools and measurements.

Pretesting of instruments and procedures: The interview schedules and behavioural scales and other types of data forms required for the study should be constructed and pre-tested.

Field operation: The full-scale field operation consists of several activities as explained in Chapter 9: *Field Work,* below. The tasks for the field workers are more varied and often more difficult than for the interviewers in a survey. The field worker must be able to enlist the cooperation of all groups in the community and also be capable of interviewing the leaders.

---

29. Newcomb, T.M., *Personality and Social Change,* New York: Dryden Press, 1943.
30. Festinger, L., S. Schachter and K. Back, *Social Pressures in Informal Groups,* New York: Harper, 1950.
31. Katz, Daniel, *Field Studies, op. cit.,* p. 65.

Analysis of materials: Data from observations and interview responses in a field study lend themselves to correlation analysis. Correlation coefficients show the nature of relationships between variables. By holding factors constant, the relationships are studied.

Advantages

There are certain natural advantages of field studies. First, a field study tends to continue over a period of time, and so it is possible to *maintain continued observation*, ascertaining the *timing* of certain variables.

Second, a field study provides opportunity for *direct observation of interaction* and of *social relationships* in their *natural occurrence*. In a survey, we can only make inferences about these factors, but cannot directly observe them.

A third advantage of a field study is the possibility of *going beyond measures* obtained from a single instrument. The correlations from a single measuring instrument may be influenced by some *halo* in its application. A field study permits the obtaining of reciprocal perceptions and interdependent reactions from different groups of people whose behaviour is interrelated to make up a social structure. Agreement in perceptions on the part of people standing at various points in the hierarchy gives greater confidence in the validity of the reporting. For example, when workers, foremen and supervisors in a department of a factory all agree about whether the foreman or supervisor has the greater power in that department, we are on a much safer ground than if we had only the foremen or the supervisors reporting on the situation.

Last, a field study facilitates *use of different independent measures:* interviews with different types of people, behavioural observations and study of available records. The relationships discovered through different methods are more convincing than if they are derived from a single method.

Thus, field studies are strong in *realism*, significance, strength of variables and reliability of findings.

Limitations

Despite these strengths, a field study has serious limitations. Its most serious weakness is its *ex post facto* character. Thus, statements of relations are weaker than they are in experimental research. The field situation always has a plethora of variables. It is difficult to *keep extraneous variables constant.*

Another methodological weakness is *lack of precision* in the measurement of field variables due to the greater complexity of field situations.

There are also potential weaknesses such as problems of feasibility, cost, sampling and time.

Usefulness

In building a science of social psychology, field studies have unique roles to play. They "can give depth of understanding to survey findings" and "rich insights and hypotheses" to the experimenter. There should be a two-way interaction between experimentation and field study. The findings of field studies may yield hypotheses, which require more rigorous experimentation. Conversely, the experimental results may require field tests for establishing their reality and external validity.

3.14 STEPS IN RESEARCH

Introduction

The task of research is a sequential process involving a number of clearly delineated steps. There are some variations in the number of steps, their names and their sequence suggested by different writers, but there is much similarity among their suggestions. No one however, claims that the research process is truly linear, moving from one step after another in an order. Some steps may be taken in a different order; some steps may have to be retraced; some may be carried on simultaneously; some may be omitted; in some projects some steps can be covered quickly, while in another cases, they may require longer time. In spite of these variations it is desirable to outline the steps involved in the task of planning and executing a project, and also the order in which they have to be taken.

Steps in Research

According to Emory, the research sequence consists of four major stages:[32]

1. Exploration of the situation: If the problem is in an area in which the investigator has previously conducted research, he may move quickly to the development of the research proposal including time and budget estimates. However, if the problem posed is an unfamiliar one, he may adopt two-stage approach; first to propose a separate exploratory study, second, to move to development of the main study after the exploratory study is over. The feasibility, the availability of data, etc. will be explored at this stage.

2. Development of the research design: At this stage, the formal research plan is developed. (For details, see Section 5.7: *Research Designs* in Chapter 5).

3. Data collection: Data are collected by adopting appropriate methods of data collection.

4. Analysis and interpretation of the results: After the fieldwork is over, the data are processed, tabulated and analysed. Then the findings are interpreted. Finally, a report is written for communicating the findings.

Pauline V. Young classifies the phases of research process into: (1) Precise formulation of the selected problem, (2) formulation of working or exploratory hypothesis, (3) observation and exploration of the problem, (4) uniform recording of the data obtained, (5) classification of the data into series, and (6) scientific generalizing.[33]

These steps are not mutually exclusive; neither are they separate and distinct. They do not necessarily follow each other in any special order. Some of them may re-enter after preliminary use of them.[34] For example, some preliminary observation is inevitable before an adequate working hypothesis can be formulated. After its formulation, systematic observation is indispensable.

Nachmias [35] identify *seven* stages in the research process: problem, hypotheses, research design, measurement, data collection, data analysis and empirical generalizations.

---

32. Emory, C. William, *Business Research Methods, op. cit.*, p. 66.
33. Young, Pauline V., *Scientific Social Surveys and Research, op. cit.*, p. 102.
34. *Ibid.*, p. 102.
35. Nachmias David, and Chava Nachmias, *Research Methods in the Social Science*, New York: St. Martin's Press, 1976, p. 10.

According to Vimal Shah, a research process involves the following major activities:[36]

1. Identification and selection of the research problem,
2. Choice of a theoretical framework for the research problem,
3. Formulation of the research problem,
4. Design of the experiment or inquiry,
5. Definition and measurement of variables,
6. Sampling procedures,
7. Tools and techniques for gathering data,
8. Coding, editing and processing of data,
9. Analysis of the data, and
10. Reporting research.

The first three activities may be considered as the planning stage of a research.

Clover and Balsley[37] present the following eleven-step outline:

1. Become aware of the problem
2. Define the problem and purpose of the research
3. Set forth hypotheses
4. Determine what information will be required
5. Decide which methods to use in collecting information
6. Collect information or evidence
7. Compile findings in a systematic form
8. Analyse findings to test hypotheses
9. Write a final research report
10. Make specific recommendation for actions
11. Conduct a follow-up, if necessary.

Roy G. Francis[38] of the university of Minnesota lists twelve steps in scientific research:

— Selection of problem area
— Acquaintance with current theory and knowledge in the area
— Definition of the problem
— Development of hypotheses
— Development of the formal argument

---

36. Shah, Vimal, *Research Designs and Strategies,* New York: The Agricultural Development Council, 1972, pp. 3-4.
37. Clover, Vernon T., and Howard L. Balsley, *Business Research Methods, op. cit.*, p. 22.
38. Francis, "Nature of Scientific Research", in John T. Doby (Ed.), *An Introduction to Social Research,* Harrisburg, The Stackploe Co., 1954, pp. 12-16.

— Delineation of the sources of data
— Creation of instruments
— Writing a 'dummy argument'
— Pretest of the instruments and possible revision
— Formal acquisition of data
— Analysis of the data
— Formal write-up of conclusion reached.

A General Model

In general, a research process consists of the following steps:

1. Identification and selection of a research problem.
2. Review of literature: Preliminary review prior to problem selection; Systematic review after selection; notes taking.
3. Formulation of the selected problem: definition of the problem, conceptual mode, delimitation of the study, formulation of the objectives of the study and the hypotheses/investigating questions.
4. Operationalisation of concepts: definition of concepts, construction of indexes/scales for measuring variables.
5. Preparation of the research plan: statement of the problem, objectives of the study, hypotheses, operational definition of the concepts, Geographical area of the study, methodology (type of research and methods of collection of data), sampling design, tools for collection of data, plan of analysis, over-view of the research report, time-schedule.
6. Construction of tools of data collection: identification of data needs, delineation of data sources, drafting observation schedule, interview schedule/guide, mailed questionnaire and/or check lists or experimental design, pre-testing and possible revision.
7. Collection of data: Experimental/field work: preparing sample frame, drawing sample of respondents; Interviewing them/mailing questionnaires to them and follow-up.
8. Processing of data: editing, coding, transcription, tabulation, construction of tables and charts.
9. Analysis of data: statistical treatment, testing hypotheses, interpretation of findings.
10. Report-writing: planning report-writing work, drafting the report and its finalisation.

The above steps or activities may be regrouped into the following three stages:

1. Planning

Selection of the problem

Formulation of the selected problem

Operationalisation of concepts

Preparation of the research design

Planning report-writing work.

2. Operation

Construction of tools of data collection

Pre-testing tools and their revision

Collection of data

Processing of data

Analysis of data and interpretation of results

3. Reporting

Drafting the report: Description of the research process; summary of findings; Suggestion for action and for further research.

Finalisation of the report.

Forwarding the report copies to the target audience/clients/users.

All the above steps involved in a research process do not constitute a time order linear sequence. There can be overlappings and recyclings depending on the nature of the study. Nevertheless one should not fail to complete the sequence of steps required in scientific procedure.

SUGGESTED READINGS

1. Festinger, Leon and Katz., Daniel, *Research Methods in the Behavioural Sciences*, New York: Holt, Rinehart and Winston, 1953.
2. Fox, David J., *The Research Process in Education*, New York: Holt, Rinehart and Winston, 1969. (Chapter 1 and 2).
3. Green, Paul, and Tull, Donald, *Research for Marketing Decisions*, Englewood, N.J., Prentice-Hall, 1970 (Chapter 1 and 2).
4. Helmastader, G.C., *Research Concepts in Human Behaviour*, New York: Appleton-Century-Crofts, 1970 (Chapter 2-4).
5. Kerlinger, Fred N., *Foundations of Behavioural Research*, Delhi: Surjeet Publications, 1983 (Part 6 and 7).
6. Selltiz, Claire *et al.*, *Research Methods in Social Relations*, New York: Holt, Rinehart and Winston, 1959. (Chapter 1 to 4).

QUESTIONS

1. Make an attempt to classify research.
2. "Any typology of research studies is inevitably arbitrary." Discuss.
3. Are different types of research sharply distinguishable? Discuss.
4. Distinguish between
   (a) Pure research and applied research
   (b) Exploratory and Diagnostic studies
   (c) Descriptive study and analytical study
   (d) Survey and case study
   (e) Action research and experimental research
   (f) Descriptive and diagnostic studies.

5. Is the distinction between pure and applied research absolute? Discuss.
6. "The terms 'pure' and 'applied' research just represent the polar ends of a continuum." — Comment.
7. Examine the interplay between pure and applied research.
8. State the meaning and need for exploratory study.
9. Explain the steps in the exploratory study.
10. Describe the meaning, nature and usefulness of descriptive studies.
11. What is a diagnostic study? How does it differ from a descriptive study?
12. State the meaning and purpose of evaluation studies.
13. Examine the criteria of evaluation research.
14. what is action research? How is it related to evaluation research?
15. Classify action research and briefly describe each type of action research.
16. What are the phases in an action research? Illustrate with an actual action research.
17. Define 'experimental research, and discuss its features.
18. What are the conditions required for an experimental study?
19. Explain the major types of experimental designs.
20. What are quasi-experimental designs? When they are relevant?
21. What are (a) one-shot case studies and (b) cross-sectional studies?
22. What is ex-post facto-design? How is it an improvement over correlational designs?
23. What is analytical study? How does it differ from an experimental study?
24. What is a historical study? What are its features?
25. What are the steps involved in historical method?
26. Examine the limitations and difficulties of historical method of research?
27. Define survey and explain its characteristics.
28. What are the purposes of survey?
29. Examine the application of survey method in different fields.
30. Evaluate survey method of research.
31. What is a case study? What are its features?
32. Evaluate case study method.
33. What is a field study? How does it differ from a survey?
34. Explain the types of field studies.
35. What are the steps involved in a field study?
36. What are the uses of field studies?
37. Evaluate field studies.
38. What are the steps involved in research process?
39. Is the research process truly linear?

❑ ❑ ❑

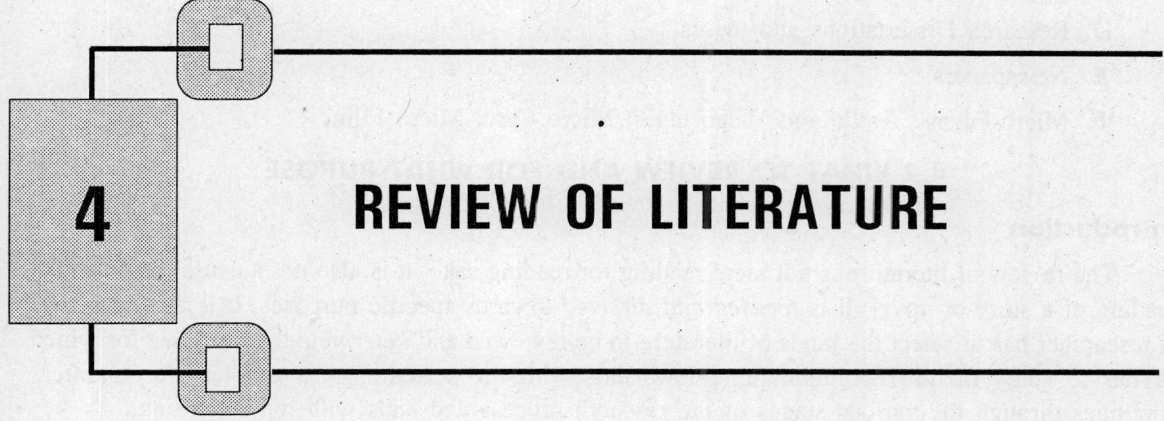

4 REVIEW OF LITERATURE

4.1 NEED FOR REVIEWING LITERATURE

Introduction

Knowledge is growing rapidly. It gets doubled in a very short span of time. Scholars, researchers and writers go on adding knowledge through their studies and writings. There is a tremendous increase in the number of publications: books and periodicals in developed and developing countries. India alone produces annually about 20,000 books.

One who is not fully conversant with what has gone before has little chance of making a worthwhile contribution. Therefore a researcher has to *survey* the available literature relating to his field of study. He must keep himself *update* in his field and related areas.

Literature

Literature in this consists of —

A. Books:

1. Encyclopedias.

   —General, e.g., Encyclopedia Britannica.

   —Specific, e.g., Encyclopedia of Social Sciences.

2. Year Books e.g., Published as supplements to Encyclopedias.
3. Textbooks.
4. Reference Books.

B. Journals: Published Monthly, Quarterly, Half yearly or Annually.

C. Reports:

1. Reports of Committees/Commissions appointed by Governments and Public institutions.
2. Seminar Reports and Conference Proceedings.

D. Research Dissertations and theses.

E. Newspapers.

F. Micro Forms: Audio and Video tapes; Micro Card; Micro Film.

4.2 WHAT TO REVIEW AND FOR WHAT PUPOSE

Introduction

The review of literature is not mere reading for reading sake; it is also not a causal reading like reading of a story or novel. It is *focused and directed* towards specific purposes. It is also *selective.* A researcher has to select the kinds of literature to be reviewed and *determine* the *purposes* for which he has to study them. The literature review starts with the selection of a problem for research, continues through the various stages of the research process and ends with report writing.

The Purposes of Review

The reasons for review of related literature are:

(1) to gain a background knowledge of the research topic,

(2) to identify the concepts relating to it, potential relationships between them and to formulate researchable hypotheses,

(3) to identify appropriate methodology, research design, methods, of measuring concepts and techniques of analysis,

(4) to identify data sources used by other researchers, and

(5) to learn how others structured their reports.

The kinds of literature to be reviewed at the various stages of the research processes and the specific purposes of the review are indicated below:

	Steps in the Research Process		*Kinds of Literatures to be Reviewed*		*Purposes of Review*
1.	Identification and selection of problem.	1.1	Source materials, encyclopedia, Textbooks, Reference books.	1.1	To gain preliminary orientation and background knowledge.
		1.2	Latest publications on the discipline.	1.2	To gain up-to-date knowledge in the field.
		1.3	ICSSR Survey of Research in Social Sciences.	1.3	To know the work already done on the subject.
		1.4	Bibliography of Doctoral Dissertations (published by Association of Indian Universities etc.)	1.4	To identify research gaps in the field.
		1.5	Theses in the selected discipline.	1.5	To avoid duplication.

2. Formulation of the selected problem.	2. Previous studies in the field. Journals, published and unpublished theses.	2 To become familiar with appropriate methodology and research techniques relevant to the study.
3. Operationalisation of concepts.	3. Same as in 2.	3 For clarifying concepts and knowing measurement techniques.
4. Preparation of Research proposals.	4.1 Illustrated Books on Methodology of research. 4.2 Published and unpublished theses.	4.1 To develop alternative designs. 4.2 For formatting hypothesis and deciding sample design, etc.
5. Construction of Tools for collection of data.	5.1 Same as 4.1 and 4.2. 5.2 Copies of tools and scales furnished in the appendix of theses.	5. For gaining a thorough knowledge of the process of tools and measurement techniques.
6. Drafting the theoretical chapters and theory parts of other chapters.	6. Journals, Textbooks, Reference books and Reports on the subject matter.	6. To take notes and compile bibliography.

4.3 LITERATURE SEARCH PROCEDURE

The above table shows that a researcher has to review the various kinds of literature relating to the selected field of study. How can he *identify the related* materials? This research procedure involves a series of steps. The exact sequence will vary depending upon the subject and the knowledge of the researcher. A *general approach* is suggested below:

1. Request learned professors, librarians or others familiar with the field to suggest relevant references.
2. Find out whether any bibliography already prepared on the subject is available in the library. See the Bibliographic index, if any, maintained in the library.
3. Consult bibliographies in the theses on the topic and related topics.
4. See the card catalogues of the library: (1) Author catalogue cards if the authors of books are known; (2) Subject catalogue cards to locate the titles and other details of the books on the subject.
5. Examine periodicals, monographs, reports and conference proceedings and other materials including microfilms available in the library.
6. Consult reference cited in the books and articles already located. Each book or article will be a means for locating additional references.
7. Consult the abstract Journal on the subject or 'Abstracts' section in the journals relating to the subject.
8. See the 'Book-Review' pages in the daily newspapers and in the journals.

(*Note:* Prepare a source (or bibliography) card[1] for each item of references located).

1. See Section 'Note-taking' in this topic, below.

Thus, one can identify many references relating to the selected topic. The problem now is to go through the references one after another and extract information relevant to the study. This is discussed in the Section 4.5 of this chapter.

4.4 SOURCES OF LITERATURE

The sources of documentary information, which can aid the process of locating literatures relating to selected research topics are:

A. Subject Catalogues of Libraries

These catalogues furnish lists of books available on various subjects. Subject Index in libraries also serves the same purpose.

B. Documentation Services

There are a number of documentation centres attached to national institutions. Some of the important centres are:

1. Social Sciences Documentation Centre of ICSSR,
2. National Documentation Centre of Mass Communication, New Delhi,
3. Small Enterprises National Documentation Centre, Hyderabad.
4. Centre for Rural Documentation, Hyderabad.
5. National Council of Applied Economic Research, New Delhi.
6. Centre for Economic and Social Studies, Hyderabad.

From these centres codified information on any topic can be obtained on payment of a nominal fee. In addition, xerox copies of pages in books or journals can also be obtained from these centres.

C. Bibliographies

Some institutes and libraries bring out bibliographies of books and papers published in India. Important bibliographies are:

1. Indian National Bibliography: This is a monthly publication of National Library, Calcutta to which copies of all books published should be delivered under the Delivery of Book Act. This publication contains a latest list of books published in all the 15 major languages of India. A five-year cumulative index is also available.

2. The Library Congress Accession List, South Asia: This is a monthly record of all publications acquired by the US Library Congress Office in New Delhi from Afghanistan, Bangladesh, Bhutan, India, Maldives, Nepal, Pakistan and Sri Lanka.

3. Asian Social Science Bibliography: This is an annual publication of the Institute of Economic Growth, New Delhi. It covers selective books, reports and papers published in English in Asia.

4. Bibliographies of Libraries: The libraries of some Universities and other educational institutions bring out bibliographies on selected subjects.

D. Lists of Books and Publishers' Bulletins

1. All leading publishers bring out periodical bulletins and list of books published and forthcoming books. Some publishers publish bulletins periodically, e.g., "Publishers Monthly"

(C.S.Chand & Co.), "The Book Maker" (Orient Longman), "Book Selection" (Allied Publishers), "Recent Indian Books" (Federation of Publishers and Booksellers' Association in India), etc.

2. Book Review Columns of Journals contain a short review of the latest books; Newspapers also give a list of latest publications in their weekly book review columns.
3. Cumulative Book Index: World List of Books in the English Language' Published since 1928 by H.W. Wilson, New York.

E. Journals

The names of journals and index of articles published in them are available from various sources. They are:

1. Index India: This is a quarterly documentation list published by the Rajasthan University Library. It consists of Newspaper Index, Index to Indian Periodicals, Index to Foreign Periodicals, Index to bibliographical Profiles, Index to Book Reviews, and Index to Theses and Documents.

2. Guide to Indian Periodical Literature: This is published as a quarterly by the Indian Documentation Centre, Gurgaon. It covers about 300 periodicals.

3. Indian Press Index: This is an index of all articles, special write-ups, editorials and letters published in 25 daily English newspapers in India.

4. Documentation Fortnightly: This is brought out by the Parliament Library with a view to keeping the members of Indian Parliament well informed of current materials contained in various documents received by the Parliament Library during the fortnight.

5. Documentation of Asia: It is an annual classified bibliography of articles on Asia, published by the Indian Council of World Affairs.

6. Indian Index Series: The Social Sciences Documentation Centre of ICSSR is bringing out Indexes of articles on various subjects published in various journals so far.

F. Government Reports

Government publishes administrative reports of various departments, reports of Commissions and Committees, " India – A Reference Annual" etc.

The sources of locating government publications include:

1. Catalogue of Government of India Civil Publications (Subject-wise analysed, 1969).
2. Catalogue of Government of India Publications, 1980.
3. Government of India Publications (by Mohinder Singh), 1982.
4. Parliament Library Bulletin (contains a separate section of government publications.)
5. Statistical Abstracts – India.

G. Research Abstracts

Abstracts of researches completed are available from the following publications:

1. ICSSR Research Abstracts: Contain abstracts of research projects funded by ICSSR.

2. Indian Dissertation Abstracts: Published by ICSSR, gives synopsis of Ph.D. theses in Social Sciences submitted to Indian Universities.

3. ICSSR Journal of Abstracts and Review: Economics: Contains abstract of selected articles and reviews of books published in Indian Economic Periodicals.

4. ICSSR Journal of Abstracts and Review: Political Science.

5. ICSSR Journal of Abstracts and Reviews: Geography.

6. Dissertation Abstracts International: 1938 to date published by Xerox University, Ann Arbor, Michigan.

H. Information on Research Done

Information on Doctoral research work already done is available from the following sources:

1. Bibliography of Doctoral Dissertations accepted by Indian universities (Social Sciences and Humanities): Published by the Association of Indian Universities: First Volume covers the period of 1957-70, second 1970-75. Thereafter, it is published as an annual publication.

2. Doctorates in Social Sciences Awarded by Indian Universities: Published by ICSSR, New Delhi in 5 Volumes; 1957-67, 1968, 1869, 1970 and 1971.

3. University News: A weekly publication of Association of Indian Universities, contains a section on dissertations accepted by Indian Universities.

4. ICSSR Survey of Research in Social Sciences: First Survey completed in 1970-71; published in 22 volumes.

5. Foreign Theses on India: A publication of Social Sciences Documentation Centre of ICSSR.

6. American Doctoral Dissertations: Published since 1957 by Xerox University Microfilms, Anna Arbor, Michigan, provides list of all doctoral dissertations accepted by American and Canadian Universities.

4.5 PLANNING THE REVIEW WORK

Proper Planning

Gathering and noting information from printed sources is often considered as a simple task and taken for granted. But it is done poorly, when it is not planned properly.

Steps

This planning involves *three* steps:

1. To decide what information is useful and what is not useful: This decision is not easy to make. The right approach is to identify the information needs of the research on hand. The researcher should draw up a *preliminary outline* of the topic with reference to the objectives of study. Even though this outline will change as he gathers more information, it serves as a guide for making the above decision.

2. To determine how to record what is gathered from a published material: Should it be noted down verbatim, outlined or paraphrased? New ideas, viewpoints, findings of earlier studies and arguments may be *outlined* in our work.

Important definitions or statements to be quoted may be recorded verbatim within inverted commas.

In a few instances, a *paraphrase* statement of the author's position may be desirable.

3. To set up an orderly recording or note-taking system: Can bounded notebooks, loose sheets or cards be used for recording notes taken from references consulted?

In this decision, the researcher must be guided by the *requirements of a good recording system.* These requirements are:

1. The recording system should facilitate *ready location* of the recorded information when required.
2. It should *allow* for more *flexible handling and organizing* of information. That is, it should permit *easy arrangement and re-arrangement,* which is a matter of great importance for the classification and analysis of information while drafting the report.
3. All notes relating to a particular concept or aspect of a topic should be available together.

Does the *traditional method* of recording information in a bounded note book meet the above requirements? No. It does not facilitate ready reference, as one has to thumb every page, every time, resulting in an awful waste of time and energy. It does not provide flexibility in organizing information i.e., it does not permit arrangement or rearrangement or information. Further, all the information relating to a particular sub-title are not available in one place in the note book. Thus, the system of recording information in a bounded note-book does not satisfy any of the requirements of a good recording system.

Even the system of loose sheets is not very much suitable. Sheets will get mutilated when handled frequently. They also do not provide much flexibility in organizing the information.

The *most suitable method of recording notes is card system.* It meets all the requirements of a good recording system. Cards are tougher and will withstand handling. They are compact. They can be easily handled. They can be stored conveniently in boxes. They promote maximum flexibility in arranging, re-arranging, grouping and classifying information. The use of cards is explained in the next Section 4.6.

4.6 NOTE TAKING

Introduction

The most suitable method of note taking, as explained earlier, is use of cards and a *tentative outline* of the key elements regarding the topic. Though the outline may undergo revision when the researcher acquires further insight into his subject, it is useful in deciding which information is needed and how various bits of information should be related.

The recording system involves use of *two sets of cards.* One set of cards (3" x 5" cards), known as *source cards,* is used for noting bibliographic information, and the second set (5" x 8" cards), known as *note cards,* is used for actual note-taking.

Source Cards

The recording of bibliographic information in the source cards should be made in proper *bibliographic format.* The following formats may be used:

For a Book

Author's name (starting with last name), *the title of the book,* place of publication: the publisher's name, year or

Author's name, *the title of the book,* the publisher's name, place, year.

Where a work has three or more authors, the abbreviation "*et al*". meaning "and other", may be used after the name of the first author, e.g., Koontz, Harold, *et al., Management,* New Delhi. McGraw-Hill International Book Company, 1980 or

Kootz, Harold, *et al., Management,* McGraw-Hill International Book Company, New Delhi, 1980. If a publication is an edited one, use the abbreviation "ed." after the name.

For an Article

Author's name, "the title of the article". *The journal's name,* place. Publisher's name, vol., Issues No., date, pages or

Author's name, "the title of the article". *The journal's name,* Publisher's name, place, vol., Issues No., date, pages or

For each reference (a book or an article or a report) taken up for reading, a *separate card* should be used. One *side* only should be used.

Source cards serve two purposes: First, they provide *documentary information* for footnotes to be given in the report. Second, they are *used for compiling bibliography* to be furnished at the end of the report.

Source cards can be coded by a simple system in order to relate them to the corresponding note cards. One useful coding system is;

On the left hand top corner, the letter 'B' or 'J' or 'R' (B = Books, J = Journal, R = Report) may be marked according to the type of reference which a card represents. This marking facilitates classification of cards into three categories: (1) Books reference cards (2) Cards relating to Articles and (3) Cards relating to Reports for compiling bibliography. When bibliography is compiled, source cards can be classified into these three groups, and cards in each group can be arranged in the alphabetical order of the authors and this bibliography can be typed.

Another code is to employ a *combination of letter and number* on the right-hand begins with 'C'..The *same code* has to be *marked on the corresponding notes card* to facilitate ready source reference for each note.

Illustrates source cards, The source cards can be preserved either in an Index box or hardboard box of suitable size.

Note Cards

Information extracted from a printed source is recorded on the note cards. It is desirable to note a *single fact or idea on each card.* This promotes *maximum flexibility. One side* only should be used.

The following format may be adopted for achieving maximum flexibility:

On the left-hand top corner the source reference code may be marked, and on the right-hand top corner the number of the researcher's proposed chapter to which the information is related may be entered.

On the space between the top edge and the first horizontal line, the *title of the broad theme,* e.g., 'corporate planning'; or 'capital budgeting' or 'demand analysis' may be written, and in the next space the *title* of the *specific idea or fact,* e.g., 'definition of planning' or 'meaning of capital budgeting' or 'elasticity of demand' may be written.

In the body of the card, first, the name of the author and the title of the book/article may be noted in order to avoid making any mistake in identifying the concerned source card.

Then the idea or fact extracted from the concerned reference is recorded. The number of the *page* of the source from which the above idea/fact has been extracted is noted on the left-hand margin of the card.

This page number has to be quoted in the footnote statement for the idea in the report.

The above system of note-taking will enable a researcher "to develop a substantial set of notes, readily sortable into new patterns of organization, and with each idea reference back to its source."[2] It facilitates arranging the notes appropriately for drafting the report.

Note cards may be preserved in a card index box as they may be useful for related researches or for writing articles.

SUGGESTED READINGS

1. Barzeen, Jacques, and Graff, Henry F., *The Modern Researcher,* New York: Harcourt, Brace & World, 1970, Chapter 4 and 5.
2. Campbell, William Giles, and Ballou, Stephen Vaughan, *Form and Style, Theses, Reports, Term Papers*, Boston: Houghton Mifflin Company, 1974.
3. Johnson, Janet Buttolph and Joslyn, Richard A., *Political Science Research Methods,* New Delhi: Prentice-Hall of India, 1989, Chapter 6.
4. Komidar, Joseph S., "Use of the Library", in Goode, William J., and Hatt, Paul K., *Methods in Social Research,* New York: McGraw-Hill Book Company, 1952, pp. 103-118.
5. Parsons C.J., *Theses and Project Work,* London: George Allen and Unwin, 1973.
6. Russell, Harold G., *et al., The Use of Books in Libraries,* Mineapolis: University of Minnesota Press, 1951.

QUESTIONS

1. What is the need for reviewing literature for research?
2. What kinds of literature should a researcher review and for what purpose?
3. How can a researcher locate available literatures relating to his topic?
4. Why should a researcher review earlier research studies relating to topic?
5. How can the literature review be planned?
6. What are the requirements of a note-taking system? Evaluate the use of (a) bounded notebook, (b) loose sheets and (c) cards for note-taking.
7. Describe the use of (a) source cards and (b) note cards in note-taking.

❑ ❑ ❑

2. Emory, C. William, *Business Research Methods, op. cit.,* p. 193.

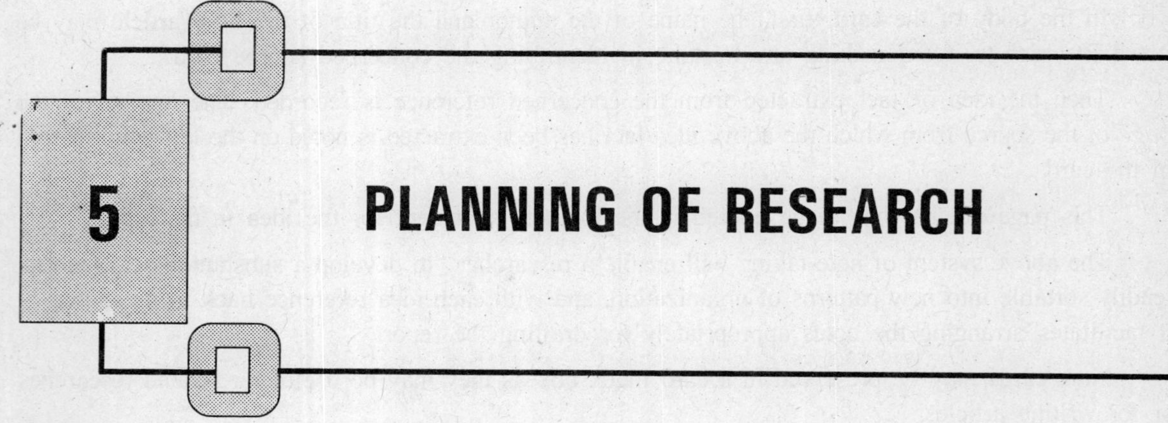

5 PLANNING OF RESEARCH

5.1 THE PLANNING PROCESS

Introduction

Research is an organized endeavour. Like any other organized work, research requires proper planning. Planning means deciding in advance. Planning of research means deciding the question or issue to be studied, setting the objectives of the study and determining the means of achieving those objectives. It is an intellectual process. It requires intellectual curiosity, intelligence, imagination and vision, and knowledge of methodology of research. *Planning systematizes* the research work. It eliminates aimless intellectual wandering. It gives direction to the work.

Planning Process

The planning stage of a research project involves the following steps:

1. Selection of a problem for research: This involves identification of a few problems and selecting one out of them, after evaluating the alternatives against certain selection criteria.

2. Formulation of the selected problem: The selected problem is defined and transformed into researchable questions.

3. Formulation of hypotheses: The propositions to be tested are set up.

4. Conceptualization: The concepts associated with the problem under study are operationally defined and measurement devices are designed.

5. Research plan or design: This plan covers all the aspects of the selected research work and serves as a blue-print for the endeavour.

All these aspects of research planning are discussed in detail in the following sections.

5.2 SELECTION OF A PROBLEM FOR RESEARCH

Introduction

The selection of a problem is the first step in research. The term *'problem'* means a question or issue to be examined. The selection of a problem for research is not an easy task; itself is a problem. It is least amenable to formal methodological treatment. Vision, an imaginative insight, plays an important role in this process.

This problem of selection arises when a student has to undertake research as a part of his course requirement. In some universities a project study is prescribed as a requirement for even undergraduate programmes. In several universities a project study is a partial requirement of postgraduate programmes like M.Com., M. B. A., M. S. W., etc. Research is an important requirement of M. Phil. and of Doctoral degree programmes.

In each of these cases, a student has to select a problem for his research.

Similarly, faculty members of colleges and universities select problems for research as an academic pursuit. In case of projects sponsored by planning bodies, departments of government, industries or other organizations, the sponsors themselves invariably suggest the problems to be studied.

The nature of the problem to be selected depends upon the level at which the research is done. A problem appropriate for undergraduate/master degree students will necessarily be a modest one. The emphasis is upon the *learning process* of a beginner. A problem to be selected for M. Phil./Ph.D. programme must be a major problem requiring comprehensive treatment. In this case, the emphasis is upon both *skill development and contribution to knowledge.*

On the other hand, a problem to be selected by an experienced academic researcher must be a complex problem meant for making a *significant contribution* to the development or refinement of theory or to policy making.

The Mode of Selection

The students who undertake research as a course requirement do their research work under the guidance of a professor. What should be the mode of selection in their cases? Should a problem be suggested by the guide or be selected by the researcher himself?

A beginner in research may, of course, prefer the first choice. He will be happy if the problem is suggested by the guide, for his problem of selection is easily solved. But is such suggestion appropriate?

The suggestion of the problem by the guide means an *imposition.* It is an attempt to get some work done rather than to train the student to do research on his own. It destroys spontaneity. The problem suggested by the guide may not be a topic in which the student is really interested. Then he may not find pleasure in studying it, and the study will become an unwanted burden to him. Therefore, it is *better to choose the problem oneself.* Of course, the guide can help the candidate to help himself. He may dig out the candidate's area of interest and show him the way. The actual selection should be choice of the candidate himself.

One with a critical, curious and imaginative mind and is sensitive to practical problems could easily identify problems for study.

Sources of Problems

The sources from which one may be able to identify research problems or develop problem awareness are:

1. **Reading:** When we critically study books and articles relating to the subject of our interest, pertinent questions may arise in our mind. Similarly, areas of research may strike to our mind when we read research reports.
2. **Academic experience:** Classroom lectures, class discussions, seminar discussions and out-of-class exchanges of ideas with fellow students and professors will suggest many stimulating problems to be studied.
3. **Daily experience:** Life is dynamic. We learn new things and undergo new experiences every day. If we are alert, inquisitive and sensitive to life situations, we may hit upon questions worth of investigation, "It is a mark of scientific genius to be sensitive to difficulties where less gifted people pass untroubled by doubts."[1]

   The story about Newton justifies to this. Though apples might have fallen on the heads of people before Newton's time, only the sensitive Newton applied his mind on this event which led to the discovery of "Law of Gravitation."
4. **Exposure to field situations:** Field visits, internship training and extension work provide exposure to practical problems which call for study.
5. **Consultations:** Discussions with experts, researchers, administrators and business executives will help a researcher to identify meaningful problems for research.
6. **Brain storming:** Intensified discussion within a group of interested persons may often be a means of identifying pertinent questions, and of developing new ideas about a problem.[2]
7. **Research:** Research on one problem may suggest problems for further research.
8. **Intuition:** Sometimes new ideas may strike to one's mind like a flash. Reflective mind is a spring of knowledge.

Process of Identification

The process of identification of problems for academic research may consist of the following *steps*:

1. Selection of the discipline: The discipline or subject in which one proposes to do research may be selected, e.g., Economics, Commerce, Management, Technology, Psychology etc. The selection of the discipline is easy. One can select any subject, which one has studied thoroughly and which has interested him most. Where one has to do research in his field of specialization (e.g., Marketing Management or Finance Management or Personnel Management in M.B.A. Programme), one has to choose the subject of one's specialization.

2. Demarcating the broad area or a particular aspect of the selected subject: The second step is to select a *particular aspect* of the selected subject. For example, if the selected subject is Financial Management, then one may select capital budgeting, financial leverage, working capital management or profit management as specific area of study.

1. Selltiz, *et al., Research Methods in Social Relations,* London: Methien & Co., 1969, p. 31.
2. Clover, Vernon T., and Howard L. Balsley, *Business Research Method, op. cit.,* p. 34.

One who says that one is willing to do research on any aspect of discipline does not mean business or does not know oneself.

One should identify his specific area of interest. Interest in a particular area of a subject develops out of educational background, reading a good book or inspiration received from a professor.

3. Identifying two or more specific topics in the selected broad area: This is the final step in *identification of problem.* This requires a grasp of the branch of the subject as a whole and awareness of work already done on it. A review of concerned literature including research theses and survey of research published by the Research Councils like Indian Council of Social Science Research, New Delhi, intensive reading and reflective thinking, and discussion with the guide will help a student in identifying specific topics or issues for research. Both an uncharted path and a *well-trodden path are dangerous* to a beginner in research. If he chooses an unexplored problem, he has to grope in the dark and may get frustrated. On the other hand, if he selects a problem, which has already been thoroughly studied, he may not learn anything new nor contribute anything to the knowledge. It is desirable for him to adopt a *via media* approach. He may identify problems on which he can get the guidance of a few articles or books.

A student cannot just select anyone of the identified problems for his research. He has to evaluate them for choosing the most appropriate one. How can this evaluation be done? Against what criteria?

Criteria of Selection

The selection of one appropriate researchable problem out of the identified problems requires *evaluation* of those alternatives against certain criteria. These criteria may be grouped into:

(a) Internal (or personal) criteria or factors, and

(b) External criteria or factors.

Internal criteria consist of (1) researcher's interest, (2) researcher's competence, and (3) researcher's own resource: finance and time.

External factors include (1) researchability of the problem, (2) its importance and urgency, (3) novelty of the problem, (4) feasibility, (5) facilities, (6) usefulness and social relevance, and (7) Research personnel.

Researcher's interest: The problem should interest the researcher and be a *challenge* to him. Without interest and curiosity, he may not develop sustained *perseverance.* Even a small difficulty may become an excuse for discontinuing the study.

Interest in a problem depends upon the researcher's educational background, experience, outlook and sensitivity.

Researcher's competence: A mere interest in a problem will not do. The researcher must be competent to plan and carry out a study of the problem. He must have the ability to grasp and deal with it. He must possess adequate knowledge of the subject matter, relevant methodology and statistical procedures.

Researcher's own resources: In the case of a research to be done by a researcher on his own, consideration of his own financial resource is pertinent. Does the cost involved in conducting the study of the problem is within the means of the researcher? If it is beyond his means, he will not be able to complete the work, unless he gets some external financial support. Time resource is more important than finance. Research is a time consuming process. What is the time that the researcher can be able to spare for the research work? Is it adequate to meet the time requirements of the problem? If not, the work cannot be completed within the prescribed time limit. As it is difficult to foresee the eventual time constraint, it is desirable to *over-estimate the time requirement and to under-estimate the time availability.* In this connection, available tidbits of time (say 5 or 10 minutes at a time) should not be counted, as nothing could be done in 5 or 10 minutes, only *large chunks* of time available should be counted.

Researchability: The problem should be researchable, i.e., amenable for finding answers to the questions involved in it through scientific method. "Although every problem in science involves a question or a series of questions, not every question qualifies as a scientific problem"[3] To be researchable a question must be one for which *observation* or other *data collection* in the real world can provide the answer. Many questions cannot be answered on the basis of information alone. They may *involve value elements,* e.g., what is merit for the purpose of employee promotion? What is 'fairness' to the workers? Some questions may not be researchable because procedures or techniques are inadequate, e.g., how will a new fiscal policy affect distributive justice? Which new management trainees have potential for top management?

Importance and urgency: Problems requiring investigation are unlimited, but available research efforts are very much limited. Therefore in selecting problems for research, their *relative importance* and significance should be considered. An important and urgent problem should be given priority over an unimportant one. For example, in industrial management today, problems of productivity, capacity utilization, motivation and industrial unrest are more important than problems of financial leverage, profit planning, vertical/horizontal integration, marketing etc. Research must be focused on useful and urgent problems.

Novelty or originality: The problem must have novelty. There is no use of wasting one's time and energy on a problem already studied thoroughly by others.

This does not mean that replication is always needless. In social sciences in some cases, it is appropriate to replicate (repeat) a study in order to verify the validity of its findings to a different situation.

Feasibility: A problem may be a new one and also important, but if research on it is not feasible, it cannot be selected. Hence feasibility is a very important consideration.

Some of the *questions* that should be considered in examining the feasibility are:

- ❖ Are suitable research techniques such as measurement devices and techniques of analysis available?
- ❖ Are accurate and reliable data available? The reliability of the findings depends upon the quality of data. In some cases, available data may be tinged by emotions. Ethnic conflicts, strikes and lockouts, poverty and affluence are examples of topics heavily weighted by emotions.
- ❖ Will the authorities of the concerned institutions extend the required cooperation in furnishing data or permit access to records? Some organizations like Commercial banks, sole proprietary

3. Merton R., *et al.,* (ed.), *Sociology Today — Problems and Prospects,* New York: Harper and Row, p. 92.

and partnership concerns and private limited companies do not easily extend cooperation to researchers.

- Will the respondents be willing to be interviewed?
- Can the study be completed within the time available?

On the basis of the consideration of the above questions, the feasibility of the problem should be determined.

Facilities: Research requires certain facilities such as well-equipped library facility, suitable and competent guidance, data processing facility, etc. Hence, the availability of the facilities relevant to the problem must be considered.

Usefulness and social relevance: Above all, the study of the problem should make significant contribution to the concerned body of knowledge or to the solution of some significant practical problem. It should be *socially relevant.* This consideration is particularly important in the case of higher-level academic research and sponsored research.

Research personnel: Research undertaken by professors and by research organizations require the services of investigators and research officers. But in India and other developing countries, research has not yet become a prospective profession. Hence, talented persons are not attracted to research projects. Employment in research projects is just considered as a stop-gap arrangement pending securing a regular placement. Therefore appropriate qualified and experienced research personnel are not easily available for the study of some problems.

Conclusion: Each identified problem must be evaluated in terms of the above internal and external criteria and the most appropriate one may be selected by a research scholar. The *overall guideline* to be followed in this selection process is:

Select a feasible and researchable problem which is interesting to you and within your competence and manageable within the available time and resources, and at the time same time has some importance and social relevance, and for which required facilities are available.

5.3 FORMULATION OF THE SELECTED PROBLEM

Introduction

The problem selected for research may initially be vague. The question to be studied or the problem to be solved may not be clear. Why the answer/solution is wanted also may not be known. Hence, the selected problem should be defined and formulated. This is a difficult process. It requires intensive reading of a few selected articles or chapters in books in order to understand the nature of the selected problem. The reading at this stage should be focused on the *'classics' and research papers* on the topic. Gunnar Myrdal's *The Challenge of World Poverty* in the study of anti-poverty programmes, Peter F. Drucker's *The Effective Executive* in the study of managerial effectiveness, Harold's paper on *Dynamic theory* in Growth Economics are a few examples of classics. The researcher should read such selected literatures, digest, think and reflect upon what is read and digested. He should also discuss with learned persons.

Then only can he gain *insight* into the chosen problem and be able to define and formulate it.

What is Formulation?

Formulation means *translating and transforming* the selected research *problem/topic* into a scientifically researchable question.[4] it is concerned with specifying exactly what the research problem is and why is it studied. The formulation should include both the *what and the why* aspects.

Merton[5] identifies three principal *components* in the progressive formulation of a problem for research:

1. The originating question (what one wants to know?)
2. The rationale (Why aspects)
3. The specifying questions (possible answers to the originating questions).

The originating question It indicates what the problem is. It may be of different kinds. It may call for discovering new and more decisive facts relating to the subject-matter of study; it may *put to question* the adequacy of certain concepts, may be related to *empirical validity;* or it may be related to the *structure* of an organisation.

Rationale of the question: Rationale is the statement of *reasons* why a particular question is posed. It states how the answer to the question will *contribute to theory and /or practice.* The rationale helps to make a discrimination between scientifically important and trivial question. In short, it "states the case for the question in the court of scientific opinion."[6]

Specifying question: The originating question is decomposed into several specific questions in order to identify the observations/data that will provide answer to them. These specific questions should be simple, pointed, clear and empirically verifiable. They are known as *'investigative' questions.* It is only such specific questions which when synthesized can afford the *solution* to the problem selected for research. This solution has implications for theory/systematic knowledge and/or for practice.

Formulation Process

The process of formulation involves the following steps:

1. Developing title: The title should be carefully worded. It should indicate the *core* of the study, reflect the *real intention* of the researcher, and show on what is the focus e.g., "Financing small-scale industries by commercial banks." This shows that the focus is on commercials banks and not on small-scale industries. On the other hand, if the title is "the Financial Problem of Small-scale industries", the focus is on small-scale industries. The title may also indicate the geographical area of the study.

2. Building a conceptual model: On the basis of our theoretical knowledge of the phenomenon under study, the *nature of the phenomenon, its properties/elements and their inter-relations* should be identified and structured into a framework. This conceptual model gives an exact *idea* of the research problem and shows its various *properties a*nd variables to be studied. It serves as a basis for the formulation of the objectives of the study and the hypotheses to be tested. In order to workout a conceptual model we must make a careful and critical study of the available literature on the

4. See topic 5-2 above.
5. Merton, *et al., op. cit.*
6. *Ibid*., p. xix.

subject-matter of the selected research problem. It is *for this reason, a research student is expected to select a problem for research in his field of specialization.* Without adequate background knowledge, a researcher cannot grasp and comprehend the nature of the research problem.

The following example[7] will illustrate the process of developing a conceptual model.

Conceptual model for a study of profitability of a commercial bank: Profit is the difference between income and expenditure. A commercial bank's main source of income is interest earned on loans and advances. It also derives some non-interest income in the form of commission, service charges, etc. Its major expenditure is interest paid on deposits; it incurs manpower and other expenses for providing services to the customers. What are the inter-relationships between these elements? (See Exh. 5.1).

The difference between interest earned and interest paid may be called "*Spread*', and the difference between the Spread and the Burden determines the net profit (or loss). By identifying the factors which influence Spread and Burden an approach for profit management can be developed.[8]

EXHIBIT 5.1

The Profitability of a Commercial Bank

Parts	*Expenses*	*Income*	*Difference*
I	a. Interest Paid	b. Interest Earned	c. Spread (b – a)
II	d. Manpower Expenses	g. Non-interest Income	h. Burden (f – g)
	e. Other Expenses		
	f. Non-interest Expenses	(d + e)	
III	i. Total Expenses (a – f)	j. Total Income (b – g)	k. Net Profit (j – i) or (c – h)

3. Defining the objective of the study: The objectives refer to the *questions to be answered* through the study. They indicate what we are trying to get from the study.

The *objectives are derived from the conceptual* model. They state *which elements* in the conceptual model – *which levels of, which kinds* of cases, *which properties,* and which *connections* among properties – are to be investigated, but it is the conceptual model that defines, describes, and states the *assumptions* underlying these elements.[9]

The objectives way aim at *description or explanation or* analysis of *causal relationship* between variables, and indicate the *expected results* or outcome of the study.

The objectives may be specified in the form of either *statements* or *questions.*

Illustration: The profitability of commercial banks tends to decline year after year, even though the volume of business — deposits and deployment of funds — is on the increase. How will a researcher formulate a problem when he encounters this situation?

---

7. This is based on a model developed by Prof. Sampath P. Singh and his associate Varsha S. Varde of National Institute of Bank Managemernt, Pune. See Varsha S. Varde and Sampath P. Singh, "Towards an Analytical Framework for Project Management in Bank", *The Chartered Accountant,* New Delhi ICAI, June, 1980.
8. Varde, Varsha S., and S.P. Singh, *op. cit.,* pp. 1065-71.
9. Riley Matilda White, *Sociological Research – Case Approach,* New York: Harcourt, Brace and World, 1963. p. 14.

(1) *Title* of the research problem: "An enquiry into the declining trend in the profitability of 'X' commercial bank."

(2) *Objectives* of the Study: In a *Statement* form:

The objectives of the study are:

(a) to identify the major factors affecting the bank's profitability,

(b) to determine the major causes of the declining trend in its profitability, and

(c) to develop a strategy for improving the bank's profitability.

The above objectives may be stated in question form as under:

The study aims at seeking answers to the following questions:

(a) What are the major factors affecting the bank's profitability?

(b) What are the major causes of the declining trend in its profitability?

(c) What strategy can be adopted for improving the bank's profitability?

The successful research will provide answers to these questions.

4. Setting investigative questions: Once the objectives of the research/or the general research questions have been defined, the formulation moves to the next level, i.e., *investigative questions.* These *sub-questions* are set up for each of the major research objectives/questions. These specific questions guide the *details* of the research efforts, including the development of *concepts, operational definitions and measurement* devices. There may be several *sub-levels* of the investigative questions, each being progressively narrower in scope and more specific.

Example: The investigative questions relating to the first objective of the previous example (Factors affecting a commercial bank's profitability) are:

A. What are the factors affecting interest earned on advances?

(1) Has the proportion of the total earning assets to deposits tended to decline?

(2) What is the composition of earning assets?

(3) What is the rate of yield on each type of asset?

B. What are the factors affecting interest paid on deposits and borrowings?

(1) Have the interest paying liabilities tended to increase?

(2) What is the composition of interest paying liabilities?

(3) What is the rate of interest on each component?

C. What are the factors affecting manpower expenses?

(1) Has the number of employees tended to increase?

(2) What are the seniority and composition of employees?

(3) What is the salary structure?

and so on.

5. Formulation of hypotheses: The hypotheses are *tentative propositions* relating to investigative questions. We formulate them to be tested in our research. They either *describe* the properties of variables or show the *relationships* between them. They aim at *answering* the research questions. They determine what facts will be sought and what research procedures will be used. For detailed discussion of hypotheses, see topic 5.4, below.

6. Operational definition of concepts: The next step in the formulation process is to define operationally the concepts involved in the title, objectives, investigative questions and hypotheses. The operational definitions specify the *measurement parameters* of the variables. Scales/indices are constructed for measuring abstract concepts.

The operational definitions of concepts and measurement devices enable us to decide exactly the *data needs* of the research. The operational definition of concepts is explained in detail in topic 5.5, below.

7. Delimiting the scope of the study: This means demarcation of the scope and dimensions of the study. A complete study of any phenomenon is well-nigh un-manageable. It would entail such an overwhelmingly large volume of data that it would require more than a student's life time to gain a glimpse of the phenomenon.

A beginner is especially over-ambitious. He is tempted to cover too wide a scope without knowing its complexities. For example, a student may propose to study the problem of unemployment in his State for his final term project. Can it be possible to complete this study on his own within a period of 3 months? The problem is complex and it is related to various categories of occupational groups. It covers several aspects: extent, causes, impacts and remedial measures. Data has to be collected from government institutions and individuals. Even a sample survey may require a large staff of field investigators. And so on.

Therefore, a research should take a *close view of the implications and dimensions* of the selected **problem and keep the *scope* of its study *within manageable limits, i.e.,*** within the ability of the mind **to grasp the implications and within the amount of time and other resources available.**

The *purpose* of this delimitation is to *avoid confusion and superficiality and promote clarification and successful completion* within time limits and available resources.

The various *aspects* that may be delimited are:

(1) the *objectives* of the study, i.e., the number and extent of questions to be investigated:

(2) the *geographical area* to be covered by the study, say, a state, a district, a taluka, a city or a village:

(3) the *reference period;* and

(4) the *magnitude* of the study; the universe to be covered; the types of sampling units to be studied; and the sample size.

The delimitation can be done from the *standpoint* of:

(1) aims and interests of the research worker or the sponsor, as the case may be,

(2) availability of relevant information,

(3) complexity of theoretical basis of the study,

(4) the extent and scope of previous research done in the field,

(5) the amount of finance, and time available, and

(6) the quantity and extent of personnel, tools, techniques and other facilities available.

The consideration of all these factors is to bring down the scope and dimensions of the study to a *manageable level* and yet to make it useful and meaningful.

Importance of Formulation

'A problem well put is half-solved'. This saying *highlights* the importance of proper formulation of the selected problem. The primary task of research is collection of relevant data and the analysis of data for finding answers to the research questions. The proper performance of this task depends upon the identification of exact data and information required for the study. The formulation serves this purpose. The clear and accurate statement of the problem, the development of the conceptual model, the definition of the objectives of the study, the setting of investigative questions, the formulation of hypotheses to be tested and the operational definition of concepts and the delimitation of the study determine the exact *data needs* of the study. Once the exact data requirement is known, the researcher can plan and execute the *other steps* without any waste of time and energy. Thus, formulation gives a *direction* and a *specific focus* to the research effort. It helps to *delimit* the field of enquiry by singling out the pertinent facts from a vast ocean of facts and thus saves the researcher from becoming lost in a welter of irrelevancies. The determination of exact information needs through the formulation process *prevents a blind search and indiscriminate gathering* of data, which my later prove irrelevant to the problem under study. The hypotheses to be tested determine the appropriate *statistical techniques* to be adopted for analysis. Thus all the *major tasks* – sampling, selecting appropriate methods of collection of data, construction of tools for data collection, designing plan of analysis – can be *planned exactly* without any waste of efforts. Hence, the saying 'a problem well put is half-solved' is true.

Researchers who do not define and formulate their research problems read and collect vast data and build up massive files without knowing which is relevant and which is not relevant and are thus lost in an aimless empirical wandering. Even after spending several months and sometimes even years, they do not get a specific direction. No wonder such researchers invariably get frustrated and discontinue their research work. Research guides have a great responsibility in helping their research scholars in making a clearcut formulation of their research problems and save them from such frustration.

5.4 HYPOTHESES

Introduction

The formulation of hypotheses or propositions as to the possible answers to the research questions is an important step in the process of formulation of the research problem as explained in the previous Section (5.3). Keen observation, creative thinking, hunch, wit, imagination, vision, insight and sound judgement are of greater importance in setting up reasonable hypotheses.[10] A thorough knowledge about the phenomenon and related fields is of great value in its process. The formulation of hypotheses plays an important part in the growth of knowledge in every science.

Meaning of Hypothesis

Hypothesis is a tentative proposition formulated for empirical testing. It is a declarative statement combining concepts. It is a tentative answer to a research question. It is tentative, because its veracity

10. Johnson, Earl S., *Theory and Practice of the Social Sciences,* New York: The Macmillan Co., 1956, p. 192.

can be evaluated only after it has been tested empirically. Lundberg defines hypothesis as "a tentative generalization, the validity of which remains to be tested."[11] Goode and Hatt define it as "a proposition which can be put to a test to determine its validity."[12]

Hypothesis — Necessary or Not

Is the formulation of useful hypotheses always necessary and possible? It is true that hypotheses are useful and they guide the research process in the proper direction. But can hypothesis be set up in all cases? In mere *fact-finding investigations,* no problems may be raised and the need for formulating hypotheses may not arise. Similarly, in *exploratory studies,* initially it may not be possible to set up any worthwhile hypotheses. In fact, the very purpose of such exploratory studies may be to formulate meaningful hypothes for further formal studies. But strictly speaking, the mere fact-finding and the exploratory studies cannot be considered to be typical research studies. In *all analytical and experimental studies, hypotheses should be set up* in order to give a proper direction to them.

Types of Hypotheses

Hypotheses are classified in several ways. With reference to their *function,* hypotheses are of two types: (a) Descriptive Hypotheses and (b) Relational Hypotheses. Another approach is to classify them into: (c) Working Hypotheses, (d) Null Hypotheses and (e) Statistical Hypotheses. Third approach is to divide them on the basis of the *level of abstraction.* Three broad levels may be distinguished: (i) simple description, (ii) logical derivation, and (iii) abstraction. Accordingly there are three types of hypotheses: (f) common-sense hypotheses, (g) complex hypotheses and (h) analytical hypotheses.

Descriptive hypotheses: These are propositions that *describe* the *characteristics* (such as size, form or distribution) of a variable. The variable may be an object, person, organisation, situation or event. Some examples are:

"The rate of unemployment among arts graduates is higher than that of commerce graduates."

"Public enterprises are more amenable for centralized planning."

"The Educational system is not oriented to human resource needs of a country."

Relational hypotheses: These are propositions, which describe the *relationship between two variables. The relationship* suggested may be positive *or negative* correlation or *causal* relationship. Some examples are:

"Families with higher incomes spend more for recreation."

"Participative management promotes motivation among executives."

"The lower the rate of job turnover in a work group, the higher the work productivity."

"Upper-class people have fewer children than lower-class people."

"Labour productivity decreases as working duration increases."

Causal hypotheses state that the existence of, or a change in, one variable causes or leads to an effect on another variable. The first variable is called the *independent variable,* and the latter the *dependent variable.* When dealing with causal relationships between variables the researcher must consider the direction in which such relationships flow, i.e., which is cause and which is effect.

---

11. Lundberg G.A., *Social Research,* New York: Longmans, Green & Co., 1942.
12. Goode, William J., Hatt, Paul K., *Methods in Social Research, op.cit.,* p. 56.

Working hypotheses: While planning the study of a problem, hypotheses are formed. Initially they may not be very specific. In such cases, they are referred to as "Working Hypotheses" which are subject to modification as the investigation proceeds.

Null hypotheses: These are hypothical statements denying what are explicitly indicated in working hypotheses. They do not, nor were ever intended to exist in reality. They state that *no difference* exists between the parameter and the statistic being compared to it. For example, even though there is relationship between a family's income and expenditure on recreation, a null hypothesis may state: "There is no relationship between families' income level and expenditure on recreation." Null hypotheses are formulated for testing statistical significance, since, this form is a *convenient approach* to statistical analysis. As the test would *nullify* the null hypotheses, they are so called.

There is some justification for using null hypotheses. They conform to the qualities of *detachment and objectivity* to be possessed by a researcher. The attempts to test hypothesis which he assumes to be true, it would appear as if he is not behaving objectively. This problem does not arise when he uses null hypotheses.

Moreover, null hypotheses are more *exact.* It is easier to reject the contrary of an hypothesis than to confirm it with complete certainty. Hence, the concept of null hypotheses is found to be very useful.

Statistical hypotheses: These are statements about a *statistical population.* These are derived from a *sample.* These are quantitative in nature in that they are numerically measurable, e.g., "Group A is older than Group B."

Statistical hypotheses may be hypotheses of *difference* or hypotheses of *association.* The latter specify the relations between variables. This association is measured by the co-efficient of correlation, e.g., if the co-efficient of correlation between bonus and productivity is +1.0, then there is a perfect positive correlation between the bonus and productivity.

As Abraham Kaplan has pointed out, "all inductive inference is based on samples ... All hypotheses might be said to be statistical hypotheses in a broad sense: statistics has the task of assessing the weight of evidence for a particular hypothesis contained in a given set of data."[13]

Common sense hypotheses: These represent the common sense ideas. They state the existence of *empirical uniformities* perceived through day to day observations. Many empirical uniformities may be observed in business establishments, the social background of workers, and the behaviour patterns of specific groups like students, e.g., "shop-assistants in small shops lack motivation."

"Soldiers from upper-class are less adjusted in the army than lower class men"; "Fresh students conform to the conventions set up by seniors."

Common sense statements are often a confused *mixture of clichés and moral judgments.* Scientists have a large-scale job in transforming and testing them. This requires three tasks: "first, the *removal of value judgement;* second the clarification of terms: and third, the application of *validity* tests."[14] 'What everybody knows' is not known until it has been tested'. The simple level hypotheses that seek empirical generalization play an important role in the growth of a science.

Complex hypotheses: These aim at testing the existence of *logically derived relationships* between empirical uniformities. For example, in the early stage Human ecology described empirical

13. Kaplan, Abraham, *The Conduct of Inquiry,* California: Chandler Publishing Co., 1964, P. 239.
14. Goode, William J., Hatt, Paul K., *Methods in Social Research, op.cit.,* p. 60.

uniformities in the distribution of land values, industrial concentrations, types of business and other phenomena. Further study and logical analysis of these and other related findings led to the formulation of complex hypotheses such as "The concentric growth circles characterize a city", "Members of minority groups suffer from oppression psychosis", etc. Such hypotheses are *purposeful* distortions of empirical exactness. Because of their removal from empirical reality, these constructs are termed as *'ideal types.'* The function of such hypotheses is to create tools and problems for further research in otherwise very complex areas of investigation."[15]

Analytical hypotheses: These are concerned with the relationship of *analytic variables.* These hypotheses occur at the *highest level of abstraction.* These specify relationship between changes in one property and changes in another. For example, the study of human fertility might show empirical regularities by wealth, education, region, and religion. If these were raised to the level of ideal type formulation, one result might be the hypotheses: "There are two high-fertility population segments in India, viz., low-income urban Muslims and low-income rural low caste Hindus." At a still higher level of abstraction, the effects of region, education, and religion on fertility might be held constant. This would allow a better measurement of the relation between the variables of wealth and fertility.

This level of hypothesizing is the most sophisticated mode of formulation and contributes to the development of 'brilliant' abstract theories.

Sources of Hypotheses

Hypotheses can be derived from various sources:

1. Theory: This is one of the main sources of hypotheses. It gives direction to research by stating what is known. *Logical deduction* from theory leads to new hypotheses. For example, profit/wealth maximization is considered as the goal of private enterprises. From this assumption, various hypotheses are derived. "The rate of return on capital employed is an index of business success"; "The optimum capital structure is that combination of debt and equity which leads to the maximum value of the firm." "Higher the earning per share, more favourable is the financial leverage."

2. Observation: Hypotheses can be derived from observation. From the observation of price behaviour in a market, for example, the relationship between the price and demand for an article is hypothesized.

3. Analogies are another source of useful hypotheses. Julian Huxley has pointed out that casual observations in nature or in the framework of another science may be a fertile source of hypotheses. For example, the hypothesis that " similar human types or activities may be found in similar geophysical regions" came from plant ecology.

4. Intuition and personal experience may also contribute to the formulation of hypotheses. Personal life and experiences of persons determine their perception and conception. These may, in turn, direct a person to certain hypotheses more quickly. The story of Newton and the falling apple, the flash of wisdom to Buddha under a Banyan tree illustrate this individual accidental process.

5. Findings of studies: Hypotheses may be developed out of the findings of other studies in order to replicate and test.

6. State of knowledge: An important source of hypotheses is the state of knowledge in any particular science. Where formal theories exist, hypotheses can be deduced. If the hypotheses are

---

15. *Ibid.*, p. 62.

rejected, theories would be modified. Where formal theories are scarce, hypotheses are generated from conceptual frameworks. In either case, the hypotheses are related to the *conceptual-theoretical level.*

7. Culture: Another source of hypotheses is the culture on which the researcher was nurtured. Western culture has induced the emergence of sociology as an academic discipline. Over the past decade, a large part of the hypotheses on American society examined by researchers were connected with violence. This interest is related to the considerable increase in the level of violence in America. In India in socio-economic and leadership studies, hypotheses based on caste and economic status are common, because Indian society is caste-ridden, hierarchical and segmental, and the Indian economic system is riddled with inequalities and privileges.

8. Continuity of research: The continuity of research in a field itself constitutes an important source of hypotheses. The rejection of some hypotheses leads to the formulation of new ones capable of explaining dependent variables in subsequent researches on the same subject.

The Functions or the Role of Hypotheses

In social science research, a hypothesis serves several important functions.

1. A hypothesis gives a *definite point* to the investigation, and it *guides the direction* on the study. Without a hypothesis, research becomes unfocussed, a random empirical wandering. The researcher would get stranded in a cross road, not knowing the direction in which to proceed. A hypothesis, thus, directs our search for the *order* among facts.
2. A hypothesis specifies the *sources of data*, which shall be studied, and in what context they shall be studied.
3. It determines the *data needs.* It defines which facts are relevant and which are not. The use of hypothesis thus prevents a blind search and indiscriminate gathering of data, which may later found to be irrelevant to the problem under study.
4. A hypothesis suggests which *type of research* is likely to be most appropriate.
5. It determines the most *appropriate technique of analysis.*
6. A hypothesis *contributes* to the development of *theory.* It links theory and investigation. A hypothesis may be deduced from theory. When it is tested through studies and found true, it forms part of the theory.

When a social scientist develops a theory to explain a phenomenon, he does not test the theory directly. He tests the hypotheses derived from it. If the tests confirm the hypotheses, the theory is accepted. Thus, hypotheses make it possible to test theories.

Occasionally, the reverse process takes place. Theory may be constructed from hypotheses.

The above point may be clear, if illustrated. Let us take the hypothesis: "Families with higher income spend more on recreation."

This shows that families belonging to the various *strata* of the people in a place have to be studied and their *family income* and *expenses* have to be studied. What is relevant is the total income and *proportion* of expenses on recreation.

As this hypothesis describes the relation between two variables, viz., income level and recreation expenditure, it is clear that appropriate research design should be used for testing it.

Characteristics of a Good Hypothesis

What is a good hypothesis? What are the *criteria* for judging it? An acceptable hypothesis should fulfill certain conditions.

1. ***Conceptual clarity:*** A hypothesis should be conceptually clear. It should consist of clearly *defined and understandable concepts.* Clarity is obtained by means of defining *operationally* the concepts in the hypothesis. (The process of Operationalisation is discussed in detail in topic 5.5, below).
2. ***Specificity:*** A hypothesis should be specific and explain the expected relations between variables and the conditions under which these relations will hold, e.g., "when there is dissatisfaction and no care is taken, deprivation will engender violence."
3. ***Testability:*** A hypothesis should be testable and should not be a *moral judgement.* It should be possible to collect *empirical evidences* to test the hypothesis. Statements like "capitalists exploit their workers"/ "Bad partners produce bad children" are common place generalizations and cannot be tested, as they merely express sentiments and their concepts are vague.
4. ***Availability of techniques:*** Hypotheses should be related to available techniques. Otherwise they will not be researchable; therefore the researcher must make sure that methods are available for testing his proposed hypotheses.
5. ***Theoretical relevance:*** A hypothesis should be related to a body of theory. A science can be *cumulative* only by building on an existing body of facts and theory. It cannot develop if each study is an isolated investigation. When research is systematically based upon a body of existing theory, a genuine contribution to knowledge is more likely to result. Therefore, a hypothesis should possess theoretical relevance.
6. ***Consistency:*** Hypotheses should be logically consistent. Two or more propositions logically derived from the same theory must not be mutually contradictory.
7. ***Objectivity:*** Scientific hypotheses should be free from value – judgement. In principle, the researcher's system of values has no place in scientific method. However, as social phenomena are affected by the milieu in which they take place, the researcher must be aware of his values and state them explicitly.
8. ***Simplicity:*** A hypothesis should be a simple one requiring fewer conditions or assumptions. But 'simple' does not mean obvious. Simplicity demands insight. The more insight the researcher has into a problem, the simpler will be his hypothesis about it.

Evaluating Hypothesis

How can hypotheses be evaluated? Clover and Basley suggest the following checklist[16] for evaluating Hypotheses:

(1) Have all the *pertinent* area or aspects of the problem been considered in the process of setting up the hypotheses?

(2) Do the hypotheses include all the pertinent possibilities to answer the research questions?

(3) Have the hypotheses been selected on the basis of such possibilities?

16. Clover, Vernon T., and Howard L. Balsley, *Business Research Methods, op cit.,* p. 42.

(4) Have the hypotheses been selected without fearing the possibility of their substantiability?

(5) Have the hypotheses been selected under conditions that allowed the researcher to set up all hypotheses having real bearing on the problem?

The above questions are concerned with the coverage of hypotheses and conditions of their selection.

Robert Bales[17] lists the following pertinent questions to be asked about hypotheses before adopting them for investigation:

(1) Are the concepts used in hypotheses specific?

(2) Is the posited relationship between variables verifiable?

(3) Is there any prior evidence as to the truth or falseness of the posited relationship?

(4) Can an appropriate research design be devised?

(5) Are the variables 'context-bound' or applicable to other situations?

(6) Are the generalizations a part of a theoretical system?

If the above sets of questions are answered satisfactorily, then the hypotheses can be considered reasonably logical and valid as guides for continuing the research process.

The Process of Setting Up Hypotheses

How can a researcher go about in setting up hypotheses for his research problem?

Once the investigative questions are set up, as explained in Section 5.3, for each of the objectives, the researcher should identify the *anticipated or possible answers* to the investigative questions. A survey of related theories and earlier studies and discussions with fellow scientists will facilitate this process.

This process "requires hunch, wit, imagination and method. It demands searching, delving, trying, failing, and trying again and coming to a conclusion."[18]

He, then, should write down those answers as appropriate types of hypotheses — descriptive, relational or causal — as the case may be.

He should evaluate these *tentative hypotheses* in terms of the characteristics of a good hypothesis and refine and record them into logical and testable hypotheses, keeping in mind the rules given below.

Rules of Constructing Hypotheses

Smith[19] suggests certain rules of constructing good hypotheses.

1. Search for *variable measurements* with the most *quantitative* characteristics available.

Precise quantitative measurement is more critical in testing theory than qualitative characteristics. Hage[20] gives *five* techniques of searching for and creating variables out of non-variable concepts.

17. Bales, Robert, *Interaction Process Analysis,* Reading, Mass: Addison – Wesley, 1950, p. 117.
18. Johnson, Earls, *Theory and Practice of the Social Sciences, op. cit.,* p. 192.
19. Smith H.W., *Strategies of Social Research — The Methodological Imagination,* Englewood Cliffs, N.J: Prentice Hall, 1975, pp. 44- 53.
20. Hage, Gerald, *Techniques and Problems of Theory Construction in Sociology,* New York: Wiley, 1972, pp. 16-28.

First, the researcher can search for *implied dimensions* underlying non-variable concepts. Campbell[21] provides a good example for this method in studying the non-variable concept "social group." He identifies four underlying dimensions of degrees of proximity, similarity, perceived common fate, and perceived spatial pattern.

Second, one can create new variables by comparing conceptual synonyms or analogies. Price[22] used the synonym technique in his study of organizational measurement; concepts like "participation in decision making", "organization control", "power" and "influence" refer to the degree of organizational centralization.

Third, one can search the literature for *rarely occurring associations* between phenomena. Cognitive dissonance theory in Sociology got its start in this manner.

Fourth, one can generate new variables through *ordering many* concepts from more to less abstract.

2. Make the variable scale properties explicit by stating all of the variable's mutually exclusive and totally inclusive *categories* by degree.

For example, a variable like 'income' may be categorized as (1) upto Rs. 500 per month, (2) Rs. 501 to 1,000, (3) Rs. 1,001 to 2,000, (4) Rs. 2,001 and above. Levels of bureaucratic structure may be defined by (1) 1 to 3 levels, (2) 4 to 10 levels, (3) 11 or more levels.

3. Describe the means used to sort observation into your variable categories in sufficient detail so that your *methods* may be evaluated and replicated by others.

"Personality disintegration" is a good example of poorly operationalized variable. It is an unreliable measure and cannot be replicated.

4. Always consider *alternative operations,* which might be more appropriate for a given variable.

5. Analyse variables through their relationships. Non-ratio one-variable distribution is arbitrary, since it has no intrinsic lower boundary.

6. *Link* two or more formal *propositions* through a shared independent or dependent variable wherever possible.

For example, form the following concrete observations —

1. Married persons are less likely than unmarried persons to commit suicide.
2. Married persons with children are less likely than married persons without children to commit suicide —

The following abstract formal hypotheses may be inductively produced:

1. Suicide rates vary directly with the degree of individualism.
2. Suicide rates vary indirectly with the degree of group cohesion.

Testing of Hypotheses

Science does not admit anything as valid knowledge, until satisfactory tests confirm its validity. Hypotheses are only hunches and *provisional* ideas. They should not be considered as facts, however

---

21. Campbell, D.T., " Common Fate, Similarity and other Indices of the Status of Aggregates of Persons as Social Entities", *Behavioural Science* 3, 1958a, pp. 14-25.
22. Price, J.I., *Handbook of Organizational Measurement*, Toronto: D.C. Health, 1972.

systematically they have been arrived at. They are just meant for '*testing*' through the research process. Only after thorough testing, they may be accepted or rejected. What should be the attitude of the researcher in testing the hypotheses?

The researcher should not start out, to "prove" his hypotheses. He should 'test' them by adopting appropriate scientific procedures and accept the negative or positive results in true scientific spirit of inquiry. He should have an *open mind,* and with a spirit of *disinterestedness* he should test them. He should not defend his hypotheses when facts prove the contrary. Hypotheses should not become a vested interest.

The process of testing hypotheses embodies the major part of the research process. It consists of operationalisation of the concepts, construction of data gathering tools, collection of data, statistical analysis of data and drawing inferences from the results. Tests of significance are applied. If the facts confirm the hypotheses, then the latter are tenable. *Two types of errors* may occur while testing hypotheses. We may reject a hypothesis, which is true and should not be rejected. Or we may accept a hypothesis, which is false and should be rejected. These errors are called *type I and type II* errors respectively. Every care should be taken at various stages of the study in order to avoid both types of errors.

The statistical procedure of testing hypotheses is discussed in detail in Chapter 11.

5.5 CONCEPTS

Introduction

The title of the research problem, the objectives of the study, the investigative questions and the hypotheses consist of concepts. Those concepts should be *precisely defined.* This is an important step in the formulation of the research problem. It is the definitions of concepts that determine the information needs of the study. Therefore, precise definitions of concepts are essential for planning the subsequent steps in the research process.

Definition

Each science attempts to investigate particular sections or aspects of reality, with an abstract system of thought to interpret those segments. So it develops its own terms or concepts for communicating its findings. For example, 'utility' in Economics represents 'the capacity of a thing to satisfy a human want'; it has no ethical or moral significance; 'responsibility' in management means 'obligation' of a subordinate to do the assigned job. A scientist abstracts meanings out of observed reality and attaches names to those meanings. Such names are concepts. They are indicated by words or phrases.

A concept is, thus, an *abstract symbol* representing an object, a property of an object or a certain phenomenon, e.g., book, person, intelligence, and meeting. It is an *abstraction from sense impressions or percepts.* A concept like 'aggression' or 'frustration' or 'political participation' represents a number of events under one general name or label. Therefore, "a concept is in reality a definition in short-hand of a *class or group of facts.*"[23] "The purpose is to present in simplified form the thinking about phenomena, events and processes."[24]

---

23. Young, Pauline V., *Scientific Social Surveys and Research, op. cit.,* p. 115.
24. *Ibid.,* p. 116.

Significance

The significance of concepts stems from their ability to transfer information in the form of images about experiences in the empirical world. By means of concepts, researchers can transmit to their colleagues and to the public a whole system of experience acquired through research."[25]

Useful concepts represent *generalized abstraction* regarding empirical phenomena. For example, the concept 'weight' represents a trait common to various physical object. 'Income' represents a trait common to different persons. The usefulness of concepts is evaluated by the extent to which they permit meaningful classification of objects or traits. "Concepts, then, are means not only of communication but also of generalizations."[26]

As generalizations, concepts are useful for *constructing assumption*. The *liking* of two or more *concepts* leads to the generation of *assumptions,* such as "if concept A, then concept B" or "the greater A, the smaller B." the combination of a number of assumption into a system leads to the *construction of formal theories*. For example, people belong to various levels of "social class" – another concept " democratic participation" an assumption — 'Democratic participation covaries with social class' — be constructed. The addition of a number of further interrelated assumptions will bring about a formal theory from which researchers may deduce propositions.

Characteristics of Concepts

Concepts have several Characteristics. It is important for a researcher to understand them.

1. Concepts are *symbols* which we attach to the bundle of meanings that we hold.
2. Concepts *represent only one part* of reality. That is, we abstract only certain meaning or implications out of the object for our use. For example, a concept like book means different things to different persons according to their needs. To the author, it is an embodiment of his organized thoughts; to the publisher and seller, it is a physical object of a given weight and volume.
3. Thus different people hold *different concepts* of the same thing.
4. Concepts also *represent various degrees of abstraction*. For example, a specific calculator, at a first level of abstraction is considered as a mechanical devise for making mathematical computations. At the third level, it may be considered as an item of office equipment. And so on. Each of these levels of concept abstraction is useful for one purpose or another. For a study of computation satisfaction, the first level is relevant; for a study of office productivity, level 2 and 3 may be of interest.

Types of Concepts

Concepts may be classified into (a) concrete concepts and (b) abstract concepts.

Concrete concepts symbolize material objects, which can be seen touched and felt, e.g., book, table, building.

Abstract concepts refer to properties or characteristics of objects, e.g., weight, height, attitude, intelligence, leadership. They are *constructs*, i.e., they *represent inferences* deduced from observable

25. Nachimias, David and Nachimias, Chava, *Research Methods in the Social Sciences,* New York: St. Martin's Press, 1976, p. 15.
26. *Ibid.*, p. 16.

events. They symbolize *inferences "at a higher level of abstraction* from concrete events and their meaning cannot be easily conveyed pointing to specific objects, individuals or events."[27]

The concrete observable events which represent the abstract concepts or constructs are called *variables.* While constructs are the abstractions, variables are representations of constructs. Any one construct (e.g., social status, power or intelligence) can be measured in many different ways, because there are a variety of concrete representations of any abstract idea.[28] For example, 'power' could represent the amount of influence a person has at his organisation, at home, in the neighbourhood, in the mass media or in the political circle. Each of these representations is a different variable, but they are all related to the construct. Taken together they are what we mean by 'power.'

Problems in Defining Concepts

The process of defining concepts is not easy. Even in defining such common place objects as 'book', or 'water', we may face difficulties. We can point these objects and show pictures of them, but to present a precise word picture is extremely difficult. Abstract concepts like 'motivation', 'intelligence', or 'frustration' are still more difficult to define. Unclear and inadequate definitions lead to lack of clarity in scientific communication. Some of the *reasons* for this problem are given below:

1. Concepts develop from a shared experience: When scientists perceive or experience particular things, they symbolise them through scientific terms. The dictionary definitions are seldom satisfactory. What a chemist means by 'titration', demographer by 'the net reproductive rate', or management expert by 'the managerial effectiveness' would require very elaborate verbal definitions. They can be best understood by participating in the *operations* to which these terms refer.

2. Term used to denote scientific concepts may also have meanings in other frames of reference: many scientific words are newly coined or taken from Greek or Latin roots, e.g., Audit from 'Audire'; cooperation from 'co-operari'. Concepts may also be named after their discoverers, e.g., "Raman's Effect". These concepts have their scientific meanings only. But many scientific terms are taken from common usage, e.g., 'mass' — a big pile of something — refers to a quality of matter in physics; 'culture' which means tillage or rearing – refers to the totality of the social heritage of a society in sociology. Such multiple meanings of concepts cause confusion.

3. A term may refer to different phenomena: For example, the term 'function' has several usages. In popular usage, it means ceremony. In economic sense, it means activity (e.g., functions of a commercial bank); in a mathematical sense, it refers to relationship, e.g., the level of living is a function of economic position. And so on. Such words cause confusion.

4. Different terms may refer to the same phenomenon: For example, the words 'enquiry', 'study', 'research', investigation', have similar meanings; 'status', rank', position' have similar meanings. A scientist may use such different words with some subtle differences in meaning, but his reader may take them as synonyms.

5. A term may have no immediate empirical referent: Some concepts may have logical relationship with other concepts, but may not be empirically measurable, e.g., 'social milieu' or 'social structure' in sociology, 'managerial effectiveness' in management are not empirically measurable.

27. Selltiz, Claire, *et al.*, *Research Methods in Social Relations,* New York: Holt, Rinehart and Winston, 1959, p. 41.
28. Kidder, Lousie H. and Charles M. Judd, *Research Methods in Social Relations,* Tokyo: CBS Publishing Ltd., 1986, p. 40.

6. The meaning of concepts may change: Terms are continuously modified, as knowledge accumulates. Definitions change and the consequent shifts in meaning confuse the reader. For example, the term 'intelligence' originally was conceived as an inherited stable intellectual potential. Now it is redefined as a 'score' made on certain types of tests.

Types of Definition of Concepts

Different levels of abstraction and the combination of abstractions into constructs are important to research. In communication, there is a constant interplay among levels of abstracting and types of meaning. Accordingly, concepts may be defined in several ways: (1) ostensive definition, (2) verbal definition, (3) descriptive definition and (4) operational definition.

Ostensive definition: A concept may be defined ostensively. Russell describes ostensive definition as "any process by which a person is taught to understand a word other than by the use of other words."[29] We may define 'elephant' by pointing to a life-like model of elephant; 'typing' may be defined by pointing to the typing work performed by a typist. This kind of definition is not suitable for verbal communication.

Verbal definition: This means definition of a *word in terms of other words* either at the same or a higher or lower level of abstraction. For example, a customer is defined as a 'patron.' This definition is of no value unless one understands the meaning of patron. Of even less value is a definition in terms of higher-level abstractions, e.g., a definition of customer as a source of business income. It says very little about the nature of customerness or patronage.

Verbal definitions are of two types: (1) descriptive definitions and (2) operational definitions.

Descriptive or Nominal definition: This is a dictionary type definition in terms of other concepts. This is also known as a *conceptual definition.* Conceptual definitions that facilitate communications have two traits. First, a concept is described by other concepts, not by itself, e.g., the definition of 'power' as 'the ability to use power' is useless. But a description in terms of *lower* level abstraction is more useful, e.g., the definition of a customer as one who buys the products or services from a given firm. Second, a *positive* definition is preferable to a negative one. For example, defining "intelligence" as "a characteristic that lacks form, colour and weight" contributes little to communication. The descriptive definitions of concepts are of little value in research where we seek to measuring concepts.

Operational definition: This is quantification of a nominal definition, i.e., it is a definition in terms of specific measuring or *testing criteria* or operations. This definition specifies the operations which observe, measure and record the phenomenon symbolized by the concept. These criteria should define a person, action, condition or phenomenon in an unambiguous manner. The criteria should also be so *objective* that any competent observer can secure the same results by using the definition. Some example of descriptive and operational definitions of concepts are given below:

Only when operational definitions are used, can variables be measured with precision and consistency, and through the corresponding empirical observations, can hypotheses and theorizes be tested.

---

29. Russell, Bertrand, *Human Knowledge – Its Scope and Limits,* New York: Simon and Schuster, 1948, p. 63.

Concept	*Descriptive definition*	*Operational definition*
1. Customer	A Patron of firm 'x' or one who buys products/services from firm 'x'	One who has purchased at least one third of his family's needs from firm 'x' during the last 3 months
2. Agriculture labour	One who works on others' farms for wages	One who earns not less than 50% of his annual income from agricultural wages.
3. Year	A period of 12 months	Calendar year, January 1 through December 31, inclusive.
4. Small-scale industrial undertaking	An industrial undertaking which manufactures some product/s on a small-scale	An industrial undertaking whose investment in plant and machinery does not exceed (say) Rs. 35 lakhs.
5. Boy	A male youth	A male of 12-16 years of age.

The important *definition criteria* of operational definition are: (1) *adequacy* of meaning, (2) *precision* of meaning, and (3) *linkability*. Linkability means combination of two or more concepts in the development of concept interrelationship such as propositions, hypotheses and theories. In this sense, "concepts are the *knots* in a network of systematic interrelations in which laws and theoretical principles form the threads."[30]

Hypothetical concepts: Concepts that cannot be given operational definitions are usually termed as hypothetical concepts."[31] Opinions regarding their role in the scientific method vary. Bridgman,[32] a founder of the operational approach, claimed that concepts which cannot be operationally defined prevent scientific progress. According to him, the sole meaning of concepts is related to their operations; "the concept is synonymous with the corresponding set of operations."[33]

This orthodox operational approach did not stand the test of time, since it was recognized that hypothetical concepts had an important role in the stage of theorizing. For example, "subconscious", a hypothetical concept, has served in developing theories of personality and behaviour.

Steps in Operationalisation of Concepts

Operational definitions of concepts are the means by which we quantify variables. They are always necessary in a research project.

The process of operationalization or defining concepts operationally is a complex task, requiring extensive knowledge and reflective thinking. It involves a series of steps or procedures to be followed to obtain a measurement. The broad steps involved in the process of Operationalisation are as follows:

The researcher should select the major concepts from the title of the research problem, the objectives of the study, the investigative questions and the hypotheses. He should attempt to operationally define each of those concepts in the following manner:

30. Hempel, Karl G., *Philosophy of Natural Science,* Englewood Cliffs, N.J. Prentice Hall, 1966, p. 94.
31. Simon, Julian L., *Basic Research Methods in Social Science,* New York: Random House, 1969, p. 16.
32. Bridgman, Percy W., *The Logic of Physics,* New York: Macmillan, 1961.
33. *Ibid.,* p. 5.

1. Examine the definition of the concept *in the published literature*-books, research articles, research reports etc.- keeping the chronology of the definitions in mind.

2. Discover the various *usage* of the concepts and *analyse* the apparent *meaning elements* of the concept, e.g., the concept of political participation' consists of such elements as (a) awareness of voting right, (b) awareness of citizen's responsibilities, (c) an analysis of the manifestoes of contesting parties and their political philosophy and economic policy, and (d) choosing a particular party and voting for it.

3. Identify the *measurement criteria* relating to the meaning element and specify appropriate quantitative measurements for those criteria. This step is relatively easier in the case of concrete concepts. For example, the maximum limit of investment in plant and machinery for defining a small-scale industrial unit is fixed as so many lakhs of Rupees. Usually the limit fixed by the government is adopted in such cases.

In the case of an *abstract concept,* identify the indirect operations which observes and measure the phenomenon symbolized by the concept, and *construct a measuring scale* by assigning appropriate score to each of them on the basis of their relative importance. (For details see topic 5.6 of Chapter 5, and topic 8.3 of Chapter 8, below).

4. Formulate a tentative definition based on the measurement dimension or the measurement scale, as the case may be.

5. Submit the definition to as wide a *critical appraisal* as possible.

6. Make final revision on the basis of the legitimate criticism received.

7. Examine the degree of congruence between the conceptual definition and the operational definition of the concept. If 'intelligence' is defined conceptually as 'the ability to think abstractly' and operationally by an 'intelligence test' what is the congruence between the two definitions? Does the score secured by an individual in the intelligence test represent everything that the concept 'intelligence' is supposed to convey?

The degree of this congruence can be evaluated with the aid of validity tests discussed in Section 5.6 and Chapter II, below.

An operational definition specifies so precisely the process of measuring a variable that any one else could repeat the steps and obtain the same measurement. However, the *limitation* of any operational definition should be recognized. "Its very specificity and concreteness limit the breadth and depth of what we are able to measure."[34] Thus, it is rarely sufficient to capture the rich and complex ideas contained in a theoretical construct. A researcher should be aware of this inadequacy and imperfection of an operational definition. He should do his best to improve his operational definition of concept.

Illustration: Let us illustrate the Operationalisation of a concept of "*Socio-Economic Development*" which is the ultimate aim of planning in developing countries like India. What is "Socio-Economic Development"? What are the relevant socio-economic criteria, which indicate development? How can 'socio-economic development' be measured? Two approaches seem to have emerged in this regard. The first is mainly associated with the work going on at the United Nations Research Institute for Social Development (UNRISD) and the other primarily with the World Bank and the Institute for Development Studies of the University of Sussex (IDS). The UNRISD studies

34. Kidder, Louise H. and Charles M. Judd, *op. cit.*, p. 41.

aim at devising unitary indices which reflect broad-based socio-economic development. As a system of interdependent variables, development is measured by building up a composite index consisting of carefully chosen socio-economic indicators.[35] This index, like the per capita output index does not reflect the quality of development.

The IDS-World Bank approach adopts an index of development[36] which in a single social welfare function combines the objectives of growth and distribution of equity. The social welfare function is conceived of as

$$G = w_1 g_1 + w_2 g_2 + w_3 g_3 + w_4 g_4 + w_5 g_5$$

Where 'G' is the index of growth of total social welfare, 'w_1' is the weight assigned to the group '$_1$', and 'g_1' is the rate of growth of income of each group (classified into quintiles by income size of assets or any other criteria).

Another very similar concept of development comes from Dudley Seers, for whom the essential criteria of development are the reduction of poverty, inequality, and unemployment.[37] The Work Bank- IDS concept of development does not specifically use the employment criterion which Dudley Seers does. While stressing such criteria as reduction of poverty inequality, and unemployment, it should not be implied that "economic" growth as well as equity, so that it is truly "socio-economic" in character, it must be based upon criteria which can measure changes over time in the aggregate output as well as the existing production potential of the economy, and also throw adequate light on the emerging style of its development. While the former would take care of the 'growth' or 'economic' aspect, the latter would account for 'equity' or 'social' aspect of development. This is, therefore, the *raison d'etre* behind a synthetic approach to the concept of development.

Sharma adopts such a synthetic approach in his study.[38]

His approach aims at measuring the following aspects of development:

1. The actual growth of the economy over time measured in terms of the GNP time-series data.
2. The growth potential level measured in terms of infrastructural indices:
   (a) demographic features like literacy ratio and trends toward urbanization, level of development of social overhead capital, level of development of human capital.
3. The extent of socio-economic structure is measured in terms of —
   (a) the share of primary, secondary and tertiary sectors in total output and employment,
   (b) the share of different commodity groups in the total labour force; and
4. The distributional parameters of actual growth is indicated by —
   (a) share of different social groups or income classes in variables like income, consumption, skills or productive assets,
   (b) level of unemployment and under-employment,

---

35. McGranaham D.V., *et al., Contents and Measurements of Socio-Economic Development,* Geneva, United Nations Research Institute for Social Development (UNRISD), Report No. 70-10, 1970, p. 12.
36. Chenery, Hollis, *et al., Redistirbution with Growth,* New York: Oxford University Press, 1974, Chapter II.
37. Dudley Seers in N.T. Uphoff and W.F. Iichman, (eds.), *The Political Economy of Development,* Berkeley, L.A: University of California Press, 1972, pp. 123-129.
38. Sharma L.R., *The Economy of Himachal Pradesh: Growth and Structure,* Delhi: Mittal Publications, 1987, pp. 12-15.

(c) degree of socio-economic integration of tribals and other depressed classes achieved, as reflected in indices like the gap between the average and the class-specific income, consumption, and skill levels.

The indicators enlisted above are only suggestive. The choice of indicators would vary from one study to another and would depend on the unit of study, the purpose of study and availability of data.

On the basis of the above conceptual model, Sharma has included the following indicators in the composite development index[39] for comparing inter-state comparison of development performance:

Development Index

I. *Aggregative Socio-Economic Features*

1. per capita income
2. per capita monthly expenditure in rural areas
3. per capita monthly expenditure in urban areas
4. unemployment rate
5. growth rate of population.

II. *Poverty Indicators*

1. per capita monthly expenditure of the bottom decile of cultivator households
2. per capita monthly expenditure of rural non-cultivating wage earner households
3. population below the poverty line (to be defined)
4. extent of – under nutrition (percentage of calorie – deficient consumer units).

III. *Household Asset Distribution*

1. proportion of rural households owning no lands
2. percentage of rural households with assets below the poverty line limit.
3. co-efficient of concentration of assets among rural households.
4. concentration ratio of area owned by rural households.
5. concentration ratio of operational land holding.

IV. *Agricultural output*

1. annual average productivity of major food crop
2. annual compound growth rate of agricultural yield
3. average annual growth rate of yield of foodgrains
4. average yield of foodgrains per hectare.

V. *Other Structural Characteristics*

1. proportion of agricultural workers in rural labour.
2. literacy percentage
3. infrastructural development
   (a) bank offices per lakh of population
   (b) road length per lakh of population
   (c) percentages of total villages electrified

39. *Ibid.*, pp. 141-143.

(d) school enrollment:

(e) share of priority sectors in bank credit

(i) as % of persons in age group 6-11

(ii) as % of persons in age group 11-14

(f) hospitals and dispensaries per 10,000 of population.

5.6 MEASUREMENT

Introduction

In social science research we have to deal with various social and psychological variables. Their measurement is one of the vital stages in the research process. The measurement of social and psychological variables is a complex and demanding task. There has been increased interest in measurement in social sciences during the past 35 years. This section is devoted to discuss the meaning and nature of measurement, the need of measurement, its functions, the level of measurement, measurement procedure and validity and reliability of measuring instruments.

What is Stevens Measurement?

Stevens[40] defines measurement as "the assignment of numerals to objects or events according to rules." Campbell[41] defines it as "the assignment of numbers to represent properties." According to Torgerson measurement is "the assignment of numbers to objects to represent amounts or degrees of a property possessed by all of the objects.[42] Suppose we desire to conduct a study of persons who seek admission to M.B.A. programme. One point of interest is to compute sex-wise percentage of applicants. We may examine the applications received and map or match the observed properties of applicants into a sex classification. The rule of correspondence is: if the applicant is a male, assign to 'O', if female, assign to '1'. Any other symbols such as 'M' and 'F' may be used, since the number codes are for identification only. Thus, measurement in its simplest form consists of assigning numerals or symbols to real objects and this process is called *mapping.* A numeral has no quantitative meaning unless one imputes to it such a meaning. Numerals can be used to label objects like individuals, events or things. Numerals that are given quantitative meaning become numbers; these enable the use of mathematical and statistical techniques for purpose of description, explanation and prediction.

The assignment of numerals or numbers to objects is done according to a rule. A rule explicates the way in which numerals or numbers are to be assigned. It is the most significant component of the measurement procedure, because it determines the quality of measurement. The range of its uses increases with the exactness of the measurement.

What is Measured?

Concepts[43] used in research consist of 'objects' and 'properties' (i.e., characteristics) of objects. For example, a person's physical properties consists of height, weight etc. In a research process, we measure the *properties* of objects – *not the objects* themselves. Abstract properties like intelligence,

---

40. Stevens S.S. "Mathematics, Measurement and Psychophysics", in Stevens S.S., ed., *Handbook of Experimental Psychology,* New York: John Wiley & Sons, 1951, p. 1.
41. Campbell, N. *What is Science?* New York: Dover, 1952, p. 110.
42. Torgerson W.S., *Theory and Method of Scaling,* New York: John Wiley & Sons, 1959, p. 19.
43. See topic 5.5 above, for detailed discussion on *Concepts.*

motivation, attitude cannot be directly observed; one must infer them from the observation of presumed indicants of the properties. We infer a child's level of intelligence from the score which he secures in an intelligence test. Thus, we actually measure *indicants*[44] of the *properties of objects*. The indicants from which properties are inferred are specified by operational definitions,[45] i.e., definitions that specify the observations of the behavioural indicants of properties.

Need for Measurement

Why do we need to measure social or psychological variables? When the researcher develops an explanation for a social phenomenon or problem, he constructs a theory. The theory is tested through the verification of a hypothesis derived from it. A hypothesis can be verified statistically, only when the variables in it are measured. Thus, the need for measurement arises.

Functions of Measurement

Measurement serves several purposes. First, it *facilitates empirical description of social and psychological phenomena.*

For example, in a study of a tribal community, the researcher has to classify and categorize the cultural patterns and behaviours he observes. Measuring devices assist him in the classification process.

Second, measurement *renders data amenable to statistical manipulation and treatment.* The application of statistical techniques for comparing groups, studying relationships between variables, etc. is possible, only when the data collected through various methods are amenable to quantification. Measurement devices make it possible to quantify variables.

Third, measurement facilitates *testing of theories and hypotheses.* Theories are formulated to explain and predict social phenomena (e.g., ethnic conflict, communal disharmony, labour unrest, delinquency, etc.) and psychological phenomena (e.g., low morale, job satisfaction, attitude, etc.) Researchers derive hypotheses from these theories and subject them to empirical test. Once the variables in hypotheses are quantified through measuring devices, the hypotheses can be tested easily.

Fourth, measurement *enables researchers to differentiate between objects or people* in terms of specific properties they possess. Do girls perform better then boys in college examinations? Does productivity vary among work groups? To deal with such questions, it is necessary to measure the concerned variables. Measurement of variables enables us to classify individuals or objects and thus to differentiate between them. In this way, measurement performs a *classificatory* function.

The above four functions are not necessarily mutually exclusive, but are inter-related, and complementary to one another.

Measurement Postulates

Since the measurement is based on numbers, the properties of numbers are relevant to measurement. These properties are; (1) identity (or equality), (2) rank order and (3) additivity. The concept of additivity implies all the four fundamental operations of addition, subtraction, multiplication and division.

---

44. According to Kerlinger an indicant is "merely a convenient word used to mean something that points to something else." See Kerlinger, Fred N. *Foundations of Behavioural Research,* Delhi: Surjeet Publications, 1983, p. 432.
45. See the last subtitle in 5.5 *Concepts,* above.

With reference to the above characteristics, there are three postulates[46] basic to measurement. They are:

1. ***Order:*** numbers are ordered. One number is greater than, less than, or equal to another.

   $a > b$ or $a < b$ or $a = b$

   if $a = b$ and $b = c$, then $a = c$

   if $a = p$ and $b = q$, then $a + b = p + q$.

2. ***Distance:*** difference between numbers are ordered. The difference between any pairs of numbers is greater than, less than or equal to the difference between any other pair of numbers.

3. ***Origin:*** the number series has a unique origin indicated by the number zero.

Levels of Measurement

Combinations of the above characteristics of order, distance and origin provide the following four levels of measurement:

Levels	*Characteristics*
Nominal	no order, distance or origin
Ordinal	order, but no distance or origin
Interval	both order and distance, but no origin
Ratio	order, distance and origin

Nominal measurement: This is the simplest and lowest level of measurement. This level involves the categorization of variable into several nominal sub-classes by assigning numerals or any other symbols to mutually exclusive sub-classes. For example, the variable 'sex' is classified into two categories: 'male' and 'female', assigning '1' to male and '2' to female; 'religion' may be classified into five categories; 1. Hindus, 2. Sikhs, 3. Muslims, 4. Christians, and 5. others: ' caste' in terms of ritual status into three categories: 1. high, 2. medium, 3. low. And so on. The numerals 1,2,3… assigned to categories of variable are just labels only and have no quantitative value.

Nominal measurement is the least powerful of the four levels. It indicates no order or distance relationship and has no arithmetic origin. The only quantification possible is counting the number of cases in each sub-class or category. For analysis, we can use mode, chi square test and co-efficient of contingency test.

Nominal measurement is useful for categorizing personal variables, types of organizations, work groups, etc.

Ordinal measurement: In this level of measurement objects or persons are ordered by rank from least to most on a continuum, with respect to an operationally defined property. Ranks are assigned in ascending or descending orders: the highest categories '1', the next '2', the third one '3' and so on or the lowest category '1', the next higher one '2', the next one '3' and so on. The numbers indicate rank order only. They do not indicate that the intervals between them are equal, nor do they indicate absolute quantities. Thus, the real difference between ranks '1' and '2' may be more or less than the difference between '2' and '3'.

---

46. A postulate is a statement assumed to be true without requiring any proof.

Various relationships may be used for ranking such as 'greater than', 'higher than', 'more desired', 'more difficult', superior to', 'happier than' and so on.

The rank order classification may be based on either *one* property or *composite* properties. For example, if we have to rank individuals according to their socio-economic level, we have to consider several variables like income, education, occupation, wealth, ritual status etc. In such cases we have to give relative weights to each variable and arrive at composite score. In terms of composite scores, individuals could be ranked.

The *procedures* used for construction of ordinal scales include rank, order, rating, paired comparison.

Most common *variables suitable* for ordinal measurement include economic status, social class, social distance, attitude, opinions, preferences, prestige ranking, ratings of organizations, and test performances.

The *statistical techniques* suitable for ordinal scales are:

Measure of central tendency	:	Median
Dispersion	:	Percentile or quartile measure
Correlation	:	Rank order coefficients
Statistical test of significance	:	Non-parametric methods

Interval measurement: This measurement has the powers of nominal and ordinal measurements plus one additional strength — the concept of equality of interval, but the numbers on an interval scale cannot be multiplied or divided because the scale does not have a true zero. It has an arbitrary zero only. Temperature gauge- Centigrade or Fahrenheit thermometer — is a typical example for interval level of measurement. In reading it we know that '40 degrees' is exactly 10 degrees warmer than 30 degrees and 10 degrees cooler than 50 degrees. Altitude based on sea level and calendar years are other examples for interval measurements.

Interval scales not only provide powerful measurement but also are quicker to complete. But it is difficult to use them for measuring socio-economic and psychological variables.

More powerful statistical techniques can be used with interval scales. The suitable *techniques of statistical* analysis are:

Measure of central tendency	:	Arithmetic Mean
Dispersion	:	Standard deviation
Correlation	:	Product moment technique
Statistical test of significance	:	't' test and 'F' test.

Ratio measurement: This is the highest and most ideal level of measurement. This is suitable for measuring properties which have natural zero points. Examples are weight, height, distance, area, money value, population counts, rate of return, etc. Since there is an absolute or natural zero, all arithmetic operations including multiplication and division are possible. Numbers on a ratio scale (e.g., weight of students in a school) indicate the actual amounts of the property under measurement. A weight of 50 Kg is twice as large as that of 25 Kg.

Behavioural and psychological properties like social participation, leadership quality, happiness, intelligence, aptitude, morale, satisfaction etc. do not have true zero points. Hence, it is not possible to use ratio scales for their measurement.

Variables that can be measured at a ratio level can also be measured at the interval, ordinal and nominal levels. As a rule, properties that can be measured at a higher level can also be measured at lower levels, but not *vice versa.*

All *statistical techniques* usable at nominal, ordinal and interval levels are usable with ratio scales. In addition, geometric and harmonic means and co-efficient of variation can be used.

The Characteristics of a Good Measurement Tool

A measurement tool must satisfy certain criteria. The most important criteria to be used in evaluating a measurement tool are described below:

1. Unidimensionality: This means the scale should measure one characteristic at a time, e.g., the ruler should measure length, not temperature also.

2. Linearity: This means that a Scale should follow the straight-line model. Some scoring system should be devised, preferably one based on inter-changeable units. In a ruler an inch is an inch whether it lies at one end of the ruler or at the other, but in altitude scales such interchangeability cannot be ensured. In such cases, ranking is preferable.

3. Validity: This refers to the ability of a scale to measure what it is supposed to measure. (For a detailed discussion *see* separate sub-title in this section).

4. Reliability: This is an attribute of consistency. A scale should give an accurate and precise measure of what we want to measure.

5. Accuracy and Precision: A tool should give an accurate and precise measure of what we want to measure.

6. Simplicity: A scale should be as simple as possible; an elaborate, complicated and over-refined scale may become unduly cumbersome, costly or even useless.

7. Practicability: This is "concerned with a wide range of factors of economy, convenience and interpretability....[47] "Some trade off is usually needed between an 'ideal' tool and that which the budget can afford. The benefit to be derived should commensurate with the cost incurred.

The tool should be easily administrable; it should contain proper instructions; it should be easily understandable and conveniently arranged for easy completion.

In order to enable others to interpret the results of a test, there is need for such aids as a statement of its function, its construction procedure and guides for interpreting the result.

Construction of a Measurement Tool

The process of constructing a measurement tool, involves the following general steps:

1. Concept identification: The first step is to gain a thorough knowledge of the topic under study through observations, a careful study of the literature and discussions with experts. The concepts of the selected problem under study should be identified.

---

47. Robert L., Throndike and Elizabeth Hagen, *Measurement and Evaluation in Psychology and Education*, New York: John Wiley and Sons, 3rd ed., p. 162.

2. Concept development: Each concept should be defined operationally. (See *"Steps in Operationalisation of Concepts"* in 5.5 *Concepts* in Chapter 5, above).

3. Concept specification:[48] By an analysis of the phenomena out of which the concept emerged, we should develop "aspects". "components", "dimension" or similar specifications. They are derived logically from the concept or empirical observations reported in studies. For example, the concept of 'corporate (or company) image' consists of such dimensions as product reputation, employer role, customer satisfaction, corporate leadership, contribution to social welfare and concern for environment. Similarly, the concept of 'buyer behaviour' consists of the following dimensions: brand advertisement recall, brand awareness, brand preference, purchase decision, and brand royalty/shift.

4. Indicator selection: The next step is to develop the indicators by which to measure each element or dimension of the concept. Indicators are specific questions, statements or other devices by which respondent's knowledge, opinions, expectations, etc. are measured. Since there is seldom a perfect or absolute measure of a concept, we should consider several possibilities. A set of questions or a scale may be used depending on the nature of the element to be measured.

For example, a company's reputation for civic responsiveness may be rated by a scale as follows:

Which of the following best describes the reputation of X company with respect its participation in community development programmes? (please check one).

— The company is a leader in these programmes

— The company is a strong supporter but not a leader in these programmes

— The company is a an average supporter of these programmes

— The company is a below-average supporter of these programmes

— The company does not support these programmes

The brand awareness may be studied by a set of questions:

1. Are you familiar with product X?
2. What brands of product 'X' are known to you?
3. Through what sources have you come to know about the brands?

— friends/neighbours

— advertisements in daily news papers

— advertisements in magazines

— advertisements in TV

— advertisements in Radio

— outdoor advertisements

— others (please specify).

On the basis of several pre-test, the questions, or items should be finalized. Care should be taken to see that they fully span the concept dimension.

48. See Paul F. Lazarfeld, *et al.,* *Continuities in the Language of Social Research,* New York: The Free Press, 1972.

5. Formation of scale: The final step is to combine the indicators into a single composite scale. This is developed by assigning scale values to the responses and summing up the scores, giving weightages in proportion to the relative importance of various elements constituting the concept under measurement. After the scale is formed, checks are made on its reliability and validity. If these prove satisfactory, the scale is then administered in the full survey. •

For a detailed discussion on various types of Scales, see topic 8.3 *Measurement Scales and Indices,* in Chapter 8, below.

Validity

Validity is an important requirement of a measuring instrument like attitude scale. Validity means the effectiveness (or success) of an instrument in measuring the specific property which it intends to measure. The measurement of physical properties like height, weight, length etc., does not pose the problem of validity, because it is direct and standardized measuring devices are available. But measurement of abstract properties like attitude, morale, motivation etc. is indirect and gives rise to the problem of validity. It becomes necessary to gather some sort of evidence to show that the concerned measuring instrument does in fact measure what it supposed to measure. The degree of validity of an instrument is determined through the application of logic and/or statistical procedures. "A measurement procedure is valid to the degree that it measures what it purports to measure."[49]

Type of validity: Validity is concerned with different aspects of the measurement situation. Accordingly, it is classified into content validity, predictive validity and construct validity. Each of these types uses either logic, statistical verification or both for determining the degree of validity and has special value under certain conditions.

Content validity: There are two forms of content validity: face validity and sampling validity. *Face Validity* is a logical type resting on the investigator's subjective evaluation as to the validity of a measuring instrument. For example, an investigator may construct a scale containing 10 or 15 statements to measure the variable "liberalism". He then evaluates each statement to assess whether its construct is related to "liberalism". He may also request some specialists (judges) to assess this. If there is an agreement among the judges, the researcher may be satisfied with the face validity of the scale. However, face validity is a poor way of determining validity; it is often a matter of opinion.

Sampling Validity refers to the *representative character* of the *content* of the instrument. Every variable has a content universe of items (statements, questions or indicators) reflecting the indicants to be measured. The measuring instrument's content must adequately represent the content universe of the property being measured. Sampling validity can be determined by comparing the instrument items with the universe of items that could theoretically be included.

The mail problem with content validity is that it has to rely entirely on subjective judgments as to the relevance of scale items and to the definition of the universe of items from which the scale is drawn. The degree of content validity thus rests primarily on the knowledge, skill and judgement of the instrument designer and/or judges, as the case may be.

Predictive validity: This refers to empirically measured association between the results produced by the instrument and the subsequent actual outcome. For example, an admission test's predictive validity may be examined by computing the correlation coefficient between the admission test scores of the freshmen and their grade-point averages during the first year of study. If this coefficient is

49. Marie Jahoda *et al., Research Methods in Social Research,* New York: The Dryden Press, 1958, p. 109.

greater than 0.50, the predictive validity of the admission test is established. However, this statistical association between predicted outcome and subsequent exhibited outcome is no conclusive indicator of the predictive validity; because the exhibited outcome might have been influenced by a different set of extraneous variables. Since behaviour varies from situation to situation, the prediction of one behaviour from another is a dangerous procedure, unless the situations in which the behaviours occur are psychologically the same. The task of prediction is, then, the forecasting of behaviour in a *specified* situation from a knowledge of the *relevant* characteristics of the persons.[50]

Construct validity: On the basis of theoretical reasoning, an investigator may perceive various kinds and degree of relationships between a property under study and other constructs (or variables). In order to determine the construct validity of a measuring instrument, the investigator has to find that these relationships in fact exits. For example, Rokeach[51] on the basis of theoretical reasoning, constructed a *dogmatism* scale. This instrument consists of statements believed to tap close-mindedness, a way of thinking presumably associated with any ideology. Rokeach theorized that the ideological orientations of individuals are related to their thought processes and behaviours, and predicted that dogmatism is related to intolerance and opinionation. He undertook an extensive series of investigations to test his theory and the construct validity of his scales. In one study he used the *known-groups method.* In this methods, groups of people with "known" characteristics are administered as instrument and the direction of difference is predicted. Rokeach found that Catholic students were more dogmatic than Protestants, as predicted. He also found that communist obtained higher scores on the dogmatism scale than did liberals.

Process of construct validity: Cronbach and Meehl[52] describe the logical process of construct validity: first, a proposition that an instrument measures a certain property – say, property A – is set forth; second, the proposition is inserted into the present theory of property A., third, working through the theory, one predicts other properties that should be related to the instrument and properties that should exhibit no relation to the instrument, finally, one collects data that empirically confirm or reject the predicted relations. If the anticipated relationships are found, the instrument is considered valid. If the predictions do not holdup, there are three (1) the instrument does not measure property A; (2) the theoretical framework that generated the predictions is incorrect; or (3) the research design failed to test the prediction properly. The researcher must then decide as to which of these three conditions has occurred by careful reconstruction of the above process of validation.

Method: The important methods used for validation are: (1) the known groups method, (2) the multitrait-multimethod matrix method, (3) factor analysis.

The known group methods: In this method, the instrument is administered to people with 'known' characteristics. It is valid if it discriminates between the groups. For example, if Communists, Naxalites and Democrats obtain different scores on a scale measuring political attitudes, then the scale is valid.

The Multitrait-multimethod matrix method: This was suggested by Campbell and Fiske.[53] This involves the convergent-discriminant conception of validity. *Convergence* means that different

50. *Ibid.*, p. 112.
51. Milton Rokeach, *The Open and the Closed Mind,* New York: Basic Books, 1960.
52. Lee J. Cronbach and Paul E. Meehl, " Construct Validity in Psychological Tests", *Psychological Bulletin* 52, 1955, pp. 281-302.
53. Donald T. Campbell and Donald W. Fiske, " Convergent and Discriminant Validation by the Multitrait-Multimethod Matrix", *Psychological Bulletin* 56, 1959, pp. 81-105.

method of measuring a particular property should yield similar results. *Discriminability* means that different properties should yield different measurement results even though a similar instrument is used. In a multitrait-multimethod analysis, at least two properties are measured and each is measured by at least two different methods. The intercorrelations among variables within and between methods are computed and analysed. Correlation coefficients among scores for a given property measured by different methods should be higher than correlations among different properties measured by different instruments.

Factor analysis is perhaps the most powerful method of construct validation. This is a statistical technique *designed to determine the basic components of a measure.* For example, the factor analysis of a measure of role clarity may show that the variable consists of three predominant factors – supervisory behaviour, seniority and group cohesiveness. (For detailed discussion on Factor analysis, see Chapter 11: *Statistical Analysis).*

Which validity test to use: A researcher is concerned as to which validity test to use in validating a given measurement instrument. Experts recommend that the validation should include all the three types of validity: content, empirical (i.e., predictive) and construct validity. In the first phase of the construction of a measuring tool, one might evaluate theories that would serve as a basis for the tool; next, a content population of items from which a representative sample to be drawn might be defined; and finally, the validity of the tool might be assessed by correlating it with an external criterion.

Reliability

Reliability means the ability of a measuring instrument to give accurate and consistent result. For example, a weighing scale is reliable, if it gives the same reading when the same object is weighed several times.

Reliability has two aspects: *Stability* and *non-variability or equivalence.* An instrument is stable if it gives consistent results with repeated measurements of the same object. The degree of stability is determined by comparing the results of repeated measurements with the same instrument. Along with repeated observations, statistical measures of dispersion and correlation tests are used. While stability is concerned with personal and situational fluctuations from one time to another, non-variability or equivalence is concerned with variations at one point in time among investigators and samples of items.

Estimation of reliability: The degree of reliability of a measure is indicated by the extent to which it contains variable errors, i.e., differences in measuring results from object to object during any one measuring instance and differences between different measurements of the same object at different time by the same instrument. Since the measurements in social sciences are indirect, the chances of having such variable errors are much greater than in physical science. Various factors such as problem of memory or recall, personal characteristics of the respondents, environmental factors, irrelevance of instrument contents, and ambiguous instructions may cause variable errors.

Each measurement, then, consists of two components: a *'true'* component and an *'error'* component and so reliability is defined as the ratio of the true-score variance* to the observed-score variance.[54] This can be expressed as

---

* The Variance is a measure of the spread of observation or scores; it is a description of the extent to which scores differ from each other. See Chapter 11.

54. David Nachmias and Chava Nachmias, *Research Methods in the Social Sciences, op. cit,* p. 65.

$$\text{Reliability} = \frac{V_t}{V_x} = \frac{V_x - V_e}{V_x}$$

Where V_x = variance of observed scores
V_t = variance of true scores
V_e = variance of errors

If the measurement involves nothing but error, then $V_x = V_e$, and the reliability is zero. On the other hand, when there is no variable error at all, $V_e = 0$ and the reliability becomes 1. Thus reliability may vary from 0 to 1. In practice, it is impossible to compute directly the true score independently of the error in any measurement. Consequently, the ratio V_t/V_x has to be estimated.

Methods of estimating reliability: There are three major methods of estimating reliability: the test-retest method, the parallel-forms technique and the split-half method.

Test-retest method: A measuring instrument is administered to the same group of person at different times. The coefficient of correlation between the two sets of scores is computed. The obtained coefficient is a measure of reliability. Higher the coefficient, higher the degree of reliability.

The test-retest method has two main *limitations*. First, the respondents may remember how they responded at the first time and respond the same way second time. This might yield a high but over-estimated reliability measure. Second, since human attributes are subject to change, it is possible that changes may have occurred in the measured attribute during the measurement interval, thus lowering the estimate of reliability. The test-retest method is thus not fool-proof.

Parallel forms technique: One way of overcoming the limitations of the test-retest methods is the use of two parallel forms of the same tool, containing different but relevant items. The two forms are administered to the same group of persons, and the two sets of scores are correlated to obtain an estimate of reliability. The main problem of this method is the difficulty in determining the equivalence of the two tools.

Split-half method: This method is designed to split the instrument into two sets halves – say, odd-numbered items as one half and the even-numbered items as second half. Each half is used as a separate instrument and the scores of both halves are correlated.

The obtained correlation coefficient is corrected by applying the Spearman-Brown Prophecy formula $r_n = 2^r h/(1+^r h)$ where r_n = the coefficient of the full scale, $^r h$ = coefficient obtained by correlating the scores to two halves. This correction assumes that an instrument 2_r items long will be more reliable than an instrument 'n' times long. Thus, the full instrument will have a higher reliability than would either half. This can be true when the full instrument is empirically a unity and each half contains sufficient items to be reliable itself.

How to improve reliability: The reliability of an instrument can be improved by (a) minimizing the external sources of variation, (b) improving internal consistency of the instrument, and (c) broadening the sample of items used. The external sources of variation can be minimized by *standardizing* the conditions under which the measurement takes place, by improving investigator consistency by using well trained investigators and by using clear and standard instructions.

The internal consistency of an instrument can be improved by item analysis as explained in "Item Analysis", a subsection in 8.3 *Measurement Scale and Indices,* below. Items which have little discriminatory power can then be dropped from the scale.

The *Sampling* base can be broadened by adding similar items to the instrument. The probability of a chance error being balanced by another opposite random error is greater when there are more items. Thus, more items increase the probability of accurate measurement.

The *adequacy* of reliability can be examined in terms of research objectives and the nature of the population under study. If our objectives call for rough estimation, then a relatively crude instrument will probably suffice. For more precise estimation, higher standards of reliability are required. In a relatively homogeneous population, a crude measure may be reliable, because variations in the data are limited. A heterogeneous population calls for a more reliable instrument.

Relationship between validity and reliability: Validity and reliability as measurement properties are significantly interrelated. An instrument that is valid, is always reliable. An instrument that is not valid may or may not be reliable. A reliable instrument need not be valid; but a non-reliable instrument is never valid, because a necessary condition of validity is reliability. Reliability is more directly demonstrated statistically and/or logically, whereas validity is often inferred by a comparison of predicted and/or measured behaviours.

5.7 RESEARCH DESIGN OR PLAN

Meaning

A research design is a logical and systematic plan prepared for directing a research study. It specifies the objectives of the study, the methodology and techniques to be adopted for achieving the objectives. It 'constitutes the blueprint for the collection, measurement and analysis of data.'[55]It is "the plan, structure and strategy of investigation conceived so as to obtain answers to research questions... The plan is the overall scheme or program of research."[56] A research design is the program that guides the investigator in the process of collecting, analyzing and interpreting observations."[57] It "provides a systematic plan of procedure for the researcher to follow."[58]

Essentials of a Good Research Design

The above definitions give the essentials of a good research design. They are:

1. It is a *plan* that specifies that objectives of the study and the hypotheses to be tested.
2. It is an *outline* that specifies the sources and types of information relevant to the research questions.
3. It is a *blueprint* specifying the methods to be adopted for gathering and analyzing the data.
4. It is a *scheme* defining "the domain of generalizability, i.e., whether the obtained information can be generalized to a larger population or to different situations."[59]

Nature of Research Design

A research design is indispensable for a research project. However, it is *not a precise and specific* plan like a building plan to be followed without deviations, but rather a *series of guideposts*

55. Philips, Bernard S., *Social Research Strategy and Tactics,* London: Macmillan Publishing Co., 2nd ed., p. 93.
56. Kerlinger, Fred N., *Foundations of Behavioural Research*, New York: Holt, Rinehart and Winston, 1973, p. 300.
57. Nachmias, David and Nachmias, Chava, *op. cit.*, p. 29.
58. Best, John, W., *Research in Education,* New Delhi: Prentice Hall of India, p. 38.
59. Nachmias, David and Nachmias, Chava, *op. cit.*, p. 20.

to keep one going in the *right direction.* It is a *tentative plan* which undergoes modification, as circumstances demand, when the study progresses, new aspects, new conditions and new relationships come to light and insight into the study deepens. For example, the scope of a study may be narrowed down, when it is discovered that certain kinds of data are not available; the sampling method may be modified from 'random sampling with probability proportional to size to simple random sampling' if a list of units of study with particulars of size is not readily available; and so on.

Besides, a research study cannot be extensive and intensive as the researcher may like it to be. It has to be geared to the availability of data and the cooperation of the informants. It has also to be kept within the *manageable limits, i.e.,* within the researcher's mental ability to grasp the implications, his competence and the amount of time and other resources available for the purpose. Thus, a research design "represents a *compromise* dictated by many practical considerations."[60]

Classification of Designs

There are a number of crucial research choices, various writers advance different classification schemes, some of which are:

1. Experimental, historical and inferential designs (American Marketing Association)
2. Exploratory, descriptive and causal designs (Selltiz, Jahoda, Deutsch and Cook)
3. Experimental, and ex-post fact (Kerlinger)
4. Historical method, and case and clinical studies (Goode and Scates)
5. Sample surveys, field studies, experiments in field settings and laboratory experiments (Festinger and Katz)
6. Exploratory, descriptive and experimental studies (Body and Westfall)
7. Exploratory, descriptive and causal (Greed and Tull)
8. Experimental, 'quasi-experimental designs' (Nachmias and Nachmias)
9. True experimental, quasi-experimental and non-experimental designs (Smith)
10. Experimental, pre-experimental, quasi-experimental designs and Survey Research (Kidder and Judd).

These different categorizations exit, because 'research design' is a complex concept. In fact, there are different perspectives from which any given study can be viewed. They are:

1. The degree of formulation of the problem (the study may be *exploratory or formalized)*
2. The topical scope – breadth and depth – of the study (a *case or a statistical* study)
3. The research environment: field setting or laboratory (*survey, laboratory experiment)*
4. The time dimension (*one-time or longitudinal)*
5. The mode of data collection (*observational or survey)*
6. The manipulation of the variables under study (*Experimental or ex-post facto)*
7. The nature of the relationship among variables (*descriptive or causal).*

The different types of designs have been discussed in Chapter 3, above.

60. Suchman E.A., "The Principles of Research Design" in John T. Doby *et al., An Introduction to Social Research,* Harrisburg Pa: Stackpole Co., 1954, p. 254.

Importance of Research Plan

A research without a pre-drawn plan is like an ocean voyage without Mariner's compass. The preparation of a research plan for a study aids in establishing *direction* to the study and in knowing exactly what has to be done and how and when it has to be done at every stage. It enables the researcher to consider beforehand the various *decisions* to be made: What are the objectives of the study? What are the investigative questions? What are the sources of data? What is the universe of the study? What sampling method is appropriate? And so on.

Without a plan, research work becomes unfocussed and aimless empirical wandering, the researcher would find it difficult, labourious and time-consuming to make adequate discriminations in the complex inter plan of factors before him; he may not be able to decide which is relevant and which is not, and may get lost in a welter of irrelevancies. The use of a research design prevents such a *blind search* and indiscriminate gathering of data and *guides* him to *proceed* in the *right direction.*

A research plan prescribes the *boundaries* of research activities and enables the researcher to channel his energies in the right work.

With clear research objectives in view, the researcher can proceed systematically toward their achievement.

The design also enables the researcher to anticipate potential problems of data gathering, Operationalisation of concepts, measurement, etc.[61]

Preparation of the Research Design

Planning involves deciding things in advance. Accordingly, the preparation of a research plan involves a careful consideration of the following *questions* and making appropriate *decisions* on them:

1. What the study is about?
2. Why is the study made?
3. What is its scope?
4. What are the objectives of the study?
5. What are the propositions to be test?
6. What are the major concepts to be defined operationally?
7. On the basis of what criteria or measurements, the operational definitions to be made?
8. When or in what place the study will be conducted?
9. What is the reference period of the study?
10. What is the typology of the design?
11. What kinds of data are needed?
12. What are the sources of data?
13. What is the universe from which the sample has to be drawn?
14. What is the sample size?

---

61. Black, James A., and Champion Dean J., *Methods and Issues in Social Research,* New York: John Wiley & Sons, 1976, p. 77.

15. What sampling techniques can be used?
16. What methods are to be adopted for collecting data?
17. What tools are to be used for collecting data?
18. How the data are to be processed?
19. What techniques of analysis are to be adopted?
20. What is the significance of the study?
21. To what target audience the reporting of the findings is meant?
22. What is the type of report to be prepared?
23. What is the time period required for each stage of research work?
24. What is the time limit within which the whole work should be completed?
25. What is the cost involved?

These questions should be considered with reference to the researcher's interest, competence, time and other resources, and the requirements of sponsoring agency, if any. "Thus, the *considerations* which enter into making decisions regarding what, where, when, how much, by what means constitute a plan of study or a study design.[62]

The Contents of a Research Plan

After making decisions on the above questions, a formal research plan is drafted, incorporating those decisions. The format may vary depending on the purpose for which the study is undertaken, but, in general, the research plan of a research student/academician may cover the following essential *sections:*

1. Introduction: The introduction of a research plan or proposal should place the research problem in its historical perspective, state the need for studying it, and the researcher's precise interests in the study of the problem.

2. Statement of the problem: The research problem should be well defined, pointing out its core nature and its importance. The issue relating to the problem may also be stated. This statement gives direction to the research process.

3. Review of the previous studies: On the selected theme, some studies might have been previously made by other. A review of available literature will bring out information on them. The salient features of those studies may be briefly described and the gaps may be pointed out. Does the selected study fill in the gap? Or is it a replication of an earlier study made elsewhere? In the later case, the justification for studying the same problem may be stated with reference to environmental differences, temporal difference, etc.

4. Scope of the study: A complete study of any problem is well nigh unmanageable. It would entail such an over-whelming volume of data that it would require more than a student's life-time to comprehend and complete the study. Therefore, the scope and dimensions of the study should be *delimited* with reference to the topical scope – breadth and depth, geographical area to be covered, reference period, the type of institutions/respondents to be studied, the issues to be analysed, etc. The *purpose of this demarcation* is to make the study manageable in terms of the researcher's aim, interest and competence and available techniques, time, finance and facilities.

Research scholars are invariably ambitious, take up a vast study, not knowing the time and other requirements, and later find it difficult to complete the work within the prescribed time limit. In their anxiety to complete the work, they are forced to sacrifice its depth and quality. Therefore, it is essential to delimit the study from the stand point of manageability. Yet it should provide the researcher with an opportunity to gain a systematic experience of planning and conducting a research study and make some contribution to the fund of knowledge.

5. Objective of the study: The specific objectives of the study should be stated clearly. These refer to the *questions* to which the researcher proposes to seek answers through the study. Although there is no limit to the number of research objectives, it is desirable to limit the objectives to a reasonable number. What is reasonable depends upon the time limitation, resource constraints, capability etc. it is wise to pick objectives that are challenging but not impossible to achieve.

The objectives may be stated as under:

To study the extent of ____________

To identify the factors which influence ____________

To examine the nature of relation between ____________ and ____________

To investigate the impact of ____________

To identify the causes of ____________

The statement of objectives should not be vague or nebulous like "to study industrial marketing in India"; "to explore unemployment in India" and the like.

These statements are vague, as they fail to specify what exactly are aimed at. The statements should be specific and indicate the exact purpose of the study. Such precise statements give functional guidelines to the research process.

The statement of objective may be followed by a statement of the *investigative* questions relating to each of the research objectives. (See Section 5.3, in Chapter 5, above).

6. Conceptual model: This section is the heart of the research plan. This is where the researcher formulates and develops the structure of relationships among the variables he is investigating. The logical connection of the variables is delineated; the assumptions, and propositions used to develop the explanatory framework are included. The entire research project rests upon the theoretical framework. (See Section 1.4 in Chapter 1, above).

7. Hypotheses: These are logically deduced from the theoretical framework above. These refer to the anticipated outcome or possible answers to the research questions. They should be conceptually clear, specific and simple. (See Section 5.4 of this Chapter, above).

8. Operational definition of concepts: The major concepts used in the title of the study, its objectives, the investigative questions and the hypotheses should be identified. Each of them should be defined in operational terms pertinent to the measurement criteria or operations. (See Section 5.5 of this Chapter, above).

9. The significance of the study: It is important to point out the relevance and significance of the investigation. What would be the value of the findings of the study for policy formulation, theory or practice? Can the findings contribute to the enrichment of theory and/or to the solution of some practical problems? A careful statement of the value of the study and the possible application of its finding helps to justify its importance and social relevance.

10. Geographical area to be covered: The territorial area to be covered by the study should be decided and specified in the plan. The area to be chosen depends on the purpose of the study and time and other resources available.

11. Reference period: This period may be one year or two or more years depending on the nature of the study and availability of data. The period should be longer, say 5 or 10 years, if the study aims at making a trend analysis of an activity like production or sale or profitability.

12. Methodology: In this section, the overall typology of the design – experimental, descriptive, survey, case study or historical study – is specified. Further the methods or methods to be adopted for collection of data – observation, interviewing or mailing – are specified.

13. Sampling plan: If the study requires collection of primary data from the field, the universe must be delineated, and the methods of sampling to be used for drawing the sample from the universe and the sample size must be stated. (See Chapter 6).

14. Tools for gathering data: In this section, the tools, to be used for gathering data – interview schedule/guide or questionnaire or check list, etc. - are listed and each of them is described. The tools chosen should be appropriate to the methods to be adopted for gathering data.

15. Plan of analysis: The statistical techniques to be used for analyzing the various techniques should be specified. The application of appropriate techniques is essential for testing hypothesis and drawing inferences.

16. Chapter scheme: The chapter scheme of the report/dissertation to be prepared for communicating the findings of the study to the academic community and the users should be outlined and the purpose of each chapter should be stated.

17. Time budget: The time period required for each stage of work and the total time duration of the study are specified. This budget may be presented in the following format:

Stages	*Time Period*
1. Initial review of literature and the selection of the problem.	XXXXX
2. Formulation of the selected problem and the preparation of the research plan	XXXXX
3. Construction of tools and pre-testing	XXXXX
4. Field work experimentation and collection of data	XXXXX
5. Processing and analysis of data	XXXXX
6. Planning and report-writing work	XXXXX
7. Drafting and finalizing the report	XXXXX
	XXXXX

(*Note:* The review of literature relevant to the research problem should be continued till the report is drafted).

18. Financial budget: This should include as estimate of the expected costs of the project under various major categories like salary (if any), printing and stationary, postage, travel expenses, computation, secretarial and typing etc.

This research plan with modifications made at the implementation stage and a description of the experiences of fieldwork will form part of the report under the title "The Design of the Study."

SUGGESTED READINGS

1. Arthur, Maurice, *Philosophy of Scientific Investigation,* Baltimore: John Hopkins University Press, 1943.
2. Carmines, Edward G., and Richard A. Zeller, *Reliability and Validity Assessment,* Beverly Hills, Calif: Sage University Papers, 1979.
3. Cohen, Morris R., and Ernest Nagel, *An Introduction of Logic and Scientific Method,* New York: Harcourt, Brace, 1934.
4. Doby, John T., (ed.) *An Introduction to Social Research,* Harrisburg, Pa: Stackpole Co., 1954.
5. Fox, David J., *The Research Process in Education,* New York: Holt, Rinehart and Winston, 1969.
6. Hagedorn, Robert and Sanford Labovitz, *Introduction to Social Research,* New York: McGraw-Hill, 1971.
7. Hempel, Carl G., *Fundamentals of Concept in Formation of Empirical Science,* Chicago: University of Chicago Press, 1952.
8. Helmstadter, G.C., *Research Concepts in Human Behaviour,* New York: Appleton-Century-Crofts, 1970.
9. Kerlinger, Fred, N., *Foundations of Behavioural Research,* Delhi: Surjeet Publications, 1983.
10. Murdick, Robert, G., *Business Research Concept and Practice,* Scranton, Pa: International Textbook, 1969.
11. Rubin, Herbert J., *Applied Social Research,* Columbus: Northern Illinois University, 1983.
12. Simon, Julian L., and Paul Burstein, *Basic Research Methods in Social Science,* New York: Random House, 1985.
13. Jhorndike, Robert L., and Hager, Elizabeth, *Measurement and Evaluation in Psychology and Education,* New York: John Wiley & Sons, 1969.
14. Tyler, Leona E., *Tests and Measurements,* Englewood, Cliffs, N.J. Prentice-Hall, 1963.

QUESTIONS

1. What are the steps involved in the planning stage of a research project?
2. Why is the selection of a problem for research a problem by itself? On what does the nature of problem to be selected depend in academic research?
3. Should a problem be suggested by the guide in academic research?
4. What are the sources from which research problems are identified?
5. Discuss the process of identification of a research problem.
6. What are the criteria or factors to be considered while selecting a research problem?
7. Both an uncharted path and a well-trodden path are dangerous to a beginner in research. Discuss.
8. What is meant by formulation of the research problem? What does it involve?
9. Why should the selected research problem be formulated?
10. What is conceptual model? How is it developed?
11. What are investigative questions? How are they set? Illustrate.
12. How does delimitation of a research problem differ from limitation of the study?
13. "A problem well stated is half-solved" — Comment.
14. What is a hypothesis? Can it be considered as a valid fact?

15. How are hypotheses set up?
16. Is hypothesis always necessary in research?
17. Explain briefly the various types of hypotheses.
18. What is a null hypothesis? Why is it set?
19. What are the characteristics of a statistical hypothesis?
20. From what sources can hypotheses be derived?
21. What is the role of hypothesis in social science research?
22. What are the functions of research hypotheses?
23. How would you evaluate hypotheses?
24. What are the characteristics of a good hypothesis?
25. Select three research studies that have appeared recently in major journals in your field. Evaluate the hypotheses set for those studies.
26. Differentiate between relational hypothesis and causal hypothesis.
27. Discuss the process of setting up hypotheses.
28. Should a hypothesis be proved? Discuss.
29. Differentiate between Type I error and Type II error in tests of hypotheses.
30. Define 'concept' and discuss its significance in a research context.
31. What are the characteristics of concepts?
32. Distinguish between
    (a) concept and construct
    (b) abstract concept and concrete concept
    (c) operational definition and descriptive definition.
33. Examine the problems in defining concepts.
34. Trace the steps in operationalizing concepts?
35. Why should concepts be operationalised in a research context?
36. You have been asked to conduct a study among current students to determine their future career expectations and objectives. What concepts would you need, and how would you define them operationally?
37. Operationalise the Concepts:
    (a) participative managements
    (b) democratic control
    (c) agricultural developments
    (d) socio-economic development
    (e) civic sense
    (f) political awareness
    (g) group cohesiveness
38. What do we measure when we measure? What is the need for measurement?
39. What can we measure about the four objects listed below?
    (a) consumer
    (b) financial health of a company

(c) employee attitude

(d) social distance

(e) performance of a cooperative society

40. What are the functions of measurement in social science research?

41. What are the measurement postulates?

42. Differentiate between nominal, ordinal, interval and ratio scales.

43. What difference does it make in research whether we measure in terms of a nominal, ordinal, interval and ratio scales?

44. Below are listed some objects of varying degrees of abstractness. Suggest properties of each of these objects which can be measured by each of the four basic types of scales (levels of measurement).

(a) customers of a retail store

(b) voter attitudes

(c) preference for a particular equity share

(d) profitability of various divisions in a company.

45. How might error distort the measurement of the objects listed in question 44?

46. What are the characteristics or criteria of a good measurement tool?

47. Discuss the process of constructing a measurement tool?

48. Is "Justice" measurable? If yes, why should it be measured?

49. What indicators would you suggest to select in constructing a measure for equity in economy? Specify the levels of measurement of each indicator.

50. You have been asked to develop an instrument which can be used to evaluate the teaching effectiveness of professors.

(a) How could you judge whether such an instrument is reliable?

(b) How can you judge its content validity? Criterion-related validity? Construct validity?

51. What is meant by validity? What are its types?

52. What is predictive validity? How is the predictive validity of a tool examined?

53. What is construct validity? How is it determined?

54. Explain the methods used for validation of an instrument.

55. You have been asked to develop an index of employee morale in an industrial undertaking.

(a) What constructs or concepts might you employ?

(b) Choose the major concepts and specify their dimensions.

(c) Select observable indicators to measure those dimensions.

(d) How would you compile these various dimensions into a single index?

(e) How would you judge the reliability and validity of these measurements?

56. What is reliability? How does it differ from validity?

57. How would you estimate the reliability of a measure?

58. Evaluate each of the various methods of estimating reliability.

59. How can the reliability of an instrument be improved.?

60. Valid measures are also reliable, but reliable measures are not necessarily valid. Discuss and bring examples that support your arguments.

61. What is a research design? Is it a specific plan like a building plan?
62. How would you classify research designs?
63. Why should a research plan be prepared for a study?
64. How is a research design prepared?
65. What are the contents of a research plan?
66. Select a research problem and prepare a research design for its study.
67. Should a research proposal be too detailed?

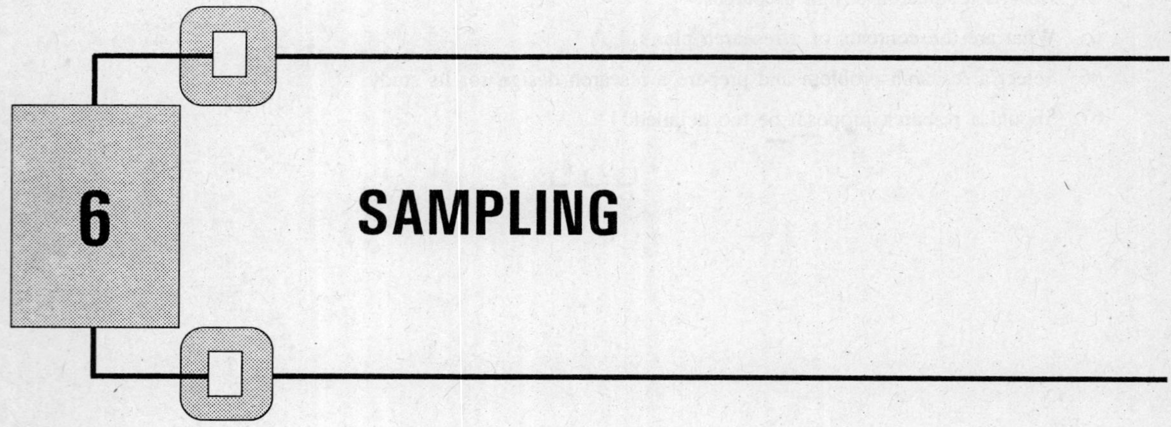

SAMPLING

6.1 INTRODUCTION

Concept

Empirical field studies require collection of first-hand information or data pertaining to the units of study from the field. The units of study may include geographical areas like districts, talukas, cities or villages which are covered by the study, or institutions or households about which information is required, or persons from whom information is required, or persons from whom information is available. The *aggregate* of all the units pertaining to a study is called the *population* or the universe. Population is the target group to be studied.

It is the aggregate of elements about which we wish to make inferences. A member of the population is an element. It is the subject on which measurement is taken. It is the *unit of study*. A part of the population is known as a sample. The process of drawing a sample from a larger population is called sampling. The list of sampling units from which a sample is taken is called the *sampling frame,* e.g., a map, a telephone directory, a list of industrial undertakings, a list of car licensees etc.

Illustration 1: A researcher desires to study the attitude of students of Master of Education of a college of education towards semester system. A student of that course is a unit of study. The total of all Master Education student of that course is a unit of study. The list of M.Ed. student from which a sample will be drawn is the sampling frame.

Illustration 2: A researcher wants to survey the brand preferences of households regarding toilet soaps in Jayanagar area of the city of Bangalore. A household is the sampling unit. The total of all households in Jayanagar area is the population. Suppose in a detailed map of Jayanagar, but list of households is not available, each block may be considered a sampling unit. A list of such blocks will be used as the frame.

Aims of Sampling

Well-selected sampling may reflect fairly accurately the characteristics of the population. For example, with a survey of a sample of voters, one can predict the voting intentions of millions of voters. A specified value of the population, such as average of variance is named *parameter;* the corresponding value in the sample is termed a *statistic.* The *chief aim* of sampling is to *make an inference* about an unknown parameter from a measurable sample statistic.

A second aim of sampling is to *test a statistical hypothesis* relating to population. A sample is drawn and the data collected from the sample informants are analysed and on the basis of the result the hypothesis may be accepted or rejected.

Census Vs. Sampling

The process of designing a field study, among other things, involves a decision to use sampling or not. The researcher must decide whether he should cover all the units or a sample of units. When all the units are studied, such a complete coverage is called a *census survey.* When only a sample of the universe is studied, the study is called a *sample survey.*

In making this decision of census or sampling, the following factors are considered:

1. ***The size of the population:*** If the population to be studied is relatively small, say 50 institutions or 200 employees or 150 households, the investigator may decide to study the entire population. The task is easily manageable and the sampling may not be required. But if the population to be studied is quite large, sampling is warranted. However, the size is a *relative* matter. Whether a population is large or small depends upon the nature of the study, the purpose for which it is undertaken, and the *time and other resources* available for it.

2. ***Amount of funds budgeted for the study:*** The decision regarding census or sampling depends upon the budget of the study. Sampling is opted when the amount of money budgeted is smaller than the anticipated cost of census survey.

3. ***Facilities:*** The extent of facilities available- staff, access to computer facility and accessibility to population elements- is another factor to be considered in deciding to sample or not. When the availability of these facilities is extensive, census survey may be manageable. Other wise, sampling is preferable.

4. ***Time:*** The time limit within which the study should be completed is another important factor to be considered in deciding the question of census or sample survey. This, in fact, is a primary reason for using sampling by academic and marketing researchers.

Characteristics of Good Sample

Whether the result obtained from a sample survey would be accurate or not depends upon the quality of the sample. The characteristics of a good sample are described below.

1. ***Representativeness:*** A sample must be representative of the population. Probability sampling technique[1] yield representative sample. In measurement terms, the sample must be valid. The validity of a sample depends upon its accuracy and precision.

---

1. See Section 6.2 of this Chapter, below.

2. ***Accuracy:*** Accuracy is defined as the degree to which bias is absent from the sample. An accurate (unbiased) sample is one which exactly represents the population. It is free from any influence that causes any difference between sample value and population value (say, average).
3. ***Precision:*** The sample must yield precise estimate. Precision is measured by the standard error or standard deviation of the sample estimate. The smaller the standard error or estimate, the higher is the precision of the sample. (See Section 6.4, below).
4. ***Size:*** A good sample must be adequate in size in order to be reliable. (For a detailed discussion of sample size, See Section 6.4, below). The sample should be of such size that the inferences drawn from the sample are accurate to the given level of confidence.

Basis of Sampling

Sampling is based on two premises. They are:

1. There is such similarity among the elements in a population that a few of these elements will adequately represent the characteristics of the total population. For example, the attitudes of postgraduate students towards the examination system can be gauged by studying the attitudes of a few representative postgraduate students in a university.
2. While the sample value (statistic) or some sample units may be more than the population value (parameter), the sample value of other sample units may be less than the population value. When the sample is drawn properly these differences tend to counteract each other. With the result, a sample value is generally close to the population value.

Thanks to these tendencies, sampling yields almost the same result as that of a census survey.

Advantages of Sampling

Why is sampling used? What are its advantages? The advantages of sampling are many.

First, sampling *reduces* the *time* and *cost* of research studies. Thanks to the use of sampling, it has become possible to undertake even national or global studies at a reasonable cost and time. Such economy in time and cost improves the viability of several field studies like credit surveys, poverty surveys and marketing surveys.

Second, sampling *saves labour*. A smaller staff is required both for fieldwork and for processing and analyzing the data.

Third, the *quality* of a study is often *better* with sampling than with a complete coverage. The possibility of better interviewing, more thorough investigation of missing, wrong or suspicious information, better supervision, and better processing is greater in sampling than in complete coverage.[2] No wonder that the accuracy of decennial population censuses in USA, India and other countries is checked by making sample surveys.

Fourth, sampling *provides* much *quicker results* than does a census. The speed of execution minimizes the time between the recognition of a need for information and the availability of that information. The speed of execution is vital in feasibility studies, evaluation studies and business research. Timely execution of a study is essential for making use of its findings.

---

2. Deming, W.E., *Sample Design in Business Research*, New York: John Wiley & Sons, 1960, p. 26.

Fifth, sampling is the *only procedure possible,* if the population is infinite, e.g., throws of dice, consumer behaviour surveys, etc.

Last, statistical sampling yields a crucial advantage over any other way of choosing a part of the population for a study. That is, when the estimates of the population characteristics are made from the sample results, the precision of these estimates can also be *gauged from the sample results* themselves. (For explanation, See Section 6.4, below).

Limitations of Sampling

Sampling is, however, not free from limitations.

1. Sampling demands a *through knowledge of sampling methods* and procedures and an exercise of *greater care;* otherwise the results obtained may be incorrect or misleading.
2. When the *characteristic* to be measured occurs only rarely in the population, a very large sample is required to secure units that will give reliable information about it. A large sample has all the drawbacks of a census survey.
3. A *complicated sampling* plan may require *more labour* than a complete coverage.
4. It may not be possible to ensure the representativeness of the sample, even by the most perfect sampling procedures. Therefore sampling results in a certain degree of sampling errors, i.e., there will be some difference between the sample value and the population value. (See Section 6.5, below).

6.2 SAMPLING TECHNIQUES OR METHODS

Classification

Sampling techniques or methods may be classified into two generic types: (a) Probability or Random Sampling, and (b) Non-probability or Non-random Sampling.

Probability sampling is of following types:

1. Simple random sampling
2. Stratified random sampling
3. Systematic random sampling
4. Cluster sampling
5. Area sampling
6. Multi-stage and sub-sampling
7. Random sampling with probability proportional to size
8. Double sampling and Multiphase sampling
9. Replicated or interpenetrating sampling.

Non-probability sampling may be classified into:

1. Convenience or accidental sampling
2. Purposive (or Judgement) sampling
3. Quota sampling
4. Snow-ball sampling

SAMPLING METHODS

Probability Sampling	*Non-Probability Sampling*
A. Simple designs	
— Simple random sampling	Convenience or accidental sampling
— Stratified random sampling	
— Systematic random sampling	Purposive or judgement sampling
B. Complex design	
— Cluster and area sampling	Quota sampling
— Multi-stage and sub-sampling	Snow-ball sampling
— Probability proportional to size sampling	
— Double sampling and Multi-phase sampling	
— Replicated sampling	

Exhibit 6.1: Sampling Methods

Each of the above sampling methods is discussed separately in subsequent pages.

Probability Vs. Non-Probability Sampling

Probability sampling is based on the theory of probability. It is also known as *random sampling.* It provides a known non-zero chance of selection for each population element.

Its characteristics are:

1. In probability sampling every population has a *chance* of being selected.
2. Such chance is a *known* probability. For instance, if a sampling frame is a list of 100 students of a specific course of study, in a simple random sample, each student has 1/100th chance of being selected.
3. Probability sampling yields a *representative* sample, and hence the findings of the sample survey are generalisable to the population.
4. The closeness of a sample to the population can be determined by estimating sampling bias or error (which we will discuss in more detail later. See Section 6.5, below). Through randomization, the danger of unknown sampling bias can be minimized. Hence, probability sampling is preferable to non-probability sampling.

Probability sampling should be used when generalization is the objective of study, and a greater degree of accuracy of estimation of population parameters is required. Cost and time required for probability sampling may be large. Hence, the benefit derived from it should justify the cost.

Non-probability sampling or non-random sampling is not based on the theory of probability. This sampling does not provide a chance of selection to each population element. The only merits of this type of sampling are simplicity, convenience and low cost.

Its merits are:

1. It does not ensure a selection chance to each population unit.
2. The selection probability is unknown.
3. A non-probability sample may not be a representative one.

4. Non-probability sampling plan does not perform inferential function, i.e., the population parameters cannot be estimated from the sample values.
5. It suffers from sampling bias, which will distort results.

Therefore, non-random is not a desirable method. Yet there are some practical reasons for using it. Those reasons are:

1. When there is no other feasible alternative due to non-availability of a list of population, non-availability of some population elements for collection of data, etc;
2. When the study does not aim at generalizing the findings to the population, but simply at feeling the range of conditions, or nature of the phenomenon;
3. When the cost required for probability sampling may be too large, and the benefit expected from it is not commensurate with such costs; and
4. When probability sampling requires more time, but the time constraints and the time limit for completing the study do not permit it.

PROBABILITY SAMPLING METHODS

Random Sampling Procedures

The importance of randomness in sampling needs no emphasis. It is a means for securing a representative sample. How can a random sample be drawn? The layman tends to think that random sampling means picking out units "at random", i.e., in a haphazard or hit-and-miss way. Experience shows that the human being is an extremely poor instrument for the conduct of a random selection. To ensure true randomness the method of *selection* must be *independent of human judgement.* There are three basic procedures.

1. The lottery method: This is the simplest and most familiar procedure of random sampling. If a sample of 10 students is to be drawn out of a list of 50 students in a section, take 50 equal size chips or slips of paper; number them from 1 to 50 each bearing only one number. Roll each slip. Put the rolled slips in a global container and thoroughly shuffle or mix them. Take 10 chips from the container one after another. Each time before drawing a chip, mix the chips in the container thoroughly. The units bearing the numbers of chips drawn constitute the random sample.

In the above sampling procedure, there are two *alternatives.* After a number is selected by draw, it may be replaced and consequently it has a chance of being selected again. Such a method is known as sampling with replacement. This is usually referred to as *unrestricted random sampling.* Alternatively, the selected number is set aside, and so in the subsequent draws; it does not get a chance of being selected again. This type of sampling is known as *sampling without replacement.* This is a form of *restricted sampling.*

Sampling with replacement *guarantees* each element an equal and independent chance of being selected in each draw. However an element previously drawn and replaced in the vessel has a chance of being drawn again. But the common procedure is not to count it again as an item of the sample. For, it is absurd to ask a respondent to fill in a questionnaire twice.

Lottery method is useful for drawing a small sample from a small population. But it would be time consuming and tedious if the population is very large.

2. The use of table of random numbers: This is a less cumbersome, but equally valid procedure of sample selection. Tables of random numbers have been developed by Kendall and Smith (1939), Fisher and Yates (1963) and Tippett (1927). One of them is usually found in a standard book on Statistics or Methodology of Research. To select a random sample out of a given frame, one should simply start to read numbers from a Table of Random Numbers at any randomly selected point and pick out numbers within the range of the frame. This procedure is illustrated below.

Let us suppose that random sample of 50 is to be selected from a college population of 500 commerce students. We can use any table of Random Numbers.

EXTRACT FROM A TABLE OF RANDOM NUMBERS

10	09	73	25	33	76	52	01
37	54	20	48	05	64	89	47
08	42	26	89	53	19	64	50
09	01	90	25	29	09	37	67
12	80	79	99	70	80	15	73
66	06	57	47	17	34	07	27
31	06	01	08	05	45	57	18
85	26	97	76	02	02	05	16
63	57	33	21	35	05	32	54
73	79	64	57	53	03	52	96

Exhibit 6.2: Sample of Random Numbers

Let us suppose, we start at the top of the left hand second column. As the population consists of a three-digit figure, read three-digit columns, i.e., read 097, 542, 422, 019 and so on. All the numbers within the range of 1 to 500 may be picked out. Then the sample will consist of:

097, 422, 019, 065, 060, 269 and so on. In the above reading, 542, 807, 573, etc. are rejected because they are over 500.

When the researcher reaches the bottom of a column, he can simply move one digit to the right and start at the top of the column again, and read numbers in three-digits: 973, 420, 226, 190, 079 and so on.

The main advantages of the use of a Table of Random Numbers are:

Easy to use and ready accessibility.

The Table of Random Numbers is ideal for obtaining a random sample from relatively small populations. When populations are quite large say lakhs or crores, drawing numbers from the table becomes tedious.

3. Use of computer: If the population is very large and if computer facilities are available, a computer may be used for drawing a random sample. The computer can be programmed to print out a series of random numbers as the researcher desires.

Simple Random Sampling

This sampling technique gives each element an equal and independent chance of being selected. An *equal chance* means *equal probability* of selection, e.g., in a population of 300, each element theoretically has 1/300th chance of being selected. In a population of 1000, each element has 1/1000th chance of being selected. Equal probability selection method is described as Epsem sampling. An *independent chance* means that the draw of one element will not affect the chances of other elements being selected.

Where some elements are purposely excluded from the sample, the resulting sample is not a random one. Hence, all elements should be included in the sample frame to draw a random sample.

Procedure: The procedure of drawing a simple random sample consists of:

- ❖ Enumeration of all elements in the population,
- ❖ Preparation of a list of all elements, giving them numbers in a serial order 1, 2, 3... so on, and
- ❖ Drawing sample numbers by using (a) Lottery method, (b) a table of random numbers or (c) a computer.

Suitability: The simple random sampling is suitable only for a small homogeneous population. It may yield a representative sample under the following conditions:

(1) Where the population is a *homogeneous group* with reference to the specified characteristics, e.g., students studying in fifth standard in a boys school form a homogeneous group as regards level of education and age group;

(2) Where the population is relatively small; and

(3) Where a complete list of all elements is available or can be prepared.

The simple random sampling is not suitable for drawing a sample from a large heterogeneous population; as it may not yield a representative sample of such population.

Advantages: Some advantages of simple random sampling are:

(1) All elements in the population have an equal chance of being selected.

(2) Of all the probability sampling techniques, simple random sampling is the easiest to apply.

(3) It is the most simple type of probability sampling to understand.

(4) It does not require a prior knowledge of the true composition of the population.

(5) The amount of sampling error[3] associated with any sample drawn can easily be computed.

Disadvantages: The simple random sampling techniques suffers from certain drawbacks.

(1) It is often impractical, because of non-availability of population list, or of difficulty in enumerating the population. For example, it is difficult to get a current accurate list of households in a city or a list of landless rural agricultural labourers who migrate from area to area in search of employment or a list of households of a nomadic tribe.

(2) The use of simple random sampling may be wasteful because we fail to use all of the known information about the population.

(3) This technique does not ensure proportionate representation to various groups constituting the population.

---

3. See Section 6.5 of this Chapter, below.

(4) The sampling error in this sampling is greater than that in other probability samples of the same size, because it is less precise than other methods.

(5) The size of the sample required to ensure its representativeness is usually larger under this type of sampling than under other random sampling techniques.

(6) A simple random design may be expensive in time and money.

These problems have led to the development of alternative superior random sampling designs like stratified random sampling, systematic sampling, etc.

Stratified Random Sampling

This is an improved type of random or probability sampling. In this method, the population is sub-divided into homogeneous groups or strata, and from each stratum, random sample is drawn. For example, university students may be dividend on the basis of discipline, and each discipline group may again be divided into juniors and seniors; and the employees of a business undertaking may be divided into managers and non-managers and each of those two groups may be sub-divided into salary –grade-wise strata.

Need for stratification: Stratification is necessary for (1) increasing a sample's statistical efficiency, (2) providing adequate data for analyzing the various sub-populations, and (3) applying different methods to different strata.[4]

Stratification ensures representation to all relevant sub-groups of the population. It is thus more efficient statistically than simple random sampling.

Stratification is essential when the researcher wants to study the characteristics of population sub-groups, e.g., male and female employees of an organisation.

Stratification is also useful when different methods of data collection, etc. are used for different parts of the population, e.g., interviewing for workers and self-administered questionnaire for executives.

Suitability: The stratified random sampling is appropriate for a large heterogeneous population.

Stratification process: This involves three major decisions:

(1) The stratification base or bases to be used should be decided. The ideal base would be the principal variable under study. For example, if the size of firms is a primary variable, the firms may be stratified on the basis of the block capital employed.

(2) The number of strata: What should be the number of strata? There is no precise answer to this question. Larger the number of strata, greater may be the degree of representativeness of the sample. The decision may be based on the number of sub-population groups to be studied and the cost of stratification. Cochran[5] suggests that there is little to be gained in estimating overall population values when the number of strata exceeds six.

(3) Strata sample sizes: There are two alternatives. First, the strata sample sizes may be proportionate to strata's shares in the total population. Second, they may be disproportionate to strata's shares. Accordingly stratified random sampling may be classified into (a) Proportionate stratified sampling and (b) Disproportionate stratified sampling.

---

4. Kish, Leslie, *Survey Sampling*, New York: John Wiley & Sons, 1965, pp. 76-77.
5. Cochran, W.G., *Sampling Techniques,* New York: John Wiley & Sons, 1963, p. 134.

Proportionate Stratified Sampling

This sampling involves drawing a sample from each stratum in proportion to the latter's share in the total population. For example, if the final year MBA students of the Management Faculty of a university consist of the following specialization groups:

Specialization stream	*No. of Students*	*Proportion of each stream*
Production	40	0.4
Finance	20	0.2
Marketing	30	0.3
Rural Development	10	0.1
	100	1.0

The researcher wants to draw an overall sample of 30. Then the strata sample sizes would be:

Strata	*Sample size*		
Production	30 × 0.4	=	12
Finance	30 × 0.2	=	6
Marketing	30 × 0.3	=	9
Rural Development	30 × 0.1	=	3
			30

Thus, proportionate sampling gives proper representation to each stratum and its statistical efficiency is generally higher. This method is, therefore, very popular.

Advantages: The principal advantages of proportionate stratified sampling are:

(1) It enhances the representativeness of the sample by giving proper representation to all sub-groups in the population.

(2) It gives higher statistical efficiency than that given by simple random sampling for a given sample size.

(3) It is easy to carry out this sample method.

(4) This method gives a self-weighing sample, the population mean can be estimated simply by calculating the sample mean.

Disadvantages: The drawbacks of the proportionate stratified random sampling are:

(1) A prior knowledge of the composition of the population and the distribution of the population characteristics are required to adopt this method.

(2) This method is very expensive in time and money. Of course its greater efficiency may offset the additional cost.

(3) The identification of the strata might lead to classification errors. Some elements may be included into the wrong strata. This may vitiate the interpretation of survey results.

Disproportionate Stratified Random Sampling

This method does not give proportionate representation to strata. It necessarily involves giving overrepresentation to some strata and under representation to others. There may be several disproportionate schemes. All strata may be given equal weight, even though their shares in the total population vary. Alternatively some substrata may be given greater weight and others lesser weight. When is such disproportionate weighing preferable?

The desirability of disproportionate sampling is usually determined by three factors, viz., (a) the sizes of strata, (b) internal variances among strata, and (c) sampling costs.

The guideline suggested by Cochran is:

In a given stratum, take a larger sample if

(a) the stratum is larger,

(b) the stratum is more variable internally, and

(c) sampling is cheaper in the stratum.[6]

If the elements of a stratum are more mixed or variable, then it would be sensible to take a larger sample from it in order to make it representative of the stratum. Similarly, if the cost per sampling unit is expected to be greater in some strata than in others, one could increase the cost effectiveness by taking a less proportionate sample in the costlier strata.

Usage: This method of disproportionate sampling is not widely used. However, it is appropriate to use it under the following circumstances:

(1) When the population contains some small but important sub-groups.

(2) When certain sub-groups are quite heterogeneous, while others are homogeneous; and

(3) When it is expected that there will be appreciable differences in the response rates of the sub-groups in the population.[7] But the above differences should be several-fold to make disproportionate sampling worthwhile.[8]

Disproportionate sampling cannot be used for population with unknown proportions of characteristics, because correct sizes of strata samples cannot be determined.

Advantages: The major advantages of disproportionate sampling are:

(1) It is less time consuming compared with proportionate sampling, because the researcher is not necessarily concerned about the proportionate representativeness of his resulting sample as in the latter method.

(2) It facilitates giving appropriate weighing to particular groups, which are small but more important.

Disadvantages: The disadvantages of disproportionate sampling are:

(1) This method does not give each stratum proportionate representation. Hence, the resulting sample may be less representative.

(2) This method requires a prior knowledge of the composition of the population, which is not always possible.

(3) This method is also subject to classification errors. It is possible that the researcher may misclassify certain elements.

---

6. *Ibid.*, p. 96.
7. Clover, Vernon T. and Balsley, Howard L., *op. cit*, p. 244.
8. Kish, *Survey Sampling, op. cit.*, p. 94.

(4) Though disproportionate sampling is a means for developing an optimal Stratification scheme, its practical feasibility is doubtful because one generally does not know the relative variability in the strata nor the relative costs.

Systematic Sampling or Fixed Interval Method

Meaning and process: This method of sampling is an alternative to random sampling. It consists of taking every k^{th} item in the population after a random start with an item from 1 to k. For example, suppose it is desired to select a sample of 20 students, from a list of 300 students, divide the population total of 300 by 20, the quotient is 15. (if there is any fraction in the quotient ignore the fraction and take the integer or whole number). Select a number at random between 1 and 15, using lottery method or a table of random numbers. Suppose the selected number is 9. Then the students numbered 9, 24 (9+15), 39 (24+15), 54 (39+15), 69, 84 ... are selected as the sample.

As the interval between sample units is fixed, this method is also known as fixed interval method.

Applications: Systematic selection can be applied to various populations such as students in a class, houses in a street, telephone directory, customers of a bank, assembly line output in a factory, members of an association, and so on.

Strictly speaking, this method of sampling is not a probability sampling. It possesses characteristics of randomness and some nonprobability traits. Hence, it is sometimes called a *'pseudo-random'* sampling.

Real systematic sampling: It is more appropriate to use the label "systematic sampling" to the procedure of drawing a sample from a frame re-arranged in a systematic order on the basis of the population's important characteristic, e.g., arranging the farm households in a village in an ascending or descending order of the size of their farms. Such systematic re-arrangement of the frame is desirable for populations with greater variability. In such a case, even stratification cannot give proper representation to all size groups. For example, for a farm management study, the farm size is a primary variable. Suppose the size of farms of farmers in the area covered by the study varies widely ranging from 0.2 hectare to 25 hectares. Even if they are stratified into 5 strata, viz., (1) upto 5 hectares, (2) 5 to 10 hectares, (3) 10 to 15 hectares, (4) 15 to 20 hectares and (5) 20 to 25 hectares, there are greater variations in each stratum. Thus, even stratified random sampling may not yield a good representative sample. But if the list of farmers is rearranged in ascending or descending order of their farm sizes, and a sample is drawn at regular intervals with a random start, all size groups get proper representation. Thus the degree of representativeness of this sample will be higher than that of a simple or stratified random sample of the same size.

Hence, it will be more appropriate to call this kind of interval sampling as systematic random sampling.

Advantages: The major advantages of systematic sampling are

(1) It is much simpler than random sampling. It is easy to use

(2) It is easy to instruct the field investigators to use this method.

(3) This method may require less time. A researcher operating on a limited time schedule will prefer this method.

(4) This method is cheaper than simple random sampling.

(5) It is easier to check whether every 'k'th has been included in the sample.

(6) Sample is spread evenly over the population.

(7) It is statistically more efficient than a simple random sample when population elements are ordered chronologically, by size, class, etc. Then systematic sampling gives a better representative sample.

Disadvantages: The primary disadvantages of systematic sampling are:

(1) This method ignores all elements between two 'k'th elements selected. Further, except the first element, other selected elements are not chosen at random. Hence, this sampling cannot be considered to be a probability sampling in the strict sense of the term.

(2) As each element does not have an equal chance of being selected, the resulting sample is not a random one. For studies aiming at estimations or generalizations, this disadvantage would be a serious one.

(3) This method may sometimes give a biased sample. If by chance, several 'k'th elements chosen represent a particular group, that group would be over-representated in the sample.

Cluster Sampling

Where the population elements are scattered over a wider area and a list of population elements is not readily available, the use of simple or stratified random sampling method would be too expensive and time-consuming. In such cases cluster sampling is usually adopted.

Meaning: Cluster sampling means random selection of sampling units consisting of population elements. Each such sampling unit is a cluster of population elements. Then from each selected sampling unit, a sample of population elements is drawn by either simple random selection or stratified random selection.

Suppose a researcher wants to select a random sample of 1,000 households out of 40,000 estimated households in a city for a survey. A direct sample of individual households would be difficult to select, because a list of households does not exist and would be too costly to prepare. Instead, he can select a random sample of a few blocks/wards. The number of blocks to be selected depends upon the average number of estimated households per block. Suppose the average number of households per block is 200, then 5 blocks comprise the sample. Since the number of households per block varies, the actual sample size depends on the block which happen to be selected. Alternatively, he can draw a sample of more blocks and from each sample blocks a certain number of households may be selected by systematic sampling.

Some illustrations of clusters are:

Population	*Elements*	*Cluster or Sampling units*
1. City	Households	Blocks
2. City	Individuals	Households
3. Affiliating University	Students	Affiliated Colleges
4. Rural areas	Households	Villages
5. Industrial areas	Industrial unit	Industrial estates

Features: What makes a desirable cluster depends on the survey's situation and resources. The individual elements are determined by the survey objectives. For example, for an opinion poll, the individual person is a population element, but for a socio-economic survey of households or a consumer behaviour survey, a household may be population element or unit of study. The cluster may be an institution or a geographical area or any other appropriate group depending on the nature of survey.

The number of elements in a cluster is called the cluster size. The clusters in most populations are of unequal size, e.g., dwellings in blocks, persons in household, employees in section, farm households in villages, etc. Clusters of equal size are often the result of planned conditions such as manufacturing, e.g., matches in match boxes, soap cakes in cases. They rarely exist in nature or society.

Cluster sampling vs. stratified sampling: How does cluster sampling compare with stratified sampling? There are certain differences between them.

Cluster sampling process: The process of cluster sampling involves the following steps:

Cluster Sampling	*Stratified Sampling*
1. The sampling unit is a cluster or a group consisting of population elements.	The population element itself is the sampling unit.
2. The population is divided into many clusters or sub-groups, each with a few elements.	The population is divided into a few sub-groups or strata, each with many elements.
3. Clustering is done on the basis of geographical areas or administrative divisions. (district/taluka) farm size etc.,	Stratification is done on the basis of variables under study, e.g., educational status, product line, of organisational unit (e.g., department/sections).
4. We try to secure heterogeneity within sub-groups and homogeneity between sub-groups.	We aim at securing homogeneity within sub-groups and heterogeneity between sub-groups.
5. We make a random selection of sub-groups or clusters.	We make a random selection of elements from each sub-group.
6. The resulting sample may give a lower degree of representativeness for a given sample size.	It yields a higher degree of representative sample for the same sample size.
7. The sampling error may be great.	The sampling error will be less.
8. The cost per element is lower.	The cost per element is higher.

1. Identify clusters: What can be appropriate clusters for a population? This depends on the nature of the study and the distribution of the population relating to it. The appropriate clusters may be area units (e.g., districts, talukas, villages, blocks of a city) or organizations/organizational units (e.g., schools, colleges, factories, sections in a school or departments in a factory).

2. Examine the nature of clusters: How homogeneous are the clusters? Clusters should not be homogeneous in internal characteristics. A sample drawn from such clusters cannot fully represent the overall population. Hence clusters should be constructed in a way as to increase intra-cluster variance. For example, contiguous villages/city blocks that contain different income/social groups may be combined into one cluster.

Should the clusters be of equal or unequal size? "The theory of clustering is that the means of sample clusters are unbiased estimates of the population mean."[9] This is generally true when clusters

9. Emory, C. William, *Business Research Methods, op. cit.*, p. 161.

are equal. But natural clusters often vary. The effects of unequal size may be reduced by 1) combining small clusters and splitting large clusters or 2) stratifying clusters by size and selecting clusters from each stratum.

3. Determine the number of stages: Shall we use single-stage or multistage clusters? This depends primarily on the geographical area of the study, the scale of the study, the size of the population and the consideration of costs. Depending on these factors, the following alternatives are possible:

(a) ***Single-stage sampling:*** Select clusters on a random basis and study all elements in each of the sample clusters.

(b) ***Two-stage sampling:*** Select clusters and then select elements from each selected cluster.

(c) ***Multi-stage sampling:*** Extend the above method to more stages. This is discussed in detail under a separate subsequent sub-heading *"Multi-stage Sampling"*, in this chapter itself.

Economy Vs. Accuracy: Cluster samples usually gives a less precise estimates than simple random samples of the same size because of social area tendencies toward homogeneity. Why then should cluster sampling be used? It is used simply because it cuts research costs and time. For example, it is simpler, more convenient and cheaper to randomly select 20 street with 30 average households each rather than to select 600 households ahead over an entire city. Interviewing units in small geographic areas is more convenient and less costly. One need not also waste lot of time in moving from one unit to another, because of their close special proximity. Thus, cluster sampling is economically more efficient in terms of time, cost and convenience.

However, the statistical efficiency to cluster samples is relatively low, because they may not fully be representative of the population.

Hence, we have to strike a balance between economic and statistical factors and consider the net relative efficiency in adopting the cluster sampling.

Applications: The applications of the cluster sampling in social science research are extensive, particularly in farm management surveys, socio-economic surveys, rural credit surveys, demographic studies, ecological studies, public opinion polls, large scale surveys of political and social behaviour, attitude surveys, and so on.

Advantages: The primary advantages of the cluster sampling method are:

(1) This method is much easier and more convenient to apply when large populations are studied or large geographical areas are covered. Even a ready list of population elements is not necessary. A researcher can simply draw a random sample of geographical sections and adopt single or multistage sampling depending on the vastness of the area covered by the study.

(2) The cost of this method is much less when compared with other sampling methods.

(3) This method promotes the convenience of field work as it could be done in compact places.

(4) Sampling under this method does not require more time.

(5) Units of study can be readily substituted for other units within the same random section.

(6) This method is flexible. Where it involves multistage sampling, it is possible to employ different types of sampling in successive stages.

Disadvantages: This method has certain disadvantages. They are:

(1) The cluster sizes may vary and this variation could increase the bias of the resulting sample. For example, if the researcher were to interview all adults in households in each selected street the number of adults would vary from house to house. There would be certain bias resulting from the large coverage of big families.

(2) The sampling error in this method of sampling is greater. Thus, this method is statistically less efficient than other probability sampling methods.

(3) Adjacent units of study (e.g., households) tend to have more similar characteristics than do units distantly apart. This affects the 'representativeness' of the sample and this effect is reflected in a greater sampling error.

Area Sampling

This is an important form of cluster sampling. In larger field surveys, clusters consisting of specific geographical areas like districts, talukas, villages or blocks in a city are randomly drawn. As the geographical areas are selected as sampling units in such cases, their sampling is called area sampling. It is not a separate method of sampling, but forms part of cluster sampling.

In a country like India where a state (previously known as a province) is divided into districts, districts into talukas and talukas into towns and villages, areas sampling is done on the basis of these administrative units in multi-stages. (See *'Multistage Sampling'*, below).

Illustration: Where the area covered by a study is a city, to draw a random sample of households, the following procedure may be adopted:

(1) Take a map of the concerned city and lay over it a transparent sheet with a grid system of lines (i.e., horizontal and vertical lines drawn at equal intervals).

(2) The grid system divides the city into squares of equal size, say 100 areas.

(3) Leave the squares occupied by non-residential business and public buildings, parks etc., — say 30 squares.

(4) Number the remaining squares in a serial order 1, 2, 3, 4, 5, ... 70 in a serpentine manner.

(5) Estimate the average number of households in each square on the basis of house counts in a few squares. Say the average number of households is 80.

(6) If the required sample of households is, say 640, determine the number of squares to be selected by dividing this total by 80, i.e., 8 squares.

(7) Select eight squares out of 80 on a simple random basis using a table of random numbers; or by adopting systematic random sampling method, i.e, every 10th (80/8 =10) square with a random start.

(8) Study all households in each of the sample eight squares. The total sample would be 8 × 80 = 640 or a little less or more.

Where different socio-economic class of households are found to be concentrated in specific areas of the city, it is desirable to stratify the areas on an identifiable basis, then

- ❖ Draw a random sample of proportionate number of areas from each strata.
- ❖ Prepare a list of households in each of the selected areas.
- ❖ Select randomly a proportionate number of households in each of these lists.

Alternatively divide each of the selected area into smaller areas of almost equal size called segments and select randomly a proportionate number of segments in each sample area and survey all households in each of the selected segments.

Area sampling invariably involves multi-stage sampling and sub-sampling. (See below).

Multi-stage Sampling

In this method, sampling is carried out in two or more stages. The population is regarded as being composed of a number of first stage sampling units. Each of them is made up of a number of second stage units and so forth. That is, at each stage, a sampling unit is a cluster of the sampling units of the subsequent stage. First, a sample of the first stage sampling units is drawn, then from each of the selected first stage sampling unit, a sample of the second stage sampling units is drawn. The procedure continues down to the final sampling units or population elements. Appropriate random sampling method is adopted at each stage.

Usage: Multi-stage sampling is appropriate where the population is scattered over a wider geographical area and no frame or list is available for sampling. It is also useful when a survey has to be made within a limited time and cost budget.

Advantages: The crucial advantages of multi-stage sampling are:

1. It results in concentration of fieldwork in compact small areas and consequently in a saving of time, labour and money.
2. It is more convenient, efficient and flexible than single-stage sampling.
3. It obviates the necessity of having a sampling frame covering the entire population.

Disadvantages: The major disadvantage of the multi-stage sampling is that the procedure of estimating sampling error and cost advantage is complicated. It is difficult for a non-statistician to follow this estimation procedure.

Sub-sampling

Sub-sampling is a part of a multi-stage sampling process. In multi-stage sampling, the sampling in second and subsequent stage frames is called sub-sampling. Suppose that from a population of 40,000 households in 800 streets of a city, we want to select a sample of about 400 households. We can select a sample of 400 individual households (elements) or a sample of 8 streets (cluster). The sample of 400 elements would be scattered over the city, but the cluster sample would be confined to 8 streets. Clustering reduces survey costs, but increases the sampling error. Sub-sampling balances these two conflicting effects of clustering. In the above case, first a sample of say 80 streets may be drawn and from each of the selected street a 10% sub sample of households may be drawn. In each of the above stages, an appropriate probability sampling-simple random/stratified random sampling/ systematic random sampling-may be adopted.

Control of Sampling Size: One of the problems of cluster sampling is the problem of greater inequality in cluster sizes. The total sample size is subject to large variation if it is based on a random selection of clusters that differ greatly in size. If we sub sample the selected clusters at a fixed rate, the total sample size of elements depends on which clusters are chosen at the first stage. With a large cluster of 10,000 a second-stage sampling fraction of 1/1000 gives a sample of 100 persons, while with a small cluster of 2,000 persons it yields only 20. The researcher needs to be able to fix the sample size within reasonable limits, therefore, the *uncontrolled random sampling* of clusters with *unequal sizes,* e.g., cities, blocks in big cities, districts, villages and establishments is *not suitable.*

Exact control of sample size is unnecessary and impossible in most situations. However, the least an approximate control is essential. The main reasons for controlling sample size are:

1. The sample should be of adequate size in order to get results of desired degree of precision.
2. The cost of data collection requires an upper limit on the overall sample size, and contractual obligation, if any, may also impose a lower limit.[10]
3. Large differences and fluctuations in the size of clusters cause administrative inefficiencies in the field work.[11]
4. Statistical efficiency tends to suffer from large inequalities of sample clusters.[12] If the random sample of clusters includes one or two very large clusters containing mostly one social, ethnic group, the survey results would become biased.

For several such reasons a reasonable control over the sample size is needed. There are some ways to control and decrease variations in ultimate sample size viz.,

1. Stratification of clusters by size and selecting a random sample in each size-group;
2. Splitting and combining natural clusters to form artificial clusters of more or less equal size; or
3. Selecting clusters with probability proportional to size (PPS) either from the overall frame of clusters or from each size group of clusters.

Sampling with Probability Proportionate Size (PPS)

The procedure of selecting clusters with probability proportional to size (PPS) is widely used. If one primary cluster has twice as large a population as another, it is given twice the chance of being selected. If the same number of persons is then selected from each of the selected clusters, the overall probability of any person will be the same. The PPS is a better method for securing a representative sample of population elements in multi-stage cluster sampling.

The selection procedure is as follows:

1. Draw a list of clusters with their size measures;
2. Cumulate the size measures in sequences;
3. Divide the list into a certain appropriate number of equal zones/ strata with reference to cumulated measure, e.g., if the cumulative total is say 600, the list may be divided into three equal zones 1-200, 201-400, 401-600;
4. Select the required equal number of sample in each zone, applying preferably systematic selection with a random start; and
5. Draw a same fixed number of population elements from each selected cluster at random.

---

10. Kish, Leslie, *op. cit.,* p. 217.
11. *Ibid.,* p. 218.
12. *Ibid.*

Illustration: Suppose the area of a survey is a State consisting of 20 districts. Out of them 4 districts are to be selected with PPS, the measure of size being population.

(a) List the district in some order and record the population of each together with cumulative population figures. (See Table 6.1);

(b) Divide the cumulative total by 2: 310/2 = 155;

(c) Divide the list into two zones: 1-155; 156-310;

(d) Make a systematic random selection of two districts in each zone;

(e) Divide the first zone total by 2: 155/2 = 77. Draw a random number between 1 and 77, say, 66. The district 8 is the first sample.

TABLE 6.1

The Scheme for Selecting Districts with PPS

District	*Population (lakhs)*	*Cumulative population (lakhs)*
1	05	05
2	06	11
3	07	18
4	08	26
5	10	36
6	11	47
7	12	59
8	13	72
9	13	85
10	14	99
11	15	114
12	16	130
13	17	147
14	18	165
15	20	185
16	21	207
17	23	230
18	24	254
19	26	280
20	30	310

(f) Add the interval 77 to the random number of 66 to give 143, to locate 13 as the second;

(g) Add the interval 77 to 143 to give 220, to locate district 17 as the third sample; and

(h) Add the interval 77 to 220 to give 297, to locate 20 as the fourth sample.

Advantages: The major advantages of PPS are:

1. Clusters of various sizes get proportionate representation.
2. PPS lead to greater precision than would a simple random sample of clusters and a constant sampling fraction at the second stage.
3. Equal-sized samples from each selected primary cluster are convenient for field work. If one interviewer is assigned to each cluster, the interviewers have equal workloads.

Limitation: PPS cannot be used if the sizes of the primary sampling clusters are not known.

Application: Since in practice, primary sampling units (clusters) generally vary considerably in size, sampling with PSS is used in all multistage sampling.

Double (or Two-Phase) Sampling and Multi-Phase Sampling

Double (or Two-Phase) sampling "refers to the subsection of the final sample from a preselected larger sample, that provide information for improving the final selection."[13] When this procedure is extended to more than two phases of selection, it is then, called Multi-phase sampling. This is also known as Sequential Sampling, as sub-sampling is done from a main sample in phases. Additional information from sub samples of the full sample may be collected at the same time or later.

Multi-phase Vs. Multi-stage sampling: Multi-phase sampling is different from multi-stage sampling. "In multi-phase sampling, the different phases of observation relate to sample units of the same type while in multi-stage sampling, the sampling units are of different types at different stages."[14]

Usage: Double or multi-phase sampling is a compromise solution for a dilemma posed by undesirable extremes. "The statistics based on the sample of n can be improved by using ancillary information from a wide base: but this is too costly to obtain from the entire population of N elements. Instead, information is obtained from a larger preliminary sample nL which includes the final sample n.[15] Multi-phase sampling is appropriate.

When it is more convenient and economical to collect certain items of general information on the whole of the units of a sample, and other items of special information from a sub-sample of cases possessing a given set of characteristics.

For example, in a consumer behaviour study relating to Television a common set of data may be collected from a larger sample of households and a set of additional data from those who posses colour TVs.

In multi-phase sampling, the general sample should be larger enough to yield adequate sub-sample or for detailed investigation.

Multi-phase sampling can result in considerable economies and reduce the burden on the respondents. Moreover, the information collected from the full sample can be used for stratification purposes in the selection of the sub-sample or for estimating the effect of non-response in the sub-sample.

Suppose we want a sample of individuals stratified by educational level, but the necessary information is not available for the population under study. A large first-phase sample may be selected and information on the educational level of sampled individuals may be collected from them. The respondents may then be stratified on the basis of educational levels. A sub-sample can then be drawn, using either proportionate or disproportionate stratified sampling.

"The use of two phase sampling for the sole purpose of increasing the precision of sub-sample results is effective, only if the cost of data collection is considerably lower for members of the first phase sample than for members of the sub-sample-by a factor of atleast, say, ten."[16]

13. Kish Leslie, *op. cit.*, p. 21.
14. UN, *The Preparation of Sampling Survey Reports,* New York: United Nations Statistical Office, 1950.
15. Kish, *op.cit.*, p. 441.
16. Moser C.A. and Kalton G., *op. cit.*, p. 122.

Replicated or Interpenetrating Sampling

A real difficulty with complex sample designs like multi-stage stratified sampling is the laboriousness of the sampling error calculations. The case of these calculations is a factor to be taken into account in designing of a sample plan. One approach to simplify the procedure of computing sampling errors is replicated or interpenetrating sampling, which Deming[17] discusses in full, with a number of illustrations.

Replicated or Interpenetrating sampling involves selection of a certain number of sub-samples rather than one full sample from a population. All the sub-samples should be drawn using the same sampling technique and each is a self-contained and adequate sample of the population.

Replicated or Interpenetrating sampling can be used with any basic sampling technique: simple or stratified, single or multi-stage or single or multi-phase sampling.

For example, in order to study the views of postgraduates students of a university on semester system a random sample of 300 students (out of a total population of 3,000 students distributed over different disciplines like Economics, Sociology, Statistics, Mathematics, Management etc.,) is to be drawn, adopting discipline-based stratified sampling.

Instead of selecting one full sample of 300 students, two sub-samples of 150 each, or five sub-samples of each may be selected. The latter procedure is replicated sampling.

Whatever may be the number and size of sub-samples, each sub-sample has to be an independent sample with the same sampling method, and must be a sample covering the complete population.

Each sub-sample may be allocated to one individual investigator or a team of investigators.

Sample errors estimates can be calculated for each of the sub-samples, and the variation between these estimates provide a means of assessing the precision of the overall estimate.

A decision to be made is the number of sub-samples to be drawn. The number may vary between 4 to 10. Mahalanobis[18] often used four replications. If it is desired to obtain simple estimates of sampling errors, more replications are desirable. For this purpose, Deming has made wide use of ten replications.

Advantages: The major advantages of Replicated or Interpenetrating sampling are:

1. It provides a simple means of calculating the sampling error.
2. It is practical. If the size of the total sample is too large to get the results ready in time, one or more of the replications can be used to get the advance results.
3. The replicated sample can throw light on variable non-sampling errors (See Section 6.5 of this chapter). If each of the sub-sample is interviewed by a different or set of interviewers, an estimation of inter-viewer variation can be obtained.

Disadvantages: A disadvantage of replicated sampling is that it limits the amount of stratification that can be employed. This limitation is a real drawback to the use of replicated sampling in a multi-stage sampling plan.

---

17. Deming, W.E., *Sample Design in Business Research,* New York: John Wiley and Sons, 1960.
18. Mahalanobis, P.C., "Recent Experiments in Statistical Sampling in the Indian Statistical Institute", *Journal of Royal Society,* 109, 1946, pp. 326-378.

NON-PROBABILITY SAMPLING METHODS

Introduction

As explained earlier, non-probability sampling does not adopt the theory of probability and it does not give a representative sample of the population. The primary methods of non-probability sampling are:

- ❖ Convenience sampling
- ❖ Purposive (or Judgement) sampling
- ❖ Quota sampling
- ❖ Accidental sampling
- ❖ Snow-ball sampling

Convenience or Accidental Sampling

This is non-probability sampling. It means selecting sample units in a just 'hit and miss' fashion, e.g., interviewing people whom we happen to meet. This sampling also means selecting whatever sampling units are conveniently available, e.g., a teacher may select students in his class.

This method is also known as accidental sampling because the respondents whom the researcher meets accidently are included in the sample.

Usefulness: Though convenience sampling has no status, it may be used for simple purpose such as testing ideas or gaining ideas or rough impression about a subject of interest. It lays a groundwork for a subsequent probability sampling. Sometimes it may have to be necessarily used. For example, when a population cannot be defined or a list of population is not available, there is no other alternative than to use convenient sampling.

Advantages:

1. Convenience sampling is the cheapest and simplest.
2. It does not require a list of population.
3. It does not require any statistical expertise.

Disadvantages:

1. Convenience sampling is highly biased, because of the researcher's subjectivity, and so it does not yield a representative sample.
2. It is the least reliable sampling method. There is no way of estimating the representativeness of the sample.
3. The findings cannot be generalized.

Purposive or Judgement Sampling

This method means deliberate selection of sample units that conform to some pre-determined criteria. This is also known as Judgement sampling. This involves selection of cases which we judge as the most appropriate ones for the given study. It is based on the judgement of the researcher or some expert. It does not aim at securing a cross section of a population.

The chance that a particular case be selected for the sample depends on the subjective judgement of the researcher. For example, a researcher may deliberately choose industrial undertakings in which quality circles are believed to be functioning successfully and undertakings in which quality circles are believed to be a total failure.

Application: The method is appropriate when what is important is the typicality and specific relevance of the sampling units to the study and not their overall representativeness to the population.

Advantages: The advantages of purposive or judgement sampling are:

1. It is less costly and more convenient.
2. It guarantees inclusion of relevant elements in the sample. Probability sampling plans cannot give such guarantee.

Disadvantages: The demerits of judgement sampling are:

1. This does not ensure the representativeness of the sample.
2. This is less efficient for generalizing when compared with random sampling.
3. This method requires more prior extensive information about the population one studies. Without such information, it is not possible to adjudge the suitability of the sample items to be selected.
4. This method does not lend itself for using inferential statistics, because, this sampling does not satisfy the underlying assumption of randomness.

Quota Sampling

This is a form of convenient sampling involving selection of quota groups of accessible sampling units by traits such as sex, age, social class, etc. when the population is known to consist of various categories by sex, age, religion, social class etc., in specific proportions, each investigator may be given an assignment of quota groups specified by the pre-determined traits in specific proportions. He can then select accessible persons, belonging to those quota groups in the area assigned to him.

"Quota Sampling is therefore a method of stratified sampling in which selection within strata is non-random. It is this Non-random element that constitutes its greatest weakness."[19]

Quotas are stratified by such variables as sex, age, social class and religion. It is easy to classify the accessible respondents under sex, age and religion, but it is very difficult to classify them into social categories, since social class usually involves a combination of factors such as occupation, income and caste and the interviewer's subjective judgement and bias play some role in the social class classification of respondents.

A model of assignment given to an interviewer is shown below:

Assignment of Quota

Sex		*Age*		*Social Class*	
Male	11	20-40	5	Higher	3
Female	9	41-50	8	Middle	10
		51-60	4	Lower	7
		61 & above	3		
Total	20	Total	20	Total	20

19. Moser, C.A. and Kalton, G., *Survey Methods in Social Investigation, op. cit.*, p. 127.

Application: Quota sampling is used in studies like marketing surveys, opinion polls and leadership surveys which do not aim at precision, but to get quickly some crude results.

Merits: The major advantages of quota sampling are:

1. It is considerably less costly than probability sampling.
2. It is takes less time.
3. There is no need for a list of population. Thus, quota sampling is a suitable method of sampling a population for which no suitable frame is available.
4. Field work can easily be organized. Strict supervision need not be required.

Shortcomings: The method of quota sampling suffers from certain major shortcomings.

1. It may not yield a *precise representative sample,* and it is impossible to estimate sampling error. The findings, therefore, are not generalizable to any significant extent.

2. Interviewers may tent to choose the most accessible persons; they may ignore slums or areas difficult to reach. Thus, they may fail to secure a representative sample within their quota groups.

3. Strict control of field work is difficult.

4. It is difficult for sampling on more than three variable dimensions. This is because the number of categories to be selected is a multiplication of the number of values in each variable. For instances, if we want to sample proportionate number of persons by sex, social status and age and these variables consist of two, three and three categories respectively, we have to select 2 × 3 × 3 = 18 categories of respondents.

5. The quota of sampling is subject to a higher degree of classification error, because the investigators are likely to base their classification of respondents' social status and economic status mostly on their impressions about them.

Snowball Sampling

This is the colourful name[20] for a technique of building up a list or a sample of a special population by using an initial set of its members as informants. For example, if a researcher wants to study the problem faced by Indians through some source like Indian Embassy. Then he can ask each one of them to supply names of other Indians known to them, and continue this procedure until he gets an exhaustive list from which he can draw a sample or make a census survey.

This sampling technique may also be used in socio-metric studies. For example, the members of a social group may be asked to name the persons with whom they have social contacts, each one of the persons so named may also be asked to do so, and so on. The researcher may thus get a constellation of associates and analyse it.

Advantages: The advantages of snowball sampling are:

1. It is very useful in studying social groups, informal group in a formal organization, and diffusion of information among professionals of various kinds.
2. It is useful for smaller populations for which no frames are readily available.

---

20. Goodman, L.A., " Snowball Sampling", *Annals of Mathematical Statistics*, 32, 1961, pp. 148-170.

Disadvantages:

1. The major disadvantages of snowball sampling is that it does not allow the use of probability statistical methods. Elements included are dependent on the subjective choice of the original selected respondents.
2. It is difficult to apply this method when the population is large.
3. It does not ensure the inclusion of all elements in the list.

6.3 SAMPLE DESIGN AND CHOICE OF SAMPLING TECHNIQUE

Sample Design

Sample design is a plan for drawing a sample from a population. This is an important part of a research design or plan. The preparation of a sample design involves making decisions on the following questions:

1. What is the relevant population?
2. What method of sampling frame shall we use?
3. What sampling frame shall we use?
4. What are the parameters of interest?
5. What should be the sample size?
6. How much will be the sample cost?

Relevant Population

The population relevant to a survey depends upon the research problem, the objectives of study, the geographical area selected for the survey, and the operational definition of the unit of study.

Some examples are:

Research Problem	*Relevant Population*
(a) A study of the operational efficiency of regulated market (This will involve a survey of regulated markets and the farmers for whose benefit they have been set up and the graders who function in them).	Regulated markets in the selected area. Farmers in the area of each sampled regulated market. Traders who make purchases in each sampled regulated market.
(b) A socio-economic survey of agricultural labourers (Agricultural labourer is one who derives not less than 50% of his total income from agricultural wages).	All regulated labourers who derive not less than 50% of their total income from agricultural wages.
(c) A study of job satisfaction of managers in a public enterprise.	Managers in various levels of the selected organization.
(d) A study of Postgraduate Student's opinion on library facilities.	Higher educational institution in the selected area. Students studying in Master degree programs.

(e) A study of corporate planning in large- scale enterprises. (This will involve a survey of enterprises which are large-scale ones as per the operational definition adopted and also a survey of executives participating in planning process).	Large-scale enterprises satisfying definition criteria. Executives in selected enterprises, who participate in the corporate planning exercise.
(f) A study of consumer behavior towards a particular brand of a toilet soap.	Households in an area selected for the survey.
(g) A survey of voter's opinion on election reform	All eligible voters in the selected area.

Sampling Frame

This is the list of population elements from which the sample is drawn. Ideally it should be a complete and correct list of population elements only. In practice, the sampling frame available may not meet the requirements of the survey. It may suffer from some shortcomings, giving rise to frame problems. In Kish's classification,[21] there are four basic kinds of frame problems. They are:

The first is the problem of non-coverage and incomplete frame. For example, the voters list in a graduates constituency may not contain the names of all eligible graduates due to non-registration by some graduates; the payroll list of a firm may not contain the names of newly recruited employees.

Such incomplete frames cannot yield representative samples. One way to deal with the missing elements in incomplete frames is to prepare a supplementary list of missing items and use that list as a separate stratum. But if the missing elements belong to different strata, they have to be listed in the respective strata. However, when such listing is costly, the coverage of the survey may be limited to the available frame, provided the survey objective permits it.

The second problem is appearing of clusters of elements in lists. This occurs when elements are listed not individually but in clusters. For example, a list of house numbers available from a municipal corporation office is only a list of houses and in each house there may be several individuals/ or households.

The possible ways of dealing with this problem are:

1. To take all the elements in the selected clusters, provided the clusters are small.
2. To select one element from each of the selected clusters, at random and to weigh it up with number of elements in the cluster.
3. To take a sample of clusters, list all their elements, and then take a sample of elements from this list.

The third problem is that of blanks or foreign elements. Some of the available lists may contain no elements of the target population or contain elements not relevant to the target population. For example, a list of members of a cooperative society may be out-of-date and some of the persons listed might have died or withdrawn membership or emigrated.

The fourth problem is duplicate listing, i.e., elements appearing more than once on the sampling frame. This problem arises when the sampling frame is made up of a combination of lists which have

21. Kish, Leslie, *Survey Sampling op. cit.,* pp. 53-59.

overlapping memberships. If the additional entries of elements can be removed before selection, then the problem of duplication can be avoided altogether. Of such removal is expensive, one of the listings may be chosen to represent the element and the others treated as blanks.

In evaluating a sampling frame, the researcher should be on the look-out for the existence of any of the above problems. If they are present, he should take appropriate remedial actions.

If no suitable frame exists, one may have to be constructed.

Method of sampling: There are various methods of sampling (See Section 6.2, below, for a detailed discussion). What method should we use? This decision depends on the aim of the study, the expected degree of accuracy of the survey result, and the sampling costs. For example, if the aim of the sample survey is to estimate certain population values in terms of ratios, percentages, average, etc., probability sampling is appropriate. Where some broad idea of population values will serve the purpose, as in the case of market surveys, a non-probability sampling method may be selected. Where the representativeness of the sample is important, an appropriate type of random sampling is appropriate? This depends upon the nature of universe and its size. For example, if the universe is heterogeneous and can be classified into a few homogeneous sub-groups then stratified random sampling method may be used. (For a detailed discussion, see "Criteria for selecting Techniques", below in this section).

Parameters of interest: The specific population parameters to be estimated should be determined. These are apparent from the investigative questions and hypothesis, e.g.,

- ❖ The average amount of savings per month.
- ❖ The percentage of consumers who prefer a particular brand of a product.
- ❖ The average rate of return on capital employed.
- ❖ The proportion of family expenditures on recreation.
- ❖ The extent of dining out by families.
- ❖ The percentage of women who read women's section in a magazine.

Such questions determine the sample design, and sample size.

Parameters may be variables or attributes. Variables like rupees, age, length, scores, family size, number of visits per month, etc., are measured by using measures of central tendency and deviation techniques. Attributes like interest, opinion, attitude etc., are measured in terms of percentage of ratio.

Sample size: The size of sample to be drawn depends upon various factors like the population size, the size of the population dispersion, the acceptable confidence level for the parameter estimate, etc., These are discussed in detail later in this chapter (See Section 6.4 in this Chapter, below).

Sample cost: Cost considerations influence decisions about the method of sampling and the sample size. Probability sampling involves listing costs, call back costs and other costs. Simple random sampling is more costly than cluster sampling. The cost per unit may be less when haphazard methods of sampling are used or when data are collected by mailing questionnaires instead of by personal interviewing.

Criteria for Selecting Sampling Techniques

In the previous Section (6.2) we have examined the various sampling methods – their features, applications and merits and limitations. Now let us examine the criteria for selecting and appropriate sampling plan for a given study. The quality of the research output, and the validity of its findings, among other things, depend upon the appropriateness of the sampling design selected for the study. The choice of a sampling plan calls for a careful consideration of various factors such as the nature of the problem, the intention of the researcher, the geographical area covered by the survey, the size of the population to be studied, the extent of the knowledge available about the population, the amount of funds and other facilities available for the study, the time factor and the desired precision or reliability of the results *vis-à-vis* the relative features and suitability of the various sampling techniques.

The decision process is complicated one. The researcher has to first identify the limiting factor or factors. Time factor, funds or non-availability of preliminary information about it may be limiting factors. He has to consider the other factors with reference to the limiting factors. Further several factors conflict. For example, there are conflicts between precision and cost; the scope of the study and the available funds and time; the area covered and the available funds and time; non-availability of population list and the researcher's intention to generalize the findings based on the sample survey; and so on. Therefore the researcher must judiciously balance the conflicting factors. The purpose of the study may call for the application of a particular method, but because of practical difficulties, it may not be possible to adopt it. For example, if the researcher aims at applying inferential statistical analysis, then probability sampling is essential. But if the nature of the population to be studied is not known and the sampling frame is not available, it is difficult to apply probability sampling. Such practical difficulties necessitate a compromise on his part.

Now let us discuss in detail the various criteria governing the choice of the sampling technique:

1. Purpose of the survey: What does the researcher aim at? If he intends to generalize the findings based on the sample survey to the population, then an appropriate probability sampling method must be selected. The choice of a particular type of probability sampling depends on the geographical area of the survey and the size and nature of the population under study.

On the other hand, if he is interested in just understanding the nature of the phenomenon under study, and does not aim at generalizing his finding, some non-probability sampling method will suffice.

2. Measurability: The application of statistical inference theory requires computation of the sampling error from the sample itself. Probability samples only allow such computation. Hence, where the research objective requires statistical inference, the sample should be drawn by applying simple random sampling method or stratified random sampling method, depending on whether the population is homogeneous or heterogeneous. All probability samples are non-measurable, e.g., selecting a single cluster, a systematic sampling from a population with periodic variation, and cluster sampling in which the primary clusters are not identified.

3. Degree of precision: Should the results of the survey be very precise, or even rough results could serve the purpose? The desired level of precision is one of the criteria of sampling method selection. Where a high degree of precision of results would serve the purpose (e.g., marketing surveys) any convenient non-random sampling like quota sampling would be enough.

4. Information about population: How much information is available about the population to be studied ? Where no lists of population and no information about its nature are available, it is difficult to apply a probability sampling method.

Then exploratory study with non-probability sampling may be made to gain a better idea of the population. After gaining sufficient knowledge about the populations through the exploratory study, appropriate probability sampling design may be adopted.

5. The Nature of the population: In terms of the variables to be studied, is the population homogeneous or heterogeneous? In the case of a homogeneous population, even a simple random sampling will give a representative sample. If the population is heterogeneous, stratified random sampling is appropriate. "Systematic sampling would, however, be preferred in those cases where the list of units of population is available or easily obtainable and where there is no periodic variation or trend present in the population."[22]

6. Geographical area of the study and the size of the population: If the area covered by a survey is very large (e.g., a country or a state) and the size of the population is quite large, multi-stage cluster sampling would be appropriate. But if the area and the size of the population are small, single stage probability sampling methods could be used.

7. Financial resources: Is the available finance a limiting factor or not? If the available finance is limited, it may become necessary to choose a less costly sampling plan like multistage cluster sampling or even quota sampling as a compromise. However, if the objectives of the study and the desired level of precision cannot be attained within the stipulated budget, there is no alternative than to give up the proposed survey. Where finance is not a constraint, a researcher can choose the most appropriate method of sampling that fits the research objective and the nature of population.

8. Time limitation: The time limit within which the research project should be completed restricts the choice of a sampling method. Then, as a compromise, it may become necessary to choose less time consuming methods like simple random sampling instead of stratified sampling/sampling with probability proportional to size; multi-stage cluster sampling instead of single-stage sampling of elements. Of course, the precision has to be sacrificed to some extent.

9. Economy Should be another criterion in choosing the sampling method. It means achieving the desired level of precision at minimum cost. "A sample is economical if the precision per unit cost is high or the cost per unit of variance is low."[23] The precisions and costs of various measurable probability sampling methods can be compared and the method which achieves the optimal balance between reliability of results and costs may be selected. This calls for much thought and ingenuity.

The above criteria frequently conflict and the researcher must balance and bend them to obtain a good sampling plan. The chosen plan thus represents an adaptation of the sampling theory to the available facilities and resources. That is, it represents a compromise between idealism and feasibility. One should use simple workable methods instead of unduly elaborate and complicated techniques.

Model Sampling Designs

Model 1: The multi-stage sampling design adopted for the All-India Rural Credit Survey[24] conducted by the Reserve Bank of India during 1951-52 (the first large-scale country-wide survey) is presented below.

---

22. Parel, Cristina P., and others, Sampling Design and Procedures, Singapore: *The Agricultural Development Council,* p. 48.
23. Kish, Leslie, *op. cit.,* p. 25.
24. The Report of the Committee of Direction of All India Rural Credit Survey, *The Technical Report,* Vol. III, Bombay, Reserve Bank of India, 1954, pp. 1-5.

The main aim of this survey was to identify the broad patterns of the working of agricultural credit, including cooperative credit in the different regions of the country.

It was decided that the working of rural credit should be studied in relation to two aspects, viz., the demand for credit from rural families and the supply of credit by credit agencies, both institutional and private; these two aspects are hereafter referred to as the 'demand' and 'supply' aspects respectively of the survey. It was decided to treat district as the unit in the investigations connected with both these aspects and to select as may as 75 districts from all over the country, representative of all the geographical and other types of regions in the country. It was considered desirable to select the districts on a random basis.

In connection with 'demand' aspect of the survey, it was decided that a sample of 600 villages, at the rate of 8 villages per district, should be selected from the 75 districts, and families in these villages should be investigated. As one of the main objectives of the survey was to study the working of cooperative credit in rural areas, it was considered desirable that half the number of villages selected should be those in which primary cooperative credit societies existed and the other half should be those where such societies did not exist.

Selection of Sample Units

Selection of districts: The survey was to cover the whole of the rural area of the country excluding Jammu and Kashmir, the Andaman and Nicobar Islands, Sikkim, Kutch and the Naga Tribal area. The 302 districts included in the area covered by the survey served as the frame for the selection of the sample of 75 districts. In making the selection it was considered desirable that the sample should be representative of the geographical and agricultural regions in the country. Two factors taken into consideration for this purpose are the percentage area under cash crops and the percentage area under irrigation. Subject to considerations regarding these two factors and geographical representativeness, the selection of the 75 districts was made at random from among the 302 districts.

The following table gives the average and the standard deviation in respect of rural population, density of population, percentage area under cash crops and percentage area under irrigation, for the 75 selected districts and for all the districts:

	Average Per District		*Standard Deviation*	
	75 Selected districts	*All districts*	*75 Selected districts*	*All districts*
1. Rural Population (000's)	10,82	9,75	6,94	6,81
2. Density of Population (rural and urban) (persons per square mile)	392	414	268	449
3. Percentage area under cash crops	22	22	13	14
4. Percentage area under irrigation.	21	20	22	20

It is seen that the averages and the standard deviations for the sample districts and for all the districts are in close agreement.

Selection of the villages: For the purpose of selecting a sample of eight villages in each selected district, lists of the villages together with their population according to the 1951 Census were obtained from the Census authorities in the different States. As it was required to select half the number of villages from among those where primary cooperative credit societies existed, lists of such societies were obtained from the Registrars of Cooperative Societies in the different states. Using both these lists, the villages in each district were divided into two groups, namely, those where primary cooperative credit societies existed and those where no such societies existed. From each of these groups four villages were selected at random, with probability of selection proportional to the population of the village.

The lists of the villages so selected were sent to the investigators and it was found during the investigation that in some villages where primary cooperative credit societies were reported to be existing no such society could be located; similarly, in some villages which were reported to be without cooperative credit societies, such societies were actually found to be existing. Substitutions were made in several of the cases by selecting fresh villages from each groups. However, it was not possible to make substitutions in those cases where the reports from the fields staff regarding such discrepancies were not received at the head office in time. Owing to this and also to the fact that in some districts there were less than four villages with cooperative credit societies, it was not possible to select exactly four villages with cooperative credit societies and four villages without such societies in every selected district. Among the 600 villages selected, 284 villages were with cooperative credit societies and the remaining 316 were without such societies. The distribution of the 75 districts according to the number of selected villages with primary cooperative credit societies is as shown below:

Number of villages with societies	*Number of districts*
Nil	4
1	1
2	2
3	6
4	54
5	4
6	3
7	1
Total	75

Selection of cultivating families: The information available in the General schedule regarding the size of the cultivated holding was used to classify all families in the village into two groups, namely, cultivators and non-cultivators. All families who cultivated any land, owned or leased, excluding small garden plots, were classified as cultivating families. Owners of tea, coffee and rubber plantations who did not cultivate other crops, were not included among cultivators.

For selecting a representative sample of cultivating families all cultivating families in each selected village were arranged in descending order of the magnitude of the size of their cultivated holding. The list of cultivating families in each village was then divided into ten deciles with roughly equal number of families in each decile, the excess of families obtained after dividing the total number by ten being adjusted by allotting them at the rate of one each to a few randomly selected deciles. For each of the first five deciles one family was selected at random and from each of the last five deciles one family was selected at random, thus giving altogether a sample of 15 cultivating families in each village. In those villages where the total number of cultivating families was less than 15, all the cultivating families were selected.

Model 2: *The Multi-stage sampling design*[25] adopted by Prof. O.R.Krishnaswami for a project sponsored by the ICSSR entitled 'Factors affecting economic conditions of agricultural labourers in Coimbatore District in the context of agrarian changes'.

The objectives of the study were:

1. To investigate into the nature of employment, the quantum of work, the wage rates, mode of payment, savings and investments and level of living of agricultural labourers in Coimbatore district;
2. To identify the factors affecting the above conditions of labourers and their migration and mobility,with particular reference to the role played by the labour organizations (formal or informal) and processes and measures like mechanization and modernization of agriculture, land reforms, labour legislations and welfare schemes, industrialization and urbanization, cropping pattern and extent of irrigation facilities and rural industrialization; and
3. To suggest measures for improving the conditions of agricultural labourers.

Keeping in mind the requirements of the above objectives, a multistage sampling design was adopted;

Sampling stage I: *Selection of Blocks*: The first stage sample units were the constituent community development blocks in the district, numbering in all, forty-one. Two blocks-one with a high degree of industrialization and urbanization, viz., Perur, situated close to the industrial city of Coimbatore and the other with a high degree of modernization of agriculture, viz., Thukkenaikenpalayam situated about 97 kms. Away from Coimbatore city — were selected for the study. The degree of industrialization and urbanization and degree of modernization of agriculture were used as the sample criteria at this stage mainly because it was considered that they are among the important external factors which influence the economic conditions of agricultural labourers. Further only at the block level rather than at other levels their impact can be studied more profitably. As far as possible the extent of irrigation facilities, cropping pattern and rural industrialization were also considered in the selection of the sample blocks.

The process of selection of the blocks was neither simple nor quick as we expected at the time of designing the study; it was more cumbersome and time-consuming. To decide upon the degree of industrialization and modernaisation of a block, various particulars like the number of industries, kind of industries, number of persons employed in industries in the block, distance of the block headquarters from the major towns and cities in the district, proportion of urban population to rural population and the number of towns in the block with over 10,000 population were required. All these were not readily available from any one source in respect of all the blocks in the district. Therefore, through the District Collector, all the concerned district level officials of the Industries Department and the Block Development Officers were contacted by post for the purpose of collecting the necessary data.

25. Krishnaswami O.R., *"How to Plan a Sampling Design for a Research Project"*, Vidya Bharathi: Bangalore University, Vol. 2 No. 1, 1976, pp. 29-36.

Only a few had responded to our request. The details supplied even by those few officials were not up-to-date, complete and reliable in many cases.

In the above circumstances, it was decided to conduct an on-the-spot study of at least those blocks which are situated around Coimbatore city, i.e., within a radius of 20 kms., and considered as having been highly industrialized and urbanized in comparison with other blocks. We found that the opinions of the concerned officials were useful. Accordingly, four blocks viz., Perur (8 kms.) Thondamuthur (14 kms.), Perianaicken Palayam (18 kms.) and Sarkarsamakkulam (19 kms.) were visited by the project staff. From the figure collected from the interviews with local officials and leaders and also by observation, it was decided to select Perur block which met more or less all the requirements of the sample design. This block being located in the industrial belt of the district and being very proximate of the city of Coimbatore is supposed to possess a high degree of industrialization and urbanization.

The personal experiences of project staff who had already conducted similar studies in the region coupled with information received from the four Divisional Agricultural Officers had helped to select another block with a high degree of modernization of agriculture with assured irrigation facilities. As such, Thukkanaickenpalayam block which is mostly irrigated by Lower Bhavani Project Canal was chosen for the study. This is the block which topped the list of six selected blocks in terms of average adoption index covered for an adoption study conducted earlier under the auspices of the Research Programmes Committee of the Planning Commission.

Sampling stage II: *Selection of Villages:* All the constituent villages of the selected blocks formed the second stage sample units of the study. Ten villages in all –five villages each – from the selected blocks were selected.

The methodology followed for the selection of the village was also not free from difficulty. Though Perur blocks viewed as a whole was highly industrialized, it was not very much true with each and every hamlet in the block. As a matter of fact, there are some industrial pockets within the block. So first of all, we selected only such of the panchayat among the nine constituent panchayats in the block which were highly industrialized and urbanized in relative terms. Secondly, within the selected panchayats, viz., Ganapathy, Perur, Sanganur, Telungupalayam and Kumarapalayam we had to visit each and every hamlet in order to select the more appropriate sample villages.

In Thukkanaickenpalayam Block also the same types of problems were faced by us. Not all the villages were equally modernized in terms of agriculture. Following a similar method as we used in Perur block, five villages were selected in this block. As far as possible, care was taken to see that only villages with varying degrees of land-labour ratio were included in the sampling process. The land-labour ratio was used as the criterion for the sampling of the villages in view of its close relation to the level of economic conditions of the farm workers. The application of this sampling procedure was believed to increase considerably the representativeness of the sample villages.

Sampling stage III: *Selection of farm families and agricultural labour households:* A list of the farm families and a list of the agricultural labour households were prepared in each of the selected villages by a quick survey. This yielded reliable data on such aspects as size of operational holding of farmers and type of labour employed, i.e., whether regular or causal, sources of income for agricultural labourers etc.,

Farm families selection: A sample of 100 farm families in all – 10 families from each village (10 × 10 = 100) – were selected for the study by *systematic sampling with probability proportional to area of* land holding. This was considered a better procedure than the ordinary systematic selection of farmers arranged on the basis of the size of holding because the latter procedure was expected to result in over-representation to small farmers (more than proportionately to their area) who cannot be expected to employ much of hired labour.

Accordingly, all the farmers belonging to a given selected village were arranged in an ascending order of the size of their farm. Then the total area of land of all the farmers was computed. Thirdly, the farmers were divided into five groups of equal area. And finally the farmers from each stratum were selected from the list. The systematic random method was used at this stage. In cases where there was none or only one in a stratum, the gap or shortage was made good by picking up a substitute from the proceeding or immediate next stratum.

As the purpose was not to build up any estimation, a sample of fixed number was found to be appropriate and convenient.

Agricultural labour households' selection: Then, a sample of 400 agricultural labour households-40 each from the selected villages — (40 × 10 = 400) were selected for the study by using stratified random sampling procedure. Firstly, the list of agricultural labour households in each village was divided into two groups, viz., casual and attached labourers. Then by using the table of random numbers, 10 attached labourers at the most and at least 30 casual labourers from each village were selected. As far as possible, only those attached labourers who were working with the selected farmers were included in the study (matched sample). This has helped to collect data more intelligently on the conditions of the attached labourers.

6.4 SAMPLE SIZE

Introduction

There are some misconceptions about the required size of a sample. One is that sample should not be less than 10% of the population. This rule, commonly known as the 1/10th rule is not relevant to large populations. Statisticians can easily illustrate that when a probability sample reaches a certain size, such as 1,000 its efficiency for estimating population parameters is not much different compared with a probability sample of 10,000 or even 1,00,000.

Another misconception is : 'larger the sample size, greater may be the accuracy of the sample results'. Although an increase in sample size will increase the precision of the sample results, a large sample size does not guarantee the accuracy of the results.

The sample size can be statistically estimated by deciding the required level of accuracy. This statistical procedure is based on some basic concepts. Let us introduce those concepts.

Basic Concepts Relevant to Sample Size

Sample value and population parameter: Suppose there are four students in a specialization stream, and they have secured 4, 9, 5 and 6 marks respectively in a test. The mean mark of the population (μ) is 6. A sample of 2 is to be drawn for estimating population.

Suppose a random draw gives a sample of 4 and 6. The sample mean is 10 2 = 5 ÷.0. This is taken as an estimate of the population mean, m. Since in this example, we know that μ is 6, it is possible for us to say that estimate is inaccurate. That is, the sample mean is not an accurate estimation of the population mean. Had the draw given a sample of 5 and 6, the estimate would have been 5.5., which is very close. Therefore, the accuracy of a sample estimate refers to its closeness to the correct population value.

In actual situations, the population value is not known, the actual accuracy of the sample estimate cannot be assessed. However, its probable accuracy can be estimated. This is explained below.

Sampling distribution of the mean: Let us consider all possible samples of size n=2 that could be selected from the above population. The possible samples and their means are:

Possible samples of marks (n=2)	*Mean (i.e., estimate of population)*
4 and 9	13 ÷ 2 = 6.5
4 and 5	9 ÷ 2 = 4.5
4 and 6	10 ÷ 2 = 5.0
9 and 5	14 ÷ 2 = 7.0
9 and 6	15 ÷ 2 = 7.5
5 and 6	11 ÷ 2 = 5.5
	Total 36.0

The distribution formed by the values of mean derived from a large number of samples drawn from the same population is called sampling distribution of the mean. The average of the estimates derived from all possible samples is 36 ÷ 6 = 6, which is equal to the population mean m.

Before proceeding further, let us examine the characteristics of a sampling distribution of the mean:

(1) The sampling distribution of the mean approximates a normal curve. By arranging sample means in a frequency polygon, we end up with the form of a normal curve.

(2) The mean of a sampling distribution of the mean (i.e., the mean of the means) is equal to the true population mean. In the above illustration, the average of means of all possible samples is 6, which is equal to the population mean.

(3) The standard deviation of a sampling distribution of the mean is smaller than the standard deviation of the population.

The variability of the sampling distribution is always smaller than the variability of the entire population. This is true because the mean scores eliminate extreme raw-score values.

The average of the estimates of a population parameter derived from an infinite number of samples of the sample population is called the expected value of the estimator (denoted by 'm'). The estimator is different from an estimate. While an estimate is the value obtained for a specific sample, the estimator is the average of the estimates.

If the expected value of the estimator is equal to the population value (as in the above illustration), the estimator is unbiased. If not, it is biased. The difference between the expected value and the true population value is called the bias. This would be the case where the larger values of the population units are used to estimate μ (statistical symbol), e.g., the expected value of the larger marks in the above illustration is

$$9 + 5 = 14 \div 2 = 7.0$$
$$9 + 6 = 15 \div 2 = 7.5$$
$$14.5$$

Average (i.e., expected value) is 14.5/2 = 7.2 which is higher than the true mean; the bias is 1.2.

Any one sample may give an inaccurate estimate on the population and the deviation may be positive or negative. But, on an average, the sample estimates are equal to the population value.

Standard deviation: In practice, a researcher does not draw several samples from a population. He estimates the population parameter (μ) on the basis of only one sample. As any two samples are likely to produce different estimates, is it not a risky procedure to estimate the m from one sample? It is not because one can estimate from any one random sample how big the differences (sampling fluctuations) are likely to be on average. What is needed is a measure to indicate the spread of the sampling distribution. The most common measure of the spread of any distribution is the standard deviation (or its square, the variance).

Standard deviation is the square root of the mean of the squares of the deviation of individual items from their arithmetic mean. This is represented by a formula:

$$\sigma = \sqrt{\frac{\Sigma x^2}{N}}$$

Where σ = Standard deviation

X = the difference between the value of each item of the series from its arithmetic mean.

Σx^2 = the sum of the squared deviations from the mean.

N = the total number of items.

Standard Error: The standard deviation of the sampling distribution of the above illustration is

$$\sqrt{\frac{(6.5-6)^2+(4.5-6)^2+(5-6)^2+(7-6)^2+(7.5-6)^2+(5.5-6)^2}{6}}$$

$$= \sqrt{\frac{0.25+2.25+1+1+2.25+0.25}{6}} = \sqrt{\frac{7}{6}} = \sqrt{1.17} = 1.08$$

This measure is called the standard error of the mean. Of course, standard error may be computed for other statistics like the median, proportion, etc.

The standard error serves as a criterion for evaluating the probable accuracy of any one estimate. This may be denoted by S.E.

S.E. can be estimated from a single sample and can be represented by the following formula:

$$\text{S.E. }(\bar{x}) = \sqrt{\frac{\sigma^2}{n} \times \frac{N-n}{N-1}}$$

where σ = standard deviation of a trait in the population (say marks secured, or age)

N = the number of units in the population

n = the number of units in the sample.

It is convenient to use a modified definition of the population standard deviation, S, rather than σ[26]. S is defined as

$$S = \sqrt{\frac{\sum_{i=1}^{n}(x^1 - \mu)^2}{N-1}}$$

With this definition,

$$\text{S.E. }(\bar{X}) = \sqrt{\frac{S^2}{n} \times \frac{N-n}{n}} = \sqrt{\frac{S^2}{n}\left(1-\frac{n}{N}\right)} \quad \ldots (6.1)$$

The factor (1-n/N) is called the *finite* population correction (f.p.c.). If the sample does not exceed about 10% of the population, the f.p.c. approximates unity and can be omitted. Then the formula becomes

$$\text{S.E. }(\bar{X}) = \sqrt{\frac{S_2}{n}} = S/\sqrt{n} \quad \ldots (6.2)$$

In the example under study, f.p.c. cannot obviously be ignored, and we calculate the standard error from (6.1) with N = 4, n = 2;

$$S^2 = \frac{(4-6)^2 + (9-6)^2 + (5-6)^2 + (6-6)^2}{(4-1) = 3}$$

$$= \frac{4+9+1+0}{3} = \frac{14}{3}$$

$$\text{S.E. }(\bar{X}) = \sqrt{\frac{14/3}{2} \times \frac{4-2}{4}} = \sqrt{\frac{14}{6} \times \frac{2}{4}} = \sqrt{\frac{7}{6}} = \sqrt{1.17}$$

Which agrees with the previous result.

26. Moser C.A. and Kalton G., *Survey Methods in Social Investigation, op. cit.*, pp. 66-67.

Samples size and variability in the population: In the formula (6.2), we note that the standard error is based on two factors:

(1) The value of 'n' i.e., sample size

(The formula shows that the standard error varies inversely to the square root of 'n', i..e., to halve the standard error requires four times a big sample. Thus larger the sample size, greater will be precision of the results) and

(2) The value of 'S' or σ i.e., the variability in the population

(This also corresponds to the above position. If the variability in the population is less, standard deviation will be smaller. If, on the other hand, the variability is more, the standard error will be larger).

Standard deviation of a trait: In practice, the value of 'S' is almost unknown. So one has to substitute for S, the standard deviation of a trait (e.g., marks secured/age/income etc). In the population calculated from the sample (to be denoted by 's' and then estimate the standard error from Formula 6.1. Thus,

$$S = \sqrt{\frac{1}{N-1}\sum_{i=1}^{n}(x_i - \bar{x})^2} \quad \text{... (6.3)}$$

Where, x_1, x_2, x_3 .....x_n are sample observations

S = standard deviation of a trait calculated from the sample

$\bar{x}$ = sample mean

The standard error calculated from 's' is an unbiased estimate of the true standard error. In order to distinguish between the two, we may use capital letters for the latter and lower-case letter for the former [s.e. $(\bar{X})$]

Interpretation of a standard error: How is an estimate of standard error to be interpreted? Suppose we have a sample of 150 students and their average mark in a test is 21 and the calculated 's' is 12; then the standard error of the mean is:

$$\text{s.e. } (\bar{X}) = \sqrt{\frac{144}{150}} = 0.98$$

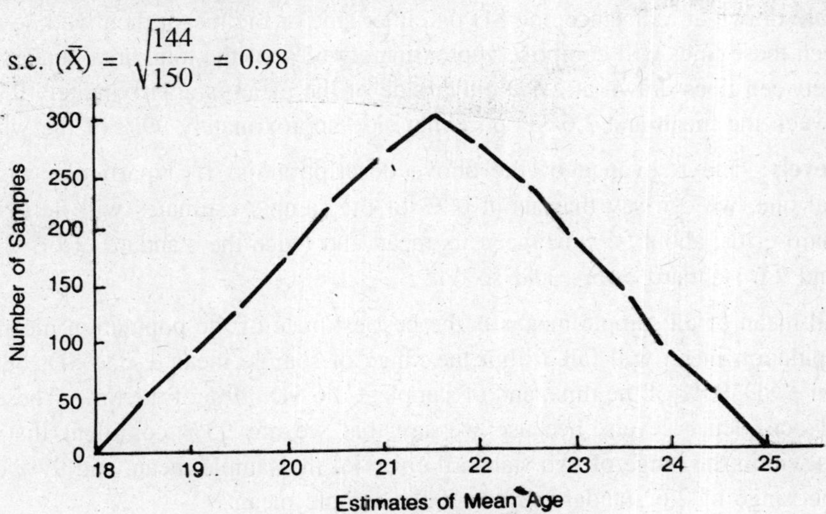

Exhibit 6.3: Sample Distribution

(the f.p.c. is ignored). What does this figure tell us about the precision of the sample estimate? We are interested in the probability that the sample mean falls in any particular range of the sampling distribution. Therefore, before the standard error concept can be utilized, we should know about the shape of the sampling distributions and about the concept of "confidence" range of the sampling distribution. Therefore, before the standard error concept can be utilized, we should know about the shape of the sampling distributions and about the concept of "confidence or probability levels".

Normal distribution: The distribution of sample means or any other statistic approximated to the normal distribution. Suppose we draw several samples of 'n' size out of say 1,000 students and estimate the mean ages of those samples; then the sample distribution is shown as under.

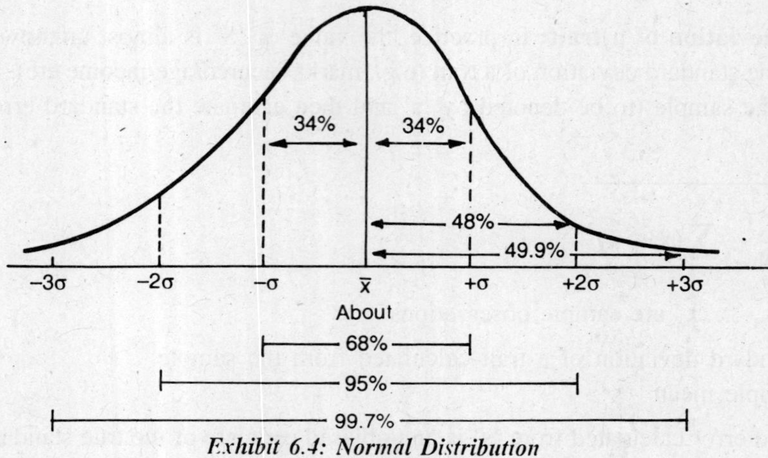

Exhibit 6.4: Normal Distribution

With reasonably large samples; the sampling distribution of any statistic approximates to the normal distribution. What are the characteristics of a normal distribution?

Normal distribution is distributed symmetrically about its mean with a large number of small deviations from the mean and a few large ones. If its standard deviation (SD) or σ is calculated and perpendicular lines are drawn at a distance one SD on either side of the mean, then we know that the area enclosed between these lines will comprise approximately 68% of the total area under the curve. Similarly the area between lines drawn at 2 SD either side of the mean is approximately 95% of the whole; the area between the mean and 2.6 SD on either side approximately 99% of the whole area.

Confidence levels: The relevance of the above description is: If a particular distribution approximated normal one, we can say that about 68% of the sample estimates will lie between its mean and one standard error; about 95% between its mean and twice the standard error, about 99% between its mean and 2.6 standard errors, and so on.

Since the grand mean of all sample means is the best estimate of the population mean, we can say that the true population mean will fall within the range of sample mean ± one SD, 68% of the time; of sample mean ± SD, 95% of the time, and of sample ± 2.6 SD, 99% of the time. These interval estimates are called confidence levels, because we say that we are 95% confident that the true population mean lies within the range of two standard errors of the sample mean, and 99% confident that it lies within the range of 2.6 standard errors of the sample mean.

Now we can deal with the sample size.

Estimation of Sample Size

If cost and other practical limitations do not enter into the decision of the sample size, there is no difficulty in determining the required size.

Recall formula (6.1) for the standard error of the mean.

$$\text{S.E. }(\bar{X}) = \sqrt{\frac{S_2}{n}\left(1-\frac{n}{N}\right)}$$

Ignoring the finite population correction, we get

$$\text{S.E }(\bar{X}) = \frac{S}{\sqrt{n}}$$

Where S = Standard deviation of the variable under study in the population

n = Sample size

Inverting we get,

$$n = \frac{S^2}{[\text{S.E.}(\bar{X})]^2} \quad \text{... (6.4)}$$

If the ratio of the calculated sample size (n) to population size (N) is large, i.e., when n/N is 0.20 or greater, the finite population correction should be included. Then the final sample size (n) is determined by

$$n' = \frac{n}{1+(n/N)} \quad \text{... (6.5)}$$

The reason for including f.p.c. is : If the ratio of an n/N is small, the standard error would be large: if the ratio is one, i.e., the sample is 100% of the population, the standard error would be zero.

In order to calculate the sample size 'n' we have to decide how big a standard error can be tolerated. Let us suppose we want to draw a random sample from a population of 10,000 units. The estimated $S^2 = 0.20$ and we desire that the standard error should be more than 0.016, then the required sample size is

$$n = \frac{0.20}{(.016)^2} = \frac{0.20}{0.00026} = 769$$

As this sample size represents a sizeable proportion of the population, f.p.c. has to be included, then the resulting sample is:

$$n' = \frac{n}{1+(n/N)} = \frac{769}{1+(769/10{,}000)} = 714$$

Practical Difficulties

Formula (6.4) and (6.5) illustrate the priciple involved in estimating the sample size. In practice, the decision on sample size is more complicated.

The first difficulty is about the precision required. The researcher must decide the required extent of precision of the sample results, i.e., how large a standard error he can tolerate.

Second, the researcher must consider the way the results are to be analysed, i.e., the sub-groups into which the sample must be divided. He can then work out roughly the numbers needed in each sub-groups to give the desired precision for it.

Third, the number of variables (or attributes) to be studied should be determined. A sample that is adequate for one variable may be inadequate for another which requires precision.

Fourth, in order to use formula (6.2), the researcher needs an estimate of S. the estimation of S is often somewhat more difficult. However, an approximate idea about the proportion of the given trait in the population will be adequate, for moderate errors in estimating this proportion will have only a small effect on the calculation of sample size.

For further discussions on the practical difficulties relating to the estimation of sample size, see (1) Leslie Kish, *Survey Sampling,* New York, John Wiley & Sons, and (2) C.A. Moser and S. Kalton, *Survey Methods in Social Investigation, op.cit.,* Section 7.1 in Chapter 7.

6.5 SAMPLING AND NON-SAMPLING ERRORS

Introduction

A survey aims at estimating or inferring selected population characteristics or parameters by studying either the entire population or a sample of the population. The research results may differ from the 'true values' of the parameters under study. Such differences are known as Errors and biases.

The errors of a survey may be classified into (a) Sampling errors, (b) Sampling biases, (c) Non-sampling errors and (d) Non-sampling biases.

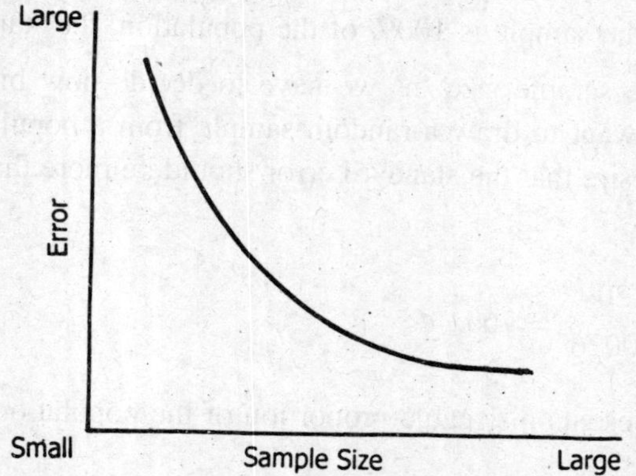

Exhibit 6.5: The Relationship between Sample size and the Sampling error

Sampling Errors

The errors which arise because of studying only a part of the total population are called sampling errors. These may arise due to non-representativeness of the samples and the inadequacy of sample size. When several samples are drawn from a population, their results would not be identical. The degree of variations of sample results is measured by standard deviation (as explained in the previous section 6.4) and it is known as the standard error of the concerned statistic. As sample size increases the magnitude of the error decreases. Sample size and sampling error are thus negatively correlated (See Exhibit 6.5).

Sampling Biases

The average of the estimates of a population parameter derived from an infinite number of samples is called the expected value of the estimator (See Section 6.4). The difference between this value and 'true value' of the parameter is the bias. Bias may arise (1) if the sampling is done by a non-random method, (2) if the sampling frame is incomplete or inaccurate and (3) if some sections of the population are not available/refuse to cooperate. Any of these factors will cause non-compensating errors which cannot be reduced by an increase in sample size. The only sure way of avoiding bias arising through the sampling method is to use a random method.[27] Randomness is an essential part of the protection against selection bias.

Non-Sampling Errors

These are errors which arise from sources other than sampling. They include errors of observation, errors of measurement and errors of responses. Data are collected through the methods of observation or interviewing. The physical procedures of observation or interviewing are subject to imperfection which cause errors. Measurement errors consist of error in processing and analysis. Errors of response include incorrect responses of the respondents, mistakes in noting their responses etc.

Non-Sampling Biases[28]

These biases pose problems for scientific measurement. They affect both the population sample values and account for the difference between the population value and the true value. They consist of biases of observation and non-observation, response biases and process biases. Biases of observation are caused by obtaining and recording observations incorrectly. Non-observation biases arise from failure to obtain observations on some segments of the population due to either non-coverage or non-response. The latter may be due to refusals, non-at-homes, lost forms, etc. response biases consist of biases arising from imperfections in field observations or interviewing. Processing biases are produced during coding, tabulating and computing.

Total Error

In sampling theory, a popular model combines sampling and non-sampling errors and biases into the Total Error. This total error is the square root of the sums of squares of variable errors and squares of bias. It is often called the root means square error (RMSE).

$$\text{Total} = \sqrt{VE^2 + \text{Bias}^2}$$

The variable errors are caused only by sampling errors, and VE equals the standard error of sampling. Bias is mostly caused by measurement biases (i.e., non-sampling errors).

The total error depends on the length of both of the legs. The sampling error/ standard error leg can be shortened by improving the sample design and by increasing the sample size. The length of

27. Moser C.A. and Kalton G., *Survey Methods in Social Investigation, op. cit.*, p. 80.
28. Kish, Leslie, *Survey Sampling, op. cit.*, p. 520.

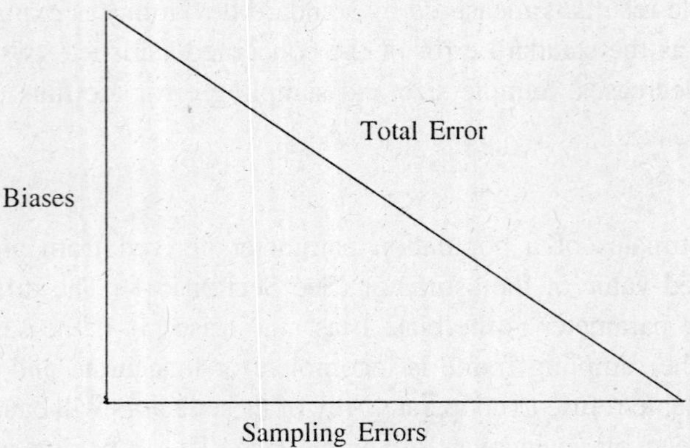

Exhibit 6.6: Total Error

biases leg may be reduced by improving the tool of data collection, the precision of methods of data collection, field work, coding, processing and analysis.

The measurement of sampling error does not pose much problem but the measurement of non-sampling errors require special procedures and it is a costly effect. Hence, the reduction of non-sampling error is a challenge to the researchers.

SUGGESTED READINGS

1. Cochran, Willian G., *Sampling Techniques,* New York: John Wiley & Sons, 1963.
2. Conway, Freda, *Sampling: An Introduction for Social Scientists,* London: George Allen and Unwin, 1967.
3. Deming, W.E., *Sample Design in Business Research,* New York: John Wiley & Sons, 1960.
4. Kaltan, Graham, *Introduction to Survey Sampling,* Beverly Hills, Calif: Sage, 1983.
5. Kish, Leslie, *Survey Sampling,* New York: John Wiley & Sons, 1967.
6. Monroe, John and A.L. Finkner, *Handbook of Area Sampling,* Philadelphia: Chilton, 1959.
7. Murthy, M.N. *Sampling Theory and Methods,* Calcutta: Statistical Publishing Society, 1967.
8. Parten, Mildred, *Surveys, Polls and Sample: Practical Procedures,* New York: Cooper Square, 1966.
9. Raj, Des, *The Design of Sample Surveys,* New York: McGraw-Hill, 1972.
10. Stephan, F.F., and McCarthy, P.J., *Sampling Opinions: An Analysis of Survey Procedure,* New York: John Wiley & Sons, 1958.
11. Sukhatme, P.V., and Sukhatme, B.V., *Sampling Theory of Surveys with Applications,* London: Asia Publishing House, 1970.
12. Som, R.K., *A Manual of Sampling Techniques,* London: Heinemann Educational Books, 1973.
13. UN Statistical Office, *A Short Manual on Sampling,* Vol. I, Elements of Sample Survey Theory, New York: United Nations, 1960,
14. Yamane, Taro, *Elementary Sampling Theory,* Englewood Cliffs, N.J., Prentice-Hall, 1967.
15. Yates, Frank, *Sampling Methods for Censuses and Surveys,* New York: Hafner, 1960.

QUESTIONS

1. What is Sampling? Why is it used in social science research?
2. What are the major considerations in deciding to sample?
3. What are the characteristics of a good sample?
4. What are the premises on which sampling is based?
5. What is meant by 'representativeness' of a sample? How is it achieved?
6. What are the limitations of sampling?
7. Differentiate probability sampling from non-probability sampling.
8. What is the importance of randomness in sampling? By what methods of selection is randomness ensured.
9. Describe the procedure of lottery method of drawing samples.
10. You plan to conduct a survey using unrestricted sampling. What are the subjectives that you must make?
11. How would you select a sample of 150 students out of 3500 graduate students in a university?
12. When and how a table of random numbers is used in sample selection?
13. How is a simple random sampling done? When is it suitable? What are its limitations?
14. What is meant by stratified random sampling? What is the need for stratification?
15. Describe the merits and demerits of proportionate stratified sampling.
16. When is disproportionate stratified random sampling desirable?
17. Can systematic sampling be treated as a form of probability sampling?
18. Discuss the merits and demerits of systematic random sampling?
19. Define cluster sampling and describe its features.
20. Differentiate cluster sampling from stratified sampling.
21. Describe the steps involved in the cluster sampling process.
22. Is cluster sampling statistically more efficient? Why or Why not?
23. Under what conditions would it be appropriate for a researcher to use cluster or area sampling?
24. What are the advantages of cluster sampling compared with simple random sampling.?
25. Is area sampling a separate method of sampling? Give an illustration for area sampling.
26. What is Multi-stage sampling? Under what conditions would it be appropriate to use it?
27. What is sub-sampling? What is its functions? How does it differ from cluster sampling?
28. Discuss the problem of control of sample size. What are the reasons for controlling sample size?
29. What are the various ways by which the ultimate sample size is controlled?
30. Describe the procedure of sampling with probability proportional to size (PPS). Illustrate it.
31. Explain double sampling and Multi-phase sampling. Differentiate Multi-phase sampling from Multi-stage sampling.
32. "Multi-phase sampling is a compromise solution for a dilemma posed by undesirable extremes" – Discuss.
33. What is replicated or interpenetrating sampling? How does it simplify the procedure of computing sampling errors?
34. What is convenience sampling? What are its limitations?
35. When is purposive or judgment sampling appropriate? What are its merits and demerits?
36. What is quota sampling? Is it related to stratified random sampling?
37. Discuss the merits and demerits of quota sampling.

38. What is snowball sampling? What are its applications?
39. Can snowball sampling be considered as a probability sampling method? Why or why not?
40. What questions are considered in drawing a sample plan for a study?
41. Discuss the problem of non-coverage and incomplete frame in sampling.
42. How is the choice of sampling techniques to be used made?
43. What are the criteria for the choice of sampling methods for a given study?
44. What are the issues involved in selecting sampling methods for a given study?
45. The chosen sample plan represents a compromise between idealism and feasibility- Discuss.
46. What are the misconceptions regarding required sample size for a study?
47. Define the following concepts:
    (a) Sample frame
    (b) Population parameter
    (c) Sample mean
    (d) Confidence levels
    (e) Finite population correction.
48. What is meant by 'sampling distribution of the mean'? What are its characteristics?
49. Why is the determination of sample size a problem?
50. What is standard error? On what two factors is it based?
51. What is normal distribution? What is the relevance of this concept to the problem of sample size?
52. How is the size of a sample for a study determined?
53. What are the practical difficulties involved in sample size decision?
54. Distinguish between:
    (a) Sample frame and population
    (b) Statistic and parameter
    (c) Restricted and unrestricted sampling
    (d) Standard deviation and standard error
    (e) Estimator and estimate
    (f) Sample precision and sample accuracy
    (g) Sampling error and sampling bias
    (h) Homogeneous and heterogeneous population
55. What are sampling errors? How do they arise?
56. Discuss the relationship between sample size and the sampling error.
57. How do sampling biases arise? How can they be avoided?
58. What are non-sampling errors and biases?
59. What is meant by 'total error'? How is it measured? Can it be reduced?
60. Discuss how the efficiency of a sample design can be increased?
61. To investigate voting intentions of various Caste groups in a small town, what sample design could yield (a) most accurate results, (b) adequate representation?

❑ ❑ ❑

7 METHODS OF DATA COLLECTION

7.1 MEANING AND IMPORTANCE OF DATA

Meaning of Data

The search for answers to research questions is called collection of data. Data are facts, and other relevant materials, past and present, serving as bases for study and analyses. Some example of data are:

- The types of Loans secured by borrowers (for a credit survey)
- The items of raw materials required for a product line (Materials management)
- The quantity of each material required for a unit of output
- The sex, age, social class, religion, income level of respondents in a consumer behaviour study
- The opinions of eligible couples on birth control devices (Family Planning Survey)
- The capital expenditure proposals considered by a firm during a year (Financial Management)
- The marks obtained by students of a class in a test on a particular subject (Performances of students)
- The opinions of people on voting in a general election (Opinion Poll)
- The types of news read by newspaper readers (Readership Survey)
- The aspirations of management trainees (The emerging Managers in Indian enterprises)
- The types and frequency of breakdowns occurred in particular brand of scooter (Post-purchase Behaviour Survey) and so on.

Types of Data

The data needed for a social science research may be broadly classified into (a) Data pertaining to human beings, (b) Data relating to organizations, and (c) Data pertaining to territorial areas.

Personal data or data related to human beings consist of-

(1) Demographic and socio-economic characteristics of individuals: Age, sex, race, social class, religion, martial status, education, occupation, income, family size, location of the household, life style, etc.,

(2) Behavioural variables: Attitudes, opinions, awareness, knowledge, practice, intentions, etc.

Organisational data consist of data relating to an organization's origin, ownership, objectives, resources, functions, performance and growth.

Territorial data are related to geophysical characteristics, resources endowment, population, occupational pattern, infrastructure, structure, degree of development, etc. of spatial divisions like villages, cities, talukas, districts, state and the nation.

Importance of data

The data serve as the bases or raw materials for analysis. Without an analysis of factual data, no specific inferences can be drawn on the questions under study. Inferences based on imagination or guess work cannot provide correct answers to research questions. The relevance, adequacy and reliability of data determine the quality of the findings of a study.

Data form the basis for testing the hypotheses formulated in a study. Data also provide the facts and figures required for constructing measurement scales and tables, which are analysed with statistical techniques. Inferences on the results of statistical analysis and tests of significance provide the answers to research questions. Thus, the scientific process of measurements, analysis, testing and inferences depends on the availability of relevant data and their accuracy. Hence, the importance of data for nay research study.

7.2 SOURCES OF DATA

The sources of data may be classified into (a) primary sources and (b) secondary sources.

Primary Sources

Primary sources are original sources from which the researcher directly collects data that have not been previously collected, e.g., collection of data directly by the researcher on brand awareness, brand preference, brand loyalty and other aspects of consumer behaviour from a sample of consumers by interviewing them. Primary data are first-hand information collected through various methods such as observation, interviewing, mailing etc. (Sec. 7.4 *Methods of Collecting Primary Data,* below).

Secondary Sources

These are sources containing data which have been collected and compiled for another purpose. The secondary sources consists of readily available compendia and already compiled statistical statements and reports whose data may be used by researches for their studies, e.g, census reports, annual reports and financial statements of companies, Statistical statements, Reports of Government Departments, Annual Reports on currency and finance published by the Reserve Bank of India, Statistical Statements relating to Cooperatives and Regional Rural Banks, published by the NABARD,

Reports of the National Sample Survey Organisation, Reports of trade associations, publications of international organizations such as UNO, IMF, World Bank, ILO, WHO, etc., Trade and Financial Journals, newspapers, etc.,

Secondary sources consists of not only published records and reports, but also unpublished records. The latter category includes various records and registers maintained by firms and organizations, e.g., accounting and financial records, personnel records, register of members, minutes of meetings, inventory records, etc.

Features of Secondary Sources: Though secondary sources are diverse and consist of all sorts of materials, they have certain common characteristics.

First, they are readymade and readily available, and do not require the trouble of constructing tools and administering them.

Second, they consist of data over which a researcher has no original control over collection and classification. Both the form and the content of secondary sources are shaped by others. Clearly, this is a feature which can limit the research value of secondary sources.

Finally, secondary sources are not limited in time and space. That is, the researcher using them need not have been present when and where they were gathered.

7.3 USE OF SECONDARY DATA

Uses

The secondary data may be used in three ways by a researcher. First, some specific information from secondary sources may be used for reference purpose. For example, the general statistical information in the number of cooperative credit societies in the country, their coverage of villages, their capital structure, volume of business, etc. may be taken from published reports and quoted as background information in a study on the evaluation of performance of cooperative credit societies in a selected district/state.

Second, secondary data may be used as bench marks against which the findings of a research may be tested, e.g., the findings of a local or regional survey may be compared with the national averages; the performance indicators of a particular bank may be tested against the corresponding indicators of the banking industry as a whole; and so on.

Finally, secondary data may be used as the sole source of information for a research project. Such studies as securities Market Behaviour, Financial Analysis of Companies, Trends in credit allocation in commercial banks, Sociological Studies on crimes, historical studies, and the like depend primarily on secondary data. Year books, statistical reports of government departments, report of public organizations of Bureau of Public Enterprises, Census Reports etc. serve as major data sources for such research studies.

Advantages

Secondary sources have some advantages:

1. Secondary data, if available can be secured quickly and cheaply. Once their source of documents and reports are located, collection of data is just a matter of desk work. Even the tediousness of copying the data from the source can now be avoided, thanks to xeroxing facilities.

2. Wider geographical area and longer reference period may be covered without much cost. Thus, the use of Secondary data extends the researcher's space and time reach.
3. The use of Secondary data broadens the data base from which scientific generalizations can be made. This is especially so when data from several environmental and cultural settings are required for the study.
4. The use of Secondary data enables a researcher to verify the findings based on primary data. It readily meets the need for additional empirical support. The researcher need not await the time when additional primary data can be collected.

Disadvantages/Limitations

The use of secondary data has its own limitations:

1. The most important limitation is the available data may not meet our specific needs. The definitions adopted by those who collected those data may be different; units of measure may not match; and time periods may also be different.
2. The available data may not be as accurate as desired. To assess their accuracy we need to know how the data were collected.
3. The Secondary data are not uptodate and become obsolete when they appear in print, because of time lag in producing them. For example, population census data are published two or three years later after compilation, and no new figures will be available for another ten years.
4. Finally information about the whereabouts of sources may not be available to all social scientists. Even if the location of the source is known, the accessibility depends primarily on proximity. For example, most of the unpublished official records and compilations are located in the capital city, and they are not within the easy reach of researchers based in far off places.

Evaluation of Secondary Data

When a researcher wants to use secondary data for his research, he should evaluate them before deciding to use them.

Data pertinency: The first consideration in evaluation is to examine the pertinency of the available secondary data to the research problem under study. The following questions should be considered:

1. What are the definitions and classifications employed? Are they consistent with our own?
2. What are the measurements of variables used? What is the degree to which they conform to the requirements of our research?
3. What is the coverage of the secondary data in terms of topic and time? Does this coverage fit the needs of our research?

On the basis of above consideration, the pertinency of the secondary data to the research on hand should be determined. As researcher who is imaginative and flexible may be able to redefine his research problem so as to make use of otherwise unusable available data.

Data quality: If the researcher is convinced that the available secondary data fit his needs, the next step is to examine the quality of the data.

The quality of data refers to their accuracy, reliability and completeness.

The assurance and reliability of the available secondary data depends on the organisation which collected them and the purpose for which they were collected. What is the authority and prestige of the organisation? Is it well recognized? Is it noted for reliability? It it capable of collecting reliable data? Does it use trained and well qualified investigators? The answers to these questions determine the degree of confidence we can have in the data and their accuracy.

It is important to go to the original source of the secondary data rather than to use an immediate source which has quoted from the original. Then only, the researcher can review the cautionary and other comments that were made in the original source.

The completeness refers to the actual coverage of the published data. This depends on the methodology and sampling design adopted by the original organisation. Is the methodology sound? Is the sample size small or large? Is the sampling method appropriate? Answers to these questions may indicate the appropriateness and adequacy of the data for the problem under study.

The question of possible bias should also be examined. Whether the purpose for which the original organisation collected the data had a particular orientation? Has the study been made to promote the organisation's own interest? How the study was conducted? These are important clues.

The researcher must be on guard when the source does not report the methodology and sampling design. Then it is not possible to determine the adequacy of the secondary data for the researcher's study.

7.4 METHODS OF COLLECTING PRIMARY DATA: GENERAL

Introduction

Primary data are directly collected by the researcher from their original sources. In this case, the researcher can collect the required data precisely according to his research needs, he can collect them when he wants them and in the form he needs them. But the collection of primary data is costly and time consuming. Yet, for several types of social science research required data are not available from secondary sources and they have to be directly gathered from the primary sources.

In such cases where the available data are inappropriate, inadequate or obsolete, primary data have to be gathered. They include: socio-economic surveys, social anthropological studies of rural communities and tribal communities, sociological studies of social problems and social institutions, marketing research, leadership studies, opinion polls, attitudinal surveys, readership, radio listening and T.V. viewing surveys, knowledge-awareness practice (KAP) studies, farm management studies, business management studies, etc.,

Methods of Primary Data Collection

There are various methods of data collection. A 'Method' is different from a 'Tool'. While a method refers to the way or mode of gathering data, a tool is an instrument used for the method. For example, a schedule is used for interviewing. The important methods are (a) observation, (b) interviewing, (c) mail survey, (d) experimentation, (e) simulation, and (f) projective technique. Each of these methods is discussed in detail in the subsequent sections in this chapter (see 7.5- 7.11).

Observations involves gathering of data relating to the selected research by viewing and or listening. Interviewing involves face-to-face conversation between the investigator and the respondent. Mailing is used for collecting data by getting questionnaires completed by respondents. Experimentation involves a study of independent variables under controlled conditions. Experiments may be conducted in a laboratory or in field in a natural setting. Simulation involves creation of an artificial situation similar to the actual life situation. Projective methods aim at drawing inferences on the characteristics of respondents by presenting to them stimuli. Even method has its advantages and disadvantages (See sections 7.5 to 7.13 below).

Choice of Methods of Data Collection

Which of the above methods of data collection should be selected for a proposed research project? This is one of the questions to be considered while designing the research plan. One or more methods has/have to be chosen. The choice of a method or methods depends upon the following factors:

1. **The nature of the study of the subject-matter:** If it is a study of opinions/preferences of persons, interviewing or mailing may be appropriate depending on the educational level of the respondents. On the other hand, an impact study may call for experimentation; and a study of behavioural pattern may require observation.
2. **The unit of enquiry:** The unit of enquiry may be an individual, household institution or community. To collect data from households, interviewing is preferable. Data from institutions may be collected by mail survey and studies on communities call for observational method.
3. **The size and spread of the sample:** If the sample is small and the area covered is compact interviewing may be preferable, but a large sample scattered over a wider area may require mailing.
4. **Scale of the survey:** A large scale may require mailing or interviewing through trained investigators.
5. **The educational level of respondents:** For a simple survey among educated persons concerned with the subject-matter of study, a mail survey may be appropriate. But for a survey of less educated/illiterate persons like industrial workers, slum dwellers, rural people, interviewing is the only suitable method.
6. **The type and depth of information to be collected:** For collection of general, simple, factual and non-emotional data, interviewing or mailing is appropriate. For an indepth survey of personal experiences and sensitive issues, indepth interview is essential. For collection of data on behaviour, culture, customs, life style etc., observational method is required.
7. **The availability of skilled and trained manpower:** In this case, even for a large general survey entailing many complicated questions, interviewing can be adopted.
8. **The rate of accuracy and representative nature of the data required:** Interviewing is the most appropriate method for collecting accurate data from a representative sample of population. Interviewing can achieve a higher response rate.

A researcher can select one or more of the methods keeping in view the above factors. No method is universal. Each method's unique features should be compared with the needs and conditions of the study and thus the choice of the methods should be decided.

Evaluation of Data Collection Methods

The appropriateness of a method of data collection may be evaluated on the basis of the following criteria:

1. The efficiency i.e., the speed and cost of data collection,
2. Data quality and adequacy i.e., response rate, accuracy and objectivity,
3. Naturalness of setting,
4. Anonymity,
5. Interviewer supervision,
6. Control of context and question order,
7. Ability to use visual aids,
8. Potential for controlling variables and
9. Dependence on respondent's reading and writing ability.

7.5 OBSERVATION

Meaning and Importance

Observation means viewing or seeing. We go on observing something or other while we are awake. Most of such observations are just casual and have no specific purpose. But observation in a method of data collection is different from such casual viewing.

Observation may be defined as a systematic viewing of a specific phenomenon in its proper setting for the specific purpose of gathering data for a particular study. Observation as a method includes both 'seeing' and 'hearing'. It is accompanied by perceiving as well.

Observation is a classical method of scientific enquiry. The body of knowledge of various natural and physical sciences such as biology, physiology, astronomy, plant ecology etc. has been built upon centuries of systematic observation.

Observation also plays a major role in formulating and testing hypothesis in social sciences. Behavioural scientists observe interactions in small groups; anthropologists observe simple societies, and small communities; political scientists observe the behaviour of political leaders and political institutions. In a sense, as the Webbs[1] have pointed out, all social research begins and ends with observation. A researcher silently watching a city council or a trade union committee or quality circle or a departmental meeting or a conference of politicians or others picks up hints that help him to formulate new hypothesis. He can test them through further observation and study.

Observation becomes scientific, when it (a) serves a formulated research purpose, (b) is planned deliberately, (c) is recorded systematically, and (d) is subjected to checks and controls on validity and reliability. Validity refers to the extent to which the recorded observations accurately reflect the construct they are intended to measure. Validity is assessed by examining how well the observations agree with alternative measures of the same construct. Reliability entails consistency and freedom from measurement error. This is usually assessed in terms of (a) the extent to which two or more independent observers agree in their ratings of the same event; and (b) the repeatability of observations over time by means of test-retest comparisons. (For detailed discussion see section 5.6 of Chapter 5).

1. Webb, Sidney and Webb, Beatrice, *Methods of Social Study,* London: Longmans Green, 1932, p. 158.

Characteristics

Observations as a method of data collection has certain characteristics.

1. It is both a physical and a mental activity. The observing eye 'catches' many things which are slighted, but attention is focused on data that are pertinent to the given study.
2. Observation is selective. A researcher does not observe anything and everything, but selects the range of things to be observed on the basis of the nature, scope and objectives of his study. For example, suppose a researcher desires to study the causes of city road accidents and has formulated a tentative hypothesis that accidents are caused by violation of traffic rules and overspeeding. When he observes the movements of vehicles on the road, many things are before his eyes: the type, make, size and colour of the vehicles, the persons sitting in them, their hair style, etc. All such things which are not relevant to his study are ignored and only overspeeding and traffic violations are keenly observed by him.
3. Observation is purposive and not casual. It is made for the specific purpose of noting things relevant to the study.
4. It captures the natural social context in which persons' behaviour occurs.
5. It grasps the significant events and occurrences that affect social relations of the participants.
6. Observation should be exact and be based on standardized tools of research such as observation schedule, social-metric scale, etc., and precision instruments, if any.

Types of Observation

Observation may be classified in different ways. With reference to investigator's role, it may be classified into (a) participant observation, and (b) non-participant observation. In terms of mode of observation, it may be classified into (c) direct observation and (d) indirect observation. With reference to the rigor of the system adopted, observation is classified into (e) controlled observation, and (f) uncontrolled observation.

Participant observation: In this observation, the observer is a part of the phenomenon or group which is observed and he acts as both an observer and a participant. For example, a study of tribal customs by an anthropologist by taking part in tribal activities like folk dance. The persons who are observed should not be aware of the researcher's purpose. Then only their behaviour will be 'natural'. The concealment of research objective and researcher's identity is justified on the ground that it makes it possible to study certain aspects of the group's culture which are not revealed to outsiders.

Advantages: The advantages of participant observation are:

(1) The observer can understand the emotional reactions of the observed group, and get a deeper insight of their experiences.

(2) The observer will be able to record context which gives meaning to the observed behaviour and heard statements.

Disadvantages: Participant observation suffers from some demerits.

1. The participant observer narrows his range of observation. For example, if there is a hierarchy of power in the group/community under study, he comes to occupy one position within it, and thus other avenues of information are closed to him.

2. To the extent that the participant observer participates emotionally, the objectivity is lost.
3. Another limitation of this method is the dual demand made on the observer. Recording can interfere with participation, and participation can interfere with observation. Recording on the spot is not possible and it has to be postponed until the observer is alone. Such time lag results in some inaccuracy in recording.

Because of the above limitations, participant observation is generally restricted to those cases where non-participant observation is not practical, e.g., a study of the functioning of a mobile library or mobile bank or tribal community etc.

Non-participant observation: In this method, the observer stands apart and does not participate in the phenomenon observed. Naturally, there is no emotional involvement on the part of the observer. This method calls for skill in recording observations in an unnoticed manner.

Direct observation: This means observation of an event personally by the observer when it takes place. This method is flexible and allows the observer to see and record subtle aspects of events and behaviour as they occur. He is also free to shift places, change the focus of the observation. A limitation of this method is that the observer's perception circuit may not be able to cover all relevant events when the latter move quickly, resulting in the incompleteness of the observation.

Indirect observation: This does not involve the physical presence of the observer, and the recording is done by mechanical, photographic or electronic devices, e.g., recording customer and employee movements by a special motion picture camera mounted in a department of a large store. This method is less flexible than direct observation, but it is less biasing and less erratic in recording accuracy. It also provides a permanent record for an analysis of different aspects of the event.

Controlled observation: This involves standardization of observational techniques and exercise of maximum control over extrinsic and intrinsic variables by adopting experimental design (see section 3.8, above) and systematically recording observations (see 7.6 *Experimentation*, below).

Controlled observation is carried out either in the laboratory or in the field. It is typified by clear and explicit decisions on what, how and when to observe. It is primarily used for inferring causality, and testing causal hypothesis.

Uncontrolled observation: This does not involve control over extrinsic and intrinsic variables. It is primarily used for descriptive research. Participant observation is a typical uncontrolled one.

Planning Observation

The use of observation method requires proper planning.

First, the researcher should carefully examine the relevance of observation method to the data needs of the selected study.

Second, he must identify the specific investigative questions which call for use of observation method. These determine the data to be collected.

Third, he must decide the observation content, viz., specific conditions , events and activities that have to be observed for the required data. The observation content should include the relevant variables.

Fourth, for each variable chosen, the operational definition should be specified.

Fifth, the observation setting, the subjects to be observed, the timing and mode of observation, recording, procedure, recording instruments to be used, and other details of the task should be determined.

Last, observers should be selected and trained. The persons to be selected must have sufficient concentration powers, strong memory power and unobtrusive nature. Selected persons should be imparted both theoretical and practical training.

Conditions of Effective Observation

These conditions consist of:

1. Observations must be done under conditions which will permit accurate results. The observer must be in vantage point to see clearly the objects to be observed. The distance and the light must be satisfactory. The mechanical devices used must be in good working conditions and operated by skilled persons.
2. Observation must cover a sufficient number of representative samples of the cases.
3. Recording should be accurate and complete.
4. The accuracy and completeness of recorded results must be checked. A certain number of cases can be observed again by another observer/another set of mechanical devices, as the case may be. If it is feasible, two separate observers and sets of instruments may be used in all or some of the original observations. The results could then be compared to determine their accuracy and completeness.

Observation Tools and Recording Devices

Systematic observation requires the use of observation schedule (or Observationnaire), diary, and various mechanical recording devices.

Schedule: The data requirements are identified by analyzing the core of the problem, the objectives of the study, the investigative questions, hypothesis and the operational definition of concepts and out of the data requirements, items of data to be colleted through observation are identified. A schedule is then constructed, covering those items of data.

It should be constructed in such a manner as to make it possible to record the necessary information easily and correctly. Enough space should be provided for recording observations for each item. The item should appear in logical groupings and in the order in which the observer would observe them.

Field observation log: This may take the form of a diary or cards. Each item of observation is recorded under appropriate sub-heading. At the time of observation, rough notings may be made, and at the end of the day, full log may be made. The card system is flexible and facilitates arrangement and re-arrangement of items in any desired order.

Mechanical devices: These may include cameras, tape recorders, videotape and electronic devices. Still, motion, sound, colour and timelapse cameras give a permanent record of events, Microscopic and telescopic lens may be used in cameras. Eye cameras are common in advertising and package research. They record eye movements while a consumer is looking at advertisements or packages. Other recording instruments are: tape, disc, and wire recorders, barometer, hygrometers, speedometers, one-way screens and mirrors, closed-circuit television, light meters, pocket calculators.

Suitability and Application

Observation is suitable for a variety of research purposes. It may be used for studying (a) the behaviour of human beings and social groups: life styles customs and manner, interpersonal relations, group dynamics, crowd behaviour, leadership styles, managerial style, other behaviours and actions; (b) the behaviour of other living creatures like birds, animals etc., (c) physical characteristics of inanimate things like stores, factories residences, etc., (d) flow of traffic and parking problems; (e) movement of materials/products through a plant.

It may be used in exploratory research to gain insights that will be subsequently tested as hypotheses. It may be used to collect supplementary data that may interpret or qualify findings obtained by other methods. Observation may be used as the primary method, e.g., anthropological studies of communities, behavioural studies of small groups.

Observation may be used in studying behaviour in 'natural' setting or in the laboratory, e.g., group formation may be studied as it occurs in a real-life situation or in the laboratory room.

Advantages

Observation has certain advantages.

1. The main virtue of observation is its directness;[2] it makes it possible to study behaviour as it occurs. The researcher need not ask people about their behaviour and interactions; he can simply watch what they do and say.
2. Data collected by observation may describe the observed phenomena as they occur in their natural settings. Other methods introduce elements or artificiality into the researched situation for instance, in interview, the respondent may not behave in a natural way. There is no such artificiality in observational studies, especially when the observed persons are not aware of their being observed.
3. Observation is more suitable for studying subjects who are unable to articulate meaningfully, e.g., studies of children, tribal, animals, birds, etc.
4. Observation improves the opportunities for analyzing the contextual background of behaviour. Furthermore verbal resorts can be validated and compared with behaviour through observation. The validity of what men of position and authority say can be verified by observing what they actually do.
5. Observation makes it possible to capture the whole event as it occurs. For example, only observation can provide an insight into all the aspects of the process of negotiation between union and management representatives.
6. Observation is less demanding of the subjects and has less biasing effect on their conduct than does questioning.
7. It is easier to conduct disguised observation studies than disguised questioning.
8. Mechanical devices may be used for recording data in order to secure more accurate data and also of making continuous observations over longer periods.

---

2. Nachmias, David and Nachmias Chava, *Research Methods in the Social Sciences, op. cit.*, p. 74.

Limitations

Observation cannot be used indiscriminately for all purposes. It has its own limitations.

1. Observation is of *no use of studying past events or activities.* One has to depend upon documents or narrations by people for studying such things.
2. It is *not suitable for studying opinions and attitudes.* However, an observation of related behaviour affords a good clue to the attitudes, e.g., and observation of the seating patterns of high caste and class persons in a general meeting in a village may be useful for forming an index of attitude.
3. Observation poses difficulties in obtaining a *representative sample.* For interviewing and mailing methods, the selection of a random sampling can be readily ensured. But observing people of all types does not make the sample a random one.
4. Observation cannot be used as and when the researcher finds it *convenient to use it. He has to wait for the event to occur.* For example, an observation of folk dance of a tribal community is possible, only when it is performed.
5. A major limitation of this method is that the observer normally *must be at the scene of the event when it takes place.* Yet it may not be possible to predict where and when the event will occur, e.g., road accident, communal clash.
6. Observation is a *slow and expensive process*, requiring human observers and/or costly surveillance equipments.

7.6 EXPERIMENTATION

Meaning

Experimentation is a research process used to study the causal relationships between variables. It aims at studying the effect of an independent variable on a dependent variable, by keeping the other independent variable constant through some type of control. For example, a social scientist may use experimentation for studying the effect of a method of family planning publicity on people's awareness of family planning techniques.

Various kinds of designs such as "after-only design", "before-after-design", etc. are used for experimentation (see 3.8 *Experimental Research,* above).

Why Experiment?

Experimentation requires special efforts. It is often extremely difficult to design, and it is also a time consuming process. Why should then one take such trouble? Why not simply observe/survey the phenomenon? The fundamental weakness of any non-experimental study is its inability to specify causes and effect. It can show only correlations between variables, but correlations alone never prove causation. The experiment is the only method which can show the effect of an independent variable on dependent variable. In experimentation, the researcher can manipulate the independent variable and measure its effect on the dependent variable. For example, the effect of various types of promotional strategies on the sale of a given product can be studied by using different advertising media such as T.V., radio and Newspapers.

Moreover, experiment provides "the opportunity to vary the treatment (experimental variable) in a systematic manner, thus allowing for the isolation and precise specification of important differences."[3]

Planning and Conducting Experiments

It is easy to conceive ideas, but difficult to translate the ideas into a workable, credible, meaningful set of experimental operations. This to a great extent depends upon the researcher's knowledge, imagination and intelligence. Yet the general procedure in experimentation may be outlined.

First, determine the hypothesis to be tested and the independent and dependent variables involved in it.

Second, operationalize the variables by identifying their measurable dimensions (see section 5.5 *Concepts* in Chapter 5 above.)

Third, select the type of experimental plan. The types of experimental design based on types of control may be classified into: (1) *one group plan,* using the same group as experimental and control group and measuring it before and after experimental treatment; (2) *matched groups plan,* consisting of two identical groups, one to be used as control group and another as experimental group, with (a) Post-test only measurement or (b) pretest-post-test measurements.

Fourth, choose the *setting*. The setting may be field or laboratory (See subsequent paragraphs for detailed discussion on these two types of experiments).

Fifth, make the *experimental conditions* as nearly the same as the expected *real life conditions.* This is essential in order to make the findings reliable.

Sixth, make a record of pre-experimental conditions.

Seventh, introduce appropriate *methods for controlling extraneous variables* that are not manipulated in the experiment.

These methods are:

1. ***Removing the variable:*** An extraneous variable may be eliminated completely. For example, observer distraction may be removed by separating the observer by a one-way glass partition. Some variables may be eliminated by selecting cases with uniform characteristics, e.g., using only male subjects removing sex as a variable.
2. ***Matching cases:*** Selecting control and experimental groups with identical characteristics. By this all variables are kept constant.
3. ***Balancing cases:*** This means assigning subjects to experimental and control groups in such as way that the means and the variances of the groups are as nearly equal as possible.
4. ***Randomization:*** This involves pure chance selection and assignment of subjects to experimental and control groups. This method eliminates systematic bias and minimizes the effect of extraneous variables.
5. ***Analysis of covariance:*** This is a statistical method of eliminating initial differences on several variables between the experimental and control groups. Pretest mean scores are used as covariates.

3. Aronson, Elliot and Carlsmith, J. Merrill, "Experimentation in Social Psychology", in G. Lindzey and E. Aronson (eds.), *Handbook of Social Psychology,* Vol. II, Mass: Addison Wesley, 1968, p. 9.

Eighth, apply the *experimental treatment* and record observations and measurements using appropriate measurement devices. If feasible, repeat the tests several times in order to insure the accuracy of results.

Ninth, analyse the results, using appropriate statistical devices.

Last, interpret the results, giving consideration to all possible extraneous conditions. No possible cause should be overlooked, as unforeseen conditions might influence the results.

Applications

The applications of experimental method are discussed under *'Laboratory Experiment'*, and *'Field Experiment'*, below.

Evaluation of Experimental Method

Experimentation has some specific advantages and disadvantages.

The advantages are:

1. Its power to *determine causal relationships* between variables *surpasses* that of all other methods. The influence of extraneous variables can be more effectively controlled in this method.
2. The element of human errors is reduced to the minimum.
3. In this method better conditions for conducting experiments may be created, than is possible in other methods.
4. Experimentation yields generally *exact measurements* and can be *repeated* for verifying results.

The disadvantages: It is difficult to establish *comparable control* and *experimental groups.*

Secondly, the scope for *experimentation* with *human beings* is extremely *limited.*

Thirdly, experiment is often difficult to design, tends to be *expensive and time-consuming*.

Fourthly, it is *artificial* to some extent and may lack realism.

Fifthly, experimentation can be used only in studies of the *present but not in studies relating to past or future.*

Sixthly, it is of *no use in determining opinions, motives and intentions* of persons.

Finally, the results observed may not be the true effects of the experimental treatment, but may be artificial, i.e., effects of some extraneous variable. For instance, an experimenter may unwillingly influence his subjects to behave in ways that confirm the hypothesis, particularly if the subjects want to please the experimenter. Laboratory experiment is especially vulnerable to such artificialities when subjects know they are being studied and want to create a good impression.

Laboratory Experiment

An experiment can be conducted either in a laboratory or in a real-life setting.

A *laboratory experiment is an investigation conducted in a setting created specifically for the purpose.* The researcher manipulates an independent variable and studies its effect on a dependent variable, keeping other variables constant.

Purpose: The purpose of laboratory experiments are: (1) to discover causal relations under uncontaminated conditions, reduce the discovered relations to functional form y = f(x) and make predictions on the basis of the functions; (2) to test the predictions derived from theory and other researches; and (3) to refine theories.

Applications or uses: This method is useful not only in physical sciences research, but also in social sciences research. Eventhough experimentation on a social science problem has special difficulties, it can be used for a variety of studies such as voting behaviour, leadership style, learning process, effectiveness of advertising media, effect of package on sales, influence of incentive schemes on labour productivity and so on.

Evaluation of this method: It has several merits. They are:

1. The chief merit of experiment method is the possibility of securing relatively *complete control over extraneous factors.*
2. The experimenter can *manipulate one or more variables* and study its or their impact on a dependent variable.
3. The experimenter in most cases can achieve a high *degree of specificity on operationalising* the variables.
4. An experiment yields *precise results* and it is replicable.

Demerits: The experimental method is not free from drawbacks.

1. The greatest weakness of this method is probably the *lack of strength of independent variables*. As the laboratory situation is artificial, the effects of experimental manipulations are usually weak.
2. This method is highly structured, thus limiting flexibility.
3. The result cannot be simply generalized to real life situations, because in the latter, various extraneous forces operate. Thus, an experimental method *lacks external validity* (see para on *Validity* below).

Nevertheless, the contributions of experimental method to theory building are so great that this method is one of man's greatest achievements.

Field Experiment

This is an experiment conducted in a real life situation in which the experimenter manipulates an independent variable in order to test a hypothesis. Compared with laboratory experiment, a field experiment incorporates less control. As it is difficult to foresee and control extraneous factors in a field experiment, its result is subject to *large uncontrolled variation.*

Application or Uses: This method is well suited to both testing of theory and finding solutions to practical social problems. It has been used for studying a variety of social action programmes such as, improving the quality of work life in assembly-lines, post offices and insurance companies and banks; the learning process in educational institutions and training centres; changing group productivity; changing organisation culture; changing superior-subordinate relationship in organisation; overcoming resistance to change through participative approach; changing attitude through social contract; changing food habits; improving the effectiveness of mass education; testing new products in markets; determining best procedures or techniques for tasks; and so on.

"Anyone who wishes to take effective social action in any setting can improve upon the uncontrolled, try out of new methods by the application of more scientific experimental procedures. Through careful measurements, better theorizing, the use of control groups, and other aspects of improved experimental design, the practical problems of social action can be solved with greater certainty, with greater accuracy, and sometimes with greater efficiency than through common-sense trial-and-error methods."[4]

The field experiment will be more successful if preceded by a field study which gives a more thorough knowledge of the setting and thus enables the experimenter to manipulate and control his variables more effectively.

Illustration: In a field experiment in a factory, Coch and French[5] manipulated participation of workers in planning and studied its effect on various dependent variables – production, resignations and aggression. The broad hypothesis tested was that resistance to change can be overcome by increased participation in decisions or processes that lead to change. Factory workers were divided into three groups. The members of the control group did not participate in any of the discussions or decisions about changes in the factory. Two experimental groups did participate in discussions and decision in different degrees: total participation and participation by representation. The results supported the hypothesis.

Evaluation of the field experimental methods: This method has some unique virtues.

1. The variables in a field experiment usually have a *stronger effect* than those of a laboratory experiment, as the field situation is real. Realism increases with strength of the variables.
2. The field experiment permits a more unequivocal *determination* of causal relations, while a mere non-experimental field study reveals only a correlation.
3. This method is particularly *appropriate* for *studying methods* of *social influence, social processes* and social changes in real life settings.
4. As the field experiment deals with the total life situation, it is well suited for studying *complex syndromes and social processes* where the interrelationships among many analytical variables are involved.

Limitations: The experimental method is not free from limitations.

1. The major limitations of this method is the *practical difficulty* involved in the manipulation of independent variables and randomization in many field situations.
2. Another weakness inherent in this method is *lack of precision*. Precise measurement in realistic situation is not so possible as in a laboratory setting.
3. A field experiment is a very *difficult process,* as it calls for social skills and good contacts on the part of the experimenter and also it is a time-consuming process. Unless the organisation where it has to be conducted and the subjects cooperate, it is not possible to conduct it.

---

4. French, John, R.P., "Experiments in Field Settings", in Festinger, Leon and Katz, Daniel, (eds.), *Research Methods in the Behavioural Sciences, op. cit.,* pp. 131-132.
5. Coch, L., and French, J.R.P., "Overcoming Resistance to Change", *Human Relations,* I, 1948, pp. 512-532.

Validity

An experiment should achieve two types of validity: *internal and external validity*. When the effects of extraneous variables are eliminated and the observed effects on dependent variable can be ascribed solely to the effect to experimented dependent variables, then the experiment has internal validity. This is generally achieved in a laboratory experiment, because in it extraneous variables are controlled.

The extent to which the results of an experiment can be *generalized* to other settings is known as *external validity*. The contribution of an experiment to the body of knowledge depends upon its external validity.

It is very difficult to achieve cent percent validity in an experiment, because there are various threats to validity. Combell and Stanley[6] list twelve *threats* to validity.

1. Maturation: This means the effects of time. Between the pre-test and the post-test, the subjects undergo various changes such as fatigue, boredom, growth or intellectual maturation which may influence their performance and so the difference between the pre-test and post-test measurements of their performance cannot be ascribed to the effect of experimental variables only. This source of invalidity is eliminated/minimized by before-after design with control group, for the control group also experiences the effects of time.

2. History: Other extraneous events may occur during experimentation and thus influence the results. These may be events that occur in the political, economic or cultural life of the people under study or other minor events such as illness of a subject, disruption in the experiment of an interruption from any unwanted source. The influence of this source of invalidity is greater in a field experiment than in laboratory experiment.

3. Testing: It is impossible that the experience gained in the pre-test may result in an increase in the post-test performance.

This testing effect is confounded with the effect of experimental variable. The before-after design with-control group guards against this source of invalidity also.

4. Instrumentation: If the tests of instruments used for measurement are not accurate or consistent, or if observers become more experienced or careless, the results will be vitiated.

5. Statistical regression: Those who scored highest on a pre-test are likely to score relatively lower on a re-test, whereas subjects who score lowest in the pre-test are likely to score higher on a re-test. Thus, their average score in re-test may be closer to the overall population average. This is merely a statistical illusion. Failure to recognize this effect may lead the researcher to arrive at erroneous conclusion on the results.

6. Differential selection: Selection bias arises when the experimental and control groups are not as identical as possible. Techniques like random selection of subjects and matching may minimize the selection bias.

7. Experimental mortality: This refers to loss of subject due to dropout, migration etc. This is more likely in a long-term experiment, and affects the comparability of pre-test and post-test results. The remedy is to omit the pre-test scores of subjects who did not take the post-test.

6. Cambell, Donald T., and Stanley, Julian, C., *Experimental and Quasi-experimental Designs for Research*, Chicago: Rand McNally & Co., 1966.

8. Selection-maturation, selection-history or selection-testing interaction: These interactions between selection and other factors arise when the effect of the other factors differs between the groups selected.

9. Reactive effect of testing: The pre-test may affect the responsiveness of the experimental group of the treatment. For example, pre-test measuring of knowledge about Denmark may sensitize the subjects; as a result, they may be more receptive to the information given out in a film about Denmark, which is the treatment under study.

10. Reactive effect of experimental arrangements: The knowledge of participation in an experiment may introduce bias in favour of the experimental group. This reactive effect is popularly known as the "Hawthrone effect", since its importance was clearly demonstrated in the famous studies conducted by Prof. Elton Mayo and his associates at the Hawthrone plant of Western Electric Company in Chicago during early 1930s. In this enquiry into the relationship between physical work conditions and productivity, the output of a group of workers under various conditions was measured. They were treated differently and they knew they were the subjects of the experiments. When light intensity was increased, the workers output increased; but when the intensity of light was reduced, there was no reduction in their output, because of the reactive effect of experimental arrangements.

11. Multi-treatment interference: In some experiment like medical experiments several types of treatments are arrived at successively on the same subject. At each stage, the residual effect of the previous treatment would interact with the effect of the next one.

12. Contamination: This is a type of bias which arises when the researcher has some previous knowledge about the subjects involved in an experiment. This may affect the objectivity of his judgement.

The researcher should be aware of the above threats and take appropriate measures like matching, randomization, etc., to minimize their effect and arrive at conclusions, keeping in view the limitations.

7.7 SIMULATION

Meaning

Simulation is one of the forms of observational methods. It is a process of conducting experiments on a symbolic model representing a phenomenon. Abelson defines simulation as "the exercise of a flexible limitation of process and outcomes for the purpose of clarifying or explaining the underlying mechanisms involved."[7] It is a symbolic abstraction, simplification and substitution for some referent sytem.[8] In other words, simulation is a theoretical model of the elements, relations and processes which symbolize some referent system, e.g., the flow of money in the economic system may be simulated in an operating model consisting of a set of pipes through which liquid moves. Simulation is thus a technique of performing sampling experiments on the model of the systems. The experiments are done on the model instead of on the real system, because the latter would be too inconvenient and expensive.

---

7. Abelson, Robert P., "Simulation of Social Behaviour", in G. Lindzey and E. Aronson (eds.), *Handbook of Social Psychology,* Vol. II Mass: Addison-Wesley, 1968, p. 275.
8. Raser, John, *Simulation and Society: An Exploration of Scientific Gaming,* Boston: Allyn and Bacon, 1969.

The Process of Simulation

First, the *process or system* to be simulated is identified.

Second, the *purpose* of this simulation is decided. It may be to 'clarify' or 'explain' the process.

Third, on the basis of the available information on the process or system- *its components and the set of conditions assumed* to operate in and between the components- *a mathematical model is developed.*

Fourth, several sets of *input data* to be used are collected. Inputs may be samples of actual data or synthetic data based on the general characteristics of real input data.

Fifth, the *type of simulation*- computer simulation or man simulation or man-computer simulation – to be used is determined.

Lastly, the simulation is *operated* with the various sets of input data, and the results are analysed to determine the best solution.

Simulation Vs. Experimentation

A real-life experiment may be too costly or may not be possible because of practical difficulties or of the complexities of the phenomenon. For example, the search for an optimal approach to the problem of inventory issue and replenishment through experimentation would disrupt operations for a certain period of time and also would be very costly; phenomena, like macro-sociological situations or business systems are so complex, that it would not be possible to manipulate independent variables, and to control extraneous variable in real-life experiments on them. Such difficulties do not arise in simulation, because it experiments with models and can artificially manipulate variables.

Further, an experiment can extrapolate to, at best a few variables, whereas simulation, particularly computer simulation may often handle many variables including intrapersonal and interpersonal processes.

Simulation, unlike experiments, is best suited to the study of a system with a set of interrelated and interdependent sub-components.

Types of Simulation

There are three types of simulation, viz., (a) man simulations, (b) computer simulations and (c) man-computer simulations.

Man Simulation: This is a game played by people in a laboratory setting to simulate people in real world. For example, number of individuals are divided into groups that are placed in a laboratory room. Each group is instructed to imagine that it represents the government of a particular nation. Simulated international situations involving treaties, alliances, threats, wars and the like are then played out by the groups.

No gaming model can serve as a universal model for all games. Each model is unique. The size of the group is important factor. The size may be two persons, three persons or more than three persons. Other important dimensions are *information level* (whether individuals have perfect information or not), and perceived goal motivation – no common interest and purely competitive or partly competitive and partly cooperative.

Computer simulation: This is an operational model programmed to generate a sequence of interactions. This requires precise definitions, storing of large amounts of data on the system to be analysed and programming of the analysis. For example, two or more sets of ratios relating to liquidity, profitability and operational efficiency may be fed into a discriminant function analysis in order to find out which set of variables has a better power to predict the financial health of an enterprise.

Man-computer simulation: In this type of simulation, persons play the role of decision-makers, while the computer is responsive to the players' activities. In this game, the computer must be provided with a script. "The script lists the messages conveyed to the player. Two kinds of messages are involved. One is simple response to the players' actions. The other is instruction to the player as to the appropriate way he can respond to the computer."[9]

The successive runs of a simulation should give similar results. Then it is said to be reliable. This is rarely a problem in computer simulation, but it may be a problem in games. The reliability in games requires that the physical equipment should not be cumbersome, the rules should be clear, simple and complete and the game should not overtax the player's span of attention.[10]

Validity refers to the generalizability of the findings of the simulation. This depends on the degree of correspondence between the operating model and its reference system.

Applications

Simulation is applicable to various categories of problems;

Behavioural and social problems, e.g., population dynamics; group behaviour; social conflicts;

(1) Political problems, e.g., predication of voting in elections; cold war conflicts; international political situations; international counteractions to specific actions like diplomatic protest, sanctions etc., study of revolutions;

(2) Economic problems e.g., study of economics under conditions of recession and inflation; developmental planning strategies; balance of payment policies; economic forecasting; urban traffic system design; water resources development; flood control system; national manpower planning.

(3) Business problems, e.g., determination of proper order quantities; production scheduling, designing complex distribution system; waiting line problems in transport services; maintenance scheduling in factories, airlines, bus service; assembly line scheduling in consumer behaviour prediction; financial forecasting; introduction of a new product; control system;

(4) War strategies and tactics.

7.8 INTERVIEWING

Definition

Interviewing is one of the prominent methods of data collection. It may be defined as a two-way systematic conversation between an investigator and an informant, initiated for obtaining

9. Inbar, M., and Stoll, C.S. (Eds.)., *Simulation and Gaming in Social Science,* New York: Free Press, 1972. p. 24.
10. *Ibid.,* pp. 279-280.

information relevant to a specific study. It involves not only conversation, but also leaning from the respondent's gestures, facial expressions and pauses, and his environment.

Interviewing requires face-to-face contact or contact over telephone and calls for interviewing skills. It is done by using a structured schedule or an unstructured guide.[11]

Importance

Interviewing may be used either as a main method or as a supplementary one in studies of persons. Interviewing is the only suitable method for gathering information from illiterate or less educated respondents. It is useful for collecting a wide range of data from factual demographic data to highly personal and intimate information relating to a person's opinions, attitudes, values, beliefs, past experience and future intentions. When qualitative information is required or probing is necessary to draw out fully, then interviewing is required. Where the area covered for the survey is a compact, or when a sufficient number of qualified interviewers are available, personal interview is feasible.

Interview is often superior to other data-gathering methods. People are usually more willing to talk than to write. Once rapport is established, even confidential information may be obtained. It permits probing into the context and reasons for answers to questions.

Interview can add flesh to statistical information. It enables the investigator to grasp the behavioural context of the data furnished by the respondents. It permits the investigator to seek clarifications and brings to the forefront those question, that for one reason or another, respondents do not want to answer.

Evaluation of Interviewing

Advantages: There are several real advantages to personal interviewing. First, "the greatest value of this method is the depth and detail of information that can be secured.[12] When used with a well-conceived schedule, an interview can obtain a great deal of information. It far exceeds mail survey in amount and quality of data that can be secured.

Second, the interviewer can do more to improve the percentage of responses and the quality of information received than other method. He can note the conditions of the interview situation, and adopt appropriate approaches to overcome such problems as the respondent's unwillingness, incorrect understanding of question, suspicion, etc.

Third, the interviewer can gather other supplemental information like economic level, living conditions etc. Through observation of the respondent's environment.

Fourth, the interviewer can use special scoring devices, visual materials and like in order to improve the quality of interviewing.

Fifth, the accuracy and dependability of the answers given by the respondent can be checked by observation and probing.

Last, interview is flexible and adaptable to individual situations. Even more control can be exercised over the interview situation.

---

11. For a comprehensive treatment, see Hyman, Herbert, *Interviewing in Social Sciences,* Chicago: University of Chicago Press, 1954.
12. Emory, Willian C., *Busines Research Methods, op. cit.,* p. 268.

Limitations: Interviewing is not free from limitations. Its greatest drawback is that it is costly, both in money and time.

Second, the interview results are often adversely affected by interviewer's mode of asking questions and interactions, and incorrect recording and also be the respondent's faulty perception, faulty memory, inability to articulate etc.

Third, certain types of personal and financial information may be refused in face-to-face interviews. Such information might be supplied more willingly on mail questionnaires, especially if they are to be unsigned.

Fourth, interview poses the problem of recording information obtained from the respondents. No foolproof system is available. Note taking is invariably distracting to both the respondent and the interviewer and affects the thread of the conversation.

Last, interview calls for highly skilled interviewers. The availability of such persons is limited and the training of interviewers is often a long and costly process.

Characteristics

Interviewing as a method of data collection has certain characteristics. They are:

1. The participants – the interviewer and the respondent – are strangers. Hence, the investigator has to get himself introduced to the respondent in an appropriate manner.
2. The relationship between the participants is a transitory one. It has a fixed beginning and termination points. The interview proper is a fleeting, momentary experience for them.
3. Interview is not a mere casual conversational exchange, but a conversation with a specific purpose, viz., obtaining information relevant to a study.
4. Interview is a mode of obtaining verbal answers to questions put verbally.
5. The interaction between the interviewer and the respondent need not necessarily be on a face-to-face basis, because interview can be conducted over the telephone also.
6. Although interview is usually a conversation between two persons, it need not be limited to a single respondent. It can also be conducted with a group of persons, such as family members, or a group of children or a group of customers, depending on the requirements of the study.
7. Interview is an *interactional process*. The interaction between the interviewer and the respondent depends upon how they perceive each other. The respondent reacts to the interviewer's appearance, behaviour, gestures, facial expression and intonation, his perception of the thrust of the questions and his own personal needs. As far as possible, the interviewer should try to be closer to the socio-economic level of the respondents. Moreover, he should realize that his respondents are under no obligation to extend response. He should, therefore, be tactful and be alert to such reactions of the respondents as lame-excuse, suspicion, reluctance or indifference, and deal with them suitably. He should not also argue or dispute. He should rather maintain an impartial and objective attitude.
8. Information furnished by the respondent in the interview is recorded by the investigator. This poses a problem of seeing that recording does not interfere with the tempo of conversation.

9. Interviewing is not a standardized process like that of a chemical technician; it is rather a flexible psychological process.

The implication of this feature is that the interviewer cannot apply unvarying standardized technique, because he is dealing with respondents with varying motives and diverse perceptions. The extent of his success as an interviewer is very largely dependent upon his insight and skill in dealing with varying socio-psychological situations.

Requirements

The requirements or conditions necessary for a successful interview are:

1. **Data availability:** The needed information should be available with the respondent. He should be able to conceptualize it in terms useful to the study, and be capable of communicating it.
2. **Role perception:** The respondent should understand his role and know what is required of him. He should know what is a relevant answer and how complete it should be. He can learn much of this from the interviewer's introduction, explanations and questioning procedure.
3. The interviewer should also know his role. He should establish a permissive atmosphere and encourage frank and free conversation. He should not affect the interview situation through subjective attitude, argumentation, etc.
4. **Respondent's motivation:** The respondent should be willing to respond and give accurate answer. This depends partly on the interviewer's approach and skill. The interview has interest in it for the purpose of his research, but the respondent has no personal interest in it. Therefore, the interviewer should establish a friendly relationship with the respondent, and create in him an interest in the subject-matter of the study.

   The interviewer should try to reduce the effect of demotivating factors like desire to get on with other activities, embarrassment at ignorance, dislike of the interview content, suspicious about the interviewer, and fear of consequences. He should also try to build up the effect of motivating factors like curiosity, loneliness, politeness, sense of duty, respect of the research agency and liking for the interviewer.

The above requirement reminds that the interview is an interactional process. The investigator should keep this in mind and take care to see that his appearance and behaviour do not distort the interview situation.

Types of Interviews

The interviews may be classified into: (a) structured or directive interview, (b) unstructured or non-directive interview, (c) focused interview, and (d) clinical interview and (d) depth interview.

Structured, Directive Interview

This is an interview made with a detailed standardized schedule. The same questions are put to all the respondents and in the same order. Each question is asked in the same way in each interview, promoting measurement reliability. This type of interview is used for large-scale formalized surveys.

Advantages: This interview has certain advantages. First, data from one interview to the next one are easily comparable. Second, recording and coding data do not pose any problem, and greater precision is achieved. Lastly, attention is not diverted to extraneous, irrelevant and time-consuming conversation.

Limitation: However, this type of interview suffers from some limitations. First, it tends to lose the spontaneity of natural conversation. Second, the way in which the interview is structured may be such that the respondent's views are minimized and the investigator's own biases regarding the problem under study are inadvertently introduced. Lastly, the scope for exploration is limited.

Unstructured or Non-directive Interview

This is the least structured one. The interviewer encourages the respondent to talk freely about a given topic with a minimum of prompting or guidance.

In this type of interview, a detailed pre-planned schedule is not used. Only a broad interview guide is used. The interviewer avoids channeling the interview directions. Instead, he develops a very permissive atmosphere. Questions are not standardized and not ordered in a particular way.

This interviewing is more useful in case studies rather than in surveys. It is particularly useful in exploratory research where the lines of investigation are not clearly defined. It is also useful for gathering information on sensitive topics such as divorce, social discrimination, class conflict, generation gap, drug-addition etc. It provides opportunity to explore the various aspects of the problem in an unrestricted manner.

Advantages: This type of interview has certain special advantages. It can closely approximate the spontaneity of a natural conversation. It is less prone to interviewer's bias. It provides greater opportunity to explore the problem in an unrestricted manner.

Limitations: Though the unstructured interview is a potent research instrument, it is not free from limitations.

One of its major limitations is that the data obtained from one interview is not comparable to the data from the next. Hence, it is not suitable for surveys.

Time may be wasted in unproductive conversations. By not focusing on one or another facet of a problem, the investigator may run the risk of being led up blind ally.

As there is no particular order or sequence in this interview, the classification of responses and coding may require more time.

This type of informal interviewing calls for greater skill than the formal survey interview.

Focused Interview

This is a semi-structured interview where the investigator attempts to focus the discussion on the actual effects of a given experience to which the respondents have been exposed. It takes place with the respondents known to have involved in a particular experience, e.g., seeing a particular film, viewing a particular programme on T.V., involved in a train/bus accident, etc. The situation is analysed prior to the interview. An interview guide specifying topics relating to the research hypothesis is used. The interview is focused on the subjective experiences of the respondent, i.e., his attitudes, and emotional responses regarding the situation under study.[13]

---

13. Merton, R.K., *et. al., The Focused Interview,* Glencoe: The Free Press, 1956.

The focused interview permits the interviewer to obtain details of personal reactions, specific emotions and the like.

Merits: This type of interview is free from the inflexibility of formal methods, yet gives the interview a set form and insures adequate coverage of all the relevant topics.

The respondent is asked for certain information, yet he has plenty of opportunity to present his views.

The interviewer is also free to choose the sequence of questions and determine the extent of probing.

Clinical Interview

This is similar to the focused interview but with a subtle difference. While the focused interview is concerned with the effects of a specific experience, clinical interview is concerned with broad underlying feelings or motivations or with the course of the individual's life experiences.

The 'Personal history' interview used in social case work, prison administration, psychiatric clinics and in individual life history research is the most common type of clinical interview. The specific aspects of the individual's life history to be covered by the interview are determined with reference to the purpose of the study and the respondent is encouraged to talk freely about them.

Depth Interview

This is an intensive and searching interview aiming at studying the respondent's opinion, emotions or convictions on the basis of an interview guide. This requires much more training inter-personal skills than structured interviewing. This deliberately aims to elicit unconscious as well as extremely personal feelings and emotions.

This is generally a lengthy procedure designed to encourage free expression of affectively charged information. It requires probing.

The interviewer should totally avoid advising or showing disagreement. Of course, he should use encouraging expressions like "uh-huh" or "I see" to motivate the respondent to continue narration. Sometimes the depth interviewer has to face the problem of affection, i.e., the respondent may hide expressing affective feelings. The interviewer should handle such situation with great care.

Interviewing Process

The interviews process consists of the following stages:

- Preparation
- Introduction
- Developing rapport
- Carrying the interview forward
- Recording the interview, and
- Closing the interview.

Preparation: The interviewing requires some preplanning and preparation. The interviewer should keep the copies of interview schedule/guide (as the case may be) ready for use. He should also have the list of names and addresses of respondents, he should regroup them into contiguous groups in terms of location in order to save time and cost in travelling.

The interviewer should find out the general daily routine of the respondents in order to determine the suitable timings for interview.

Above all, he should mentally prepare himself for the interview. He should think about how he should approach a respondent, what mode of introduction he could adopt, what situations he may have to face and how he could deal with them.

The interviewer may come across such situations as respondents' avoidance, reluctance, suspicion, diffidence, inadequate responses, distortion, etc. The investigator should plan the strategies for dealing with them. If such preplanning is not done, he will be caught unaware and fail to deal appropriately when he actually faces any such situation. It is possible to plan in advance and keep the plan and mind flexible and expectant of new development.

Introduction: The investigator is a stranger to the respondents. Therefore he should be properly introduced to each of the respondents. What is the proper mode of introduction? There is no one appropriate universal mode of introduction. Mode varies according to the type of respondents.

When making a study of an organization or institution, the head of the organization should be approached first and his cooperation secured before contacting the sample inmates/employees.

When studying a community or a cultural group, it is essential to approach the leader first and to enlist his cooperation.

For a survey or urban households, the research organization's letter of introduction and the interviewer's identify card can be shown. In these days of fear of opening the door for a stranger, residents' cooperation can be easily secured, if the interviewer attempts to get him introduced through a person known to them, say a popular person in the area e.g., a social worker.

For interviewing rural respondents, the interviewer should never attempt to approach them along with someone from the revenue department, for they would immediately hide themselves, presuming that they are being contacted for collection of land revenue or subscription to some government bond. He should not also approach them through a local political leader, because persons who do not belong to his party will not cooperate with the interviewer. It is rather desirable to approach the rural respondents through the local teacher or social worker.

After getting himself introduced to the respondent in the most appropriate manner, the interviewer can follow a sequence of procedures as under, in order to motivate the respondent to permit the interview:

- With a smile greet the respondent in accordance with his cultural pattern
- Identify the respondent by name
- Describe the method by which the respondent was selected
- Mention the name of the organization conducting the research
- Assure the anonymity or confidential nature of the interview
- Explain their usefulness of the study
- Emphasize, the value of respondent's cooperation, making such statements as. "You are among the few in a position to supply the information." "your response is invaluable." I have come to learn from your experience and knowledge."

The following short introduction will serve as an illustration:

Interviewer: "I'm from the department of Management Studies of Bangalore University. People talk of Japanese Style of management, American style of management and so on. What is the style of management in Indian enterprises? Is it just an imitation of Western style or is it based on our culture and value system? We should know the nature of our style of management. Is it not? This study is done throughout the country and the results will contribute to management thought and profession."

"The respondents for interview chosen may entirely change. The interview will just take about half-an-hour. All information is entirely confidential, of course."

A respondent often has reservations about being interviewed. He may suspect that the interviewer is a disguised salesman, bill collector, tax official or the like. The interviewer should skillfully clear such suspicion by establishing his identity.

The respondent may also feel incompetent or fear that he may not be able to answer questions relating to the study. Allay such kind of anxiety by reassuring him: "There are no right or wrong answers. This is not a quiz. We are trying to find how persons like you feel."

Developing rapport: Before starting the research interview, the interviewer should establish a friendly relationship with the respondent. This is described as "rapport." It means establishing a relationship of confidence and understanding between the interviewer and the respondent. It is a skill which depends primarily on the interviewer's commonsense, experience, sensitivity, and keen observation.

Start the conversation with a general topic of interest such as weather, current news, sports event, or the like perceiving the probable interest of the respondent from his context.

Such initial conversation may create a friendly atmosphere and a warm interpersonal relationship and mutual understanding of the other. However the interviewer should "guard against the over-rapport" as cautioned by Herbert Hyman.[14] Too much identification and too much courtesy result in tailoring replies to the image of a "nice interviewer." The interviewer should use his discretion in striking a happy medium.

Carrying the interview forward: After establishing rapport, the technical task of asking questions from the interview schedule starts. This task requires care, self-restraint, alertness and ability to listen with understanding, respect and curiosity.

In carrying on this task of gathering information from the respondent by putting questions to him, the following guidelines may be followed:

1. Start the interview. Carry it on in an informal, natural conversational style.
2. Ask all the applicable questions in the same order as they appear on the schedule without any elucidation and change in the wording. Ask all the applicable questions listed in the schedule. Do not take answers for granted.
3. If interview guide is used, the interviewer may tailor his questions to each respondent, covering, of course, the areas to be investigated.

---

14. Hyman, Herbert. "Interviewing as a Social Process," in Daniel Lerner and Harold Lasswell, *The Policy Sciences,* Standard University Press, 1951, p. 214.

4. Know the objectives of each questions so as to make sure that the answers adequately satisfy the question objectives.
5. If a question is not understood, repeat it slowly with proper emphasis and appropriate explanation, when necessary.
6. Take all answers naturally, never showing disapproval or surprise. When the respondent does not meet with interruptions, denial, contradiction and other harassment, he may feel free and may not try to withhold information. He will be motivated to communicate when the atmosphere is permissive and the listener's attitude is non-judgement and is genuinely absorbed in the revelations.
7. Listen quietly with patience and humility. Give not only undivided attention, but also personal warmth. At the same time, be alert and analytic to incomplete, nonspecific and inconsistent answers, but avoid interrupting the flow of information. If necessary, jot down unobtrusively the points which need elaboration or verification for later and more timely probing.

   The appropriate technique for this probing is to ask for further clarification in such a polite manner as: "I am not sure I understood fully. Is this....what you meant?"
8. Neither argue nor dispute.
9. Show genuine concern and interest in the ideas expressed by the respondent, at the same time, maintain an impartial and objective attitude.
10. Should not reveal your own opinion or reaction. Even when you are asked for your views, laugh off the request, saying "Well, your opinions are more important than mine."
11. At times the interview "runs dry" and needs restimulation. Then use such expressions as "Uh-huh" or "That's interesting" or "I see," "can you tell me more about that?" and the like.
12. When the interviewee fails to supply his reactions to related past experiences, represent the stimulus situation, introducing appropriate questions which will aid in revealing the past. "Under what circumstances did such and such a phenomenon occur?" or "How did you feel about it and the like.
13. At times, the conversation may go off the track. Be alert to discover drifting, steer the conversation back to the track by some such remark as, "You know, I was very much interested in what you said a moment ago. Could you tell me more about it?"
14. When the conversation turns to some intimate subjects, and particularly when it deals with crises in the life of the individual, emotional blockage may occur. Then drop the subject for the time being and pursue another line of conversation for a while so that a less direct approach to the subject can be made later.
15. When there is a pause in the flow of information, do not hurry the interview. Take is as a matter of course with an interested look or a sympathetic half-smile. If the silence is too prolonged, introduce a stimulus saying "You mentioned that....What happened then?"

Additional sittings: In the case of qualitative interviews involving longer duration, one single sitting will not do, as it would cause interview weariness. Hence, it is desirable to have two or more sittings with the consent of the respondent.

Recording the interview: It is essential to record responses as they take place. If the note-taking is done after the interview, a good deal of relevant information may be lost. Nothing should be made in the schedule under respective question. It should be complete and verbatim. The responses should not be summarized or paraphrased. How can complete recording be made without interrupting the free flow of conversation? Electronic transcription through devices like tape recorder can achieve this. It has obvious advantages over note-taking during the interview. But it also has certain disadvantages. Some respondents may object to or fear "going on record." Consequently the risk of lower response rate will arise especially for sensitive topics.

> If the interviewer knows short-hand, he can use it with advantage. Otherwise, he can write rapidly by abbreviating word and using only key words and the like. However, even the fast writer may fail to record all that is said at conversational speed. At such times, it is useful to interrupt by some such comment as "that seems to be a very important point, would you mind repeating it, so that I can get your words exactly." The respondent is usually flattered by this attention and the rapport is not disturbed.

The interviewer should also record all his probes and other comments on the schedule in brackets to set them off from responses.

With the pre-coded structured questions, the interviewers task is easy. He has to simply ring the appropriate code or tick the appropriate box, as the case may be. He should not make mistakes by carelessly ringing or ticking a wrong item.

Closing the interview: After the interview is over, take leave off the respondent, thanking him with a friendly smile.

In the case of a qualitative interview of longer duration, select the occasion for departure more carefully. Assembling the papers for putting them in the folder at the time of asking the final question sets the stage for a final handshake, a thank-you and a good-bye. If the respondent desires to know the result of the survey, note down his name and address so that a summary of the result could be posted to him when ready.

Editing: At the close of the interview, the interviewer must edit the schedule to check that he has asked all the questions and recorded all the answers and that there is no inconsistency between answers. Abbreviations in recording must be replaced by full words. He must ensure that everything is legible.

It is desirable to record a brief sketch of his impressions of the interview and observational notes on the respondent's living environment, his attitude to the survey, difficulties, if any, faced in securing his cooperation and the interviewer's assessment of the validity of the respondent's answers.

Interview Problems

In personal interviewing, the researcher must deal with two major problem, inadequate response, non-response and interviewer's bias.

Inadequate response: Kahn and Cannel[15] distinguish five principal symptoms of inadequate response. They are: partial response, in which the respondent gives a relevant but incomplete answer; non-response, when the respondent remains silent or refuses to answer the question; irrelevant response, in which the respondent's answer is not relevant to the question asked; inaccurate response, when the reply is biased or distorted; and the verbalized response problem, which arises on account of respondent's failure to understand a question or lack of information necessary for answering it.

One possible approach to deal with an inadequate response is to allow a brief expectant pause with an expectant glance. Another way to encourage the respondent is to use such expressions as, "I see?" "Is it?" or to put a supplementary neutral question as "What do you mean?", "Can you tell me more about that?" or "Can you explain little more fully?"

If the respondent's answer is ambiguous or inexplicit, probes like "How do you mean?" or "In what way?" can be used to clarify his answer. For exploring other aspects of the respondent's opinion, if any, probes like "Is there anything else?" or "Are there any other reasons?" can be used.

For a 'don't know' answer, over-probing is counter-productive. If motivational probing fails, no further probing should be attempted.

The problem of inaccurate response is common in economic surveys. The respondents have difficulty in furnishing accurate information on 'sensitive' matters like asset holdings, income, expenditure, saving and investments. It is difficult to deal with this problem. Perhaps one possible approach is to use indirect questions instead of direct questions for securing information on above matters, and to cross-check with information furnished on other related questions. For example, data on income can be verified with the details on occupation.

Interviewer's bias: The interviewer is an important cause of response bias. He may resort to cheating by 'cooking up' data without actually interviewing.

The interviewers can influence the responses by inappropriate suggestions, word emphasis, tone of voice and question rephrasing. His own attitudes and expectations about what a particular category of respondents may say or think may bias the data.

The respondent's perception of the interviewer's characteristics (education, apparent social status, etc) may also bias his answers.

Another source of response bias arises from interviewer's perception of the situation. If he regards the assignment as impossible or sees the results of the survey as a possible threat to personal interests or beliefs he is likely to introduce bias.

As interviewers are human beings, such biasing factors can never be overcome completely, but their effects can be reduced by careful selection and training of interviewers, proper motivation and supervision, standardization of interview procedures (use of standard wording in survey questions, standard instructions on probing procedure an so on) and standardization of interviewer behaviour. There is need for more research on ways to minimize bias in the interview.

Non-response

Non-response refers to failure to obtain responses from some sample respondents. There are many sources of non-response; non-availability, refusal, incapacity, inaccessibility.

15. Kahn, R.L., and Cannel, E.F., *The Dynamics of Interviewing: Theory, Technique and Cases,* New York: John Wiley & Sons, 1957, pp. 217-18.

Non-availability: Some respondents may not be available at home at the time of call. This depends upon the nature of the respondent and the time of calls. For example employed persons may not be available during working hours. Farmers may not be available at home during cultivation season. Selection of appropriate timing for calls could solve this problem. Evenings and weekends may be favourable interviewing hours for such respondents. If someone is available, then the respondent's hours of availability can be ascertained and the next visit can be planned accordingly.

A respondent may be too busy, tired or out of station.

Call-backs to find the not-at-homes increase the overall response rate.

Refusal: Some persons may refuse to furnish information because they are ill-disposed, or approached at the wrong hour and so on. Although a hardcore of refusals remain, another try or perhaps another approach may find some of them cooperative.

Incapacity or inability may refer to illness which prevents a response during the entire survey period. This may also arise on account of language barrier.

Inaccessibility: Some respondents may be inaccessible. Some may not be found due to migration and other reasons.

Non-responses reduce the effective sample size and its representativeness.

Methods and aims of control of non-response: Kish[16] suggests the following methods to reduce either the percentage of non-response or its effects:

(1) Improved procedures for collecting data are the most obvious remedy for non-response. Improvements advocated are (a) guarantees of anonymity, (b) motivation of the respondent to cooperate, (c) arousing the respondents' interest with clever opening remarks and questions, (d) advance notice to the respondents.

(2) Call-backs are most effective way of reducing not-at-homes in personal interviews, as are repeated mailings to no-returns in mail surveys.

(3) Substitution for the non-response is often suggested as a remedy. Usually this is a mistake, because the substitutes resemble the responses rather than the non-responses. Nevertheless beneficial substitution methods can sometimes be designed with reference to important characteristic of the population. For example, in a farm management study, the farm size is an important variable and if the sampling is based on farm size, substitution for a respondent with a particular size holding by another with the holding of the same size is possible.

Attempts to reduce the percentage or effects on non-responses aim at reducing the bias caused by differences on non-respondents from respondents. The non-response bias should not be confused with the reduction of sample size due to non-response. The latter effect can be easily overcome, either by anticipating the size of non-response in designing the sample size or by compensating for it with a supplement. These adjustments increase the size of the response and the sampling precision, but they do not reduce the non-response percentage or bias.

Telephone Interviewing

Telephone interviewing is a non-personal method of data collection. It may be used as a major method or supplementary method.

16. Kish, Leslie, *Survey Sampling op.cit.,* pp. 548-54

Uses: It will be useful in the following situations:

1. When the universe is composed of those persons whose names are listed in telephone directories, e.g., business houses, business executives, doctors, other professionals.
2. When the study requires responses to five or six simple questions, e.g., Radio or Television programme survey.
3. When the survey must be conducted in a very short period of time, provided the units of study are listed in telephone directory.
4. When the subject is interesting or important to respondents, e.g., A survey relating to trade conducted by a trade association or a chamber of commerce, a survey relating to a profession conducted by the concerned professional association.
5. When the respondents are widely scattered and when there are many call backs to make.

Evaluation Advantages: The advantages of telephone interview are:

1. The survey can be completed at very low cost, because telephone survey does not involve travel time and cost and all calls can be made from a single location.
2. Information can be collected in a short period of time. 5 to 10 interviews can be conducted per hour.
3. Quality of response is good, because interviewer bias is reduced as there is no face-to –face contact between the interviewer and the respondent.
4. This method of interviewing is less demanding upon the interviewer.
5. It does not involve field work.
6. Individuals who could not be reached or who might not care to be interviewed personally can be contacted easily.

Disadvantages: Telephone interview has several limitations.

1. It is limited to persons with listed telephones. The sample will be distorted, if the universe includes persons not on phone. In several countries like India only a few persons have phone facility and that too in urban areas only. Telephone facility is very rare in rural areas. Hence, the method is not useful for studying the general population.
2. There is a limit to the length of interview. Usually, a call cannot last over five minutes. Only five or six simple questions can be asked. Hence, telephone cannot be used for a longer questionnaire.
3. The type of information to be collected is limited to what can be given in simple, short answers of a few words. Hence telephone is not suitable for complex surveys, and there is no possibility of obtaining detailed information.
4. If the questions cover personal matters, most respondents will not cooperate with the interviewer.
5. The respondent's characteristics and environment cannot be observed.
6. It is not possible to use visual aids like charts, maps, illustrations or complex scales.
7. It is rather difficult to establish rapport between the respondent and the interviewer.
8. There is no possibility to ensure the identity of the interviewer and to overcome suspicions.

Group Interviews

Meaning and nature: A group interview may be defined as a method of collecting primary data in which a number of individuals with a common interest interact with each other. In a personal interview, the flow of information is multi-dimensional.

The group may consist of about six to eight individuals with a common interest. The interviewer acts as the discussion leader. Free discussion is encouraged on some aspect of the subject under study. The discussion leader stimulates the group members to interact with each other.

The desired information may be obtained through self-administered questionnaires or interview, with the discussion serving as a guide to ensure consideration of the areas of concern. In particular, the interviewers look for evidence of common elements of attitudes, beliefs, intentions and opinions among individuals in the group. At the same time, he must be aware that a single comment by a member can provide important insight.

Samples for group interview can be obtained through schools, clubs and other organized groups.

Uses: The group interview technique can be employed by researchers in studying people's reactions on public amenities, public health projects, welfare schemes, etc. It is a popular method in marketing research to evaluate new product or service concepts, brand names, packages, promotional strategies and attitudes. When an organization needs a great variety of information inasmuch detail as possible at a relatively low cost and in a short period of time, the group interview technique is more useful. It can be used to generate primary data in the exploratory phase of a project.

Evaluation: Advantages: The advantages of this technique are:

1. The respondents comment freely and in detail.
2. The method is highly flexible. The flexibility helps the research work with new concepts or topics which have not been previously investigated.
3. Visual aids can be used.
4. A group can be interviewed in the time required for one personal interview.
5. The client can watch the interview unobserved.
6. Respondents are more articulate in a group than in the individual interview.
7. The technique eliminates the physical limitations inherent in individual interviews.

Disadvantages: This method is not free from draw backs.

1. It is difficult to get a representative sample.
2. There is the possibility of the group being dominated by one individual.
3. The respondents may answer to please the interviewer or the other members in the group.

Nevertheless, the advantages of this technique outweigh the disadvantages and the technique is found to be useful for surveys on topics of common interest.

Selection and Training of Interviewers

The quality of data collected depends ultimately upon the capabilities of interviewers. Hence, careful selection and proper training of interviewers is essential. (See for detailed discussion, 9.2 *"Selection of Training of Investigators"* in chapter 9, below).

7.9 PANEL METHOD

Meaning

The panel method is a method of data collection, by which data is collected from the same sample respondents at intervals either by mail of by personal interview. This is used for longitudinal studies on economic conditions, expenditure pattern, consumer behaviour, recreational pattern, effectiveness of advertising, voting behaviour, and so on. The period over which the panel members are contacted for information may spread over several months or years. The time interval at which they are contacted repeatedly may be 10 or 15 days, or one or two months depending on the nature of the study and the memory span of the respondents.

Characteristics

The basic characteristic of the panel method is successive collection of data on the same items from the same persons over a period of time.

The type of information to be collected should be such facts that can be accurately and completely furnished by the respondent without any reservation.

The number of item should be as few as possible so that they could be furnished within a few minutes, especially when mail survey is adopted. The average amount of time that a panel member has to spend each time for reporting can be determined in a pilot study.

The panel method requires carefully selected and well-trained field workers and effective supervision over their work.

Need for Panel Study

When sample respondents — particularly households or individuals-are contacted once only, they may not be able to recall exactly what have occurred during a longer time period, say a year because their memory span is short. Therefore they will not be able to give correct information on such facts as cash inflow, source-wise income, expenditure pattern, purchases, savings, recreation pattern and so on. But when they are contacted successively at short intervals of 10 or 15 days, they would to able to give accurate information on happenings between two successive contacts, as the time span is short and well within the memory span. In this way, data are collected repeatedly at intervals, and computations for the required period like a year can be easily made and the data so collected will be more reliable.

Illustration

The author of this book adopted the panel method for collection of data for a major research project (funded by ICSSR) entitled "The Factors affecting the Economic Conditions of Agricultural Labourers in Coimbatore District" (1971-72).[17] This study involved collection of primary data from a sample farmers and sample labourers. The sample farmers were contacted 36 times in the year 1971-1972 once every ten days and data on their farm operations, number of labourers employed, wages paid etc. were collected. Similarlythe sample labourers were contacted repeatedly once every ten days and data on the number of days employed, type of work, wage earned and item-wise expenditure, etc.

17. Krishnaswami, O.R., "Economic Conditions of Agricultural Labourers in Coimbatore," *ICSSR Research Abstracts Quarterly,* Vol. IV, No. 142, pp. 111-125.

were collected. On the completion of the entire field work, annual data were compiled from the ten-day long data.

Types of Panels

The panel may be static or dynamic. A static or continuous panel is one in which the membership remains the same throughout the life of the panel, except for the members who drop out. The dropouts are not replaced.

The static panel is appropriate when the purpose is to study changes in a given group of persons over a period of time. The main drawbacks of the static panel are:

1. Due to dropouts, it ceases to be representative of the original universe after a time.
2. The size of the reporting panel may become too small for satisfactory results.

In a dynamic panel, to keep the panel representative of the current population in the area covered by the universe, replacement are found for the members who drop out. A dynamic panel may also be a rotating one, in which members are systematically replaced at specified time intervals.

The dynamic panel is most useful when it is important to keep the panel representative of the population at all times. The main problem connected with its use is the cost and difficulty of recruiting new members to replace the dropouts.

Evaluation

Advantages: The advantages of panel method are:

1. This method facilitates collection of more accurate data for longitudinal studies than any other method, because under this method event or action is reported soon after its occurrence.
2. This method makes it possible to have before-after designs for field-based studies. For example, the effect of public relations or advertising campaigns or welfare measures can be measured by collecting data before, during and after the campaign.
3. The panel method offers a good way of studying trends in events, behaviour or attitudes. For example, a panel enables a market researcher to study how brand preferences change from month to month; it enables an economics researcher to study how employment, income and expenditure of agricultural labourers change from month to month; a political scientist can study the shifts in inclinations of voters and the causative influential factors during an election; it is possible to find out how the constituency of the various economy and social strata of society changes through time; and so on.
4. A panel study also provides evidence on the casual relationship between variables. For example, a cross-sectional study of employees may show an association between their attitude to their jobs and their positions in the organization, but it does not indicate which came first — favourable attitude or promotion. A panel study can provide data for finding an answer to this question.
5. If facilitates depth interviewing, because panel members become well acquainted with the field workers and will be willing to allow probing interviews.

Limitations: The major limitations or problems of the panel method are:

1. This method is very expensive. The selection of panel members, the payment of premiums, periodic visits of investigators and supervisors, and the costs involved in replacing dropouts, all add to the expenditures.
2. It is often difficult to set up a representative panel and to keep it representative. Many persons may be unwilling to participate in a panel study. In the course of the study, there may be frequent dropouts. The dropouts may be replaced by persons with similar characteristics. But there is no guarantee that the emerging panel would be a representative one.
3. A real danger with the panel method is "panel conditioning", i.e., the risk that repeated interviews may sensitize the panel members and they become untypical as a result of being on the panel. For example, the members of a panel study of political opinions may try to appear consistent in the views they express on consecutive occasions. In such cases, the panel becomes untypical of the population it was selected to represent. One possible safeguard to panel conditioning is to give members of a panel only a limited panel life and then to replace them with persons taken randomly from a reserve list.
4. The quality of reporting may tend to decline due to decreasing interest after a panel has been in operation for some time. Cheating by panel members or investigators may be a problem in some cases.

7.10 MAIL SURVEY

Definition

The mail survey is another method of collecting primary data. This method involves sending questionnaires to the respondents with a request to complete them and return them by post. This can be used in the case of educated respondents only. The mail questionnaires should be simple so that the respondents can easily understand the questions and answer them. It should preferably contain mostly closed-end and multiple-choice questions so that it could be completed within a few minutes.

The distinctive feature of the mail survey is that the questionnaire is self-administered by the respondents themselves and the responses are recorded by them, and not by the investigator as in the case of personal interview method. It does not involve face-to-face conversation between the investigator and the respondent. Communication is carried out only in writing and this requires more cooperation from the respondents than does verbal communication.

Procedure

The researcher should prepare a mailing list of the selected respondents by collecting the addresses from the telephone directory of the association or organization to which they belong.

A covering letter should accompany a copy of the questionnaire. Exhibit 7.1 is a copy of a covering letter used by the author in a research study on 'Corporate Planning.' It must explain to the respondent the purpose of the study and the importance of his cooperation to the success of the project. Anonymity may be assured.

BANGALORE UNIVERSITY DEPARTMENT OF COMMERCE AND MANAGEMENT STUDIES

Dr. O.R. Krishnaswami
Professor and Chairman

City Campus,
Bangalore-560 001

19...

Dear respondent,

My we ask you a favour that takes only a few minutes of your time?

We are conducting a study of Corporate Planning in Public and Private sector enterprises in India with a view to knowing the status of this managerial function in India.

We solicit your cooperation in completing the enclosed questionnaire. Your reply will be kept strictly confidential, of course, and the result of the study will be shown in statistical form only.

At your earliest convenience, please return the completed questionnaire in the enclosed self-addressed stamped envelope.

We thank you for your cooperation.

Sincerely yours,

O.R. KRISHNASWAMI

Encl: 2

Exhibit 7.1

A Covering Letter used for a Study on 'Corporate Planning'

The sponsor's identity may be revealed. However when such information may bias the results, it is not desirable to reveal it. In the later case, a disguised organization name may be used.

A self-addressed stamped envelope should be enclosed in the covering letter.

After a few days from the date of mailing the questionnaires to the respondents, the researcher can expect the return of completed ones from them. The progress in return may be watched and at the appropriate stage follow-up efforts can be made.

Alternative Modes of Sending Questionnaires

There are some alternative methods of distributing questionnaires to the respondents. They are: (1) personal delivery, (2) attaching questionnaire to a product. (3) advertising questionnaire in a newspaper of magazine, and (4) news stand inserts.

Personal delivery: The researcher or his assistant may deliver the questionnaires to the potential respondents with a request to complete them at their convenience. After a day or two he can collect the completed questionnaires from them. Often referred to as the self-administered questionnaire method, it combines the advantages of the personal interview and the mail survey.

Alternatively, the questionnaires may be delivered in person and the completed questionnaires may be returned by mail by the respondents.

Attaching questionnaire to a product: A firm test-marketing a product may attach a questionnaire to a product and request the buyer to complete it and mail it back to the firm. The respondent is usually rewarded by a gift or a discount coupon.

Advertising the questionnaire: The questionnaire with the instructions for completion may be advertised on a page of a magazine or in a section of newspapers. The potential respondent completes it tears it out and mails it to the advertiser. For example, the committee on Banks Customer Service used this method for collecting information from the customers of commercial banks in India. This method may be useful for large-scale on topics of common interest.

News-stand inserts: This method involves inserting the covering letter, questionnaire and self-addressed reply-paid envelope into a random sample of newsstand copies of a newspaper or magazine.

Improving the Response Rate in a Mail Survey

The response rate in mail surveys is generally very low,. More so in developing countries like India. Certain techniques have to be adopted to increase the response rate. They are:

1. ***Quality printing:*** The questionnaire may be neatly printed in quality light coloured paper so as to attract the attention of the respondent.
2. ***Covering letter:*** The covering letter should be couched in a pleasant style so as to attract and hold the interest of the respondent. It must anticipate objections and answer them briefly. It is desirable to address the respondent by name.
3. ***Advance information:*** Advance information can be provided to potential respondents by a telephone call or advance notice in the newsletter of the concerned organization or by a letter. Such preliminary contact with potential respondents is more successful than follow-up efforts.
4. ***Incentives:*** Money, stamps for collection and other incentives are also used to induce respondents to complete and return mail questionnaires.
5. ***Follow-up-contacts:*** In the case of respondents belonging to an organization, they may be approached through some one in that organization known to the researcher.
6. ***Larger sample size:*** A larger sample may be drawn than the estimated sample size. For example, if the required sample size is 1000, a sample of 1500 may be drawn. This may help the researcher to secure in effective sample size closer to the required size.

Evaluation of Mail Surveys

Advantages: The advantages of mail surveys are:

1. They are less costly than personal interviews, as cost of mailing is the same throughout the country, irrespective of distances.
2. They can cover extensive geographical areas.
3. Mailing is useful in contacting persons such as senior business executives who are difficult to reach in any other way.
4. The respondents can complete the questionnaires at their conveniences.
5. Mail surveys, being more impersonal, provide more anonymity than personal interviews.

6. Mail surveys are totally free from the interviewers bias, as there is no personal contact between the respondents and the investigator.
7. Certain personal and economic data may be given more accurately in an unsigned mail questionnaire.

Disadvantages: The disadvantages of mail surveys are:

1. The scope for mail surveys is very limited in a country like India where the percentage of literacy is very low.
2. The response rate of mail surveys is low. Hence, the resulting sample will not be a representative one.
3. It is also difficult to determine the degree of representativeness of a sample obtained by mail.
4. The causes for inadequate and non-responses cannot be known, and no probing is possible.
5. Information on the personal characteristics of the respondent and his environment cannot be secured.
6. Respondents may not cooperative if the mail questionnaire is long or complex.
7. Several returned questionnaires may contain unanswered questions and incomplete responses.

7.11 PROJECTIVE TECHNIQUES

The direct methods of data collection, viz., personal interview, telephone interview and mail survey rely on respondents' own report of their behaviour, beliefs, attitudes, etc. But respondents may be unwilling to discuss controversial issues or to reveal intimate information about themselves or may be reluctant to express their true views fearing that they are generally disapproved. In order to overcome these limitations, indirect methods have been developed. Projective techniques are such indirect methods. They became popular during 1950s as a part of motivation research.

Meaning

Projective techniques involve presentation of ambiguous stimuli to the respondents for interpretation. In doing so, the respondents reveal their inner characteristics. The stimuli may be a picture, a photograph, an ink blot or an incomplete sentence.

The basic assumption of projective techniques is that a person projects his own thoughts, ideas and attributes when he perceives and responds to ambiguous or unstructured stimulus materials. Thus, a person's unconscious operations of the mind are brought to a conscious level in a disguised and projected form, and the person projects his inner characteristics.

Functions

Projective techniques can help to overcome some of the following psychological barriers:

1. ***The barrier of unawareness:*** People are often unaware of their motives and attitudes. For example, a lonely woman may keep cats as some kind of substitute for children, but also might be unaware of such need.
2. ***The barrier irrationality:*** Our society places a high premium on sensible, rational and logical behaviour. Most of us tend to rationalize. We invent logical reasons for actions whose origins are far from rational.

3. ***The barrier of inadmissibility:*** We find it difficult to admit our failure to meet social norms or expectations.
4. ***The barrier of self-incrimination:*** It concerns those aspects of behaviour and feelings that might lower the respondent's self-esteem such as communal prejudice, superstition, etc.
5. ***The barrier of politeness:*** People often prefer not to say negative or critical views. They tend to say 'all right' for everything.

Whenever the pilot study shows the existence of the above barriers with respect to the problem under study, then the use of projective technique should be considered.

Approaches

The commonly used approaches are:

1. ***Association:*** "Say-the-first-thing comes into your mind" approach is based on the assumption that a fast response to a stimulus word, picture or question will be less 'guarded' and therefore more 'revealing of underlying attitudes and motives.
2. ***Fantasy:*** The respondent is asked to guess or tell a story or discuss a picture in imaginary terms. In doing this he is likely to reveal his own attitudes and experiences.
3. ***Ambiguous stimuli:*** Whenever a subject is asked to respond to a relatively ambiguous stimulus, he will reveal something about himself when making his response.
4. ***Conceptualizing:*** The way a respondent names, orders or groups things may reflect his attitudes.

All these approaches rely on spontaneity or interpretation, and on ambiguity in the stimulus. They should be as non-directive as possible so as not to bias the responses. They also require a certain amount of interpretation on the part of the researcher. The influence may vary from observer to observer. Thus, projective methods lack objectivity and the reliability and validity are rather shaky. Yet they yield best results when interpreted by tainted psychologists, in terms of some pre-established psychological conceptualization. In fact, projective tests serve as a major tool for understanding human personality, and for measuring achievement motivation as well. "If we have to penetrate deeper, below the level of conscious awareness or being the individual's social façade, then indirect projective techniques have to be used."[18]

Types of Projective Techniques

Projective Techniques may be divided into three broad categories: (a) visual projective techniques, (b) verbal projective techniques, and (c) Expressive techniques.

(a) Visual Projective techniques involve use of visual (pictorial) stimuli. They include (1) Rorschach Tests, (2) Thematic Apperception Test (TAT), (3) Rosenzweigh Test, (4) Picture Frustration Test, and (5) Holtzman Inkblot Test (HIT).

(b) Verbal Techniques involve use of words both for stimulus and for response. They consist of (1) Word Association Test, (2) Sentence Completion Test and (3) Story Completion Test.

---

18. Oppenheim, A.N., *Questionnaire Design and Attitude Measurement,* London: Heinemann Educational Books, p. 161.

(c) Expressive Techniques: The subject is required to form some sort of product out of the given material. But the emphasis is on the manner in which he does the work and not on the end product. "The subject expresses his needs, desires, emotions and motives through working with, manipulating and interacting with materials, including other persons, in a manner or style that uniquely expresses his personality."[19]

The principal expressive methods are (1) play, (2) drawing, (3) finger painting, and (4) role playing.

Rorschach test: This was first developed by a Swiss scientist Herman Rorschach and was used for diagnostic investigation of the personality as a whole. This test uses association approach. It consists of ten cards. On each card is printed an ink blot the subject is asked to tell what he sees-what the blot represents.

This test studies the imagination of an individual. It is also used as a supplementary test to study mental qualities of an individual. This test requires very high skill on the part of its administrator.

Thematic Apperception Test (TAT): This test was first developed by Murray and his associates at the Howard Psychological Clinic. In contrast to ink-blot techniques, the TAT presents highly structured stimuli and requires more complex and meaningfully organized verbal responses.

The TAT material consists of 19 cards containing vague pictures in black and white and one black card. The subject is shown each card and is asked to make up a story to fit each picture, telling what led up the event shown in the picture, what is happening at the moment and what the outcome would be. In the case of the black card, the subject is asked to imagine some picture on the card, describe it and then tell a story about it.

The content of the story is analyzed, the themes developed by the subject, the way in which each card is perceived, the roles ascribed to the characters, emotional tones expressed, speed of responses, length of stories, etc., are considered. On the basis of qualitative scoring schemes and rating scales relating to them, the interpretation is made.

The TAT is used extensively in personality research, attitude surveys, executive appraisal, etc.

Rosenzweigh test of Cartoon test: This was first developed by Rosenzweig. The test consists of a series of cartons. In each cartoon are portrayed two characters; one is represented as saying something which is stated in a speech balloon over the character; the other character is provided with an empty speech balloon. The respondent is asked to write in the empty balloon what the second character would probably say. The answer of respondents can be classified according to the attitudes, frame of reference and role perceptions that they reflect.

The cartoon characters should be so developed as to represent the situation pertinent to the subject matter under investigation. It is important to maintain the neutrality of cartoon characters, because it helps the respondent to identify with a character.

The administration of cartoon test requires trained investigator and the interpretation must be done with the assistance of trained psychologists.

Picture frustration test: This is an adaptation of Rozenzweig test. It consists of 24 sets of cartoon pictures in pair. In each pair there is a picture depicting a frustrating situation accompanied

19. Kerlinger, Fred N., *Foundations of Behavioural Research,* Delhi: Surjeet Publications, 1983. p. 518.

by verbal remarks. A blank space is provided for the respondent to write what the frustrated person would reply.

The responses are classified with reference to the direction of aggression and type of aggression. The direction of aggression is scored as extra punitive (aggression turned outward), intra punitive (turned inwards), and impunitive (turned off to evade situation or gloss over it). The type of aggression includes obstacle dominance, emphasizing frustrating object, ego defence, focusing attention on the constructive solution of the frustrating problem. In scoring this test, the percentage of responses falling into each of these categories is compared with the corresponding normative percentage.

The P.F., being highly structured and relatively objective in its scoring procedure, lends itself better to statistical analysis than many other projective techniques. It is used for research on a variety of problems such as attitude towards minority group, consumer response to products, reactions of disabled towards their disability etc.

This test calls for a thorough knowledge of psychology and skill in interviewing.

Holtzman Inkblot Test (HIT): This test, developed by W.H.Holtzman, is a modification of the Rorschach Test. This test consists of 45 inkblot cards based on colour, movement, shading and other factors. Only one response per card is obtained from the respondent and his responses are interpreted at three levels of form appropriateness. Form responses are interpreted for knowing the accuracy or inaccuracy of respondent's percepts: shading and colour for ascertaining his affectional and emotional needs; and movement responses for assessing the dynamic aspects of his life.

Word association test: This is the oldest and simplest test. The interviewer administering the test reads a list of 25 to 100 words, one at a time. Emotionally-tinged words are mixed up with neutral words. The respondent is asked to respond with the first matching word that comes to his mind, in two or three seconds. As he reads the words, the interviewer records the response and the time taken by the respondent to react to each word.

A word which provokes and immediate response is more likely to be noticed and remembered than that which provokes a slow response. Speediness of response also indicates attitude strength or intensity.

If the respondent takes more than three seconds to respond with a matching word then it is called 'hesitation.' Hesitation indicates his emotional involvement in finding a suitable word. In some cases, the respondent may "block' or give no answer, because the test word or what it symbolizes to him is highly charged with emotion. A high hesitation rate and low response rate to a word indicate that the respondent is concerned about what the word means to him.

The list of words should be selected carefully so that the researcher can uncover the patterns of responses, motives and attitudes of individuals.

The 'word association' test is easy to administer and does not need highly trained interviewers. However the interpretation requires someone trained in psychology.

This technique is frequently used in marketing research to find out the appropriate words to be used for advertising.

Sentence completion test: This is an extension of word association test. It is administered and interpreted in the same manner. The respondent is exposed to the first parts of incomplete sentences and asked to complete them. The completion of sentences requires the respondent to take a position or express his attitudes.

The objective of the test is to provoke spontaneous response from the respondent and the first answer reveals his attitudes or motives.

Story completion test: This test is an extended version of the sentence completion test. The interviewers provides the respondent with the beginning of a story and asks him to complete. It is assumed that in completing the story, the respondent will reveal his own attitudes and other characteristics.

This test is of great help in identifying and devaluating specific psychogenic needs that cannot be uncovered by simple projective techniques.

Highly trained interviewers are required to administer this test and the assistance of psychoanalyst is needed for interpretation of data. The data obtained are qualitative and cannot be analysed by quantitative methods.

Play technique: This is used often in studying children's attitudes through manipulation of dolls. A set of dolls representing a miniature life situation is given to children who are allowed to play with them freely. The manner in which the children organize dolls would indicate their attitude towards the subject under study.

Finger painting: This is a rich expressive method. A set of pots of a special type of paint is given to the respondent who is told to draw what he likes with the paints, using his fingers and hands. Variables can be measured by counting numbers of certain kinds of manipulative and approach behaviour. Alper, Blans and Adams' study[20] is an excellent example. Sixteen aspects of finger painting were measured: time to begin painting, use of whole hand, finger tip approach, washing-up behaviour, and so on. Significant differences were found between middle-class and working-class children in most of the tasks.

Role playing: is the acting-out of assigned specific roles for a brief period by two or more individuals. This is used in behavioural research. An observation system may be used to measure the variables under study. Group processes, interpersonal interaction, authoritarianism, prejudice and other variables can be studied.

Evaluation

"The attractiveness of projective devices lies in the fact that they seem to go below the surface, that they can give us 'insights' and provide us with 'revealing information."[21] When used with great care, they can be useful tools of psychological and educational research. However they do not adequately satisfy the scientific canons of reliability, validity and objectivity, because they are inadequately standardized with respect to administration and scoring and standard norms are not available. Hence, the projective instruments need not be used, if we have a more objective instrument to measure the variables under study.

---

20. Alper T., Blans H., and Adams B., "Reactions of Middle and Lower Class Children to Finger Paints as a Function of Class Differences in Child-Training Practices," *Journal of Abnormal and Social Psychology,* LI, 1955, pp. 439-448.
21. Oppenheim A.N., *op. cit.,* p. 166.

7.12 SOCIOMETRY

Definition

Sociometry is "a method for discovering, describing and evaluating social status, structure, and development through measuring the extent of acceptance or rejection between individuals in groups."[22] Franz defines sociometry as "a method used for the discovery and manipulation of social configurations by measuring the attractions and repulsions between individuals in a group."[23] It is a means for studying the choice, communication and interaction patterns of individuals in a group. It is concerned with attractions and repulsions between individuals in a group. In this method, a person is asked to choose one or more persons according to specified criteria, in order to find out the person or persons with whom he will like to associate.

Helen Jennings describes sociometry "as a means of presenting simply and graphically the entire structure of relations existing at a given time among members of a given group. The major lines of communication, or the pattern of attraction and rejection in its full scope, are made readily comprehensive at a glance."[24]

Origin

The basic principles and techniques of sociometry were first embodied in a volume entitled who shall survive? By J.L.Moreno, first published in 1934.[25] An enlarged revised edition of this book published in 1953 covers the history, theory, terminology, techniques, bibliography and applications of sociometry.[26]

Sociometry Test

The basic technique in sociometry is the "sociomteric test." This is a test under which each member of a group is asked to choose from all other members those with whom he prefers to associate in a specific situation. The situation must be a real one to the group under study, e.g., 'group study.' 'play,' 'class room seating' for students of a public school.

A specific number of choices, say two or three to be allowed is determined with reference to the size of the group, and different levels of preferences are designated fo reach choice.

Suppose we desire to find out the likings and disliking of persons in a work group consisting of 8 persons. Each person is asked to select 3 persons in order or preference with whom he will like to work on a group assignment. The levels of choices are designated as: the first choice by the number 1, the second by 2, and the third by 3. The result may be tabulated as under:

---

22. Urie Bronfenbrenner, "A Constant Frame of Reference for Sociometric Research," *Sociometry,* VI, pp. 363-372.
23. Franz, J.G., "Survey of Sociometric Techniques with an Annotated Bibliography," *Sociometry*, II. pp. 76-90.
24. Jennnigs, Helen Hall, *Sociometry in Group Relations,* Washington, DC., American Council on Education, 1948, p. 11.
25. Cf. J.L. Moreno, "Contributions of Sociometry to Research Methodology in Sociology," *American Sociological Review,* XII, pp. 287-292.
26. J.L. Moreno, *Who Shall Survive?* New York: Beacon Press, 1953.

TABLE 7.1

Sociometric Choices in a Group of 8 Persons

		Chosen							
		A	*B*	*C*	*D*	*E*	*F*	*G*	*H*
	A				3	1	2		
	B	2		1		3			
	C								
Chooser	D		3	1			2		
	E			3	2			1	
	F		2		1	3			
	G	3		1		2			
	H								
1st choice		—		3	2				1
2nd choice		1	1	—	1	2	1		
3rd choice		1	1	2		1	1		
Total		2	2	5	3	3	2		1

The requirements of the Sociometric Test are:

1. The limits of the group should be indicated to the subjects.
2. The number of choices allowed should be specific and it depends on the size of the group tested.
3. Each subject should be permitted to make his choices and rejections privately without the presence of the other members of the group.
4. A specific criterion for choice should be used, with reference to the functional activity of the group.
5. Different levels of preference should be designated for each choice.

Types of choice: Sociometric choice may mean 'choice of persons.' 'choice of lines of communication,' or 'choice of lines of influence.'

Scoring sociometric choices: One method is to count the number of times an individual is chosen, disregarding the order of choice. This is the most simple method and is widely used. The main draw back of this method is that it is insensitive, for it does not distinguish between first and third choice.

Another method is to score the order of choices: say, 3 points to first choice, two to second choice, and one point to third choice. The weakness of this scoring plan is that it treats the difference between a third choice and no choice as identical to the difference between first and second choices, and that between second and third choices.

A third plan is to use a rating scale. Each subject may be asked to rate each one of the other members in a five point scale: 4, 3, 2, 1, 0. In this scale 4 means "would like to work with him very much," and O means "would not want to work with him at all," and other numbers representing intermediate degrees of linking to work with him.

The results of a sociometric test may be augmented by personal interviews in order to discover motivation for attraction and rejection — sympathy, fear, anger, jealousy etc.

Methods of Analysis of Sociometric Data

There are three important methods of sociometric analysis: sociometric matrix, sociogram and sociometric index.

Sociometric matrix: A matrix is a rectangular array of numbers of other symbols. Sociometric matrix is a square or n x n matrix, 'n' being the number of persons in a group.

Suppose a group of six members responds to a sociometric questions: "With whom would you like to work on such and such a project during the next three months? Choose any three individuals." The responses are choices. If a member chooses another member, the choice is denoted by 1. If a member does not choose another, the non-choice is denoted by O. (If rejection has been called for, -1 would be used). The sociometric matrix of choices of the above group is given in table 7.2.

TABLE 7.2

Sociometric choice matrix: Six members Group and three-choice question

	A	*B*	*C*	*D*	*E*	*F*
A	0	1	0	1	0	1
B	1	0	0	0	1	1
C	0	0	0	1	1	1
D	0	1	0	0	1	1
E	1	0	0	1	0	1
F	0	1	0	1	1	0
Total	2	3	0	4	4	5

The table can be read by rows (left to right): A chooses B, D and F; D chooses B, E and F and so on. It can also be read by columns (vertical). A is chosen by B and E; C is not chosen by any one. The sum at the bottom indicate the number of choices each member receives.

The matrix is analyzed by studying the pattern of choices. There are three kinds of choice. A simple one-way choice is where one member chooses another member, but the latter does not choose the former, e.g., in Table 7.2 A chose D, but D did not choose A. A mutual choice is where one chooses another and the latter also chooses the former. In Table 7.2 A chose B and B chose A; D chose E and E chose D. F is 'popular,' as he was chosen by all the other members; C is not popular; no one chose him.

The advantages of the matrix are:

1. It is inclusive, i.e., the relationship between every single pair is specifically recorded.
2. Joint relationships among pairs are recorded.
3. Only one interrelation (criterion) is recorded on each matrix and is thus isolate for scientific study.
4. Matrices may be combined and compared. Hence, they are valuable in mathematical analysis and synthesis.

The shortcomings of the matrix are:

1. It is not suitable for a large group, as it is difficult to comprehend the complexities of the choice relations in it.
2. It is a poor graphic device.
3. It is a poor tool for detecting cliques, mutual choices and other aspects of group structure.

Sociogram is a graphic representation of the sociometric choice relations of a group. A graph of the data shown in 7.2 is given in Exhibit 7.2.

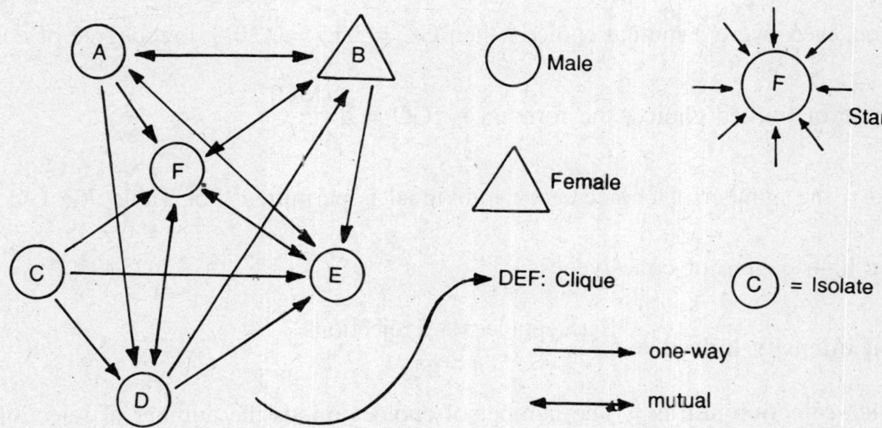

Exhibit 7.2: Sociogram of choices

The symbols of those chosen most often are placed nearest to the centre of the diagram and those chosen less often are placed progressively outward. Those not chosen are on the outside.

One-way choice is represented by a single-pointed arrow, a mutual choice by a double-edged arrow. A member chosen by most others is a leader and referred to as star. A member not chosen by another is an isolate. A small group consisting of members who mutually choose each other is a clique.

Advantages

1. The sociogram is a superior to the matrix as a graphic device.
2. It gives a birds eye view of all aspects of group structure.

Sociometric indices: Sociometric choices or other relations are also measured by indices. A large number of indices are possible.

1. Choice status index: $CS_A = \frac{\Sigma CA}{n-1}$

Where CS_A = the choice status of person A: ΣCA = the sum of choices in column A and n = the number of individuals in the group. (n – 1) is used, because one cannot choose oneself. In Table 7.2 $CS_A = \frac{2}{5} = 0.4$; $CS_F = \frac{5}{5} = 1.0$. How well or how poorly chosen an individual is revealed by his choice status index.

2. Group cohesiveness index: $GC = \dfrac{\Sigma(MC)}{\dfrac{n(n-1)}{2}}$

Where GC = Group cohesiveness; ΣMC = sum of mutual choices or pairs; n = the number of individuals in the group. GC index is the proportion of mutual choices to the total number of possible pairs. In six member group the total number of possible pairs is $\dfrac{6(6-1)}{2} = 15$. If in an unlimited choice situation, there were 3 mutual choices, then GC = 3/15 = 0.20, a low degree of cohesiveness.

In the case of limited choice, the formula is: $GC = \Sigma \dfrac{(MC)}{dn/2}$

Where d = the number of choices each individual is permitted. For Table 7.2, $GC = \dfrac{5}{3 \times \dfrac{5}{2}} = \dfrac{5}{7.5} = 0.67$, a high degree of cohesiveness.

3. Social intensity indeed $= \dfrac{\Sigma \text{ acceptances} + \Sigma \text{ rejections}}{n-1}$

4. Choice-rejection status = The number of choices minus the number of rejections received or ΣC – ΣR.

5. Criswell in her study of race cleavages suggests the index of self preference, based on the actual ratio between in-group and out-group choices and the expected ratio based on the total number in each group.[27]

Zeleny[28] has developed indices of sociation, social status and morale. Lundbeng and Steele have developed indices of interaction and cohesion.[29]

Applications

Sociometric techniques are widely used by sociologists, psychologists and psychiatrists in the study of group structure, status, personality traits, leadership, morale and social adjustment. They make more explicit and precise the configuration of group relationships, the characteristics and composition of cliques and other elements in a larger group, the social position of individual members in a group and the streams and points of influence within and among groups.

Sociometric studies of communities, fraternities, schools, college student bodies, camps, armed forces, and factories have been made.

With matrix methods, one can discover cliques in groups, communication and influence channels, patterns of cohesiveness, connectedness, hierarchization and so on.

---

27. Criswell, J.H., "Sociometric Methods of Measuring Group Preferences," *Sociometry,* VI, pp. 398-408.
28. Zeleny, L.D, "Measurement of Sociation," *American Sociological Review,* VI, pp. 173-188.
29. Lundberg and Steele, "Social Attraction Patterns in a Village," *Sociometry,* I, pp. 375-419.

Sociometric techniques are highly useful in identifying leadership, small group behaviour, prejudice, attitudes and values. They are also useful in classifying individuals and groups.

A number of sociogram over a period of time may be constructed to measure changes resulting from efforts to bring isolates into closer group relationships or to transform cliques into more general group membership. Thus, the effectiveness socializing can be measured by the changes revealed in the sociogram.

Evaluation

Sociometry is a simple, economical and naturalistic method of observation and data collection. It can usually be used for studying human actions in group situations. It has considerable flexibility. It can be adapted to a wide variety of research in the laboratory and in the field. Its qualification and analysis possibilities are rewarding. Indexes and scoring devices are extensively used in sociometric studies.

Since sociometry is a peer rating, rather than a rating by superiors, it adds another dimension to the understanding of members of a group.

However, the difficulty of securing reliable information from sociometric tests and their statistical limitations have to be recognized. They have to be used with discrimination and carefully adapted to each situation.

The sociometric measures are one of the multiple means of studying inter-personal relations. Hence, they should be supplemented by other means of gathering information on such relations. For example, the use of spontaneity tests and interviews and the study of the pattern of acquaintance pattern yield clues to the determinants of sociometric responses. The importance of selecting an appropriate criterion for sociometric questions should be recognized.

7.13 CONTENT ANALYSIS

Meaning

Content analysis is a research technique for making inferences by objectively and systematically identifying specified characteristics of contents of documents. This is a method of data collection and analysis. This is used for gathering data from archival records, documents, newspapers, diaries, letters, minutes of meetings and the like. The content of the written materials serves as a basis of inference. The analysis is made objectively and systematically. Objectivity refers to making analysis on the basis of explicit rules which enable different researchers to obtain the same results from the same documents. Systematic analysis refers to making inclusion or exclusion of content according to consistently applied criteria of selection; only materials relevant to research's hypothesis are examined.[30]

Content analysis, as a method of studying communications was developed in the United States as a branch of social psychology known as 'Communications research.'[31]

Content analysis can be applied to available materials such as letters, diaries, newspaper articles and editorials, etc. and to materials like stories or essays especially produced for a particular research problem.

30. Holsti, Ole R., "Content Analysis," in Gardner Lindzcy and Elliot Aronson, eds., *The Handbook of Social Psychology, Reading,* Mass: Addison-Wesley, 1968, p.598.

31. See Brelson, Bernard, *Content Analysis in Communication Research,* Glencoe, III: Free Press, 1942.

Procedure

Significant content analysis begins with some systematic problem which requires specific data from content analysis. The researcher must conceptualize the variables that are relevant to his problem.

The procedure of content analysis involves certain steps.

The first step is to define the universe of content that is to be analysed, e.g., the editorials of newspapers on the subject-matter of the problem (say 'sati') under study; the publications of an author; the issues of a newspaper for a given period. If the volume of materials to be examined is too large, a representative sample of documents may be selected for analysis.

The second step is to specify the content characteristics to be measured. On the basis of these characteristics, the universe is divided into categories.

Before discussing the general procedures for categorization, it is necessary to specify the major units of analysis or recording units and to differentiate recording units from context units. The recording unit is the smallest element of content in which the appearance of a reference is counted. The context unit is a larger body of the content that may be examined in characterising a recording unit. For example, the recording unit may be a single term; but in order to note whether the term is treated favourably or unfavourably, one has to consider the entire sentence in which the term appears. The sentence is the context unit.

Recording units: Five major recording units are frequently used in content analysis. They are: words (terms), themes, characters, paragraphs and items. The word is the smallest unit. The words are counted and a list of frequencies of selected words is prepared. For example, Lasswell[32] in a study on propaganda detection, reports that the Moscow News frequently used twenty-seven key political terms (bourgeois, class struggle, red army, the people, revolution etc.)during 1938-39.

The theme is a proposition about something. It is usually in the form of a sentence, clause or passage. Themes are most frequently employed in the study of propaganda, attitudes, images and values.

The character is an individual in a literary production. This is used as a unit in analyzing stories for studying the traits of characters appearing in them.

The paragraph as a unit of analysis is rarely used because of difficulties in classifying various things discussed in it.

The item is the whole document. It may be an entire article, a book or a speech.

The third step in content analysis is categorization. Categorization is an important part of content analysis, because it reflects the purpose of the study and spells out the variables of the hypothesis to be tested. Eventually recording units are classified and coded into categories. For example projective stories written by children in response to a picture may be categorized into 'creative' or 'non-creative.' Categories must relate to the research objectives and be exhaustive and mutually exclusive. Exhaustiveness ensures that every recording unit relevant to the study can be classified. Mutual exclusivity means that no recording unit can be included in more than one category. The indicators or criteria for classifying recording units into respective categories should be explicitly specified. This enables replication, which is an essential requirement of objectivity.

32. Lasswell, Harold, D., "Detection: Propaganda Detection and the Counts," in Harold D. Lasswell, *et al., The Language of Politics: Studies in Quantitative Semantics,* Cambridge, Mass.: MIT Press, 1965.

The last step in content analysis is to quantify the materials in any appropriate form. One form of quantification is counting the number of objects in each category. A second form of quantification is ranking. Judges can be asked to rank the objects according to a specified criterion. The next form of quantification is rating scale. This is generally employed in quantifying attitudes, and values. For example, the degree of creativity may be rated as 'very high, high, average, low, very low.'

Applications

Content analysis is used for various purposes such as (a) to analyze their attributes, antecedents or effects; (b) to infer personality traits of speakers from logical and cognitive characteristics of their verbal communications; (c) to infer aspects of culture and cultural change from contents of literatures; (d) to understand the role of the mass media in molding public opinion on occasions like general election; (e) to study newspapers stand towards current issues like Sati, terrorism in Punjab, India's peace-keeping force's role in Sri Lanka etc; (f) to determine the philosophy of saints like Sri Ramakrishna, Swami Vivekananda of Sri Aurobindo and of great national leaders like Mahatma Gandhi, Gopal Krishna Gokhale or Jawaharlal Nehru; (g) to determine themes and values of novels and short stories; (h) to determine socio-cultural life in ancient times from classical literatures; (i) to measure behaviour variables like need, values, attitudes, authoritarianism, creativity and so on through an analysis of both available materials and deliberately created materials of projective kind; (j) to study the propaganda techniques adopted by propagandists to influence the public; (k) to identify the literary style, concepts or beliefs of a writer, e.g., Mahatma Gandhiji's concept of trusteeship; (l) to explain the possible causal factors related to some outcome or action or event, e.g., the influence of editorials upon the action of the parliament on an economic legislation; and so on.

Content analysis of available materials should not be used indiscriminately. If a researcher can gather data directly through interviewing, mailing or projective techniques, so much the better. If there is no such possibility, then available materials can be used.

SUGGESTED READINGS

1. Atkinson, J., *A Handbook for Interviewers,* (Govt. Social Survey No.M 136), London: H.M.S.O., 1967.
2. Berelson, Bernard, *Content Analysis in Communication Research,* Glencoe, III.: Free Press, 1942.
3. Campbell, Donald T., and Stanley, Julian C., *Experimental and Quasi-Experimental Design for Research,* Chicago: Rand McNally & Co., 1963.
4. Edwards, Allen L., *Experimental Design in Psychological Research,* New York: Holt Rinehart and Winston, 1972.
5. Erdos, Paul L., *Professional Mail Surveys,* New York: McGraw-Hill Book Co., 1970.
6. Glazer, Myron, *The Research Adventure: Promise and Problems of Field Work,* New York: Random House, 1972.
7. Hyman, Herbert H., *et al., Interviewing in Social Research,* Chicago: University of Chicago Press, 1954.
8. Kahn, Robert I., and Cannell Charles F., *The Dynamics of Interviewing,* New York: John Wiley and Sons, 1957.
9. McCall, George J., and J.L. Simmons, *Issues in Participant Observation, Reading,* M.A.: Addison-Wesley, 1969.
10. Merton, R.K., Fiske, M., and Kendall, P.L., *The Focused Interview: A Manual of Problems and Procedures,* Glencoe, III.: Free Press, 1956.

11. Mize, Joe H., and Cos, J.Grady, *Essentials of Simulation,* Englewood, Cliffs, N.J.: Prentice-Hall, 1968.
12. Moreno, Jacob L., *The Sociometry Reader,* New York: Free Press, 1960.
13. Murstein, Bernard I., Ed., *Handbook of Projective Techniques,* New York: Basic Books, 1966.
14. Northway, M., *A Primer of Sociometry,* Toronto: University of Toronto Press, 1952.
15. Richardson, S.A., Dohrenwend, B.S., and Klein, D., *Interviewing: Its Forms and Functions,* New York: Basic books, 1965.
16. Schmidt, J.W., and Taylor, R.E., *Simulation and Analysis of Industrial Systems,* Homewood, III.: Richard D.Irwin, 1970.
17. Selltiz, Claire, *et al., Research Methods in Social Relations,* New York: Holt, Rinehard and Winston, 1959.
18. Survey Research Centre, *Interviewer's Manual,* An Arbor: Institute for Social Research, University of Michigan, 1969.
19. Webb, E.J., *et al., Unobtrussive Measures; Non-reactive Research in the Social Sciences,* Chicago: Rand Mcnally, 1966.
20. Webb, Eugene J., *et al., Non-reactive Measures in the Social Sciences,* Boston: Houghton-Miffin, 1981.

QUESTIONS

1. Define 'data.' Give some examples. Discuss the importance of data.
2. Differentiate primary sources of data from secondary sources.
3. Name some research situations in your discipline where secondary data sources are probably the only ones feasible.
4. What are the uses of secondary data and what are their advantages and limitations?
5. How should a researcher evaluate secondary data before deciding to use them?
6. Name the different methods of data collection and discuss the factors upon which the choice of a method/s for a given research project depend.
7. How can the appropriateness of a method of data collection be evaluated?
8. Define 'observation' as a method of data collection. What are its characteristics? When does observation become scientific?
9. Distinguish between (a) participant observation and (b) non-participant observation.
10. For what research purposes would you recommend (a) participant observation? (b) non-participant observation? Why?
11. How should the use of observation method be used?
12. What are the conditions of effective observations?
13. Evaluate observation as a method of data collection.
14. What is experimentation? Why is it used in research?
15. Outline the general procedure in experimentation.
16. Evaluate the experimental method of Investigation.
17. Distinguish between laboratory experiment and field experiment.
18. For what research purposes would you recommend (a) laboratory experiment? (b) field experiment? Why?
19. Evaluate (a) laboratory experimental method and (b) field experimental method.
20. What are the types of validity? How is it difficult to achieve cent per cent validity in an experiment?
21. State the twelve threats to validity of an experiment.

22. Of the various methods of achieving validity in experimentation, which is most important? Why?
23. Define 'simulation' and describe its process.
24. Distinguish between simulation and experimentation.
25. Describe briefly three types of simulation.
26. For what research purposes would you recommend the application of simulation?
27. Would you recommend an experimentation or a simulation for each of the following? In each case how would you design it?
    (a) Testing three methods of compensation of factory workers: hourly wage, incentive pay, and weekly salary.
    (b) The effects of various levels of advertising effort and price reduction on the sale of branded consumer non-durables.
28. What is 'interviewing'? As a method of data collection? What is its importance?
29. Evaluate interviewing as a method of data collection.
30. How is interview an interactional process? What are its Implications?
31. Discuss the characteristics of interview method.
32. What are the requirements of a successful interview?
33. Classify interviews and describe briefly each type of interview.
34. Differentiate between directive interview and non-directive interview.
35. What is clinical interview? How does it differ from focused interview?
36. Describe the various stages in interviewing process.
37. How should an investigator introduce himself to a respondent?
38. How can a respondent be motivated for interview?
39. Describe the Process of Interviewing a respondent.
40. What are the do's and don'ts in interviewing a respondent?
41. How do environmental factors affect response rates in personal interviews? How can we overcome these problems?
42. Under what circumstances are personal interviews desired?
43. How would you deal with the problems of inadequacy and interviewer's bias in personal interviews?
44. What are the sources of non-responses in personal interviews? How would you control non-responses?
45. In what situations is telephone interview useful? What are its merits and demerits?
46. In the following situations would you use a personal interview, telephone interview or mail survey? Give your reasons.
    (a) A survey of the residents of a new extension on why they happened to select that particular area and on their likes and dislikes about it.
    (b) A poll of students at a university on their preferences among three candidates who are running for the presidency of the student union.
    (c) A survey of manufacturing companies scattered over Southern India on their wage policies.
    (d) A survey of financial analysis of merchant bankers to learn their predictions on capital market developments in India in 2000 A.D.
47. Describe the meaning and nature of group interviews and evaluate them.
48. Define panel method and describe its characteristics.
49. What is the need for panel study? What are its advantages and disadvantages?

50. Distinguish between static panel and dynamic panel.
51. What problems are met in the administration of panel study?
52. Describe the procedure of a mail survey.
53. You propose to conduct a mail survey of accounting practices followed in large manufacturing companies over the country. How you would improve the response rate of such a survey?
54. Evaluate the mailing method of data collection.
55. What are projective techniques? What types of psychological barriers can they help to overcome?
56. What are the approach used in projective techniques?
57. Describe the features and applications of —

    (a) Rorschach test, (b) Thematic Apperception test, (c) Rosenzweig test, (d) Picture Frustration test, (e) Holtzmann Inkblot test.
58. Describe the procedure and uses of-

    (a) Word association test, (b) Sentence completion test, (c) Story completion test.
59. For what purposes would you use (a) play technique, (b) finger painting, (c) role playing?
60. Evaluate projective technique of data collection.
61. Define sociometry and describe sociometric test.
62. What are the requirements of the sociometric test?
63. Describe the sociometric matrix method and evaluate it.
64. What is sociogram? What are its advantages and disadvantages?
65. State the major socio-metric indices and their uses.
66. Examine the applications of sociometric techniques and also evaluate them.
67. What is meant by content analysis? What are the steps involved in it?
68. What are the major types or recording units used in content analysis?
69. For what purposes is content analysis used? What are its limitations?

8 TOOLS FOR DATA COLLECTION

8.1 TYPES OF TOOLS

Tools

The various methods of data gathering involve the use of appropriate recording forms. These are called tools or instruments of data collection. They consist of-

- Observation schedule or observationnaire
- Interview guide
- Interview schedule
- Mailed quesionnaire
- Rating scale
- Check list
- Opinionnaire
- Document schedule/data sheet
- Schedule for institutions
- Inventories

Each of the above tools is used for a specific method of data gathering: Observation schedule for observation method, interview schedule and interview guide for interviewing, questionnaire and optionnaire for mail survey, and so on.

Functions

The tools of data collection translate the research objectives into specific questions/items, the responses to which will provide the data required to achieve the research objectives. In order to achieve this purpose, each question/item must convey to the respondent the idea or group of ideas required by the research objectives, and each item must obtain a response which can be analyzed for fulfilling the research objectives.

Information gathered through the tools provide descriptions of characteristics of individuals, institutions or other phenomena under study. The characteristics may help to explain differences in behavioural pattern and performance of objects under study.

Information gathered through the tools serve another purpose also. It is useful for measuring the various variables pertaining to the study. The variables and their interrelationships are analysed for testing the hypothesis or for exploring the content areas set by the research objectives.

A brief description of the various tools of data collection is given below.

Observation Schedule or Observationnaire

This is a form on which observations of an object or a phenomenon are recorded. The items to be observed are determined with reference to the nature and objectives of the study. They are grouped into appropriate categories and listed in the schedule in the order in which the observer would observe them.

The items are structured with possible alternatives. Space is provided against each unit observation for encircling or checking, or recording, as the case may be.

Provision is made for the correct identification of each case observed and of the observer.

The schedule should be so constructed as to make it possible to record the observations easily and correctly, and to tabulate and analyze effectively.

A sample of observationnaire is given in Exhibit 8.1.

The schedule must be so devised as to provide the required verifiable and quantifiable data and to avoid selective bias and misinterpretation of observed items. The units of observation must be simple, and meticulously worded so as to facilitate precise and uniform recording.

Interview Guide

This is used for non-directive and depth interviews. It does not contain a complete list of items on which information has to be elicited from a respondent; it just contains only the broad topics or areas to be covered in the interview.

Interview guide serves as a suggestive reference or prompter during interview. It aids in focusing attention on salient points relating to the study and in securing comparable data in different interviews by the same or different interviewers.

There is considerable flexibility as to the manner, order and language in which the interviewer asks the questions. If the interviewer has to refer the guide very often, it would defeat its own purpose. The interviewer cannot listen closely and analytically if his attention rests on the guide. He may fail to respond to the cues and implications of the interviewee's remarks.

Interview Schedule and Mailed Questionnaire

Both these tools are widely used in surveys. Both are complete lists of questions on which information is elicited from the respondents. The basic difference between them lies in recording responses. While a schedule is filled out by the interviewer, a questionnaire is completed by the respondent. (See topic 8.2 below for a comprehensive discussion on these two tools).

OBSERVATION SCHEDULE FOR PHYSICAL CHARACTERISTICS OF OFFICE ROOMS

Name of the Organization:

Date of Observations: ...Time: ....A.M./P.M.

Name of Observer:

1. Purpose for which the room is used:
   Chief Executive's room ________
   Section head's room ________
   Open Office ________
   Other (specify) ________
2. Dimensions of room (in meter and centimeter):
   (a) Floor space: Length ________ Width ________
   Total square meter ________
   (b) Height of ceiling ________
3. Windows:
   (a) Number of windows
   (b) Measurement of each window: Height ____ Width ______
   (c) Window doors: Wooden ______ Glass: Clear _____ Tinted ______
   (d) Panes: Single ______ Double ______
   (e) Frames: Wood _____ Metal ______
4. Lighting: Fluorescent _____ Incandescent ______
   Direct ______ Indirect ______
5. Temperature control: Cooling
   Central cooling system for building ______
   Room cooler ______ None _______
   Temperature at time of observation ______
6. Floor covering: Wood _____ Carpet (Wall to wall) ______
   Carpet partial ______
   Linoleum ______ Other (specify) ______
   None ______

Exhibit 8.1: Observation Schedule

Rating Scale

This is a recording form used for measuring individual's attitudes, aspirations and other psychological and behavioural aspects, and group behaviour. (For detailed discussion see 8.3 *Measurement Scales and Indexes,* below).

Check List

This is the simplest of all the devices. It consists of a prepared list of items pertinent to an object or a particular task. The presence or absence of each item may be indicated by checking 'yes' or 'no' or multipoint scale. The use of a check list ensures a more complete consideration of all aspects or the object, act or task. A check list contains terms which the respondent understands and which more briefly and succinctly express his views than answers to open-ended question.[1] It is a crude device, but careful pre-test can make it less so. It is at best when used to test specific hypothesis.[2] It may be used as an independent tool or as a part of a schedule/questionnaire.

Its main drawback is that items may be responded in different ways. They may try to create a favourable impression of themselves by checking those qualities that they regard as socially desirable.[3]

Given below is a check list taken from a Questionnaire designed for University lady students to study their marriage aspirations:

Would you please give your opinions on the following attributes of a prospective husband? Check (✔) appropriate columns.

	Very Important	*Important*	*Indifferent*	*Undesirable*
1. Good looks				
2. Fair complexion				
3. Kindness				
4. Economic status				
5. Higher. education				
6. Dependability'				
7. Family background				
8. Sense of humour				
9. Ambition				
10. Moral character				
11. Domesticity				
12. Intelligence				
13. Good health				
14. Physique				

A check list given under *"Question Construction"* in topic 8.2 is another example.

Opinionnaire

This is a list of questions or statements pertaining to an issue or program. It is used for studying the opinions of people. It is commonly used in opinion polls. People are asked to express their responses to the listed questions or reactions to the listed statements.

1. Oppenheim A.N., *Questionnaire Design and Attitude Measurement,* London: Heinemann Educational Books Ltd., 1973, p. 81.
2. *Ibid.,* p. 82.
3. *Ibid.,* p. 83.

Documents Schedule/Data Sheet

This is a list of items of information to be obtained from documents, records and other materials. In order to secure measurable data, the items included in the schedule are limited to those that can be uniformly secured from a large number of case histories or other records. For example, a study of annual returns and financial statements filed by joint-stock companies with the Register of joint-Stock Companies may include such items as age of the company, membership, capital structure, capital employed, net worth, volume of business, income and expenditure, gross profit, net profit before tax and net profit after tax.

Schedule for Institutions

This is used for survey of organizations like business enterprises, educational institutions, social or cultural organizations and the like. It will include various categories of data relating to their profile, functions and performance. These data are gathered from their records, annual reports and financial statements.

Inventories

"An inventory is essentially a list that the respondent is asked to mark or check in a particular way." Some example of inventories are.[4]

1. **Lists of interest:** The respondents are asked to check those things that interest them a lot.
2. **List of personality traits:** People are asked to check which of these apply to them.
3. **List of spare-time activities:** One has to check the activity engaged most often.
4. **Perceived effects of T.V:** (Stimulation of Activities): The respondents may be asked to check 'true' or 'untrue' the following items:
   (a) I have copied the way the people dress on TV.
   (b) I have made things after they have been shown on TV.
   (c) I have purchased a particular brand after seeing its advertisement on TV.
   (d) I have gone to an art gallery after seeing it on TV. And so on.

Uses: Inventories can be constructed with various purposes in mind or to test particular hypothesis. They invariably form part of a Questionnaire/Schedule.

8.2 CONSTRUCTION OF SCHEDULES AND QUESTIONNAIRES

Schedule Vs. Questionnaire

Schedules and questionnaires are the most common instruments of data collection. These two types of tools have much in common. Both of them contain a set of questions logically related to a problem under study; both aim at eliciting responses from the respondents; in both cases the content, response structure, the wordings of questions, question sequence, etc. are the same for all respondents. Then why should they be denoted by the different terms: 'schedule' and 'questionnaires"? This is because the methods for which they are used are different. While a schedule is used as a tool for interviewing, a questionnaire is used for mailing.

4. *Ibid.*, p. 94.

This difference in usage gives rise to a subtle difference between these two recording forms. That is, a schedule is filled by the interviewer in a face-to-face interviewing, whereas a questionnaire is filled in by the respondent himself. Hence the need for using two different terms..

The tool is referred to as a schedule when it is used for interviewing; and it is called a questionnaire when it is sent to a respondent for completion and return.

The Process of Construction

The process of construction of a schedule and a questionnaire is almost same, except some minor differences in mechanics.

This process is not a matter of simply listing questions that comes to researcher's mind. It is a rational process involving much time, effort and thought. It consists of the following major steps:

1. Data need determination: As an interview schedule or a mailed questionnaire is an instrument for gathering data for a specific study, its construction should flow logically from the data required for the given study. Hence the data need determination is the first step in the instrument design process. How the data requirement can be determined?

The data required for a specific study can be determined by a deep analysis of the research objectives, the investigative questions relating to each of the research objectives, hypothesis, and the operational definitions of the concepts used in them.

What data are required to answer the research questions and to test the hypothesis? What questions should be put to the respondents to elicit these data?

The outcome of this exercise in analytical reasoning depends upon researcher's perception of the research problem and his insight into it. If he has no thorough knowledge of the full dimensions of the subject, then it is necessary to do an exploratory 'pilot study' to gain it.

2. Preparation of 'Dummy' tables: We are concerned with adequate coverage of the information required for the study and also with securing the information in the most usable form. The best way to ensure these requirements is to develop "dummy" tables in which to display the data to be gathered. The adequacy of the dummy tables for describing the possible distributions or relationship related to the problem or hypothesis should be examined. This will help to identify gaps and duplications in the instrument and enable the designer to make appropriate additions, corrections and deletions.

3. Determination of the respondents' level: Who are our respondents? Are they persons with specialized knowledge relating to the problem under study? Or are they lay people? What is their level of knowledge and understanding? The choice of words and concepts depends upon the level of the respondents' 'knowledge.'

4. Data gathering method decision: At this stage we must choose the method of collection of data to be used. Which communication mode is most appropriate – face-to-face interview or mailing? The choice of question structure depends largely on the communication mode chosen. For example, it is necessary to use structured questions for a mail survey, to the extent possible.

5. Instrument drafting: After determining the data required for the study, first, a broad outline of the instrument may be drafted, listing the various broad categories of data. For example, the outline of a questionnaire for a survey of consumer behaviour towards colour televisions may consist of such sections as (a) Identification data, (b) Brand awareness, (c) Brand choice, (d) Purchase decision, (e) Brand loyalty, (f) Post-purchase behaviour, and (g) Personal information.

Second, the sequence of these grouping must be decided. They must be arranged in a logical order — For example, in the questionnaire outline given above 'brand choice' cannot precede 'brand awareness,' because the choice is made out of brands known. (For further details see *'Question Sequence'* in the next sub-title, below).

Third, the questions to be asked under each group heading must be listed. All conceivable items relevant to the 'data need' should be compiled. The goal of this listing is to ensure that all questions that are required to obtain the needed data are compiled. In compiling his draft, the content, wording and other aspects should be considered. (For details, see the next topic: *Question Construction,* below).

6. Evaluation of the draft instrument: In consultation with other qualified persons, the researcher must rigorously examine each questions in the draft instrument. This evaluation may be done in terms of the following criteria:

(a) The relevance of each question to the research objectives and investigative questions.

(b) The appropriateness of the type of question: open ended or structured.

(c) The clarity and unambiguity of the question.

(d) The practicability of the question: i.e., it should not demand knowledge and information that the respondent does not possess, it should not test his memory span and also should not embarrass him.

(e) The validity of the question: i.e., it should not be a leading or loaded question.

The logical and psychological order of the questions, their clarity and content, and the length of the instrument and other aspects of its structure should also be considered. The length of the questions is likely to influence the response rate and test-weary level, but the length in itself need not be the guiding factor in the design. The important consideration is that the instrument adequately covers the subject, but does not include irrelevant items.

In the light of the above evaluation, the draft instrument should be revised.

7. Pre-testing: The revised draft must be pre-tested in order to identify the weaknesses of the instrument and to make the required further revisions to rectify them. (For a detailed discussion on pre-testing see topic: 8.4 *Pre-test* and *Pilot Study,* below).

8. Specification of procedures/instructions: After the instruction is finalized after pre-tests, the procedures or instructions, relating to its use must be specified. If the instrument is an interview schedule, then it is necessary to specify the procedures for its use. This specification is one way to ensure that different interviewers will deal with specific questions in a standardized manner. The definitions of concepts and variables should be given. The procedure for recording responses and approaches to deal with various interview situations must also be specified. The efficiency of field handling is the operating consideration in the case of an interview schedule. If the instrument is meant for mail survey, instructions regarding the mode of answering should be specified at the top of the first page. The anonymity should be assured.

A good covering letter should also be drafted. (See topic 7.10 *Mail Survey*, in Chapter 7, above).

The questionnaire itself should be carefully and clearly laid out, using bold types and capitals to emphasize particular words and instructions. It should be neatly printed in quality paper, as the primary consideration in questionnaire design is attractiveness and clarity. (See sub-heading *"Mechanics of the Schedule and Questionnaire,"* below in this topic).

9. Designing the format: The format should be suited to the needs of the research. The instrument should be divided into different sections relating to the different aspects of the problem. Each section heading should be printed in thick/bold letters. There must be more space for the answer of each open-ended question. There should be space between one question and another so that the interviewer/respondent will not easily confuse the line from which he is reading.

There may be questions for which answers are 'ýes' or 'no.' If the respondent answers ýes' to such a question, then a series of questions is offered, which is different from the series offered to 'no' answer. Such series must be set off spatially by indentation, asterisks or some other technique, so that there is no confusion between the two series. (See *"Mechanics of the Schedule and Questionnaire,"* below).

Question Construction

A survey instrument – interview schedules or questionnaire – is useful for collecting various types of information, viz, (a) factual information – facts about the respondents: sex, age, marital status, education, religion, caste or social class, income and occupation; and facts about events and circumstances, (b) psychological information such as attitudes, opinions, beliefs, and expectations, and (c) behavioural information, like social participation, and so on.

Once the information needed is determined as explained in the previous topic we can begin question construction. This involves four major decision areas. They are: (a) question relevance and content, (b) question wording, (c)response form, and (d) question order or sequence.

Question Relevance and Content

Any question to be included in the instrument should pass certain tests. Is it relevant to the research objectives? Can it yield significant information for answering an investigative question? If not, it should not be included in the instrument.

If a question passes the relevance test, we should then consider its coverage. Is it of proper scope? If it covers two separate ideas, then it is a double-barreled question requiring splitting. An example of this type of question is: Are you satisfied with the service conditions and the promotional policy of your employer? It is better to break this into two separate questions.

Another test of coverage is: Does the question provide the information needed to interpret the response fully? If we have to ask about the operational efficiency of X enterprises, a single question about it cannot provide adequate information to judge the operational efficiency. We should ask several questions on the various dimensions of this variable.

Another test is to consider whether the respondents know the answer to the question. Respondents may prefer to give some answer even if they are not aware of a topic. General public cannot be expected to know the correct meanings of technical concepts, like net reproductive rate, Sanskritization, social structure, gross margin, gross block, etc. The question designer should consider the respondent's information level when determining the content and appropriateness of a question. A question should not call for more information than the potential respondent's ability and willingness to provide.

A question should not overtax the respondent's recall ability. Most of us cannot recall much that has happened in the past. This limitation should be kept in mind in framing questions on past events.

Another aspect of adequacy relates to a balance between generality and specificity. For example, to ask about average annual movie attendance is an unrealistic demand for generalization. It may be better to ask about attendance for the last month.

The main difficulties with factual questions are to ensure that they are understandable and convey to the respondents precisely what facts are wanted.

The difficulties with opinion questions are much more fundamental. A person's opinion on any issue is many-sided. For example, opinions on 'sati,' there are moral, religious, legal, social and other aspects. There is also the problem of intensity. To estimate the opinions on an issue, an opinion statement may be given and the respondents may be asked to say whether they agree with it or not. Alternatively, a number of opinion statements may be given and the respondents may be asked to check the particular statement which best describes their opinion.

However, if their attitudes have to be measured an attitude scale (see 8.3 *Measurement Scales and Indices,* below) has to be constructed.

The most important guideline for asking about behaviours of respondents is that the question should be specific. For example, Questions like "what brand or brands of coffee do you have in the house today? Do you usually buy that brand?" are preferable to a more general question like "what brand of coffee do you usually use?

Finally, it must be determined whether questioning would secure the required information or not. If we find that through questioning we cannot succeed in securing the needed information, we should think of other alternatives. For example, in a survey of magazines read by respondents, an unusually high rate was reported for prestige magazines and an unusually low rate for pulp magazines. The method of data collection as changed: Instead of interviewing the respondents, they were asked to contribute their older magazines to a charity drive. This collection gave a much more realistic estimate of readership of both types of magazines.

Question Wording

This is a difficult task. The function of a question in a schedule/questionnaire is to elicit a particular information without distortion. "Questioning people," says Oppenheim, is more like trying to catch a particular elusive fish, by hopefully casting different kinds of bait at different depths, without knowing what goes on beneath the surface."[5] As the meaning of words differs from person to person, the question designer should choose words which have the following characteristics:

(a) ***Shared vocabulary:*** The collection of data is ultimately an exchange of ideas between the investigator and the respondent. The exact understanding between them calls for the use of vocabulary common to both parties. Each must understand what the other says. Each word should mean the same thing to all respondents.

(b) ***Exactness:*** The words should be exact or precise, reflecting what the question content is intended to mean. Such words as 'small,' frequently,' 'good,' 'beautiful,' and 'usually,' are intrinsically vague and should be avoided in favour of numerical ranges when possible. Even a word like income' should be stated exactly as 'family income per month' or individual income per month.

5. *Ibid,* p. 49.

(c) ***Simplicity:*** The words should be simple. Many commonly used words like 'nationality,' 'marital status, 'bureaucrat' are frequently misunderstood. Such words should be avoided and simpler equivalents used or clarified in detail. For example, a question worded as "What is your marital status?" may elicit feelings about marital life or marital problems. It is better to word it as Are you currently married, widowed, divorced" or separated or unmarried?

Similarly, the questions should also be simple. Instead of designing a single complex question on a complicated subject it is desirable to compile a series of simple questions.

(d) ***Neutrality:*** Words that cause undue influence of prestige or bias can result in inaccurate answers. Suppose we ask a customer "would you patronize a high-class aristocratic café?" This practically would force the respondent to answer in a certain way. Such wordings should be avoided. The words to be used must be neutral ones, i.e., free from the distorting influence of fear, prestige, bias or emotion.

Certain other problem areas of question wording are:

(a) ***Unwarranted assumptions:*** The questions designer should not assume that the respondents know or understand key words or phrases or abstract concepts. Unless words have concrete referents, their meanings are too vague for a research tool. Example of such words are 'business,' 'society,' 'culture' and 'social justice.'

(b) ***Personalization:*** It is necessary to decide whether a question should be worded in a personalized form or not; should we ask "what would you do about...?" The responses to personalized and impersonal questions will vary. We should choose that form which is likely to present the issue more realistically. Indirect questioning is widely used for opinions in sensitive topics. It is likely that the respondent will reply in terms o his on attitudes and experiences.

(c) ***Presumptions:*** Questions should not presume anything about the respondent. They should not imply that he engages in the activity about which he is being asked or necessarily possesses any knowledge on the survey matter. Questions like: "How many times a day do you drink coffee?" or "Are you satisfied with the performance of your colour TV?" should be preceded by a filter question: "Are you used to drink coffee everyday?" or "Do you have a colour TV in your house? As the case may be.

(d) ***Hypothetical question:*** Hypothetical questions like: "Would you like to...?" or "What would you do if....?" Are of very little value to predict behaviour?

(e) ***Embarrassing questions:*** People do not like to discuss in public private matters or to admit socially unacceptable behaviour and attitudes. For example, many respondents would probably refuse to answer or distort their answers to questions on premarriage sexual experience, frequency of taking a bath, or cheating in examination and the like.

Some of the approaches to deal with this problem are: (i) to express the question in the third person; instead of asking the respondent for his views, he is asked about the views of others: (ii) to use a drawing of two persons in a certain setting with 'balloons' containing speech coming from their mouths, as in a cartoon – leaving one person's balloon empty and asking the respondent to put himself in the position of that person and to fill in the missing words; and (iii) to use sentence completion tests. (See topic 7.11 *"Projective Technique"* in Chapter 7, above).

The question designer should be aware of question wording problems and take every care to develop unbiased and unambiguous questions. After developing them, he should test and revise them two or more times in order to improve the quality of their wordings. The general rules are that questions should be brief and simple, without compound phrases; they should be clear, having few or no adjectives; and they should be positive rather than negative.

Response Form or Types of Questions

The third major area in question construction is the types of questions to be included in the instrument. They may be classified into open questions and closed questions. Closed questions may be dichotomous, multiple choice or declarative ones.

Determinants: The choice between open and closed questions depends on the situation. Kahn and Cannel[6] point out five situational factors that determine this decision.

They are:

(1) Objectives of the interview,

(2) Respondent's level of information about the topic,

(3) Respondent's thinking through the topic,

(4) Ease of communication and motivation of respondent to talk, and

(5) The investigator's awareness of the above factors.

If the objective of interview/mailing is to classify the respondents' characteristics/view points is into some specific categories, then the closed form of question is preferable. For example, the age of the respondents may be structured as 'up to 20 years, 20 to 40 years. 40 to 60 years; and 60 years and above.' Open questions are appropriate when the objective is to discover opinions and degrees of knowledge, or to seek suggestions and more information.

When the subject matter of a question is likely to be outside the range of the respondent's experience, the open questions may be the better way to learn his level of information. Open questions are also preferable for determining the depth of feelings and expressions of intensity. Where the respondent has not yet thought through the topic, an open question may give him a chance to think through it. Closed questions require less motivation than open ones.

Finally, it is better to use open questions when the investigator has no clear idea of respondents' level of information. This situation is likely to prevail in exploratory research or the pilot stage of a study.

Open-ended questions: These are unstructured ones, providing free scope to the respondents to reply with their own choice of words and ideas, e.g., what you propose to do after graduation? Open responses are useful in studies where discovery is the objective. Response freedom encourages a variety of frames of references which may provide unanticipated insights.

Open questions of general type may be included in the opening part of the tool in order to arouse the interest of the respondents. Open questions are also useful to start a depth interview. However, they make compilation and classification of responses difficult.

---

6. Kahn, Robert L., and Cannel, Charles F., *Dynamics of Interviewing,* New York: John Wiley & Sons, 1957, p. 132.

Closed questions are structured ones with two or more alternative responses from which respondent can choose. They contain standardized answers and they are simple to administer and easy to compile and analyze. As the alternative responses are designed with reference to the requirements of the study, the chances of securing relevant answers are better.

However, closed questions suffer from certain disadvantages. They force a statement of response couched in the researcher's terms rather than the respondent's. The respondent may be led to choose a response, even when he has no knowledge of it, or the limited alternatives may not cover his viewpoints. It is also possible that different respondents will interpret the same words and statements differently.

Dichotomous or two-choice questions: A dichotomous question can be answered in one of the two responses such as 'yes' or 'no'. For example, 'Do you own a watch'? Yes ____ No. _____. Do you own or rent your house? Own _____ Rent ______. It is necessary to realize that in many two-choice questions there may be potential alternatives beyond the stated two. For example, a respondent may answer 'do not know' or 'no opinion' or even 'in-between', e.g., a question like "Do you propose to buy NS Certificates?" requires three choices: 'yes', 'no' and 'undecided.'

Multiple choice questions: These questions contain more than two alternatives, e.g., Why have you preferred this brand of two wheeler?

— Reasonable price

— Fuel-efficient

— Sturdy

— Riding comfort

— Others (please specify)

The list may not necessarily be all-inclusive. To solve this problem, we should add the category "others (please specify)" to provide for any other options.

The multiple-choice questions should satisfy the following requirements:

1. The list of alternative choices should be exhaustive, i.e., it should contain all the possible choices that the respondents would like to have. The category of "others (please specify)" should be included to provide for unanticipated choices.
2. They should not contain overlapping choices.
3. There should be a fair balance in choices.
4. All alternatives should be reasonable, e.g., in a survey of industrial workers, suppose the following choices are presented under "What is your monthly total wages?"

   — upto Rs. 1,000

   — Rs. 1,001 to Rs. 2,000

   — Rs. 2,001 to Rs. 3,000

   — Rs. 3,001 to Rs. 5,000

   — Rs. 5,001 to Rs. 10,000

   — Rs. 10,001 and above.

It is obvious that the last three choices are not reasonable in the light of our general knowledge about industrial wages in India.

5. The choices should be logically consistent, i.e., they should not mix-up causes and effects, e.g., in your opinion what are the two main causes for industrial sickness?

   — (a) inefficient management

   — (b) inadequate capital

   — (c) obsolete technology

   — (d) technical insolvency

   — (e) others, please specify.

   Item (d) is the effect of (b), and hence not consistent.

6. The choices should be conceptually unidimensional, i.e., they should refer to the different aspects of the same conceptual dimension, e.g., for a question relating to low labour productivity, the list of alternatives should not include items like (a) insufficient capital, (b) lack of demand for the product, and (c) severe competition which represent conceptual dimensions different from "labour productivity."

The actual process of designing satisfactory alternative responses to multiple choice questions calls for repeated pre-tests and revisions.

Declarative questions: A declarative question is a type of multiple choice question in which a series of statements about a given subject is given. The respondent is asked to check one of them which represents his view, e.g.,

Which of the following statements best describes your company's philosophy?

- A business firm is responsible for making a profit and helping to solve social problems which it may directly create.
- A business firm is responsible for making profit while abiding by legal requirements.
- In addition to making profit, a firm should help to solve social problems, as long as there is some profit potential.
- In addition to making a profit, a firm should help to solve social problems around it, even if there is probably no profit potential.

When the responses are best expressed in degrees of agreement or disagreement or like or dislike, the declarative form should be considered.

Types of Questions to be Avoided

The question designer should avoid the following types of questions:

(a) ***Leading questions:*** A leading question is one that is worded in such a way as to influence the respondent to give a certain answer. It does not elicit an accurate answer or correct view point of the respondent. Examples of leading questions are:

"Are you against giving too much power to the trade unions?"

"You would like to own a new Maruthi Car, wouldn't you?"

"Don't you think that yesterday's T.V. drama was thrilling"?

"Do you think that the Government should get involved in...?"

(b) ***'Loaded' questions:*** A 'loaded' question is one that contains words which are emotionally coloured and suggests an automatic feeling of approval or disapproval. Words such as 'starvation', 'bureaucracy', 'terrorist,' etc., make respondents react not so much to the issue posed by the question as to the loaded phrase itself. Consider the following two questions: "Mahatma Gandhi has always advocated religious harmony. Do you think that we should maintain religious harmony?" and "Fundamentalists have advocated religious harmony. Do you think we should maintain religious harmony?" These two questions are loaded in different directions. More respondents will tend to agree with the first. Another example: "Have you ever tried to get special favours from a business establishment by pressuring them? Yes ____ No _____." The respondent cannot answer 'yes' without putting himself in a bad light.

(c) ***Ambiguous questions:*** An ambiguous question is one that does not have a clear meaning. It may mean different things to different people, e.g., Are you interested in a small house? What does the word 'interested' mean: to own or to hire? What does the word 'small' mean?

(d) ***Double-barreled questions:*** "They contain two or more different ideas or references, e.g., Do you favour or oppose increased job security and productivity-linked wage system? This should be split up into two questions: (1) Do you favour or oppose increased job security? (2) Do you favour or oppose productivity-linked wage system?

(e) ***Long questions:*** When questions become long they often become ambiguous and confusing. For example, the question "Do you have any impairments or handicapped conditions, even though they may not interfere with your usual activities?" causes confusion. It can be split into two points.

(f) ***Avoid double negative:*** A question with a double negative will cause confusion. Hence, double negative construction should be avoided.

Question Order or Sequence

The order in which questions are arranged in a schedule/questionnaire is as important as question wording. It has two major implications. First, an appropriate sequence can ease the respondent's task in answering. Second, the sequence can either create or avoid bias due to context effects, i.e., the effects of preceding questions on the response to later questions.

Should the sequence decision be determined by the research process (i.e., the needs of analysis) or by the logic of the respondent? The nature and needs of the respondent must determine the sequence of questions and the organization of the schedule. This is the basic principle governing sequence decision.

Emory suggests the following guidelines[7] to implement this principle of respondent orientation:

1. The question process must quickly awaken respondent's interest and motivate him to respond willingly and fully.
2. The respondent should not be confronted by early requests for personal information.

---

7. Emory, C.William, *Business Research Methods, op. cit.,* p. 222.

3. The questioning process should begin with simple items and move to the more complex, and from general items to the more specific.
4. Changes in frame of reference should be minimal and should be clearly pointed out.

In other words, there should be a logical progression[8] such that the respondent is (1) drawn into the questioning process by awakening his interest, (2) not affronted by an early and sudden request for personal information, (3) easily brought along items which are simple to answer to those which are complex, (4) never asked to give an answer which could be embarrassing without being given an opportunity to explain, and (5) brought smoothly from one frame of reference to another rather than made to jump back and forth.

The question sequencing has two dimensions: (1) overall sequence, i.e., the sequence among topical areas within the instrument, and (2) intra sequence, i.e., sequence within a topical area.

Overall sequence: The researcher is a stranger to respondents, and the latter are under no obligation to oblige. They may also have some doubts about their competence to answer research questions. Therefore, the investigator's first challenge is to awaken the respondents' interest in the study and motivate participation. In order to bring this about, the instrument should begin with attention-catching non-controversial and simple but interesting questions. If these questions have human interest value so much the better. In fact, the first few questions may set the tone of the entire questioning process.

Two forms of error are common in this respect. One is the common practice of beginning the instrument with easy-to-answer background information like age, education, religion, occupation, marital status etc. This practice is not correct, because people do not normally like to furnish such data to a stranger. These items should be put at the end. At that stage respondents are ordinarily more willing to give such personal information, and even if they are not, nothing much would be lost, as data on vital items would have been furnished.

Another practice of listing private or sensitive questions at the start is also dangerous. Then more respondents will either refuse to answer or furnish incorrect or evasive responses.

Some examples of reasonable opening questions are given below:

(i) (For a study involving household financial matters): "There has been a lot of talk about rising prices. We are interested in knowing how people are getting along financially these days. To what extent your financial position has been hit by rising prices? - Very much, somewhat, not too much or not at all?"

(ii) (For a study involving dealership survey): "There has been much talk about industrial deregulation and the emerging competitive market situation. It is said that industrial marketing has become highly challenging. We are interested in knowing how long-standing dealers like you manage this challenging task. How do you find this emerging scenario? Highly competitive, moderately competitive? Is it both an opportunity and a challenge?"

Questions like these may invoke the respondent's interest, put him at ease and build up his confidence and motivate his participation.

---

8. Goode, William J., and Hatt, Paul K., *Methods in Social Research, op. cit.*, pp. 136-137.

Following a few general initial questions of the sort just described, the main questions should be arranged in a logical manner, moving from topic to topic.

The principle of logical progression should be followed in arranging the topics, i.e., to place simple topics first and to move progressively to more complex ones and sensitive topics may be kept at the end.

Questions related to a particular topic should be kept together. The respondents are confused and angered if questions skip around from topic to topic, as when one question about tax policy, the next about job satisfaction and the next about investment preference. The respondent's comprehension and ability to answer the questions will be facilitated by keeping topically related questions together. Moreover each topic area should be linked in the respondent's mind to the overall purpose of the study. Questions with no connection to the topic are bound to arouse suspicion and resentment.

The next aspect is transition from one topic to another. This transition should be smooth and meaningful. Where one topic ends, it is advisable to give a sentence or two indicating the break and the relevance of the new topic to the study purpose. Such transitional statements should be simple and appropriate, e.g., (1) "We have been talking so far about your profession. Now I would like to learn about your association with social organisation." (2) "An important part of understanding people's attitude towards social security has to do with their feelings about achievement from work. So next I would like to ask some questions about your thoughts and plans on retirement." To introduce the personal background items like age, education, income etc., the following transitional statement may be used:" In study of this type, it is desirable to compare the people's opinions, or attitudes with their characteristics like age, religion, education etc. So finally I would like to ask some questions about yourself to help interpret the study results." Sensitive questions demand particular attention to transitions to ensure that respondents understand their relevance to the research purpose.

Where the schedule/questionnaire is long, the problem of respondent fatigue will arise. This usually sets in within a period of 15 to 20 minutes or after about 90 items. When the respondent experiences fatigue, he may fail to recall the latter items and hence give negative or 'don't know' responses. The best solution to this problem is to have more than one sitting with the respondent at his convenience.

Intra sequence: There are two general patterns in arranging the questions within a specific topical area. They are: the funnel sequence and the inverted funnel sequence. The funnel sequence refers to the procedure of listing the most general question first and following it with increasingly specific and detailed questions. The general question introduces the general subject and from the respondent's answer to it, we can probably infer his frame of reference. Each successive question is related to the previous question and it is progressively more specific. For example, if one were interested in finding out how the job and working conditions influence workers' attitude towards, wage structure, the following questions can form a funnel sequence: (1) "What is the job you hold? (2) What are the activities involved in it? (3) Do you find your job pleasant or tedious? (4) Under what working conditions do you perform those activities? (5) Do you find the working conditions conducive to work? (6) What is the wage structure pertaining to your job? (7) Do you find it commensurate with the nature of the job and working conditions?"

The objective of funnel approach is to learn the respondent's frame of reference and to extract the full range of desired information without the distortion effect of earlier questions on latter ones.

In the inverted funnel sequence, narrower questions are followed by broader ones. If the purpose is to obtain a generalization in the form of a judgement regarding a concrete situation, and it seems that the respondents do not hold considered opinions about it, then it is helpful to begin with specific questions which are easier to answer, and in answering them, the respondent is led towards forming a considered opinion on the broad question.

Another requirement in arranging questions is to avoid context effects, i.e., the influence of one question on another. For example, in a survey made for determining the relative popularity of a certain brand of a product, if an earlier question mentions the name of that brand or in any way indicates that the makers of that brand are interested in the findings, all the answers to the remaining questions are likely to be biased towards favouring that brand, because, ordinarily respondents would prefer to be pleasant to the investigator. Such sequence effect should be kept in mind in arranging questions. Any question that will prejudice the answers of other related questions should not precede the latter.

Check list: Kornhauser[9] has prepared a useful checklist of points to be considered while evaluating the questions constructed. An outline of those points is given below:

Questions Content

Is this question necessary for clear understanding; just how will it be used?

Are several questions needed on the subject matter of this one question?

Do the respondents have the information necessary to answer the question?

Does the question need to be more concrete, more specific and more closely related to respondent's experience?

Is the question content sufficiently general and free from spurious concreteness and specificity?

Is the question content biased or loaded in one direction – without accompanying questions to balance the emphasis?

Question Wording

Do the questions contain difficult or unclear phrases tending toward misunderstanding?

Do the questions adequately express the alternatives with respect to choices of responses?

Are the questions misleading by reason of unstated assumptions or unseen implications?

Is the wording biased? Is it emotionally loaded?

Is the question wording likely to be objectionable to the respondents?

Would a more personalized or less personalized wording of the question produce better results?

Can the question be better asked in a more direct of more indirect form?

Question Sequence

Are the answers to the questions likely to be influenced by the content of the preceding questions?

Are the questions led up to in a natural way? Are they in correct psychological order?

9. Kornhauser, Arthus, "Questionnaire Construction and Interview Procedure" in Claire Selltiz *et al., Research Methods in Social Relations,* pp. 552-574.

Do some questions come too early or too late from the point of view of arousing interest and receiving sufficient attention, avoiding resistance and inhibitions?

In the light of the above evaluation, the draft questions should be revised and improved.

Reason Analysis

The construction of questions to determine the 'reasons for' an action or opinion poses a challenge to the question designer. A simple "Why" question, though easy to use, is totally inadequate for the purpose. One effective approach for determining causal factors is 'reason analysis.' This is defined as "a set of procedures used in survey research to construct a causal explanation for the actions, decision, or intentions of individuals."[10] Reason analysis can be used in studying the subjective factors in any course of individual action.

To employ reason analysis, a researcher must analyze the research objectives and the type of actions of opinion under study. In the context of this analyst he should set up an accounting scheme. This scheme is an organized list of factors that are believed to be relevant causes or influences upon some action, opinion or intention. Zeisel refers to these factors as "dimensions of the action or attitude under study."[11] For example, purchase propositions can be analyzed with a three-dimension accounting scheme: (1) respondent's motives prior to the decision to buy, (2) attributes of the product – its quality, its usefulness, pricc etc., (3) influences that affect the course of the decision.

The accounting scheme must reflect the specific objectives of the study and also include the time element. Questions, then, may be designed covering the various dimensions of the accounting scheme. When done in this manner, substantial causal information can be secured.

Mechanics of the Schedule and Questionnaire

In addition to question wording and question construction, the mechanics of the form should also be considered in the design of a schedule/questionnaire. The mechanics of the form has several aspects; items of the form, instruction, pre-coding, sectionalization, spacing, paper, printing, margins, etc.

Items of the form: The following items are mandatory for schedules and questionnaires.

1. The name of the organization collecting the data should appear at the top of front page. The name of the sponsor, of the study, if any should also be shown. If the instruments are to be returned by mail, the address to which they are to be sent must be clearly specified.
2. The title of the study should appear in large print next to the name of the organization on the first page. Below this title, the title of the tool – e.g., 'Schedule for consumers' – may be noted.
3. The confidentialness of the data should be made clear.
4. A place for writing the date of filling in the form should be provided.
5. A serial number to each copy of the tool may be assigned.
6. The pages of the instrument should be numbered.

---

10. Kadushin, Charles, "Reason Analysis," in David L, Sills, (ed.), *The International Encyclopedia of the Social Sciences,* Vol. 13, New York: Macmillan Co., p. 338.
11. Zeisel, Hans, *Say it with Figures,* New York: Harper & Brothers, Publishers, 1957, p. 138.

Instructions: In the face sheet below the title of the questionnaire, a brief statement of the objective of the study, the confidentialness of the data, and instructions relating to answering the questions may be provided.

Pre-coding: Items in the tool should be pre-coded so as to facilitate transcription of data. For example, items in Section 1 may be numbered as 1.1, 1.2, 1.3 and so on, and in Section 2 as 2.1, 2.2, 2.3…. and so on. Sufficient space may be left for coding the responses to the open-ended questions.

Sectionalization: There should be a separate section for each topical area. For example, a questionnaire for studying the management of distribution channels in an equipment manufacturing industry may consist of sections entitled (1) Production, (2) Marketing channels: General, (3) Company's own Sales outlets, (4) Marketing through Dealers, (5) Marketing through agents, (6) General Information. Section heading may be printed in thick/block letters. Sections should be given serial numbers: 1, 2, 3…and so on.

As noted earlier, in order to make the shift from one section to another, it is desirable to insert transitional statements, such as "we have been talking about…, now, would you mind letting me ask a few questions about…?" Any such statements should be set off spatially or a different type face used, in order to draw the attention of the interviewer/respondent to the item.

Spacing: For each open-ended question, an adequate space should be provided for answer. There should be indeed more space than seems necessary, for some interviewers/respondents may write in a large script for legibility. Moreover, liberal spacing is a stimulus for the questionnaire respondent to write more fully. Even short-answer questions should be spaced, so that the interviewers/ respondent will not easily confuse the line, from which he is reading.

At times, there are additional facts to be recorded after the interviewers leave the respondent: the type of dwelling or neighbourhood, the respondent's response, etc. For recording such items of information in a systematic manner the face sheet or end sheet of the schedule may be set aside. In the case of a mailed questionnaire, in the end sheet space may be provided under 'General remarks' with a note: "Please furnish any other information relevant to the study."

Paper: The paper used for mimeographing/printing should be of good quality.

Printing: Mailed questionnaire should necessarily be printed in order to make it attractive and to minimize the postal expenditure. If a large number of copies are required, then even interview schedule may be printed. Printing has its own advantages. The letter size and colour may be varied in printing with advantageous effects. For example, section headings, could be printed in bold-type, questions in one colour, instructions in another colour and so on.

Margins: One inch margin on the left side of the sheet and one-half inch margin on other sides may be provided. If the instrument is to be bound, left-side margin should conform to the type of binding used.

Indentation: This is required for 'yes' or 'no' questions. If the respondent's answer is 'yes', then a series of questions is offered. If the answer is 'no' a different series of questions is offered. Such series must be set off spatially as under:

If yes then please answer the following questions.

If your answer is 'No' to Question…

The above demarcation avoids confusion between the two series.

Note of thanks: A final note or comment of thanks for the cooperation of the respondent should be included at the end of the instrument.

Concluding Remarks

Question designing remains primarily a matter of common sense and experience and of avoiding known pitfalls, as there are no hard and fast rules relating to it. Hence, alternative versions of questions must be rigorously tested in pre-tests. Test-revision-retests play a crucial role in questionnaire construction.

Summary of Characteristics of a Good Schedule/Questionnaire

The construction and use of schedules and questionnaires has been discussed at length in this and the preceding chapter. A summary of the main characteristics of a good schedule/questionnaire is given below:

1. It asks for and obtains all the information required for achieving the research objectives.
2. It contains questions relevant to the study and does not include any irrelevant and unimportant questions.
3. It does not aim at obtaining any information which can be more accurately and effectively obtained by other data-gathering methods like observation.
4. It contains no questions that are unclear, ambiguous, double, leading, loaded or uninformative, and long.
5. It contains no open-ended or discussion questions unless they are absolutely necessary.
6. It does not contain questions which are beyond the memory span of respondents.
7. It contains questions that can be answered as quickly and easily as possible.
8. It avoids unwarranted presumptions about the respondents.
9. It does not restrict the choices of answers so as to bias or distort replies to be given.
10. Choices to closed questions are adequate, reasonable, unidimensional and logically consistent.
11. Each question is limited to a single idea or single reference.
12. No embarrassing questions are given without providing an opportunity to explain.
13. Appropriate balance between personalization and indirect form is maintained.
14. Filter questions are used wherever necessary.
15. Topics and questions are arranged in a logical and psychological sequence that is natural and easy for the respondent.
16. Transition between one section and another is smooth.
17. Inter-related questions are so positioned as to avoid context effects.
18. Questions seeking 'reasons for' are based on reason analysis.
19. Questions and alternative answer choices are properly coded.
20. Design requirements like margin, spacing etc. are taken care of.
21. Appropriate introduction and instructions are included.
22. The instrument has been adequately pre-tested and revised so as to be a satisfactory tool for the particular survey.

8.3 MEASUREMENT SCALE AND INDICES

Introduction

Scales are devised for measuring variables in social science research. During the past few decades thousands of scales have been designed by researchers in sociology, psychology, education, psychiatry, ethics, behavioural science, economics, administration and other fields.[12]

Indices and scales are often used interchangeably to refer to all sorts of measures, absolute or relative, single or composite, simple or elaborate. "Scaling" refers to the procedure by which numbers or scores assigned to the various degrees of opinions, attitude and other concepts.

Scales Classification

Scales may be classified in many ways"[13] in terms of (a) subject matter, (b) scaling methods or techniques, (c) scale function, (d) levels of measurement, and (e) number of dimensions. However, there is no widely accepted system of classification.

Subject matter: Scales are designed to measure (1) attitude, (2) social distance, (3) socio-economic status, and (4) other variables.

Scaling techniques: In terms of techniques, scales may be classified into (a) Arbitrary Scales, (b) Judgement Scales, (c) 'Item analysis' Scales, (d) Rating Scales, (e) Ranking Scales, (f) Cumulative Scales, and (g) Factorial Scales.

Scale functions: Scales may have either predictive powers or reproductivity. Scales which have powers to predict an external criterion are *Predictive Scales*. Aptitude tests and prediction of marital adjustment are examples of this type of scale. Reproductive Scales are designed to arrange sets of data in such fashion that if the research is given a single score, he can reproduce all items in the scale. Louis Guttman has designed scales of this type.

Levels of measurement: In terms of this property, scales may be classified as *nominal, ordinal, interval or ratio scales*. (See *"Levels of Measurement"* in 5.6 Measurement, above).

Number of dimensions: Scales are either unidimensional or multidimensional. Unidimensional scale measures only one attribute of the respondent or object, e.g., attitude, opinion, job satisfaction, durability and so on. Most of the scales used in research are of this type. Multidimensional scale measures several dimensions of an object.

Arbitrary Scales

An arbitrary scale is constructed by assigning arbitrarily numerical values to the responses to a set of questions appropriate to a given attribute. The values are summed up to secure the attribute scale. For example, a company's image among its employees may be measured through the following items:

---

12. See Edward B. Greena, *Measurement of Human Behaviour,* Odyssey Press, 1952; Raymond B. Cattell, *Description and Measurement of Personality,* World Book Company, 1946; Anne Anastasi, *Psychological Testing*, Macmillan Co., 1961; Leona E. Eyler, *Tests and Measurements,* Prentice-Hall, 1963; Marvin E.Shah and Jack M.Wright, *Scales for Measurement of Attitudes,* New York McGraw-Hill, 1967.
13. For a discussion of various scale classification, see W.S.Torgerson, *Theory and Methods of Scalings*, New York: John Wiley & Sons, 1958, Chap. 3.7.

How do you regard your company's reputation

1. as a place to work? Bad- - - - - - - good
2. as a pay master? Bad- - - - - - - good
3. as a provider of promotional opportunities Bad- - - - - - - good
4. For concern for employee welfare? Bad- - - - - - - good

Each of these may be scored from 0 to 4 according to the degree of favourableness reported.

The total of scores of all respondents for each item may be made and studied. The overall image may also be studied by combining the scores of each respondent for the five items.

Merits: Arbitrary scales have certain merits: easy and quick to construct, specific to the content of interests, inexpensive and quite adequate.

Weaknesses: Arbitrary scales are based on the respondent's subjective logic, and scoring is arbitrary.

Judgement scaling: Thurstone Differential Scale

In judgement scaling a large number of items (statements) are constructed. A number of edges are asked to evaluate the items and determine their relevance to the topic area, clarity and degrees of favourableness towards the object. The most widely known example for this type is the Thurstone Differential Scale.

L.L. Thurstone's technique,[14] is one of the most important methodological contributions to attitude scale construction.

This scale consists of a number of statements whose position on the scale has been determined previously to be a ranking operation performed by judges. 3 to 7 point scale is used. The respondent is asked to make a (x) mark in the particular column against each statement, which best describes his feeling.

Procedure: The steps in constructing a Thurstone attitude scale are:

1. Select the issue (say, religion, democracy, socialism, morality) about which people's attitude is to be measured.
2. Prepare an outline indicating the areas of attitude to be measured.
3. Define the dimensions of attitude to be measured.
4. Design and collect 100-150 attitudinal statements from literature, interview etc. covering the entire range of attitudes from 'most favourable' through neutral ones and to 'least favourable' statements.

   Keep in mind the following points while writing the attitudinal statements:

   ***Avoid**

   (a) factual statements, (b) past-tense,
   (c) multiple interpretations, (d) irrelevant ones,
   (e) non-distinguishers, (f) all, always, none, never
   (g) double negatives, (h) long statements, and
   (i) slang.

14. L.L. Thurstone and E.J. Chave, *The Measurement of Attitude,* Chicago: University of Chicago Press, 1929. p. 5.

* Write simple, clear and direct statements.

— Each statement should express only one thought or idea.

— Each statement should be free from confusing concepts.

5. Assign arbitrary numbers to the statements for identification.
6. Reproduce the statements on uniform individual slips of paper.
7. Select 50 or more judges and give to each judge a complete set of items with clear, simple instructions to sort them into several piles, usually 7 or 11 (seven or eleven) which represent a graduated series of attitudes from "most favourable" to "least favourable." The intervals between the categories should be regarded as subjectively equal. The job of a judge is to place each statement in a particular category according to its meaning, ignoring his own agreement or disagreement with the statement. Each judge will record on each statement the number of pile in which he has placed it.
8. Assemble all the judgements for each statement and tabulate the sortings (a frequency table) to determine the distribution of judgements for each item, i.e., the number of times each statement is included in the several piles. Suppose 50 judges have sorted say, a statements No.98 as follows: 2 judges placed it in pile No.6; 3 in pile 7;9 in pile 8; 12 in pile 9; 15 in pile 10; and 9 in pile 11. This can be tabulated as under:

TABLE 8.1
Distribution of Judgements for Statement No.98

Pile No. (Category)	*No. of slips in each (judgements)*	*Percentage to total*	*Cumulative percentages*
1	0	—	—
2	0	—	—
3	0	—	—
4	0	—	—
5	0	—	—
6	2	4%	4%
7	3	6%	10%
8	9	18%	28%
9	12	24%	52%
10	15	30%	82%
11	9	18%	100%
Total	50	100%	

9. Draw up a cumulative graph for the cumulative frequencies for each statement. Place the eleven categories along the bottom line, and the percentages along the perpendicular line. Plot the cumulative percentages, and draw lines to connect these percentage points. This will give a steeply rising Ogive or cumulative percentage frequency curve.
10. Draw lines across the graph for the median (50% of the total frequencies) and the first and the third quartiles (25% and 75% respectively). Note the points at which these lines cross the Ogive curve and drop perpendiculars to the base-line at those three points (See Exhibit 8.2).

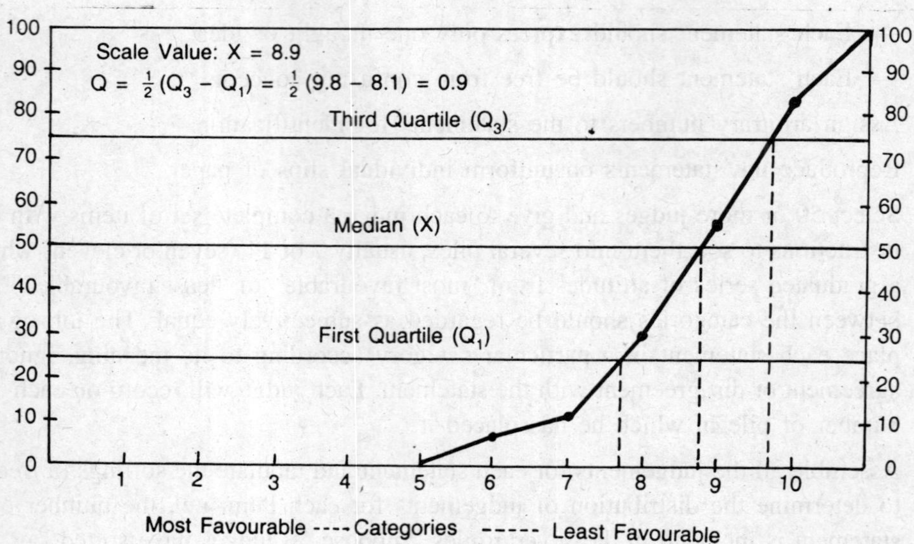

Exhibit 8.2 Cumulative-frequency graph for statement No. 98

11. Record the median, i.e., the value of the central perpendicular, Calculate Q = the semi-inter quartile range, i.e., half of the scale value of the third perpendicular – the scale value of the first perpendicular. The median value represents the scale value of the statement and the Q-value or co-efficient of ambiguity represents the spread of judgement.
12. Eliminate statements with excessive spread (Q – values). Out of the remaining ones, select those statements whose medians (i.e., scale values) are nearest to scale points 1.5, 2.0, 2.5, 3.0, 3.5, 4.0… In this way, build up the final scale consisting of 20 to 30 statements with equal-appearing intervals.
13. Rearrange the statement in random order and print them without scale values. The scale is now ready for administration to the population whose attitudes are to be measured.
14. Administer the scale to a sample of respondents with instructions to tick the statements with which they agree.
15. Analyze the result to check on the internal consistency of the statements. If respondents who agree with a statement say, with a scale value of 2-0 have also checked other statements with widely differing scale values say 7.0 or 8.0, the statement has to be rejected as an irrelevant one. After eliminating such irrelevant items, the scale is finalized.

Scoring system: Two alternative scoring procedures are used: the score for a respondent may be either (1) the arithmetic mean of the scale-values of the agreed statements or (2) the median value of the agreed statements. These two alternatives give substantially the same results.

If all goes according to plan, respondents should only agree with a very few statements. For example, if a respondent is mildly positive in his attitude, then he should disagree with items that are strongly positive, neutral or negative.

In Thurstone's procedure, we are dealing not with equal, but with equal-appearing intervals, which are psychological rather than numerical units. Hence numerically the scale values may or may not be equal. Moreover, the division of the continuum into eleven units is arbitrary. Therefore, we should not think of a score of eight as numerically twice as high as a score of four and so on.

One may wonder whether different groups of judges produce the same scale values. Experimental investigations have shown that the scale values obtained from different groups of judges correlate highly with one another, provided judges with extreme views are excluded. In practice, judges who place more than one-third of items in the same category should be excluded. All judges will be influenced by their own attitudes, but in most cases the effect will be small and barely affect the order of the statements. It is advisable to use as judges people similar ot the respondents in the research sample.

Thurstone's scales are time-consuming to construct, but simple to administer and score. They are primarily useful in attitude measurement.

Social Distance Scale

This was first developed by Emory S.Bogardus.[15] This scale like Thurstone's scale depends to a large extent on the ratings of a panel of judges in determining scale graduations. This method can be applied to various types of social groups such as ethnic minorities, social classes, communities, tribes and occupational groups.

Procedure: The steps involved in constructing this type of scale are:

1. Develop a number of social distance items;
2. Get them judged by a number of judges (50 to 100) in terms of an increasing degree of social farness or of decreasing degree of social nearness.
3. Select five or seven of those items evenly spaced according to the judges' ratings of increasing social distance (farness).
4. Arrange vertically the list of social groups (cultural groups, religions, occupations or communities, towards which a person's reactions/attitudes to be discovered) in the left-hand column of the scale.
5. Write the selected five or seven scale items on the right-side horizontally. The scale is ready for administration to a sample of persons belonging to the selected social group. The sample scale given below illustrates this procedure.

SOCIAL DISTANCE SCALE

(To discover Hindu's attitude towards other religious groups)

Directions: 1. Remember to give your first reactions in every case.

2. Give your reactions to each religion as a group. Do not give your reactions to the best or to the worst members that you have known, but think of the picture of stereotype that you have of the whole religion.

15. Emory S. Bogardus, *Immigration and Race Attitudes,* Boston: Heath, 1928.

3. Put a cross (x) after each religion in as many of the five columns as your feelings dictate.

Religious Groups	*Would have marriage relationships*	*Would have as regular friends*	*Would live in same neighbourhood*	*Would have mere speaking acquaintances*	*Would debar from my neighbourhood*
Christians					
Muslims					
Anglo-Indians					
Parsees					

Exhibit 8.3: A Social Distance Scale

Scoring: The most practical methods to assign arbitrarily values 1 to 5 to the scale items from left-end item through the right-end item (position). Then the percentage of responses to each group at each position may be multiplied by the value of that position. The sum of the values thus secured would be the score for the group. The groups can be assumed to stand in a rank order according to their scores. The Bogardus scale's assumption of equal intervals between scale points is questionable. The scale may not also satisfy the criterion of unidimensionality. However, reliability of the scale is found to be satisfactory, and there is also some positive evidence of its validity.

Item Analysis: Likert's Summated Scale

In the procedure of its analysis, each item is evaluated on the basis of how well it discriminates between those persons whose total score is high and those whole score is low. The most popular scale using this approach is Likert Scale of Summated rating.

Rensis Likert[16] was instrumental in developing Summated Rating scale based on item analysis. Likert Scale is by far the most popular of all measurement scales. It is meant for measuring ordinal attributes like attitudes. It is designed to measure the intensity with which an attitude is expressed.

This scale consists of a number of statements which express either a favourable or unfavourable attitude towards the object of study. The respondent is asked to respond to each statement in terms of 5 degrees of agreement (three and seven point scales are also used). A few examples from a job satisfaction scale developed by Brayfield and Rothe[17] are:

	Strongly Agree	*Agree*	*Undecided*	*Disagree*	*Strongly Disagree*
My Job is like a hobby to me	5	4	3	2	1
I consider my job rather unpleasant	1	2	3	4	5

The numbers in the above examples indicate the scale values for different degrees of agreement: "I" indicating the least favourable degree and "t" the most favourable. For positive statements 5 to 1 scores are assigned and for negative statements 1 to 5 scores are assigned. While administering,' these scores are not printed on the instrument; they are later adopted while computing the scores for respondents. Each person's response values are summed up to obtain his score. Hence, this scale is called "summated" scale.

16. Rensis Likert, "A Technique for the Measurement of Attitudes," *Archieves of Psychology,* No. 140, 1932.
17. A.H. Brayfield and H.F.Rothe, "An Index of Job Satisfaction," *Journal of Applied Psychology,* Vol. 35, No. 5, October 1951, pp. 307-11.

Procedure: The development of Likert-type scale consists of the following steps:

1. Compose an item pool of 50 or more statements relevant to the attitude being studied and expressing either favourable attitude or unfavourable attitude;
2. List the items (statements) in a five-point scale: Strongly agree, agree, undecided, disagree and strongly disagree; strongly approve, approve, undecided, disapprove, strongly disapprove;
3. Adminster the item pool to a sample of respondents, say 100 or more, who are similar to those who are going to be studied for the survey; ask them to check one of the five positions in the scale against each item;
4. Score the responses of each respondent to each item using scale value of 5 to 12 for a positive statement and 1 to 5 for a negative one;
5. Add up the item scores to obtain a total score for each respondent, for example, if there are 150 items in the item pool, then each respondent's total score will range from 150 to 750 (5 × 150);
6. Carry out an item analysis to decide which are the best statements for the final scale; one approach to item analysis is to calculate correlation co-efficients for each item with the total score (minus the score for the item in question), and to retain items with highest correlations. This is known as the internal consistency method of analysis.

   Here is an example. Suppose we want to make the analysis of item 9 in the item pool, the hypothetical scores of respondents can be tabulated as under:

   TABLE 8.2

   Analysis of Item 9 in the Item Pool

Respondent (*1*)	*Total Score* (*2*)	*Score on Item 9* (*3*)	*Total Score minus Item 9* (*4*)
A	145	5	140
B	142	5	137
C	135	4	131
D	135	4	131
E	120	2	118
F	140	4	136
G	133	3	130
H	139	4	135

   (*Note:* The correlation coefficient for figures in columns (3) and (4) will be calculated).

   Another approach to item analysis is: Array the total scores of respondents from the lowest to the highest scores; select the top 25 per cent of the scores and the bottom 25 per cent of scores; select the top 25 per extreme groups as criterion groups for evaluating individual statements; calculate the mean scores for each statement among the high scores and the low scores; Test the significance of difference between the item mean of the high-score group and that of the low-score group by calculating 't' value; retain items which have the greatest 't' values (i.e., high discriminatory power);
7. Select 20 to 25 items from among the retained items with the highest correlations or 't' values and design the final scale.

Items in the final scale have no scale values such as in the Thurstone scale; all items carry equal weights.

Likert's scale Vs. Thurstone's Scale: The Likert Scale is lesser laborious than the Thurstone Scale. Likert scale requires fewer items than Thurstone scale to reach a given level of reliability. Since respondents answer each item, the Likert scale is more reliable than the Thurstone scale and also provides a greater volume of data than does the latter. The Likerts' scale makes no pretence at equal-appearing intervals, but by using the internal consistency method of item selection it approaches unidimensionablity.

Advantages: The Likert scale has many advantages which account for its popularity. It s easy and quick to constract. It is easy to use this scale. It provides more precise information about a respondent's degree of agreement. It is unidimensional, i.e., all items measure the same thing. It does not require the use of judges. It is flexible. The researcher is at liberty to include as many or as few items in the scale. It lends itself to ordinal measurement.

Weaknesses or limitations: The most serious weakness of the Likert scale is its lack of reproducibility: the same total score may be obtained in many different ways. Hence, the raw score has little meaning or two or more identical scores may have totally different implications. Often, for this reason, the pattern of responses becomes more interesting than the total score.

Another limitation is that the scale offers no metric or interval measures. It also lacks a neutral point; one cannot know where scores in the middle, range from mildly negative.

It is assumed that all items in the Likert scale have equal weights. This is not necessarily a valid assumption. Certain statements compared with others may have greater meaning to a person. Different individuals may possess a given attitude to the same degree, yet they may respond differently to the item on the scale. Nevertheless, the Likert scale is highly reliable for rough ordering of people with regard to a particular attitude.

Rating Scale

Rating means measuring an attribute of objects or persons by judgement in a continuum. It gives a measure of one's actual position on the judgement continuum. For example, school marks or grades; performance appraisal rating of an employee in an organization.

Forms of rating scales: A rating scale may be either a graphic rating scale or an itemized scale.

Graphic rating scale: This is a common and simple form to use. In this form of scale, the judge checks response to an item along a continuum. For example, two items of graphic form taken from a teacher rating scale are:

You are asked to rate your teacher on the indicated qualities by placing a check mark (Ö) at the point on each line which best describes your feeling about him. Each line is a continuum, so you place your rating anywhere along the line.

1. Is the teacher interested in his subject?

Intensely interested	Mildly interested	Rather more disinterested than interested	Subject boring to him

2. How does the teacher act towards students?

Courteous	Considerate	Occasionally cutting	Sarcastic

Itemized scale: This form of rating scale presents a series of statements (5 to 7) from which a respondent selects one as best reflecting his evaluation. The statements, are listed in a graded manner. An example of an item taken from an employee rating scale is:

— How well does the employee get along with his fellow workers?

— He is almost always involved in some friction or argument with a fellow worker.

— He is often at odds with one or more of his fellow workers.

— He sometimes gets involved in friction.

— He rarely becomes involved in friction with others, definitely less often than most of the men.

— He almost never gets involved in friction situations with fellow workers.

This form is more difficult to develop, but provides more information and meaning to the rater.

Number of scale points: In designing a rating scale the number of scale points to use has to be decided. The general guideline is: more points on a scale provides for greater sensitivity of measurement and accommodates various shades of opinion. Often five to seven points are used. The choice between an odd or even number depends on whether or not respondents are to be forced to decide the direction of their attitude; with an odd number there is a middle item representing a neutral position, but with an even number, there is no middle point so that respondents are forced to decide the high or low side to which they belong.

Phrasing of degrees of judgement: Some of the common phrasings[18] used to indicate the degrees of judgement in surveys are:

Three-point Scales

Greater- Above average-	Equal- Average-	Less- Below average-

Four-point Scales

Many- Excellent- Highest-	Some- Good- Next highest-	Few- Fair- Next lowest-	None- Poor- Lowest-

Five-point Scales

Strongly approve- Much greater- Like very much-	Approve- Somewhat greater- Like somewhat-	Undecided- Neutral- Neutral-	Disapprove- Somewhat less- Dislike somewhat-	Strongly disapprove- Not at all- Dislike very much

Longer Scales

Good ┼┼┼┼┼┼┼┼┼┼┼┼┼┼ Bad

Modern ┼┼┼┼┼┼┼┼┼┼┼┼┼┼ Old

Fair ┼┼┼┼┼┼┼┼┼┼┼┼┼┼ Unfair

18. Mildred Parten, *Surveys, Polls and Samples: Practical Procedures,* New York: Harper & Brothers, 1950, pp. 190-92.

When objective assessment is wanted, it is dangerous to give such labels as 'frequently', 'moderately', 'often', etc.

Problems in using rating scales: The respondents' ratings may be subject to some errors like the error of central tendency, leniency and halo effect.

First, the respondents may avoid extreme positions and this leads to the error of central tendency. Measures to counteract this error are: (1) to make sure that raters have the necessary information, (2) to adjust the strength of descriptive adjectives, (3) to provide greater differences in meaning between steps near the ends of the scale than between the steps near the centre, and (4) to use more points in the scale.

Second, certain respondents may be "easy" raters and cause the error of leniency, while others may be "hard" raters who may commit the error of severity. One way to deal with the tendency to positive leniency is to adopt an asymmetrical scale with one unfavourable descriptive term and four favourable terms (poor, fair, good, very good, excellent).

The third major problem is the halo effect, i.e., the systematic bias arising out of the respondent's overall feeling of like or dislike, e.g., if a respondent likes a particular make of T.V., he will give it high rating for all its characteristics such as performance, appearance, picture clarity etc. One way to counteract halo is to rate one trait at a time for al subjects or to have one trait per page rather than one subject per page.

Another serious danger lies in the ease with the respondents can be influenced by variables which they are not aware of. For example, when a child is rated by his teacher on attributes like imitability, shyness, obedience etc., we may find differences because the teacher unknowingly compares him with other children, i.e., the rates have different frame of references. The respondents are also influenced by what they think is the purpose of rating procedure.

Uses: The ratings may be used (1) as objective assessments, e.g., ratings of the quality of furnishings in a home by the interviewer, (2) in a subjective projective way to tell us something about the rater, his perception, and his attitude, and (3) as self-rating of personality traits or attitudes. Rating scales are widely used in business research, psychological studies and opinion surveys.

Merits: The results obtained with careful use of ratings scales compare favourably with alternative methods. They are simple to design and operate; they require less time; and they are more sensitive and informative than a straight yes/no choice of answers. They may be used with a large number of attributes or variables.

Ranking Scale

A ranking scale is meant for arranging objects or persons in order from most to least with regard to some attribute, e.g., ranking students according to their performance in an examination, paintings in the order or merit, two wheelers in the order of fuel efficiency, etc. The basis on which ranking is done should be stated clearly.

Ranking tells us the order or sequence, but does not indicate the differences or 'distances' between ranks.

Methods of ranking: There are several methods of ranking: (1) Simple ranking, (2) Paired comparison method, (3) Method of Successive categories.

Simple ranking: In this method, the respondents are asked to rank their choices, as 1, 2, 3.... For example, in a consumer survey, respondents may be asked to rank to attributes of an automobile car, which they consider while choosing a particular brand:

Attributes	**Ranks (1, 2....)**
Price	...
Fuel efficiency	...
Riding comfort	...
Seating capacity	...
Appearance	...
Maker's image	...

The ranks may be assigned score values in the reverse order, i.e., if six items/stimuli are to be ranked, the first rank is assigned a score of 6, the second rank, a score of 5.... And the sixth rank a score of '1'. In order to study the relative importance given to the attributes, for each attribute, the rank values may be multiplied by the corresponding frequencies (number of respondents) and summed up. The total scores indicate the comparative rankings of attributes (see Table 8.3).

TABLE 8.3

Frequency Distribution of Ranks Marked by Respondents (Hypothetical)

N = (say) 100

Ranks Attributes	*First* *S.V.6*	*Second* *5*	*Third* *4*	*Fourth* *3*	*Fifth* *2*	*Sixth* *1*	*Total*	*Rank*
Price	20 × 6	40 × 5	15 × 4	10 × 3	8 × 2	7 × 1	403	4
Fuel efficiency	40 × 6	20 × 5	20 × 4	9 × 3	8 × 2	3 × 1	406	1
Riding comfort	30 × 6	25 × 5	20 × 4	20 × 3	3 × 2	2 × 1	453	2
Seating capacity	15 × 6	10 × 5	30 × 4	35 × 3	5 × 2	5 × 1	380	5
Appearance	25 × 6	20 × 5	40 × 4	10 × 3	2 × 2	3 × 1	447	3
Maker's image	10 × 6	15 × 5	20 × 4	30 × 3	10 × 2	15 × 1	360	6

Note: S.V = Scale value.

The method of simple ranking is usually easier and more motivating to the respondents, but the number of stimuli to be handled should be less than 5 or six, because respondents may grow quite careless in ranking more items. Further, the rank ordering is an ordinal scale with all of its limitations.

Paired comparison method: In this method, stimuli are presented in pairs to judges and the judges are asked to select the better one in each pair. For example, a sample of 100 persons may be asked to select the more desirable occupation for women from each of the pairs. The five occupations to be considered are: office employee (A), nurse (B), sales woman (C), farm laborer (D), and domestic servant (E). The 10 pairs of the occupations are so arranged that each occupation appeared first in pairs as many times as it appears second. No occupation is repeated in any two succeeding pairs. The pairs are:

1. Farm labourer (D): Nurse (B)
2. Domestic Servant (E): Office employee (A)

3. Nurse (B): Sales women (C)
4. Office employee (A): Farm labourer (D)
5. Sales woman (C): Domestic servant (E)
6. Nurse (B): Office employee (A)
7. Sales woman (C): Farm labourer (D)
8. Domestic servant (E): Nurse (B)
9. Office employee (A): Sales woman (C)
10. Farm labourer (D): Domestic servant (E)

(*Note:* Each respondent will prefer one from each of the ten pairs. Hence, the total preference of 100 respondents will be 100 ×10 = 1,000).

TABLE 8.4

Response Patterns of 100 Persons' Paired Comparison of Five Occupations for Women

Occupations	*Number of respondents preferring occupations*					*Total*
	A	*B*	*C*	*D*	*E*	
A	—	82 *	69	25	35	211
B	18	—	27	07	15	67
C	31	73	—	16	25	145
D	75	93	84	—	59	311
E	65	85	75	41	—	266
Total	189	333	255	89	134	1000
Rank order	3	1	2	5	4	
M_p	.478	.766	.610	.278	.368	
Z_j	–.06	.73	.28	–.59	–.34	
R_j	.65	1.32	.87	.00	.25	

* Read 82 respondents preferred occupation B (column) to occupation A (row).

The Data may also be Tabulated as under

Occupations	*Number of preferences*	*Rank*
A	189	3
B	333	1
C	255	2
D	89	5
E	134	4
Total	1,000	

The consistency in responses must be examined. For instance, if occupation B is preferred to C, and C is preferred to D, then B will be preferred to D, but if occupation D is preferred to C or B, the response is then inconsistent. Such inconsistencies may be rectified/eliminated. The hypothetical data of preferences of 100 respondents are shown in Table 8.4.

By a comparison of the total number of preferences stated for each occupation, it is apparent that B is the most popular.

While a paired-comparison provides ordinal data, Guilford[19] has developed a method by which such data may be coveted into an interval scale. It is called the comparative-standard method and is illustrated here.

The steps involved are: First, using the data in Table 8.4, the columns are calculated using the equation:

$$M_p = \frac{P + .5N}{nN} = \frac{189 + .5(100)}{5 \times 100} = 0.478$$

Where

M_p = the mean proportion of the columns

P = the total number of preferences for a given stimulus

n = number of stimuli

N = Number of respondents

Guilford points out, "The correction .5N in the numerator is for the assumed number of choices the stimulus would have received if it had been compared with itself.... It is assumed that the standard is the composite of all the stimuli in the series and that M_p is the proportion of times any given stimulus is chosen in preference to that standard."[20]

The calculated means are shown in Table 8.4. The Z values for M_p are secured from the normal curve tables. When the proportion (M_p) is less than 0.5 the Z value is negative, while all proportions over 0.5 are positive. These values are also shown in Table 8.4 as "Z_j." Since this scale is an interval scale the zero is an arbitrary value. We can eliminate negative scale values by giving the value of zero to the lowest scale value and then adding the absolute value of this lowest scale value to all other items. (D: -.59 = .0; A:.06 + 0.59 + .65; B.73 + .59 = 1.32; C:.28 + .59 = .87; E: .59 -.34 = -.25)

This scale (R_j) is shown in Exhibit 8.4.

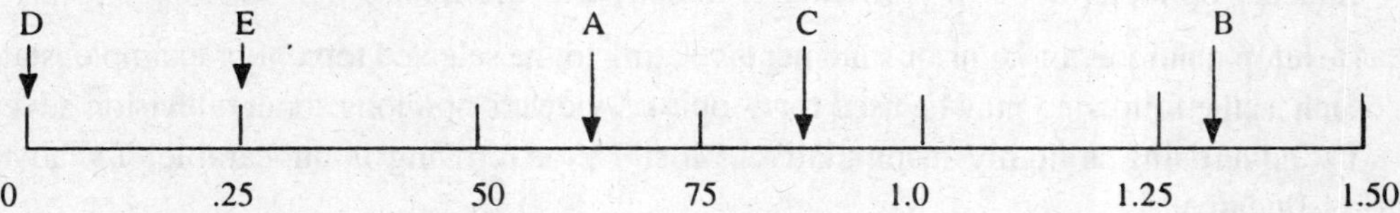

Interval scale derived from Paired Comparison Data using the Composite-standard method.

Exhibit 8.4

Method of successive intervals: When the number of items to be considered is large, this method is used. In this method, the subject is asked to sort the items (usually one per card) into 7 or 11 categories ranging from "most favourable" to "least favourable." From these sorting an interval scale can be developed. (See *"Judgement Scaling"*, above).

Ranking scales are used for stimulus-centred scaling. They are also the response form of choice with all types of scale construction techniques.

19. J.P. Guilford, *Psychometric Methods,* New York: McGraw-Hill Book Company, 1954.
20. *Ibid.*, p. 170.

Cumulative Scale of Scalogram: Guttman Scale

Under this method, from a respondent's total score, it is possible to know which items he has answered positively. This method was developed by Guttman[21] for scaling qualitative data.

Scalogram analysis is a procedure for determining the unidimensionality and reproducibility of a set of items. A scale is unidimensional if the responses fall into a pattern in which endorsement of the item reflecting the extreme position results also in endorsing all items which are less extreme. If there are, say, five items in a scale, representing different degrees of favourable attitude and if a respondent agrees to the 'most favourable' statement, he also agrees to the other statements. In such a scale, from a respondent's score we know exactly which items (or statements) he endorsed. This quality of reproducing the responses to each item, knowing only the total score is called reproducibility.

Likert and Thurstone scale also contain items associated with the attitude in question, but they do not necessarily form a unidimensional scale. Different respondents may have the same score and yet react differently to the different dimensions of the scale. For example, A and B may secure identical job satisfaction score. A may like his pay, and type of supervision, but he may dislike the nature of the job and his work group. On the other hand, B may like the challenge of the work, and his work group, but may dislike his pay, and type of supervision. Thus, a given total score can be secured by widely divergent answer patterns, bringing the meaning of the total score into question. This problem is best met by using scalogram.

Guttman and his associates have developed four techniques of scale analysis to determine the unidimensionality of an attitude scale. Of them, the "Cornell" Technique of scalaogram analysis[22] is the best-known and most useful one.

Steps: The Cornell Technique involves the following steps.[23]

1. Define the universe of content with reference to the problem under study, e.g., people's attitude towards a minority social group; people's opinions about television advertising, students opinions about a particular textbook; and the like.
2. Develop a number of items or statements relating to the selected topic. For example, statements such as the following may be used for a topic on viewers opinions about television advertising; TV advertising is highly manipulative. Most TV advertising is unbearable. TV advertising is educative.
3. Pre-test the statements to determine whether the topic is scalable. (Guttman suggests that a pre-test should include 12 or more items and 20 or 30 respondents, but the final scale testing should involve 100 or more respondents).
4. Ask pre-test respondents to record their opinions on all items (statements, using "agree'disagree." (Yes/No) scale or 3 or five point scale ranging from "strongly agree" to "strongly disagree."
5. Tabulate the responses giving one score for each 'Yes' answer (see Table 8.5).

---

21. Louis Guttman, "A Basis for Scaling Qualitative Data," *American Sociological Review*, Vol. 9, 1944, pp. 139-50.
22. Louis Guttman, "The Cornell Techniques for Scale and Intensity analysis," *Educational and Psychological Measurement*, Vol. 7, 1947, pp. 247-280.
23. For an Excellent Manual on Unidimensional Scale, see Raymond L. Gordon, *Unidimensional Scaling of Social Variables*, Riverside N.J., Free Press, 1977.

TABLE 8.5
Model Table for Pre-test Responses

Respondents \ Items		*1*	*2*	*3*	*4*	*5*	*6*	*7*	*8*	*Score*
A	..	1	1	1	1	1	—	.1	—	6
B	..	1	—	—	—	1	—	1	1	4
C	..	1	1	—	—	1	—	1	1	5
D	..	—	—	—	—	1	—	1	—	2
E	..	1	—	—	—	1	—	1	—	3
F	,,	1	—	—	—	1	—	1	1	4
G	..	1	1	—	1	1	1	1	1	7
H	..	1	—	—	1	1	—	1	—	4
I	..	1	1	—	1	1	1	1	1	7
J	..	1	1	—	1	1	—	1	1	6
K	..	—	—	—	—	—	—	—	1	1
L	..	—	—	—	—	—	—	1	—	1
Total (yes)		9	5	1	5	10	2	11	7	

6. Rearrange the table, by placing the respondents in the order of their total scores from top to bottom, and the statements in the order of the number of yes-answers from left to right (see Table 8.6).

TABLE 8.6
Rearranged model Table of responses

Respondents \ Items	*7*	*5*	*1*	*8*	*2*	*4*	*6*	*3*	*Score*
G	1	1	1	1	1	1	1	-	7
I	1	1	1	1	1	1	1	-	7
A	1	1	1	-	1	1	-	1	6
J	1	1	1	1	1	1	-	-	6
C	1	1	1	1	1	-	-	-	5
B	1	1	1	1	-	-	-	-	4
F	1	1	1	1	-	-	-	-	4
H	1	1	1	-	-	1	-	-	4
E	1	1	1	-	-	-	-	-	3
D	1	1	-	-	-	-	-	-	2
K	-	-	-	1	-	-	-	-	1
L	1	-	-	-	-	-	-	-	1

7. Locate any deviations from the perfect scale pattern. For example, respondent H has given a yes-response to item 4 instead of the item 8. Similarly A and K show deviations. Such deviations are called "errors."
8. Calculate the coefficient of reproducibility in order to test the unidimensionality. The formula suggested by Guttman is:

$$\text{Reproducibility} = 1 - \frac{\text{No. of errors}}{\text{No. of responses}}$$

(The number of responses = No. of items × the number of respondents).

If the reproducibility is below 0.9 then the scale is not considered unidimensional.
9. Discard statements at the tail to discriminate between favourable and unfavourable respondents, i.e., items with errors. For instance, in the above illustration we may drop items 8 and 3.
10. Discard also items with less than 20 percent or more than 80% endorsement in order to guard against spuriously high estimates of reproducibility.
11. If two or more items have the same popularity, retain one of them and drop others. It is appropriate to choose items with popularities close to 20, 40, 60 and 80 per cent.

Customarily, scalogram analysis is carried out on one or more samples of 100 each. The number of items tested may be several dozen. After repeated trials they are whittled down to 4 to 8 items that from the final scale. The above procedure is naturally very tedious and fraught with errors. This is led to the development of scalogram boards by Guttman and others. These are mechanical devices that enable us to move whole columns of responses in one operation, without needing to rewrite the whole matrix. The use of scalogram boards has been described in detail by Suchman.[24]

Advantages: Scalogram analysis has several advantages.

1. It assures unidimensionality of items in measuring attitude.
2. A person's response pattern can be reproduced, given his total score on the scale.
3. The scale is determined by respondents, not by researcher's subjective judgement.
4. As the final scale contains a small number of items, it is easy to administer it.
5. The scale is highly reliable, as a rule.

Disadvantages: Some of the disadvantages of scalogram are:

1. The task of designing this scale is both tedious and complex.
2. It is not suitable for measuring attitude towards complex variables like job satisfaction with several dimensions.
3. The criterion of reproducibility insisted by Guttman is valuable, but not an essential property.
4. The standard or reproducibility (a coefficient of not less than 0.9) set by Guttman is some what arbitrary.
5. The scale does not have equal or equal-appearing intervals.

24. See Chapter 4 by Suchman in Stouffer S.A., and Others, *Measurement and Prediction,* New York: John Wiley & Sons, 1950.

6. There is no guarantee that the items will scale and that items that do scale generally cover a narrow universe of content, as the item analysis may lead to the rejection of items in a way that leaves a scale of homogeneous items.

Application: In view of the above limitations, Guttman scale is perhaps more appropriate for scaling ordered behaviour like attitude towards minorities, students' reactions to the teaching process etc., than less structured and broader based attitudes.

Factor Scaling

This is another basic scale construction technique developed to identify the multi-dimensions of a complex attitude. The factor-analysis is a statistical technique based on inter-correlations among all the items in a scale in order to uncover the underlying (latent) dimensions or factors. There are three types of factors: (1) a general factor that contributes to all the items in the scale, (2) a group factor contributes to two or more, but not to all items; and (3) a specific factor contributes to just one item. The group and general factors are termed common factors. (See chapter 11 for illustration).

Uses:[25] Factor-analysis is used to examine a set of developed attitude items in order to eliminate items that do not belong and to keep items that have high loadings on the attitude to be measured. It is also used to show how a seemingly unified attitude complex in fact "breaks up" into several independent factors.

When applied to a single scale, it can throw light on its unidimensionality. When applied to a battery of scales administered to the same respondents, it can reveal their similarities and differences and the underlying attitudes or value systems as well. For instance, Eysenck[26] shows that opinions on sovereignty, abortion law, corporal punishment, and religious education have the same underlying attitude structures. Factor-analysis then becomes a tool for theoretical investigation and new discoveries.

Factor-analysis is widely used with Likert and Semantic Differential items at the pilot study in order to examine the dimensions of the attitude under study.

Limitation: Factor-analysis is a laborious process. For instance, a factor-analysis of a pool of only 20 items would involve as a first step computation of 190 correlation co-efficients. Often, therefore, it is applied not to the original items pool, but to a finished scale.

Semantic Differential Scale (SD Scale)

This scaling method, based on factor-analysis, was developed by Osgood[27] and his associates. It attempts to measure the psychological meanings of a concept to individuals. It is based on the proposition that a concept (e.g., father, Mahatma Gandhi, United Nations, Socialism) can have several implied meanings that can be located in multidimensional semantic space.

The SD method consists of a set of bipolar rating scales, usually seven-point, by which groups of subjects are asked to rate one or more concepts relevant to the selected research problem. Examples of scale items are:

25. A.C. McKennell, *Some Uses of Factor Analysis in Social Survey Work*, London: Government Social Survey (No. M.125), 1966.
26. H.J. Eysenck, *The Psychology of Politics*, London: Poutledge and Kegans Paul, 1954.
27. Charles F. Osgood, *et al.*, *Measurement of Meaning*, Urbana: The University of Illinois Press, 1957.

good	——:	——:	——:	——:	——:	——:	——:	Bad
strong	——:	——:	——:	——:	——:	——:	——:	Weak
fast	——:	——:	——:	——:	——:	——:	——:	Slow

Subjects are asked to place a check-mark in one of the spaces on each scale to indicate their rating of the concept's position with respect to the objectives involved. The positions are assigned scores 1 to 7.

Factors or dimensions: Each scale measures one or two or three major underlying dimensions or factors, viz., Evaluation, Potency, Activity. These may be called clusters of adjectives.

Adjective-pairs may be evaluative, share strength (or potency) ideas or express motion and action (or Activity). Examples of adjective pairs identified with these factors are:

Evaluation	Potency	Activity
Good – bad	Large – small	Active – passive
Positive – negative	Hard – soft	Fast – slow
Clean – dirty	Strong – weak	Hot – cold

Osgood gives a list of 50 scales with their factor identifications. Researchers can develop scales using these and other appropriate adjective pairs.

Steps: The construction of SD scale involves the following steps:

1. Select the concepts to be studied in terms of the nature of the research problem: concepts tend to be nouns or noun phrases. E.g., for studying educational environments as perceived by teachers, we may use concepts like school, pupil, teaching, head master/principal, discipline. Concepts must elicit varied responses from different individuals and they should cover, to some extent, the semantic space.
2. Select the appropriate scales or adjective pairs. The criteria for selecting scales are:
   (a) *Factor composition to the concepts used:* The common practice is to use at least three adjective pairs for each factor or dimension and to calculate an average factor score.
   (b) *Relevance of scales to the concepts:* It is important to choose adjectives that permit connotative perceptions, e.g., adjective pairs like good-bad, young-old, lovable-hatable are suitable for a concept of 'Father', pairs like original stereotyped, systematic disorganized, responsible-irresponsible may be relevant to the concept 'Teacher.'
   (c) Scales should be *stable* across subjects and concepts.
   (d) Scales should be *linear* between polar opposites, e.g., a pair like "rugged – delicate" fails this test, because it is non-linear relative to evaluation.
3. Use a separate page for each concept. Write the title of the concept at the top and list under it the adjective pairs in mix-up order in relation to the factors and reverse polar adjectives at random to counteract response bias tendencies. See the illustration given below:

LEADERSHIP

(E)	Sociable	.	.	.	.	.	.	Unsociable
(P)	Weak	.	.	.	.	.	.	Strong
(A)	Active	.	.	.	.	.	.	Passive
(E)	Progressive	.	.	.	.	.	.	Regressive
(P)	Yielding	.	.	.	.	.	.	Tenacious
(A)	Slow	.	.	.	.	.	.	Fast
(E)	True	.	.	.	.	.	.	False
(P)	Heavy	.	.	.	.	.	.	Light
(A)	Hot	.	.	.	.	.	.	Cold
(E)	Unsuccessful	.	.	.	.	.	.	Successful

The letters before the adjective pairs indicate the factors: Evaluation (E), Potency (P), and Activity (A). In the actual scale the letters should be omitted.

Concepts to the rated may be single words like "Teacher", "School', "Socialism" or phrases like "the kind of person you are," "by what you think they mean to teachers."

4. *Develop the scoring plan:* To give a score of 7 to 1 or 1 to 7 to scales depending on the order in which they run, starting the unfavourable and with '1', and ending the favourable end with '7' e.g.,

Good	7:	6:	5:	4:.	3:	2:	1	Bad
Weak	1:	2:	3:	4:	5:	6:	7	Strong

A scoring system of + 3, + 2, + 1, 0, – 1, – 2, – 3, may also be used. This has the advantage of having zero at the neutral point. But this advantage is more than offset by the disadvantage of dealing with negative numbers.

A respondent's total score is the measure of his attitude. Thus, SD like a Likert scale is a summated rating scale.

The average of the scores of a group of individuals will represent the concept mean. The difference between the concept means may be tested by tests of significance. A more detailed analysis can also be made using factor or cluster analysis to measure the different dimensions involved.

Application or uses: SD technique is widely used in brand image and other marketing studies, institutional images, political issues and personalities, organization morale, attitude-conditioning studies, study of emotions, measurement of attitudes and values.

Advantages: The SD has several advantages. It is an efficient and easy method of studying attitudes of a large sample of respondents. It is a standardized technique and free from the problems of response distortion. "It is good, it is active, it is potent."[28]

Attitude Scales

An attitude is a tendency to act or react in a certain manner when confronted with certain stimuli. It is the degree of positive or negative feelings about an object or issue. Attitude is not directly observable, but is inferred from one's behaviour, both verbal and non-verbal. It can be

28. J. Carroll's, *Review of The Measurement of Meaning,* by Cosgood and others, in Language, XXXV, 1959, p. 77.

described by its content (what the attitude about), by its direction (positive, neutral or negative feelings about the object or issue in question) and by its intensity..

An attitude is said to have three components:

(1) An affective component consisting of an individual's feelings about the object in question.

(2) A cognitive component which refers to an individual's knowledge about the object, and

(3) A behavioural component which is the individual's predispositions to act towards the attitude object in a particular way.

Attitudes are measured by attitude scales consisting of 5 to 25 attitude statements with which the respondents are asked to agree or disagree. An attitude cannot be measured by a single statement, because it may give rather one-sided result, but by having several statements we can reduce one-side effects.

Attitude scales are relatively crude measuring instruments and their main function is to divide the respondents into a number of broad groups with regard to a particular attitude. "Such scales cannot by themselves be expected to provide us with subtle insights in an individual case. They are techniques for placing people on a continuum in relation to one another, in relative and not in absolute terms."[29]

The major types of scales for measuring attitudes are (a) Likert Scale, (b) Thurstone Scale, (c) Cumulative Scale (Guttman Scale) and (d) Semantic Differential Scale. These scales have been discussed in detail in the previous pages of this Chapter.

Each method has important desirable features. If we wish to study the attitude-patterning or explore theories of attitudes, the Likert Scale is the most relevant. If we wish to study the hierarchical structure of an attitude then Guttman's scale is preferable. If we study group differences, then Thurstone method is preferable.

Attitude scales and Prediction of behaviour: Can attitude scales predict behaviour? Behaviour does not have a simple one-to-one relationship with one type of inner determinant as attitude. Behaviour is a complex factor and it is a function of the interaction between a person's all inner determinants such as temperament, attitudes or character traits and all the environmental factors perceived by him. Behaviour has a complex relationship with its various inner determinants because of the influence of perceived environmental factors. Therefore, we cannot use it as a measure of index of inner determinants and we cannot accurately infer attitudes from behaviour. For the same reasons, we cannot predict over behaviour merely from one determinant such as a score on an attitude scale. Other determinants including conflicting attitudes and effects of environmental factors may play a part. For example, an attitude scale may indicate a person's inclinations towards cheating, but he would probably act honestly if he thinks he will be found out. "Behaviour is a compromise, a resultant of the interaction of multiple forces."[30]

Socio-economic Status Scale

The measurement of socio-economic status of individuals or families is of much importance, since this status is correlated with several variables like opinions, attitudes, family welfare practices, voting behaviour, value system and others. This scale may cover such socio-economic indicators as

29. A.N. Oppenheim, *op. cit,* p. 121.
30. *Ibid.*, p. 153.

ritual status (high, medium and low caste), social participation (membership and positions in social organizations), educational status, occupational ranking, source of income, annual income, net wealth, living environment (type of house, built-in-area, facilities in house, etc), and other material possessions.

In scoring the various items, arbitrary values may be assigned. For example, if a certain factor like telephone is present, it is given a value of '1' and if it does not exist, it is assigned a value of 'O'. In cases where the factor is graduated into levels, an arbitrary value is assigned to each level. For example, educational status graded into (a) illiterate, (b) up to primary level, (c) up to secondary, (d) graduate, (e) post-graduate and the values of 0, 1, 2, 3 and 4 respectively may be assigned to them.

8.4 PILOT STUDIES AND PRE-TESTS

Pilot Study

The need for pilot study: It is difficult to plan a major study or project without adequate knowledge of its subject matter, the population it is to cover, their level of knowledge and understanding and the like. What are the issues involved? What are the concepts associated with the subject matter? How can they be operationalized? What method of study is appropriate? How long the study will take? How much money it will cost? These and other related questions call for a good deal of knowledge of the subject matter of the study and its dimensions. In order to gain such pre-knowledge of the subject matter of an extensive study, a preliminary investigation is conducted. This is called a pilot study.

Meaning: A pilot study is a "small scale replica"[31] of the main study. It is the rehearsal of the main study. It covers the entire process of research: Preparation of a broad plan of the study, construction of tools, collection of data, processing and analysis of data and report-writing.

Functions of a Pilot Study

A pilot study fulfils one or more of the following purposes:

1. It provides a better knowledge of the problem under study and its dimensions.
2. It provides guidance on conceptualization – identification and operationalization of concepts relating to the study.
3. It assists in discovering the nature of relationship between variables and in formulating hypothesis.
4. It shows the nature of the population to be surveyed and the variability within it. This is of importance in determining an efficient sample design.
5. A pilot study shows whether the available sampling frame from which sampling is to be drawn is adequate, complete, accurate, up to date and convenient.
6. It provides data on the relative suitability of alternative methods of collection of data - observation, mailing, interviewing – their relative cost, accuracy and response rates to make a sensible choice.
7. It shows the adequacy of the tool for data collection.
8. It also helps in discovering mechanical problems relating to interviews/mailing.
9. It assists in developing better approaches to target population – as regards introduction, rapport etc.

31. C.A. Moser and G. Kalton, *Survey Methods in Social Investigation, op. cit.*, p. 48.

10. It provides information for structuring questions with alternative answers.
11. It helps the researcher to develop an appropriate plan of analysis.
12. It enables the researcher to identify field problems to be encountered and suggests remedial approaches.
13. It provides information for estimating the probable cost and duration of the main study and of its various stages.
14. Above all, it helps the researcher to determine whether or not a more substantial study is warranted. In the light of the results of the pilot study, the researcher will be able to take a pragmatic view on the main study's potentialities and feasibility.

Size and Design of Pilot Study

The size, scope and design of the pilot study is a matter of convenience, time and money. It should be large enough to fulfill the above functions and the sample should be of a comparable structure to that of the main study. It should be designed so as to ensure a testing of alternative methods of data collection, ordering the questions, wording and the like. It should succeed in disclosing the significant difficulties to be guarded against.

In the light of the outcome of the pilot study, if it is found that the main study is worth undertaking, then it is adequately designed on the basis of the results of the pilot study and the lessons drawn from its experience.

Pre-test

Meaning: While a pilot study is a full-fledged miniature study of a problem, pre-test is a trial test of a specific aspect of the study such as method of data collection or data collection instrument – interview schedule, mailed questionnaire of measurement scale.

Need for Pre-testing

An instrument of data collection is designed with reference to the data requirements of the study.[32] But it cannot be perfected purely on the basis of a critical scrutiny by the designer and other researchers. It should be empirically tested. As emphatically pointed by Goode and Hatt, "no amount of thinking, no matter how logical the mind or brilliant the insight, is likely to take the place of careful empirical checking."[33] Hence pre-testing of a draft instrument is indispensable. Pre-testing means trial administration of the instrument to a sample of respondents before finalizing it.

Purposes of Pre-testing

Pre-testing has several purposes: (1) to test whether the instrument would elicit responses required to achieve the research objectives, (2) to test whether the content of the instrument is relevant and adequate, (3) to test whether wording of questions is clear and suited to the understanding of the respondents, (4) to test the other qualitative aspects of the instrument like question structure and question sequence, and (5) to develop appropriate procedure for administering the instrument with reference to field conditions.

---

32. See 8.2 *Construction of Schedules and Questionnaries,* above.
33. William J.Goode and Paul K. Hatt, *Methods in Social Research, op. cit,* p. 145.

Pre-test Procedure

A broad guideline is suggested below for pre-testing of an instrument. The first testing of a draft instrument can be done among one's colleagues in order to find out its shortcomings. After this "in-house" testing, it should be revised and tested in the field. The instrument may be administered to 15 or 20 sample respondents drawn from the universe relating to the planned survey. They may be interviewed or copies of the instrument mailed to them, depending on the method selected for data collection. Test mailings are useful, but it is quicker to use a substitute procedure. That is, copies of the draft questionnaires may be handed over to a few respondents with a request to complete them. The researcher may meet them later and request them to comment on question clarity and other aspects of the questionnaire. This appeal for advice may elicit their cooperation, and the researcher can get constructive suggestions for revising the questionnaire. Whatever be the mode of pre-testing, it is important to conduct the field test under actual field conditions.

The pre-test responses should be carefully examined and analysed in order to identify the weaknesses of the instrument. The researcher should look for signs or indicators of weaknesses. As pointed by Goode and Hatt,[34] the signs may include: (1) lack of order in the answer which may be caused by a poor conceptualization; (2) "all-or-none" responses, i.e., questions eliciting mere stereotyped responses; (3) a high proportion of "don't know" or "don't understand" answers, which indicate that the questions are improperly drawn or vague or a bad sampling design has been used; (4) a great number of qualifications or irrelevant comments, indicating the inadequate listing of alternative answers; (5) a high proportion of refusals to answer indicating out of context of the question or poor transition from one subject area to another; (6) inconsistencies in answers, (7) problem of space and the like.

Necessary corrections, deletions, additions and changes in question wording and sequences should be made to eliminate the imperfections discovered.

Often, several pre-testing with different sets of new respondents are required until a workable instrument is achieved. The importance of 'rest-revise' retest cycle' needs no emphasis. Any failure to take this step will lead to poor research results. Testing is the hallmark of a scientific research.'

SUGGESTED READINGS

1. Berdie, Douglas R., and Anderson, John F., *Questionnaire: Design and Use,* Metuchen, N.J.: The Scarecrow Press, 1974.
2. Bonjean, Charles M., *et al., Sociological Measurement: An inventory of Scales and Indices,* San Francisco: Candler Publishing Company, 1967.
3. Cantril, H., ed., *Gauging Public Opinion,* Princeton: Princeton University Press, 1944.
4. Edwards, A.L., *Techniques of Attitude Scale Construction,* New York: Appleton-Century-Crofts, 1957.
5. Guilford, J.P., *Psychometric Methods,* New York: McGraw-Hill Book Co., 1936.
6. Harman, H.H., *Modern Factor Analysis,* Chicago: University of Chicago Press, 1967.
7. Jahoda M., and Warren, N., eds., *Attitudes: Selected Readings,* Harmonds Work, Middlesex: Penguin Books, 1966.
8. Kahn, R.L., and Cannell, C.F., *The Dynamics of Interviewing: Theory, Technique and Cases,* New York: John Wiley & Sons, 1957.

34. *Ibid.*, pp. 157-161.

9. Miller, Delbert C., *Handbook of Research Design and Social Measurement,* New York: Longman, 1983.
10. Oppenheim, A.N., *Questionnaire Design and Attitude Measurement,* London: Heinemann Educational Books, 1973.
11. Osgood, Charles E., *et.al.. The Measurement of Meaning,* Urbana, III: University of **Illinois**, 1971.
12. Parten, Milred, *Surveys, Polls and Samples: Practical Procedures,* New York: Harper & Brothers. Publishers, 1950.
13. Payne, S.L.B., *The Art of Asking Questions,* Princeton: University Press, 1951.
14. Richardson, S.A., *et.al., Interviewing: Its Forms and Functions,* New York: Basic Books, 1965.
15. Stouffer, S.A., and others, *Measurement and Prediction,* Princeton: University Press, 1950.
16. Summers, G.F., ed., *Attitude Measurement,* Chicago: Rand McNally & Co., 1970.
17. Thurstone, L.L., and Chave, E.J., *The Measurement of Attitudes,* Chicago: University of Chicago Press, 1929.
18. Torgerson, W.S., *Theory and Methods of Scaling,* New York: John Wiley & Sons, 1958.
19. Zeisel, Hans, *Say it with Figures,* New York: Harper & Brothers, Publishers, 1957.

QUESTIONS

1. Describe the functions of data collection tools.
2. Distinguish between observationnaire and checklist.
3. Differentiate between interview guide and interview schedule.
4. What is an inventory? What are its uses?
5. Distinguish between Schedule and Questionnaire.
6. What are the major steps involved in the process of construction of a schedule/questionnaire?
7. What are the major decision areas involved in question construction?
8. What are the tests to be passed by any question to be included in a schedule/questionnaire?
9. What should be the characteristics to be possessed by words chosen for question construction?
10. How can one go about finding the best wording for a question on a questionnaire?
11. Examine the major problem areas of question wording.
12. State the various kinds of questions. Briefly describe each of them with an example.
13. What are the factors which determine the choice between open and closed questions in questionnaire construction?
14. In what situations is the open-ended question most useful?
15. What special problems do open-ended questions have? How can these be minimized?
16. State the requirements of multiple-choice questions?
17. List and describe the types of questions to be avoided with examples.
18. Below are five questions which might be found on questionnaires. Comment on each as to whether or not it is a good question. If nct, tell why?

    (a) Do you read the Reader's Digest regularly?

    (b) What per cent of your time is spent on attending meeting in your organization?

    (c) How much discretionary buying power do you have per year?

(d) When did you **first start** smoking?

(e) Why did you change to a Maruthi car?

19. What is the order in which questions are listed in an instrument important?
20. Should the questions' sequence decision be determined by the needs of analysis or by the logic of the respondent?
21. What are the principles governing sequence of questions on a schedule?
22. What are your suggestions regarding overall sequence in an instrument?
23. Discuss the two general patterns of intra sequence in questionnaires.
24. Describe the meaning and the objective of funnel sequence in arranging questions on an instrument.
25. How would you evaluate the questions constructed when designing an instrument?
26. How does the construction of questions to determine the 'reasons for' an action or opinion pose a challenge to the question designer?
27. Develop an accounting scheme to determine why organizations depute their managers for manager development programmes.
28. Construct a schedule/questionnaire for one of the following surveys:

    (a) TV viewers' opinions on weekly program on 'Mahabharat.'

    (b) Political affiliation of college students.
29. Discuss the various aspects of mechanics of a schedule/questionnaire.
30. What are the major characteristics of a good instrument?
31. How is an arbitrary scale constructed? What are its merits and demerits?
32. Describe the procedure of constructing a Thurstone attitude scale.
33. Thurstone Scale is a judgement scale, a differential scale and a method of equal-appearing intervals. Justify this description.
34. What is a Social Distance Scale? How is it constructed?
35. What is the nature of Likert type rating scale? Why is it called a scale of summated rating?
36. How is 'item analysis' made in a scale construction?
37. How is a Likert-type scale developed?
38. Compare and contrast Likert-type scale with Thurstone scale.
39. What are the advantages and limitations of a Likert Scale?
40. Which method - Thurstone scale or Likert scale would you recommend for constructing a 'political morality' attitude scale?
41. What is a rating scale? In what alternate forms can it be designed? What are its merits and demerits?
42. Examine the problems in using rating scales and discuss how can they be overcome.
43. One of the problems in developing rating scales is the choice of response terms to use. Below are samples of some widely used scaling codes. Do you find any problems with them?

    (a) Yes _______ Depends _____ No _______

    (b) Excellent _____ Good _____ Fair ______ Poor _______

    (c) Excellent _____ Good _____ Average _____ Fair _____ Poor _____.

    (d) Strongly approve ______ Approve ______ Uncertain _______ Disapprove ______ Strongly disapprove _______.

44. Distinguish between
    (a) Error of central tendency and error of leniency.
    (b) Graphic rating scale and Itemized Scale
45. Describe the following methods of ranking used in ranking scales:
    (a) Simple ranking
    (b) Paired comparison method
    (c) Method of successive categories
46. How can ordinal data be converted in to an interval scale?
47. Discuss some of the weaknesses of Guttman Scale in comparison with Likert type scale.
48. What are the functions of scalogram analysis? What are its advantages and disadvantages?
49. What is meant by a unidimensional scale? It is preferable to a multidimensional one? Why or why not?
50. What are the characteristics of a cumulative scale?
51. Describe the process of Cornell Technique of Scale analysis.
52. Discuss the nature and the uses of Factor-scaling technique.
53. Under what conditions would the following scales be useful:
    (a) Likert
    (b) Thurstone
    (c) Guttman
    (d) Semantic Differential Scale
54. What is Semantic Differential Scale? What does it measure?
55. Explain the three major underlying dimensions measured by a Semantic Differential Scale.
56. Describe the steps involved in the construction of Semantic Differential Scale.
57. What is an attitude? What are its components? By what types of scales an attitude is measured?
58. Can attitude scales predict behaviour?
59. Construct a socio-economic status scale for a survey of rural households.
60. Discuss the meaning and the functions of a pilot study.
61. When and why is a pilot study desirable?
62. Why is it desirable to pre-test survey instruments? What information can you secure from such a pre-test.
63. What is the need for pre-testing? What are its purposes?
64. Describe the procedure of pre-testing an instrument.
65. Distinguish between a pilot study and a pre-test.
66. Discuss the importance of *'test-revise retest cycle'* in developing a workable instrument for data collection.

❑ ❑ ❑

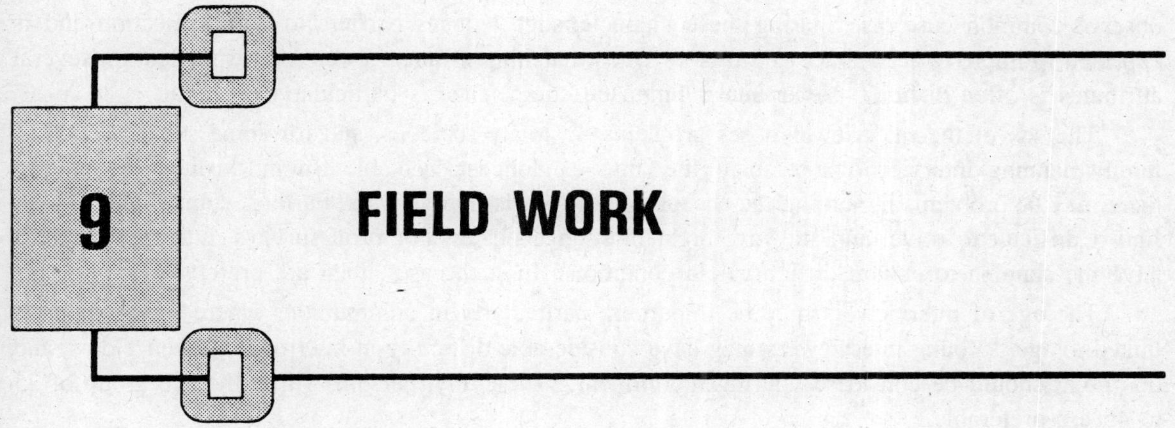

9 FIELD WORK

9.1 THE NATURE OF FIELD WORK

The Need for Fieldwork

Census and sample surveys, and field studies of life situations and communities involve fieldwork for collection of data. Initial fieldwork is done for pre-testing tools for data collection, such as observation schedule or interview schedule and measurement scales. Main fieldwork is launched after the tools are ready for use.

Nature of Fieldwork

Fieldwork requires proper planning and administration. It consists of several activities: (1) selection and training of investigators, (2) selection of the geographical area where the study is to be conducted or the community to be studied, as the case may be, (3) locating and securing sampling frames and selection of sample units in the case of a sample survey, (4) preparation of lists of names and addresses of the selected respondents, (5) planning fieldwork logistics, (6) field operation for data collection by observation and/or interviewing, and (7) field administration.

9.2 SELECTION AND TRAINING OF INVESTIGATORS

Selection Criteria

The quality of data collected in any survey depends ultimately upon the capabilities and skills of investigators. Who does the interviewing is therefore a vital consideration. The kinds of persons employed as interviewers, will vary from country to country, cultural group to cultural group, type of areas (urban or rural) and subject-matter of the study. Nevertheless, careful consideration should be given to certain characteristics in recruiting investigators.

In multilingual or ethnically diverse areas, ability to speak the language of the respondent is essential, and membership of the same ethnic group is desirable. The task of interviewing is easier, as pointed out by Hursh-Cesar and Roy, "when the interviewers and respondents are alike in terms of social origin, religion, language and dialect, geographical area and can understand, appreciate and observe common customs. Sharing these characteristics reduces barriers to communication and is expected to improve acceptance and trust."[1] Such matching of interviewer and respondent on several attributes is often difficult. Nevertheless linguistic competence is particularly essential.

The sex of the interviewer poses problems. In many societies, and for some subjects such as family planning, interview by a person of the same sex alone is acceptable. But in Muslim communities, there may be problems in gaining the acceptance of female interviewers. Further women interviewers find it difficult to travel and stay overnight in strange places. For rural surveys, interviewers must have the stamina to endure difficult field conditions. In such cases, men are preferable.

The age of interviewers may be important, particularly in communities where social status is linked to age. "Young interviewers may have considerable difficulty in interrogating their elders, and this point should be considered during recruitment."[2] Generally, persons within the age group of 25 to 45 are preferable.

Personal qualities are also important. The following qualities can be considered when selecting candidates:

Honesty: Interviewers must be honest and sincere. These characteristics cannot be easily assessed at the selection stage, but selected persons who are found to be dishonest should be immediately terminated.

Interest in the work is highly desirable. The quality of most investigators' work deteriorates after a time. Hence it is desirable to keep this work as occasional assignment rather than as full-time work.

Accuracy: Interviewers should be accurate in following instructions, understanding the objectives of questions and in recording or answers.

Adaptability: The investigators should be able to easily adapt themselves to varying circumstances. Persons with strong prejudices against certain subjects and groups of population are obviously unsuitable.

Personality and temperament: Investigators' personality should be neither over-aggressive nor over-sociable. Pleasantness and a business-like manner are the ideal combination.

Intelligence: Fieldwork does not call for extraordinary intelligence. What is needed is sufficient intelligence to understand and follow even complicated instructions and to record meaningful answers.

Communication skill: The investigators should possess interviewing ability. Working knowledge of respondents' language and dialect, common sense and ability to make the interview interesting are essential.

Education is important, but there is no necessary correlation between more education and better interviewing. A basic knowledge of statistics is desirable.

From what groups — secondary school products, university students, teachers, social workers, extension workers, unemployed school leavers/graduates.... Can interviewers be recruited? Practices vary. Experiences in several countries suggest that for fieldwork in urban areas unemployed graduates

1. G. Hursh-Cesar and P. Roy, *Third World Surveys,* Delhi: Macmillan of India, 1976, p. 305.
2. Martin Bulmer, "Interviewing and Field Organization" in M. Bulmer and D.P. Warwick, eds., *Social Research in Developing Countries,* New York: John Wiley & Sons Ltd., 1983, p. 215.

or university students may be used. But the use of university students for field work in rural areas is often disastrous. Most of them are 'elitist.' They cannot adapt themselves to rural conditions and have difficulty in establishing rapport with illiterate, subsistence-level rural people; school leavers in rural areas, rural extension workers and village school teachers are more effective and know the region, and its local dialect and mores well.

Selection Procedures

The selection procedure, may usually consist of: (1) *Selection test* designed to measure reading comprehension, arithmetic ability and ability to follow instructions and accuracy in recording, summarizing, checking and classifying data.

(2) *Trial interview:* Each candidate who passes the selection test may be asked to interview a few strangers with an interview schedule. How they establish rapport and interview should be observed.

(3) *Personal interview:* The candidates who complete trial interviews satisfactorily may be called for a personal interview to study their personality, manners and temperament.

Training

Though the training methods may vary from institution to institution, the training process should necessarily consist of three components:

(1) orientation course, (2) practice of mock interviews in the office, and (3) interviews in the field.

The orientation course may last for four or five days. The selected candidates should be oriented to the background of the organization and its general work. They should be told about the objectives of the survey, its design, sampling, the type of respondents from whom data have to be collected and other aspects of the study. The importance of the interviewers' role in collecting accurate data should be explained to them.

Then the techniques of interviewing should be taught to them with audio-visual aids. This may be followed by specific instructions on the schedule of the survey on hand. Important questions in the schedule should be discussed separately, giving the trainees some insight into the purpose of the questions, examples of adequate and inadequate responses and the common problems that arise from interviews and the possible approaches to deal with them. Written instructions should be provided.

After the instruction sessions are over, experienced interviewers can give demonstration interviews. Then the candidates can practice mock interview in the presence of experienced investigators and evaluate the interviews.

Finally, the candidates have to conduct interviews in the field which have to be evaluated and discussed. In the light of the evaluation,. Further instructions may be given to the investigators for improving the quality of their work. When the field work is in progress, once or twice conferences of investigators may be held to review their experiences, to identify their problems and to find solutions for those problems. It is also desirable to conduct short re-orientation training.

Compensation

Fair and competitive compensation should be offered to the investigators. It may include fixed salary per month, travelling allowance and some incentive linked to productivity. Part-time investigators may be paid hourly wage and travelling allowance.

9.3 SAMPLING FRAME AND SAMPLE SELECTION

Locating Sampling Frame

The sample design of a study may envisage a multi-stage sampling. This may involve, in the case of an urban area, (a) selection of a sample of divisions/blocks of the selected city, (b) selection of certain number of streets in the selected blocks, and (c) selection of households in the selected streets. In the case of a rural area study, sampling may involve (a) selection of districts, (b) selection of talukas in selected districts, (c) selection of villages in the selected talukas, and (d) selection of households in the selected villages. Sampling at each sampling stage calls for a sampling frame or list. The available lists are obtained from the offices of the concerned local administration. The adequacy, completeness, accuracy and updateness of the lists should be examined. If there are problems of missing elements, duplication, inaccuracy, etc., then appropriate steps should be taken to deal with them. If no suitable frame exists, for any stage of sampling, it has to be constructed through field enumeration.

Sample Selection

Sample selection is done as per the planned sampling design. A list of names and addresses (door numbers or any other identification information) of selected households/persons for each selected block/village should be prepared and kept ready for use. Local guides or informants can be very helpful in this task. Care must be taken in selecting the guides. Persons who are reasonably well-known and trusted are most suitable.

It is unwise to let investigators to enumerate households from which the sample is to be drawn or select sample respondents without careful on-the-spot supervision. Whichever method of sampling (probability, sociometric, purposive) is used, investigators (i.e., interviewers) should have complete written instructions on the exact procedure to be followed for sampling in order to ensure sample validity and uniformity. The supervisors should make the sampling themselves or carefully observe the interviewers performing the task.

9.4 FIELD OPERATIONS

Logistics

Before starting data collection work, the field operation logistics have to be planned. Planning of interviewing logistic envisages several aspects, such as transportation, interview strategy, food, stay, timing of interview, privacy in interview and the like.

Transportation, food, and stay do not pose much problems in urban field work; but they become difficult problems in rural areas. Cluster sampling[3] may minimize these difficulties to some extent. Some villages could be reached only by foot or bicycle. If the field work requires several days, the place where the investigators can stay has to be decided. It is desirable to stay in a central village and cover the villages around one after another, rather than shifting the camp from village to village.

Interview Strategies

There are two alternate interview strategies: One, to use all interviewers as a team to cover selected villages intensively in turn, and second, to leave single or pairs of interviewers in particular villages for several days to complete the work gradually. The first approach is called the 'invasion'

---

3. For detailed discussion, see 6.2. *Sampling Techniques*, in Chapter 6, above.

method, and the second in 'immersion' method. The invasion method is usually adopted in large-scale surveys, partly for operational reasons, and partly for reducing changes for feedback between those interviewed and those still to be interviewed, and for avoiding rumors to build up. On the other hand, the immersion method permits interviewers to gain familiarity with local conditions and to develop rapport with respondents.

Period Suitable for Interviews

The period suitable for fieldwork should be identified. In rural areas, the rainy reason, planting period, harvest season, and religious festival seasons should be avoided. The time of the day convenient for the respondents should be identified. Untimely contacts may lead to non-response and refusals.

Cooperation of Local Leaders

The strategy for obtaining the cooperation of the contact leaders should be decided. In the case of organizations, the cooperation of the head can be sought through a letter of introduction. In rural areas, knowledgeable informant like the school headmaster or village level extension worker is a good source of information for identifying contact leaders. Often a letter of introduction or personal introduction by a local school teacher or extension worker will prove useful for establishing rapport with local leaders.

Information on Survey

After securing the consent of the local leaders, the information about the study and its basic purpose, the sampling procedure and the usefulness of the study to the community should be given to the people of the community. This can be done by arranging for a village meeting preferably with a film show to attract people.

Privacy

Although privacy is preferable for interviewing a respondent, it is difficult to secure privacy in a rural area. A number of ways of overcoming this problem is used. Interviewing is often done in pairs in order to get privacy. For example, a pair of female interviewers may work together with one to interview the house-wife and the other to segregate the mother-in-law, engaging her in *pseudo* interview. Interviewing respondents where they work (e.g., in the fields) is another way of getting more privacy. Sometimes the presence of a third party may be useful for improving the quality of data, for the third party will assist the respondent by providing information that the latter is not able to recall (e.g., date of birth/marriage).

Fieldwork Briefing

Another aspect of field operation planning is field work briefing. This generally covers how to locate the respondents, how to deal with non response, how to open the interview, ask questions and record answers, whom to contact in the case of problems and what to do with the completed schedules. Personal briefing and discussion of doubtful points are preferable to impress upon interviewers the operational details of their task.

Interviewing and Statistical Information

Then the actual work of interviewing is taken up by the investigators. Apart from collecting data from the respondents, the statistical information relating to the area under study has to be collected from the local administration office. Infrastructure facilities in the place – communication, school, health centre etc. – may be observed and noted down in the area of profile data sheet.

Diary and Time-recorded Schedule

Each investigator should be required to maintain (1) a diary to note the nature of cooperation received from respondents, difficulties and problems faced during fieldwork, and (2) a daily time-recording, schedule to note time spent on various operations of fieldwork – journey, listing of households, contacting persons, interviewing, number of interviews conducted and other work.

Their experiences and difficulties may be reviewed at periodical review meetings and appropriate remedial/corrective actions taken up. The time-record schedules are useful for studying time-requirements for various operations and planning the programme of work accordingly.

9.5 FIELD ADMINISTRATION

Introduction

"Successful fieldwork," observe Warwick and Lininger,[4] "requires not only a theoretical understanding of the interview and a command of practical techniques, but also a carefully organized system of field administration."

Field administration involves (1) fieldwork scheduling and monitoring, (2) supervision, and (3) fieldwork review.

Scheduling and Monitoring

The various operations of fieldwork – enumeration of households, contacting persons, interviewing, checking of filled in schedules and the like and the tour programme of the field staff should be planned properly and monitored.

Supervision

"The quality of the data is no better than the quality of the field organization."[5]

Some supervision of fieldwork is essential. Each compact region may be placed in charge of a supervisor. He has to perform various tasks: briefing the field staff locally, directing the sample selection, scheduling fieldwork, allotting work to field staff, attending to their queries and difficulties, supervise the fieldwork by surprise check of fieldwork, and receiving the completed schedules from the investigators. Weekly meetings may be held to discuss cases, exchange experiences, and to find solutions to problems.

Fieldwork Review

The quality and productivity of the fieldwork should be kept under constant review. The main objects of this review is to test (a) whether all the interviews claimed by an interviewers were in fact made: (b) the interview output, i.e., the rate of interviews conducted per day and the response rate: and (c) the quality of interviewing.

The first check can be made by a test check with respondents or by sending postcards to a sample of respondents asking them whether they are interviewed.

---

4. D. Warwick and C. Lininger, *The Sample Survey: Theory and Practice,* New York: McGraw-Hill, 1975, p. 220.
5. *Ibid.*, p. 220.

In the second type of check, the output of each interviewers and the response rate (i.e., proportion of completed schedules to the number of assigned interviews) are studied. If an Interviewer's output and response rate are consistently lower than those of others, it may be time to terminate his services. Certain operational standards may be laid down in terms of interviews per day, response rate, rate of refusals, rate of "don't know" replies, rate of incomplete answers and the like. The performance of each investigator can be reviewed against the performance standards.

The check on the equality of interviewing is the most difficult of all checks. The quality refers to the right way of asking questions and correct interpretation and recording of answers. The major strategies for this quality control are: (1) careful scrutiny of completed schedules, (2) re-interview of some respondent by high grade interviewers or supervisors and comparing the two sets of results, (3) observing interviewers at work, (4) recording the interviews mechanically, (5) checking of answers to survey questions against other related data.

In the light of review outcome, appropriate remedial action should be taken. The remedial action may take several forms: revision of instructions, re-orientation/re-training of investigators, intensive supervision or dismissal as a last resort.

All possible efforts should be made to improve the quality of fieldwork through effective field administration.

SUGGESTED READINGS

1. Atkinsons, J., *A Handbook for Interviewers* (Government Social Survey, No. M.136), London: H.M.S.O., 1967.
2. Bulmer, Martin, "Interviewing and Field Organization," in Martin Bulmer and Donald P. Warwick, *Social Research in Developing Countries*, New York: John Wiley & Sons Ltd., 1983.
3. Edwards F., ed., *Readings in Market Research,* London: The British Market Research Bureau, 1956.
4. Hursh-Cesar, G., and Roy, P., *Third World Surveys,* Delhi: Macmillan of India, 1976.
5. Parten, Mildred, *Surveys, Polls, and Samples: Practical Procedures,* New York: Harper & Row, Publishers, 1950.
6. Rudolph, and Rudolph, S.H., "Surveys in India: Field Experience in Madras State," *Public Opinion Quarterly,* 22, pp. 235-44.
7. Steinkamp, S.W., "The Identification of Effective Interviewers," *Journal of the American Statistical Association,* 59, pp. 1165-74.
8. Survey Research Center, *Field Methods in Sample Interview Surveys,* Ann Arbor, Michigan: University of Michigan, 1951.
9. Survey Research Center, *Interviewers' Manual*, Ann Arbor, Michigan: Institute for Social Research, University of Michigan, 1969.
10. Warwick, D., and Lininger, C., *The Sample Survey: Theory and Practice.* New York: McGraw-Hill, 1975.

QUESTIONS

1. Discuss the need for, and nature of fieldwork.
2. What are the selection criteria to be considered in recruiting investigators?
3. What are the personal qualities to be possessed by investigators?
4. Describe the procedure of selecting investigators.
5. How are investigators trained?
6. Discuss the nature of fieldwork relating to sampling frame and sample selection.
7. What are the various aspects of planning of field operation for data collection?
8. Distinguish between 'invasion' method and 'immersion' method of interviewing.
9. What strategies can be adopted for securing privacy in interviewing?
10. How can the quality of interviewing be checked?

❑ ❑ ❑

10 PROCESSING OF DATA

10.1 INTRODUCTION

Data in the real world often comes with a large quantum and in a variety of formats that any meaningful interpretation of data cannot be achieved straightaway. Social science researches to be very specific draw conclusions using both primary and secondary data. To arrive at a meaningful interpretation on the research hypothesis, the researcher has to prepare his data for this purpose. This preparation involves the identification of data structures, the coding of data and the grouping of data for preliminary research interpretation. This data preparation for research analysis is termed as processing of data. Further selection of tools for analysis would to a large extent depend on the results of this data processing.

Data processing is an intermediary stage of work between data collection and data interpretation. The data gathered in the form of questionnaires/interview schedules/field notes/data sheets is mostly in the form of a large volume of research variables. The research variables recognized is a result of the preliminary research plan, which also sets out the data processing methods beforehand. Processing of data requires advance planning and this planning may cover such aspects as identification of variables, hypothetical relationship among the variables and the tentative research hypotheses.

The various steps in processing of data may be stated as:

(a) Identifying the data structures

(b) Editing the data

(c) Coding and classifying the data

(d) Transcriptions of data

(e) Tabulation of data.

10.2 PREPARATION FOR ANALYSIS

In the data preparation step, the data are prepared in a data format, which allows the analyst to use modern analysis software such as SAS or SPSS. The major criterion in this is to define the data structure. A data structure is a dynamic collection of related variables and can be conveniently represented as a graph whose nodes are labeled by variables. The data structure also defines and states the preliminary relationship between variables/groups of variables that have been preplanned by the researcher. Most data structures can be graphically presented to give clarity as to the framed research hypotheses. A simple structure could be a linear structure, in which one variable leads to the other and finally to the resultant end variable. Graphically, it may be shown as below:

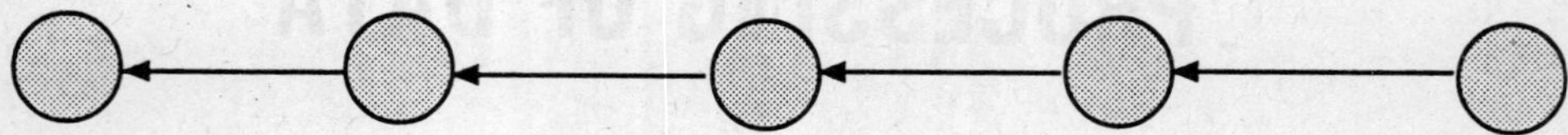

Alternatively, a more serial data structure could be drawn as follows:

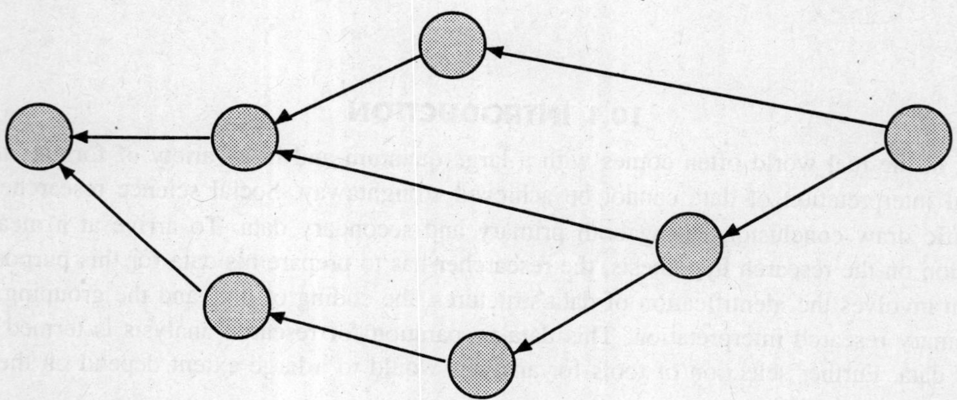

The identification of the nodal points and the relationships among the nodes, could sometimes be a complex task than estimated. When the task is complex, which involves several types of instruments being collected for the same research question, the procedure for drawing the data structure would involve a series of steps. In several intermediate steps, the heterogeneous data structures of the individual data sets can be harmonized to a common standard and the separate data sets are then integrated into a single data set.

However, the clear definition of such data structures would help in the further processing of data.

10.3 EDITING

The next step in the processing of data is editing of the data instruments. Editing is a process of checking to detect and correct errors and omissions.

Data editing happens at two stages, one at the time of recording the data and second at the time of analysis of data.

Data Editing at the Time of Recording of Data

Documented editing and testing of the data at the time of data recording is done considering the following questions in mind.

- Do the filters agree or are the data inconsistent?
- Have "missing values" been set to standardized values, which are the same for all research questions?
- Have variable descriptions been specified?
- Have labels for variable names and value labels been defined and written?

All editing and cleaning steps are documented, so that the redefinition of variables or later analytical modification requirements could be easily incorporated into the data sets.

Data Editing at the Time of Analysis of Data

Data editing is also a requisite before the analysis of data is carried out. This ensures that the data is complete in all respect for subjecting them to further analysis. Some of the usual check list questions that can be had by a researcher for editing data sets before analysis would be:

- Is the coding frame complete?
- Is the documentary material sufficient for the methodological description of the study?
- Is the storage medium readable and reliable?
- Has the correct data set been framed?
- Is the number of cases correct?
- Are there differences between questionnaire, coding frame and data?
- Are there undefined and so-called "wild codes" or duplicate cases?
- Comparison of the first counting of the data with the original documents of the researcher.

The editing step checks for the completeness, accuracy and uniformity of the data set created by the researcher.

(a) Completeness: The first step of editing is to check whether there is an answer to all the questions/variables set out in the data set. If there were any omission, the researcher sometimes would be able to deduce the correct answer from other related data on the same instrument. If this is possible, the data set has to be rewritten on the basis of the new information. For example, the approximate family income can be inferred from other answers to probes such as occupation of family members, sources of income, approximate spending and saving and borrowing habits of family members' etc. If the information is vital and has been found to be incomplete, then the researcher can take the step of contacting the respondent personally again and solicit the requisite data again. If none of these steps could be resorted to the marking of the data as "missing" must be resorted to.

(b) Accuracy: Apart from checking for omissions, the accuracy of each recorded answer should be checked. A random check process can be applied to trace the errors at this step. Consistency in response can also be checked at this step. The cross verification to a few related responses would help in checking for consistency in responses. The reliability of the data set would heavily depend on this step of error correction. While clear inconsistencies should be rectified in the data sets, fake responses should be dropped from the data sets.

(c) Uniformity: In editing data sets, another keen look out should be for any lack of uniformity in interpretation of questions and instructions by the data recorders. For instance the responses towards a specific feeling could have been queried from a positive as well as a negative angle. While interpreting the answers, care should be taken as to record the answer as a "positive question" response or as "negative question" response. In all, uniformity checks for consistency in coding throughout the questionnaire/interview schedule response/data set.

The final point in the editing of data sets is to maintain a log of all corrections that have been carried out at this stage. The documentation of these corrections help the researcher to retain the original data set.

10.4 CODING AND CLASSIFICATION

The edited data are then subject to codification and classification. Coding process assigns numerals or other symbols to the several responses of the data set. It is therefore a pre-requisite to prepare a coding scheme for the data set. The recording of the data is done on the basis of this coding scheme.

The responses collected in a data sheet varies, sometimes the responses could be the choice among a multiple response, sometimes the response could be in terms of values and sometimes the response could be alphanumeric. At the recording stage itself, if some codification were done to the responses collected, it would be useful in the data analysis. When codification is done, it is imperative to keep a log of the codes allotted to the observations. This code sheet will help in the identification of variables/observations and the basis for such codification.

The first coding done to primary data sets are the individual observations themselves. This response sheet coding gives a benefit to the research, in that, the verification and editing of recordings and further contact with respondents can be achieved without any difficulty. The codification can be made at the time of distribution of the primary data sheets itself. The codes can be alphanumeric to keep track of where and to whom it had been sent. For instance if the data consists of several public at different localities, the sheets that are distributed in a specific locality may carry a unique part code which is alphabetic. To this alphabetic code a numeric code can be attached to distinguish the person to whom the primary instrument was distributed. This also helps the researcher to keep track of who the respondents are and who are the probable respondents from whom primary data sheets are yet to be collected. Even at a latter stage, any specific queries on a specific response sheet can be clarified.

The variables or observations in the primary instrument would also need codification, especially when they are categorized. The categorization could be on a scale i.e., most preferable to not preferable, or it could be very specific such as Gender classified as Male and Female. Certain classifications can lead to open-ended classification such as education classification, Illiterate, Graduate, Professional, Others, please specify. In such instances, the codification needs to be carefully done to include all possible responses under "Others, please specify". If the preparation of the exhaustive list is not feasible, then it will be better to create a separate variable for the "Others, please specify" category and record all responses as such.

Numeric coding: Coding need not necessarily be numeric. It can also be alphabetic. Coding has to be compulsorily numeric, when the variable is to be subject to further parametric analysis.

Alphabetic coding: A mere tabulation or frequency count or graphical representation of the variable may be given an alphabetic coding.

Zero coding: A coding of zero has to be assigned carefully to a variable. In many instances, when manual analysis is done, a code of 0 would imply a "no response" from the respondents. Hence, if a value of 0 is to be given to a specific response in the data sheet, it should not lead to the same interpretation of "no response". For instance, there will be a tendency to give a code of 0 to a "no" answer. However, if the respondent had not chosen "yes" or "no", then a different coding than 0 should be given in the data sheet. An illustration of the coding process of some of the demographic variables is given in the following table.

Question Number	*Variable/Observation*	*Response Categories*	*Code*
1.1	Organization	Private	Pt
		Public	Pb
		Government	Go
3.4	Owner of Vehicle	Yes	2
		No	1
4.2	Vehicle performance	Excellent	5
		Good	4
		Adequate	3
		Bad	2
		Worst	1
5.1	Age	Up to 20 years	1
		21 - 40 years	2
		40 - 60 years	3
		Above 60 years	4
5.2	Occupation	Salaried	S
		Professional	P
		Technical	T
		Business	B
		Retired	R
		Housewife	H
		Others	*

* Could be treated as a separate variable/observation and the actual response could be recorded. The new variable could be termed as "Otherocc".

The coding sheet needs to be prepared carefully if the data recording is not done by the researcher, but is outsourced to a data entry firm or individual. In order to enter the data in the same perspective, as the researcher would like to view it, the data coding sheet is to be prepared first and a copy of the data coding sheet should be given to the outsourcer to help in the data entry procedure. Sometimes, the researcher might not be able to code the data from the primary instrument itself. He may need to classify the responses and then code them. For this purpose, classification of data is also necessary at the data entry stage.

Classification

When open-ended responses have been received, classification is necessary to code the response. For instance, the income of the responded could be an open-ended question. From all responses, a suitable classification can be arrived at. A classification method should meet certain requirements or should be guided by certain rules.

First, classification should be linked to the theory and the aim of the particular study. The objectives of the study will determine the dimensions chosen for coding. The categorization should meet the information required to test the hypotheses or investigative questions.

Second, the scheme of classification should be exhaustive. That is, there must be a category for every response. For example, the classification of martial status into three-category viz., "married", "single", and "divorced" is not exhaustive, because responses like "widower" or "separated" cannot be fitted into the scheme. Here, an open-ended question will be the best mode of getting the response. From the responses collected, the researcher can fit a meaningful and theoretically supportive classification. The inclusion of the classification "Others" tends to fill in the cluttered, but few responses from the data sheets. But "others" categorization has to carefully used by the researcher. However, the "other" categorization tends to defeat the very purpose of classification, which is designed to distinguish between observations in terms of the properties under study.[1] The classification "others" will be very useful when a minority of respondents in the data set give varying answers. For instance, the reading habits of newspapers may be surveyed. The 95 respondents out of 100 could be easily classified into 5 large reading groups while the 5 respondents could have given a unique answer. These given answers rather than being separately considered could be clubbed under the "others" heading for meaningful interpretation of respondents' reading habits.

Third, the categories must also be mutually exhaustive, so that each case is classified only once. This requirement is violated when some of the categories overlap or different dimensions are mixed up.

The number of categorization for a specific question/observation at the coding stage should be maximum permissible. Since, reducing the categorization at the analysis level would be easier than splitting an already classified group of responses. However, the number of categories is limited by the number of cases and the anticipated statistical analysis that are to be used on the observation.

10.5 TRANSCRIPTIONS OF DATA

When the observations collected by the researcher are not very large, the simple inferences that can be drawn from the observations can be transferred to a data sheet, which is a summary of all responses on all observations from a research instrument. The main aim of transition is to minimize the shuffling process between several responses and several observations. Suppose a research instrument contains 120 responses and the observations has been collected from 200 respondents, to prepare a simple summary of one response from all 200 observations would require a shuffling of 200 pages. The process is quite tedious if several summary tables are to be prepared from the instrument. The transcription process helps in the presentation of all responses and observations on data sheets, which can help the researcher to arrive at preliminary conclusions as to the nature of the sample collected etc. Transcription is hence an intermediary process between data coding and data tabulation.

Methods of Transcription

The researcher may adopt a manual or computerized transcription. Long work sheets, sorting cards or sorting strips could be used by the researcher to manually transcript the responses. The

1. Paul F. Lazarfeld and Allen Barton, *"Quantitative Measurement in the Social Sciences: Classification, Typologies and Indices"*, in Daniel Larner and Harold D.Lasswell, (Eds.), *The Policy Sciences*, Stanford, California: Stanford University Press, 1951, pp. 155-92.

computerized transcription could be done using a data base package such as spreadsheets, text files or other databases.

The main requisite for a transcription process is the preparation of the data sheets where observations are the rows of the database and the responses/variables are the columns of the data sheet. Each variable should be given a label so that long questions can be covered under the label names. The label names are thus the links to specific questions in the research instrument. For instance, opinion on consumer satisfaction could be identified through a number of statements (say 10). The data sheet does not contain the details of the statement, but gives a link to the question in the research instrument through variable labels. In this instance the variable names could be given as CS1, CS2, CS3, CS4, CS5, CS6, CS7, CS8, CS9 and CS10. The label CS indicating Consumer Satisfaction and the number 1 to 10 indicates the statements measuring consumer satisfaction. Once the labelling process has been gone through for all the responses in the research instrument, the transcription of the responses is done.

Manual Transcription

When the sample size is manageable, the researcher need not use any computerization process to analyze the data. The researcher could prefer a manual transcription and analysis of responses. The choice of manual transcription would be when the number of responses in a research instrument is very less, say 10 responses, and the number of observations collected are within 100. A transcription sheet with 100 x 50 (assuming each response has 5 options) row /column can be easily managed by a researcher manually. If, on the other hand the variables in the research instrument are more than 40 and each variable has 5 options, it leads to a worksheet of 100 x 200 size which might not be easily managed by the researcher manually. In the second instance if the number of responses are less than 30, then the manual worksheet could be attempted manually. In all other instances, it is advisable to use a computerized transcription process.

Long Worksheets

Long worksheets require quality paper, preferably chart sheets, thick enough to last several usage. These worksheets normally are ruled both horizontally and vertically, allowing a response to be written in the boxes. If one sheet is not sufficient, the researcher may use multiple ruled sheets to accommodate all the observations. Headings of responses which are variable names, and their coding (options) are filled in the first two rows. The first column contains the code of observations. For each variable, now the responses from the research instrument are then transferred to the worksheet by ticking the specific option that the observer has chosen. If the variable cannot be coded into categories, requisite length for recording the actual response of the observer should be provided for in the worksheet.

The worksheet can then be used for preparing the summary tables or can be subject to further analysis of data. The original research instruments can be now kept aside as safe documents. Copies of the data sheets can also be kept for future references. As has been discussed under the editing section, the transcript data has to be subject to a testing to ensure error free transcription of data.

A sample worksheet is given below for reference:

Sl. No.	*Vehicle Owner*		*Occupation*							*Vehicle Performance*					*Age*			
	Y	N	S	P	T	B	R	H	Otherocc	1	2	3	4	5	1	2	3	4
1	x					x							x				x	
2		x	x							x						x		
3	x							x				x						x
4	x						x							x				x
5	x				x						x				x			
6		x		x									x				x	
7		x							Student				x		x			
8	x								Artist				x			x		

Transcription can be made as and when edited instruments are ready for processing. Once all schedules/questionnaires have been transcribed, the frequency tables can be constructed straight from the worksheet.

Other methods of manual transcription include adoption of sorting strips or cards.

In olden days data entry and processing were made through mechanical and semi auto-matic devices such as key punch using punch cards.The arrival of computers has changed the data processing methodology altogether.

10.6 PRELIMINARIES FOR COMPUTERIZED DATA PROCESSING

When the sample size is large and/or when the variables studied is vast and interrelated, data can be transcribed to the computer for further easy processing. Many data base software packages are available using which data can be easily transcribed. The database software shows a worksheet similar to the manual worksheet prepared above. Some important points that can be kept in mind while preparing the 'coding' for computerized data entry are:

(a) *Use a 'natural' coding scheme:* Logical ordering of responses would be preferable. For instance, when the response is "very high" "more than once", "only once", "nil", the coding could be in the integer format of "4", "3", "2", "1". The alphabetical coding could also be used such as "H", "F", "O", "N". The use of numbers would help in further netric evaluations of that variable, while the alphanumeric codes would be amenable only for categorical analysis. If they are to be used as a metric measure, recoding of these variables into numeric format should be carried out using the software packages.

(b) *Avoid the use of blank space as a coding category:* Many computer software programs may not distinguish between blank space and zero unless otherwise specifically marked. Sometimes blank space may also be inferred as "no response"/"no information" by the software packages. When using alphanumeric coding also the use of blank space would differentiate it as an altogether separate response. Thus, in an alphanumeric coding the entry "KBALA" will be different from entry "K BALA". The blank space between A and B makes it a unique response though the researcher might have erroneously used it.

(c) *Do not use the "-", "+" symbols:* These would be taken as a numeric expression indicating negative and positive integers. Hence, avoidance of these symbols as a code is recommended.

10.7 TABULATION

The transcription of data can be used to summarize and arrange the data in a compact form for further analysis. The process is called tabulation. Thus, tabulation is a process of summarizing raw data and displaying them on compact statistical tables for further analysis. It involves counting the number of cases falling into each of the categories identified by the researcher.

Tabulation can be done manually or through the computer. The choice depends upon the size and type of study, cost considerations, time pressures and the availability of software packages. Manual tabulation is suitable for small and simple studies.

Manual Tabulation

When data are transcribed in a classified form as per the planned scheme of classification, category-wise totals can be extracted from the respective columns of the work sheets. A simple frequency table counting the number of "Yes" and "No" responses can be made by easily counting the "Y" response column and "N" response column in the manual worksheet table prepared earlier. This is a one-way frequency table and they are readily inferred from the totals of each column in the worksheet. Sometimes, the researcher has to cross tabulate two variables for instance the age group of vehicle owners. This requires a two-way classification and cannot be inferred straight from the worksheet. For this purpose, tally sheets are used. This process of tabulation is simple and does not require any technical knowledge or skill. If one wants to prepare a table showing the distribution of respondents by age, a tally sheet showing the age groups horizontally is prepared. Tally marks are then made for the respective group i.e., 'vehicle owners', from each line of response in the worksheet. After every four tally, the fifth tally is cut across the previous four tallies. This represents a group of five items. This arrangement facilitates easy counting of each one of the class groups. Illustration of this tally sheet is presented below:

Age Groups	*Tally Marks*	*No. of Responses*
Below 20	||	2
20-39	~~||||~~ ~~||||~~ ~~||||~~ ~~||||~~ |||	23
40-59	~~||||~~ ~~||||~~ ~~||||~~	15
Above 59	~~||||~~ ~~||||~~	10
Total		50

Although manual tabulation is simple and easy to construct, it can be tedious, slow and error-prone as responses increase.

Computerized tabulation is easy with the help of software packages. The input requirement will be the column and row variables. The software package then computes the number of records in each cell of the row/column categories. The most popular package is the Statistical Package for Social Sciences (SPSS). It is an integrated set of programs suitable for analysis of social science data. This package contains programs for a wide range of operations and analysis such as handling missing data, recoding, variable information, simple descriptive analysis, cross tabulation, multivariate analysis and non-parametric analysis.

10.8 CONSTRUCTION OF FREQUENCY TABLE

Frequency tables provide a "shorthand" summary of data. The importance of presenting statistical data in tabular form needs no emphasis. Tables facilitate comprehending masses of data at a glance; they conserve space and reduce explanations and descriptions to a minimum. They give a visual picture of relationships between variables and categories. They facilitate summation of items and the detection of errors and omissions and they provide a basis for computations.

It is important to make a distinction between the general-purpose tables and specific tables. The general-purpose tables are primary or reference tables designed to include large amounts of source data in convenient and accessible form. The special purpose tables are analytical or derivate ones that demonstrate significant relationships in the data or the results of statistical analysis. Tables in reports of government on population, vital statistics, agriculture, industries etc., are of general-purpose type. They represent extensive repositories of statistical information. Special purpose tables are found in monographs, research reports and articles and are used as instruments of analysis. In research, we are primarily concerned with special purpose tables.

Components of a table: The major components of a table are:

A. Heading
- (i) Table Number
- (ii) Title of the Table
- (iii) Designation of units

B. Body
- (i) Stub-head: Heading of all rows or blocks of stub items
- (ii) Body head: Headings of all columns or main captions and their sub-captions
- (iii) Field/body: The cells in rows and columns

C. Notations
- (i) Footnotes, wherever applicable
- (ii) Source, wherever applicable

The format of a Frequency Table is Presented below:

TABLE NUMBER

TITLE OF THE TABLE

Designation in units

Stub-head	Caption or Column head			Box head
	Y	N	Total	
1 ...				
2 ...				
3 ...	Sub captions			Field/body
4 ...				(Data only)

Notations:
Footnotes:
Source:

Principles of Table Construction

There are certain generally accepted principles of rules relating to construction of tables. They are:

(a) Every table should have a title. The title should represent a succinct description of the contents of the table. It should be clear and concise. It should be placed above the body of the table.

(b) A number to facilitate easy reference should identify every table. The number can be centred above the title. The table numbers should run in a consecutive serial order. Alternatively tables in Chapter 1 be numbered as 1.1, 1.2, 1., …., in Chapter 2 as 2.1, 2.2, 2.3…. and so on.

(c) The captions (or column headings) should be clear and brief.

(d) The units of measurement under each heading must always be indicated.

(e) Any explanatory footnotes concerning the table itself are placed directly beneath the table and in order to obviate any possible confusion with the textual footnotes such reference symbols as the asterisk (*) dagger (+) and the like may be used.

(f) If the data in a series of tables have been obtained from different sources, it is ordinarily advisable to indicate the specific sources in a place just below the table.

(g) Usually lines separate columns from one another. Lines are always drawn at the top and bottom of the table and below the captions.

(h) The columns may be numbered to facilitate reference

(i) All column figures should be properly aligned. Decimal points and 'plus' or 'minus' signs should be in perfect alignment.

(j) Columns and rows that are to be compared with one another should be brought close together.

(k) Totals of rows should be placed at the extreme right column and totals of columns at the bottom.

(l) In order to emphasize the relative significance of certain categories, different kinds of type, spacing and identifications can be used.

(m) The arrangement of the categories in a table may be chronological, geographical, alphabetical or according to magnitude. Numerical categories are usually arranged in descending order of magnitude.

(n) Miscellaneous and exceptional items are generally placed in the last row of the table.

(o) Usually the larger number of items is listed vertically. This means that a table's length is more than its width.

(p) Abbreviations should be avoided whenever possible and ditto marks should not be used in a table.

(q) The table should be made as logical, clear, accurate and simple as possible.

Text references should identify tables by number, rather than by such expressions as "the table above" or "the following table". Tables should not exceed the page size by photo stating. Tables that are too wide for the page may be turned sidewise, with the top facing the left margin or binding of the script. Where should tables be placed in a research report or thesis? Some writers place both special purpose and general-purpose tables in an appendix and refer to them in the text by numbers. This practice has the disadvantage of inconveniencing the reader who wants to study the tabulated data as the text is read. A more appropriate procedure is to place special purpose tables in the text and primary tables, if needed at all, in an appendix.

Frequency Distribution and Class Intervals

Variables that are classified according to magnitude or size are often arranged in the form of a frequency table. In constructing this table it is necessary to determine the number of class intervals to be used and the size of the class intervals.

A distinction is usually made between continuous and discrete variables. A continuous variable has an unlimited number of possible values between the lowest and highest with no gaps or breaks. Examples of continuous variables are age, weight, temperature etc. A Discrete variable can have a series of specified values with no possibility of values between these points. Each value of a discrete variable is distinct and separate. Examples of discrete variables are gender of persons (male/female), occupation (salaried, business, profession), Car Size (800cc 1000cc 1200cc).

In practice, all variables are treated as discrete units, the continuous variables being stated in some discrete unit size according to the needs of a particular situation. For example, length is described in discrete units of millimeters or a tenth of an inch.

Class intervals: Ordinarily, the number of class intervals may not be less than 5 nor more than 15, depending on the nature of the data and the number of cases being studied. After noting the highest and lowest values and the features of the data, the number of intervals can be easily determined.

For many types of data, it is desirable to have class intervals of uniform size. The intervals should neither be too small nor too large. Whenever possible, the intervals should represent common and convenient numerical divisions such as 5 or 10, rather than odd division such as 3 or 7.

Class intervals must be clearly designated in a frequency table in such a way as to obviate any possibility of misinterpretation or confusion. For example, to present the age group of a population, the use of intervals of 1-20, 20-50, and 50 and above would be confusing. This may be presented as 1-20, 21-50, and above 50.

Every class interval has a midpoint. For example, the midpoint of an interval 1-20 is 10.5 and the midpoint of class interval 1-25 would be 13. Once class intervals are determined, it is routine work to count the number of cases that fall in each interval.

One-way tables: One-way frequency tables present the distribution of cases on only a single dimension or variable. For example, the distribution of respondents of gender, by religion, socio-economic status and the like are shown in one-way tables. Table 10.1 illustrates one-way tables. One-way tables are rarely used, since the result of frequency distributions can be described in simple sentences. For instance, the gender distribution of a sample study may be described as: "The sample data is represented 58% by males and 42% of the sample are females."

TABLE 10.1

Distribution of Respondents by Gender

Gender	*Number of Respondents*	*Percent to Total*
Male	116	58%
Female	84	42%
Total	200	100%

Two-way tables: Distributions in terms of two or more variables and the relationship between two variables are shown in two-way tables. The categories of one variable are presented one below another, on the left margin of the table and those of another variable at the upper part of the table, one by the side of another. The cells represent particular combinations of both variables. To compare the distribution of cases, raw numbers are converted into percentages based on the number of cases in each category. Table 10.2 and Table 10.3 illustrate two-way tables.

TABLE 10.2

Member's Democratic Participation

Category Members	*Extent of Participation*						
	Low No. of respondents	*%*	*Medium No. of respondents*	*%*	*High No. of respondents*	*%*	*Total*
Ordinary	65	41.9	83	56.8	2	1.3	155
Committee	4	10.3	33	84.6	2	5.1	39

(*Source:* Krishnaswami O.R., Cooperative Democracy in Action, Mumbai: Somaiya Publications, 1976, p. 82).

Another method of constructing a two-way table is to state the percent of representation as a within brackets item rather than as a separate column. Here, special care has to be taken as to how the percentages are calculated, either on a horizontal representation of data or as a vertical representation of data. Sometimes, the table heading itself provides a meaning as to the method of representation in the two-way table.

TABLE 10.3

Economic Status of Members and their Democratic Participation

Economic Status	*Democratic Participation*			
	Low	*Medium*	*High*	*Total*
Low	6(35.3)	11(64.7)	0(0.0)	17
Medium	13(38.2)	18(53.0)	3(8.8)	34
High	6(62.5)	10(62.5)	0(0.0)	16
Very High	2(33.3)	3(50.0)	1(16.7)	6
Total	27	42	4	73

(*Note:* Figures in brackets represent percentages to the respective totals horizontally).

(*Source:* Krishnaswami O.R., Cooperative Democracy in Action, Mumbai: Somaiya Publications, 1976, p. 131).

10.9 GRAPHS/CHARTS/DIAGRAMS

In presenting the data of frequency distributions and statistical computations, it is often desirable to use appropriate forms of graphic presentation. In addition to tabular forms, graphic presentation involves use of graphics, charts and other pictorial devices such as diagrams. These forms and devices reduce large masses of statistical data to a form that can be quickly understood at a glance. The meaning of figures in tabular form may be difficult for the mind to grasp or retain. "Properly constructed graphs and charts relieve the mind of burdensome details by portraying facts concisely, logically and simply."[9] They, by emphasizing new and significant relationships, are also useful in discovering new facts and in developing hypotheses.

The device of graphic presentation is particularly useful when the prospective readers are non-technical people or general public. It is useful to even technical people for dramatizing certain points about data for important points can be more effectively captured in pictures than in tables. However, graphic forms are not substitutes for tables, but are additional tools for the researcher to emphasize the research findings.

Graphic presentation must be planned with utmost care and diligence. Graphic forms used should be simple, clear and accurate and also be appropriate to the data. In planning this work, the following questions must be considered.

What is the purpose of the diagram?

What facts are to be emphasized?

What is the educational level of the audience?

How much time is available for the preparation of the diagram?

What kind of chart will portray the data most clearly and accurately?

Types and General Rules

The most commonly used graphic forms may be grouped into the following categories:

(a) Line Graphs or Charts

(b) Bar Charts

(c) Segmental Presentations

(d) Scatter Plots

(e) Bubble Charts

(f) Stock Plots

(g) Pictographs

(h) Chesnokov Faces

The general rules to be followed in graphic representations are:

(a) The chart should have a title placed directly above the chart.

(b) The title should be clear, concise and simple and should describe the nature of the data presented.

(c) Numerical data upon which the chart is based should be presented in an accompanying table.

(d) The horizontal line measures time or independent variable and the vertical line the measured variable.

(e) Measurements proceed from left to right on the horizontal line and from bottom to top on the vertical.

(f) Each curve or bar on the chart should be labelled.

(g) If there are more than one curve or bar, they should be clearly differentiated from one another by distinct patterns or colours.

(h) The zero point should always be represented and the scale intervals should be equal.

(i) Graphic forms should be used sparingly. Too many forms detract from rather than illuminate the presentation.

(j) Graphic forms should follow not precede the related textual discussion.

Line Graphs

The line graph is useful for showing changes in data relationships over a period of time. In this graph, figures are plotted in relation to two intersecting lines or axes. The horizontal line is called the abscissa or X-axis and the vertical, the ordinal or Y-axis. The point at which the two axes intersect is zero for both X and Y-axis. The 'O' is the origin of coordinates. The two lines divide the region of the plane into four sections known as quadrants that are numbered anti clockwise. Measurements to the right and above 'O' are positive (plus) and measurements to the left and below 'O are negative (minus). Exhibit 10.1 is an illustration of the features of a rectangular coordinate type of graph. Any point in the plane of the two axes is plotted in terms of the two axes reading from the origin 'O'. Scale intervals in both the axes should be equal. If a part of the scale is omitted, a set of parallel jagged lines should be used to indicate the break in the scale. The time dimension or independent variable is represented by the X-axis and the other variable by Y-axis.

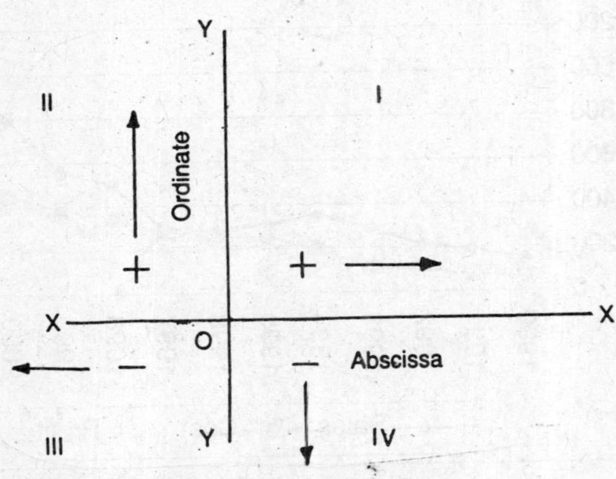

Exhibit 10.1: Line Graph Dimensions

A sample line chart is provided in Exhibit 10.2. Each variable can be given a separate colour coding or style differentiation. A think, thick, or broken lines could distinguish the variables in terms of their line style.

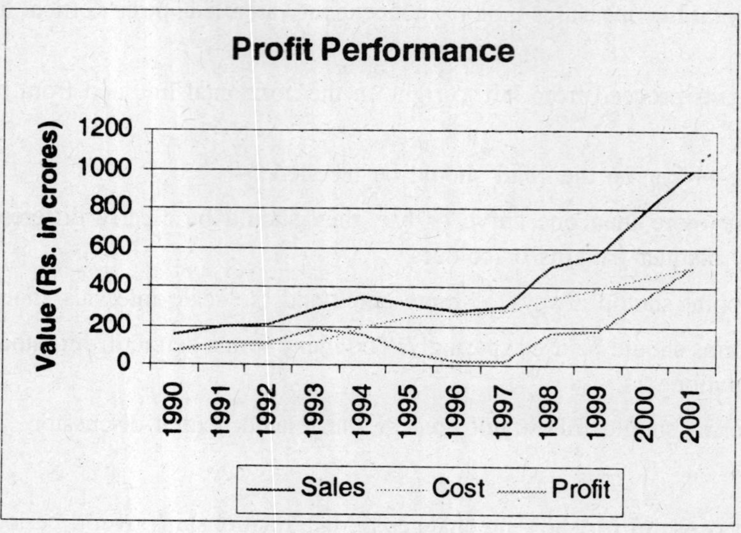

Exhibit 10.2: Simple Line Graph

The line graph can also provide markers for each data point. The marker for each variable can be different to distinguish it from other variables. Exhibit 10.3 gives an illustration of a line graph with markers to distinguish between the variables. The markers also highlight the value at any specific point. It distinctly points out the values that have been joined together to form the line graph. The horizontal lines drawn across the body of the line graph is called the grid lines. The grid lines help in identifying the scale differences across the graph at a glance.

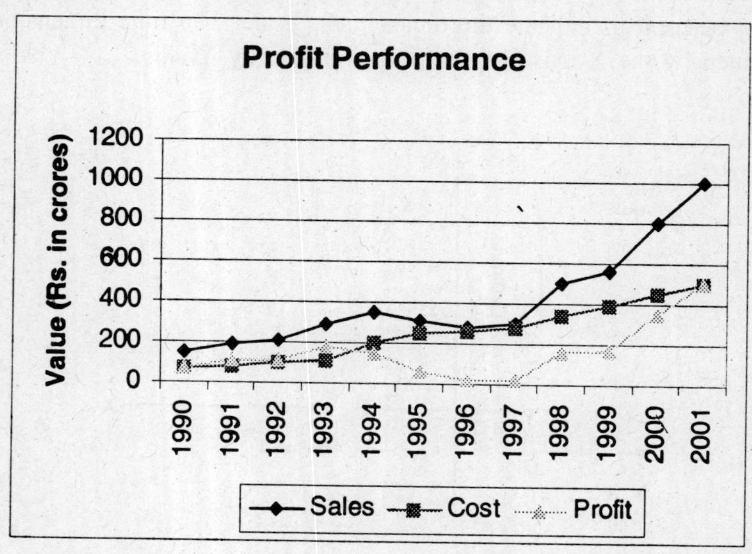

Exhibit 10.3: Market Line Graph

Histogram

This is another form of line chart used for presenting a frequency distribution. It is constructed by erecting vertical lines on the limits of the class intervals marked on the base line. The vertical lines so drawn form a series of contiguous rectangles or columns. The width of each rectangle represents its class interval and the height represents the class frequency. Exhibit 10.4 illustrates the histogram.

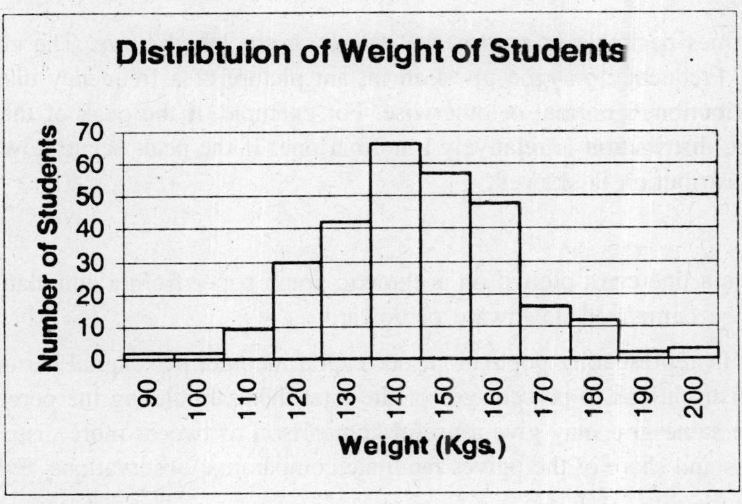

Exhibit 10.4: Histogram

Frequency Polygon

It is often more convenient to draw a frequency polygon instead of drawing a histogram of a distribution. In laying out a frequency polygon, the frequency of each class is located at the midpoint of the interval and straight lines then connect the plotted points. If two or more series are shown on the same graph, the curves can be made with different kinds of ruling. If the total number of cases

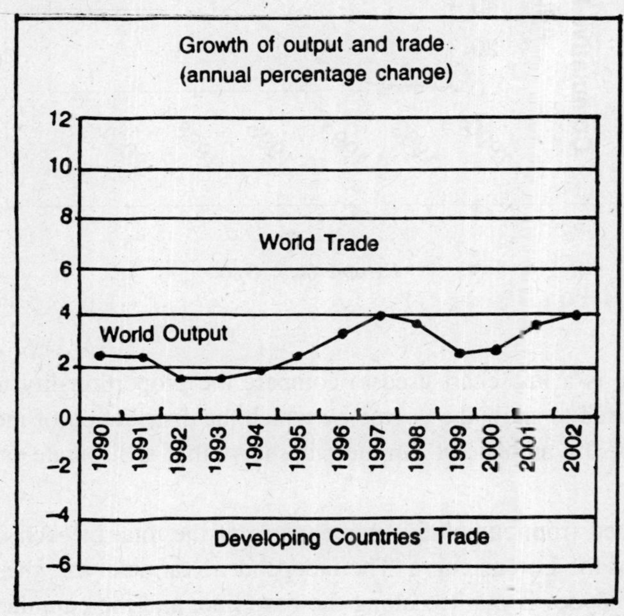

Exhibit 10.5: Frequency Polygon

in the two series is of different size, the frequencies are often reduced to percentages. The frequency polygon is particularly appropriate for portraying continuous series. Exhibit 10.5 illustrates a frequency polygon.

It is sometimes desirable to portray the data by a smoothed curve. The chart is then called a frequency curve. Frequency polygon gives an instant picture of a frequency distribution and shows whether the distribution is normal or otherwise. For example, if the peak of the frequencies occurs in the middle, the distribution is relatively a normal one. If the peak occurs towards one end or the other, then the distribution is skewed.

Ogive

The ogive is a line chart plotted on arithmetic graph paper from a cumulative frequency distribution that may be cumulated downward or upward.

It is useful in representing population, per capita income, per capital earnings etc. Converting the data of the distributions to percentages of the total then cumulating the percentages and plotting the ogives on the same grid may give a useful comparison of two or more distributions. The differences in steepness and share of the ogives facilitate comparative observations. Exhibit 10.6 illustrates the ogive.

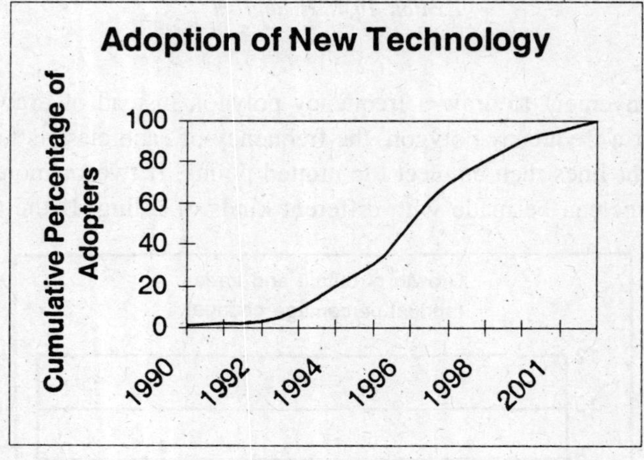

Exhibit 10.6: Ogive

Lorenz Curve

The Lorenz curve is a line chart used to compare the proportionality in two quantitative variables. It is commonly used to show the degree by which the distribution of income per family departs from the distribution of the number of families; it shows that a disparate proportion of the income goes to a few families.

The curve is plotted from cumulative percentages of the total of each of the variables. Exhibit 10.7 is an illustration of the Lorenz curve. The independent variable viz., the cumulative percentages of total number of employees is marked along the base line, and the cumulative percentages of total income (i.e., dependent variable) are plotted on the vertical line. The "line of equal distribution" is a line that would have been obtained if the two distributions had been proportional. The line designated 'actual distribution' reveals that the distribution of income is unequal compared to the distribution of the number of employees. The more the 'actual distribution' line departs from the 'line of equal distribution', the more unequal is the Y-variable in terms of the X-variable and the more disproportionate is the relationship.

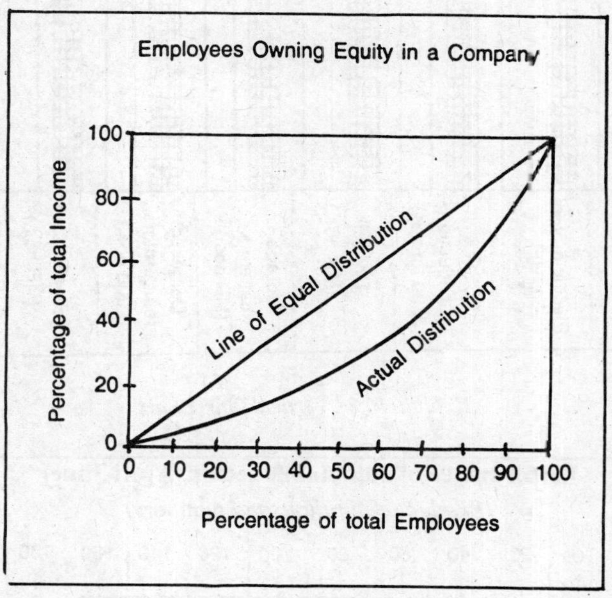

Exhibit 10.7: Lorenz Curve

Bar Charts

These charts consist of either vertical or horizontal bars to represent variables. The length of the bars varies corresponding to the values of the variable. Bar charts are the most effective pictorial device for comparing data. The bars may be depicted in solid blocks or in patterns of dots, dashes etc. They may be of different forms: (1) linear or one-dimensional, (2) a real or two-dimensional, and (3) cubic or three dimensional. The actual numerical values may be shown on the X-axis or Y-axis, as the case may be, or at the immediate ends of the bars.

Vertical Bar Charts consists of vertical bars or columns erected on the horizontal line and the values of the bars are shown on the Y-axis. Exhibit 10.8 illustrates a typical vertical bar chart.

The vertical bar charts are commonly used for presenting time series data.

Horizontal Bar Charts are commonly used for presenting qualitative and geographical distributions. They are also used for discrete quantitative distributions. Exhibit 10.9 is an illustration of horizontal bar chart.

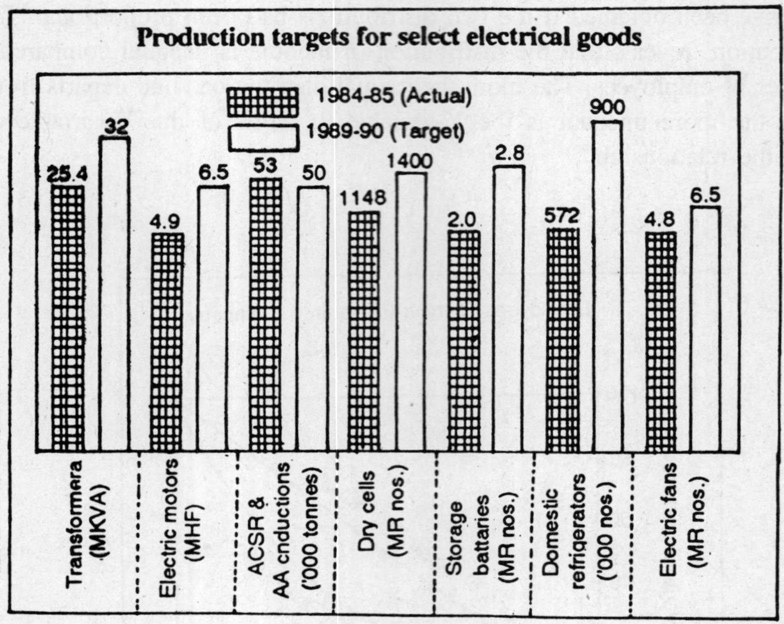

Exhibit 10.8: Vertical Bar Chart

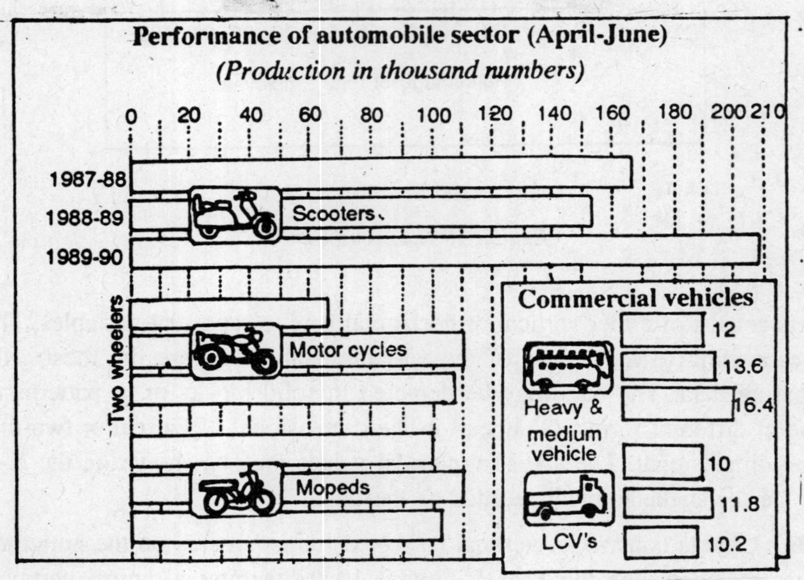

Exhibit 10.9: A Horizontal Bar Chart

Component Bar Chart

This is employed to show comparisons involving two or more variables on a single chart (see Exhibit 10.10). This may consist of either horizontal bars or vertical bars. This type of chart shows not only variations in total values, but also components of the respective totals.

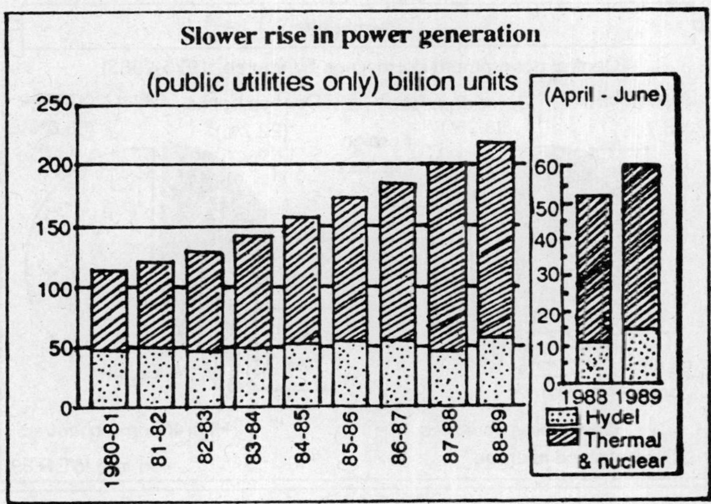

Exhibit 10.10: Component Parts Bar Chart

Principles of Designing Bar Charts

In constructing bar charts the following principles should be adopted:

1. The bars should be arranged in some systematic order: in chronological order in a presentation of time series; according to magnitude, starting with the largest, in other cases.
2. The bars should be of uniform width and properly adapted to the over-all size, proportion, and other features of the chart.
3. A scale should be included in every bar chart. The number of intervals on the scale should be adequate for measuring distances but not too numerous to cause confusion. The intervals should be indicated in round numbers.
4. The status or designations for the various categories of a bar chart should be clearly indicated to the left of the vertical base line.

Pie or Circle Charts

The circle or pie chart is a component parts bar chart. The component parts form the segments of the circle. (See Exhibit 10.11). The circle chart is usually a percentage chart. The data are converted to percentage of the total; and the proportional segments, therefore, give a clear picture of the relationship among the component parts.

The name of each segment and its percentage are placed inside its own area. When a segment is too small, an arrow is drawn to it and the legend is placed outside, in a horizontal position. The pie chart is commonly used for presenting the sectoral distribution of national income, the cost structure of a firm, or any other type of simple percentage distribution.

Pictograms

A pictogram is a variation of the bar chart. In it the values are represented by identical symbol or pictures. Each one represents a fixed size of the variable. The symbols used may be appropriate to the type of data. For example, pictures of human beings can be used for depicting population data.

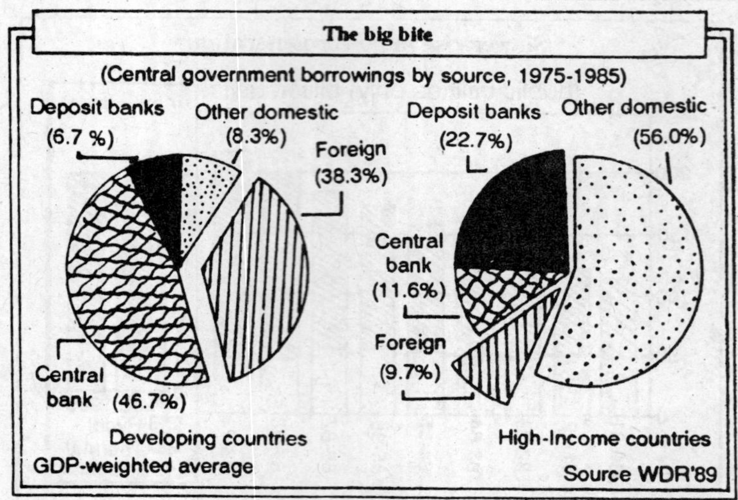

Exhibit 10.11: Component Parts Pie Chart

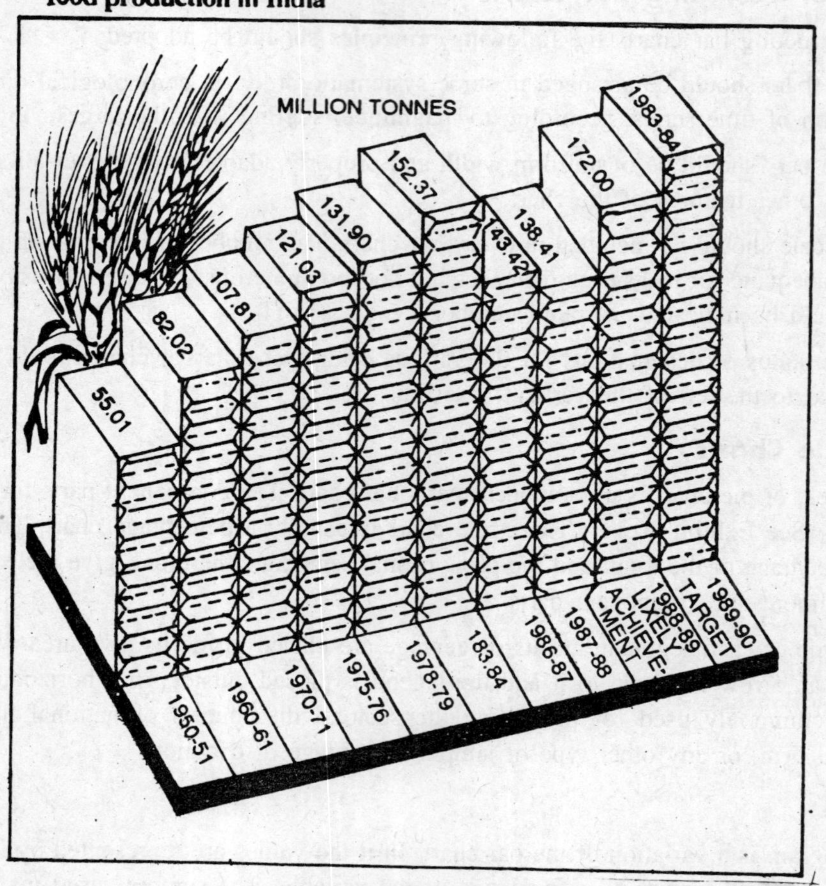

Exhibit 10.12: Pictogram

(See Exhibit 10.12). The pictogram is used for qualitative distributions and for time series distributions as well.

The following rules should be observed in developing a pictorial chart:

1. The symbols should be self-explanatory.
2. Each symbol should represent a convenient sum of units.
3. The chart should be made as simple and clear as possible.
4. The chart should give only an over-all picture; it should not show minute details.
5. Comparison in terms of one dimension only should be charted.

Conclusion

Whatever the graphic devices we use to represent our data, we must draw them accurately; otherwise, we may allow the readers to infer unintended meanings.

For comparing two or more items, the bar chart is ideal. The chart should be designed so that only linear comparisons are made. With linear comparison, the eye is not deceived with two or three dimensions, accurate comparisons are more difficult.

SUGGESTED READINGS

1. Hull, J.E., *Introduction to Computing,* Englewood Cliffs, N.J.; Prentice-Hall, 1986.
2. Janda, Kenneth, *Data Processing*, Evanston, 111.: North-Western University Press, 1965.
3. Modley, Rudolph, *et.al., Pictographs and Graphs,* New York: Harper & Row, Publishers, 1952.
4. Parten, M.S., *Surveys, Polls and Samples: Practical Procedures,* New York: Harper & Brothers, Publishers, 1950.
5. Rosenberg, Morris, *The Logic of Survey Analysis,* New York: Basic Books, 1968.
6. Sanders, Donald H., *Computers Today*, Singapore: McGraw-Hill Book Co., 1988.
7. Schmid, Calvin F., *Handbook of Graphic Presentation,* New York: Ronald Press, 1954.

QUESTIONS

1. What is data Processing? What does it involve?
2. What is editing? For what is it done?
3. Why are responses categorized? What are the requirements of categorization?
4. You are planning to conduct a survey among final year students of master degree courses at the local university concerning the types of work they would prefer for their lifetime careers.
   (a) Define what you think might be a satisfactory category set for classifying their answers, when they use your set as a checklist.
   (b) How would this differ from the category set which you might develop to code responses to the open-end question: "What type of work do you prefer for your lifetime career?
5. Prepare a non-structured schedule on a topic of interest. Interview at least ten respondents.
   (a) Construct a coding scheme for all items.
   (b) Construct a codebook that will include the code for each item.

6. What is meant by 'transcription'? Why is it done?
7. Compare and contrast (a) long work sheets and (b) sorting strips as methods of transcription.
8. Describe the procedure of transcribing data in long work sheets.
9. What are sorting strips? How are they superior to long work sheets for transcription of data?
10. Describe the procedure of using sorting strips for transcription of data.
11. How are data transferred to punch cards?
12. What are the rules relating to coding for punch cards?
13. How are magnetic tapes and disks used for computerization of data processing?
14. How is hand tabulation of data done?
15. How is machine tabulation of data done?
16. Suppose you are planning to conduct a survey of about 70 persons, in which you will secure about 50 different items of data, which are easily coded. You expect to do a number of cross tabulations of the results. What type of hand tabulation would you recommend? Why?
17. How are computers used for data processing and analysis?
18. What is a statistical table? What are principles of table construction?
19. Draw a table and show its components.
20. Why is graphic representation of data desirable?
21. What are the general rules relating to graphic representation?
22. Explain the use of different types of line graphs and charts.
23. What is Lorenz Curve? How is it used?
24. Describe the use of different types of bar charts.
25. Describe the use of Pie Chart and Pictograms.

❑ ❑ ❑

11 STATISTICAL ANALYSIS OF DATA

11.1 STATISTICAL ANALYSIS

The analysis of data is the most skilled task in the research process. It calls for the researcher's own judgement and skill. Analysis means a *critical examination* of the assembled and grouped data for studying the *characteristics* of the object under study and for determining the patterns of *relationships* among the variables relating to it. Both quantitative and non-quantitative methods are used. However, social research most often requires quantitative analysis involving the application of various statistical techniques.

Purpose of Statistical Analysis

Statistical analysis of data serves several major purposes. First, it *summarizes* large mass of data into understandable and meaningful form. This is the role of *descriptive statistics*. The reduction of data facilitates further analysis.

Second, statistics makes *exact descriptions* possible. For example, when we say that the educational level of people in a district is very high, the description is not specific; but when statistical measures like the percentages of literate among males and females, the percentages of degree holders among males and females are available, the description becomes exact.

Third, statistical analysis facilitates *identification* of the *causal factors* underlying complex phenomena. What are the factors that determine a variable like labour productivity or academic performance of students? What are the relative contributions of the causative factors? Answers to such questions can be obtained from statistical *multivariate* analysis.

Fourth, statistical analysis aids the *drawing* of reliable *inferences* from observational data. Data are collected and analyzed in order to *predict* or make *inferences* about situations that have not been measured in full. What would be the growth rate of industrial production during the coming year?

What would be the probable demand for a particular product in the coming year? Questions of this kind require predictions of future states to be made on the basis of current knowledge. Such predictions are essential in any strategic decision relating to management of an enterprise or the national economy or a social action program. The statistical prediction is one of the functions of *inferential statistics.*

Fifth, statistical analysis also helps making *estimations* or *generalizations* from the results of sample surveys. This is another function of *inferential statistics*. Sample statistics based on probability samples may give good estimates of particular population parameters. Any estimate will deviate from the true value due to sampling error. The process of statistical inference enables us to evaluate the accuracy of the estimates.

Last (inferential) statistical analysis is useful for assessing the significance of *specific sample results* under assumed population conditions. This type of analysis is called *hypothesis testing*.

Approach to Statistical Analysis

The general approach to statistical analysis consists of several different aspects:

The *first aspect* is what is called *descriptive analysis*. This involves construction of *statistical distributions* and calculation of simple measures like averages, percentages and measures of dispersion for describing the features of the research queries.

It is common to begin the analysis by showing the distribution of respondents by each of the pertinent variables. For example, if the respondents are persons, their distribution by gender, age, social class, income level etc., are worked out. If the respondents are institutions, their distributions by form, size, age, type, efficiency etc., are shown. Then some average value that represents the distribution is computed by using the appropriate *measure of central tendency* — the mode, the median or the arithmetic mean.

The *second aspect* of analysis is to *compare* two or more distributions or two or more sub-groups within a distribution. Any comparison by measures of central tendency only would be misleading for they do not give a complete indication of the nature of distributions. Hence measures of *dispersion* are also used. The latter indicate the pattern of the spread of individual values. The measures of dispersion include the range, the standard deviation and the coefficient of variation. These measures are used to compare the relative wideness of spread in any two or more frequency distributions. (See Section 11.3, below).

Other methods like *ratios, proportions* and *percentages* are also used for comparing distributions or sub-groups. Ratios show the relation between one figure and another. They can also be expressed as proportions and percentages. These are *relative measures* and permit the comparison of groups of unequal size, *e.g.,* liquidity and turnover ratios and return on investment are used for inter-firm and intra-firm comparisons.

The *purpose* of *using percentages* (and ratios and proportions) is to simplify the problem of comparison. It is important to note what their use implies. First, they serve to *put qualitative characteristics into numerical form.* For example, the performance of two similar firms may be compared in terms of their rates of return on investment. Second, percentages reduce two frequency distributions to a *common base*, thus making comparisons much simple. However, this obscures *absolute* comparisons that are sometimes more important.

The *third* aspect of analysis is to study the *nature of relationships* among variables. The coefficients of correlation, partial and multiple correlation and regression are used for this analysis. In order to know the effect of one or more independent variables on the dependent variable, regression analysis is made. Once this relationship is established it is used for *prediction* purposes.

In survey research, it is not always possible to study all the units in the population for drawing generalizations about it. Hence, a representative sample is drawn and the population characteristics are estimated from the results of the sample survey. But the results of a sample may have some errors. Hence, the validity of inferences drawn from sample survey results has to be tested. *Parametric tests of significance* such as 't' test, 'F' test etc., and *non-parametric* tests like chi-square test, K S test, Sign test etc., are used for this purpose. These tests are also used for testing the hypothesis relating to variables.

Another *aspect* of analysis is to find out the *factors* that explain the relationship between a set of variables. Factor analysis is used for this purpose.

Types of Statistical Analysis

Statistical analysis is used for estimating the values of unknown characteristics (parameters) of the population and for testing hypothesis for drawing inferences. Analysis may therefore be broadly classified into (1) descriptive analysis and (2) inferential analysis.

Descriptive Analysis

This type of analysis describes the nature of an object or phenomenon under study. This analysis provides us with profiles of organisations, work groups, persons and other subjects on any of a multitude of characteristics such as size, compositions, efficiency, preferences etc.

This sort of analysis may describe data on one variable, two variables or more than two variables. Accordingly it is called *univariate analysis, bivariate analysis* and *multivariate analysis* respectively.

Multivariate analysis consists of (*a*) multiple regression analysis, (*b*) multiple discriminant analysis, (*c*) cannonical analysis, (*d*) multivariate analysis of variance and (*e*) factor analysis.

(*a*) **Multiple Regression Analysis** is made when one dependent variable is presumed to be a function of two or more independent variables.

(*b*) **Multiple Discriminant Analysis** is appropriate when the dependent variable cannot be measured but can be identified with a particular group on the basis of several predictor variables.

(*c*) **Cannonical Analysis** is used for simultaneously predicting a set of dependent variables from their joint covariance with a set of independent variables.

(*d*) **In Multivariate Analysis of Variance,** the ratio of 'among group variance' to 'within group variance' is worked on a set of variables. This is useful for testing hypothesis concerning multivariate differences among group responses to experimental manipulations.

(*e*) **Factor Analysis** is useful for grouping a large number of variables into a few independent factor dimensions.

Inferential Analysis

Inferential analysis is concerned with drawing inferences and conclusions from the findings of a research study. There are *two areas* of statistical inference, *viz.,* (*a*) statistical estimation and (*b*) the testing of hypothesis.

(*a*) **Statistical estimation** involves estimation of the population parameters from the results of sample data analysis. In order to arrive at accurate estimates of parameters, the researcher has to effectively deal with three problems: (*i*) the precise definition of population, (*ii*) the determination of adequate sample size, and (*iii*) the selection of a representative sample.

(*b*) **Testing Hypothesis:** Hypotheses are tested with tests of significance. This testing involves the assessment of the probability of specific sampling results under assumed population conditions. Assumptions about the population parameters are made in advance and the sample then provides the test of these assumptions. An inference is also drawn about the relationships among variables.

Inferential analysis enables us to make *decisions* and draw *conclusions* from studies which could otherwise not be feasible because of the size of the universe or of prohibitive costs of a census survey or of destructive testing procedures as in quality control.

Inferential analysis involves an estimate of the accuracy of the inference called *reliability*. The reliability is expressed in terms of probability determined from the relevant statistical distribution *i.e.,* confidence levels.

Types of Statistical Measures

The statistical measures used in statistical analysis may be categorised into:

(*a*) *Measures of central tendency* — mean, median, mode,

(*b*) *Measures of dispersion* — ranges, deviation, standard deviation,

(*c*) *Measures of association/relations* — correlation, regression, chi-square test, factor analysis, discriminant analysis, cluster analysis, cannonical analysis

(*d*) *Analysis of variance* — one-way ANOVA, two-way ANOVA, MANOVA and analysis of covariance and

(*e*) *Time series analysis* — seasonal, cyclical, trend and erratic variations.

Each of these measures is discussed in detail in the following sections.

Computerized Analysis

Computer software packages are available for applications of various statistical techniques like correlation coefficients, regression, multivariate analysis and the like. They facilitate complex analysis with great ease and tremendous speed. It is not always necessary for researchers to know computer languages or to write programs. They just have to learn how to use the appropriate programs as per the instructions contained in them.

Computers can be used for generating formal models of social systems for simulating the behaviour of persons, groups of nations and for retrieving large amounts of documentary materials such as abstracts of journal articles.

The availability of computers has shifted the emphasis in social sciences from the study of univariate and bivariate problems to the study of multivariate problems. To be efficient predictors, social science theories generally need to be stated in multivariate terms. Before computer utilities, multivariate techniques were so tedious that they were not commonly used. The computers have now made these techniques accessible and practical and the potential uses of computers for research analysis stagger the imagination.

11.2 MEASURES OF CENTRAL TENDENCY

Introduction

A useful way to describe a set of observations is to find a single value that represents the 'average' characteristic of its frequency distribution. Such a value is known as a *measure of central tendency* since it is generally located toward the *centre* of the distribution. The three most commonly used measures of central tendency are the mode, the median and the arithmetic mean. Each of these measures is a *descriptive measure* of central location and provides a way of reducing a large mass of data to a single representative value.

Need

The measures of central tendency are necessary for two reasons:

1. The average represents *all* the measurements made on a group and gives a *concise* description of the group as a whole.
2. When two or more groups are measured, the central tendency provides the basis of *comparison* between them.

Mode

The mode is the simplest of all averages. It is a measure that occurs most *frequently* in a distribution. Consider the distribution of discipline categories of applicants in Table 11.1.

TABLE 11.1

Distribution of applicants for admission to M.B.A. by discipline

Discipline	*Frequency (No. of applicants)*
Engineering	210
Commerce	180
Arts	110
Science	90
Others	50
Total	640

The engineering category is the most predominant. This is the mode of the distribution. Note that the mode is not 210, which is the frequency of the modal category. The mode need not be expressed numerically. It can refer to a qualitative variable as in Table 11.1.

Grouped data: The procedure for finding the mode of a set of grouped data is described below:

- Find the category or the class interval which has the greatest frequency
- The midpoint on this category is the mode.

For example, in Table 11.2, we find that the modal frequency is 54, which is associated with the modal class interval of 41-60. The midpoint of this class interval is 50.5. Hence, the mode of this distribution is 50.5.

Most distributions are *unimodal*, *i.e.,* they contain only one mode, but some distributions are *bimodal*. For example, the distribution of heights of adults consisting of both men and women can be bimodal, because each gender class has a typical height.

TABLE 11.2

Distribution of Respondents by Age

Age Group	*Frequency*	*Cumulative Frequencies*
1 - 20	15	15
21 - 40	32	47
41 - 60	54	101
61 - 80	30	131
81 - 100	19	150
Total	150	

Use: The mode is an especially useful measure for *qualitative* data. It is the only appropriate measure of central tendency for *nominal* level of data. Example of application of mode can be in distributions like ethnic classification of occupational classification. For finding out the *typical category*, the mode is the appropriate measure.

Evaluation: The mode is easily calculable, but it is quite unstable, because its position shifts when categorization is altered. It is a *positional* average and is not affected by extreme items. It is a *dead-end* statistic as it is not amenable for any further arithmetic manipulation.

Median

The median is a *positional average* that divides a distribution into two equal parts so that one half of items fall above it and the other half below it. For example, in the series 3,4,6,7,8,9,10, the median is 7.

If the number of cases (n) is odd, the median is the middle item. If n is even, the median is the midpoint of the distance between the two middle most items, *e.g.,* in the distribution 2,3,4,6,7,8, the median is midpoint between 4 and 6 *i.e.,* 5.

Grouped Data: The same logic governs the computation of the median for grouped data. The number of cases (n) in Table 11.2 is 150. Hence, the median is that point which has (n/2 = 75) 75 cases above it and an equal number below it. From the cumulative frequency column, it can be seen that 75th case falls in the class interval of 41-60. The median can be computed by applying the following formula:

$$\text{Median} = l + \left(\frac{n/2 - cf}{f} \times (i) \right) \quad \text{... (11.1)}$$

Where '*l*' is the lower limit of the median category, 'cf' is the cumulative frequency up to but not including the median category; 'f' is the frequency of the median category; and 'i' is the size of the median class interval. For the data in Table 11.2,

$$\text{Median} = 41 + \frac{75-47}{54} \times 20 = 41 + 10.4 = 51.4$$

Uses: The median can be used for *ordinal* or *interval level* data, but not for nominal level data. It can be used very effectively when extreme items are likely to unduly affect the mean.

Evaluation: The median is a simple concept. It is the central point in a distribution. Like the mode, it cannot be manipulated arithmetically. But is it relatively stable, as it is not influenced by grouping procedures. There is only one median for any set of data.

Related Measures: Quartiles, Deciles and Centiles

At times we may be interested in positions other than middle one. The most common non-middle positions are quartiles, deciles and centiles.

Quartiles are measures of location which divide a distribution into four equal parts. The first quartile, Q_1, is the point which has 25% of the cases below it and 75% above it. The second quartile is of course the median. The third quartile Q_3, has 75% of the cases below it and 25% of the cases above it. The following formulas are used for computing Q_1, and Q_3.

$$Q_1 = 1 + \left[\frac{n/4 - cf}{f} \times (i)\right] \quad \text{... (11.2)}$$

$$Q_3 = 1 + \left[\frac{3n/4 - cf}{f} \times (i)\right] \quad \text{... (11.3)}$$

where 'l' is the lower limit of the first and the third quartile classes respectively; f = frequency of the first and third quartile classes respectively. For the data in Table 11.2 Q_1, and Q_3 are worked out as follows:

$$Q_1 = 21 + \left[\frac{37.5 - 15}{32} \times 20\right] = 21 + 14 = 35$$

$$Q_3 = 61 + \left[\frac{112.5 - 101}{30} \times 20\right] = 61 + 7.6 = 68.6$$

iles are measures that divide a distribution into ten equal parts. The first decile, D_1 has 10% s below it and 90% above. The third decile D_3 has 30% of the cases below it. The fifth the median. The ninth decile D_9 has 90% of cases below it. The formulas for D_1 and D_9

$$1 + \left(\frac{n/10 - cf}{f} \times (i)\right) \quad \text{... (11.4)}$$

$$cf \times (i) \quad \text{... (11.5)}$$

class (the first or the ninth decile class as the case may

divide a distribution into one hundred equal parts.

As an illustration, let us compute C_{85} (the point

$$C_{85} = 1 + \left(\frac{.85n - cf}{f} \times (i) \right)$$

$$C_{85} = 61 + \left(\frac{127.5 - 101}{30} \times 20 \right) = 61 + 17.6 = 78.6 \qquad \text{... (11.6)}$$

Arithmetic Mean

This is what is commonly known as the 'average'. It is the average of all values in a distribution. The mean of a set of an ungrouped data is the sum of all values divided by the number of items. For example, the mean of a series 2,5,8.6,9 is 30/5 = 6. In statistical notation, the mean is usually designated by the symbol $\overline{x}$ (read as X-bar) and its simple computational formula is:

$$\overline{x} = \frac{\Sigma(fx)}{n} \qquad \text{... (11.7)}$$

where $\overline{x}$ = the arithmetic mean

x = any value

f = the frequency of a value

Σ = the sum total of all categories

n = the number of values

TABLE 11.3

Distribution of Daily Wages of Farm Labourers

Daily Wages (Rs.)	*Frequency (f)*	*Fx*
6	4	24
7	8	56
8	6	48
9	12	108
10	7	70
12	4	48
15	2	30
Total	[illegible]	

$\overline{x}$ = 384/43 = 8.9

In the case of a grouped data (example Table 11.4), the midpoin multiplied by its frequency. The *midpoint* can be computed by divid highest scores in any interval by 2. For example, the midpoint c 96/2 = 48. The formula for computing the arithmetic mean fro

$$\overline{x} = \frac{\Sigma fm}{n}$$

where $\overline{x}$ = the arithmetic mean,

m = the midpoint of each class-interv

f = the frequency of a value

fm = a midpoint multiplied by its frequency

n = the number of cases

TABLE 11.4

The Computation of Mean from a Grouped Frequency Distribution

Scores	*Frequency (f)*	*Midpoint (m)*	*fm*
11 - 15	3	13	39
16 - 20	4	18	72
21 - 25	7	23	161
26 - 30	3	28	84
31 - 35	2	33	66
36 - 40	1	38	38
Total	20 = n		460 = Σfm

$\bar{x}$ = 460 / 20 = 23

In Table 11.4 each midpoint (m) was multiplied by its corresponding frequency (f). Then the total of the multiplied figures was computed. This total was divided by the total number of cases (n) to get the mean.

Evaluation: Unlike the mode and the median, the arithmetic mean is based on all the values in the distribution. Hence, it is sensitive to extreme values. The mean will thus be a misleading measure when *extreme* values are present. But it is *amenable* to *mathematical* calculations.

Choice of an appropriate average

It is important to know when and where to use the different measures of central tendency. The choice depends upon the consideration of several *factors*: (1) the level of measurement; (2) the shape of the data distribution, and (3) the research objective.

Level of measurement:* Since the *mode* requires only a frequency count, it can be applied to any set of data at the nominal, ordinal or interval level of data.

The *median* requires an ordering of items from the highest to the lowest or *vice versa*. Hence it can be obtained from an ordinal or interval level of data and not from nominal data (like party affiliation, caste or religion).

The use of *mean* is exclusively restricted to interval (and ratio} data such as income, age, wage rate, and test score.

Shape of the distribution

In a perfectly symmetrical, unimodal distribution, the mode, the median and the mean will be identical.

In a skewed distribution, the mode falls closest to the 'peak' of the curve; the mean falls closest to the 'tail'; and the median somewhere between the mode and the mean. It is this characteristic that kes the *median* the *most desirable* measure of central tendency for describing a skewed distribution ta.

detailed discussion see "Levels of Measurement" in 5.6 Measurement, above.

When the researcher works with a symmetrical distribution, his choice of measure of central tendency is chiefly based on his particular research purpose and the data's level of measurement.

To describe bimodal distributions, it is necessary to identify both modes; the use of either median or mean will obscure the important aspects of such distributions.

Research objective: What is the purpose of the measure to be used? What does the researcher expects to do with his measure of central tendency? If he seeks a *simple crude* descriptive measure he can use the mode. If he wants to find out the most common or the *typical* category (*e.g.,* the most common caste or the typical income level or test score), the *mode* is the most appropriate measure. If an *average* figure is required for further mathematical manipulations, the *arithmetic mean* is the most appropriate measure. To describe a skewed distribution, the median is preferable. It is also used when the midvalue is to be identified. For a precise measure of symmetrical distributions, the mean is preferable over the median, as the mean is more stable than the median and amenable for advanced statistical analysis.

11.3 MEASURES OF DISPERSION

Introduction

The measures of central tendency indicate the central value of a distribution. However, the central value alone is not suficient to fully describe the distribution. In addition to the measures of centrality, we require a measure of the spread of the actual scores. The extent of such spread may vary from one distribution to another. For example, two income distributions may have the identical mean, but they may present different patterns of distributon: in one most incomes may cluster around the mean, and in another, the incomes may be widely dispersed, *i.e.,* one distribution has less variability than another. The extent of such variability is measured by *measures of dispersion.* The most common mesures of dispersion are: the range, the mean, absolute deviation, the variance, the standard deviation, and the coefficient of variation.

Range

The range (R) measures the *difference* between the *highest* and *lowest* scores of a distribution. For example, in a set of values 3, 5, 7, 9, 12, the range is the difference between 12 and 3, *i.e.,* 12 – 3 = 9. This measure requires ordering of scores according to size. It can thus he applied in cases where the distributionn is at least on an ordinal level of measurement.

Evaluation: The range is easy to compute and understand. It is a useful device for gaining a quick impression of dispersion. It is useful for *computation* of the standard deviation, the most important measure of deviation. As illustrated in Exhibit 11.1 (below) six standard deviations cover almost the entire distance, from the highest to lowest score in a distribution. Hence, the size of the standard deviation is approximately one sixth of the size of the range. This rule is useful in checking the calculation of the standard deviations. However, it is a *crude* measure of dispersion, because it suffers from several limitations. First, as it is based on the two extreme values only, even if one of the extreme value changes, the range will fluctuate sharply. It is thus, *sensitive* to extreme value[illegible] Second, the ranges *cannot be compared* with each other unless they are based on a similar nu[illegible] of observations. Third, the range *does not give* us any information about the pattern of vari[illegible]

Intermediate Ranges

An alternative lo the range is an intermediate range like interquartile range or interdecile range.

The *interquartile range* is the difference between the third and the first quartiles ($Q_3 - Q_1$). It measures the spread in the *middle half* of the distribution, and is less affected by extreme values. It is thus a more stable measure of dispersion that is the range. Consider the data in Table 11.2. The Q_3 and Q_1 for those data are 68.6 and 35.0 respectively. Hence the interquartile range for them is 68.6 – 35.0 = 33.6.

The principle of the interquartile range can be applied to any parts of the distribution. For example, one can calculate the range between the ninth and first deciles (D_9 and D_1).

The great virtue of the above intermediate ranges is that they reduce the influence of extreme scores.

Measures of Aggregate Dispersion

The range, the interquartile range and other forms of range have a major drawback in that, being based on two values alone, they reflect only the dispersion in some defined section of the distribution, but not the aggregate dispersion in it. To overcome this drawback, some measures of aggregate dispersion have been devised. They include: the mean deviation, the variance, the standard deviation and the co-efficient of variance.

In these measures, the deviations of *all* scores in the distribution from some norm are computed. Any of the measures of central tendency can be chosen as a norm. However, the *arithmetic mean* is *most commonly* used because of its mathematical properties.

Mean Absolute Deviation (MD)

This is one of the measures of *aggregate* dispersion based on *all* values in a distribution. It is computed as follows:

* Calculate the difference between each score or item and the mean, $\bar{x} = (X - \bar{x})$
* Sum up the absolute values of these differences ignoring the plus and minus signs, $\Sigma \mid \bar{x} \mid /n$
* Divide the sum by the number of cases, $\Sigma \mid x \mid /n$
* The result is the mean deviation, MD.

The above procedure is expressed as a formula:

$$MD = \frac{\Sigma|\bar{x}|}{n} \quad \text{... (11.9)}$$

Where MD = the mean absolute deviation

$|x|$ = the absolute deviation of each score from the mean ignoring plus or minus sign.

n = the total number of scores

To illustrate, take a set of scores 4,6,8,10,12. Their mean is 40 ÷ 5 = 8; the deviation of each of the scores from the mean: – 4, – 2, 0, +2, +4. We must ignore the plus and minus signs, because the sum of actual deviations using signs is always zero. The plus and minus deviations cancel themselves out, and therefore cannot be used to describe or compare the variability of distributions. The sum of absolute deviations without signs is 12, which is divided by the number of scores: 12 ÷ 5 = 2.4. Thus the mean deviation is 2.4.

The mean deviation can also be computed from the median or the mode.

The relationship between the mean, the range and the mean deviation is illustrated in Table 11.5.

TABLE 11.5

Income Distributions

	A	*B*	*C*
$\overline{x}$	20	20	20
R	0	6	30
MD	0	1.7	8.7
Inference:	no variability	moderate variability	high variability

When the ranges and the mean deviations of distributions with identical means vary, the variability of the distributions will be low or high, corresponding to the value of tbe range and the mean deviation.

Evaluation: The MD takes into account all values in a distribution, and so represents the aggregate or overall dispersion. However, the absolute values, on which the MD is based, are not amenable to mathematical manipulations. Hence the MD is *not useful* for *advanced* statistical *analysis*. Moreover, the MD does not provide us with much information about a distribution.

The variance (V) and the Standard Deviation (SD)

These measures of dispersion are based on the *square deviations* of all values (or scores) from the mean. These measures thus eliminate the drawback of the MD. The computation of the variance (V) and the standard deviation (SD) is similar to that of MD, except that deviations of scores from the mean are squared and then summed up and divided by n, the total number of observations.

The *variance* is the *means* of the *squared deviations* from the *mean* of a distribution.

The formula for computing variance is

$$\sigma^2 \text{ or } s^2 = \frac{\Sigma x^2}{n} = \frac{\Sigma(X - \overline{x})^2}{n} \quad \text{... (11.10)}$$

where σ^2 or s^2 = variance

x = the deviation of each score from the mean ($X - \overline{x}$)

n = the number of observations

Table 11.6 illustrates the procedure.

Evaluation: The variance expresses the *average dispersion* not in the original units of measurement but in *squared units*. This problem is solved by taking the square root of variance. This transforms the variance into the standard deviation.

The *standard deviation* (SD) is the *square root* of the *mean* of the *squared deviation* from the *mean* of a distribution. The SD is a measure which, unlike the variance, expresses dispersion in the original scores. It is usually denoted by σ, the Greek letter sigma or S. The formula for computing SD is

$$\sigma \text{ or } S = \sqrt{\frac{\Sigma x^2}{n}} \qquad \text{... (11.11)}$$

Table 11.6 illustrates the computation of the SD.

Implication: What is the implication of the standard deviation? The larger the standard deviation, the greater the variability around the mean of the distribution.

TABLE 11.6

Computation of the variance and the SD

(X) Scores (N = 6)	$\bar{x}(X-\bar{x})$	x^2	x^2
3	–5	25	9
5	–33	9	25
7	–1	1	49
9	1	1	81
10	2	4	100
14	6	36	196
Total 48		$\Sigma x^2 = 76$	$460 = x^2$

$$\text{Arithmetic average } \bar{x} = \frac{48}{6} = 8$$

$$S^2 = \frac{\Sigma x^2}{n} = \frac{76}{6} = 12.6$$

$$\sigma \text{ or } S = \sqrt{\frac{\Sigma x^2}{n}} = \sqrt{12.6} = 3.5$$

An *alternative easier* method is to compute the V and the SD directly with the raw scores without obtaining deviations.

The formulas are:

$$V = \sigma^2 = \frac{x^2}{n} - \bar{x}^2 \qquad \text{... (11.12)}$$

$$SD = \sigma = \sqrt{\frac{x^2}{n} - \bar{x}^2 s} \qquad \text{... (11.13)}$$

where Σx^2 = the sum of the squared raw scores (each raw score is squared and then the products are added)

$\bar{x}^2$ = the mean squared

By applying these formulas to Table 11.6, we get the same results.

$$V = \sigma^2 = \frac{460}{6} - 8^2 = 76.6 - 64 = 12.6$$

$$SD = \sigma = \sqrt{\frac{460}{6} - 8^2} = \sqrt{12.6} = 3.5$$

When *data are grouped,* the procedure for computing the V and the SD is similar to that used for the mean, *i.e.,* the formulas are modified to account for the frequencies and the size of class intervals. The formulas thus become:

$$V = \sigma^2 = \frac{\Sigma fm^2}{n} - \bar{x}^2 \qquad \text{... (11.14)}$$

$$SD = \sigma = \sqrt{\frac{\Sigma fm^2}{n} - \bar{x}^2} \qquad \text{... (11.15)}$$

where f = frequency in a class interval

m = the mid-point of a class interval

n = the total number of scores

$\bar{x}^2$ = the mean squared

Alternative formulas are:

$$Va = \sigma^2 = \frac{\Sigma f(m - \bar{x})^2}{n} \qquad \text{... (11.16)}$$

$$SD = \sigma = = \sqrt{\frac{f(m - \bar{x})^2}{n}} \qquad \text{... (11.17)}$$

where $\bar{x}$ = the mean

Table 11.7 illustrates the application of the above formulas.

TABLE 11.7

Calculation of V and SD from Grouped Data

Scores	*f*	*Midpoint m*	*fm*	*fm²*
4-6	1	5	5	25
7-9	2	8	16	128
10-12	4	11	44	484
13-15	3	14	42	588
16-18	1	17	17	289
19-21	1	20	20	400
Total	n = 12		Σfm = 144	Σfm² = 1914

$$\bar{x} = \frac{144}{12} = 12$$

$$\Sigma^2 = \frac{\Sigma fm^2}{-n} - \overline{x}^2 = \frac{1914}{12} - 144 = 159.5 - 144 = 15.5$$

$$\sigma = \sqrt{15.5} = 3.9$$

By applying the alternative formulas to data in Table 11.7 we get

m	*f*	*m* – $\bar{x}$	$(m-\bar{x})^2$	$f(m-\bar{x})^2$
5	1	–7	49	49
8	2	–4	16	32
11	4	–1	1	4
14	3	+ 2	4	12
17	1	+ 5	25	25
20	1	+ 8	64	64
	n = 12			$\Sigma f(m - \bar{x})^2 = 186$

(*Note:* Is the size of the type changed so often due to some technical difficulty?

$$\sigma^2 = \frac{\Sigma f(m - \bar{x})^2}{n} = \frac{186}{12} = 15.5$$

$$\sigma^2 = \sqrt{\frac{\Sigma f(m - \bar{x})^2}{n}} = \sqrt{\frac{186}{12}} = \sqrt{15.5} = 3.9.$$

Evaluation: The SD is more useful than other measures of dispersion. The reasons are: (1) The SD is more stable from sample to sample. (2) Its mathematical properties makes it possible to obtain standard division for two or more groups combined. (3) It is more *useful* in more *advanced* statistical *analyses* especially in statistical inferences. (See Section 6.5 of Chapter 6, above; Sections 11.6 and 11.7 of this Chapter, below).

Co-efficient of Variation

The standard deviations cannot be compared in absolute magnitudes when the distributions compared have very different means. A standard deviation of 2, for instance, would convey a different meaning in relation to a mean of 7 than to a mean of 75. Therefore the degree of variability must be calculated in relation to the mean of the distribution. This is measured by a measure called the *co-efficient of variation* (CV). The CV indicates the relative variation. It is computed by the following formula.

$$CV = \frac{\sigma}{\bar{x}} \times 100 \qquad \text{... (11.18)}$$

where CV = the co-efficient of variation

σ = the standard deviation

$\bar{x}$ = the arithmetic mean

Table 11.8 illustrates the application of CV.

Table 11.8

Democratic participation in four co-operatives

Co-operative	*A(160)*	*B(150)*	*C(190)*	*D(170)*
Mean	4.7	5.4	2.9	5.6
SD	2.7	2.9	2.8	2.7
CV	57.0%	54.0%	96.5%	48.0%

(*Note:* The figures is parentheses denote the number of persons interviewed in each group).

In absolute magnitudes (see Table 11.8) there are no significant differences among the standard deviations in the four co-operatives. However, there are substantial differences between the means, indicating the varying degrees of democratic participation in each co-operative. CVs show that the relative deviation from the mean is higher in C than in other co-operatives, reflecting the lower degree of homogeneity in democratic participation (i.e., the higher degree of variability in democratic participation in it).

Standard Deviation and the Normal Distribution

The standard deviation is the most important measure of dispersion. This importance arises from its *special* relationship with the normal distribution.

A *normal distribution* is unimodal and symmetric. (Sec Section 6.4, above). When graphed as a frequency curve, this distribution takes the familiar bell-shaped curve which can be used as an approximation of the distribution of numerous variables like IQ scores, heights of males, measurement errors, sampling distributions and others.

In a normal distribution, the proportion of the area lying under the curve between any two points can be specified. For example, the distance between lhc mean and ± one standard deviation (σ) occupies 34.13% the area under curve: therefore the distance between –σ and + σ includes 61.26% of the arèa; the dislance between +2σ and –2σ includes 95.44% the area of; and the distance belween –3σ and +3σ includes 99.7% areas. (See Exhibit 11.1)

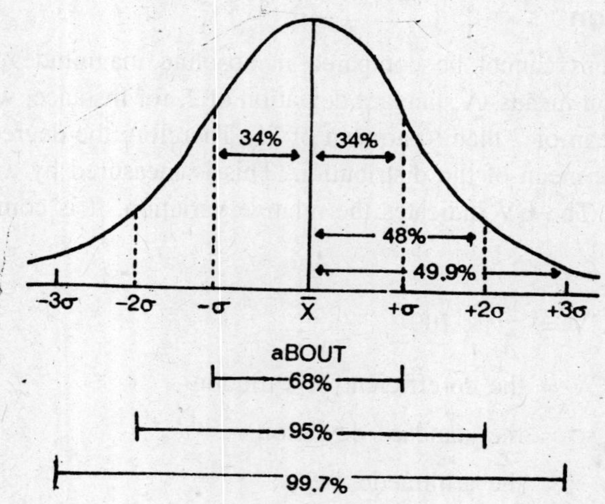

Exhibit 11.1: Standard Deviation and Normal Distribution

We can similarly define the area corresponding to the distance between any two points, when those points are expressed as standard deviation units.

Standard Deviation Units or Standard Scores

The standard scores provide a method of expressing any score in a distribution in terms of its distance from the mean in standard deviation units. There are two common types of standard scores: (1) z–score and (2) Z or T – score.

z-scores: A z-score is a measure of deviation from the mean relative to the standard deviation; that is, it is a deviation score expressed in standard deviation units.

Symbolically,

$$z = \frac{X - \bar{X}}{\sigma} = \frac{*}{\sigma} \quad \text{... (11.19)}$$

where X = any raw score

$\bar{X}$ = the arithmetic mean

σ = the standard deviation

* = the deviation of raw score from the mean.

A z-score thus expresses any raw score as being so many standard deviations above or below the mean. Suppose we have a normal distribution whose mean is 20 and the standard deviation is 4. If one of the scores in this distribution is 28, this score 8 units above the mean. If we divide this deviation score, *2 = 8 =(28 – 20), by the standard deviation, we obtain a z-score of +2. In other words, the raw score of 28 lies two standard deviation units above the mean.

We can convert any normal distribution into a *standard normal distribution* by converting the raw scores into Z-scores. A *standard normal distribution* is a normal distribution with a mean of zero and a standard deviation and variance of one. All z-scores have some of the properties of a standard normal distribution, *i.e.*, the mean of the z-scores is zero, and the standard deviation and variance of z-scores are equal to one.

z-scores make it easier to compare groups of scores or variables on an equally weighted basis. They are also useful in hypothesis testing, determination of percentile ranks and probability judgement.

Z - score: Another version of a standard score is Z or T-score. This has been devised to avoid some confusion resulting from the negative z-score (below the mean) and also to eliminate decimal values.

The Z-score is obtained by adding 50 to the mean and multiplying the z-score by 10.

$$Z = 50 + 10\left(\frac{x - \bar{x}}{\sigma}\right) = 50 + 10z \quad \text{... (11.20)}$$

Thus we get positive numbers. Z-scores are always rounded to the nearest whole number; *e.g.*, a z-score of +1.27 would be converted into a Z-score of 63:

$$Z = 50 + 10\,(+\,1.27) = 50 + 12.70 = 62.70 = 63.$$

11.4 MEASURES OF ASSOCIATION/RELATIONSHIP

Bivariate Analysis

Once the data relating to single variables are summarized and their pattern of distribution studied, the researcher's next task is to examine the pattern of relationship between the variables under study. This section examines the important measures of association/ relationship between two variables.

The Concept of Relationship

In the world around us, we observe association between things. As children grow, their weight increases; application of fertilizers increases crop yield; cities tend to be more polluted than rural areas; when the demand for a commodity expands, its price tends to rise up; and so on. Each of these observations is a statement of relationship: between age and weight; fertilizer application and crop yield; degree of urbanization and pollution; demand and price. To state a relationship between X and Y, is to say that certain categories of variable X go with certain categories of variable Y. This is the *principle of covariation* and it is basic to the notion of association or relationship.

In examining the relationship between variables, we have to consider *certain* questions: Is there a relationship between the variables under study? If so, what is the *direction* and *degree* of their relationship? Is the relationship a *causal* one? Is the relationship statistically significant? The answers to these questions are provided by different statistical techniques and the related tests of significance. The most important measures of association between two variables are: (*a*) cross tabulation and percentage difference, (*b*) association coefficients: Lamda, Goodman and Kruskal's tau, Gamma, Kendall's tau and Somer's d, (*c*) correlation coefficient, and (*d*) regression analysis.

Cross tabulation and percentage difference, Lambda and Goodman & Kruskal's Tau are used for measuring association between nominal level[1] variables. Gamma, Kendall's tau-b, Somer's d, and Spearman's Rank-order Correlation Coefficient (Rho) are used for ordinal variables. When both the independent and the dependent variables are interval or ratio level measures, correlation or regression analysis is used. The correlation analysis shows whether there is association between the variables, whereas the regression analysis helps in judging causal relationship.

Cross Tabulation and Percentage Difference

The percentage difference in a cross table is used for measuring association between nominal level variables. Nominal variables are purely qualitative and can be categorized only.

A two-way table (Table 11.9) is prepared. The values for one variable are put along one side of the table and the values of the other variable along the other side of the table. Each variable is categorized into two or more categories; and the variables are cross-tabulated for those sub-categories. The percentages are computed for them. On the basis of the percentages, conclusions are drawn.

TABLE 11.9

Preference for Brand X and Age (Hypothetical)

Brand Preference	*Age*		
	Youth	*Adult*	*Total N*
Yes	120 (60%)	120 (60%)	240
No	80 (40%)	80 (40%)	160
Total	200	200	400

(*Note:* Figures in brackets represent percentages to respective column totals).

In Table 11.9 the variables of preference for Brand X and age are independent *i.e.,* not associated, because proportionately as many youths as adults prefer brand X.

TABLE 11.10

Preference for Brand Y and Age (Hypothetical)

Brand Preference	*Age*		
	Youth	*Adult*	*Total*
Yes	140 (70%)	20 (10%)	160
No	60 (30%)	180 (90%)	240
Total	200	200	400

(*Note:* Figures in brackets represent percentages to respective column totals).

In Table 11.10 the variables are associated, because higher proportion of youths prefer brand Y than adults.

When a researcher finds that a relationship exists between two variables, he must investigate its *direction*. When one variable increases, the other also increases; a direct or positive relationship exists between them. Example, relationship exists between income and education; children's age and weight. When one variable increases, the other decreases, there is a *negative* or inverse relationship between them, example, supply and price; socio-economic status and family size.

The *strength* of a relationship is determined by the pattern of differences between the values of variables. If there are marked percentage differences between the different categories of the variables, the relationship between them is strong, if the differences are slight the relationship is weak. In Table 11.10, we find that the relationship between the variables is strong.

The *statistical significance* of a relationship is determined by using an appropriate test of significance. The tests of significance are discussed in a separate section in this chapter. The stronger a relationship is the more likely it is to be statistically significant.

Prediction and Proportional Reduction of Error (PRE)

The notion of prediction is inherent in the concept of covariation. When two variables covary, it is possible to use one to predict the other.

Suppose we have a group of fifty farmers and we know that twenty of them have a record of loan delinquency, while thirty have no such record. Suppose we are asked to guess the delinquency status of each farmer. Since our information is minimal, the best prediction is to use the mode. Here the mode is delinquent and the modal frequency is thirty. By guessing that each of the fifty farmers is delinquent we will be correct in thirty cases and wrong in twenty cases. Our prediction based on the mode has resulted in 20 errors in prediction or an error rate of 20/50 *i.e.,* 40%. But suppose we add a second variable and thus have a second piece of information; twenty-six of the farmers are members of Farmers' Association and twenty-four are not. Let us arrange the data in a cross-table (Table 11.11).

TABLE 11.11

Association membership and Loan Delinquency (Hypothetical)

Loan repayment (X)	*Association Membership (Y)*		
	Member	*Non-member*	*Total*
Delinquent	22	8	30
Non-delinquent	4	16	20
Total	26	24	50

Let us predict delinquency on the basis of association membership status of eaci. farmer. Our prediction rule is to use *within category* mode. For the twenty-six farmers who are members of Farmers' Association, the within-category mode is delinquent and if we guess all members are delinquent, our prediction results in four errors or an error rate of 4/26 = 15%. Similarly, for the twenty-four farmers who are not members of Farmers' Association, we predict non-delinquent (since within the category of non-member, the mode is non-delinquent) and make eight errors in prediction or an error rate of 8/24 = 33%. In total we have made 4 + 8 errors, and our error rate is (4+8)/(26+24) = 12/50 = 24%.

We can now know the advantage of using another variable (association membership). It reduces our error rate from 40% to 24%. This is known as the *Proportional Reduction of Error* (PRE). This is defined as

$$PRE = (E_1 - E_2) / E_1 \qquad \text{... (11.21)}$$

where E_1 = original number of errors based on the dependent variable's mode.

E_2 = new number of errors after employing independent variable as a predictor.

The PRE is thus achieved when we shift from one prediction rule to another. These rules are:

PR 1: To predict the dependent variable, use its own mode.

PR 2: To predict the dependent variable, use the within category modes of the independent variable.

A measure of association can be developed on the basis of the above PRE mod·l.

Lambda (λ)

This measure of relationship was developed by Louis Guttman.[2] It is also known as the Guttman Co-efficient of Predictability. It is suitable for measuring association between nominal variables. It is based on PRE model discussed earlier.

Lambda is defined as the co-efficient of reduction of prediction error achieved by shifting from one prediction rule (overall mode) to another (within-category modes).

$$\lambda = (E_1 - E_2) / E_1 \qquad \text{... (11.22)}$$

Where E_1 = Error of prediction based on Rule 1

E_2 = Error of prediction based on Rule 2

2. Guttman Louis, "An Outline of the Statistical Theory of Prediction," in Paul Horst (Ed.), *The Prediction of Personal Adjustment,* New York: Social Science Research Council, Bulletin 48, 1941.

For the data in Table 11.11

λ_{xy} = (20 – 12)/20 = 8/20 = 0.40

In this case, the value λ_{xy} was computed by predicting loan delinquency (X) from our knowledge of association membership (Y). Similarly we can compute λ_{yx} by predicting association membership from the knowledge of delinquency.

λ_{yx} = (24 – 12)/24 = 12/24 = 0.50.

A similar formula for computing lambda is:

$$\lambda_{xy} = \frac{\Sigma f_y - F_x}{n - F_x} \quad \text{... (11.23)}$$

where f_y = the modal frequency within each category of independent variable (Y)

F_x = the modal frequency of the marginal total of the dependent variable (X)

N = the total number of cases

Applying formula in 11.23 for data in Table 11.11 we get

λ_{xy} = [(22 + 16) – 30]/(50 – 30) = 8/20 = 0.40.

The Lambda is an asymmetric measure of association. A measure of association is said to be asymmetric if for a given contingency table, two values of that measure can be computed: one with variable X conceived as in independent variable, and a second value with variable Y conceived as an independent one. A *symmetric measure*, on the other hand, yields only a *single computed value* either way.

A symmetric measure always describes one-way as opposed to mutual association. Whether a measure is asymmetric or symmetric is a question of *statistical* formulation, while the question of one-way versus mutual associations is a *logical* one.

Interpretation: The Lambda may vary from 0.0 to 1.0. It cannot be negative. A value of 1.0 means that knowledge of the independent variable enables us to perfectly predict the dependent variable. A value of 0.40 means that in shifting the prediction rule 1 to 2, we reduce the error by 40%. The value of 0.0 does not necessarily mean that there is no association between the variables. It just means that the shift in prediction rule is of no help. When within the category modes are identical to each other and to the overall mode there will be no difference in prediction error and hence lambda will be zero. To illustrate let us consider Table 11.12.

TABLE 11.12

Association Membership and Loan Delinquency (Hypothetical)

Loan repayment (X)	*Association Membership (Y)*		
	Member	*Non-member*	*Total*
Delinquent	26	13	39
Non-delinquent	0	11	11
Total	26	24	50

λ_{xy} = [(26 + 13) – 39]/(50 – 39) = 0/11 = 0.0.

In such situations, the Lambda is said to be insensitive. In these cases, any other measure of association such as Goodman & Kruskal's Tau[3] must be used.

Goodman & Kruskal's Tau

This is a PRE and *asymmetric* measure of association for nominal data. It can be applied when Lambda is inappropriate.

The main difference between Lambda and GK's Tau lies in the method of computing errors. Whereas the prediction rules for Lambda are based on modes, the prediction rules for Tau are based on the concept of *random assignment* of subjects within the table. The prediction rules for Tau are:

PR 1: All *n* cases are to be randomly assigned to categories of the dependent variable.

If, in Table 11.12, we randomly assign eleven of the fifty cases to the delinquent category of the dependent variable, we will make on the whole on average, (11) × (39/50) = 8.58 errors. Similarly the random assignment of thirty-nine cases to the non-delinquent category will yield on average (39) × (11/50) = 8.58 errors. Therefore, E_1, the number of errors made from using PR^1 is (8.58 + 8.58) = 17.16.

PR 2: Within each category of the dependent variable, each case is to be randomly assigned to a category of the dependent variable.

In Table 11.12, we have twenty-six cases within the category of association member. If we randomly assign these twenty-six cases to non-delinquent category we will make (26) × (0/26) = 0 errors in prediction. If we assign the twenty-six cases to the delinquent category we will make (0) × (26/26) = 0 errors. In non-member category there are twenty-four cases. If we randomly assign these twenty-four cases to the delinquent category, we will make on the average (13) × (11/24) = 5.96 errors. If we assign them to the non-delinquent category, we will make on the average (11) × (13/24) = 5.96 errors. Therefore E_2, the number of errors made from using PR^2 is (0 + 0 + 5.96) = 11.92.

Using the general formula we can now determine the value of Tau:

$$\text{Tau} = (E_1 - E_2)/E_1 = (17.16 - 11.92)/17.16 = 5.24/17.16 = 0.31$$

Tau ranges from 0 to 1.00 with '0' implying no reduction in error and 1.0 indicating prediction with no error.

Measuring Association between Ordinal Level Variables

The ordinal level variables have rank order differences. The most common measures of association between ordinal variables are Gamma, Kendall's tau, Somer's *d* and Spearman's rank –order correlation coefficient (Rho).

Gamma

Gamma is a measure of association developed by Goodman and Kruskal.[4] It is a symmetric measure, *i.e.*, it yields only a single computed value for a given contingent table. It measures association

---

3. Goodman & Kruskal's Tau (A measure of association for nominal variables) should not be confused with Kendall's Tau which is a measure of association for ordinal data.
4. Goodman Leo A., and William H.Kruskal, "Measures for Cross Classification," *Journal of the American Statistical Association*, 49, December 1954, pp. 734-764.

between two *ordinal level* variables. It measures *one-way* association *i.e.,* it uses information about one variable to tell us something about a second one, and it is based on *pair-by-pair comparison.*

Let us introduce the logic of pair-by-pair comparison. Suppose two respondents X and Y are asked to rank the product characteristics that they would consider while buying a scooter. Three possible sets of rankings are given in Table 11.13.

TABLE 11.13

Ranking of Product Characteristics by Two Respondents (three hypothetical examples)

Characteristics	*Respondent X*	*Respondent Y*
(*a*) Fuel efficiency (F)	1	1
Price (P)	2	2
Mechanical Efficiency (M)	3	3
Riding comfort (R)	4	4
Style (S)	5	5
(*b*) F	1	5
P	2	4
M	3	3
R	4	2
S	5	1
(*c*) F	1	1
P	2	2
M	3	4
R	4	5
S	5	3

In (*a*) there is a perfect positive agreement between the two respondents, in (*b*) a perfect negative agreement between them, but in (*c*) there are both agreement and disagreement among the sets of ranks, example, in terms of pair-by-pair comparison the ranking of F-P pair is similar and that of R-S pair is dissimilar.

After counting the number of similar and dissimilar pairs, the level of association between the two sets of ranks is computed by the ratio of the preponderant type of pairs (similar or dissimilar) to the total number of similar and dissimilar pairs. This value is Gamma (G or γ). The simple formula for computing Gamma is

$$G = \frac{n_s - n_d}{n_s - n_d} \quad \text{... (11.24)}$$

Where n_s = the number of similar pairs

n_d = the number of dissimilar pairs

Let us list the pairs of ranks of Table 11.13 in Table 11.14 and also record for each of the three examples, whether a given pair is similar (S) or dissimilar (D).

TABLE 11.14

List of Pairs for Table 11.13

Pair	11.13(*a*)	11.13(*b*)	11.13(*c*)
FP	S	D	S
FM	S	D	S
FR	S	D	S
FS	S	D	S
PM	S	D	S
PR	S	D	S
PS	S	D	S
MR	S	D	S
MS	S	D	D
RS	S	D	D

Note: S = Similar; D = Dissimilar

For (a) $n_s = 10; n_d = 0$
(b) $n_s = 0; n_d = 10$
(c) $n_s = 08; n_d = 02$

All possible ten pairs in (*a*) are similar; all ten in (*b*) are dissimilar, and in (*c*) eight are similar and two are dissimilar. Applying the formula 11.25 we can now compute Gamma for the data in Table 11.14.

For (*a*) G = (10 – 0) / (10 + 10) = 10/10 = +1.0
(*b*) G = (0 – 10) / (0 + 10) = – 10/10 = – 1.0
(*c*) G = (8 – 2) / (8 + 2) = 6/10 = + 0.60

A coefficient of +1.0 indicates the perfect positive association between the variables in terms of pair-by-pair comparison, G = – 1.0 indicates the perfect inverse association and + 0.60 the preponderance of similar pairs over dissimilar ones.

At times, a judge may be unable to decide the ranks of some attributes. Suppose in Table 11.12 (*c*) the respondent X assigns the same rank 4 to R and S, then RS is a *tied* pair. With Gamma, *tied* pairs are *excluded.*

When the number of cases under analysis is large, the listing of similar and dissimilar pairs becomes cumbersome. To avoid this, it is usual to group the data into categories (see Table 11.15).

TABLE 11.15

Education and Civic Sense

Civic Sense (Y)	*Education (X)*			
	Low	*Medium*	*High*	*Total*
Low	9	4	2	15
Medium	2	10	8	20
High	1	4	10	15
Total	12	18	20	50

To find n_s in a bivariate table, the frequency in every cell is multiplied by the total of all frequencies in the cells below it and to its right and the products are added.

For Table 11.15

$n_s = 9(10 + 8 + 4 + 10) + 4(8 + 10) + 2(4 + 10) + 10(10) = 288 + 72 + 100 + 100 + 448$

To calculate n_d the frequency in each cell is multiplied by the total of all frequencies in the cells below it and to its left and the products are added up.

For Table 11.15

$n_d = 2(10 + 2 + 4 + 1) + 4(2 + 1) + 8(4 + 1) + 10(1) = 34 + 12 + 40 + 10 = 96$

To find the number of tied pairs in X (T_x) the frequency in each cell is multiplied by the total of all the frequencies in the cells in that column and the products are added up.

For Table 11.15

$T_x = 9(2 + 1) + 4(10 + 4) + 2(8 + 10) + 2(1) + 10(4) + 8(10) = 27 + 56 + 36 + 2 + 40 + 80 = 241$

To find the number of tied pairs in Y (T_y), the frequency in each cell is multiplied by the sum of frequencies in the cells in that row and the products are added up.

For Table 11.15

$T_y = 9(4 + 2) + 4(2) + 2(10 + 8) + 10(8) + 1(4 + 10) + 4(10) = 72 + 8 + 36 + 80 + 14 + 40 = 250$

We can now compute Gamma

$G = (448 - 96)/(448 + 96) = 352/544 = 0.65$

Interpretation: If $G = \pm 1.0$ there is perfect association between the variables. If G is 0.0, there is no association. Gamma can be viewed as a PRE measure as well.

Evaluation: The main weakness of Gamma is the *exclusion of ties* from its computation. Hence it will reach a value of ± 1.0 even under conditions of less than perfect association. This problem is especially acute in 2 × 2 tables, where the proportion of untied pairs will be small.

Kendall's Tau

When ties are many, Kendall's Tau is used. Kendall[5] had described three symmetric measures of mutual association for ordinal data. They are known as Kendall's Tau, Tau-a, Tau-b, and Tau-c. All three, like Gamma, are based on the logic of pair-by-pair comparison.

The three Tau measures and Gamma involve the computation of n_s and n_d. All involve $n_s - n_d$ in the numerator of the computational formula. However, these four measures differ in the determination of the maximum possible number of pairs used in the denominator.

For Gamma, the maximum number of pairs is $(n_s + n_d)$, ties being excluded.

Tau-a takes the total number of pairs including ties. It is the maximum number of pairs. Its formula is

$$\text{Tau} - a = \frac{n_s - n_d}{\frac{1}{2}n(n-1)} \qquad \text{... (11.25)}$$

where n = total number of cases

n_s = the total number of similar pairs

n_d = the total number of dissimilar pairs

5. Kendall, Maurice G., *Rank Correlation Methods*, London: Charles Griffin, 1962.

Tau-b has a correction factor for ties in its denominator (T_y and T_x). Its formula is

$$\text{Tau-b} = \frac{n_s - n_d}{\sqrt{(n_s + n_d + T_y)(n_s + n_d + T_x)}} \quad \text{... (11.26)}$$

$$\text{Tau-b} = \frac{n_s - n_d}{\left(\frac{1}{2}\right)\sqrt{(n^2 - \Sigma F_r^2)(n^2 - \Sigma F_c^2)}} \quad \text{... (11.27)}$$

Where Fr and Fc are the row totals and column totals respectively.

Tau-b is applicable only to tables with the equal *number of rows (r) and columns (c)*. For rectangular tables, Tau-c, a variant of Tau-b is used. Its formula is

$$\text{Tau-c} = \frac{n_s - n_d}{\left(\frac{1}{2}\right)N^2}[(m-1)/m] \quad \text{... (11.28)}$$

where 'm' is the smaller of the number of rows or number of columns

Let us compute Tau measures for Table 11.15.

$$\text{Tau-a} = \frac{n_s - n_d}{\frac{1}{2}N(N-1)} = \frac{488-6}{25(50-1)} = \frac{392}{1225} = 0.32$$

$$\text{Tau-b} = \frac{488-96}{\left(\frac{1}{2}\right)\sqrt{[50^2 - (15^2 + 20^2 + 15^2)][50^2 - (12^2 + 18^2 + 20^2)]}}$$

$$= \frac{392}{\frac{1}{2}\sqrt{(2500-850)(2500-868)}} = \frac{392}{\frac{1}{2}\sqrt{(1650)(1632)}}$$

$$= 0.48$$

$$\text{Tau-c} = \frac{488-96}{\left(\frac{1}{2}\right)2500\left(\frac{3-1}{3}\right)} = \frac{392}{\frac{1}{2}\times 2500\times\frac{2}{3}} = \frac{392}{833.3}$$

Evaluation: The measures like Gamma are symmetric measures of association, but while they measure mutual association, Gamma measures one-way association. Tau-a is used only in cases where ties do not exist. Tau-b is used where the number of rows equals the number of columns. Tau-c applies to cases where $r \neq c$.

Somers' d

Somers[6] had introduced a measure of association for ordinal data. It is known as Somers' d. Like Gamma and Kendall's Tau, Somers' d is based on pair-by-pair comparison. It is an asymmetric measure.

6. Somers, Robert H., "A New Asymmetric Measure of Association for Ordinal Measures", *American Sociological Review*, 27, December 1962, pp. 799-811.

Somers' *d* is very similar to Gamma with one important exception, viz., the denominator includes tied pairs on the dependent variable only, but excludes tied pairs on the independent variable only and tied ones on both variables. The computing formulas are:

$$d_{yx} = \qquad \ldots (11.29)$$

$$d_{xy} = \frac{n_s - n_d}{\frac{1}{2}\left(n^2 - F^2{}_y\right)} \qquad \ldots (11.30)$$

where F_x and F_y are column and row totals of the X and Y variables.

The *interpretation of 'd'* is analogous to that of Gamma. But Somers' *d* does not have a distinct PRE interpretation.

Comparison: All six measures discussed thus far (G, Tau-a, Tau-b, Tau-c, d_{yx}, d_{xy}) are similar in that all are based on the logic of pair-by-pair comparison. But they differ on the treatment of tied pairs. Gamma completely eliminates all tied pairs. Tau-a includes all tied pairs. Tau-b and Tau-c treat all pairs as if they have complete mutual association and exclude all tied pairs. Somers' *d* exclude tied pairs on the independent variables only.

Choice: Which of these measures should be used? It is not easy to make this decision. Gamma is always the preferred measure. But it does not measure mutual association. If we wish to measure mutual association, one of the Tau measures is preferable. Somers' *d* gives us an asymmetric measure but lacks a clear conceptual interpretation.

Testing for significance: All the above measures are subject to tests of significance. This is discussed in Section 11.7, Tests of Significance.

Spearman's Rank-order Correlation Coefficient (Rho)

This is the oldest of the frequently used measures of ordinal association. Rho (ε) is a measure of the extent of agreement of disagreement between two sets of ranks. It is a nonparametric measure and so it does not require the assumption of a bivariate normal distribution. Its value ranges between –1.0 (perfect negative association) and + 1.0 (perfect positive association)

The underlying logic of Rho centres on the difference between ranks. Rho is measured by

$$\text{Rho or } \varepsilon = 1 - \left[\frac{6\Sigma D^2}{n\left(n^2 - 1\right)}\right] \qquad \ldots (11.31)$$

where D = the difference between X, Y ranks assigned to an object

n = the number of observations

For the data given in Table 11.13 (b)

X rank	*Y rank*	*D*	*D^2*
1	5	– 4	16
2	4	– 2	4
3	3	0	0
4	2	2	4
5	1	4	16
			$\Sigma D^2 = 40$

$$e = 1 - \frac{6(40)}{5(25-1)} = 1 - \frac{240}{120} = 1 - 2 = -1.0$$

This value −1.0 indicates that there is perfect negative association between the two sets of ranks.

If there are any ties in ranking two objects, the mean values of the tied ranks is assigned to each object.

Rho is simpler than Kendall's Tau, but Kendall's Tau is generalizable to partial correlation coefficient, while Rho is not.

Requirements for using Rho: The following conditions should be satisfied for using Rho :

1. A straight-line correlation should exist between the variables.
2. Both X and Y variables must be ranked or ordered.
3. Sample members must have been taken at random from a larger population.

Research Examples:

Sarveswara Rao (1972),[7] in a study of two-factor theory of job satisfaction, used Rho. Ranks were given to perceived needs for supervisors and clerks on each job factor according to the magnitude of mean scores, and Rho was calculated, The calculated value was significant (Rho = 0.86, $p < 0.01$) indicating similarity between the two groups in their perceived need importance.

Sridharan and Radhakrishnan (1978),[8] used Kendall's rank correlation coefficient to test whether there was any shift in the cropping pattern during 1966 to 1976 in the selected district. Ranks were assigned to each crop on the basis of its percentage to the total cropped area. Rank coefficients of correlation were worked out for each pairs of successive years. All coefficients were significant at .01 level, which indicated that there was no shift in the cropping pattern.

Sharma (1987)[9] computed rank-order correlation coefficients for ranks of nine dimensions (labour-management relations, grievance handling, participative management, etc.,) between (*a*) multinationals and non-multinationals, (*b*) multinationals and public enterprises, and (*c*) non-multinationals and public enterprises. He also computed rank-order correlation coefficients between ranks for different dimensions of organizational climate and psychological climate (Rho = .9667; df = 7; t = 9.9890; $p < .001$).

Anbalagan (1989),[10] used rank-order correlation technique for examining the relationship between the perceived importance of the values of supervisors and workers in his study on 'Value Systems of Supervisors and Workers.' He ranked the values perceived by the supervisors and workers on the basis of their average response scores (see Table 11.16).

---

7. Sarveswara Rao G.V., *A Study of the Two-factor Theory of Job Satisfaction,* (unpublished doctoral thesis), Bangalore, Department of Management Studies, Indian Institute of Science, 1972, p. 58.
8 Sridharan B., and S.A. Radhakrishnan, "A Study of Factors Affecting Changes in the Cropping Pattern in Nilgiris District," *Indian Journal of Agricultural Economics,* Vol. XXXIII, No. 4, Oct.-Dec., 1978, pp. 14-21.
9. Sharma Baldev R., *Not by Bread Alone,* New Delhi: Shri Ram Centre for Industrial Relations and Human Resources, 1987, pp. 137, 146.
10. Anbalagan, "Value Systems of Supervisors and Workers", *Business Sprectrum,* Vol.1, No.2, April 1989, p. 15-29.

TABLE 11.16

Rank-order correlation between the Importance of the Values perceived by Supervisors and Workers

Values	*Supervisors rank assigned (R_1)*	*Workers Rank assigned (R_2)*	*$D^2 = (R_1 - R_2)^2$*
Self-confidence	1	1.5	0.25
Experience	2	1.5	0.25
Job satisfaction	3	9	36
Recognition	5	12	49
Status	5	6	1
Growth	5	8	9
Achievement	7	7	0
Creativity	8.5	10	2.25
Change	8.5	3.5	25
Affiliation	11	11	0
Money	11	5	36
Hard work	11	3.5	56.25
Competition	13	13	0
Independence	14	14	0
Promotion	15	16	1
Job security	16	15	1
			$\Sigma D^2 = 217$

Rho = +0.6728 $r^2 = 0.453$

He applied t-test to examine the value of Rho showed that it is significant at 5% level of significance. The coefficient of determination (r^2) is 0.4527 which explains 45% of variation in relationship between supervisors and workers in the importance of perceived values.

Correlation Analysis

When both the independent and dependent variables are *interval* or *ratio* level measures *correlation analysis is used* for measuring relationships and testing hypotheses.

The correlation coefficient measures the *degree of association* between variables. The correlation could be positive or negative. When two variables move in the same direction, their association is termed positive correlation. When they move in the opposite direction, their association is said to be *negative* or *inverse* correlation. There are also other types of correlation such as linear correlation, non-linear correlation, simple correlation, multiple correlation and partial correlation.

Linear correlation refers to a positive or negative straight-line relationship. *Non-linear correlation* refers to the curved line-type relationship. Simple correlation shows the relationship between two variables, whereas multiple correlations is concerned with simultaneous correlation among three or more variables. Partial correlation refers to the correlation between any two out of multiple variables while the remaining variables are held constant.

The correlation analysis involves three main aspects: (1) measuring the degree of association between the two variables, (2) testing whether the relationship is significant and (3) establishing the cause and effect relationship, if any.

Pearson Product Moment Correlation Coefficient

The most common measure of correlation is the Karl Pearson product moment coefficient of correlation *(r)*. This measure expresses both the strength and direction of linear correlation. This is measured by the formula:

$$r = \frac{N\Sigma XY - (\Sigma X)(\Sigma Y)}{\sqrt{\left[N\Sigma X^2 - (\Sigma X)^2\right]\left[N\Sigma Y^2 - (\Sigma Y)^2\right]}} \qquad \ldots (11.32)$$

where r = the Pearson correlation coefficient

N = the total number of pairs of X and Y

X = raw score on the X variable

Y = raw score on the Y variable

To illustrate let us examine the relationship between period of education (X) and religious prejudice (Y) for a sample of six respondents.

TABLE 11.16A

Correlation between Period of Education (X) and Religious Prejudice (Y) (N = 6)

X	X^2	Y	Y^2	XY
3	9	1	1	3
6	36	7	49	42
8	64	3	9	24
9	81	5	25	45
10	100	4	16	40
2	4	2	4	4
$\Sigma X = 38$	$\Sigma X^2 = 294$	$\Sigma Y = 22$	$\Sigma Y^2 = 104$	$\Sigma XY = 158$

$$r = \frac{6(158) - 38(22)}{\sqrt{\left[6(294) - (38)^2\right]\left[6(104) - (22)^2\right]}} = \frac{112}{211.66} = 0.53$$

The correlation coefficient ranges from – 1.0 to + 1.0. The value –1.0 indicates perfect negative correlation, the value + 1.0 perfect positive correlation, 0.00 no correlation and ± 0.5 moderate positive/negative correlation.

Requirement for using ‘r’: In order to use Pearson correlation coefficient, the following requirements must be satisfied:

1. The distributions of X and Y should have a linear relationship.
2. The data should be expressed in interval or ratio level measures.
3. Sample members must have been drawn on a random basis.
4. The distribution should be normal, especially for small samples. This requirement is of minor importance when the sample size is 30 or above.

For measuring the correlation between curvilinear variables, Pearson 'r' is inappropriate; an alternative measure called **Eta-square** is used. The procedure for calculating eta-square is not described here. The interested researcher can consult: Mueller, John H., Karl F.Schuessler and Herbert L.Costner, *Statistical Reasoning in Sociology,* Boston: Houghton Mifflin, 1970 and Freeman Linton C., *Elementary Applied Statistics,* New York: John Wiley and Sons, 1965.

Evaluation: While the correlation analysis can determine the degree of association between variables, it cannot show the existence of casual relationship. Only on the basis of the thorough conceptual knowledge and reasoning we can arrive at some conclusion on the casual relationship.

Regression Analysis

In social sciences, most relationships are linear in nature and can be fitted into a linear function. A function is said to be linear when pairs of X, Y values fall into a function that can be plotted as a straight line. This line is represented by the equation

$$Y = a + bX \quad \text{... (11.33)}$$

where X and Y = values of X and Y variables respectively.

a = Y-intercept or the place at which the line crosses the Y-axis or the amount of Y when X = 0.

b = slope of the line across the group, expressing the number of units of change in Y accompanying one unit of change in X.

For example, there is a perfect linear relationship between the distance and the time that a car travels at a fixed speed. Exhibit 11.2 shows the interrelationship between distance and time.

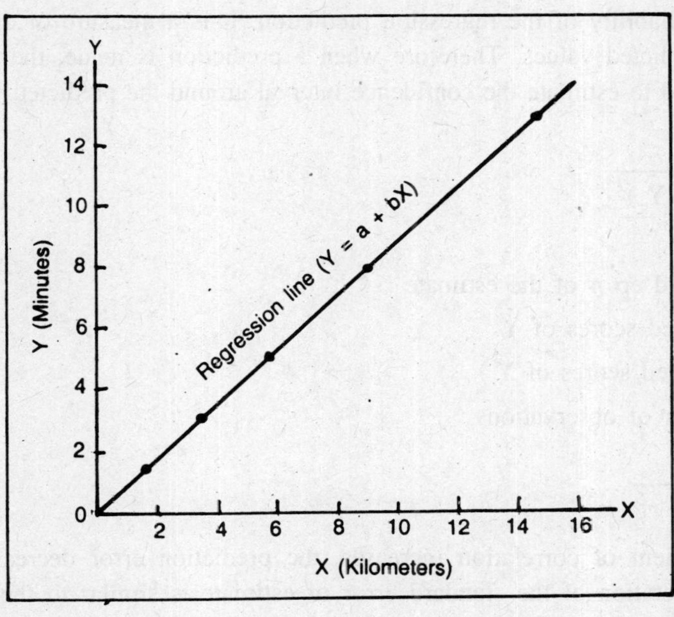

Exhibit 11.2: Regression of Y on X

The regression equation performs some *functions*. First, it describes the nature of association. The slope of the regression line (Y on X) is a geometric representation of the rate of change of Y with respect to X. Second, the regression equation is useful for predicting or estimating an unknown value of one variable for a given value of the other variable. The goal is to construct such an equation that the error of prediction will be at a minimum. The criterion of *least squares* achieves this goal. According to this criterion, 'a' and 'b' in the regression equation can be calculated by the following formulas:

$$b = \frac{N(\Sigma XY) - (\Sigma X)(\Sigma Y)}{N(\Sigma X^2) - (\Sigma X)^2} \quad \text{... (11.34)}$$

$$a = \bar{Y} - b\bar{X} \quad \text{... (11.35)}$$

After 'b' and 'a' are determined for a set of given data of X and Y variables, the regression line is fitted to the data by means of the technique of *least squares*. The least squares line of best fit minimizes the squared differences between the observed and predicted values of Y. Computer programs relating to regression analysis accomplish these calculations quickly and accurately.

We can predict any value of Y by using the straight line equation.

Y_e (the estimated value of Y) = a + bX.

The Standard Error of the Estimate

The values of Y estimated by the regression equation may not exactly be equal to the observed value. Thus the estimates may be in error. This is due to the fact that variations in Y may not be exactly due to variations in X.

A measure for estimating this prediction error is known as the standard error of estimate. It is a measure of the reliability of the regression prediction. It is a measure of dispersion of observed values from the predicted values. Therefore when a prediction is made, the standard error of the estimate may be used to estimate the confidence interval around the predicted value. The formula to be used is

$$Sy = \frac{\sqrt{(Y - Y_e)^2}}{n} \quad \text{...(11.36)}$$

where Sy = standard error of the estimate

Y = observed scores of Y

Y_e = estimated scores of Y

n = number of observations

Or

$$Sy = \sigma y \sqrt{1 - r^2} \quad \text{... (11.37)}$$

As the coefficient of correlation increases, the prediction error decreases. When r = ±1.0, Sy = 0. The interpretation of the standard error of estimate is similar to the interpretation of the standard deviation. If r = ± 0.60, the standard error of estimate of Y would be 0.80 σy. An actual score of Y would probably fall within a band of ± 0.80 σy from the predicted Y in about 68 out of

100 predictions. In other words, the probability is that the predicted score would not be more than one standard error of estimate from the actual score in about 68% of the predictions.

Research Examples for Correlation and Regression Analysis

see under "Multiple correlation and Regression" in section 11.5, below.

11.5 MULTIVARIATE ANALYSIS

Introduction

In the previous section we described techniques used for analyzing the relationships between two variables. The bivariate measures of relationship have a limited function of establishing covariation and its direction. An observed correlation between two variables does not, of itself, permit making causal relationships. A bivariate relationship may be the result of chance or it may exist because the variables are related to a third, unrevealed variable. Moreover the phenomenon under study may be multivariate in nature and cannot be explained by a single independent variable. In either case, the *need* for analyzing multiple variables arises. The analysis of multiple variables of a phenomenon is known as *multi-variate analysis,* and it involves *simultaneous analysis* of more than two variables. Multivariate analysis provides more *complete explanations* for complex phenomena and permit assessing *causal relationships* through statistical control.

The Concept of Control

A correlation between an independent variable and a dependent variable is not a sufficient basis for inferring causal relationship between them. The relationship between them might be caused by a third variable that is the cause of both the independent and dependent variables. Only by eliminating the possible effects of such other variables the original bivariate association can be validated. A process called *control*, a basic principle in all research designs achieves this.

In experimental research, control is accomplished by dividing subjects into experimental and control groups. The controlled experimentation assures control over extraneous variables. It is difficult to introduce experimental control in studies of social problems. In these cases, *control* is achieved through statistical methods that include cross tabulation; multiple correlation, partial correlation, multiple regression and factor analysis.

Cross Tabulation

This is one of the simplest methods of analyzing more than two variables at a time. The process of this method is as follows:

We establish first the relationship between an independent variable and a dependent variable through bivariate analysis. We then select a *third* variable associated with the independent variable and use it as a *control variable.* The sample is then divided into *sub-groups* according to the categories of the control variable. The bivariate association is then reassessed within each sub-group. We may find an entirely different result:. the disappearance/weakening of the original strong relationship, or emergence of a new relationship or existence of a strong relationship under one control condition but not under another. The following example illustrates this process of control through cross tabulation.

Suppose a sample of 900 persons is selected from urban and rural areas to test the hypothesis that urban people are politically more aware than rural people. The hypothetical data are presented in Table 11.17. 11 is observed that 50 per cent of urban respondents have higher level of political awareness compared with only 28 per cent of the rural respondents. Thus, it may be concluded that political awareness is related to place of living. Whether this relationship is real or is just based on an accidental relatiòn with a third variable (in which case the relationship is not real or spurious). One such additional variable might be educational level which is associated with political awareness and place of living (see Tables 11.18 and 11.19).

TABLE 11.17

Political Awareness by place of living (Hypothetical data)

Political Awareness	*Place of living*	
	Urban	*Rural*
High	200 (50%)	140 (28%)
Low	200 (50%)	360 (72%)
Total	400 (100%)	500 (100%)

TABLE 11.18

Place of living by educational level

Place of living	*Educational level*	
	High	*Low*
Urban	300 (75%)	100 (20%)
Rural	100 (25%)	400 (80%)
Total	400 (100%)	500 (100%)

TABLE 11.19

Political awareness by educational level

Political Awareness	*Educational level*	
	High	*Low*
High	240 (60%)	100 (20%)
Low	160 (40%)	400 (80%)
Total	400 (100%)	500 (100%)

To control for educational level, the 900 respondents are divided into two groups according to their level of education (high, low). Within each group, urban-rural living is cross-tabulated with political awareness. The original bivariate association is then estimated in each of the sub-groups (Table 11.20).

TABLE 11.20

Political awareness by place of living, controlling for educational level

Political awareness	*High Education*		*Low Education*		
	Urban	*Rural*	*Urban*	*Rural*	*Total*
High	180 (60%)	60 (60%)	20 (20%)	80 (20%)	340
Low	120 (40%)	40 (40%)	80 (80%)	320 (80%)	560
Total	300 (100%)	100 (100%)	100 (100%)	400 (100%)	900

In Table 11.20 educational level completely 17 accounts for the relationship between place of living and political awareness, for there is no difference between rural and urban respondents in their level of political awareness within either of the two educational groups. The overall association between the independent and dependent variables is completely accounted for by the association of each with educational level, as in Exhibit 11.3.

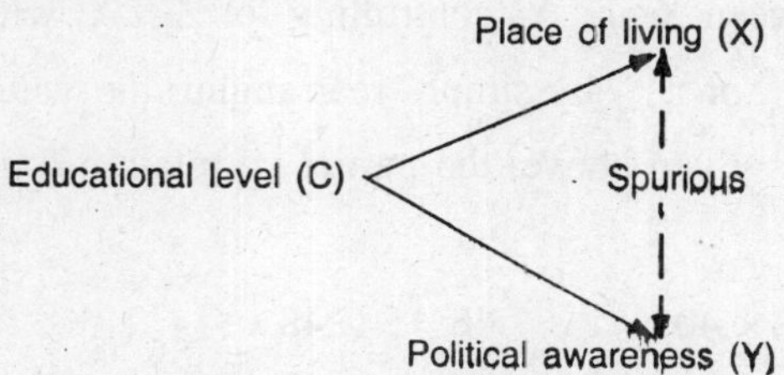

Exhibit 11.3: Association between variables

Educational level determines both political awareness and place of living. That is, people who are educated tend to live in urban areas and are generally politically aware. There is no inherent link between political awareness and place of living and the association between them is *spurious* or unreal.

Alternatively the introduction of control variables may lead to a different result also. If they do not change the original bivariate association then the original relationship between the independent and dependent variables may be considered to be *real*. Of course, one can never be completely sure that all relevant variables have been introduced into the analysis. However, the more relevant factors controlled for, the greater is the confidence that the relationship is not spurious.

Evaluation: The cross-tabulation method is popular in empirical research and it is applied to all levels of measurement. However, this method is a *tedious* process. It also suffers from a serious *limitation*. That is, it necessitates a *subdivision* of the sample into progressively *smaller* sub-groups for measuring association and thus rendering its validity and *reliability questionable.* The partial correlation method overcomes these drawbacks.

Partial Correlation

The partial correlation is a statistical method designed to measure the relation between an *independent* variable and a *dependent* variable by holding *all other related variables constant.* It cancels out the effect of the control variables on the independent and dependent variables and thus shows the *unmarred direct association* between them.

Suppose a correlation of r = 0.60 is found between variables X and Y. To test the nature of association between them, a third variable Z which is related to both X and Y is introduced. We compute the correlation between Z and X and that between Z and Y and get the r values of 0.30 and 0.40 respectively. These zero-order correlation coefficients can then be statistically manipulated to reveal the true relationship between X and Y with the effect of the third variable *'partialled out'* or removed. The formula for computing partial correlation is given below:

$$r_{xy.z} = \frac{r_{xy} - (r_{xz} X^{ryz})}{\sqrt{(1 - r_{xz}^2)(1 - r_{yz})}} \qquad \text{... (11.38)}$$

where X = independent variable

Y = dependent variable

Z = control variable

$r_{xy \cdot z}$ = the correlation between X and Y, controlling for Z (*i.e.*, with the effect of Z removed)

We could also compute $r_{xz \cdot y}$ or $r_{zy \cdot x}$ by simply rearranging the values in the above formula.

On the basis of the r values given above, the partial correlation for X and Y, controlled for Z can be now computed.

$$r_{xy.z} = \frac{.60 - (.30 \times .40)}{\sqrt{1 - .30^2)(1 - .40^2)}} = \frac{.48}{\sqrt{.764}} = \frac{.48}{.87} = .55$$

A partial correlation with one control is referred to as a first-order correlation, a partial correlation with two controls is known as second-order correlation and so on. The formula may be extended to control more than one variable. The controlling for variables 3 and 4 would be expressed as $r_{12.34}$; controlling for variables 3,4 and 5 expressed as $r_{12.345}$ and so on. The formulas for second-order and third-order partial correlation coefficients are:

$$r_{12.34} = \frac{r_{12.3} - (r_{14.3})(r_{24.3})}{\sqrt{(1 - r_{14.3}^2)(1 - r_{24.3}^2)}} \qquad \text{... (11.39)}$$

$$r_{12.345} = \frac{r_{12.34} - (r_{15.34})(r_{25.34})}{\sqrt{(1 - r_{15.34}^2)(1 - r_{25.34}^2)}} \qquad \text{... (11.40)}$$

Interpretation: The partial r is similar in measurement and interpretation to the simple Pearson r. Its value varies from –1.00 to +1.00. If the value of partial correlation is not very much different from the correlation of the independent and dependent variables, the original association between them may be considered as real. If on the other hand, the partial correlation is far below the original zero-order correlation, the original association is found to be spurious when control is removed.

Research Examples

See under *Multiple Regression,* below.

Multiple Correlation

The multiple correlation (R) shows the combined effects of two or more independent variables on a dependent variable. The formula commonly used for determining multiple R for two independent variables is:

$$R_{x.yz} = \frac{\sqrt{r_{xy}^2 + r_{xz}^2 - 2(r_{xy} \times r_{xz} \times r_{yz})}}{1 - r_{zy}^2} \quad \text{... (11.41)}$$

This formula can be extended to three or more independent variables.

Suppose three variables age (X), income (Y) and education (Z) are related to each other as:

$r_{xy} = {}^\circ 70$; $r_{xz} = -{}^\circ 20$, $r_{yz} = {}^\circ 50$

The combined effect of age and education on income is:

$$R_{x.yz} = \frac{\sqrt{{}^\circ 70^2 + {}^\circ 50^2 - 2(.70)(.50)(-.20)}}{1-(-.20^2)} = \sqrt{\frac{{}^\circ 88}{{}^\circ 96}} = \sqrt{{}^\circ 9167} = {}^\circ 96$$

The squared value of $R_{y.xz} = {}^\circ 96^2 = {}^\circ 92$. The interpretation of this value is: 92% of the variance in income (Y) can be explained by age and education.

The measure of R^2 is termed the *Coefficient of Multiple Determination*. The value of R^2 may vary from –0.00 to +1.00 with a value of +1.0 indicating that the independent variables perfectly predict the dependent variable, and a value of zero indicating that there is no linear relationship between the dependent variable and the combined independent variables.

R always reaches maximum value relative to the zero-order coefficients when the independent variables are not inter-correlated. Hence to improve the prediction, one should introduce the greatest possible number of relevant independent variables that are independent of each other.

Correlation for sample error: If the above formula (11.41) is used on population data the computed value of R will be accurate. However, if sample data are used, the computed value of R will be an overestimate. This bias can be corrected by the following formula:

$$R_c = \sqrt{1 - \frac{n-1}{n-k}(1 - R^2)} \quad \text{... (11.42)}$$

where R_c = the corrected value of R

n = the sample size

k = the number of independent variables

(For example, see under *Multiple regression,* below)

Multiple Regression

The simultaneous effect of several independent variables on a dependent variable can be assessed by constructing a multiple regression equation presented by the following formula:

$$Y_1 = a_{1.23} + b_{12.3} X_2 + b_{13.2} X_3 \quad \text{... (11.43)}$$

where Y_1 = the dependent variable

X_2 and X_3 = the independent variables

$b_{12.3}$ and $b_{13.2}$ = the partial regression coefficients denoting the slopes of the regression line for each independent variable, controlling for the other.

The $b_{12.3}$ thus reflects the amount of change in Y_1, associated with a given change in X_2, holding X_3 constant.

The regression coefficients ($b_{12.3}$, $b_{13.2}$) become less reliable as the degree of inter-correlation between the independent variables increases. This problem is described as multicollinearity. Therefore care should be taken in selecting independent variables so as to reduce the multicollinearity to the minimum.

The computing formulas for $b_{12.3}$, $b_{13.2}$ and $a_{1.23}$ are presented below:

$$b_{12.3} = \frac{b_{12} - (b_{13})(b_{32})}{1 - b_{23}b_{32}} \quad \text{... (11.44)}$$

$$b_{13.2} = \frac{b_{13} - (b_{12})(b_{23})}{1 - b_{32}b_{23}} \quad \text{... (11.45)}$$

$$a_{1.23} = \bar{Y}^1 - b_{12.3}\bar{X}^2 - b_{13.2}\bar{X}^3 \quad \text{... (11.46)}$$

Since the b coefficients reflect the net effect of each variable on the dependent variable, they can be compared to find the relative importance of the independent variables.

However, since each variable may be measured on a different scale in different units, b's in the formula must be standardized by converting them into beta weights (β). The beta weights are obtained by multiplying b by the ratio of the standard deviation of the independent variable to the standard deviation of the dependent variable. Thus $b_{13.2}$ would be expressed as:

$$b_{13.2} = b_{13.2} (S_3/S_1) \quad \text{... (11.47)}$$

where S_1 = standard deviation of the dependent variable Y_1

S_3 = standard deviation of the independent variable X_3

Just as with simple regression, one needs to estimate how well the multiple regression rule fits the actual data. This fit (or the relative reduction of error) is measured by the measure R^2 (the coefficient of multiple determination) described under multiple correlation.

Computer programs are available for the multiple correlation and regression analysis. They are useful in making the computations quickly and correctly.

Research Examples for Simple, Partial and Multiple Correlation and Regression analysis

Dhingra, Pandey and Paliwal (1969)[11] conducted an action research to identify the dominant psychophysical traits essential for efficient performance of a weaver's job and to develop appropriate

11. Dhingra O.P., S.K.D. Pandey and T.R. Paliwal, "Action Research: Selection Techniques for Trainee-Weavers", *Indian Journal of Industrial Relations,* Vol. 4, No. 3, January 1969.

tests to assess these traits. A set of five elemental tests (for two-hand coordination, finger dexterity, eye-hand coordination, visual acuity, and disparate attention) and another integrated tests are tried. The actual production efficiency figures of plain loom weavers and the average efficiency scores of award winner automatic loom wavers were taken as criterion scores. Coefficients of correlation between (*a*) elemental test scores and criterion variables, (*b*) integrated test scores and criterion scores, (*c*) each of five variables (two-hand coordination, finger dexterity, eye-hand coordination, visual acuity, and disparate attention) and the criterion scores were computed. The inter-correlations were also computed. The tests, which showed high correlations with criterion scores were picked up and multiple correlations were run and its significance, were tested. Partial correlations were also computed and their significance was tested. The results showed that finger dexterity and two-hand coordination tests are adequate predictors for selecting trainee weavers.

Rangaswamy, Ramaswamy and Guruswamy (1972),[12] studied the relationships of farmers' value dimensions (success-security, secular-scared; individualism-familism, future-past) education, and size of holdings to the adoption of new agricultural technology by computing *simple correlation* coefficients and tested their significance by t-test and found the coefficients significant at .01 level.

To find out the relationship of each of the above independent variables with adoption, when the effects of other variables were controlled, *partial correlation* coefficients were calculated and their significance was tested by applying t-tests. The partial correlations of education and four value dimensions were significant.

Multiple *regression* was fitted with adoption as the dependent variable. The significance of multiple regression was tested by the ANOVA. The F-value of 64.2482 was significant at .01 level, and R^2 was .212. The results showed that the factors that substantially contributed to the variation in adoption in the order of importance were educational level, success-security, value, future-past value, and secular-scared value.

Prasada Rao (1973),[13] used least squares *multiple regression technique* to determine the factors and their relative importance in influencing the level of borrowing. The independent variables examined were consumption expenditure, operating expenses, capital expenditure and assets owned. Regression coefficients of the independent variables and coefficient of *multiple determination* for all samples and for each farm type (general, hog, dairy, crop farms) were computed and their significance were tested by t-tests. The results show that operating expenses and capital expenditure are the most important factors determining the level of borrowing and borrowing do not increase with consumption.

Krishnaswami (1976),[14] in his study of democratic control in cooperatives, studied the relationship of each of the dependent variables: members' socio-economic status, business participation, cooperative knowledge, knowledge of own society, identification, and satisfaction with the dependent variable 'democratic participation' by computing *correlation coefficients* and their significance was tested by t-tests. All the coefficients were significant at .01 level.

In order to find out the net influence of each of the above six variables on democratic participation when all other variables were kept constant, *partial correlation coefficients* were computed and

12. Ramaswamy and P.A.Guruswami, *India's Changing Farmers,* Allahabad, Kitab Mahal, 1972, pp. 158, 162, 163, 164.
13. Prasada Rao B., *The Economics of Agricultural Credit-use in Southern Brazil,* Waltair: Andhra University, 1973.
14. Krishnaswami O.R., *Cooperative Democracy in Action, Op.cit.,* pp. 111-116.

applying t-tests tested their significance. The results showed that there was highly significant and positive relation between democratic participation and three factors, *viz.,* cooperative knowledge, member-identification, and socio-economic status. These three variables were put into *multiple regression analysis and* the regression was tested by ANOVA. The value of F was 225.8 significant at .01 level. R_2 = .817. Thus the socio-economic status, cooperative knowledge and member-identification together accounted for 81.76% of variation in participation behaviour. The standard regression coefficients indicated that member-identification was the most important factor and cooperative knowledge and socio-economic status come next in order.

Sain (I978)[15] in his economic analysis of shifting cultivation in North-East India, computed *correlation coefficients* between (*a*) operational size of farm (x) and per hectare yield of paddy (y), (*b*) crop mixture (x) and operated area (y), each of the selected villages, (*c*) farm size (x) and farm return (y) in selected villages, and (d) annual return per farm (x) and percentage of annual expenditure on food (y), and tested the significance of the correlation coefficients by 't'-tests. He also calculated the *regression coefficients* of Y on X and tested them by t-tests.

Nagaraju and Raghavendra (1981)[16] used *multiple regression analysis* to estimate veneer recovery from logs of different characteristics in the plywood industry. With veneer output as the dependent variable and a set of independent variables (length, girth, crookedness, taper, ovalness, knots and splits), *stepwise regression* was made. F-test at .05 level was used for testing the significance. The result was very significant (R^2 = 0.968). Except ovalness and splits, all other variables significantly contribute to the variability in veneer output.

Klein (1987)[17] tested three alternative models of the conditions necessary for employee ownership to positively influence employee attitudes. The models tested were: (1) intrinsic satisfaction (pride of ownership), (2) extrinsic satisfaction (financial benefits) and (3) instrumental satisfaction (worker participation). Data were collected from 2804 employee-stock owners in 37 companies. *Correlation coefficients* between employee outcome measures (satisfaction with the ownership plan, organizational commitment, and turnover intention) and the Employee Stock Ownership Plan (ESOP) characteristics (percentage of company stock owned, stock return, voting rights, reasons for the plan, employee ownership philosophy and strategies of communication about the plan).

Hierarchical (Step-wise) regression analyses of employee ownership philosophy and ESOP communications, (controlling for perceived worker influence were made). Further *multiple regression analyses* were made to examine the overall effects of the significant independent variables (contribution, employee ownership philosophy, and ESOP communications) on the employee outcomes. The results indicate that, on the average, employees are most satisfied with employee ownership and most committed to their companies when the company makes large contribution to the ESOP and the management is highly committed to the concept of employee ownership.

---

15. Sain K., "Economic Analysis of Shifting Cultivation," *Indian Journal of Agricultural Economics,* Vol. 32, No. 4, October-December 1978, pp. 8-13.
16. Nagarajan S., and B.G.Raghavendra, "Multiple Regression Analysis in Log Quality Factors and Veneer Yield," A Paper presented at the *Canadian Conference of Applied Statistics,* Concordia University, Montreal, April-May, 1981.
17. Klein Katherin, "Employee Stock Ownership and Employee Attitude," *Journal of Applied Psyschology,* Vol. 72, No. 2, May 1987, pp. 319-332.

Steele (1982),[18] used Pearson *product-moment correlation analysis* in a study of compensation problems; problem of salary compression (*i.e.,* the compensation gap between managers and their subordinates becoming narrower and narrower) and the inability to adequately reward meritorious performance, reduction in real salary-income on account of inflation. One theory was that companies avoid compression problems by offering new college graduates lower salaries so as to maintain a desired salary difference between supervisors and subordinates. To get a deeper insight into this problem, the data were analyzed by separate academic discipline: engineering, business administration, marketing, production, and data processing. Each organization's previous four-year merit increase program was correlated with its increases in offers to college graduates. Organizations with compression problems showed a slight to moderate correlation (all significant at .02 level or better) between the two sets of data for each discipline every year. Organizations without compression problems showed no relationships that were significant at the .02 level.

Sharma (1987)[19] used *multiple regression technique* to identify the critical determinants of supervisor-management relations (SMR) in industries in India. The ten variables — safety and security, monetary benefits, grievance/handling, participative management, objectivity and rationality etc., — selected for the study were correlated with one another and with SMR. These 45 correlation coefficients were put into a multivariate analysis using step-wise multiple regression technique. The analysis showed that 'grievance handling' and 'objectivity and rationality' were the major determinants of SMT.

Raghavendra Sai (1988)[20] used *step-wise multiple regression technique* to investigate the simultaneous influence of the rainfall at several rain gauge stations (independent variables) on the inflow to the reservoir (dependent variable) and used F-test for testing the significance of overall regression relationship and t-tests for testing the significance of the regression coefficients of each one of the independent variables.

In a study of relationship between dividend policy and share prices in selected industries, Murali and Krishnaswami[21] computed the *coefficient of correlation* between the dividend payout ratio and the average market price of equity shares for each of the firms for each year of the reference period of 1976-1986. The correlation coefficients were tested by t-tests at .05 level. The results showed that there was no significant correlation between dividend payout ratios and equity share prices.

A similar analysis was made for examining the relationship between rates of dividend and equity share prices. The results showed that in cement, pharmaceutical, tea and paper industries, there was significant and positive correlation between dividend rates and share prices.

In a study of self-concept of teachers and their emotional adjustment, Chadda[22] examined the relationship between the self-concept and emotional adjustment scores of various groups of teachers

18. Steele, James W., *Paying for Performance and Positions,* New York: American Management Associations, 1982.
19. Sharma Baldev R., *op. cit.* pp. 110-112.
20. Raghavendra Sai, Vissa, *Statistical Models for Rainfall Data Analysis of Reservoir Systems,* (unpublished dissertation), Bangalore, Dept. of Management Studies, Indian Institute of Science, 1988, pp. 27-32.
21. R. Murali and O.R. Krishnaswami, *A Study of the Relationship Between Dividend Policy and Share Prices in Selected Industries,* (unpublished dissertation), Bangalore, Dept. of Commerce and Management, Bangalore University, 1988.
22. Chadda D.K., "Self Concept of Teachers and their Adjustment," *Indian Educational Review,* Vol. XXIII, No. 1, January 1988.

(male, female, rural, urban groups) by computing *correlation coefficients* and found them statistically not significant.

Narayanasamy and Krishnasami (1989)[23] studied the relationship of capacity utilization, degree of operating leverage and turnover ratios to profitability to cooperative sugar mills and spinning mills by computing the *coefficients of correlation* and tested their significance by t-tests. After analyzing the inter-correlations among independent variables, they made a *multiple correlation* and *regression analysis* to determine the contribution of independent variables to the total variance in the dependent variable. The multiple regression coefficients were tested by F-test. The results showed that turnover ratios made significant contribution to profitability.

Chinnappa, Venkataram and Keshava (1987)[24] employed *multiple linear regression analysis* in a study made for identifying the causes for overdue of loans among farmers. The multiple linear regression function was fitted separately for marginal, small and large farmers with the average overdue amount per farmer as dependent variable and non-farm income, capital investment, family size, non-farm expenditure, debt to asset ratio and net farm income as independent variables. For the regression equation, non-farm income, capital investment, debt to asset ratio and net farm income were the independent variables. The regression coefficients on non-farm income, capital investment, debt to asset ratio and net farm income and R^2 were significant at .01 level. T-test was used as a test of significance.

Mander and Grewal (1988)[25] used *multiple regression analysis* in estimating the contribution of various inputs: land, human labour, manure and fertilizers, irrigation, expenditure on tractor, and expenditure on other capital assets to agricultural output in tractor and non-tractor farms and tested the significance of regression coefficients of various inputs and coefficient of *multiple determination* by t-tests at .01 level. The purpose of the analysis was to evaluate the rationale of resource use. The use of resources other than tractor was found to be rational. The investment on tractor was economically justified only on farms of 20 acres and above.

Subba Rao and Nagabhushanam[26] used *partial regression analysis* to study the role of manures and supplementary feeds in increasing fish output in inland fish farms. The partial regression coefficients of manure and feeds were computed for small, large and combined farm size-groups and their significance was tested by F-test at .01 level. The coefficients were positive and highly significant highlighting the significant contribution of this input to fish output.

Somasekhara (1975)[27] used the *multiple regression analysis* in a study of the efficacy of industrial estates. In order to estimate the elasticity of output with respect to capital and labour, production

23. N. Narayanasamy and O.R. Krishnaswami, *A Study of Factors Influencing the Relatioship Between Capital Structure and Cost of Capital in Larger Cooperatives, op. cit.*, pp. 234, 235, 243, 244.
24. Chinnappa Reddy B.V., J.V. Venkataram and T.R. Keshava Reddy, "An Economic Analysis of Overdues Among Farmers in Srinivaspur Taluk, Kolar District," *Land Bank Journal,* Vol. XXVI, No. 2, December 1987, pp. 1-10.
25. Mander G.S., *and* S.S. Grewal, "Economic Rationale of investments on Punjab Farms with Special Reference to Tractorisation," *Indian Journal of Agricultural Economics,* Vol. XLIII, No. 1, October-December 1988, pp. 613-623.
26. Subba Rao D.V., and T.D.J. Nagabhushanam, "Resource Management of Inland Fish Breeding-cum-Rearing Farms in Andhra Pradesh", *Indian Journal of Agricultural Economics,* Vol. XL, No. 4, October-December 1985. pp. 556-563.
27. Somasekhara N, *The Efficacy of Industrial Estates in India,* Delhi: Vikas Publishing House P. Ltd, 1975, pp. 38-39, 51-52.

functions of the Cobb-Douglas type were fitted for the industrial estates and their control groups. By the application of the multiple regression analysis the elasticities of output were estimated. The coefficients of multiple determination were tested for significance at .05 level by t-tests. The results showed that labour was more productive compared to capital in four out of seven industrial estates studied.

Canonical Analysis

What is the relation between two *sets* of data with several independent and dependent variables? Canonical analysis studies this relationship: It is a regression analysis of data with 'k' independent variables and 'm' dependent variables. Through least-squares analysis, two linear composites are formed: one for the independent variables, and another for the dependent variables. The correlation between these two composites is called *canonical correlation.* And like R, it will be the maximum correlation possible.

In addition to the canonical correlation, sets of regression weights for both the independent and dependent variables are calculated. The relative weights may be computed from the individual regression results by squaring the standardized regression (beta) coefficients and then dividing them by the R^2. The weights can be used to determine which of the independent and dependent variables are more closely associated.

Research Examples

Pandey (1986)[28] in his study of organizational and individual characteristics of R and D organisations, has made a set of *canonical analyses* to substantiate the multivariate nature of the conceived functional model of R and D organisations. In each set of analysis, the data matrix was arranged to form a "two-set" case, namely, independent variable set (predictor) and dependent variable set (criterion). The major objective was to explore the relationship between two given sets, three commitment variables (namely, organisational commitment, job involvement and professional commitment) and three rated performance measures (namely, contribution to the organisational goal achievement, contribution to science and technology, and perceived efficiency of the scientist) were taken as the set of criterion variables. Micro- and macro-organisation-climate, total scores and the four personality variables were taken together as the predictor set. Canonical correlations for different combinations of two sets of variables were computed. To test the statistical significance of a set of canonical correlations, Wilks' Lamba test was used. The strength of relationship between the two sets of variables, the mean square of the canonical correlation was computed.

Patnaik (1988),[29] in his study of the pattern in the integration of groundnut markets in Rayalaseema region of Andhra Pradesh (India), used the *canonical correlation analysis* to find out the product identification in inter-market integration. The data of monthly prices of the groundnut pod, kernel, oil and cake of selected six markets for pre- and post-regulation period, *i.e.,* 1963-71 and 1972-81 respectively were used for the analysis. For each market for pre- and post-regulation periods the canonical variates of various compositions were computed. The canonical correlation between the two sets were calculated. These correlations in all markets were nearly one. Lambda values were computed.

28. Pandey Subrata, *A Study of Organizational Individual Characteristics in R & D Organisations,* (unpublished Doctoral Thesis), Bangalore, Dept. of Management Studies, Indian Institute of Science, 1986.
29. Patnaik, Uma Shankar K., "A Changing Pattern in the integration of Groundnut Markets," *Indian Journal of Applied Economics,* Vol. XLIII, No. 4, October-December 1988, pp. 631-642.

The chi-square values in all cases were found to be statistically significant. The results show that inter-market integration was achieved by flow of price information.

Discriminant Analysis

How can individuals or members of a sample be best assigned to groups on the basis of a set of independent variables? Discriminant analysis deals with this question. A discriminant function is a *regression equation* with a *dependent variable* that represents group membership This function maximally discriminates the members of the group; it tells us to which group each member probably belongs. It can be used to assign individuals to groups on the basis of their scores on two or more measures. From those scores, the 'best' composite score based on least-squares is calculated. Then the higher R square is the better predictor of the group membership.

One can use discriminant analysis to *classify objects* into *two groups* delinquent/non-delinquent; success/failure; default/non-default, etc. One can extend it to more than two groups. Cooley and Lohnes,[30] for example, describe the discrimination among three career-plan groups. For the application of discriminant analysis the discriminatory variables must be *normally distributed.*

The discriminant analysis has been applied in various empirical studies in psychology, behavioural science, finance and so on. In finance, it has been used in consumer credit evaluation, earnings ratio classification, standard investment categories, rate of return prediction, and prediction of corporate failure. The discriminant analysis has been used in the prediction of corporate success/failure by Altman, Deakin, Blum, Tamer and Tisshaw, Kaveri, Sarma and Rao, Ramanathan and Krishnaswami and so on.

Research Examples

Michael Etgar (1976)[31] made a comparative study of the operational efficiencies of administratively coordinated and market-based vertical market systems in the property and casualty insurance industry. The market-based system operates through 'independent insurance agents' and the centrally coordinated system through 'direct writing system.' The hypotheses state: compared with a market-coordinated vertical marketing system, the centrally coordinated system will exhibit: (1) Less intensive contacts among system members, (2) Less duplication of activities. (3) Higher degree of standardization of activities, (4) Reliance on fewer product lines, (5) Faster intrasystem flows, (6) Better intrasystem communications, (7) Lower risk of operation for system members, (8) More adoption of advanced technologies, (9) Higher productivity. The discrete record keeping between insurers and distributors, extent of use of managerial techniques, use of mass media in promotion and use of electronic data processing were analysed by a discriminant analysis. This analysis was designed to achieve two goals: (1) to indicate the overall power of all to differentiate between the two groups of distributions (*a*) independent agents and (*b*) the direct writing distributors) and (2) to find out the relative importance of each of those variables in describing the two groups of distributors. Twenty measurement components of the variables were introduced into discriminant function. The discriminant coefficients were computed for all the measurements, the centroid value for each of the two groups was arrived at and significance was tested by Wilk's lambda. The derived discrimination function reflects a relatively high differentiating

30. Cooley W., and P.Lohens, *Multivariate Procedures for the Behavioural Science,* New York: JohnWiley and Sons, 1962, pp. 119-123.

31. Etgar Michael, "Effects of Administrative Control on Efficiency of Vertical Marketing Systems," *Journal of Marketing Research,* Vol.XIII, February 1976, pp. 12-24.

power. The results show that 18 measurements have signs as predicted by the hypotheses. Of them 9 were found to have significant coefficients.

George W.Gau (1978)[32] used three multivariate techniques for developing taxonomic model for the default risk of residential mortgages. Factor analysis provided a method of combining the mortgage variables into linearly independent factor dimensions. Discriminant analysis was used to form functions that indicated the relative importance of the factor dimension as discriminators between the default and non-default mortgages. Discriminant coefficients were computed for the factor functions. F-tests were used for testing the significance of the discriminatory power of the functions.

Kalyankar (1983)[33] made discriminant function analysis to classify the defaulters of cooperative societies into wilful and non-wilful defaulters. The results showed that wilful defaulters were farmers with higher level of income, higher proportions of educated members in the family and high caste.

Katharine R. Parkes (1987)[34] used the *cannonical discriminant* analysis to examine the effects of the predictor variables in a longitudinal study of relative weight, smoking and mental health as predictors of sickness and unauthorized absence from work among student nurses (n=185). Two discriminant functions were derived for a three-factor discriminant model. The cannonical correlations were calculated for the two functions; discriminant coefficients for the three predictor variables were computed and evaluated at the means of three sickness groups. The results showed that high relative weight and high somatic symptoms distinguished high level sickness group from no sickness and little sickness groups.

Dhyani and Tewari (1988)[35] used *discriminant analysis* for identifying the discriminatory variables of defaulters and non-defaulters of agricultural production credit. The variables that turned out to be significant discriminators based on discriminant analysis and step-wise regression are behavioural characteristics (borrower's attitude towards savings, loan and indebtedness, litigation; motivation towards farming and business risks), irregularity of borrower in bank customership, farming efficiency (ratio of gross farm expenses to gross farm income), other outstanding debts in the year, per acre value of farm assets including land, and social status. The results suggest that higher farming efficiency and greater employment of farm assets per unit of land make a prospective borrower a good credit risk, whereas poor attitude towards saving, loan etc., irregularity in bank customership, other outstanding debts and higher social status, make a prospective borrower a bad credit risk.

Fern Avila and Grewal (1989),[36] in their study on sales force turnover in a large computer manufacturing company, examined the relationship between three sets of variables (1. demographic and personal characteristics, 2. work-related factors, and 3. performance indicators). *Canonical discriminant analysis* was used to determine which variables were most important in explaining the

---

32. Gau George W., A Taxonomic Model for the Risk Rating of Residential Mortgages, *Journal of Business,* Vol. 51, No. 4, 1978, pp. 687-706.
33. Kalyankar S.P., *Crop Loan Overdues of Cooperative Finance,* Coimbatore: Rainbow Publications, 1983.
34. Parkes Katherine R., "Relative Weight, Smoking and Mental Health as Predictors of Sickness and Absence from Work," *Journal of Applied Psychology,* Vol. 72, No. 2, May 1987, pp. 275-86.
35. Dhyani B.L. and S.K. Tewari, "Predicting Good and Bad Risks in Agricultural Production Credit: An Application of Numerical Evaluation System," *Indian Journal of Agricultural Economics,* Vol. 43, No. 2, April-June 1988, pp. 126-139.
36. Fern, Edward F., Ramon A. Avila and Dhruv Grewal, "Sales force Turnover: Those Who Left and Those Who Stayed," *Industrial Marketing Management,* 18, 1989, pp. 1-9.

differences between those who remained with the company and those who left. The 26 independent variables were: company rating, job security, seven job satisfaction dimensions, four role conflict dimensions, four role ambiguity dimensions, and nine measures of sales performance. The dependent variable was the dichotomy between those who stayed and those who left. Because the purpose of the research was to explain how the two groups differed — and not prediction — step-wise analysis was not done. Discriminant coefficients for the 26 variables were computed and the canonical loadings for them were calculated. The canonical correlation, an index of discrimination (R = 0.4572), was significant (Wilks' Lambda = 0.7909, F(26, 173) = 1.7588, p = 0.0180). The result indicates that the variables discriminate between those who left and those who stayed. The canonical loadings determine the rank order of importance of the variables. Satisfaction with the job and promotional opportunities were the two most important discriminators followed by job security.

Factor Analysis

The factor analysis is another multivariate technique. It is an extremely powerful and useful analytic approach to psychological. behavioural, financial and other types of data. It is a statistical technique for determining the *underlying factors* or forces among a large number of interdependent variables or measures. It is a method for extracting common factor variances from a set of observations. It groups the number of variables into a smaller set of uncorrelated factors potentially conveying a great deal of information. It tells us what variables belong together — which ones virtually measure the same thing.

The factor analysis is an *appropriate* technique *for cases* where the *variables* have a ***high degree of intercorrelation.*** A *factor* is a construct, a hypothetical entity that is assumed to underlie tests, scales, items or any other measures. For example, a number of factors underlie intelligence: verbal ability, numerical ability, reasoning, memory and others.

If a test measures one factor only, it is said to be factorially "pure." To the extent that a test measures a factor it is said to be *loaded* on the factor or saturated with the factor. Some measures are so complex that it is difficult to tell just what they measure, *e.g.,* grades secured by students. If a test contains more than one factor, it is said to be factorially complex.

We need an objective method to determine the number of factors, the variables loaded on the various factors and the magnitude of the loadings.

Methods of Factor Analysis: There are several methods of factor analysis. The important methods are: (*a*) the centroid method, and (*b*) the principal components method.

Let us first state the meanings of some of the basic concepts relating to factor analysis.

Factor: A factor is an underlying dimension of several related variables. There can be one or more factors in a phenomenon depending upon its nature and the number of variables involved in it.

Factor loadings: These are values that explain how closely the variables are related to each one of the factors discovered. They are factor-variable correlations. It is the absolute size of the loadings that is important in the interpretation of a factor.

Communality (h^2): It shows how much of each variable is accounted for by the underlying factors taken together. It is computed as under:

h^2 of a variable = (its factor loading of Factor A)^2 + (its factor loading of Factor B)^2 + ...

Eigen value (or Latent Root) is the sum of squared values of factor loadings relating to a factor. It indicates the relative importance of each factor in accounting for the particular set of variables under study.

Total sum of squares: When Eigen values of all factors are totalled, the resulting value is called the total sum of squares.

Rotations reveal different structures in the data. If the factors are independent, orthogonal rotation is done, and if they are correlated an oblique rotation is made.

Factor score represents the degree to which each respondent gets high scores on the group of item that load high on each factor. Factor scores are used in several other multivariate analysis.

Now we can take up the important methods of factor analysis.

1. **Centroid method:** This method was developed by L.L.Thrustone. It tends to maximize the sum of loading for each factor. It was frequently used before the advent of high speed computers. For a detailed description of this method, see Nunnally Jum C., *Psychometric Theory,* New York: McGraw-Hill, 1978, pp.349-357.
2. **The Principle Components method:**[37] This was developed by H.Hotelling. This is the most popular method used after the advent of high speed computers.

The steps involved in this method are:

1. Compute the correlation coefficients (by the product moment method) between the pairs of k variables..
2. Layout the above coefficients in a correlation matrix called R.

The R matrix is always a square and symmetric array. This is because the lower half of the matrix below the diagonal (from upper left to lower right) is the same as the upper half of the matrix. The top row is the same as the first column, the second row the same as the second column and so on. By inspecting the R matrix, we can determine the underlying factors (i.e., common to the variables). If we find two or more clusters of high value of r, they indicate the common factors underlying the variables.

	X_1	X_2	X_3	....	X_k
X_1	r_{11}	r_{12}	r_{13}	....	r_{1k}
X_2	r_{21}	r_{22}	r_{23}	....	r_{2k}
X_3	r_{31}	r_{32}	r_{33}	....	r_{3k}
....	....	....	....	....	....
....	....	....	....	....	....
X_k	r_{k1}	r_{k2}	r_{k3}	....	r_{kk}

3. Obtain the sum of coefficients in each column of the matrix. The vector of these sum *is* called as U_{al}.

37. L. Thurstone, *Multiple Factor Analysis*, Chicago: University of Chicago Press, 1947, Chapter II and G.Thompson, *The Factorial Analysis of Human Ability,* Boston: Houghton-Mifflin, 1951, Chapter VII for A Simple Exposition of the Principle Factor Method.

4. Square and sum up the column sums and compute the square root of these sums. This square root is termed as normalizing factor.
5. Divide each element in Ual (obtained in step 3) by the normalizing factor to get the Vector (V_{al}).
6. Multiply accumulately elements in V_{al} by the first row of R to obtain the first element in a new vector U_{a2}. That is multiply the first element in V_{al} by the r_{11} value in the first row of R, second element in V_{al} by X r_{12} value, the third element in V_{al} by r_{13} value, and so on. The total of these products would be the first element in U_{a2}.
7. Repeat the same process for the second and other rows of R to get the second and subsequent elements in U_{a2}.
8. Normalize U_{a2} to obtain V_{a2}.
9. Compare V_{al} and V_{a2}. If they are nearly identical, then convergence is said to have occurred. (If convergence does not occur one should go on computing, V_{a3}, V_{a4} and so on until convergence occurs. Suppose it occurs at V_{a6}, in which case V_{a5} will be taken as V_a (the *Characteristic* vector).
10. Multiply each element of V_a by its normalizing factor.

    The resulting figures are the loadings on the first principal component on factor A.
11. Obtain the first residual matrix, R_l by multiplying the loadings for each pair of variables on factor A, and repeat the above procedure to obtain factor B.
12. Repeat the above procedure again and again to obtain successive factors, C, D, etc.
13. Select the factors to be retained in the study. Kaiser's criterion is often used for this purpose. According to this criterion, the factors having latent root greater than one are considered essential and should be retained.
14. Construct a *factor matrix,* a table of correlation coefficients between the variables and retained factors.
15. Rotate the retained principal components from their beginning positions to enhance interpretability of the factors.
16. Work out communality (h^2), which shows how much of each variable is accounted for by the underlying factors taken together. The amount of variance explained (sum of squared loadings) by each factor is equal to the corresponding characteristic root. When these roots are divided by the number of variables, they show the characteristic roots as proportions of total variance explained.
17. Regress the variables against each factor loading and the resulting regression coefficients are used to generate what are known as factor scores.

The factor scores are used in further analysis as inputs.

Rotation Principles: To guide the factor analyst in his rotations, Thrustone has laid down five principles or rules of simple structure.[38] The rules are applicable to both orthogonal and oblique methods of rotations. The rules are as follows:

38. Thurstone, *op.cit.,* p. 335.

1. Each row of the factor matrix should have at least one loading close to zero.
2. For each column of the factor matrix, there should be at least as many variables with zero or near zero loadings as there are factors.
3. For every pair of factors (columns) there should be several variables with loadings in one factor (column) but not in the other.
4. When there are four or more factors, a large proportion of the variables should have negligible (close to zero) loadings on any pair of factors.
5. For every pair of factors (columns) of the factor matrix there should be a small number of variables with appreciable loadings in both columns.

These criteria call for as 'pure' variables as possible, *i.e.*, each variable loaded on as few factors as possible. In this way, the simple possible interpretation of the factors can be achieved. Thus, rotation to achieve a simple-structure is a fairly objective way to achieve simplicity or to reduce variable complexity.

R-type and Q-type Factor Analyses: Factor analysis may be R-type analysis or Q-type analysis. In *R-type analysis* high correlations occur when respondents who score high on variable 1 also score high on variable 2, and respondents who score low on variable 1 also score low on variable 2. Factors emerge when there are high correlations within groups of variables.

In *Q-type factor analysis* the correlations are computed between pairs of respondents, instead of pairs of variables. High correlations occur when respondent 1's pattern of responses on all variables is much like respondent 2's pattern of response. Factors emerge when there are high correlations within groups of people. Q-type analysis is useful when the objective is to sort out people into groups based on their simultaneous responses to all the variables.

Factor analysis is used in developing psychological tests, media readership profiles of people, for condensing and simplifying multivariate data, for providing a classification scheme for clustering products, media or people and so on.

Research examples

Ramanathan and Krishnaswami (1985)[39] used factor analysis as a part of multivariate analysis employed for a study on the prediction of financial health of business corporations. In order to determine what particular form of profitability measure can serve as the best predictor of sickness 25 different profitability ratios representing different dimensions of earnings' position were empirically tested for their predictive accuracy. Another set of 31 balance sheet ratios were also selected for testing and experimentation. Each ratio measures directly or indirectly the strength of equity base, liquidity, intensity of asset utilization or the asset condition. Thus, a total of 56 ratios were tested.

In order to derive a smaller set of important variables having independent direction and uncorrelated with each other, factor analysis was employed to the 56 ratios for each of the sample failed and non-failed companies. The inter-correlations between the 56 ratios were factorially analysed using the principle component method and the varimax rotation of factor analysis. The analysis was

39. Ramanathan S., O.R. Krishnaswami, *Development of an Analytical Model for the Prediction of Financial Health of Business Corporations,* (unpublished dissertation), Bangalore, Department of Commerce and Management, Bangalore University, 1988.

carried out on WIPRO PC?XT, an IBM compatible personal computer system. The programs were developed in fortran following the IBM/SAS Packages and were run under MS-FORTRAN environment.

The solutions produced the variance-covariance matrix, the rotated factor matrix, the Eigen values of each factor and the percentage of total variance in the data explained by each factor (Table 11.20A).

TABLE 11.20A

The Eigen values of factors and the variance in the data explained by each of them

Group I: Failed Companies				*Group II: Non-failed Companies*			
Factor	*Eigen value*	*Portion*	*Cum.portion*	*Factor*	*Eigen value*	*Portion*	*Cum.portion*
F-1	12.8015	0.360	0.360	F-1	11.7031	0.342	0.342
F-2	10.4673	0.242	0.602	F-2	11.2848	0.269	0.611
F-3	7.6892	0.125	0.727	F-3	9.8476	0.175	0.786
F-4	5.4489	0.110	0.837	F-4	8.4894	0.151	0.937
F-5	2.5959	0.089	0.926	F-5	8.3027	0.051	0.988
F-6	1.4450	0.044	0.970	F-6	7.9430	0.010	0.998
F-7	0.8976	0.013	0.983	F-7	6.0770	0.001	0.999
F-8	0.1103	0.008	0.991	F-8	6.0665	0.001	1.000
F-9	0.0934	0.006	0.997	F-9	5.1129	0.000	1.000
F-10	0.0172	0.002	0.999	F-10	4.2988	0.000	1.000
F-11	0.0115	0.001	1.000	F-11	3.5578	0.000	1.000
F-12	0.0004	0.000	1.000	F-12	2.5825	0.000	1.000
F-13	0.0001	0.000	1.000	F-13	2.4614	0.000	1.000

From the rotated factor matrix (Table 11.20B) four factors in each group accounting for 83.7% and 93.7% respectively of the total variance in the data were extracted. The variables found to load 0.30 or higher on a factor were selected as its domain in both groups. The contributions of each factor ranged from 36% to 11% in group-1 and from 34.2% to 15.1% in group-2. It may be noted that if six factors were chosen instead of the four selected in the study (the choice was limited to four due to time constraints), they would have accounted for 97 per cent and 99.8 per cent of the total variance in the data. The smaller subset of ratios so arrived at were used for discriminant analysis.

TABLE 11.20B

Rotated Factor Loadings Pattern of Variables

		Group-I		*Group-II*	
Factor	*Variable*	*Loading*	*Factor*	*Variable*	*Loading*
F-1	R-1	0.797	F-1	R-2	0.515
	R-13	0.843		R-13	0.653
	R-23	0.643		R-24	0.491
	R-26	0.971		R-26	0.873
	R-34	0.970		R-41	0.427
	R-41	0.969		R-43	0.672
	R-43	0.832			
	R-56	0.476			

F-2	R-2	0.449	F-2	R-6	0.979
	R-19	0.684		R-18	0.490
	R-24	0.072		R-26	0.450
	R-29	0.630		R-30	0.632
	R-31	0.833		R-40	0.708
	R-34	0.820		R-55	0.652
	R-42	0.652		R-56	0.931
	R-48	0.697			
F-3	R-4	0.645	F-3	R-4	0.754
	R-13	0.934		R-13	0.876
	R-24	0.953		R-26	0.527
	R-26	0.453		R-32	0.933
	R-30	0.574		R-36	0.803
	R-36	0.921		R-43	0.929
	R-38	0.894		R-48	0.318
				R-52	0.757
				R-54	0.893
				R-56	0.997
F-4	R-1	0.794	F-4	R-1	0.836
	R-22	0.514		R-12	0.449
	R-40	0.980		R-22	0.741
	R-42	0.444		R-36	0.521
	R-45	0.740		R-42	0.664
				R-46	0.992
				R-51	0.560
				R-54	0.552

Note: Patterns of the variables from the Rotated Factor Matrix.

Sarveswara Rao (1972)[40] used factor analysis in a study made for testing the two-factor theory of job satisfaction in Indian context. The inter-correlation analysis was made for six motivators (achievement, responsibility, independence, recognition, promotions, ability utilisation, work itself) and seven hygienes (salary, job status, working conditions, supervision-personal relations, supervision-technical, company policies and practices, job security). This analysis failed to reveal context-content dichotomy as hypothesised by the two-factor theory. In order to gain a better understanding factor analysis was made. The principal components analysis was done for the thirteen job variables to extract the factors and the same were rotated by varimax analytical rotation. The loadings of the first factor suggest that it is a hygiene factor. The second factor has high loading on mostly motivator variables and hence a motivator factor. The third factor is a mixed one. Regarding clerks, the first factor appears to be a motivator one, the second factor is a mixed one as it has high loadings on the some of both hygiene and motivator variables. The third factor is clearly a motivator one. The fourth is hygiene factor. For skilled workers, the first factor is a motivator, while the second and third factors

40. Sarveshwara Rao G.V., *A Study of the Two Factor Theory of Job Satisfaction, op.cit.,* pp. 131-37.

are mixed ones. These results show that the variables could not be classified distinctly as motivators and hygienes.

Gau (1978)[41] employed factor analysis along with discriminant analysis in a study made for developing a taxonomic model for risk rating of residential mortgages. The total sample of 212 default and 873 non-default mortgages was subjected to a principal component analysis of 64 variables relating to financial aspects, property mortgages and socio-economic characteristics of the borrower. Twenty-eight factors were retained for a varimax rotation and further anlaysis factors accounting for 78% of the original variance in the mortgage sample. After a rotation of the 28 factors, the rotated factor loading matrix of factor scores was constructed. The factor scores were derived through a least square solution. The factor loadings were correlation coefficients showing the relationship among the original variables and the derived factors — the higher a specific loading, the stronger the relationship between the variable and the factor. For example, factor 1 had high loadings for five mortgage variables: monthly payment on mortgage, monthly payment on property, purchase price, primary borrower's income and total family income. These variables represent 'financial standing' dimension. The other dimensions so identified include: financial obligations, property, job security and the like. The factor scores were then used in a discriminant analysis.

Gunasekaran, Pisharoti and Ramachandran[42] used *factor analysis* in a study of infant mortality in rural India.. The correlation matrix pertaining to ten independent variables (per capita income, percentage of female literate, percentage of schedule caste, etc.) were factor analyzed using the principal components method and varimax rotation procedure. Three factors were extracted and used for linear regression analysis.

Mandal and Sengupta (1982)[43] used *factor analysis* in study of generation gap in value system existing between the old and young industrial-workers. Self ranking profile of two sets of values (Instrumental and terminal, i.e., A1 and A2 developed by Rokeach) and an attitudinal scale (Likert type) were used as tools for data gathering. The sixteen variables in the value set A1 (ambitious, capable, cheerful, clever, courageous etc.) and the sixteen variables in the value set A2 were subjected to factor analysis and six factors in each set were derived and used in discriminant analysis.

Similarly the scores of attitude towards the factors of job success and job related environment of the sample workers were subjected to factor analysis and three factors were derived. The factor loadings were later used for discriminant analysis.

Pandey (1986)[44] used *factor analysis* as one of the multivariate analysis in a study of organizational and individual characteristics in R & D organisations, A 13-item scale was constructed to collect data from sample respondents. Factor analysis on the questionnaire was carried out to check the dimensionality and the amount of true variance present in the test. The principal component analysis

41. Gau, George, W., "A Taxonomic Model for the Risk-rating of Residential Mortgages," *Journal of Business*, pp. 687-707.
42. Gunasekaran S., K.A. Pisharoti and L.R. Ramachandran, A Study of Variations in Infant Mortality in Rural India — A Factor Analysis, *Research Compendium* (164-87), Gandhigram Institute of Rural Health and Family Welfare Trust, pp. 36-38.
43. Mandal J., and S.Sengupta, Generation Gap — Its Effect on a Large Industrial Unit: A Case Study, *Indian Journal of Psychology*, 1982, Vol. 57, 161-171.
44. Pandey Subrata, *A Study of Organizational and Individual Characteristics in R & D Organizations* (unpublished doctoral thesis), *op. cit.*

with specification of eigen values greater than 1.00 revealed, five factors. The 'total variance' extracted in the process was 62%, indicating the upper limit of reliability as .78 for the test. One item which had insignificant loading in all the factors was deleted. Varimax rotation of the five factor solution did not reveal and interpretable factor structure. However, a three factor solution and subsequent rotation showed evidence of three interpretable factors, which may be called 'internalized professional value', 'calculative involvement', and 'major satisfaction of life.' The factor analysis revealed that the scale has considerable amount of true-variance (62%) and its internal consistency (after excluding one item) was acceptable for use in research.

Miller and Droga (1986)[45] in a study of the psychological and traditional determinants of organization structure of business firms, used *factor analysis* for identifying structural dimensions. They performed an orthogonal, exploratory factor analysis of nine structural variables (structural liaison devices, liaison in decision-making, formalization, controls, specialization, centralization, proportion of managerial personnel to total personnel, number of operating sites, vertical span), using varimax rotation to exclude the least consistent structural dimensions. The four composite dimensions of the variables examined were formulation, complexity, centralization and integration. The factor loadings on complexity variables were below .30. Hence, the complexity dimension was dropped and the other three were used as inputs in further analysis.

Mount and Thompson (1987)[46] studied the effects of cognitive categorization of raters on accuracy, leniency, and halo of performance evaluation of managers in an organization. The questionnaire used by them consisted of three sections: background information, behavioural performance and perceived role congruence scale. The section on behavioural performance contained 14 behavioural items (processing paper-work, developing new solutions, documenting decision, etc.) designed to measure managerial job performance. These fourteen items were inter-correlated. The matrix of intercorrelations (14 × 14) was subjected to matrix. The *factor analysis* was performed on mean ratings across raters for each manager on each of the 14 behavioural dimensions. First, the subordinate ratings for each item were averaged for each manager. Then the three rating constituencies (supervisor, self and subordinate) were unit weighted, summed and divided by three. The resulting valued were used as the data for the factor analysis. The principal-components method was used. Three factors (general supervision, motivation" expertise) with Eigen values greater than 1.0 were extracted and used as variables in further analysis.

Akhtar and Nishat (1988)[47] used *factor analysis* in a study of variations in cotton yields in the Tharparkar district of Sind province (Pakistan). Initially 57 variables pertaining to cultural practices, input usage, extension service, tenancy and land use characteristics and the farmer's education were employed to search for a meaningful factor solution. However, the determinant of correlation matrix was nearly singular (.9728 D-10). A second look at the data and their correlation matrix revealed that the correlation of several variables with yield was near to zero, and the variability in a few others was negligible. Such variables were excluded and the remaining 40 variables were included in the final

---

45. Miller Danny and Correlia Droga, Psychological and Traditional Determinants of Structure, *Administrative Science Quarterly,* 31, December 1986, pp. 539-60.
46. Mount Michael K., and Durane E. Thompson, Cognitive Categorization and Quality of Performance Ratings," *Journal of Applied Psychology,* Vol. 72, No. 2, May 1987, pp. 240-46.
47. Akhtar Sajjad and Mohammed Nishat, Explaining Variations in Cotton Yields: A Factor Analysis Approach, *Indian Journal of Agricultural Economics,* Vol. 43, No. 4, October-December 1988, pp. 603-12.

factor solution. It yielded 16 factors. Out of them four factors which account for 45 per cent of the aggregate variation in the data and also account for 77 per cent of the total variation in cotton yields explained by 16 factors. 14 variables have significant factor loadings with one or the other of the selected four factors. These variables include per acre use of urea at flowering stage, the proportion of area hand and plough-weeded, the number of sprays, ownership pattern, the proportion of cotton area sharecropped, the farmer's education, and farmer's visits to the extension staff. These variables are positively related to yields.

Gupta (1988)[48] employed *factor analysis* to find out whether the dimensions of fluency, flexibility, originality, elaboration, seeing problems, inquisitiveness and persistency were fundamental dimensions of creativity; Five different creativity tests were administered to a sample of 200 graduate students to test the above four dimensions of creativity. The raw scores 5 × 4 kg 20 dimensions were normalized on the T-scale and then correlations were computed. The correlation matrix was put into factor analysis using Thurstone's centroid method. Oblique rotation was made and the method of extended vectors was used. The results show that creativity is patterned on the model of 'structure of intellect' given by Guilford. Different types of creative abilities are needed in different field of activity for producing different products in different ways.

Cluster Analysis

Cluster analysis is a method for classifying variables into clusters. A *cluster consists* of *variables* that *correlate highly with one another* and have comparatively low correlations with variables in other clusters. The objective of cluster analysis is to determine how many mutually and exhaustive groups or clusters, based on the similarities of profiles among entities, really exist in the population and then to state the composition of such groups.

The cluster analysis is found useful in market research studies. This analysis is useful for segmenting the market for a product on the basis of the various characteristics of the customers. For a detailed discussion of cluster anlaysis, see Tryon R.C., and D.E. Bailey, *Cluster Analysis,* New York: McGraw-Hill, 1970.

Research Example

Gau (1978)[49] used *cluster analysis* in developing a taxonomic model for risk-rating residential mortgages. First factor dimensions were extracted through factor analysis. Second, discriminant analysis was made to determine the relative importance of the factor dimensions as discriminators between the defaulters and non-defaulters. With the factor dimensions as defining characteristics and the discriminant coefficients as weights, cluster analysis was then applied, employing the MIKCA Cluster Program. Cluster analysis provided a classification procedure for grouping the mortgages into a small number of mutually exclusive categories based on the similarity of the characteristics of the mortgages as measured through a distance function. The groupings of the mortgages on the basis of the factor dimensions allowed for the elimination of the effects of the scale and multicollinearity on the cluster's distance measures.

---

48 Gupta G.S., Fundamental Dimensions of Creativity, *Indian Educational Review,* Vol. 13, No. 1, January 1988, pp. 51-54.

49. Gau George W., "A Taxonomic Model for the Risk-rating of Residential Mortgages," pp. 696-700.

Latent Structure Analysis

This analysis shares both of the objectives of factor analysis, *viz.*, to extract *latent* factors and express relationship of *observed* (manifest) variables with the latent factors as their indicators and to classify a population of respondents into pure types. This analysis is appropriate when the variables involved in a study do not possess dependency relationship and happen to be non-metric.

Path Analysis

The term 'path analysis' was first introduced by a biologist Sewall Wright in 1934 in connection with decomposing the total correlation between any two variables in a causal system. This analysis is based on a series of multiple regression analysis with the assumption of causal relationship between independent and dependent variables. This analysis lays emphasis on the heuristic use of visual diagram (described as a path diagram and uses standardised partial regression coefficients) (known as beta weights) as effect coefficients.

The main *principle* of path analysis is that a *correlation* coefficient between two variables can be decomposed into a series of paths: separate paths of influence leading through an intermediate variable to which both the correlated variables have links. This analysis makes explicit the assumptions underlying the causal connections and elucidates the indirect effect of the explanatory variables. For a fuller discussion see Takeuchi K., *et al., The Foundations of Multivariate Analysis,* New Delhi: Wiley Eastern Ltd., 1982.

Analysis of Variance (ANOVA)

The significance of the difference between the means of two categories (*e.g.*, males and females; trained and untrained; liberals and conservatives) can be evaluated by the z-test or the t-test.[50] But when the comparison among three or more categories or samples has to be made simultaneously, the use of t-test is not only tedious, but also increases the probability of making type I error. To overcome this difficulty, a method known as the *analysis of variance (ANOVA)* has been developed.

The ANOVA is very much useful in researches in social sciences and other disciplines. It is appropriate to situations where more than two categories have to be compared, *e.g.*, the crop yield from several varieties of seeds, the fuel efficiency of several brands of cars, the attitude of persons belonging to various religions on family planning, and the like.

The ANOV A is designed to test whether a significant difference exists among the three or more sample means. In this analysis, the total variance in a set of data is divided into variation *within-groups,* and variation *between-groups.*

The ANOVA used for studying the differences among the influence of various categories of *one* independent variable on a dependent variable is called *one-way ANOVA,* and that used for studying the influence of two independent variables on a dependent variable is called *two-way ANOVA.*

The ANOVA technique is based on the concept of *sum of squared deviations* from a mean. Corresponding to the total variance and its two components, we have the *total sum of squares* (SS_t), *between-groups sum of squares* (SS_b), and *wilhin-groups sum of squares* (SS_w).

Suppose we want to determine the influence of religious affiliation on child-health-care awareness. We might compare Hindus, Muslims, Sikhs and Christians.

50. See Section 11.7, Tests of Significance for a Description of z-test and t-test.

Null Hypothesis: The Hindus, Muslims, Sikhs and Christians do not differ in child-health-care awareness.

Research Hypothesis: The Hindus, Muslims, Sikhs and Christians differ in child-health-care awareness.

Assume we had interviewed four women in each religious category and obtained awareness scores (ranging from 1 to 5). (see Table 11.21)

Table 11.21

Child Health care awareness of religious groups

Christians (n = 4)			*Muslims (n = 3)*		
X_1	$d(=X - \overline{X})$	d^2	X_2	d	d^2
1	–.50	.25	1	–1	1
2	.50	.25	.3	1	1
1	– .50	.25	2	0	0
2	.50	.25	2	0	0
$\Sigma X = 6$		$\Sigma d^2 = 1.00$	$\Sigma X = 8$		Σd^2 12.0
$X^1 = 6 + 4 = 5$			$X^2 = 8 + 4 = 2.0$		
Sikhs (n = 4)			*Hindus (n = 4)*		
X_3	d	d^2	X_4	d	d^2
1	– .75	.56	3	+ 1.25	1.56
2	.25	.06	2	.25	0.06
2	.25	.06	1	–.75	.56
2	.25	.06	1	–.75	.56
$7 = \Sigma X$		$\Sigma d^2 = .74$	$\Sigma X = 7$		$Sd^2 = 2.74$
$\overline{X}_3 = 7 + 4 = 1.75$			$\overline{X}_4 = 7.4 = 1.75$		
	$\overline{X}_t = 28 \div 16$ 17.5				

The within-groups sum of squares (SS_w) is obtained by combining the sums of squares (*i.e.,* the squared deviations of every raw score from its sample mean). The formula used is:

$$SS_w = \Sigma d_1^2 + \Sigma d_2^2 + \Sigma d_3^2 + \Sigma d_4^2 + ... + \Sigma d^2 n$$

Where d = a deviation of every raw score of a category from its sample mean.

For the data in Table 11.21, SS_w = 1.0 + 2.0 + 0.74 +2.74 = 6.48 or 6.50

The between-groups sum of squares (SS_b) is obtained as under: Calculate the difference between each sample mean and the total mean. Square this difference. Multiply it by the sample size in the concerned category and add these quantities. The formula is:

$$SS_b = \Sigma[\overline{X} - \overline{X}_t)^2 \times n] \qquad ... (11.48)$$

Where $\overline{X}$ = any sample mean

$\overline{X}_t$ = the total mean (the mean of all raw scores from all samples combined)

n = the number of scores in any sample

SS_b = the between-groups sum of squares

For the data in Table 11.21, we get

$$SS_b = (1.50 - 1.75)^2 \times 4 + (2.0 - 1.75)^2 \times 4 + (1.75 - 1.75)^2 \times 4 + (1.75 - 1.75)^2 \times 4$$
$$= (-.25)^2\ 4 + (.25)^2\ 4 + + (0)\ 4$$
$$= .24 + .24 = 0.48 \text{ or } 0.50$$

The total sum of squares (SS_t) is equal to a sum of within and between groups sum of squares.

$$SS_t = SS_b + SS_w \qquad \text{... (11.49)}$$

Alternatively $SS_t = \Sigma(X - X_t)^2$ ... (11.50)

where X = a raw score in any sample

x_t = the total mean

SS_t = the total sum of squares

For the data in Table 11.21, $SS_t = SS_b + SS_w = 6.48 + 0.44 = 6.96$

Simple Formulas

The computation of sums of squares using the above formula is a time-consuming and tedious process. The following simple formula may be used:

$$SS_t = \Sigma X_t^2 - \frac{(\Sigma X_1)^2}{n_t} \qquad \text{... (11.51)}$$

$$SS_b = \left(\Sigma\frac{(\Sigma\bar{X})^2}{n}\right) - \frac{(\Sigma X_t)^2}{n_t} \qquad \text{... (11.52)}$$

where n_t = the total number of scores in all samples combined

n = the total number of scores in any sample

x^2 = the square of each score in any sample

Mean square: The value of the sums of squares tends to become larger as variation increases and also as sample size increases. Therefore, the sum of squares cannot be regarded as a satisfactory 'pure' measure of variation, unless it is controlled for the sample size. This is achieved by a measure of variation called the *mean square* (or variance) that is obtained by dividing SS_b or SS_w by the appropriate degrees of freedom:

$$MS_b = SS_b/df_b \qquad \text{... (11.53)}$$
$$MS_w = SS_w/df_w \qquad \text{... (11.54)}$$

where MS_b = the between-groups mean squares

MS_w = the within-group mean squares

df = the degrees of freedom.

The degrees of freedom are obtained by:

$$df_b = k - 1$$
$$df_w = n_t - k$$

Where k = the number of samples (groups)

n_t = the total number of scores in all samples combined

For the data from Table 11.21, the degrees of freedom work out to

$$df_b = 4 - 1 = 3$$

$$df_w = 16 - 4 = 12$$

We get the mean squares:

$$MS_b = .50/3 = 0.17$$

$$MS_w = 6.5/12 = 0.54$$

The F-ratio: The analysis of variance yields an F ratio that is a ratio between-groups variation and within-groups variation. The F ratio indicates the size of the difference between groups relative to the size of the variation within each group.

For Table 11.21, $F = MS_b/MS_w = 0.17/0.54 = 0.31$

Having obtained an F ratio, we must now determine whether it is larger enough to reject the null hypothesis. If the calculated F ratio is larger than the corresponding table value, the null hypothesis is rejected and the research hypothesis is supported. If the calculated F ratio is less than the table value, the null hypothesis is accepted. For the data in Table 11.21 the table value of F for degrees of freedom of 3 and 12 respectively at 0.05 level of significance is 3.49. As the calculated value is only 0.31, the null hypothesis is accepted. Thus, we can conclude based on the data in Table 11.21 that there is no difference in child health care awareness among women of different religious groups.

The results of our analysis can be presented in a summary table (Table 11.22).

TABLE 11.22

Analysis of Variance

Variation	*df*	*SS*	*MS*	*Calculated F*	*Table F at 0.5 level*	*Significant or not*
Between groups	3	.50	.17	.31	3.49	No
Within	12	6.5	.57			

The **two-way ANOVA** and other techniques used for analyzing the impact of two or more independent variables are described in advanced texts such as Edwards, Allen L., *Statistical Analysis,* New York: Holt, Reinhart and Winston, 1974, Winter B.J., *Statistical Principles in Experimental Design,* New York: McGraw-Hill Book Co., 1962.

Multivariate Analysis of Variance (MANOVA)

This analysis is an extension of bivariate ANOVA, in which the ratio of among-group variance to within-group variance is calculated on a set of variables instead of on a single variable. This analysis is useful for a study involving several metric dependent variables along with many non-metric explanatory variables. It is specially applied when a researcher wants to test hypotheses concerning multivariate differences in group responses to experimental manipulations *e.g.,* use a MANOVA in an experiment using one test market and one control market to examine the effect of an advertising campaign on sales as well as on awareness, knowledge and attitudes.

Analysis of Covariance (ANOCOVA)

This analysis is used as a procedure for the statistical control of an uncontrolled variable in an experiment. The influence of the uncontrolled variable is usually removed by simple linear regression method and the residual sums of squares are used to provide variance estimates. In other words, from each individual score is subtracted the portion of that score which is predictable from uncontrollable variable. Then the usual analysis of variance is made on the resulting scores.

Research Examples

Rangaswamy, Ramasamy and Guruswami (1972),[51] in their study of adoption of new technology in agriculture used ANOVA to study whether small (0-5 acres), medium (5-10) and large (above 10 acres) farmers differ in average adoption and computed F value for testing the significance (.01 level). The result showed that the groups differed significantly in average adoption.

They also made similar ANOVA analysis for studying differences in adoption among different groups of farmers classified according to (*a*) their tenurial status, (*b*) credit scores, (*c*) yield scores, (*d*) educational status, and (*e*) training in new technology.

Gautam and Narayan (1985),[52] in their case study on organizational effectiveness in a public sector enterprise, used *one-way ANOVA* to test the null hypothesis: The differences in mean satisfaction scores were due to chance. The responses of executives relating to (1) Pay, (2) Promotion avenues, (3) Working conditions, (4) Team work, (5) Autonomy and (6) Recognition for good work were considered. Two independent estimates of the common variance were made: first is a weighted average of the variances within each of the separate samples based on executive levels; and the second is the variance of the separate sample means, treated as individual scores. The calculated F-value of 4.15 was significant at .05 level, leading to rejection of Ho- A similar ANOVA analysis was also made to test the H_0 relating to workers' satisfaction with salary, hours of work, team work, etc. In this case also the obtained F-value was significant at .05 level.

Krishnaswami and Seshaiah (1985)[53] used ANOVA for assessing the variation among districts and sectors (agriculture, small-scale industries and services) in respect of budgeted advances and actual advances made under the first round district credit plans by commercial banks in Andhra Pradesh.

Pappuraj (1986)[54] tested the null hypothesis that there is no significant variation between the executives' opinions, the firm's current philosophy and the suggested level of responsiveness towards employees by *ANOVA* in his study relating to corporate social responsibility. The result led to the rejection of Ho. He also made similar analyses for responsibility towards (1) customers, and (2) the society at large.

Shanthi Srinivas and Motowidlo (1987)[55] in a study of the effects of raters' stress on the dispersion and favourability of Performance Ratings, used a *multivariate analysis of variance*

51. Rangaswamy P., A.S. Ramasamy and P.A. Guruswami, *India's Changing Farmers, op.cit.,* pp. 105, 109, 131, 136, 147.
52. Gautam, Vinayashil and S.Narayan, A Socio-technical Systems Perspective for Understanding Organisational Effectiveness, *Public Enterprise* (Yogoslavia), Vol.6, No.1, November 1985, pp.41-48.
53. Krishnaswami O.R., and K.Seshaiah, *The Lead Bank Scheme, op.cit.,* pp. 111-12.
54. Pappuraj Antony A., *Executive Perception of Corporate Social Responsibility, op.cit.,* pp.73,97,121.
55. Shanti Srinivas and Stephen J.Motowidlo, Effects of Raters' Stress on the Dispersion and Favourability of Performance Ratings, *Journal of Applied Psychology,* Vol. 72, No. 2, 1987, pp. 247-51.

(MANOVA) with hostility, depression, anxiety, subjective stress, and pulse rate as dependent variables and sex, orders of information presentation, and work load as independent variables. F-tests were used for testing the significance of multivariate effects of independent variables. Another three-way MANOVA was also conducted with favourability and dispersion as dependent variables.

Sharma (1987)[56] used *one-way ANOVA* to find out whether inter-rater agreement exists among supervisors in perceiving each organisational climate dimension. The supervisors' scores on the various OC dimensions (scope for advancement, grievance handling, participative management, recognition and appreciation, etc.) were used for the analysis. For each of the nine dimensions of OC, between-company mean square was substantially larger than within-company mean square, and F-ratio was statistically significant ($p < .001$) in each case. Thus for the sample as a whole there was adequate inter-rater agreement in perceiving each climate dimension. He also used a similar ANOVA analysis for examining the inter-rater agreement in the assessment of supervisor-management relations.

Karakaya and Stahl (1989)[57] used ANOVAs in a study relating to market entry barriers. Whether there are differences in the importance of barriers in market entry decisions was tested by performing *multivariate analysis of variance* (MANOVA) on relative weights associated with six barriers (cost advantages of incumbents, product differentiation of incumbents, customer switching costs, access to distribution channels, government policy) for four decisions (early entry and late entry in consumer goods market and industrial goods markets).

Wilks' Lambda was computed and its significance tested by F-test. Four one-way ANOVAs were also made to compare the relative weights of market entry barriers for four decisions.

Howell and Frost (1989)[58] employed ANOVA in a study of charismatic leadership. This study examines the interactive influence of three different styles of leadership (charismatic, structuring and considerate), and two levels of group productivity norms (low and high) on individuals' adjustment and performance on a decision-making task. The data pertaining to adjustment and performance measures were submitted to 3 (Leadership style) × 2 (group productivity norms) *univariate ANOVA* and F ratios were computed. Due to the large number of F ratios, an experiment wise alpha level of .05 was used. The ANOVA results indicate highly significant effects for leadership style, group productivity norms, and the leadership style X group productivity norm interaction on role conflict, specific satisfaction, and general satisfaction.

11.6 HYPOTHESIS TESTING

The meaning, characteristics, types and functions of hypotheses have been discussed in Section 5.4 of Chapter 5, above. Hypotheses are tentative propositions relating to the phenomenon under study. They have to be *tested* empirically before we can accept or reject them. The various aspects of testing hypotheses are discussed in this Section.

Meaning

Hypothesis testing means *subjecting* a hypothesis to an appropriate *empirical scrutiny* and *statistical test* to determine its *validity*. A researcher has to do a number of things as *pre-requirements*

56. Sharma Baldev R., *op.cit.*, pp. 100-101.
57. Karakaya Fahri and Michael J.Stahl, Barriers to Entry and Market Entry Decisions in Consumer and Industrial Goods Market, *Journal of Marketing*, Vol. 53, April 1989, pp. 80-91.
58. Howell Jane M., Peter J.Frost, A Laboratory Study of Charismatic Leadership, *Organizational Behaviour and Human Decision Processes*, 43, 1989, pp. 243-69.

for testing a hypothesis. He should see that the hypothesis is *testable, i.e.,* amenable for empirical investigation. The variables used in the hypothesis should be *amenable* to *measurement.* The researcher has to establish *decision rules* pertaining to the level of significance and specify *the type* of *sampling distribution* to be used. He has then to select a *real* social *situation* that will be sufficient as a reasonable testing ground for the hypothesis. For example, if the hypothesis is concerned with consumer behaviour, the researcher should select a sample of consumers, and collect the relevant data needed for verifying his hypothesis, and analyze them. All these are pre-requirements for hypothesis testing.

Testing Approaches

There are *two* approaches to hypothesis testing. They are: (1) the classical or sampling theory approach, and the Bayesian approach. The *classical approach* is an established one and is widely used in research. In this approach, the decision-making rests totally upon an analysis of sampling data. A hypothesis is set up and tested on the basis of sample data.

The *Bayesian Approach* is based on an older theorem known as Bayes Theorem. It also uses sampling data, but it goes beyond them, and takes into consideration all other available information for making decisions. Most of the additional information consists of subjective probability estimates about the various states of nature. Decision rules are established, and cost and other estimates are made. The expected outcomes of combinations of these elements are made. On the basis of them, decision alternatives are judged. The Bayesian approach has emerged as an alternative testing procedure since the mid-1950s. It is likely to gain a significant place in applied statistical inference, but its acceptance in research practice has been slow.

The Logic or Hypothesis Testing

Our first task is to *state* the *hypothesis* in *statistical terms.* Suppose we are studying the impact of a rural employment scheme on the level of income of rural people. The hypothesis may be stated as: the average level of income of rural people has increased due to the employment scheme. We draw a random sample of rural people in the villages covered by the scheme and collect income data for testing the hypothesis.

We develop a *null hypothesis* (H_0) for statistically testing the hypothesis. The null hypothesis is specifically formulated for testing for possible rejection or nullification. Hence the name null hypothesis. It is accompanied by an *alternative hypothesis* (H_a), *i.e.,* our regular research hypothesis which is the logical opposite of the null hypothesis. Let us state the null hypothesis as: the implementation of the employment scheme has not led to an increase in the average rural income level.

The *null* hypothesis is always a *statement* of *no change* or *no difference* or *no relationship.* Both the null hypothesis and the research hypothesis are *expressed* in *terms* of the population *parameters,* not in terms of the sample statistics. It is the *null hypothesis that is tested directly;* the research hypothesis is supported when the null hypothesis is rejected.

The *need* for a *null hypothesis* arises out of a *logical* necessity. The null hypothesis is based on a negative inference in order to avoid the fallacy of affirming the consequent. That is, it is easy to reject a false hypothesis rather than to accept a real hypothesis.

Since a sample is likely to vary somewhat from its population, the sample result is subject to sampling error and therefore, it does not always reflect the true population value. Accordingly, the sample result cannot be interpreted directly; a *decision rule* is needed to enable us to reject or accept a hypothesis on the basis of a sample result. We should determine whether the sample result falls within a range that can occur by chance or could not possibly by a result of chance.

Significance levels

When does the sample result justify the rejection of the null hypothesis? The answer is: when it could not be a result of chance, *i.e.,* when it is highly improbable. Statisticians generally consider that an event is statistically improbable, only if it is among the extreme 5 per cent or 1 per cent of the possible outcomes. The 5 per cent (or 1 per cent) value defines the proportion of a sampling distribution[59] that contains the specified highly improbable outcomes. This proportion of the distribution is called the *region of rejection,* and the 5 per cent (.05) and 1 per cent (0.01) are called the *levels of significance or levels of confidence.* (See exhibit 11.4). These are levels of probability at which, the null hypothesis can be rejected with confidence. For example, 0.05 level of significance means that we are willing to reject the Ho, if the sample statistic occurs by chance only 5 times or less out of 100 times. The significance levels commonly used are .001, .01, and .05.

Thus, the decision rule is specified in terms of a specific level of significance. If the obtained sample result falls within the specified region of rejection, the null hypothesis is rejected at that level of significance. The rejection of the null hypothesis supports the research hypothesis.

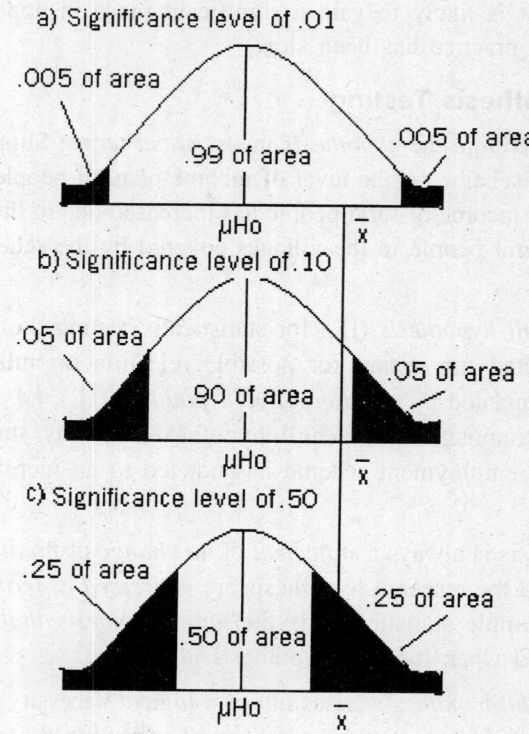

Exhibit 11.4: Different Levels of Significance

59. Sampling distribution is a probability distribution of all the possible values of statistic may take on for a sample of given size from a population.

Type I and Type II Errors

In statistical hypothesis testing as the entire population is not measured directly, the statistical test can never prove whether the null hypothesis is really/actually true or false. The only thing it shows is whether the sample result is sufficiently likely or unlikely to justify the decision based on the sample evidence to reject or not to reject the null hypothesis. The null hypothesis can be actually true or false. If a null hypothesis which is actually true is rejected, the decision based on the sample evidence is wrong. Such an error is called a Type I error. If the null hypothesis is false but is not rejected, then the error is called a Type II error (see Exhibit 11.5).

Decision	*The Null Hypothesis* (H_0)	
	True	*False*
Reject H_0	Type I Error	No Error
Accept H_0	No Error	Type II Error

Exhibit 11.5: Type I and Type II Errors

Interpreting the Significance Level

The probability of rejecting a true hypothesis – a type I error – is equivalent to the level of significance. Thus, a researcher employing the 5% level of significance has 5% probability of falsely rejecting the true null hypothesis. Exhibit 11.6 illustrates how to interpret a 5% level of significance. Note that 2.5 of the area under the normal curve is located in each tail. 95% of the area under the normal curve is covered by an interval extending 1.96 standard deviation on either side of the mean. (This is valid for the normal distribution). In this area there is no significant difference between the sample statistic and the population parameter. Hence, in this area we would accept the null hypothesis. In the remaining 5% area, a significant difference between them exists and so here we would reject the null hypothesis. Even if the sample statistic falls in the non-shaded region, it does not prove that the Ho is true, it simply does not provide statistical evidence to reject it.

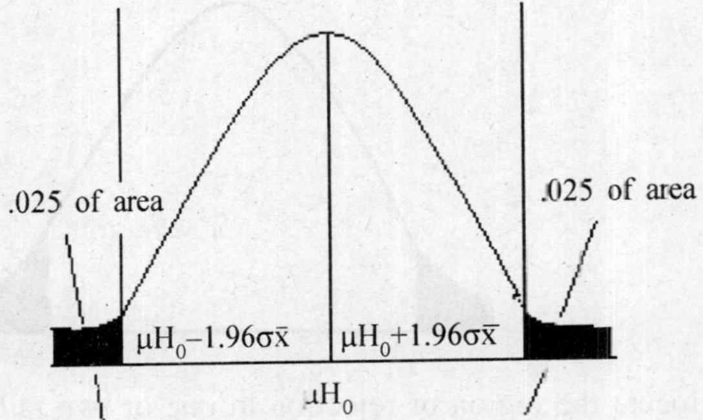

Exhibit 11.6: Interpreting Significance Level

The higher the significance level, the higher the probability of rejecting s true null hypothesis. Therefore to minimize the probability of rejecting a true hypothesis, the significance level should be as low as possible.

The choice of significant level is determined by the type of problem under study and the consequence of rejecting a true hypothesis or retaining a false one. If the practical implications of rejecting a true hypothesis are more severe than those of retaining a false one. If would be preferable to minimize the significance level to say 0.01. When a study does not have practical implications the choice of level will usually be governed by accepted conventions.

One-tailed and Two-tailed Tests

A statistical test used for hypothesis testing may be one-tailed or two-tailed. In an one-tailed test, the region of rejection is located at either the left or the right tail of sampling distribution (Exhibit 11.7). In a two-tailed test, the region of rejection is located at both the left and right tails i.e. a two-tailed test will reject the null hypothesis if the sample mean is significantly highei than or lower than the hypothesized population mean, suppose a manufacturer of light bulbs wants to produce bulbs with a mean life of 1,200 hours. If the lifetime is shorter, the cost of production increases. So the manufacturer does not want to deviate significantly from 1,200 hours in either direction. A sample of output can be tested for the null hypothesis, H_o=1200 and may use a two-tailed test. Ho is rejected if the mean life of bulbs in the sample is either too far above 1,200 hours or too far below 1,200 hours.

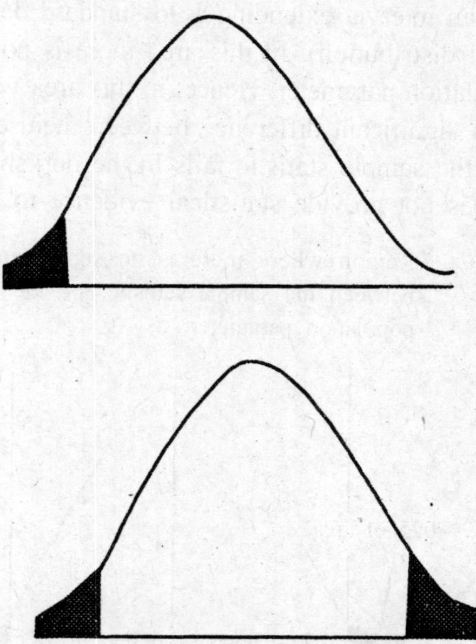

The decision to locate the region of rejection in one or two tails will depend upon whether the research hypothesis (H_a) implies a specific direction to the predicted result and where it specifies large or small values. When Ha predicts large value, the region of rejection will be located at the right tail of the sample distribution. When H_a implies lower values, the left tail is selected.

A research hypothesis, which indicates a direction of difference (higher or lower) rather than the mere existence of a difference, is a *directional hypothesis*, example, educated couples have a lower number of children than that of the general population. A directional hypothesis requires the use of non-tailed test. When the direction of the research hypothesis cannot be predicted, the two-tailed test is used.

Degrees or Freedom

This is another concept relating to hypothesis testing. The degree of freedom in a distribution is the number of observations or values that are independent of each other, and cannot be deduced from each other, *i.e.*, the number of values which we can choose freely. When a mean is computed from a number of values, there are no restrictions placed on the data. The sum is calculated and divided by n. However, when we compute a standard deviation, one restriction is imposed, *viz.*, the sum of the deviations from the mean must be zero. This restriction uses up one degree of freedom and so the denominator of the formula is n-l, rather than n.

Suppose we have two values 'a' and 'b' and we know their mean is 15. What values 'a' and 'b' can take on in this situation? They can be any two values whose sum is 30, because 30 ÷ 2 = 15. Suppose we find that 'a' has a value of 9. Now 'b' is no longer free to take on any value, but must have the value of 21(30-9) only. In this distribution of two values with a given mean, we are free to specify only one of the values. Thus, we have one degree of freedom.

Suppose there are six values in a sample with a mean of 18. In this case the degree of freedom or the number of values we can specify freely, are 6 – 1 = 5. We are free to give any values to five observations, and the value of the sixth one is determined automatically. To generalize, if the sample size is n, then the degree of freedom is n – 1.

The strength of prediction of a population parameter from a sample statistic is increased, as the number of independent observations or the degree of freedom is increased.

Statistical Testing Procedure

The statistical testing of a hypothesis consists of the following steps:

1. **State the null hypothesis and the (alternative) research hypothesis.** The hypotheses should be stated clearly, example,

   H_o: Educated and uneducated persons have the same level of political awareness.

   H_a: Educated persons have higher level of political awareness than uneducated persons.

2. **Select the appropriate statistical test.** There are various tests of significance such as 't'-test, z-test, chi-squire test, etc. (See the next Section 11.7 for a detailed description of test of significance). An appropriate test must be selected with reference to the nature of the population studied, the method of sampling used, the level of measurement of data and the like. This problem of test selection will also be discussed in Section 11.7, below.

3. **Select the desired level of significance.** The most common level is .05; .01 is also widely used. The exact level to choose is largely determined by how much a risk of Type-I Error we are willing to accept, and the effect that this choice has on the risk of committing the Type-II Error.

4. **Compute the appropriate statistic from the sample data.** A random sample has to be selected as per the sample design decided, and for the collected data, the appropriate statistic or measure (*e.g.*, mean, standard deviation or correlation) with reference to the research question, type of hypothesis to be tested and the level of measurement of the data. (See Sections 11.2, 11.3 and 11.4, above).

5. **Select the correct type of probability distribution.** The probability distributions are theoretical distributions that describe how outcomes are *expected* to vary. They are different from frequency distributions. While a frequency distribution is a listing of the *observed* frequencies of all the actual outcomes occurred, a probability distribution is a listing of the *probabilities* of all the possible anticipated outcomes. Probability distributions are mathematically derived and can be based on theoretical considerations (the tosses of a coin), or on subjective estimates or on experience. Since these distributions deal with expectations, they are useful models in making inferences and decisions under conditions of uncertainty.

   In hypothesis testing, generally the choice is between the normal distribution and the 't' distribution. The *normal distribution* is a theoretical or *ideal* model. As described in Section 6.4 of Chapter 6 - *Sampling,* above, the normal distribution is unimodal and symmetrical. The total area under the normal curve contains 100 per cent of values in the given distribution, and approximately 99.7 per cent of all the values in a normally distributed population lie within 3 standard deviations on either side from the mean.

   The *'t' distribution* is based on theoretical work done by W.S. Gossett (pen name 'Student'). The 't' distribution is flatter than the normal distribution, and there is a different 't' distribution for every possible sample size. As the sample size gets larger, the shape of the t distribution loses its flatness, and approximately equal to the normal distribution. In fact, for sample sizes of more than 30, the 't' distribution is so close to the normal distribution. Therefore, the normal distribution is the appropriate probability distribution when the sample size is larger than 30. The use of t-distribution is appropriate when the sample size is 30 or less and the population standard deviation is not known. It is also necessary to use the finite population multiplier (see Section 6.4 of Chapter 6, above) whenever the population is finite in size, sampling is done without replacement, and the sample is more than 5 per cent of the population.

6. **Compute the significance test value.** After the sample statistic is calculated, the formula for the selected significance test is used to obtain the calculated test value (t, r or other measure, as the case may be).

7. **Obtain the critical test value.** We must locate the critical value in the Table concerned with the selected probability distribution (normal or t) for the given level of significance for the appropriate number of degrees of freedom. The critical value so located in the Table is commonly known as Table value.

8. **Make the decision.** For most tests, if the calculated test value is larger than the corresponding critical (*i.e.,* table) value, we reject the null hypothesis and conclude that the research hypothesis is supported. If the table value is larger than the calculated value, the research hypothesis is not supported. (See example given in the next Section).

11.7 TESTS OF SIGNIFICANCE

The Parametric Tests

The tests of significance used for hypothesis testing are of two types: the parametric and non-parametric tests. The *parametric tests* are more powerful, but they depend on the *parameters* or characteristics of the population. They are based on the following *assumptions:*

1. The observations or values must be independent, *i.e.,* the selection of one item must not depend upon the selection of any other item.
2. The population from which the sample is drawn on a random basis should be normally distributed.
3. The population should have equal variances.
4. The data should be measured at least at interval level so that arithmetic operations can be used.

The important parametric tests are: the z-test, the t-test and the F-test.

The z-test

Prof. R.A. Fisher has developed the z-test. It is based on the normal distribution; it is widely used for testing the significance of several statistics such as mean, median, mode, coefficient of correlation and others. This test is used even when binomial distribution or 't' distribution is applicable on the presumption that such a distribution tends to approximate normal distribution as the sample size (n) becomes larger.

The relevant test statistic, z, is calculated and compared with its probable value (to be read from the normal distribution table) at a specified level of significance for judging the significance of the measure concerned.

For Formulas, see *"Applications of the Tests of Significance"*, below.

Research Example

Rama Kapur[60] in her study on Role conflict among employed housewives computed Z values pertaining to the differences between mother role and other sub roles of housewives (overall) and also for each occupational group. The Z values showed that respondents experienced difficulty in their role as mothers and also in their relationship with parents and relatives.

The t-test

The t-test was developed by W.S. Gosset around 1915. Since he published his finding under a pen name 'Student', it is known as *Student's t-test.* It is suitable for testing the significance of a sample mean or for judging the significance of difference between the means of two samples, when the samples are less than 30 in number and when the population variance is not known. When two samples are related, the *paired t-test* is used. The t-test can also be used for testing the significance of the coefficients of simple and partial correlations.

The relevant test statistic, t, is calculated from the sample data, and it is compared with its corresponding critical value in the t-distribution table for rejecting or accepting a null hypothesis.

For formula, see *"Applications of the Tests of Significance"*, below.

---

60. Rama Kapur, *Role of Conflict Among Employed Housewives,* New Delhi: *Shri Ram Centre for Industrial Relations,* pp. 11, 13.

Research Examples

Krishnaswami and Seshaiah (1985)[61] used t-test to examine the significance of linear and compound growth rates of branch expansion of banks in India in the post-nationalisation period, and also that of linear and compound growth rates of deposits and advances of banks and found them significant at .01 level.

Rajkishor Panda (1986)[62] in his study on the use of water in a canal irrigation system in Puri district, Orissa, tested the significance of differences in yield-rate of selected crops among farm size groups at different locations of the canal system by using t-tests at .01 level and found the yield rate differences significant. The yield rates were higher for the small farms than those for the large farms.

The F-test

The F-test is based on F-distribution (which is a distribution skewed to the right, and tends to be more symmetrical, as the number of degrees of freedom in the numerator and denominator increases). The F-test is used to compare the variances of two independent samples. It is also used in analysis of variance (ANOVA) for testing the significance of more than two sample means at a time. It is also used for judging the significance of multiple correlation coefficients. (See Section 11.5, above).

Research Examples

See under ANOVA in Section 11.5 above.

The Nonparametric Tests

The *non-parametric tests* are population-free tests, as they are not based on the characteristics of population. They do not specify normally distributed populations or equal variances. They are easy to understand and to use. The non-parametric tests are the only ones usable with nominal data; they are also the most appropriate technically correct tests to use with ordinal data.

To understand the important place of non-parametric tests in social science research, we must understand the statistical concept of power. *The power of a test* is the probability of rejecting the null hypothesis when it is actually false and should be rejected. The power varies from one test to another. The most powerful tests are the tests that have the most rigorous requirements to satisfy. These are parametric tests. Hence, social researchers would ideally prefer to use parametric tests of significance. However, it is often not possible to satisfy their requirements, because much of the data of social science research are at the ordinal or nominal level, and we cannot be sure of the normal distribution of the properties under study.

When the requirements of a test are not met, it is not possible to know the power of the test. Under such circumstances, the non-parametric tests are relevant and hence their importance in social science research.

The important non-parametric tests are: the chi-square test, the Median test, the Mann-Whitney U test, the sign test, the Wilcoxin matched-pairs test (or signed ranks test), and Kolmogorow Smirnov (KS) test.

---

61. Krishnaswami O.R., and K. Seshaiah, *The Lead Bank Scheme: An Empirical Evaluation*, Coimbatore: Rainbow Publications, 1985, pp. 60, 62, 76.
62. Rajkishor Panda, Anomaly in the Use of Water in a Canal Irrigated System, *Indian Journal of Agricultural Economics,* Vol. XLI, No. 4, October-December 1986, pp. 528-33.

The Chi-square Test (χ^2)

The Chi-square test is the most popular non-parametric test of significance in social science research. It is used to make comparisons between two or more *nominal* variables. Unlike the other tests of significance, the chi-square is used to make comparisons between *frequencies* rather than between mean scores. This test evaluated whether the difference between the observed frequencies and the expected frequencies under the null hypothesis can be attributed to chance or actual population differences. A chi-square value is obtained by the formula:

$$\chi^2 = \sum \frac{(f_o - f_e)^2}{f_e} \quad \text{... (11.55)}$$

where f_o = the observed frequency

f_e = the expected frequency in terms of the null hypothesis.

Suppose we want to examine the relationship between education and income and the frequency data obtained are summarized in Table 11.23.

TABLE 11.23

Distribution of Income by Education

Income	*Education*		
	Low	*High*	*Total*
Low	30	12	42
High	10	28	38
Total	40	40	80

Null Hypothesis: There is no difference between the two education categories in their pattern of income level. (That is, persons with low education and persons with high education are expected to have the same proportion of low or high income level).

Research Hypothesis: There is a relation between educational and income levels.

We can compute the expected frequencies with the observed ones. The greater the differences between them, the larger will be the value of χ^2.

To compute the expected frequency for any cell, the following formula is used:

$$f_e = \frac{\text{(row total) (column total)}}{\text{n(total number)}} \quad \text{... (11.56)}$$

The expected frequencies so computed are shown in brackets in Table 11.24.

TABLE 11.24

Income by Education: Observed and Expected Frequencies

Income	*Education*		
	Low	*High*	*Total*
Low	30 (21)	12 (21)	42
High	10 (19)	28 (19)	38
Total	40	40	80

Note: Figures in brackets are expected frequencies.

To compute χ^2, the expected frequency of each cell is subtracted from the observed one, squared, divided by the expected frequency of the cell and then all quotients are added up.

$$\chi^2 = \frac{(30-21)^2}{21} + \frac{(12-21)^2}{21} + \frac{(10-19)^2}{19} + \frac{(28-19)^2}{19}$$

$$= \frac{81}{21} + \frac{81}{21} + \frac{81}{19} + \frac{81}{19}$$

$$= 3.86 + 3.86 + 4.26 + 4.26 = 16.24$$

$$= 16.24$$

To evaluate the obtained X^2 value (16.24), we have to compare it to the critical value of sampling distribution of X^2 and to find whether the value of 16.24 is large enough to reject the null hypothesis. The sampling distribution of x^2 is determined by (1) the level of significance and (2) the number of degrees of freedom.

Let us select for the problem under illustration a level of significance of .01, which means that only if the calculated χ^2 is larger than what would be expected in not more than 1 out of 100 samples, will the null hypothesis be rejected.

The number of degrees of freedom of the χ^2 distribution is set by the number of cells for which the expected frequencies can be selected freely. For any bivariate table, the cells that can be determined freely are limited by the marginal total of both variables. Thus in a 2 × 2 table, there is only one cell that is free to vary, the three others being predetermined by the marginal total.[63] The formula used is:

$$df = (r - 1) \times (c - 1) \qquad \text{... (11.57)}$$

where r = the number of rows

c = number of columns

Thus in a 2 × 2 table df = (2 – 1) (2 – 1) = 1.

In a 3 × 3 table df = (3 – 1) (3 – 1) = 4 and so on.

For our example, with 1 degree of freedom and 0.01 level of significance the table value of χ^2 is 6.635. Our obtained χ^2 value (16.24) is much larger than the table value. Hence, the null hypothesis is rejected and the research hypothesis is supported *i.e.,* we may conclude that there is significant relationship between education and income.

Yate's correction

If the expected frequency is less than 10 (but not below 5) in any one cell of a 2 × 2 table, the χ^2 formula may yield an inflated chi-square value. In order to reduce the overestimate, a correction known as Yate's correction is applied. This correction is the difference between each set of obtained and expected frequencies is reduced by 0.50.

The *important requirements* for using the chi-square as a test of significance are:

1. There should be at least a 2 × 2 table
2. The data should be nominal *i.e.,* frequencies only

63. Marginal total means the total of respective column or row in the table.

3. The sample should have been selected on a random basis
4. For a 2 × 2 table, no expected frequency should be smaller than 5. Yate's correction formula should be used for a 2 × 2 table in which an expected cell frequency is smaller than 10. For a comparison of three or more categories in each variable (*i.e.*, 3 × 3 or 4 × 5 etc.) there is no hard and fast rule regarding the minimum cell frequencies.

Evaluation: The χ^2 test compares frequencies only, not ordinal, interval data, or other forms of data. The χ^2 statistic does not lend itself to comparison with other statistics and unless the values of n are equal, even two chi-square values cannot meaningfully be compared with each other, because the value of χ^2 is a function of *n*.

Research examples

Krishnaswami (1976)[64] in his study on democratic control and management in agricultural co-operative credit structure used χ^2 test for studying the following relationships:

Variables	*Calculated* χ^2	*df*	*Table value*	*Significance level*
Education and Democratic Participation (DP)	24.159	8	20.09	.01
Caste and DP	9.91396	4	13.28	.05
Occupation and DP	17.536	2	9.21	.01

Pappuraj (1986)[65] used χ^2 test in his study on executive perception of corporate social responsibility of testing whether the following variables are dependent on each other or not:

Variables	*Calculated* χ^2	*Table value at 5% level*	*Significance*
Age of firm & its responsiveness to employees (RR)	12.35	28.869	Not significant
Nature of firm and RCR	5.8	16.919	Not significant
Executive's education & RR	19.01	24.996	Not significant
Executive position and RR	8.68	24.996	Not significant
Age of the firm and responsiveness to customers (RC)	12.27	28.869	Not significant
Nature of firm & RC	10.2	16.919	Not significant
Executive's education & RC	12.38	24.996	Not significant

Kher (1984)[66] in his study on the profile of industrial workers used χ^2 test for testing whether the following variables are related to one another or not:

64. Krishnaswami O.R., *Co-operative Democracy in Action*, Bombay: Somaiya Publications, 1976, pp. 86, 88, 91.
65. Pappuraj Antony A., *Executive Perception of Corporate Social Responsibility* (unpublished dissertation) Madras: Department of Commerce, Madras University, 1986, pp. 74-78; 98-100.
66. Kher Manik, *Profile of Industrial Workers*, Pune: The Times Research Foundation, 1984, pp. 29-77.

Variables	*Computed* χ^2	*Significance at .10 level*
Workers' age and no. of jobs changed	5.27	No
Workers' age and dissatisfaction with job factors	25.43	Yes
Workers' education and satisfaction with job factors	55.151	Yes
Workers' age and choice of union leaders	5.416	Yes
Workers' education and choice of union leaders (CUL)	12.802	Yes
Workers' relations with supervisor and CUL	7.629	No
Workers' relations with management and CUL	26.895	Yes
Factory size and CUL	5.945	Yes
Workers' opinion on adequacy of welfare measures & CUL	5.103	Yes

Rama Kapur[67] in her study on role conflict among employed housewives used χ^2 to test the differences between degrees of difficulty in family sub-roles of employed housewives and the differences between degrees of difficulty in family sub-roles for each professional group (nurses, research workers and social workers) and found them satisfactorily significant at 0.05/0.01 level.

Narayanasamy and Krishnaswami[68] in their study on relationship between capital structure and cost of capital in cooperatives used the χ^2 to test the significance of relationship between business success and leverage and found it significant at 0.01 level in both cooperative sugar mills and spinning mills.

The Median Test

The chi-square test is applicable to two or more independent samples measured at the nominal level. For ordinal data also, the *median test* is useful. It determines the significance of the difference between the medians of two or more random samples. It is meant for determining whether the samples have been taken from populations with the same median. The median test compares the medians. The procedure for computing the median of two or more samples is as follows:

1. Find the median of the two or more samples combined.
2. Count the number of values in each sample falling above the combined median and items that are not above the median and prepare a contingent table
3. Perform a chi-square test for the 'above median' cases and 'not above median' cases so counted
4. Determine the degrees of freedom.
5. Compare the calculated χ^2 value with the corresponding table value of χ^2 at the specified degrees of freedom at the specified level of significance.
6. Make the decision.

If the calculated value equals or exceeds the table value we can reject the null hypothesis.

67. Rama Kapur, *Role of Conflict Among Employed Housewives,* New Delhi: Shri Ram Centre for Industrial Relations, pp. 11, 12, 16.
68. Narayanasamy N., and Krishnaswami O.R., *A Study of Factors Influencing the Relationship Between Capital Structure and Cost of Capital in Cooperatives,* (unpublished doctoral thesis), Gandhigram: Gandhigram Rural Institute, 1989, p. 266.

The Mann-Whitney U Test

This test belongs to a family of rank sum tests. It uses ranking information rather than pluses and minuses and therefore, is more powerful than the median test. The U test is designed to determine whether two independent samples have been drawn from the same population or from two different populations having the same distribution.

To apply the U test to a set of two samples (example, the average grades of students at two colleges of a university), the values of the combined samples n_1 and n_2 are ranked from the lowest to the highest rank irrespective of the samples, rank 1 to the lowest score, rank 2 to the next in order and so on indicating beside each the identification of the sample. Then the ranks of each sample group are summed separately and the sums are represented as R_1 and R_2. Then the value of U statistic is computed using the formula given below:

$$U = n_1 \times n_2 + \frac{n_1(n_1+1)}{2} - R_1 \qquad \text{... (11.58)}$$

Where n_1 = the number of items in sample 1

n_2 = the number of items in sample 2

R_1 = the sum of ranks of the items in sample 1

If the null hypothesis that the $n_1 + n_2$ observations came from identical populations is true, then the U statistic has a sampling distribution with a mean of:

$$\text{U mean or } \bar{U} = \frac{n_1 \times n_2}{2}$$

$$\text{and standard error (SD)} = \sigma u = \frac{\sqrt{n_1 n_2 (n_1 + n_2 + 1)}}{12}$$

Hence the Z-value of U can be determined by the formula:

$$Z = U - \bar{U} / \frac{\sqrt{n_1 n_2 (n_1 + n_2 + 1)}}{12} \qquad \text{... (11.59)}$$

If the calculated Z-value equals or exceeds the table Z value, the null hypothesis is rejected.

The Sign Test

The sign test is one of the earliest non-parametric tests. Its name comes from the fact that it is based on the *direction* (plus or minus signs) of a pair of observations and not their numerical magnitude. It is useful for evaluating the effectiveness of two types of methods whose effects cannot be quantified but can only be judged as superior/inferior or good/bad or preferable/not preferable, example, evaluation of two types of teaching methods by a set of students. The evaluation of the two methods are converted into signs: a plus means preference for the first method, a minus means preference for the second method and a zero represents a tie (no preference). We count (+) signs and (–) signs and exclude tie evaluations.

H_o: There is no difference between the two methods.

H_a: There is difference between the two methods.

Using the Z critical value of the normal distribution, the H_o is tested. The following formula is used.

$$Z = \frac{(p \pm .50) - n/2}{\sqrt{n/4}} \qquad \text{... (11.60)}$$

Where p = the number of plus signs

n = the total of plus and minus signs (zero signs excluded)

when p < n/2, use (0 +.50) in the formula

when p > n/2 use (0 – .50) in the formula

If the calculated Z value is higher than the table value, the null hypothesis is rejected.

Evaluation: The sign test is appropriate for determining the difference between dependent, not independent samples. It is somewhat insensitive for it does not reflect the amount of difference.

The Wilcoxon Matched-pair Test (Signed Rank Test)

This test not only tests the direction, but also the magnitude of differences between matched pairs (example, husband and wife, twins, output of two similar machines, or the results of a before-after experiment).

The *procedure* of calculation is as follows:

1. Find the difference (d) between each pairs of scores.
2. Rank the d's without regard to sign, giving a rank 1 to the smallest difference, 2 to the next in order and so on.
3. Then to each rank affix sign of difference.
4. Total the ranks with plus signs and total the ranks with minus signs.

The pairs whose scores are equal are dropped from the calculation. When two or more pairs have the same d value, their ranks are averaged. The sum of the ranks of the smaller sign group is designated as T.

A z formula is then applied:

$$Z = \frac{\text{T-mean}}{\text{Standard deviation}} = \frac{T - \left[\frac{n(n-1)}{4}\right]}{\sqrt{\frac{n(n+1)(2n+1)}{24}}} \qquad \text{... (11.61)}$$

Where n = number of pairs ranked (excluding no-difference pairs)

T = the sum of ranks of the smaller sign group

If the computed value exceeds the table value for a two-tailed test at the specified level of significance, the null hypothesis is rejected.

Kolmogorov Smirnov Test (KS Test)

This test is used when the data are at least ordinal and the research situation calls for a comparison of an observed sample distribution with a theoretical distribution. The KS one-sample test is more powerful than the χ^2 test and can be used for very *small* samples when the χ^2 test cannot be applied. The KS test is a test of goodness-of-fit in which we specify the *cumulative* frequency distribution which would occur under the theoretical distribution and compare that with the observed cumulative frequency distribution. The theoretical distribution represents our expectations under Ho. The point of greatest divergence between the observed and the theoretical distribution is determined and this value is identified as D (maximum deviation). The value for D is calculated as follows:

$$D = \text{maximum} \mid F_o(X) - F_t(X) \mid \quad \text{... (11.62)}$$

where $F_o(X)$ = the observed cumulative distribution of a random sample of n observations where X is any possible score.

$F_0(X) = k/n$, where X is any possible score,

$F_t(X)$ = the theoretical frequency distribution specified under H_0.

The calculated D value is compared with the table D value and decision on significance is made.

Other non-parametric Tests

McNemar test is used when the data are nominal and related to two related samples.

When there are k related samples with nominal data, the Cochran Q test can be used.

When the data are at least ordinal, we may also use the Friedman two-way analysis of variance test.

The details of calculation procedures for these tests are found in many books on Statistics. (See Seigel, *Non-parametric Statistics;* or Hays W.L, *Statistics for the Social Sciences*).

The Choice of a Significant Test

The selection of a particular significance test for the given case is determined by the following criteria:

1. The power efficiency of the test: A more powerful test provides a given level of significance with a smaller sample than with a less powerful test. Hence, the more powerful parametric tests are preferable to non-parametric tests, provided the requirements of parametric tests are satisfied. However, when those requirements are not met, the non-parametric tests have to be used.

2. The nature of the population: When the population is normally distributed and its variance is known, the z-test is used, but when the population variance is unknown and the sample size is small, the t-test is used.

3. The sampling method used: One of the requirements of parametric tests is that the sample should have been drawn on a random basis. This requirement equally holds good in several non-parametric tests also.

4. The number of samples involved: When the samples to be compared are two, the z-test, t-test, or the U-test, depending on the nature of distribution and the sample size is used. When three or more samples are to be compared the ANOVA test or χ^2 test is used, depending on whether the population is normally distributed or not.

5. The sample size: In the case of a small sample of less than 30, drawn from a normal distribution, the t-test is used; and for larger samples, the z-test is used.

6. The measurement levels or data: If the data are nominal, the non-parametric tests are used. When the data are at least interval ones, the parametric tests are used.

Applications or the Tests of Significance

The applications of appropriate significance tests in different research situations are explained below:

1. Testing the Significance of a Mean

When a single sample is drawn from a particular population and some measure of central tendency like mean is calculated, we wish to determine the statistical significance between the sample mean and the population mean. There are different situations for such testing:

(i) *Population normal, but infinite, sample size large or small but population variance known*

The z-test is used, applying the following formula;

$$z = \frac{\bar{x} - \mu H_o}{\sigma p / \sqrt{n}} \quad \text{... (11.63)}$$

where $\bar{x}$ = the mean of the sample

μH_o = Hypothesised mean for the population

σp = Standard deviation of the population

n = the number of items in a sample.

(ii) *Population normal and finite sample size large or small but population variance known*

The z-test is used with finite population multplier.

$$z = \frac{\bar{x} - \mu H_o}{\sigma p / \sqrt{n} \times \sqrt{N - n)(N - 1)}} \quad \text{... (11.64)}$$

where N = the population size.

(iii) *Popuiation normal and infinite, sample size small (n < 30) and population variance unknown*

The t-test is used, applying the formula

$$t = \frac{\bar{x} - \mu H_o}{\sigma s / \sqrt{n}} \text{ with d.f. (n – 1) and}$$

$$\sigma s = \frac{\sqrt{\Sigma (X - \bar{x})^2}}{n - 1} \quad \text{... (11.65)}$$

where σs = SD of the sample

(iv) *Population normal and finite, sample size < 30, and population variance unknown.*

The t-test is used with finite population multiplier and with d.f. = (n–1).

(v) *Population may not be normal but sample size lage, population variance known or unknown.*

The z-test is used (formula as in (i) above)

(vi) *When data are nominal.*

The *nonparametric binomial test* is used when the population is viewed as only two classes such as male and female, buyer and nonbuyer etc., and the size of the sample is so small that the χ^2 cannot be used.

Where persons, events or objects are classified into two or more nominal categories and each expected frequency is not less than 5 and when d – f = 1, the (non-parametric) χ^2 test is used for testing the significance of the sample mean.

2. Testing the Differences between Two Means

Many hypotheses in social science research involve a comparison between two populations. The difference between them may be studied by comparing their sample means. Does the obtained difference between the two sample means represent a true difference between their populations' means? Examples of such situations are: studies of output of male and female workers, the test performance of two sections of students, the comparison of the test and control groups in an experiment, and the like.

(a) Two Independent Samples: When the means of two different samples (*e.g.*, two samples of employees, two samples of consumers, etc.) have to be compared, the following situations may arise:

(i) Samples are larger ($n > 30$)

The z-test is used for testing the difference between the means.

(ii) *Samples are small* ($n < 30$)

The *t-test* is often used; the F-test can also be used.

(iii) *When the requirements of parametric test are not met, and the data are at least ordinal*

The *Mann-Whitney* U test is an alternative to t-test; the median test can also be used.

(iv) *When data are nominal.*

The χ_2 test is used.

(v) *When data are ordinal* the *KS two-sample test* is used.

(b) Two Related Samples: These are concerned with situations where the difference between closely matched pairs such as husband and wife, experimental and control groups, etc. are studied. The following situations may arise:

(i) *Population normal and samples small*

The *paired t-test* is used.

(ii) *Observations nonmeasurable but judged as superior/inferior, etc.* The sign test is used for determining the direction of difference between the matched pairs. For determing both the direction and magnitude of difference, the Wilcoxon Matched-pairs test is used.

(c) Three or more Independent Samples: We have often to test for significance in cases with three or more independent samples.

The *anlysis of variance* is used to test the significance of the sample means when conditions are appropriate for parametric tests. When the data of the samples are nominal the χ^2 is the test of choice.

When the data are at least *ordinal* we can use *Kruskal-Wallis test* which is more powerful than χ^2.

(d) Three or more related samples: When there are three or more *matched* samples (*e.g.*, the impact of three different trade discount rates on sales), *a two-way ANOVA* is employed with *F-test*.

Research Examples

Sarveswara Rao (1972)[69] used t-tests to test the significance of differences in *means* of dificiency scores of clerks and supervisors in a job satisfaction study. These differences were in respect of seven motivating factors (achievement, responsibility, etc.) and nine hygiene factors (salary, working conditions, etc.). He also used t-tests for testing the significance of difference between mean of motivators and mean of hygienes in respect of clerks and supervisors separately.

Rangaswamy, Ramasamy and Guruswami (1972),[70] in their study of factors influencing adoption of improved agricultural practices by farmers in Coimbatore district, used to test the significance of difference in average adoption scores between different farm-size holders, between owners and tenants, between farms with adequate irrigation and farms with inadequate/average irrigation, between higher and lower education groups, trained and untrained farmers, and between different value dimensions.

Sharma (1987)[71] used t-test for comparing the mean scores of supervisor-management relations and organisational climate betwcen private sector and public sector enterprises.

Mohanasundaram (1988),[72] in his study of the impact of minor irrigation scheme on Small farmers, used t-tests to examine the significance of *mean values* of percentage of area under HYV crops and percentage of area under cash crops to the total area cultivated before and after the implementation of the irrigation scheme in the selected blocks.

Fern, Avila and Grewal (1989),[73] in their study on *Salesforce turn-over,* used *t-test* to test the significance of (a) *mean differences* in job satisfaction, (b) mean differences in role conflict and ambiguity, and (c) mean differences in sales performance of those who stayed (n = 162) and those who left (n = 39).

A Testing Proportions

(a) **The significance of Proportions:** In qualitative phenomena, we have data on the basis of presence or absence of an attribute. With such data the sampling distribution may take the form of binomial probability distribution. For example, the human resources director of a company may report to the chairman that 70 per cent of the employees are 'promotable.'

A special committee assesses a sample of employees and finds only 60 per cent of the sample are qualified for promotion.

---

69. Sarveswara Rao G.V., *A Study of the two-factor Theory of Job Satisfaction* (unpublished doctoral thesis), Bangalore: Dept. of Management Studies, Indian Institute of Science, 1972, pp. 56-57.
70. Rangaswamy P., A.S. Ramaswamy and P.A. Guruswami, *India's Changing Farmers,* Allahabad, Kitab Mahal, 1972, pp. 109-58.
71. Sharma, Baldev R., *Not by Bread Alone,* New Delhi: Shri Ram Centre For Industrial Relations and Human Resources, 1987, pp. 107, 127, 147.
72. Mohansundaram V., "Minor Irrigation Scheme and its Impact on Small Farmers: a Study in Tamil Nadu", *Land Bank Journal,* Vol. XXVI, No. 3, March 1988, p. 38.
73. Fern, Edward F., Ramon A. Avila and Dhruv Grewal, "Salesforce Turnover: Those Who Left and Those Who Stayed," *Industrial Marketing Management,* 18, 1989, 1-9.

The significance of such proportions is tested by the use of z-test with the following formula:

$$z = \frac{\hat{p} - p}{\sqrt{\frac{p.q}{n}}} \quad \text{... (11.66)}$$

where $\hat{p}$ = the sample proportion

$\hat{p}$ = the population proportion

$q = 1 - p$

n = the size of the sample

The observed z-value is compared with the table value and the significance is judged.

(b) **Differences between Proportions:** When two samples are drawn from two different populations, one may wish to know whether the difference between their proportions is significant or not. For example, the success of two different drugs developed for reducing blood pressure may be tested by experiment.

The *z-test* is used with the following formula:

$$z = \frac{\hat{p}_1 - \hat{p}_2}{\sqrt{\frac{\hat{p}_1 - \hat{q}_1}{n_1} + \frac{\hat{p}_2 . \hat{q}_2}{n_2}}} \quad \text{... (11.67)}$$

where $\hat{p}_1$ = proportion of success in sample one

p_1 = proportion of success in sample two

$\hat{q}_1 = 1 - \hat{p}_1$

$\hat{q}_2 = 1 - \hat{p}_2$

n_1 = size of the sample one

n_2 = size of the sample two

The observed value is compared with the table value for judging the significance of the sample result.

Research Example

Fern, Avila and Grewal (1989)[74] used X^2-test for testing the significance of demographic *differences* (age, marital status, education level, and life cycle stage) between those who left (n = 39) and those who stayed (n = 162), and for testing the differences in experience, company rating, job security and sales performance between these two groups.

4. Testing Variances

(a) **Comparing a Vriance to some hypothesized Population Variance:** The X^2 *test* is used for this purpose.

74. Fern, Edward F., Roman A. Avila and Dhruv Grewal, "Salesforce Turnover: Those Who Left and Those Who Stayed," *Industrial Marketing Management,* 18, 1989, pp. 1-9.

(b) **Variances of two normal Populations:** The equality of vaiances of two normal populations is tested by the F-test.

5. Testing Correlation Coefficients

When the correlation coefficient of two variables is computed on the basis of sample data, we have to test the significance of the correlation coefficient. We use the following tests for the purpose:

(a) *Simple Correlation Coefficient*

The test is used with the following formula:

$$t = r_{yx}\sqrt{\frac{n-2}{1-r_{yx}^2}} \quad \text{with d.f.} = (n-2) \qquad \text{... (11.68)}$$

(b) *Partial Correlation Coefficient*

The *t-test* is used and the test statistic is calculated as under:

$$t = r_p \sqrt{\frac{(n-k)}{1-r_p^2}} \quad \text{with d.f.} = (n-k)$$

where n = the number of paired observations
k = the number of variables involved
r_p = the coefficient of partial correlation

(c) *Multiple Correlation Coefficient*

This is tested by using *F-test*, employing the following formula:

$$F = \frac{R^2(k-1)}{(1-R^2)/(n-k)} \qquad \text{... (11.69)}$$

where R = the multiple coefficient of correlation
k = the number of variables involved
n = the number of paired observations

(d) *Spearman's Rank Correlation*

When we compute this correlation coefficient for two variables, we have to test its significance The testing device depends on the value of n. For small values of n ($n < 30$), the table showing the values for Spearman's rank correlation to determine the acceptance and rejection regions may be used.

If the sample size exceeds 30, then the sampling distribution of r is approximately normal, we can then use the normal distribution table to find the appropriate z value for testing hypotheses about the population rank correlation and draw inference as usual.

Research Examples

See under Multiple Regression in Section 11.5, above.

11.8 TIME SERIES ANALYSIS

Time Series

In economic and business research, researchers often obtain data relating to a phenomenon over a time period. Such data are called a time series. A *time series* is a set of ordered observations of a quantitative variable taken at successive points in time in terms of years, months, weeks, day or hours, *e.g.*, annual data of industrial production in a country, crop production data over a period of time, weekly sales figures of a company, daily sales in a drug store, and the like.

A time series is influenced by a variety of forces which operate continuously, at recurring intervals or at random. The data of the series are decomposed to study each of these influences in isolation. This study is known as *Time Series Analysis.* This analysis identifies four kinds of change or variation in the given phenomenon, *viz.,* (1) secular trend (T), (2) cyclical fluctuation (C), (3) seasonal variation (S), and (4) irregular variation (I).

Secular trend shows the direction of the series in a *long-period of time.* The trend is the long-term movement of the series, reflecting either continuous growth, stagnation or decline. For example, the cost of living index has been steadily increasing over the years.

Cyclical fluctuation refers to wave-like *recurring rises* and *declines* in an activity. The typical example is the business cycle which moves through four phases: prosperity, recession, depression and recovery.

Seasonal variation refers to recurring *changes within a year e.g.,* fall in agricultural prices in the harvest season, and rise in their prices in the off-season; increasing demand for electric fans and air-cooling equipment in summer and declining demand for them in winter. The seasonal variation is caused by changes in climatic conditions and social customs within a year.

Irregular Variation is a non-recurring unpredictable variation taking place at random. It stems from several sources such as natural calamities, political developments, war and the like.

The combined influence of all the four components is often represented by a *multiplicative* model-

$$Y = T \times C \times S \times I \text{ or}$$

an *additive model*—

$$Y = T + C + S + I$$

where Y = observed values of a time series T = Trend, C = cyclical fluctuation,

S = Seasonal variation, and 1 = Irregular variation.

The time series analysis aims at measuring each of these four kinds of variations. When one kind of variation is measured, the other kinds are eliminated from the series.

Trend Analysis

Of the four kinds of variation in a time series, the secular trend represents its long-term direction. The past trend may be used to evaluate the success or failure of a policy or program, and also to predict the future patterns. A trend may be linear, curvilinear or straight line.

Methods or Measuring Trend: There are various methods of isolating the trend from the given series, *viz.,* the free hand method, semi-average method, moving average method and the method of least squares. The last two methods are more important. They are described below.

The Moving Average Method: This method of measuring trend is based upon the idea that if the values of the series for a sufficient period of time are averaged, the influence of shorter-term fluctuations will be eliminated. This is one of the methods aiming at elimination of seasonal variations. A moving average is *computed* by adding the values for some number of years both before and after to the value for the year for which the average is being obtained, and then dividing the total value by the total number of years included.

The period chosen for calculating moving averages should be long enough to eliminate the effect of recurring variations in the series. This period should be identical with the length of the cyclical movements in the data. Generally 3-year or 5-year period is taken to compute the moving averages. When we calculate 3-yearly average, the first three years' values are added, and their total and average are noted against the second year. Next, we drop the first year's value and add the next three year's values and note the total and the average against the third year and so on. The averages so calculated are plotted on a graph. The curve joining the points shows the rising or declining trend. See Table 11.25.

TABLE 11.25

Three-year Moving Average of Production in thousand quintals of a sugar factory

Year	*Production in thousand quintals*	*3-year Moving total*	*3-years' moving average (Trend)*
1981	80	—	—
1982	90	262	87.3
1983	92	265	88.3
1984	93	269	89.6
1985	94	276	92.0
1986	99	285	95.3
1987	92	—	—

In this case there is a rising trend in production over the years.

The moving average is *appropriate* for trend computation only when (1) the purpose of the investigation does not call for current analysis or forecasting, (2) the trend is linear, and (3) the cyclical variations are regular both in periods and quantities.

Method of Least Squares

This method is the most popular method of computing the secular trend in a time series. This is used for fitting a line curve of best fit. (See *Regression Analysis* in Section 11.4, above). The least squares method gives a formula for getting the straight line that will best fit the data. The equation of a straight line is expressed as:

$$Y_c = a + bx \quad \text{... (11.70)}$$

where Y_c = the calculated value of the trend

a = the intercept of Y or the height of the line at the origin, *i.e.,* when X == 0, a = Y

b = the amount by which the slope of the tiend line rises or falls, *i.e.,* the rate of increase in Y for a unit change in X.

X = the number of units of time each given year lies away from the middle year of the period

(The middle of the time series is used as the origin for convenience in computation. If an even number of year is given, the origin falls between the two middle years. Any other — say first or last — may also be used as the origin.)

The values of a and b for a least squares straight-line are found by solving the following equations:

$$a = \frac{\Sigma Y}{N} \quad \text{... (11.71)}$$

$$b = \frac{\Sigma XY}{\Sigma X^2} \quad \text{... (11.72)}$$

where Y = the actual values of the series for the period
N = the number of values included
X = the values assigned to each time period

The procedure of computing the trend line is illustrated in Table 11.26, in which the middle year 1983 is assigned the zero x value.

TABLE 11.26

Computation of the least squares Trend line for the production in an Engineering Factory

Year	*Production in thousand units Y*	*Deviation from 1983 X*	X^2	*XY*	*Trend value* Y_c
1980	12	−3	9	−36	10.75
1981	10	−2	4	−20	11.50
1982	14	−1	1	−14	12.25
1983	11	0	0	0	13.00
1984	13	+1	1	+13	13.75
1985	15	+2	4	+30	14.50
1986	16	+3	9	+48	15.25
Total ΣY = 91		ΣX = 0	$\Sigma X^2 = 28$		21 = ΣXY

$$N = 7 \quad a = \frac{\Sigma Y}{N} = \frac{91}{7} = 13 \qquad b = \frac{\Sigma XY}{\Sigma X^2} = \frac{21}{28} = 0.75$$

The required straight-line equation is

$$Y_c = 13 + 0.75X$$

when X = −3,

$$Y_c = 13 + .0.75\,(-3) = 10.75$$

and so on.

The Y_c values are plotted on a graph to get the trend line.

Extrapolation of the Trend: The least squares method is objective and gives us the most satisfactory results. The resultant equation is useful for *forecasting* further levels by *extrapolation*. For example, the trend of production computed in Table 11.26 may be extended to 1993 by assigning X the value of 10. When the equation $Y_c = 13 + .75\ (10)$ is solved, we get 20.5. Care must be taken in interpreting such a forecast. It is a forecast of trend only. First, actual values may be expected to diverge from it because of cyclical and random factors. Second, the forecast has meaning, only if the *same basic influences* which shaped the trend in the past can be expected to be operating in the future.

Research Example

Swarup and Sikker (1983)[75] used *exponential equation* for calculating compound growth rates of area under cultivation, production and productivity for important crops keeping 1966-67 as the base year in order to assess trends in area, production and productivity. The agricultural production is determined by three factors, *viz.*, area, yield and cropping pattern. In order lo determine the relative contribution of each component to total production an additive model was used for this component analysis.

SUGGESTED READINGS

1. Anderson, T.W., *Introduction to Multivariate Statistical Analysis,* New York: John Wiley & Sons, 1958.
2. Blalock, Hubert M. *Social Statistics,* New York: McGraw-Hill Book Co., 1972.
3. __________, *Causal Inference in nonexperimental Research,* Chapel Hill: University of North Carolina Press, 1964.
4. Brooks, B.C., and Dick, W.F.L., *Introduction to Statistical Method,* London: Heinemann, 1969.
5. Chou, Ya-Lun, *Statistical Analysis,* New York: Holt, Rinehart and Winston, 1975.
6. Cooley, W.W., and Lohnes, P.R., *Multivariate Procedures for the Behavioural Sciences,* New York: John Wiley and Sons, 1962.
7. Draper, N.R. and Smith, H., *Applied Regression Analysis.* New York: John Wiley and Sons, 1966.
8. Elifson, Kirk W., Runyon, RichardP., and Haber, Audrey, *Fundamentals of Social Statistics,* Reading, Mass: Addison-Wesley, 1982.
9. Freeman, Linton C., *Elementary Applied Statistics,* New York: John Wiley & Sons, 1965.
10. Harman, H.H., *Modern Factor Analysis,* Chicago: University of Chicago Press, 1960.
11. Hays, William L., and Winkler, Robert L., *Statistics: Probability Inference and Decision,* New York: Holt, Rinehart and Winston, 1975.
12. Hays, William L., *Statistics for Psychologists,* New York: Holt, Rineherat and Winston, 1963.
13. __________, *Statistics for the Social Sciences,* New York: Holt, Rinehart and Winston, 1973.
14. Hirchi, T., and Selvin, H.C., *Delinquency Research: An Appraisal of Analytic Methods,* New York: Free Press, 1967.
15. Huck, Suchyler W., Cormier, William H., and Bounds, William G., *Reading Statistics and Research,* New York: Harper Row, 1974.
16. Kerlinger, F.N. and E. Pedhazer, *Multiple Regression in Behavioural Research,* New York: Holt, Rinehart and Winston, 1973.
17. Levin, Richard 1., *Statistics for Management,* New Delhi: Prentice-Hall of India P. Ltd., 1986.
18. Loether, Herman J., and Tavish, Donald G., *Inferential Statistics for Sociologists,* Boston: Allyn & Bacon, 1974.
19. Morrison, D.F., *Multivariate Statistical Methods,* New York: McGraw-Hill Book Co., 1967.
20. Mueller, John H., Schuessler Karl F., and Costner, Herbert L. *Statistical Reasoning in Sociology,* Boston: Houghton Mifflin, 1970.

---

75. Swaroop R. and R.K. Sikker, *Agricultural Development in Himachal Pradesh,* New Delhi: Agricole Publishing Academy, 1983.

21. Niel, Norman H., *et al., Statistical Package for the Social Sciences,* New York: McGraw-Hill Book Co., 1975.

22. Overall, J.E. and C. Klett, *Applied Multivariate Analysis,* New York: McGraw-Hill, 1973.

23. Phillips, Bernard S., *Social Research,* New York: Macmillan Co., 1971, Chapters 13-16.

24. Rosenberg Morris, *The Logic of Survey Analysis,* New York: Basic Books Publishers, 1968.

25. Scheffe, H.A., *The Analysis of Variance,* New York: John Wiley & Sons, 1959.

26. Siegel, Sidney, *Nonparametric Statistics for the Behavioural Sciences,* New York: McGraw-Hill Book Co., 1956.

27. Thorndike R.M., *Correlational Procedures for Research,* New York: Gardener Press, 1978.

QUESTIONS

1. What are the purposes of statistical analysis of research data?
2. What is descriptive analysis? What is its purpose?
3. What is inferential statistics? What are its two main areas?
4. What are the characteristics of mean, mode and median? When and why each of these averages can be used?
5. Give two examples of problems in which (*a*) the mean is the best measure of central tendency; (*b*) the mode is the best one; (*c*) the median is the best measure.
6. Give the mean, median and mode of the following distribution: 22,40,42,57, 32,21,20,38.
7. The following is the income distribution of a group of industrial employees:

Income per month (Rs.)	*Frequency*
2,000	6
3,050	3
3,500	3
4,000	2
10,000	1

   (a) Which measure of central tendency would you use to represent the above income distribution?

   (b) Compute that measure.

8. Describe the uses of percentages in comparing samples.
9. The table given below describes the employment status of women in two communities. What conclusions can be drawn from the absolute numbers? From the percentages?

Employment Status of Women

Status	*Community A*	*Community B*
A. Employed profession	1,000 2%	1,000 5%
skilled	3,000 6%	1,600 8%
semiskilled	5,000 10%	2,000 10%
unskilled	15,000 30%	2,000 10%
B. not in employment	26,000 52%	13,400 67%
Total	50,000 100%	20,000 100%

10. On what does the choice of an appropriate average depend?
11. How does the variance differ from the mean absolute deviation?
12. What is standard deviation? What are its uses?
13. Suppose you obtain a set of scores of attitudes towards widow marriage from a group of respondents and that the standard deviation of this set of scores is zero. What does this imply about the group?
14. Attitudes towards authority often can be treated as an interval variable. Suppose this variable is normally distributed with a mean score of 60 and a standard deviation of 10.

    (*a*) What proportion of cases has a score between 60 and 63?

    (*b*) What proportion has a score less than 48?

    (*c*) What proportion is between 72 and 83? 52 and 55?
15. What is the special relationship of standard deviation with the normal distribution?
16. The X Boot Company runs two assembly lines in its plant. The production manager is interested in improving the consistency of the line with the greatest variation. Line A produces a monthly average of 10,280 units, with a standard deviation of 1051.5. Line B produces a monthly average of 9,935 with a standard deviation of 1020.8. Which line has the greater relative dispersion?
17. A car distributor's sales data are given below. Calculate the absolute deviation, variance, and standard deviation and comment on what your calculations tell you about his sales record.

    Average cars sold per day for each month

    3.28 3.21 3.10 2.33 2.05 2.68 3.05 2.91 2.87 2.55
18. What are standard scores? How z-scores and T-scores are computed?
19. Distinguish between

    (*a*) symmetric and asymmetric measures

    (*b*) one-way and mutual associations
20. Discuss the concept of relationship between variables in terms of proportional reduction of error.
21. Give an example of a bivariate nominal distribution for which lambda is not suitable as a measure of relationship. What measure would you use instead?
22. The table given below is a bivariate distribution of alienation by social status. By making a percentage comparison, and by using a suitable measure of relationship, assess the following hypothesis: As status increases, the degree of alienation decreases. What other measures of relationship can be used to test this hypothesis?

Alienation by Social Status

	Social Status			
Alienation	*Low*	*Medium*	*High*	*Total*
High	90	40	10	140
Medium	75	75	50	200
Low	65	125	140	670
Total	230	240	200	670

23. Discuss the applications of (a) Lambda, (b) Goodman and Kruskal's tau, and (c) Gamma.
24. Examine the uses of three measures of Kendall's Tau.
25. What are the features of Somer's d? How does it differ from Gamma?

26. What are the requirements for using Rank-order correlation? What are its uses?

27. What is correlation? What are the various types of correlation and their uses?

28. Suppose the correlation r = .29 exists between social class and higher education intentions. Analyse the meaning of this correlation.

29. From the following data investigate the relationship between unemployment rates and other variables. Which of the independent variable is most closely related to unemployment? Base your assessment on appropriate measures.

Country	*Unemployment rate*	*Political stability*	*Level of Economic Development*	*Rate of urbanization*
A	3.1	8.0	2.32	1.7
B	3.0	8.5	1.70	0.8
C	2.1	8.6	1.41	1.2
D	2.5	8.1	.82	0.6
E	5.1	3.1	.46	0.9
F	3.7	8.1	.40	0.8
G	4.7	7.2	.80	0.6
H	7.1	5.0	.02	0.2
I	7.2	2.6	1.45	1.1
J	7.7	2.1	.08	0.9

30. Below are ratings of aggressiveness (X) and amount of sales in the last year (Y) for 8 salespersons. Is there a significant rank correlation between the two measures? Use 0.05 significance level.

X	30	16	35	28	42	25	19	34
Y	35	30	40	46	50	32	33	41

31. What is regression analysis? What are its uses?

32. A study on the effect of bus-ticket prices upon the number of passengers produced the following results:

Ticket price (paise)	20	25	30	40	50	60
Passengers per 100 KM	450	430	460	370	340	360

(a) Plot these data on a graph.

(b) Develop the estimating equation that best describes these data.

(c) Predict the number of passengers per km if the ticket price were 35 paise.

33. What is multivariate analysis? How does it differ from bivariate analysis?

34. Distinguish between descriptive and inferential statistics.

35. Discuss the concept of control in multivariate analysis.

36. What are the uses of partial correlation, multiple correlation and multiple regression?

37. We obtain the following bivariate correlation matrix by correlating three variables X, Y and Z.

	X	Y	Z
X	1.0	.7	.8
Y		1.0	.7
Z			1.0

(a) What is the meaning of r^2yz?

(b) What is the meaning of $r^2xy.z$?

(c) What is the meaning of Rxyz?

38. A coffee manufacturer wanted to know the differences in the pattern of consumption of granuled coffee. A sample survey showed the following results. Is there a significant difference among age groups in the consumption of this type of coffee?

Age group	*Number of Respondents*	*Users of granulated coffee*
65 and above	20	10
45-64	20	8
30-44	25	7
below 30	25	6

39. What is coefficient of multiple determination? What does it indicate?
40. What is meant by multicollinearity? How does it affect multiple regression?
41. Illustrate the research uses of multiple regression analysis.
42. What is cannonical analysis? Why and when is it used? Illustrate.
43. What is discriminant analysis? When and why is it made? Illustrate.
44. What is the factor analysis? What are its purposes? Indicate its research applications.
45. Describe the principal component method of factor analysis.
46. Distinguish between R-type and Q-type factor analyses.
47. What are (a) cluster analysis and (b) path analysis? What are their purposes?
48. What is ANOVA? How and why is it made?
49. Distinguish between ANOVA and ANOCOVA.
50. On the following random samples of social class, test the null hypothesis that neighbourliness does not vary by social class. (Higher scores indicate greater neighbourliness).

Lower	*Working*	*Middle*	*Upper*
8	7	6	5
4	3	5	2
7	2	5	1
8	8	4	3

51. Test for the significance of differences among means of the following random samples of scores:

Sample 1	*Sample 2*	*Sample 3*
12	6	3
6	5	2
8	7	5
7	5	3
6	1	1

52. What is hypothesis testing? What is the logic of hypothesis testing?

53. What is null hypothesis? What is the need for it? How is it tested?

54. Distinguish between the null hypothesis and alternative hypothesis.

55. What is meant by level of significance? How is it interpreted?

56. What are Type 1 and Type II errors? How do they arise? How can the probability of these errors be reduced?

57. What are one tailed and two-tailed tests? How could you decide whether to use one-tailed test or two-tailed test?

58. A manufacturer guaranteed that a particular type of steel cable had a mean. tensile strength of 2,000 pounds with a standard deviation of 200 pounds. In a shipment, 16 lengths of the cable were subjected to a test for breaking strength. The mean breaking strength was 1900 pounds. Using a one-tailed test at the .05 level of significance, determine whether the shipment met the manufacturer's specifications.

59. In a survey of brand preference of high school students for soft drink, the following result was obtained:

	Brand A	*Brand B*	*Brand C*
Boys	25	30	52
Girls	46	22	28

Was there any relationship between the brand preference and the gender of the consumers? Use a two-tailed test at the .05 level of significance.

60. Two samples of mathematics students took an engineering aptitude test. Using a two-tailed test at the .05 level of significance, determine whether the two groups were random samples from the same population:

Group A	Group B
n = 25	n = 30
M = 80	M = 88
S = 8	S = 9

61. Suppose you interview all the junior and senior graduate students and find that 66 per cent of the juniors and 63 per cent of the seniors favour a certain social reform. Is this difference significant?

62. An investigator is testing the following two hypotheses: (a) the brakes on my car are safe; (b) the brakes on my car are too old to be safe. Regarding the decision on each of these hypotheses, which error (type I or type II) would have the most dangerous implications?

63. What are degrees of freedom? How are they determined?

64. Explain "decision criteria" in hypothesis testing? Why are they used?

65. Describe the hypothesis testing procedure.

66. Distinguish between parametric and nonparametric tests.

67. What is meant by the power of a test? How can it be measured?

68. Discuss the uses of z-test, t-test and F-test.

69. A machine was used to put out 16 defective products in a sample of 500. After it is overhauled, it puts out three defective products in a batch of 100. Has the machine improved? test at the 5% level of significance.

70. A university librarian suspects that the average number of books borrowed per student per visit has changed recently. In the past an average of 3.5 books were borrowed. However, a sample of 20 students averaged 4.2 books per visit, with a standard deviation of 1.8 books. At the .05 level of significance, has the average borrowing changed?

71. A personnel manager hypothesized that 15 per cent of the company employees work over time every week. If the observed proportion is.17 for a sample of 200 of the 2,000 employees, test whether his hypothesis can be accepted at the .10 level.
72. Explain the place of nonparametric tests in social science research.
73. What is chi-square test? When and why is it used?
74. What are the requirements for using χ^2 test?
75. To determine whether different income groups have different purchasing habits concerning a certain brand, a marketing researcher asked 4 income groups, "Do you always purchase the brand, never purchase it or sometimes purchase it?" The results of the survey were:

	2,000	*Rs. 2,000-2,999*	*Rs. 3,000-3,999*	*Rs.4,000+*	*Total*
Always	25	40	46	45	156
Never	68	40	75	58	251
Sometimes	37	30	19	37	123
Total	130	120	140	140	530

Is there any association between income level and purchasing habit?
76. What is median test? When and for what purpose is it used?
77. Discuss the respective uses of (a) Mann-Whitney U test, (b) the Sign test, (c) Signed rank test, and (d) KS test.
78. A group of 50 college fresh students was randomly assigned to experimental and control groups to determine the effectiveness of a counselling program upon academic performance averages. Use the Mann-Whitney test to test the null hypothesis that there was no difference between the academic performance of the experimental and control groups at the .05 level of significance.

Experimental	*Control*	*Experimental*	*Control*
2.10	2.01	2.66	3.34
3.00	2.69	2.56	2.31
1.96	3.07	2.50	3.05
2.04	2.14	3.77	2.67
3.27	2.82	2.40	1.96
3.60	2.57	3.20	1.70
3.80	3.44	1.71	1.57
3.75	4.00	3.04	1.39
1.98	3.01	3.04	1.39
2.00	2.55	2.06	2.09
2.98	2.77	2.86	3.68
3.10	3.09	3.02	2.11
3.69	2.72	1.88	2.83

79. The following ratings were made by people who used 2 detergents for 3 weeks. Test the hypothesis that the users found no difference in the two products. Use the 0.5 level of significance.

Product A	4	4	5	5	3	2	5	3	1	2	5	3	4	5	5
Product B	2	3	3	3	3	3	4	3	2	2	3	2	2	3	3

80. How is the choice of a particular significance test determined for a given case?
81. What tests of significance are applied for testing (a) a mean, (b) differences between means, (c) proportions?
82. A sample of size 40 has a mean of 12.2 and a standard deviation of 3.6. A second sample of 60 has a mean of 13 and a standard deviation of 3. Test the hypothesis that the means of the two populations are equal, assuming that their variances are equal. Use a two-tailed test at the .01 level of significance.

83. In a test given to two groups of students, the marks secured by them were:

Group A	18	20	35	50	49	35	34	50
Group B	30	28	26	35	30	44	45	

Test the significance of difference between mean marks at .05 level of significance.

84. The means of two random samples of 1,000 and 2,000 are 67.5 and 68.0 inches respectively. Can the samples be regarded to have been drawn from the same population of standard deviation 9.5 inches. Test at .05 level of significance.

85. What tests of significance are used for testing (a) variances, and (b) various types of correlation coefficients?

86. A random sample of 300 persons were asked to rate Company A on an 11-point scale as to its responsibility towards the local community. A second group of 200 persons rated Company B on the same scale, with the following results. Is there a significant difference at the .05 level?

Scale value	*A*	*B*
+ 5	36	24%
+ 4	21	16%
+ 3	16	20%
+ 2	10	8%
+ 1	7	11%
0	4	7%
− 1	0	4%
− 2	1	1%
− 3	1	3%
− 4	0	1%
− 5	4	5%
	100%	100%
n	300	200

87. What is time series analysis? What kinds of variations are identified by it?

88. Describe the important methods of measuring the trend in a time series.

89. How are growth rates of a phenomenon like production are computed?

90. The sales of a mini-car over the last five years were:

Year	1984	1985	1986	1987	1988
No. of cars sold	795	864	930	1010	1150

(a) Find the linear equation that describes the trend in the number of cars sold.

(b) Estimate the number of cars that can be expected to be sold in 1989.

91. The quarterly figures of accounts receivable of a company for the last five years (figures in Rs. thousands).

Quarter	*1*	*2*	*3*	*4*
1984	101	118	90	80
1985	107	120	95	82
1986	110	125	96	86
1987	113	130	102	90
1988	120	140	108	97

(a) Calculate a 4-quarter centred moving average.

(b) Find the percentage of actual to moving average for each period.

❑❑❑

12.1 INTRODUCTION

The final and a very important step in a research study is to write its report. The research report is a means for communicating our research experiences to others and adding them to the fund of knowledge. This chapter discusses the purpose of research reports, types of reports, planning report-writing, research report format, principles of writing, drafting and finalising the report, and evaluation of a research report.

Meaning and Purpose of a Research Report

A research report is a formal *statement* of the *research process* and its *results.* It narrates the problem studied, methods used for studying it and the findings and conclusions of the study.

The *purpose* of a research report is to *communicate* to interested persons the methodology and the results of the study in such a manner as to enable them to understand the research process and to *determine* the *validity* of the conclusions. The aim of the report is not to convince the reader of the value of the result, but to *convey* to him what was done, why it was done, arid what was its outcome. It is so written that the reader himself can reach his *own conclusions* as to the adequacy of the study and the validity of the reported results and conclusions.

Characteristics of a Report

A research report is a *narrative* but *authoritative* document on the outcome of a research effort. It presents a highly specific information for a clearly *designated audience.* It is *nonpersuasive* as a form of communication. Extra caution is shown in advocating a course of action even if the findings point to it. Presentation is subordinated to the *matter* being presented. It is a *simple, readable* and *accurate* form of communication.

Functions of a Research Report

A well written research report performs several functions.

1. It serves as a means for *presenting* the *problem* studied, methods and techniques used for collecting and analysing data, the findings, conclusions and recommendations in an organised manner.
2. It serves as a basic *reference material* for future use in developing research proposals in the same or related area.
3. A report serves as a *means for judging the quality* of the completed research project.
4. It is a means for *evaluating* the *researcher's ability* and *competence* to do research.
5. It *provides factual base* for formulating policies and strategies relating to the subject-matter studied.
6. It provides *systematic knowledge* on problems and issues analysed.

12.2 TYPES OF REPORTS

Research reports may be classified into (1) technical report, (b) popular report, (c) interim report, (d) summary report, (e) research abstract, and (f) research article. These types of reports vary from one another in terms of the degree of formality, physical form, scope, style and size.

Technical Report/Thesis

This is a *comprehensive full* report of the research process and its outcome. It is primarily meant for *academic community,* i.e., the scientists of the researcher's discipline and other researchers. It is a *formal long* report covering *all* the *aspects* of the research process: a description of the problem studied, the objectives of the study, methods and techniques used, a detailed account of sampling, field and other research procedures, sources of data, tools of data collection, methods of data processing and analysis, detailed findings and conclusions and suggestions. There is also a technical appendix for methodological details, copies of measuring instruments and the like. It is so comprehensive and complete that the study can be *replicated* by others.

The technical report is essentially technical in nature and scope and couched in *technical language.* It follows a *specified pattern* and consists of several prefatory sections with appropriate headings and paragraphs.

Popular Report

This type of report is designed for an audience of executives/administrators and other *non-technical users.* The requirement of this audience is different. The reader is less concerned with methodological details, but more *interested* in studying quickly the major findings and conclusion. He is interested in *applying* the findings to decisions.

The organization of this report is very important. The presentation can be more *forceful* and persuasive without, of course, any distortion of fact. It should be clear, brief and straightforward. Complicated statistical techniques and tables need not be used. Instead *pictorial devices* may be extensively used.

The format of this report is different from that of a technical report. After a brief introduction to the problem and the objectives of the study, an *abstract* of the findings, conclusions and recommendations is presented. The methodological details, data analysis and their discussion are presented in the second part. More headlines, underlining, pictures and graphs may be used. Sentences and paragraphs should be short. There can be a liberal use of margins and blank space.

The style may be more *journalistic* but be precise and it should encourage *rapid reading* and quick comprehension.

Interim Report

When there is a long time lag between data collection and the presentation of the results in the case of a sponsored project, the study may lose its significance and usefulness and the sponsor may also lose interest in it. One of the most effective ways to avoid such eventualities is to present an interim report.

This short report may contain either the *first results* of the analysis or the final outcome of the analysis of some aspect/s completely analysed. Whatever may be the coverage of the interim report, it fulfils certain functions. It facilitates the sponsoring agency to take action without waiting for the full report. It helps to *keep alive* the agency's interest in the study and prevent misunderstandings about the delay. In addition, it serves to spread over a longer period the time consuming process of discussion of research findings and their implications. The report also enables the researcher to find the appropriate style of reporting.

The interim report contains a narration of what has been done so far and what were its outcome. It presents a summary of the findings of that part of analysis which has been completed.

Summary Report

A summary report is generally prepared for the consumption of the lay audience, *viz.,* the *general public*. The preparation of this type of report is desirable for any study whose findings are of *general interest.* It is written in non-technical, simple language with a liberal use of pictorial charts. It just contains a brief reference to the objective of the study, its major findings and their implications. It is a *short report* of two or three pages. Its size is so limited as to be suitable for publication in daily newspapers.

Research Abstract

This is a *short summary* of the *technical report*. It is usually prepared by a doctoral students on the eve of submitting, his thesis. Its copies are sent by the University along with the letters of request to the examiners invited to evaluate the thesis. It contains a brief presentation of the statement of the problem, the objectives of the study, methods and techniques used and an overview of the report. A brief summary of the results of the study may also be added. This abstract is primarily meant for enabling the examiner-invitees to decide whether the study belongs to the area of their specialization and interest.

Research Article

This is designed for *publication* in a *professional journal*. If a study has two or more aspects that can be discussed independently, it may be advisable to write separate articles rather than to crowd too many things into a single article.

A research article must be clearly written in concise and unambiguous language. It must be logically organised, progressing from a statement of the problem and the purpose of study, through the analysis of evidence, to the conclusions and implications.

A professional journal may have its own *special format* for reporting research. It is important to find out in advance whether the publication does have specific format requirements. For example, the research articles submitted for publication in the *Journal of Applied Psychology* should be prepared according to the Publication Manual of the American Psychological Association. The preferred format is:

1. *Introduction:* A statement of the nature of the problem and a brief review of previous studies pertinent to the development of the specific questions or hypotheses to be tested.

2. *Method:* A brief statement of what was done, where and how it was done, and a statement of the specific techniques and tools used.

3. *Results:* A presentation of the salient findings with tables or charts.

4. *Discussion:* A discussion of the findings in relation to the hypotheses or questions originally posed.

5. *Conclusion:* A presentation of the contribution of the study to theory and/or practice and the broad implications of the findings.

The article must be accompanied by an abstract of 100-150 words typed on a separate sheet of paper.

Any reference to an article or other source is to be identified at an appropriate point in the text by the last name of the author, year of publication and pagination where appropriate, all within parentheses, *e.g.*, Sherman (1980); Heller (1976, p.701). No footnote is to be used for purpose of citation.

All references are to be listed alphabetically by author in an appendix titled "Reference', *e.g.*,

Grove, A.S. (1983), *High Output Management,* New York: Random House.

Tannenbaum, A., & Schmidt, W. (1958). How to choose a leadership pattern. *Harvard Business Review,* 36, 95-101.

Similarly, the *Indian Society of Agricultural Economics,* Bombay has prescribed guidelines for submission of papers for publication in the *Indian Journal of Agricultural Economics.* The preferred format is: 1. Introduction, 2. Methodology, 3. Results and Discussion; and 4. Policy implications/ conclusion, followed by references. Only cited works should be included in the reference list. The style of citations to be followed is:

A.S. Kahlon and K. Singh: *Managing Agricultural Finance: Theory and Practice,* Allied Publishers Private Limited, New Delhi, 1984.

Jairam Krishna, "Focus on Wasteland Development: Degradation and Poverty," *The Economic Times,* April 13, 1986.

C.H. Hanumantha Rao, "Current Agrarian Scene: Policy Alternatives," *Economic and Political Weekly,* Vol. XXIII, No. 13, March 26, 1988.

An abstract not exceeding 100 words should be submitted along with the paper. The length of the article is limited to 20 (double space) typed pages (8½ × 11").

Regardless of the format followed, however, the style of writing should be the same as that used for a technical report thesis.

12.3 PLANNING REPORT WRITING

Steps in Planning Report Writing

After the data analysis is over, report writing cannot be started abruptly. It requires careful *pre-planning*. This planning process involves the following considerations and steps:

As a research report is a means of communication, we have to consider some basic questions which determine the effectiveness of communication, namely, *'who'* says *"what'* to *'whom'* in *'which way'* and with *'what effect.'*

1. The Target Audience: The *first step* in planning report writing is to determine the target audience. The form and style of reporting and other aspects depend upon the type of the reader, for whom the report is intended. The identification of the target audience depends on who is the researcher and what is his intention.

The *target audiences,* may be classified into (1) the academic (or scientific) community, (2) the sponsors of research, and (3) the general public.

The *academic* or *scientific community* will be the primary target audience in the following cases: (1) when the research is undertaken as an academic exercise for a Master's degree, or M.Phil. Degree or Ph.D. degree (in this case the thesis evaluation committee members will be the immediate target audience); (2) when a research student or social scientist plans to publish his research output in the form of a research Monograph; (3) when a researcher plans to write research articles based on his research for publication in professional journals. (In the last two cases, the referees, and the fellow-scientists interested in the study will be the target audience).

The *Sponsors of Research* may consist of two categories: (1) *research promotion bodies* like Indian Council of Social Science Research, the University Grants Commission, and educational foundations which provide financial support to social scientists working in universities and colleges for undertaking research with a view to encouraging them to do research; and (2) government department, industrial and other organizations which sponsor research for their *own use* in policy making and the like.

If the research is sponsored by a research promotion organization, the reporting has to follow its prevalent norms. In general, a full-fledged technical report is expected, along with an abstract of the report. When the research is sponsored by an organisation for its own use, it has to be reported according to its requirements. It is to be written as a private documents, emphasizing the findings and recommendations rather than methodology.

The *general public* is viewed as a cross-section of the society. This lay audience may be interested in the broad findings and the implications of research studies on socio-economic problems. The reporting for this audience may be in the form of a *summary report* or an article written in non-technical journalistic language.

Can one multipurpose report aiming at *all* categories of target *audiences* be *written*? The *communication characteristics,* viz., the level of knowledge and understanding, the information needs and the kind of language to which one is accustomed, are *not the same.* They vary from one type of audience to another. The preferences and the requirements of different audiences differ widely and cannot be reconciled. Hence *it is neither possible nor desirable to attempt to write one multipurpose report.* A separate report tailored to the needs of each type of audience has to be written when there is a need for communicating to different types of audiences.

2. The Communication Characteristics of the Audience: The second step in planning report writing is to consider the selected audience's communication characteristics. What is their *level of knowledge* and *understanding*? What is the *gap in knowledge* on the subject between the readers and the writer? The greater the knowledge gap, the more difficult it is to convey the full findings meaningfully and concisely.

What is the *kind of language* — scientific or journalistic — that which the readers are accustomed? What do they need to know about the study? Or, what is likely to be of *interest* to them? How can the needed information be *presented best* — verbal, a combined tabular or pictorial presentation? These questions determine the scope, form and style of reporting. The underlying purpose of a report should be noted. The purpose of report is not communication *with oneself,* but communication with the *target audience.* Hence we must constantly keep in mind the needs and requirements of the target audience.

3. The Intended Purpose of the Report: What is the intended purpose of the report? Is it meant for *evaluation* by experts for the award of a degree or diploma? It is to be used as a *reference material* by researchers and fellow scientists? Or it is meant for implementation by a user-organization? This intended purpose also determines the type of the report and its contents and form of presentation.

4. The Type of Report: With reference to the intended use, the type of report to be prepared should be determined. When the research is undertaken to fulfil the requirements of a degree or diploma, or funded by a research promotion agency, the report is prepared as a comprehensive technical report. When it is sponsored by a user-organization, it is written as a popular or summary report.

5. The Scope of the Report: The next step is to determine the scope of the contents with reference to the type of the report and its intended purpose. For example, a research thesis or dissertation to be submitted for award of a degree or diploma should narrate the *total research* process and experience; the state of the problem, a review of previous studies, objectives of the study, methodology, findings, conclusions and recommendations.

6. The Style of Reporting: What should be the style of reporting? Should it be simple and clear or elegant and pompous? Should it be technical or journalistic? These questions are decided with reference to the target audience. For a detailed discussion on style, see Section 12.5 *Principles of Writing,* below.

7. The Format of the Report: The next step is to plan the format of the Report, which varies according to the type of report. See Section 12.4: *Research Report Format,* below.

8. Outline/Table of Contents: The final step in planning report writing is to prepare a detailed outline for each of the proposed chapters of the Report. An outline lends cohesiveness and direction to report writing work. Until an outline is prepared, the researcher does not know that he has to do and how to organise the presentation.

A table of contents flows from the nature of the problem under study and the objectives of the study, the hypothesis to be tested and the variables studied.

Styles of Outlining

There are *two styles of outlining:* (1) topic outline and (2) sentence outline. In the topic outline, the topic heading and the sub-topic headings are noted and the points to be discussed under each subheading may be denoted by one or two key words.

In the *sentence outline* the essential ideas to be discussed under each subtopic are stated. This requires more thought and decisions on what to include and how to say it. It guards against later forgetting certain specific points that one wanted to make.

Topic outline *Democratic Control in Primary Cooperatives*	*Sentence outline* *Democratic Control in Primary Cooperatives*
1. Extent of members' participation — measurement — categorisation 2. Factois influencing Democratic Control (a) Members' characteristics and democratic participation — Age — Formal education	1. Extent of Members' participation — measured by a scale — on the basis of the score respondents categorised into activists, non-activists and medium participants — reasons for low participation 2. Factors influencing democratic control (a) Members' Personal characteristics and Democratic participation • a Person's social participation influenced by his personal characteristics like age, education etc. It is expected that the older, better educated and higher status persons will be activists in social organization Does this hold good in sample members? • Age and democratic participation — Age, as a correlate of the membership, likely to influence participation — Testing this relationship — Presentation of the table and the result of Chi-square Test — Interpretation of the result

Exhibit 12.1: Styles of Outlining

Obviously, it is more *difficult* to write a sentence outline than a topic outline, but it is *more useful* than the latter. A report "writes itself if it is based upon such an outline. Since it is much easier to change the outline than to change the rough draft of the report, it is *preferable to write a sentence outline* before drafting the report. Major omissions and commissions in the drafting stage can be avoided if writing is based on a detailed outline. Of course, an outline should not be considered as a rigid scheme to be strictly followed. It is a tentative one and is likely to undergo changes while the report writing work proceeds. Exhibit 12.1 illustrates the two styles of outlining.

Arrangement of Materials

After the detailed outline is developed, it should be studied carefully to see whether all aspects have been fully covered and arranged in a logical sequence.

The *notes cards* have to be sorted out and grouped topicwise. The groups of cards have to-be then arranged in the order in which the respective topics have been listed in the outline. Similarly the *statistical tables a*nd tables of statistical computation results have to be arranged in the order in which the related variables have been ordered in the outline. With these arrangements, the planning stage of report writing ends.

12.4 RESEARCH REPORT FORMAT

In this Section, the format of a comprehensive technical report or doctoral thesis is discussed.

Report Outline

A technical report has a number of clearly defined sections. While the headings of the sections and their order may vary form one situation to another, the following is suggested as a broad sequence of contents of a research report.

Report Outline

A. *Prefactory items*

1. Title page
2. Researcher's declaration
3. The certificate of the research Supervisor
4. Preface/Acknowledgements
5. Table of contents
6. List of tables
7. List of graphs and charts
8. Abstract or Synopsis

B. *Body of the report*

1. Introduction
   - (a) Theoretical background of the topic
   - (b) Statement of the Problem
   - (c) Review of Literature
   - (d) The Scope of the Present study
   - (e) The Objectives of the study
   - (f) Hypotheses to be tested
   - (g) Definition of concepts
   - (h) Model, if any

2. The design of the study
    (a) Methodology
        — Overall typology
        — Methods of data collection
    (b) Sources of data
    (c) Sampling plan
    (d) Data Collection instruments
    (e) Filed work
    (f) Data Processing and analysis plan
    (g) An overview of the report
    (h) Limitations of the study
3. Results: Findings and Discussion
4. Summary, Conclusions and Recommendations

C. *Terminal items*

1. Bibliography
2. Appendix
    (a) Copies of data collection instruments
    (b) Technical details on sampling plan
    (c) Complex tables
    (d) Glossary of new terms used in the report

A. PREFACTORY ITEMS

Title Page

The title page is the first page of a research report. It carries: (1) the title of the study, (2) the name of the degree for which it is submitted, (3) the name of the author, (4) the name of the institution on which the report is submitted and the date of presentation.

The title should be precise and reflect the core of the problem under study. It should be printed in capital letters and centered in the page. Exhibit 12.2 shows a sample of a title page.

Researcher's Declaration

In the case of a research undertaken by a student in fulfillment of the requirements of a Degree, he may be required to make a declaration as shown in Exhibit 12.3.

EFFECTIVE ORGANIZATIONAL DEVELOPMENT THROUGH PARTICIPATION AND COMMUNICATION PROGRAMME

A Thesis submitted for the award of Ph.D. Degree

By

K. B. AKILESH

Department of Management Studies

INDIAN INSTITUTE OF SCIENCE, BANGALORE

December 1980

Exhibit 12.2: Sample of Title Page

DECLARATION

I declare that the thesis entitled *"A Study of the Factors influencing the relationship between Capital Structure and cost of Capital in selected larger Cooperatives in Tamil Nadu"* is a record of independent research work carried out by me under the supervision and guidance of Prof. O.R. Krishnaswami. This has not been previously submitted for the award of any diploma, degree, associateship or other similar title.

Gandhigram,
February 9, 1989 N. Narayanasamy

Exhibit 12.3 Declaration by Research Student

Research Supervisor's Certificate

In the case of a student's research work, his research supervisor has to certify that it was a record of independent research work done by the student. See Exhibit 12.4 for an illustration.

CERTIFICATE

I certify that this thesis entitled *"A Study of the Factors influencing the Relationship between Capital in selected larger Cooperatives in Tamil Nadu"*, submitted to the Gandhigram Rural Institute, Gandhigram for award of Ph.D. Degree, is a record of independent research work carried out by Mr. N. Narayanasamy, Lecturer in Cooperation, Gandhigram Rural Institute, under my supervision and guidance. This has not been previously submitted for the award of any degree, diploma, associateship or other similar title.

Bangalore O.R. Krishnaswami
February, 9, 1989 Research Supervisor

Exhibit 12.4 Supervisor's Certificate

Acknowledgements

In this section, the researcher acknowledges the assistance and support received from individuals and organizations in conducting the research. It is thus intended to show his gratitude. Good taste calls for acknowledgements to be expressed simply and nicely.

In the case of a research undertaken by a nonstudent researcher, acknowledgements may be made in the preface itself, where a brief background of the study is given.

Table of Contents

A Table of contents gives an outline of the contents of the report. It contains a list of the chapters and their sub-titles with page numbers. It facilitates ready location of topics in the report. The chapter headings may be typed in capital letters and the subtitles in small letters. For a model, see Exhibit 12.5.

3. *DEMOCRATIC CONTROL IN PRIMARY COOPERATIVES*		Pages 40-81
3.1.	Introduction	40-43
3.2.	Social background of the sample cooperatives	43-45
3.3.	Characteristics of members	45-52
3.4.	General meetings	52-68
3.5.	Election of Director	68-70

Exhibit 12.5 A Sample of Table of Contents

List of Tables

This comes after the Table of Contents. It is presented in the following format:

Table number The title of the table page

All the tables may be numbered serially as 1, 2, 3, 4, ... in one continuous series, or Tables in each chapter may be given a separate serial order, as I.1, 1.2, 1.3,... for tables in chapter 1; 2.1,2.2,2.3., 2.4... for tables in chapter 2; and so on.

List of Graphs and Charts

If there are many graphs and charts or other exhibits they should also be listed after the list of tables, as under:

Number Title of the graph/chart page

Abstract

An abstract is a succinct *statement* of the *findings* of the project. It should be as brief as possible and run about one or two pages. It is placed at the prefactory part of the report so that a reader can get a quick overview of the report. It contains a brief and precise statement of the purpose and the scope of the study and the method used for the investigation, and a bare *summary* of the *findings* or the results of the investigation. The style of writing this abstract "places a premium on directness, conciseness and condensation."[1] There should be no overemphasis of minor points, but important conclusions should be given adequate treatment.

B. BODY OF THE REPORT

After the prefactory items, the body of the report is presented. It is the major and main part of the report. It covers the formulation of the problem studied, methodology, findings and discussion and a summary of the findings and recommendations. In a comprehensive report, the body of the report will consist of several chapters.

1. Introduction

This is the first chapter in the body of a research report. It is devoted for introducing the theoretical background of the problem, its definition and formulation. It may consist of the following sections.

(a) Theoretical Background of the Topic: The first task is to introduce the background and the nature of the problem so as to place it into a *larger context* to enable the reader to know its significance in a proper perspective. This section summarises the theory or *conceptual framework* within which the problem has been investigated. For example, the theoretical background in the thesis entitled, "A Study of Social Responsibilities of Large-scale industrial units in India.[2] discusses: The nature of the Indian economy, the objective of India's Constitution to establish an egalitarian social order, the various approaches to the concept of social responsibility — property rights approach, trusteeship approach, legitimacy approach, social responsibility approach — and their implications for industries in the Indian context. Within this conceptual framework, the problem was defined, the

1. Anderson C.R., *et al., Business Reports,* New York: McGraw-Hill Book Company, 1957, p. 307.
2. Ranganathan, M., *A Study of Social Responsibilities of Large-scale Industrial Units in India,* (an unpublished Ph.D. thesis), Bangalore: Department of Commerce and Management, Bangalore University, 1980.

objectives of the study were set up, the concept of social responsibility was operationalised and the methodology of investigation was formulated.

Similarly, the theoretical background in another doctoral thesis[3] on "the relationship between capital structure and cost of capital in larger cooperative undertakings", deals with an overview of the financial management decisions, the characteristics of cooperatives, the irrelevance of wealth-maximization goal to cooperatives and the alternative 'capital-cost-minimisation' objective of financial management in cooperatives. The problem under study was formulated within this conceptual framework.

(b) The Statement of the Problem: In this section, why and how the problem was selected are stated, the problem is clearly defined and its facets and significance are pointed out.

(c) Review of Literature: This is an important part of the introductory chapter. It is devoted for making a brief review of previous studies on the problem and significant writings on the topic under study. This review provides a summary of the *current state of knowledge* in the area of investigation. Which aspects have been investigated, what *research gaps* exist and how the present study is an attempt to fill in that gap are highlighted. Thus the underlying purpose is "to locate the present research in the existing body of research on the subject and to point out what it contributes to the subject."[4]

(d) The Scope of the Present Study: The dimensions of the study in terms of the geographical area covered, the designation of the population being studied and the level of generality of the study are specified.

(e) The Objectives of the Study: The objectives of the study and the investigative questions relating to each of the objectives are presented.

(f) Hypotheses: The specific hypotheses to be tested are stated. The sources of their formulation may be indicated.

(g) Definition of Concepts: The reader of a report is not equipped to understand the study unless he can know what concepts are used and how they are used. Therefore, the operational definitions of the key concepts and variable's of the study are presented, giving justifications for the definitions adopted. How those concepts were defined by earlier writers and how the definitions of the researcher were an improvement over earlier definitions may be explained.

(h) Models: The models, if any, developed for depicting the relationships between variables under study are presented with a review of their theoretical or conceptual basis. The underlying assumptions are also stated.

2. The Design of the Study

This part of the report is devoted for the presentation of all the aspects of the methodology and their implementation, *viz.,* overall typology, methods of data collection, sample design, data collection instruments, methods of data processing and plan of analysis. Much of this material is taken from the research proposal plan. The revisions, if any, made in the initial design and the reasons therefor should be clearly stated.

---

3. Narayanasamy, N., *A Study of the Factors influencing the Relationship between Capital Structure and Cost of Capital in Selected Larger Cooperatives in Tamil Nadu,* (unpublished thesis), Gandhigram: Gandhigram Rural Institute, February 1989.
4. Kerlinger, Fred N., *Foundations of Behavioural Research, op. cit.,* p. 696.

If *pilot study* was conducted before designing the main study, the details of the pilot study and its outcome are reported. How the outcome of the pilot study was utilised for designing the final study is also pointed out.

The details of the study's design should be so meticulously stated as to fully satisfy the criterion of replicability. That is, it should be possible for another researcher to reproduce the study and test its conclusions.

Technical details may be given in the Appendix. Failure to furnish them could cast doubts on the design.

(a) Methodology: In this section, the overall typology of research (*i.e.,* experimental, survey, case study or action research) used, and the data collection methods (*i.e.,* observation, interviewing or mailing) employed are described.

The sources of data, the sampling plan and other aspects of the design may be presented under separate subheadings as described below.

(b) Sources of Date: The sources from which the secondary and or primary data were gathered are stated. In the case of primary data, the *universe* of the study and the unit of study are clearly defined. The limitations of the secondary data should be indicated.

(c) Sampling Plan: The size of the universe from which the sample was drawn, the sampling methods adopted and the sample size and the process of sampling are described in this section. What were originally planned and what were actually achieved and the estimate of *sampling error* are to be given. These details are crucial for determining the limitations of generalisability of the findings.

(d) Data-collection Instruments: The types of instruments used for data collection and their contents, scales and other devices used for measuring variables, and the procedure of establishing their validity and reliability are described in this section.

How the tools were *pre-tested* and finalised are also reported.

(e) Field Work: When and how the field work was conducted, and what problems and difficulties were faced during the field work are described under this sub-heading. The description of field experiences will provide valuable lessons for future researches in organising and conducting their field work.

(f) Data Processing and Analysis Plan: The method — manual or mechanical — adopted for data processing, and an account of methods used for data analysis and testing hypotheses must be outlined and justified. If common methods like chi-square test, correlation test and analysis of variance were used, it is sufficient to say such and such methods were used. If an unusual or complex method was used, it should be described in sufficient detail with the formula to enable the reader to understand it.

(g) An Overview of the Report: The *scheme* of subsequent *chapters* is stated and the purpose of each of them is briefly described in this section in order to give an overview of the presentation of the results of the study.

(h) Limitations of the Study: No research is free from limitations and weaknesses. These arise from methodological weaknesses, sampling, imperfections, non-responses, data inadequacies, measurement deficiencies and the like. Such limitations may vitiate the conclusions and their generalisability.

Therefore a careful statement of the limitations and weaknesses of the study should be made in order to enable the reader to judge the validity of the conclusions and the general worth of the study in the proper perspective. A *frank statement of limitations* is one of the hallmarks of an honest and competent researcher.

3. Results, Findings and Discussion

This is the major part of the report. It should be an organised presentation of the results of investigation and not a clutter of tables and charts.

It may be divided into several chapters depending upon the number of objectives of the study, each being devoted for presenting the results pertaining to art objective. The chapters should bewell-balanced, mutually related and arranged in logical sequence.

The results should be reported as accurately and completely as possible, showing how they bear on the research questions/hypotheses.

Each chapter should be given an appropriate *heading*. For example, if one of the objectives of a study is to study the relationship between the socio-economic characteristics of consumers and their brand preferences, the chapter devoted to this objective may be given a heading of "Socio economic variables and brand Preferences."

Each aspect of the topic of a chapter may be dealt with under an appropriate *paragraph heading* in the following manner and order:

1. A brief description of theory or classification pertaining to it.
2. A citation of the relevant findings of previous significant studies.
3. A presentation of the summary table relating to the subject-matter.
4. Presentation of the findings and the inference drawn from it, stating how does the finding compare with the findings of earlier study/s and whether the hypothesis is accepted or rejected.

The entire verbal presentation should run as an *independent* stream and such expressions as "As seen from the above Table "or "As the following table shows " need not be used. The table number can be just referred to as" (See Table...)" in the appropriate place. Exhibit 12.6 illustrates the above points.

Every table/chart should be a *self-contained and setf-explanatory* unit within the body of the report, and the presentation should be so clear that the reader be able to grasp the finding either by reading the text or by looking at the table/chart.

Age and Democratic Participation

The age of a member of a Cooperative as a correlate of the period of his membership is likely to influence his democratic participation. An older member with his longer period of membership is likely to be an activist. The study of Ostergaard and Halsey, on "Power in Cooperatives" (1965), confirms this proposition. Therefore this proposition is tested in this study. Age is classified into three categories: young (18 to 35 years), middle (36 to 50 years), and old (51 and above).

TABLE 12.1

Age of Sample Members and Democratic Participation

Age group	*Number of members*	*Average Democratic Participation Score*
Young	41	4.54
Middle	93	4.89
Old	60	5.18
Total	194	4.91

The average participation score of the 'middle' age group is higher than that of the 'young' age group, and that of the 'old' age group is higher than that of the 'middle' age group (See Table 12.1).

To test the significance of these differences the analysis of variance test was adopted. The test was not significant. The relationship between age and democratic participation was further analysed by Chi-square' test. The value of XZ is 5.92202, while the table value at 5% level is 9.49. Hence there is no relation between age and democratic participation for this sample. The unexpected result may be due to the fact that interest in the affairs of cooperatives might not grow with advancement of age, but might depend on other factors like participation in business, cooperative knowledge, etc. Moreover, age is not necessarily a correlate of membership period."

(*Source:* Krishnaswami O.R., Cooperative democracy in Action, *op. cit.,* pp. 84-85.)

Exhibit 12.6 A Model for Presentation of Results

Negative or *unexpected results* should also be stated *frankly* without a tortured attempt to explain them away.

Each Section or chapter should end with a *summary* and lead into the next section or chapter with a smooth transition sentence.

4. Summary, Conclusions and Recommendations

The presentation of analysis and results is followed by a separate final chapter. This chapter is more extensive than the abstract given in the beginning of the report.

This chapter should be a *self-contained summary* of the whole report, containing a summary of essential background information, findings and inclusions, and recommendations.

After a brief statement of the problem, the purpose of the study and the methodology used in the investigation, the findings and conclusions are presented. This summary may be more or less a reproduction of the topical sentences of the various findings and conclusions presented in the main body.

Findings are statements of factual information based upon the data analysis, *e.g.,* "The average democratic participation of members increases with an increase in the level of cooperative knowledge."

On the other hand, *conclusions* are *inferences/generalisations* drawn from the findings and relate to hypotheses. They are the answers to the research questions or the statements of acceptance or rejection of hypotheses, *e.g.,* "The coefficient of correlation between cooperative knowledge and democratic participation is significant at 1% level, which shows that cooperative knowledge is strongly and positively related to democratic participation. The hypothesis relating to this is proved. That is, *Cooperative knowledge promotes* democratic participation in cooperatives.[5]

The formulation of conclusions is the most difficult aspect of report-writing, A researcher sometimes may be tempted to overgeneralize on the basis of his limited data or previously held convictions, not tested by the analysis. It is, therefore, essential to cultivate the qualities of skepticism and modesty.

Conclusions on Methodology: An investigation may throw out valuable lessons on the practical methodology — efficacy or otherwise of approaches and methods and tools adopted for collection of data, ordering items in data collection instruments, field work and the like. These lessons will be of immense use in planning and conducting similar studies in future. Hence a section may be devoted for presenting the methodological experiences. If such experiences are not reported, every researcher may have to learn by trial and error with no cumulative build-up of knowledge.

The Recommendations for Policy/Action: These should flow from the findings and conclusions. These are the actions suggested to the policy makers/users of the research findings. Recommendations made by other researchers or study teams/committees, however important they may be, should not be reproduced if they are not related to the findings of the present study.

The recommendations should be specific and should not be mere vague statements like "Member education should be organised;" "State regulation should be liberalised." They should rather indicate 'what', 'how' and other aspects of the action suggested.

Suggestions for further research: In the course of conducting research, new questions may arise or new problems may be uncovered. It is appropriate to indicate them along with suggestions for appropriate methodology for studying them.

C. TERMINAL ITEMS

Bibliography

This is the first of the terminal items presented at the end of the research report. The bibliography lists in *alphabetical order* all published and unpublished references used by the writer in preparing the report. All books, articles and reports and other documents may be presented in one common list in the alphabetical order of their authors. Alternatively, the bibliography may be classified into three or four sections: (a) Books, (b) Articles, (c) Reports, and (d) other documents, and in each section relevant references may be arranged in alphabetical order.

The purpose of bibliography is *different from that of footnotes.* While the bibliography gives a list of materials relating to the topic under study as a ready reference to the reader, the footnotes, found at the bottom of the respective pages or at the end of a section/chapter, specifically cite the exact sources and pages where quoted or paraphrased materials are found.

Format: Bibliography listing should be done with proper format in order to serve its purpose. For details see Section 12.6 *Footnotes and Bibliography* Format, below.

---

5. Krishnaswami O.R., *Cooperative Democracy in Action, op. cit.,* pp. 98-99.

Appendix

The following documents are included in appendix: (a) Copies of data collection instruments like interview schedules or questionnaires used for the study, (b) technical details on sampling plan, (c) complex and long primary tables, (d) statistical computations, (e) supporting documents and any other evidence that may be important as backup details for the report.

A glossary of new terms used in the report may also be furnished under appendix.

12.5 PRINCIPLES OF WRITING

The writing of a research report is governed by certain principles or standard practices. These are described below:

Organization of the report

A research report requires clear organization. Each chapter may be divided into two or more sections with appropriate headings and in each section margin headings and paragraph headings may be used to indicate subject shifts. Headings serve as pointer to where the discussion is going.

Standard usage in paragraphing and in giving headings to topics and subtopics should be followed. The general grouping is from "Centered section headings" to "marginal headings" to "paragraph headings' then to individual paragraphs. (See Exhibit 12.7).

Physical presentation is another aspect of organization. A page should not be fully filled in from top to bottom. Wider margins should be provided on both sides and on top and bottom as well.

Style

A research report requires a style different from other academic writings like essay, fiction or poetry. In the latter, the richness of words usage is often desirable to achieve beautiful effects. But a research report, being a formal presentation of an objective, unbiased investigation should be written at a formal level of standard English.

CENTERED SECTION HEADING

The centered section heading is placed in the centre of the page and is usually in solid capitals. It is separated from other textual material by two or three lines' space.

Marginal Heading

This heading is used for a subdivision in each Section. It starts from the left side margin without leaving any space. No punctuation mark like full-stop or semicolon is used at the end of this heading. The matter is presented below the heading and not along its line.

Paragraph Heading: This is used to head an important aspect of the subject matter discussed in a subdivision. There is some space between the margin and this heading. The matter is presented as a continuation of the heading along the same line.

The matter presented under each paragraph heading may be grouped under several paragraphs without separate headings, each dealing with a unified topic or idea.

A chapter may contain several sections with centered headings; each section may contain several marginal headings, and under each marginal heading there may be two or more paragraph headings.

Exhibit 12.7 Organic of a Research Report

It dues not require elegant word usage and allusion. It just needs a *plain discourse* with accuracy, clarity, coherence, conciseness and readability.

Accuracy the first requirement of the style in report writing. The report should be factual with objective presentation. Exaggerations and superlatives should be avoided.

Clarity is another requirement of presentation. It is achieved by using familiar terms and common words and unambiguous statements, explicitly defining concepts and unusual terms and by taking care of logical flow of ideas and sequence of sentences.

Coherence is an essential part of clarity. Each sentence must be so linked with other sentences that the writer's thoughts move smoothly and naturally from one statement to the next.

Guidelines for ensuring coherence:

— Arrange sentences within a paragraph in a logical sequence.

— Arrange paragraphs in a logical sequence.

— Place at the beginning of a paragraph the *topic sentence* to link it with the one before it and to prepare the reader for what is to follow.

— Use conjunctions, adverbs and phrases as connectives, *e.g.* but, because, therefore;... on the other hand, on the contrary.

Conciseness refers to the absence of waste wordage. Statements must be succinct and precise. Useless and meaningless words and verbose explanations should be avoided, without, of course, omitting pertinent information. Conciseness calls for repeated review, revision and condensation.

Readability is an important requirement of good communication. Even a technical report should be easily understandable. Technicalities should be translated into language understandable by the reader interested in the results of the study. The readability may be achieved by using (*a*) active verbs rather than passive verbs, (*b*) correct and exact names, references, facts and figures, (*c*) simple words and (*d*) sentences. The style of presentation should be such as to encourage rapid reading and quick comprehension.

The writer should keep in mind the reading ability of the target audience, have concern for the meanings of words, and try to humanize the writing style in keeping with the topic and occasion. He should also avoid unclear writings.

Unclear writings

Clarity and readability call for *avoiding* the following types of unclear writings:

- Avoid the *jargon*, and *pretentious* and pompous style, *e.g.*, a sentence taken from an unnamed work and quoted by Goode and Halt (1952, p. 366):

These concepts can hold only for ranges of variation of circumstances not too large to invalidate the assumption that for practical purposes the particular constant relations between the values of analytical elements which these type concepts in concrete case represent, will not be so unreal as to exceed an acceptable margin of error. Such unclear writing arises out of unclear thinking.

- Avoid *offensive* words, *e.g.*, adding the suffix "wise" to a noun, or adding "ize" to nouns or adjectives to make verbs.

- Omit *needless* words that cause verbosity, *e.g.*,

Instead of	Say
A large number of	many
in the course of	during
an adequate amount of	enough
with regard to/with reference to	about/concerning
in connection with	for
in large number of cases	often
a small number of	a few
it is generally believed	many think
it has been reported by a	As reported
begin to initiate	start

- Avoid *superfluous* phrases such as

  Authorities agree that ....

  It is a well-known fact ....

  Although certainly not a new finding, it is important to point out

- Avoid *abstract* words and use the concrete, *e.g.,*

Instead of	Say
(1) The position in regard to the supply of coal may become serious.	There may be a serious coal shortage.
(2) The *situation* with reference to the supply of skilled engineers is not likely to improve.	The shortage of skilled engineers is likely to continue
(3) Conditions with regard to employment are more favourable than for many years past.	Employment prospects are better than for many years past.

- Avoid words that *exaggerate* such as stupendous, immeasurable, gigantic, awfully, dreadfully...
- Avoid *tautology* or repetition, e.g,, in the phrases, '*joint* partnership', 'return *back*', 'declined to *accept*', 'the *true* facts', the words in italics are redundant and should be omitted.
- Avoid *smothered* verbs and instead use vigorous verbs.

A verb is smothered when it is buried inside another word and thus loses its power to state a clear relationship. You can restore the power of the verb by linking an idea to it, and by removing the suffixes like 'tion', 'ion', 'ment', 'ency' added to the verbs for converting them into nouns. For example, the following rewritten sentences replace the smothered verbs with action verbs:

Smothered verbs	Vigorous action verbs
It has been pointed out that in a training institution, careful initial selection and classification are important procedures in eliminating potential maladjusted personnel.	If a training institution selects and classifies personnel carefully, it will have few misfits
Safety helps in the prevention of injuries.	Safety helps prevent injuries.
It is currently our belief that consideration should be given to possibilities of failure of equipment now seeming to function without difficulty.	We believe that we should consider that this equipment may fail later.

Avoid cliches or stereotyped phrases such as,

— as a rule

— be that as it may

— bear in mind

— by and large

— conspicuous by its absence

— it goes without saying

— last but not least

— in the first place

— to all intents and purposes

- Avoid using slang, *i.e.*, language of a colloquial type, such as 'on the dot'; 'cushy'; 'posh'; 'had it; 'fallen for if; etc.

Grammar

Presentation should be free from spelling and grammatical errors. If the writer is not strong in grammar and correct language usage, he should get his manuscript corrected by a language expert.

The research writer should consult a good handbook of language usage (see the "Suggested Readings" at the end of this chapter).

A summary of important *rules of grammar* is given below:

Spelling: Each word must be spelled correctly.

1. Use preferred spelling found in a standard dictionary.
2. Refer to the best available authority for correct spelling of proper names not found in a dictionary.
3. Distinguish between singular and plural forms of anglicized nouns of foreign origin; for example:

Analysis - analyses	appendix - appendices
basis - bases	index - indexes (or indices)
hypothesis - hypotheses	stratum - strata
thesis - theses	matrix - matrices

Punctuation: Some desk dictionaries contain rules of punctuation, and good language usage books contain detailed explanations and rules. Carefully observe the rules of punctuations.

Capitalization: Standard practices for capitalizing words in English should be followed when writing in English or when quoting English titles.

Principal words of titles and parts of specific works are capitalized. Principal words in captions of tables and exhibits are also capitalized.

Person: A research paper embodies the results of a scientific investigation and is not of a personal nature. Most authorities, therefore, believe it should be written in the third person, and the first and the second person pronouns (I, me, we, our, your etc.) should be avoided. When the writer has to refer to himself, such expressions as "the researcher", or "the writer" are preferred.

Voice: *Active voice is preferable* to passive voice, because the passive reverses the normal order of ideas and tends to slow down reading and understanding. Avoid such expressions as "It is estimated ...", "It can be foreseen ...", "There has existed ...", and the like.

Tense: Use the past tense for

(a) citing findings of others (*e.g.*, Srinivas found that....)

(b) describing how you conducted the study (*e.g.*, A structured interview schedule was developed and pie-tested....) and

(c) reporting specific past behaviours of your subjects (*e.g.*, Some of the sample respondents were not readily available...).

Use *present* tense for

(a) presenting the findings of your study (*e.g.*, the factors which consumers consider most in selecting brands are ...) and (*b*) stating generalizations (*e.g.*, "one of the most important conclusions to emerge from the World Fertility Study is that it is feasible to conduct surveys based on strict probability samples in most developing countries.")

Gender: Do not use masculine nouns and pronouns when the content refers to both genders. The generic use of 'man', 'he', 'his' and 'him' to refer to both men and women is not only misleading in many instances but also make the readers visualize and think of male persons.[6] To avoid this confusion,

- Use male pronouns when referring to males.
- Use female pronouns when referring to females.
- Use plural when referring to mixed group (*e.g.*, The individual who display prejudice in their personal relations...).

Numerals

Numerals: Arabic and Roman numerals should be used as follows:

Arabic

1. Chapter
2. Edition
3. Figures
4. Footnote number
5. Issue of periodical
6. Page
7. Section
8. Table
9. Volume of periodical
10. Exhibit

---

6. Martyna, W., "What does 'He' mean?" *Journal of Communication,* 1978, 28, pp. 131-138.

Roman

Upper-case	*Lower-case*
1. Act in a play	1. Preliminary page
2. Division of a paper	2. Scene in a play
3. Part of a volume	
4. Volume of a book in a series	

Words and Numerals: There are certain conventions that determine how and when to use numbers and when to use words.

1. Use words to state numbers in the following cases:
    1. numbers smaller than one hundred
    2. round numbers (*e.g.,* multiplies of one hundred)
    3. a fraction (*e.g.,* the twenty-fifth anniversary...)
    4. ordinal numbers (*e.g.,* the twenty-fifth anniversary...)
    5. the number at the beginning of a sentence (*e.g.,* Forty-five of the 897 participants were Christians) as no sentence should begin with a number.
2. Use the word *'present' as one word with a number,* and the word, *'percentage'* without reference to a number.
3. Use the percent *symbol (%) only in tables* and *figures.*
4. Use *numerals* to express page, street, telephone number, dates, and quantities combined with abbreviations and symbols. In dates B.C. follows the year and A.D. precedes it. (*e.g.,* 1800 B.C., A.D. 1890).
5. Use Arabic numerals to express decimals and percentages, even when they are smaller than one hundred (*e.g.,* The records show that 35 percent of members had attended the general meeting.)
6. Express references to table and exhibit/figure numbers numerically.
7. Express *textual reference* to *numbers taken from figures and tables* in the form of numerals and not in words even if the numbers are small, (*e.g.,* Table 7 shows that only 19 tests were run.)

Enumeration

Items or points can be given special emphasis by listing them in one of the following forms of enumeration: (1) textual and (2) tabular enumeration.

1. *Textual enumeration* is used when the items are so brief that they can easily be woven into the text, e.g.,

The essential characteristics of style in research writing are (1) accuracy, (2) clarity, (3) coherence, (4) conciseness, and (5) readability.

2. *Tabular enumeration* is preferable when the length and/or number of items would make a cumbersome sentence if run into the text or when items are long phrases or complete sentences *e.g.,*

The following are some specific suggestions made for ethically acceptable cross-cultural studies:

(1) Research should avoid actions violating the ethical standards of the group being studied.

(2) Studies should show sensitivity to each political and cultural situation.

(3) Research participants should be informed of the general purposes and sponsorship of the project.

(4) The study should ensure informed consent and avoid invasions of privacy.

(5) The research experience should not cause physical, mental, social or political harm to participants.

Quotations

In a research report, as in most other writings, quotations are used to cite definitions, view points, conclusions, etc. of other writers and authors. As a research study is an original critical analysis of data and information, and not a mere compilation of the words of other writers, quotations should be used sparingly. Certain types of reports, however, such as an analysis of the works of some author, require more quotations than others.

Unless the contrary is clearly stated, the citation of another's opinions or conclusions often signifies the writer's acceptance of them as his own. Therefore a careful investigation of the grounds for the validity of such citations is essential.

Forms of Quotations: Quotations may be direct (verbatim) or indirect (paraphrased).

Direct (verbatim) quotations should be employed:

(1) When giving the wording of laws, official rulings, and important edicts;

(2) When citing mathematical, scientific and other formulas;

(3) When citing the definitions of concepts; and

(4) When a well expressed significant idea is quoted.

Any matter that is directly quoted must be reproduced exactly in all details: wording, spelling, capitalisation, punctuation, and paragraphing Careful comparison with original sources should be made to check the accuracy of direct quotations.

Some rules to be observed:

1. Use *double quotation* marks to enclose direct quotations run into the text, *e.g.,*

"The power of concentration," says Swami Vivekananda, "is the only key to the treasure-house of knowledge."

2. Use *single quotation* marks for a quotation within a short, run-in quotation, *e.g.,*

In a review of a book of essays on fiction, Moore agreed with Robbe-Grillet that "at for things, 'all our literature has not yet succeeded in eroding their smallest corner, in flattening their slightest curve' —"....

3. Fit short direct quotations not over three type-written lines in length with quotation marks into the text itself, *e.g.,*

In his *Essays on Gita,* Sri Aurobindo writes, "The Gita is not a weapon for dialectical warfare; it is a gate opening on the whole world of spiritual truth and experience it maps out, but it does not cut up or builds walls or hedges to confine our vision."

4. If a direct quotation is more than three typewritten lines in length, *set it off* from the text in a separate paragraph, or paragraphs, *single-spaced.* Opening and closing quotation marks are *omitted e.g.,*

In his lectures delivered on his 'Master', Sri Ramakrishna, in New York and England in 1896, Swami Vivekananda said:

This is the message of Sri Ramakrishna to the modern world: Do not care for doctrines, do not care for dogmas, or sects, or churches, or temples; they count for little compared with the essence of existence in each man, which is spirituality; and the more this is developed in a man, the more powerful is he for good. Earn that first, acquire that, and criticise no one, for all doctrines and creeds have some good in them. Show by your lives that religion does not mean words, or names, or sects; but that it means spiritual realisation. (*The Complete Works*, Vol. iv, p. 187.)

Indirect Quotation means paraphrasing a given passage of another writer in our own words. This must involve genuine rephrasing. An example is given below:

On the issue of the ethics of policy research, Warwick and Pettigrew emphasize that social scientists should adhere strictly to the standards of the craft of research whatever be their own and their sponsor's value convictions. (In D. Callahan and B. Jennings(eds.), *Ethics, the Social Sciences and Policy Analysis,* New York: Plenum Press, 1982.)

Documentation: Every quotation used, either direct or indirect, should be *acknowledged* through a footnote.

Capitalization and punctuation: Although the rule requires that the capitalization and punctuation of quoted materials be reproduced exactly, good grammatical practice calls for an exception:[7]

Unless the first word of a quotation is a proper noun or adjective, it should not be capitalised, if it forms a grammatical whole with what precedes it, *e.g.,*

"Swami Vivekananda defines education as 'the manifestation of the perfection already in man.' "

If, however, the quotation is considered to be a grammatical whole by itself, the first letter is capitalised as in the original, *e.g.,*

Commenting on the term 'model', Rigby said, "An organization chart may be a recipe or a set of instructions rather than a model."

Ellipses: Omissions in quoted matter are permitted if the original meaning is not altered. Such omissions are to be indicated by the sign of ellipsis (...) See the previous example. Omission of one or more paragraphs of prose is indicated by a full line of ellipsis.

Adding Italics: The italicizing of any part of a quotation not italicized in the original must be indicated by the insertion of a phrase — italics not in the original — within square brackets. [ ].

Interpolation: Any corrections or remarks by the person quoting should be inserted in square brackets.

7. Campbell, William Giles, and Ballou, Stephen Vaughan, *Form and Style: Theses, Reports Term Papers,* Boston: Houghton Mifflin Company, 1974, p. 42.

Abbreviations

Do *not abbreviate* words in the text; spell out them in full (except decorations like Dr., Rev., and Hon. preceding proper names; Esq., Sr., and Jr. following proper names; and *measurement denominations* such as 16 mm., 250 cc., and 4 feet 10 in.)

This rule does not apply to materials included in the footnotes, appendices, bibliographies, tables and figures where abbreviations are rather desirable.

Statistical Test Results

A researcher may make use of various mathematical and statistical techniques like matrices, correlation, regression equations, multivariate analysis, significance tests and the like for analysing data and testing hypotheses, depending on the needs of the study. Naturally he presents the results of such analyses in the report. How should this presentation be made is significant. A mere statement of the results in technical form such as

$$X^2 = 9.74; \quad r = 0.84; \quad R^2 = 0.64$$

will not do. What such results mean in terms of the subject matter of the study should be brought out. Above all, the *statistical limitations* of the analyses should be clearly pointed out. For example, a few extreme cases will bias sharply the arithmetic mean; percentages based on meagre samples may lead to misleading comparisons, if the samples are not representative of the population, the findings cannot be generalised. Such limitations should be identified and openly reported without any reservation.

Presentation of Tables, Charts and Graphs

Tables, Charts, Graphs and other forms of visual aids are used to provide a basis for discussion in the text or to illustrate and classic points made in the text. Graphs and charts help the reader to understand even the more complex tabulations. Hence their presentation in the report requires special care. A reader reads these materials in a frame of mind different from that in reading the verbal matter. In his mind tables and other exhibits are set apart from the verbal presentation. Recognising this factor, tables should be presented as self-contained and self-explanatory units. This is achieved by giving accurate, clear and simple headings and footnotes to the tables and other exhibits. All these illustrative materials should be as simple and as clear as possible. They should not be cramped. Too much detail in a single table or chart or graph will make it difficult to understand. Then the very purpose of using it as an easy and simple means of conveying information is defeated.

All illustrative materials must be clearly labelled and numbered. Different types of illustration should be separately numbered serially: Table 1,2,3...; Exhibit 1,2,3 Graph 1,2,3....

12.6 DOCUMENTATION: FOOTNOTES AND BIBLIOGRAPHY

Documentation

The ethics of scholarship require proper acknowledgement of all source materials by the writer. This is a matter of intellectual honesty and validation of his work as well. Credit for borrowed words, ideas, symbols or other forms of expression should be given and their sources should be stated in the text or footnotes. Source cards prepared while reviewing literature provide the information required for this documentation.

There are two alternative models for documenting sources of ideas and information: (1) footnotes and (2) references — cited format.

Footnotes

Footnotes are of two kinds: content and reference. *Content notes* contains explanatory materials. *Reference notes* serve as documentation of sources or as means for cross-references (*see* below):

Purposes: Footnotes serves several purposes:

1. *To acknowledge indebtedness:*

   This acknowledgement is necessary when an exact quotation is used or when a passage of another writer is paraphrased. Common facts of general knowledge require no citation.

2. *To amplify or clarify the ideas or information presented in the text:*

   The footnotes used for this purpose are called content footnotes. They are used to clarify thoughts or concepts presented in the text without complicating the presentation. These notes may include explanatory material, technical details, incidental comments, additional information and the like. Of course, value and significant facts, and directly relevant ideas should not be transferred to footnotes, but should be included in the text itself.

3. *To establish the validity of evidence:*

   All important statements of fact must be supported by evidence of their validity. Reference is given in footnotes to the source of such evidence.

4. *To refer the reader to further sources of information on the subject under discussion.*

5. *To give the original version of material that has been translated in the text.*

6. *To provide cross-reference to various parts of the thesis:*

   Reference to materials appearing in an appendix or in earlier or later portions of the report facilitate cross-reference or location of related ideas. These references are made in the footnotes, as well as in the text.

Placement: A footnote citation is indicated by placing an index number, *i.e.,* a superscript or numeral, at the point of reference. This may be immediately following an author's name, a title, a sentence or a paragraph. In the case of a directly quoted or a paraphrased except, the superscript must appear at the end of the quotation or paraphrase.

The superscript numeral must appear at the top of the line both in the text and in a footnote. No mark of punctuation is used after the superscript numeral, ether in the text or in a footnote.

Footnotes are single-spaced, with double spacing between two consecutive citations. Footnotes are numbered consecutively within each chapter or throughout the entire report, if they are a few in number. Exhibit 12.8 illustrates the process of footnoting.

Superscripts may be confusing for mathematical or scientific formulas; in their cases, symbols like asterisk (*), daggers (†), double dagger, two asterisks, etc. may be used.

Footnote contents: Footnote citations for reference should contain full information for identification, viz., author's name, the title of the publication, place of publication, publisher's name, year and page number(s). A mere citation of the author's name and title only will not do.

Basic Format: Author's name, *title of the work,* place of publication: Publisher's name, Year, page no. (s). Note the punctuations. Page number to be preceded by "p" if single or "pp". if two or more pages. Title has to be underlined.

The first reference to a work should contain all the above details. If the immediate next reference, i.e.,

---

Krishnaswami defines Management by Objective (MBO) as "a system of participative management on the basis of position-wise result-oriented, measurable and time-bound objectives integrated with the organizational objectives, and with the environment."[1]

Drucker[2] lays great stress on the concept of self-control. Control, according to him means "the ability to direct one-self and one's work"[3] on the basis of objective.

The objectives at one level are the means for the objectives at the higher level; and the end for the objectives at the lower level. This chain of *means-end-sequence continues.* It emphasizes that objectives at different levels in the hierarchy must be balanced and integrated *and be* consistent one with another.[4]

An analysis of the environment[5] is an important step in establishing the organization's strategic and long-term goals.

Consecutive reference is also from the same work, then simply use the Latin abbreviation *'Ibid'* (meaning in the same work) and write the page numbers. (For abbreviations that can be used in footnotes and reference, see Section 12.7, below).

If the same work is cited after one or more citations from other publications, then write the author's name, abbreviation *'op.cit.'*, and the page numbers.

When a second but non-consecutive reference is made to the exact source (*i.e.,* the same work and page) previously cited, *'loc.cit.'* ('the place cited') is substituted for *'op. cit.'* the author's name is given to identify the work, but page numbers are not mentioned, because they are unnecessary.

Examples of footnotes for citing various types of materials, books, articles, Government publications, etc. are given below. The writer should carefully note the formats, punctuation, abbreviations and other details.

Author's name in Footnote: As per the general practice in vogue, the name starts with the *first name* in footnotes, but in a bibliography it starts with the *second* or *surname*. This variation may cause some difficulty and confusion, because the source of details for both footnotes and bibliography is the *same, viz.,* source cards. In source cards the names are noted starting with the surnames. I, therefore, suggest that the *same format* (*i.e., the surname format) may be adopted for both footnotes and bibliography* in order to avoid the confusion arising out of the conventional practice.

---

1. Krishnaswami, O.R., *Concept and Methodology of Management By Objectives,* Annamalainagar: Annamalai Univereity, 1983, p. 1.
2. Peter F. Drucker, *The Practice of Management,* London: Pan Books Limited, 1955, p. 150
3. *Ibid.*, p. 161.
4. Paul Mali, *Management by Objectives*, New York: Wiley Inter-Science, 1972, pp. 22-29.
5. For a useful model for Environmental Analysis, See Eli Segev, "How to use Environmental Analysis in Strategy Making", *Management Review*, March 1977, pp. 4-13.

EXAMPLES OF FOOTNOTES

For Citing Books

Single Volume Works

1. Mann, R.S., *Social Change and Social Research*, New Delhi: Concept Publishing Company, 1988, p. 27.

2. *Ibid.,* pp. 80-85.

3. Dube, S.C., *India's Changing Villages,* London: Routledge and Kegan Paul Ltd., 1958, p. 76.

4. Mann, *op. cit.,* p. 138.

5. Bandyopadhyaya, Jayantanuja, *The Poverty of Nations,* Ahmedabad: Allied Publishers Private Ltd., 1988, p. 48.

   Multiple author book with more than three authors use "and others' or "et al. ' after the first name.

6. Sheridan, Martin C. and others. *The Motion Picture and the Teaching of English,* New York: Appleton-Century-Crofts, 1965, p. 37.

   For quoting again from a previous reference, say cited in 5, same page:

7. Bandyopadhyaya, *loc. cit.*

Chapter in an edited multiple-author book

8. Warwick, Donald P., "The Politics and Ethics of Field Research," in Bulmer, Martin and Donald Warwick, (eds.). *Social Research in Developing Countries,* Chickester: John Wiley & Sons, 1983, pp. 315-30.

Editor as an author

9. Warwick, Donald, P. and Osherson, S. (Eds.), *Comparative Research Methods,* Englewood Cliffs, NJ.; Prentice Hall, 1973, p. 86.

An Article in an Encyclopedia

10. Banta, Richard E., "New Harmony", *Encyclopedia Britannica,* Chicago: William Benton, 1968, 16: p. 305.

Publications of Government and Public Organizations

11. Government of India, *India 1986:* A Reference Annual, New Delhi: Publications Division, 1987, p. 127.

12. World Bank, *Rural Development*, Sector Policy Paper, Washington D.C., 1975, p. 26.

Quoting from Secondary Sources

13. Gand, William S., "Foreign Aid : What it is; how it works; why we provide it," *Department of State Bulletin,* 59, No. 1537, 1958, quoted in Todaro, Michael P., *Economic Development in the Third World,* New York: Longman, 1981, p. 40.

For Citing Journals

The footnote format for citing articles from scholarly journals is:

Author's name, title of article enclosed in quotation marks, name of the journal underlined, volume number, issue number, the date of publication, page numbers. (The place of publication and publisher's name are not given).

14. Goel Ranjan, "Achievement Through Human Engineering," *Indian Management,* 28, No. 8, July, 1988, pp. 14-16.

15. Drucker Peter F., "What Business can Learn from Nonprofits," *Harvard Business Review*, 4, July-August 1989, pp. 88-93.

Newspaper Articles

16. Kumar, Naresh, "Exploring Sea for Economic Progress," *The Economic Times* (Bangalore), August 7, 1989, p. 5.

17. Editorial, *Deccan Herald* (Bangalore), August 5, 1989, p. 8.

For Citing Thesis or Dissertation

18. Pandey, Subrata, *A Study of Organizational and Individual Characteristics in R & D Organizations,* unpublished Ph.D. Thesis, Bangalore: Indian Institute of Science, 1986.

For Citing Semimar Paper

19. Krishnaswami O.R., "Towards Excellence in Cooperative Management," (Paper presented at a Seminar on *"Excellence in Management,* Cooperative Training College, Bangalore, July 1989).

Typing Instructions for Footnotes

1. No space intervenes between the word, or the mark of punctuation, and the superscript that follows it.
2. No mark of punctuation is used after the superscript numeral, either in the text or in the footnote.
3. Footnotes may be numbered 1,2,3.... in each chapter.
4. All footnotes for citations on a page are listed at the bottom of the page, without, of course, intruding into the bottom margin.
5. At the bottom of a page, draw a *dividing line* one and one-half inches long, one double space below the last line of textual material, beginning at the left margin.
6. The first footnote is put a double space below the above line.
7. Each footnote begins with its superscript, is indented as a paragraph, and is single-spaced.
8. When two or more footnotes appear at the bottom of a page, a double space is left between them.
9. For the sake of balanced appearance of a typed page, two or more consecutively numbered short footnotes are put on one line. e.g,,

   [12]Roy, op. cit., p. 40.[14] Ibid.
10. A footnote to a table or chart is placed one double space below it, without a dividing line.

Reference-cited Format

The *reference-cited format* of documentation consists of a single listing of research references at the end of a paper or thesis. This is preferred in most scientific writings. It is most often headed *"Reference Cited"* or *"References."* Sources are referred to in the text by author and year publication, and page number. References are listed in alphabetical order at the end of the report/paper without numbering. They include page numbers, if page numbers are not mentioned in the references cited in the text.

Examples of sources cited in the text and their listing under References are given below:

Citation in the text

Becker and Geer (1975) suggested that participant observation was to be preferred to interviewing....

Martin Trow (1957) argued that one method was not inherently superior over another.

Proponents of survey research are the first to admit the problems of bias and error which can occur (see Schuman, 1982).

"It is not that the numbers are necessarily false but that they draw the inquirer's attention away from what is of crucial significance", (Leach, 1967, p. 82).

"No amount of statistical sophistication can set right the distortions and falsifications introduced by wrong data" (Srinivas, Shaw and Ramaswamy, 1979, p. vii).

Gerald Berreman (1972, pp. xvii-lvii) has ably highlighted the problems of sample surveys in his essay on his field experiences in the Himalayas.

Computers are now universally used in the industrial world to handle quantitative social data, while their use in the developing world is less general. (For an excellent review of the practical and technical aspects of data processing, see Hursh-Cesar and Roy, 1976, pp. 347-98).

The listing of above references under "References"

REFERENCES

Becker, H.S. and Geer, B,, "Participant Observation and Interviewing," *Human Organization,* 16, 1957, pp. 28-32.

Berreman, G.D., *Hindus of the Himalayas: Ethnography and Change,* Berkeley, University of California Press, 1972.

Hursh-Cesar, G. and Roy, P. (Eds.), *Third World Surveys: Survey Research in Developing Nations,* Delhi: Macmillan of India, 1976.

Leach, E.R., *"An anthropologist's reflections on a social survey,"* in D.G. Jongmans and P.C.W. Gutkind (Eds.), *Anthropologists in the Field,* Assen, Netherlands: Van Gorcum, 1967, pp. 75-88.

Schuman, H,, "Artifacts are in the mind of the Beholder," *American Sociologist,* 17, 1982, pp. 21-28.

Srinivas, M.N., Shah A.M. and Ramaswamy, E.A., *The Fieldworker and the Field: Problems and Challenges in Sociological Investigation,* Delhi: Oxford University Press, 1979.

Trow, Martin, "Comment on 'Participant Observation and Interviewing' by Becker and Geer," *Human Organization,* 16, 1957, pp. 33-35.

If a cited author, say Arul had published more than one article in 1986, the citation for a particular reference would be Arul (1986 b: 25-28) indicating that this was the second entry with a publication date of 1986 for Arul.

There are *acceptable variations* in footnote *formats*. For example, in some, the place of publication is cited after the name of the publisher, in some, the place of publication and publisher's name are enclosed in brackets; in some, the year enclosed in parentheses appears immediately after the author's name and so on. What is important is *use of a particular format consistently* in a paper/thesis.

Bibliography

The Bibliography is a list of references relating to a topic or subject. It is located at the end of the main body of the report. It contains all the information found in a first footnote relating to a work.

The *function* of *bibliography* is *different* from *that* of *footnotes*. While footnotes are used to cite authority for specific statements quoted or paraphrased, the bibliography lists in alphabetical order references used by the writer. The footnotes designate the exact place (*i.e.,* page/s) where the quoted matter is located. But the bibliography just gives identification details for the works, as a whole. There may be several footnotes to a work, but there is only one entry for it in bibliography. The footnote appears only when a specific matter from a work is cited, whereas, a work may be listed in the bibliography even if it is not quoted in the report, provided it is related to the subject of the study.

Format: The formats for bibliographical listing for books, reports, articles etc. are same as the formats for footnotes except one difference. That is, no page number is stated in the case of books and reports listed in the Bibliography.

Another difference is often indicated: While in the first footnote relating to a work, author's name begins with the first name (*e.g*,, Peter F. Drucker), in the bibliography, name begins with the second or the surname (*e.g.,* Drucker, Peter F.). As the information required for the footnotes and the bibliography is secured from the same source, *viz.,* source cards, the author-surname format may be used in both cases, as explained earlier.

Classification: References may be grouped according to their form of publications; for examples, books may be listed in one group; periodicals in a second group, and reports in another group. In each group references should be arranged in *alphabetical order* of the *surnames* of authors or by initial letter of the first words of listing.

A bibliography containing less than *twenty* titles reed not be sub-divided into categories.

When there are two or more works by the same author repetition of his name is avoided by substituting for it an unbroken line eight spaces in length, beginning with the left margin, *e.g.,* Good Carter V. ed., *Dictionary of Education,* New York: McGraw-Hill. 1973.

— *Essentials of Educational Research,* New York: Appleton-Century-Crofts, 1966, and Douglas E. Scates, *Methods of Research,* New York: Appleton-Century-Crofts, 1954.

SOME EXAMPLES OF BIBLIOGRAPHICAL FORMS

A. Books

Brislin, R.W. *et al., Cross-cultural Research Methods,* New York: John Wiley & Sons, 1973.

Bulmer, Martin (Ed.), Sociological Research Methods, London: Macmillan, 1977.

Campbell, D.T. and Stanley, J.C., *Experimental and Quasi-Experimental Designs for Research,* Chicago: Rand McNally Cp., 1963.

B. Journals (or Periodicals)

Becker, H.S. and Geer, B., "Participant Observation and Interviewing," *Human Organisation,* 16, 1957, pp. 28-32.

Neale, W.C., "The Limitations of Indian Village Survey Data," *Journal of Asian Studies,* 17, 1958, pp. 383-402.

Roy, P. and Fliegel, F.C., "The Conduct of Collaborative Research in the Developing Nations: the insiders and the outsiders," *International Social Science, Journal,* 22, 1970, pp. 505-523.

C. Report

UNCTAD, *The Least Developed Countries: 1984 Report,* New York: United Nations, 1984.

United Nations (ESCAP), *Problems and Methods of Collecting Statistics of Distributive Trades for Household and Small-scale Enterprises,* Document E/CN. 11/ASTAT/SDT/L.4., Bangkok: ESCAP, 1966.

World Bank, *World Development Report* 1987, Washington D.C, 1987.

Annotated Bibliography

In this bibliography, each entry is followed by a one-sentence or one paragraph description of the content of the work cited. Some examples are:

Bandyopadhyaya, Jayantanuja, *The Poverty of Nations,* Ahmedabad: Allied Publishers, 1988.

The first attempt by a Third World Scholar to offer a global perspective of the problem of mass poverty in the South and its solution.

Bulmer, Martin and Donald P. Warwick, *Social Research in Developing Countries: Surveys and Censuses in the Third World,* Chichester John Wiley & Sons. 1983.

A critical overview of the methodological and contextual assumptions of standard survey and census design and practice related to research in developing countries.

Typing Instructions for Bibliography/List of References

1. The heading BIBLIOGRAPHY or REFERENCES is placed an inch space below the top of the paper. It is centered between the margins. No terminal punctuation is used after it.

2. The first entry is placed a double space below the title. If, however, there is a category heading, the heading is placed a triple space below the title, and the first entry is placed a double space below the category heading.

3. The entries are arranged in an underhung, single-spaced form, with double spacing between items. Each entry begins flush with the left margin, and the second and ensuing lines, if any, are indented four spaces.

4. Where there are two or more works by the same author listed consecutively, repetition of his name is avoided by substituting for it an unbroken line eight spaces in length, beginning flush with the left margin and followed by a period (*i.e.,* two-letter space).

5. In the case of annotated bibliography, the annotation should begin on the next line below bibliographical entry, with the first line indented another four spaces from the underhung indention (a total of eight spaces from the margin). Ensuing lines should be indented four spaces from the usual margin.

Abbreviations

In bibliography and footnotes, English and Latin abbreviations are used to avoid repetition and to conserve space. The most common abbreviations are:

anon.	anonymous
ante	before
art., arts	article
bk., bks.	book, books
cf.,	compare
ch.	chapter
col., cols.	column, columns
div.	division
ed., eds.	editor, editors
edn.	edition
et al.	and others
e.g.	exampli gratia: for example
et seq.	et sequens: and the following
et passin	and here and there
ex.	example
f.,ff.	and the following (*e.g.,* "pp 5 ff" = 5 and the following pages)
fig., figs.	figure, figures
fn.	footnote
ibid.	ibidem: in the same reference
idem.	same person
i.e.,	that is
illus.	illustrated

infra.	below
|., ||	line, lines (e.g., |.8; ||.10-14)
loc. cit	loco citato, the same place and same page
MS, MSS	Manuscript, Manuscripts
n.d.	no date given
n.p.	no place given
no., nos.	number, numbers
NB	Nota bene – taken notice
op. cit.	opera citato; in the work cited
p., pp.	page, pages
passim.	here and there
post.	after
rev.	revised
Sec.	Sections
supra	above, earlier in this writing
trans. or tr.	translated
v. or vide	see
viz.	namely
vol., vols.	volume, volumes
Vs.,	versus; against
(....)	omissions in quoted matter up to one paragraph in length

(All Latin abbreviations are bold)

12.7 WRITING THE REPORT

Introduction

No researcher, however experienced, can write a research report in final form in one draft. The report needs several revisions and rewriting. This hard fact has to be kept in mind while starting the writing work. The writer should arrange the following materials in an order and keep them on the table ready for use:

1. The detailed outlines for chapters
2. Note cards arranged in the order of chapters
3. Source cards arranged in an alphabetical order
4. Statistical tables, charts and results of analysis, each in a separate sheet and
5. Plain sheets of paper and a good pen.

The writer should overcome the *initial inertia* — the tendency to put off beginning to overcome this tendency, the writer should set aside a section of free time for the report writing work. If this can be as long as an entire morning, so much the better. He should establish a regular schedule for writing until the work is done. He should begin drafting as soon as some thoughts on the topic crystallizes in his mind. Once he starts writing, he should keep going, and maintain a psychological momentum. He should plan for an atmosphere of quiet and isolation. I recall what I did when I wrote my doctoral thesis. I was used to get up at 4.30 AM and concentrate on writing in my study room without any disturbance and similarly on weekends. I used to go to my room in the college and concentrate on writing. Any serious writing requires free mind, and free atmosphere.

First Draft

On what the writer should concentrate in the first draft stage? He should concentrate on substance, *i.e.,* fullness of facts, as per the planned outline. In writing the first draft, maintaining a flow of ideas is more important than choosing exact words. Hence the entire first draft work should be completed without any stopping for editing.

The points to be kept in mind in writing the first draft are:

1. Keep in mind that you are writing for communicating with the target audience.
2. Keep the purpose of each chapter, section and paragraph in mind.
3. Expand the outline and put all ideas that occur on paper.
4. Do not hesitate to write in any order those sections of your total work that seem to have grown ripe in your mind.
5. Do not struggle for words and phrases. Write down something that occurs. As Barzun and Graff have aptly said, "Paper is not granite, and in a first draft you are not carving eternal words in stone."[8] Inappropriate words can be replaced while revising the draft.
6. When any idea, word or phrase refuses to come to mind, leave it blank. It will arise easily on revision.
7. Write different sections and major ideas on *separate sheets* to facilitate additions and cuttings.
8. Write on *one side* of the sheet leaving larger margin (say 2") on the left side.
9. Leave *double space* between *lines* to provide for corrections.
10. Do not copy the tables on the text, just pin them in the appropriate places. This is necessary for avoiding recopying tables at every revision.
11. Document each borrowed idea or information — whether quoted exactly, paraphrased or summarised — by a footnote on the same page (See *"Footnotes"* in Section 12.6, above).
12. Give appropriate headings to chapters, sections and paragraphs.
13. When the first draft is completed, make sure that all research *objectives* have been analysed and discussed adequately, all research *questions* have been answered adequately, and all the *hypotheses* have been tested adequately.
14. Ensure the correctness of facts and citations.

---

8. Barzun, Jacques and Henry F. Graff, *The Modem Researcher,* rev. ed, New York: Harcourt Brace & World, 1970 quoted in Embry, C. William, *Business Research Methods, op. cit.,* p. 429.

After the first draft work is over, keep the matter in a cupboard and forget it for some days. Later take it up for reading and revision with a fresh outlook.

Revisions

The first draft should be read carefully again and again and edited thoroughly and revised. Any writing improves upon revision. In revising the first draft, the attention should be given to *form, language, readability, clarity* and *lucidity.* With an open and critical mind the researcher must correct, carve, cut, add and polish. The following *points* may be *kept in mind:*

1. Keep in mind the requirements of a research report (See Section 12.1 in this chapter, above; and the principles of report writing). (See 12.5, above).
2. Fill in the blanks with appropriate ideas, words or phrases.
3. Reorganize ideas wherever necessary.
4. Eliminate gaps in continuity and unclear statements.
5. Replace inappropriate words by exact and apt words.
6. Omit needless words and expressions such as "as a matter of fact", "owing to the fact that ....." etc.
7. Simplify sentences and improve their effectiveness.
8. Cut off repetitions by giving cross references.
9. Improve the readability and clarity of the writing.
10. Correct the spelling and grammatical errors.
11. Make a *critical evaluation* of the draft as if you are evaluating another writer's draft, using the following *Test Questions:*

    Evaluations of the draft report: Test Questions

Methodological aspects

(1) Has the research plan — as originally drawn up and as ultimately realised — been presented in detail? (This will enable the reader to know the difficulties faced by the researcher and take a correct view of his findings and conclusions).

(2) Does the report fulfil the aims of the study?

(3) Does the title reflect the core of the problem studied?

(4) Have the observational and reading background which led to the hypotheses been given?

(5) Are the hypotheses and operational definitions of concepts specific and clear?

(6) Have the problem and hypotheses been stated in scientific terms?

(7) Is the chapter scheme relevant to the objectives of the study?

(8) Are the hypotheses tested appropriately and adequately?

(9) Are the findings and inferences clear and substantiated by data evidences?

(10) Are the conclusions effective, logical and based on the findings?

(11) Are the recommendations flow from the findings and conclusions?

(12) Are the recommendations specific, practical, weighty and convincing?

(13) Does the summary really summarize and point to further research?

Organization and Form

(14) Has the target audience been kept in mind?

(15) Is the division of the report into chapters and sections appropriate and logical?

(16) Is there a smooth development from the introduction to recommendations?

(17) Are there order and proportion in the paragraphs, sections and chapters?

(18) Are the quotations accurate?

(19) Is the technical information up-to-date?

(20) Have you given the techniques for the development of scales and indexes?

(21) Are the tables and charts accurate and self-contained?

(22) Are the footnotes complete and correct?

Language and Style

(23) Does the language conform to prevailing standard of usage?

(24) Is the presentation accurate, clear, crisp, logical and complete?

(25) Are the opening sentences of chapters, sections and paragraphs attractive?

(26) Is the style smooth and coherent?

(27) Is the expression strong, vigorous and dignified and free from grammatical and spelling errors?

(28) Has every word been weighed and used for its exact meaning and function?

(29) Are the findings and arguments concise?

(30) Are there no jargons and vague words?

(31) Are you sure that you have done a good job, and are you, as your own critic, satisfied with the report?

(32) Rectify the flaws, imperfections and weaknesses discovered in the course of the above critical evaluation, and improve the presentation.

(33) Get the revised draft read by your colleagues/guide, as the case may be, and invite their constructive criticism. It may be hard to take criticism, but as a researcher you must learn to take it with open mind.

(34) Give each criticism serious, careful and objective attention.

(35) Revise the draft in the light of valid criticism and suggestions made by the readers.

Final Stage

The final stage of the work consists of (a) *Adding* the following *elements* to the report:

(1) title page, (2) acknowledgement/preface, (3) table of contents, (4) list of tables and charts, (5) bibliography and (6) appendices (See 12.4 *Research Report Format,* above) and (b) the final

editing of the revised and completed report. In the *final editing, your* attention should be focused on the *relationship between* the original *research questions* and the report once more. Look at the introduction and the conclusion. Are those sections adequate in every way? Did you stay on the track? Are all investigative questions fully developed? Does the entire report read smoothly, with transitions that carry the reader along from one idea to the next? Is the report *complete* in all respects? Are *all* the *elements* — the title page, table of contents, list of tables and charts, bibliography and appendices — have been *added*? Are they complete and correct? Does the report *justify* the time, energy and thought you have invested on it? If the answer to all these questions is "Yes", your report is ready for *final proofreading.*

Set aside the final draft for a few days, and then take it up for *final reading* with a fresher outlook. Do not rush through. Read word by word. All *data* should be *checked* against the original, and *computations* should be checked and cross-checked to ensure absolute accuracy. The sequence of page numbers, table numbers, footnote numbers should be checked. The footnotes and bibliographical entries should be checked carefully against the original. The correspondence of captions and numbers of tables and charts in the text and in the list of tables and charts should be checked. Your *aim* is to give *finishing touches* and correct all grammatical errors and deficiencies in punctuation, spelling, word choice, and sentence structure. Of course, there is no limit to perfection. One can go on improving the report. Your final satisfaction and fulfilment that you had done all that you should do to your report serves as an indicator to complete the work.

12.8 TYPING THE REPORT

Introduction

The final manuscript of the report should be given for typing preferably to a professional typist with experience in typing research reports. The required number of multiple copies may be produced either by the traditional method of typing an original and three or four carbon copies or by the modern method of xeroxing multiple copies from a single original typed in an electronic typewriter. The later method is preferable, because the quality of reproduction will be excellent.

The writer is expected to submit an accurate and acceptable draft to the typist. The final should be correct in all grammatical conventions: capitalization, punctuation, spelling, compound words, hyphenation, and paragraphing. The writer should give clear *instructions* on requirements of margins, word division, indentions, documentation placement, spacing, headings, tables and charts, and quotations. The typist should use a new black medium-inked ribbon, superior grade black carbon sheets and good quality bond papers.

Typing Instructions

Paper: Most universities require the thesis or dissertation typed on quality bond paper of sixteen — or twenty—pound weight and 8½ × 11 inches in size. Only one side of the sheet should be typed.

Margin: The left-side margin should not be less than 1½ inches (or 40 mm), the right, top and bottom margins one inch (or 25 mm).

Centering: The material on any page should be symmetrically arranged with reference to the centre of the typed matter. To facilitate the proper placement of copy on the page a guide sheet may be constructed, showing the proper margins, centre of the copy portion, and the number of lines from the top and bottom margins. This sheet should be ruled in black ink and placed beneath the first sheet, so that the markings show through.

Spacing: The text of the thesis should be *double-spaced* and *indented quotations* and *footnotes* should be *single-spaced.*

Words Division: When the division of word is necessary to avoid great marginal unevenness, the break should come between two syllables, for example, "thirty-six" rather than "thirty-six." Do not divide words of one syllable. Do not also divide a word at the end of a page.

Proper names: When there is occasion to use both given name and surname, or initials and surname, they should preferably be all on the same line; very long names will, of course, require an exception.

Indivisible items: Letters of a government agency, the dates, parts of an equation, monetary expressions, and hours of the day should not be divided and run over to a second line; examples are

BBC IFC	March 10,1989	6x + 4y = 27
Rs. 1,487.10	524 B.C	8.00 a.m.

Alignment of Numerals: Numericals are often arranged in vertical lists, and aligned on the right side, for example, columns of figures should appear as follows:

5
8
27
485
15,364

Headings and titles: Chapter *headings* and Section headings should be *capitalised* and *centered.* Subdivision headings should be typed from the left-hand margin in lower-case and underlined. A section within a chapter should normally be commenced on a new page. The titles of appendices should be capitalized and centered on the page. The titles of tables and charts should also be capitalised, centered and placed above the material to which they refer.

Paragraphs should be indented seven spaces for pica type, nine for elite.

Tables, Graphs and Diagrams: They should be placed as near as possible to the text to which they refer. Short tables can be included in the body of the text. The table number (e.g., TABLE 2.5) should be separated from the text by two or three spaces. Two spaces below, the heading should be typed in capitals. If an explanatory note to a time is necessary, an asterisk should be used. The note should be placed immediately below the table. If the writer is quoting a table, the sourcer should be indicated below the table preceded by the word 'Source.'

Quotations: Direct quotations not over three typewritten lines in length are included in the length are enclosed in quotation marks. Quotations of more than three lines are set off from the text in a single-spaced paragraph and indented four spaces from both left and right margins without quotation marks.

Footnotes: *See* Section 12.6, above.

Bibliography: See Section 12.6, above.

Pagination: Pages of the text are numbered continuously in Arabic numerals; prefactory material in small Roman numerals.

Corrections: Strikeovers, crossovers, insertions and erasures are not permitted. Corrections by pen are never permissible. Either the error should be corrected on the typewriter, or the page should be retyped. White correction fluid may be used for carrying out the corrections.

Proofreading

The typed script should be carefully read. This proofreading should consist of a word-by-word search for misspelling, mispunctuation, and typing errors. All the errors should be corrected on the typewriter, using correction fluid. Pages with noticeable erasures should be retyped. The final typed script should be accurate, neat, clear and attractive.

Binding

The research students must consult department regulations relating to binding. Binding should be neat and attractive. The writer should make sure the pages are in the correct order before copies are sent to the binder.

12.9 BRIEFING

Meaning

A researcher may have to present his research output in a 'briefing.' This involves an *oral presentation* of the lengthy complex report in a condensed summarized form. The presentation may take 15 to 30 minutes followed by questions and discussion.

Situations

The briefing is generally made in the following situations:

1. A researcher may be asked to present his findings *before* the *top executives* of the *organization* which had sponsored the study; the executives are too busy to find time to studying a lengthy written report. Hence they prefer to listen to the researcher's brief oral presentation and interact with him. This briefing is a presentation before *user-executives* with practical experience and expertise.

2. A doctoral student may be asked to give a *seminar* on his research in the *Department* before the faculty, and other research students. He may be required to give this briefing while the study is in progress and also later after the study is completed. In the first case he gets an opportunity to receive valuable critical comments on his work and constructive suggestions for improving it. In the second case, he gets an opportunity to share his experience with his professors and co-researchers. This type of briefing is an academic exercise.

3. A doctoral student is often asked by the *viva-voce board* to give a *brief presentation* about his research work before questions are put to him. In this case the audience consists of expert examiners, and other academicians and students as observers.

The Scope of Briefing

The scope of the briefing varies according to its situation and purpose. In the case of a briefing before the executives of the sponsor-organisation, the focus of presentation will be on the *conclusions* based on the *findings* and the recommendations. The user-executives may not be directly interested in the details of the methodology as such. Their primary concern is to determine the usefulness of the results of the study to their decision making and planning.

In an *academic presentation,* the focus will be on the *entire research process* in general and the methodology in particular and on the *contribution* of the study to the wealth of knowledge. The academic people are keenly interested in knowing the problem formulation and conceptualisation, sampling, methods of, and tools for data collection, their validity and reliability and the plan of analysis and the reliability of the findings.

Preparation

A briefing requires a thorough preparation on the following lines:

1. Studying the *expected audience:* What do they expect to know from the study?
2. Finding the *time available* for presentation.
3. Anticipating the *criticisms* and the *questions* likely to be raised by the audience.
4. Developing an *outline* of the presentation:
   (i) *introduction* to state the nature of the study, how it came about and what it attempted to do.
   (ii) *main ideas:* conclusions based on findings and recommendations, if the audience consists of user-executives; methodology, the research process and the results, if the audience consists of academic persons.
   (iii) *Concluding* part.
5. *Organizing* the *material* for presentation.
6. Noting down the points in cards or a small (quarter-size) spiral note book.
7. Preparing the needed *audio-visual* aids in keeping with the needs and nature of the audience in order to make the communication effective.

The audio-visual aids may include transparencies for overhead projector, flow charts, slides and videotapes.

8. Anticipating *briefing problems* such as stage-fear, distracting mannerisms and the like, and devising approaches to avoid them.
9. *Rehearsing* the entire briefing 3 or more times, and cutting the material, if necessary, to stay within about 80% of the expected time allotted.

   This would allow a time cushion for elaborating vital points and adding insights that might arise at the moment.
10. Checking to see that *all materials* and aids are ready. The preparation on the above lines would facilitate better presentation.

Delivery

A skilful presentation captivates the audience. The delivery should be regulated. The speed of delivery, clarity of enunciation, pauses and gestures all play a part. The following *guidelines* deserve consideration:

1. to reach the venue ahead of time
2. to arrange and set audio-visual aids
3. to start on time
4. to keep your eye contact with the audience
5. to speak loudly, clearly and slowly
6. to change the tone of your voice to keep the audience's attention
7. to avoid showing nervous mannerism
8. to use visual aids for presenting models, sampling design, statistical tables, charts and graphs
9. to complete the presentation on time
10. to answer questions appropriately and clarify points raised by the audience
11. to summarise main points and sum up aptly.

In short, a briefing should be planned carefully, organised well and presented effectively. Good presentation adds luster to both the research and the researcher's reputation.

12.10 EVALUATION OF A RESEARCH REPORT

Introduction

There are a few *situations* in which a research report may be *evaluated* or *reviewed.*

1. A *doctoral research* thesis or dissertation submitted to a university for award of Ph. D. Degree is evaluated by a *Board of examiners* consisting of academic experts in the concerned field of study. This evaluation aims at judging the research competence of the researcher — how well he planned and executed the study — and the contribution of his study to knowledge, policy and action. This evaluation embraces *all aspects* of the research process — from problem selection to reporting.

2. *A critical analysis* of research reports may be prescribed as an *assignment* to research students. Research reports for this purpose may be selected from the published research reports, unpublished theses or dissertations found in the university library, or research abstracts published in journals. Through a critical analysis of research reports, a student may gain some insight into the research problem formulation, research designs, difficulties inherent in the research process, measurement techniques, construction of data-gathering instruments, processing and analysis of data, interpretation of results and the form, organization and presentation of the research report.

3. *Research promotion bodies* like ICSSR are interested in the quality of reports of research studies funded by them. They often refer the research reports to one or two references before releasing the final instalment of the research grant.

4. Many Ph. D. scholars seek from funding agencies like UGC, ICSSR, etc. *financial assistance for publishing* their reports. A funding agency refers the reports submitted for publication grants to *experts for review* and recommendation. This evaluation is meant for ascertaining whether the report represents a significant contribution to knowledge and whether it is worthy of publication.

Evaluation Criteria

On what basis a research report can be evaluated or reviewed? There is no universally accepted set of standards for evaluating a research report. However, the following *checklist* will serve as a *general guideline* for a critical evaluation or analysis of a research report:

1. The appropriateness of the title

(a) Does the title exactly indicate the core of the study?

(b) Is it clear and concise?

(c) Does it promise no more than what the study can provide?

2. Importance of the Problem

(a) Is the research problem topically important?

(b) Is it socially relevant in terms of its contribution to knowledge and/or solution to the burning problem of the day?

3. Problem formulation

(a) Is the problem clearly defined?

(b) Is it properly delimited?

(c) Are the research questions (objectives) clearly stated?

(d) Are they specific and related to the selected theme?

(e) Are hypotheses pertinent to research questions?

(f) Are they clearly stated and testable?

(g) Are the concepts in the title, objectives and hypotheses operationally defined?

(h) Are the operational definitions valid and reasonable?

(i) Has the researcher demonstrated the usefulness of his study?

(j) Are assumptions and limitations stated?

(k) Does the problem formulation reflect the researcher's mastery of the subject matter of the study?

4. Review of related literature and earlier studies

(a) Is this review covered adequately?

(b) Is it well organized and documented?

(c) Has the research gap been identified?

(d) Does the present study fill in the gap?

5. Soundness of Methodology

(a) Are the type of research and sources and methods of data collection described in detail?

(b) Are the above methods appropriate to the problem under study and the respondents?

(c) Does the research design appropriate to test adequately the hypothesized relationships?

(d) Is the sampling design appropriate and described in detail?

(e) Are the methods adopted for sampling scientific?

(f) Is the sample size adequate?

(g) Are relevant variables recognized, defined, inter-related and measured?

(h) Are data-gathering instruments appropriate?

(i) Are the validity and reliability of the instruments established?

(j) Are the details of methodology adequate for replicability?

6. Data Analysis

(a) Is the analysis objective and deep?

(b) Is the statistical treatment appropriate?

(c) Is appropriate use made of tables and charts?

(d) Is their format proper and complete?

(e) Have the hypotheses been adequately tested?

(f) Is the analysis of data relationship logical and perceptive?

(g) Is the significance of statistical results tested properly?

(h) Are the statistical results interpreted and presented without any bias?

7. Contribution of the Study and conclusions and recommendations

(a) Are their findings of the study stated clearly?

(b) Are the findings generalizable?

(c) Does the study test a theory or develop a new theory, a new model or new tool or contribute to methodology in any other way?

(d) Are the conclusions logical and justified by the empirical evidence?

(e) Are the implications of the results for policy and action explicitly pointed out?

(f) Are the recommendations flowing from the findings?

(g) Are the recommendations specific and practical?

8. Presentation

(a) Is the format of report appropriate?

(b) Does the report have headings and subheadings that facilitate the reading and understanding of it?

(c) Is the chapter scheme based on the objectives of the study?

(d) Is the textual discussion clear, concise and convincing?

(e) Is the style of writing smooth and simple?

(f) Is the presentation logical and objective?

(g) Is it free from spelling and grammatical errors?

(h) Are the footnotes/references containing full details of the sources?

(i) Is the bibliography exhaustive?

Evaluation Report

The evaluator has to give an evaluation report on the thesis or dissertation evaluated by him. There is no standard format for this report. The evaluator is expected to comment on (1) the importance of the study; (2) soundness of the methodology; (3) quality of analysis; (4) significance of the findings, and (5) format and style of presentation. It is not necessary for him to summarize the contents of the thesis. But he must point out the strengths and weaknesses of the work. He should give his final recommendation in *clear* terms — the thesis be accepted or rejected. If the thesis needs revision and resubmission, the evaluator recommends that the thesis be revised and resubmitted. In this case, he should offer specific suggestions for the revision.

Viva Voce Examination

In most of the universities, a doctoral student is required to appear for an oral examination conducted by a Board consisting of the chairman of the student's Department, external examiners and the research guide. The faculty members of the Department and research scholars may attend the 'viva' meeting as observers. In some universities the viva is open to public. Anybody present may put questions to the doctoral student.

The student is expected to defend his thesis in the viva voce examination. This examination has several *purposes*:

1. To establish the *authenticity* of the thesis, *i.e.,* the student has in fact carried out the research described in the thesis. (To this end he may be questioned closely on the problem formulation, methodology and other aspects of the study);
2. To test the student's *knowledge* of his *subject*;
3. To seek *clarification* or explanation from the student upon points made in the thesis; and
4. To provide the student with an opportunity to know the weaknesses and shortcomings of his thesis.

To prepare for the viva voce, the student should re-read the thesis, anticipate any points the examiners are likely to make. He should plan the defences to be offered for them.

During the viva, the student should *stay confident* and relaxed. He should answer all questions as fully and clearly as possible. But he should not, however, try to defend valid criticism.

For a student who has carried out his research systematically and presented the results carefully, the oral examination does not pose any problem. It may turn out to be a pleasant exchange of thoughts between the student and experts in the field.

SUGGESTED READINGS

1. Ballou, Stephen, V., *A Model for Theses and Research Papers,* Boston: Houghton Mifflin, 1970.
2. Barzun, Jacques and Henry F. Graff, *The Modem Researcher,* New York: Harcourt, Brace & World, 1970. Chapters 12-16.
3. Berenson, Conrad and Raymond Colton, *Research and Report Writing for Business and Economics,* New York: Random House, 1971 Chapters 8 to 17.
4. Bernstein, Theodore, *The Careful Writer: A Modem Guide to English Usage,* New York: Atheneum, 1965.
5. Bowers, Fredson, *Principles of Bibliographical Description,* New York: Russell & Russell, 1949.

6. Campbell, William Giles and Stephen Vaughan Ballou, *Form and Style: Theses, Reports, Term Papers,* Boston: Houghton Mifflin Co., 1974.
7. Corbett, Edward P.J., *Classical Rhetoric for the Modern Student,* New York: Oxford University Press, 1971.
8. Dawe, Jessamon, *Writing Business and Economics Term Papers, Theses and Dissertations,* Totowa, N.J.: Littlefield, Adams and Co., 1965.
9. Flower, H.W., *A Dictionary of Modern English Usage,* New York: Oxford University Press, 1965.
10. Gallagher, William J,, Report *Writing for Management,* Reading, Mass: Addison Wesley Publishing Co., 1969.
11. Jonis, J.Harold, *The Business Research Paper,* New York: Hobbs, Dorman & Co., 1967.
12. Kapp, R.O., *The Presentation of Technical Information,* London: Constable, 1948.
13. Strunk, William, Jr., and E.B. White, *The Elements of Style,* New York: Macmillan, 1972.
14. Jurabian, Kate L., *A Manual for Writers of Term Papers, Theses and Dissertations,* Chicago: University of Chicago Press, 1971.
15. University of Chicago, *A Manual of Style,* Chicago: University of Chicago, 1969.
16. Zeisel, Hans, *Say it with Figures*, New York: Harper, & Row, Publishers. 1957.

QUESTIONS

1. Define a research report and explain its purpose.
2. What are the characteristics of a research report? What functions does this report perform?
3. Distinguish between:
   (a) a technical report and a popular report
   (b) an interim report and a summary report
   (c) a research abstract and a research article
   (d) a topic outline and a sentence outline.
4. What may be the format requirements of a research article to be published in a professional journal?
5. Describe the considerations and steps involved in planning report writing work.
6. What are the various categories of target audience for research reports? What may be their requirements?
7. Can a single mulitipurpose report aiming at all categories of target audiences be written? Why or why not?
8. Describe the layout or format of a research report.
9. Why is a 'review of literature' included in a research report? What is its purpose?
10. Describe briefly the various elements included in a research report.
11. Compare and contrast the findings and the conclusions of a research study.
12. Narrate the precautions that a researcher should take while interpreting his findings.
13. What is a bibliography? What is its purpose?
14. What are the principles relating to the organization of a research report.
15. Describe the desirable characteristics of style in writing a research report.
16. List the types of unclear writings to be avoided. Give illustrations to each type.
17. Describe briefly how a research report should be presented.
18. Narrate the principles relating to the grammatica' aspects in research writing.

19. Why quotations are used in a research report?
20. What are the two forms of quotations? When each of them is used? How?
21. State the importance of documentation and describe modes for documenting sources.
22. Distinguish between (a) footnotes and reference-cited format, and (b) content and reference footnotes.
23. What are the purposes of footnotes? What are the kinds of footnotes?
24. Distinguish between footnotes and bibliography.
25. What are the points to be kept in mind in writing the first draft?
26. What are the points to be kept in mind in revising the draft report?
27. How a researcher can make a critical evaluation of his draft report?
28. What is 'briefing' of a research report? In what situations is it done?
29. How would you plan for a briefing of your research report?
30. On what basis a research report can be evaluated?
31. Select a report of a research study in your area of interest, and critically evaluate it.
32. Why is an oral examination conducted for a doctoral student?

❑ ❑ ❑

APPENDIX

SELECTED STATISTICAL TABLES

TABLE 1

Proportion of the Area under the Normal Curve with Values as Extreme as the Observed Values of z

z	*.00*	*.01*	*.02*	*.03*	*.04*	*.05*	*.06*	*.07*	*.08*	*.09*
0.	.5000	.4960	.4920	.4880	.4840	.4801	.4761	.4721	.4681	.4641
1.	.4602	.4562	.4522	.4483	.4443	.4404	.4364	.4325	.4286	.4247
2.	.4207	.4168	.4129	.4090	.4052	.4013	.3974	.3936	.3897	.3859
3.	.3821	.3783	.3745	.3707	.3669	.3632	.3594	.3557	.3520	.3483
4.	.3446	.3409	.3372	.3336	.3300	.3264	.3228	.3192	.3156	.3121
5.	.3085	.3050	.3015	.2981	.2946	.2912	.2877	.2843	.2810	.2776
6.	.2743	.2709	.2676	.2643	.2611	.2578	.2546	.2514	.2483	.2451
7.	.2420	.2389	.2358	.2327	.2296	.2266	.2236	.2206	.2177	.2148
8.	.2119	.2090	.2061	.2033	.2005	.1977	.1949	.1922	.1894	.1867
9.	.1841	.1814	.1788	.1762	.1736	.1711	.1685	.1660	.1635	.1611
1.0	.1587	.1562	.1539	.1515	.1492	.1469	.1446	.1423	.1401	.1379
1.1	.1357	.1335	.1314	.1292	.1271	.1251	.1230	.1210	.1190	.1170
1.2	.1151	.1131	.1112	.1093	.1075	.1056	.1038	.1020	.1003	.0985
1.3	.0968	.0951	.0934	.0918	.0901	.0885	.0869	.0853	.0838	.0823
1.4	.0808	.0793	.0778	.0764	.0749	.0735	.0721	.0708	.0694	.0681
1.5	.0668	.0655	.0643	.0630	.0618	.0606	.0594	.0582	.0571	.0559
1.6	.0548	.0537	.0526	.0516	.0505	.0495	.0485	.0475	.0465	.0455
1.7	.0446	.0436	.0427	.0418	.0409	.0401	.0392	.0384	.0375	.0367
1.8	.0359	.0351	.0344	.0336	.0329	.0322	.0314	.0307	.0301	.0294
1.9	.0287	.0281	.0274	.0268	.0262	.0256	.0250	.0244	.0239	.0233
2.0	.0228	.0222	.0217	.0212	.0207	.0202	.0197	.0192	.0188	.0183
2.1	.0179	.0174	.0170	.0166	.0162	.0158	.0154	.0150	.0146	.0143
2.2	.0139	.0136	.0132	.0129	.0125	.0122	.0119	.0116	.0113	.0110
2.3	.0107	.0104	.0102	.0099	.0096	.0094	.0091	.0089	.0087	.0084
2.4	.0082	.0080	.0078	.0075	.0073	.0071	.0069	.0068	.0066	.0064
2.5	.0062	.0060	.0059	.0057	.0055	.0054	.0052	.0051	.0049	.0048
2.6	.0047	.0045	.0044	.0043	.0041	.0040	.0039	.0038	.0037	.0036
2.7	.0035	.0034	.0033	.0032	.0031	.0030	.0029	.0028	.0027	.0026
2.8	.0026	.0025	.0024	.0023	.0023	.0022	.0021	.0021	.0020	.0019
2.9	.0019	.0018	.0018	.0017	.0016	.0016	.0015	.0015	.0914	.0014
3.0	.0013	.0013	.0013	.0012	.0012	.0011	.0011	.0011	.0010	.0010
3.1	.0010	.0009	.0009	.0009	.0008	.0008	.0008	.0008	.0007	.0007
3.2	.0007									
3.3	.0005									
3.4	.0003									
3.5	.00023									
3.6	.00016									
3.7	.00011									
3.8	.00007									
3.9	.00005									
4.0	00003									

TABLE 2
Table of Critical Values of t

	Level of Significance for One-Tailed Test					
	.10	.05	.025	.01	.005	.0005
	Level of Significance for Two-Tailed Test					
df	.20	.10	.05	.02	.01	.001
1	3.078	6.314	12.706	31.821	63.657	636.619
2	1.886	2.920	1.4303	6.965	9.925	31.598
3	1.638	2.353	3.182	4.541	5.841	12.941
4	1.533	2.132	2.776	3.747	4.604	8.610
5	1.476	2.015	2.571	3.365	4.032	6.859
6	1.440	1.943	2.447	3.143	3.707	5.959
7	1.415	1.895	2.365	2.998	3.499	5.405
8	1.397	1.860	2.306	2.896	3.355	5.041
9	1.383	1.833	2.262	2.821	3.250	4.781
10	1.372	1.812	2.228	2.764	3.169	4.587
11	1.363	1.796	2.201	2.718	3.106	4.437
12	1.356	1.782	2.179	2.681	3.055	4.318
13	1.350	1.771	2.160	2.650	3.012	4.221
14	1.345	1.761	2.145	2.624	2.977	4.140
15	1.341	1.753	2.131	2.602	2.947	4.073
16	1.337	1.746	2.120	2.583	2.921	4.015
17	1.333	1.740	2.110	2.567	2.898	3.965
18	1.330	1.734	2.101	2.552	2.878	3.922
19	1.328	1.729	2.093	2.539	2.861	3.883
20	1.325	1.725	2.086	2.528	2.845	3.850
21	1.323	1.721	2.080	2.518	2.831	3.819
22	1.321	1.717	2.074	2.508	2.819	3.792
23	1.319	1.714	2.069	2.500	2.807	3.767
24	1.318	1.711	2.064	2.492	2.797	3.745
25	1.316	1.708	2.060	2.485	2.787	3.725
26	1.315	1.706	2.056	2.479	2.779	3.707
27	1.314	1.703	2.052	2.473	2.771	3.690
28	1.313	1.701	2.048	2.467	3.763	3.674
29	1.311	1.699	2.045	2.462	2.756	3.659
30	1.310	1.697	2.042	2.457	2.750	3.646
40	1.303	1.684	2.021	2.423	2.704	3.551
60	1.296	1.671	2.000	2.390	2.660	3.460
120	1.289	1.658	1.980	2.358	2.617	3.373
∞	1.282	1.645	1.960	2.326	2.576	3.291

Source: **Abridged from Table III of Fisher and Yates, Statistical Tables for Biological, Agricultural and Research, 6th ed., published by Oliver and Boyd Ltd., Edinburgh, 1963, by permission of the publishers.**

TABLE 3
Critical Values of Chi Square (X^2)

df	*Probability under Ho that $X^2 \geq$ Chi Square*					
	.99	.98	.95	.90	.80	.70
1	.00016	.00063	.0039	.016	.064	.15
2	.02	.04	.10	.21	.45	.71
3	.12	.18	.35	.58	1.00	1.42
4	.30	.43	.71	1.06	1.65	2.30
5	.55	.75	1.14	1.61	2.34	3.00
6	.87	1.13	1.64	2.20	3.07	3.83
7	1.24	1.56	2.17	2.83	3.82	4.67
8	1.65	2.03	2.73	3.49	4.59	5.53
9	2.09	2.53	3.32	4.17	5.38	6.39
10	2.56	3.06	3.94	4.86	6.18	7.27
11	3.05	3.61	4.58	5.58	6.99	8.15
12	3.57	4.18	5.23	6.30	7.81	9.03
13	4.11	4.76	5.89	7.04	8.63	9.93
14	4.66	5.37	6.57	7.79	9.47	10.32
15	5.23	5.98	7.26	8.55	10.31	11.72
16	5.81	6.61	7.96	9.31	11.15	12.62
17	6.41	7.26	8.67	10.08	12.00	13.53
18	7.02	7.91	9.39	10.86	12.36	14.44
19	7.63	8.57	10.12	11.65	13.72	15.35
20	8.26	9.24	10.85	12.44	14.58	16.27
21	8.90	9.92	11.59	13.24	15.44	17.18
22	9.54	10.60	12.34	14.04	16.31	18.10
23	10.20	11.29	13.09	14.85	17.19	19.02
24	10.86	11.99	13.85	15.66	18.06	19.94
25	11.52	12.70	14.61	16.47	18.94	20.37
26	12.20	13.41	15.38	17.29	19.82	21.79
27	12.88	14.12	16.15	18.11	20.70	22.72
28	13.56	14.85	16.93	18.94	21.59	23.65
29	14.26	15.57	17.71	19.77	22.48	24.58
30	14.95	16.31	18.49	20.60	23.36	25.51

Source: Abridged from Table IV of fisher and Yates, Statistics for Biological, Agricultural, and Medical Research, published by Oliver and Boyd Ltd., Edinburgh, 1963, by permission of the publishers.

.50	.30	.20	.10	.05	.02	.01	.001
.46	1.07	1.64	2.71	3.84	5.41	6.64	10.83
1.39	2.41	3.22	4.60	5.99	9.21	9.21	13.82
2.37	3.66	4.64	6.25	7.82	9.84	11.34	16.27
3.36	4.88	5.99	7.78	9.49	11.67	13.28	18.46
4.35	6.06	7.29	9.24	11.07	13.39	15.09	20.52
5.35	7.23	8.56	10.64	12.59	15.03	16.81	22.46
6.35	8.38	9.80	12.02	14.07	16.62	18.48	24.32
7.34	9.52	11.03	13.36	15.51	18. 17	20.09	26.12
8.34	10.66	12.24	1 A	16.92	19.68	21.67	27.88
9.34	11.78	13.44	15.99	18.31	21.16	23.21	29.59
10.34	12.90	14.63	17.28	19.68	22.62	24.72	31.26
11.34	14.01	15.81	18.55	21.03	24.05	26.22	32.91
12.34	15.12	16.98	19.81	22.36	25.47	27.69	34.53
13.34	16.22	18.15	21.06	23.68	26.87	29.14	36.12
14.34	17.32	19.31	22.31	25.00	28.26	30.58	37.70
15.34	18.42	20.46	23.54	26.30	29.63	32.00	39.29
16.34	19.51	21.62	24.77	27.59	31.00	33.41	40.75
17.34	20.60	22.76	25.99	28.87	32.35	34.80	42.31
18.34	21.69	23.90	27.20	30.14	33.69	36.19	43.82
19.34	22.78	25.04	28.41	31.41	35.02	37.57	45.32
20.34	23.86	26.17	29.62	32.67	36.34	38.93	46.80
21.34	24.94	27.30	30.81	33.92	37.66	40.29	48.27
22.34	26.02	28.43	32.01	35.17	38.97	41.64	49.73
23.34	27.10	29.55	33.20	36.42	40.27	42.98	51.18
24.34	28.17	30.68	34.38	37.65	41.57	44.31	52.62
25.34	29.25	31.80	35.56	38.88	42.86	45.64	54.05
26.34	30.32	31.91	36.74	40.11	44.14	46.96	55.48
27.34	31.39	34.03	37.92	41.34	45.42	48.28	56.89
28.34	32.46	35.14	30.09	42.56	46.69	49.59	58.30
29.34	35.53	36.25	40.26	43.77	47.96	50.89	59.70

TABLE 4
Critical Values of D in the Kolmogorov-Smirnov One-Sample Test

Sample Size N	*Level of Significance for D = Maximum [Fo (X) — SN(x)]* .20	.15	.16	.05	.01
1	.00	.925	.950	.975	.995
2	.684	.726	.776	.842	.929
3	.565	.597	.642	.708	.828
4	.494	.525	.564	.624	.733
5	.446	.474	.510	.565	.669
6	.410	.436	.470	.521	.618
7	.381	.405	.438	.486	.577
8	.358	.381	.411	.457	.543
9	.339	.360	.388	.432	.514
10	.322	.342	.368	.410	.490
11	.307	.326	.352	.391	.468
12	.295	.313	.338	.375	.450
13	.284	.302	.325	.361	.433
14	.274	.292	.314	.349	.418
15	.266	.283	.304	.338	.404
16	.258	.274	.295	.328	.392
17	.250	.266	.286	.318	.381
18	.244	.259	.278	.309	.371
19	.237	.252	.272	.301	.363
20	.231	.246	.264	.294	.356
25	.21	.22	.24	.27	.32
30	.19	.20	.22	.24	.29
35	.18	.19	.21	.23	.27
Over 35	$\frac{1.07}{\sqrt{N}}$	$\frac{1.14}{\sqrt{N}}$	$\frac{1.22}{\sqrt{N}}$	$\frac{1.36}{\sqrt{N}}$	$\frac{1.63}{\sqrt{N}}$

Source: F. J. Massey, Jr., "The Kolmogorov-Smirnov Test for Goodness of *Fit*," *Journal of the American Statistical Association*, vol. 46, p. 70. Adapted with kind permission of the publisher.

TABLE 5
Critical Values of Tin the Wilcoxon
Matched Pairs Test

N	*Level of Significance for One-Tailed Test* *.025*	*.01*	*.005*
	Level of Significance for Two-Tailed Test *.05*	*.02*	*.01*
6	0	–	–
7	2	0	–
8	4	2	0
9	6	3	2
10	8	5	3

11	11	7	5
12	14	10	7
13	17	13	10
14	21	16	13
15	25	20	16
16	30	24	20
17	35	28	23
18	40	33	28
19	46	38	32
20	52	43	38
21	59	49	43
22	66	56	49
23	73	62	55
24	81	69	61
25	89	77	68

Source: Adapted from Table I of F. Wilcoxon, ***Some Rapid Approximate Statistical Procedures*** (New York: American Cyanamid Company, 1949), p. 13, with kind permission of the publisher.

TABLE 6
Critical Values of D in the Kolmogrov Smirnov Two — Sample Test (small samples)

N	*One-Tailed Test**		*Two-Tailed Test †*	
	α =.05	α = .01	α =.05	α =.01
3	3	–	–	–
4	4	–	4	–
5	4	5	5	5
6	5	6	5	6
7	5	6	6	6
8	5	6	6	7
9	6	7	6	7
10	6	7	7	8
11	6	8	7	8
12	6	8	7	8
13	7	8	7	9
14	7	8	8	9
15	7	9	8	9
16	7	9	8	10
17	8	9	8	10
18	8	10	9	10
19	8	10	9	10
20	8	10	9	11
21	9	10	9	11

22	9	11	9	11
23	9	11	10	11
24	9	11	10	12
25	9	11	10	12
26	9	11	10	12
27	9	12	10	12
28	10	12	11	13
29	10	12	11	13
30	10	12	11	13
35	11	13	12	
40	11	14	13	

**Source:* Abridged from I. A. Goodman, "Kolmogorov-Smirnov Tests for Psychological Research," Psychological Bulletin, vol. 51,1951, p. 167, copyright 1951 by the American Psychological Association. Reprinted by permission.

† *Source:* Derived from Table 1 of F. J. Massey, Jr., "The Distribution of the Maximum Deviation Between Two Sample Cumulative Step Functions," *Annals of Mathematical Statistics*, vol. 23,1951,126-127, with kind permission of the publisher.

TABLE 7
Critical Values of D in the Kolmogorov-Smirnov Two-Sample Test for Large Samples (two-tailed test)

Level of Significance	*Value ofD So large As To Call for Rejection of Ho at the Indicated Level of Significance, Where D = Maximum* $\mid S_{n1}(x) - S_{2}(x) \mid$
.10	$1.22\sqrt{\frac{n_1+n_2}{n_1n_2}}$
0.5	$1.36\sqrt{\frac{n_1+n_2}{n_1n_2}}$
.025	$1.48\sqrt{\frac{n_1+n_2}{n_1n_2}}$
.01	$1.63\sqrt{\frac{n_1+n_2}{n_1n_2}}$
.005	$1.73\sqrt{\frac{n_1+n_2}{n_1n_2}}$
.001	$1.95\sqrt{\frac{n_1+n_2}{n_1n_2}}$

* Adapted from N. Smirnov, "Table for Estimating the Goodness of Fit of Empirical Distributions", Annals of Mathematical Statistics, *vol. 18,1948, pp. 280-81, with kind permission of the publisher.*

TABLE 8

Partial Table or Critical Values of U in the Mann-Whitney Test

Critical Values for One-Tailed Test at α = .025 or a Two-Tailed Test at α = .05

$n_1 \backslash n_2$	?	10	11	12	13	14	15	16	17	18	19	20
1												
2	0	0	0	1	1	1	1	1	2	2	2	2
3	2	3	3	4	4	5	5	6	6	7	7	8
4	4	5	6	7	8	9	10	11	11	12	13	13
5	7	8	9	11	12	13	14	15	17	18	19	20
6	10	11	13	14	16	17	19	21	22	24	25	27
7	12	14	16	18	20	22	24	26	28	30	32	34
8	15	17	19	22	24	26	29	31	34	36	38	41
9	17	20	23	26	28	31	34	37	39	42	45	48
10	20	23	26	29	33	36	39	42	45	48	52	55
11	23	26	30	33	37	40	44	47	51	55	58	62
12	26	29	33	37	41	45	49	53	57-	61	66	69
I?	28	33	37	41	45	50	54	59	63	67	72	76
14	31	36	40	45	50	55	59	64	67	64	78	83
15	34	39	44	49	54	59	64	70	75	80	85	90
16	37	42	47	53	$9	64	70	75	81	86	92	98
17	39	45	51	57	03	67	75	81	87	93	99	105
18	42	48	55	61	67	74	80	86	93	99	106	112
19	45	52	58	65	72	78	85	92	99	106	113	119
20	48	55	62	69	76	83	90	98	105	112	119	127

Critical Values for One-Tailed Test at α = .05 or a Two-Tailed Test at α =10

n_1/n_2	9	10	11	12	13	14	15	16	17	18	19	20
											0	0
2	1	1	1	2	2	2	3	3	3	4	4	4
3	3	4	5	5	6	7	7	S	9	9	10	11
4	6	7	8	9	10	11	12	14	15	16	17	18
5	9	11	12	13	15	16	18	19	20	22	23	25
6	12	14	16	17	19	21	23	25	26	28	30	32
7	15	17	19	21	24	26	28	30	33	35	37	39
8	18	20	23	26	28	31	33	36	39	41	44	47
9	21	24	27	30	33	36	39	42	45	48	51	54
10	24	27	31	34	37	41	44	48	51	55	58	62
11	27	31	34	38	42	46	50	58	57	61	65	69
12	30	34	38	42	47	51	55	60	64	68	72	77
13	33	37	42	47	51	56	61	65	70	75	80	84
14	36	41	46	51	56	61	66	71	77	82	87	92
15	39	44	50	55	61	66	72	77	83	88	94	100
16	42	48	54	60	65	71	77	83	89	95	MM	107
17	45	51	57	64	70	77	8P	89	96	102	109	115
18	48	55	61	68	75	82	88	.95	102	109	116	123
19	51	58	65	72	80	87	94	101	109	111S	123	130
20	54	62	69	77	84	92	100	107	1.15	123	130	138

Source: Abridged from D. Auble, "Extended Tables from the Mann-Whitney Statistic," ***Bulletin of the Instiute of Educational Research*** at Indiana University, vol.1, no. 2, with permission. For tables for other size samples consult this source.

TABLE 9

Critical Values of F Distribution for Alpha (α) Equal to 5 Percent

n_2	1	2	3	4	5	6	7	8	9	10	12	15	20	24	30	40	60	120	∞
1	16.14	19.95	21.57	22.46	23.09	23.85	23.68	23.89	24.09	24.39	24.39	24.59	24.80	24.91	25.01	15.11	25.22	25.33	24.33
2	18.51	19.00	19.16	19.25	19.30	19.33	19.35	19.37	19.38	19.40	19.41	19.43	19.45	19.45	19.46	19.47	19.48	19.49	19.50
3	10.13	9.55	9.28	9.12	9.01	8.94	8.89	8.85	8.81	8.79	8.74	8.70	8.66	8.64	8.57	8.59	8.57	8.55	8.53
4	7.71	6.94	6.59	6.39	6.26	6.09	6.04	6.00	5.96	5.91	5.86	5.80	5.77	5.75	5.72	5.69	5.66	5.63	5.
5	6.61	5.79	5.41	5.19	5.05	4.95	4.88	4.82	4.77	4.74	4.68	4.62	4.56	4.53	4.50	4.46	4.43	4.40	4.36
6	5.99	5.14	4.76	4.53	4.39	4.28	4.21	4.15	4.10	4.06	4.00	3.94	3.87	3.84	3.81	3.77	3.74	3.70	3.67
7	5.59	4.74	4.35	4.12	3.97	3.87	3.79	3.73	3.68	3.04	3.57	3.51	3.44	3.41	3.38	3.34	3.30	3.27	3.23
8	5.32	4.46	4.07	3.84	3.69	3.58	3.50	3.44	3.30	3.35	3.28	3.22	3.15	3.12	3.08	3.04	3.01	2.97	2.93
9	5.12	4.26	3.86	3.63	3.48	3.37	3.29	3.23	3.18	3.14	3.07	3.01	2.94	2.95	2.86	2.87	2.75	2.71	2.71
10	4.96	4.10	3.71	3.48	3.33	3.22	3.14	3.07	3.02	2.98	2.91	2.85	2.77	2.74	2.70	2.66	2.62	2.58	2.54
11	4.84	3.98	3.59	3.36	3.20	3.09	3.01	2.95	2.90	2.85	2.79	2.72	2.65	2.61	2.57	2.53	2.49	2.45	2.40
12	4.75	3.89	3.49	3.26	3.11	3.00	2.91	2.85	2.80	2.75	2.69	2.62	2.54	2.51	2.47	2.43	2.38	2.34	2.30
13	4.67	3.81	3.41	3.18	3.03	2.92	2.83	2.77	2.71	2.67	2.60	2.53	2.46	2.42	2.38	2.34	2.30	2.25	2.21
14	4.60	3.74	3.34	3.11	2.96	2.85	2.76	2.70	2.65	2.60	2.53	2.46	2.39	2.35	2.31	2.27	2.22	2.18	2.13
15	4.54	3.68	3.29	3.06	2.90	2.79	2.71	2.64	2.59	2.54	2.48	2.40	2.33	2.29	2.25	2.20	2.16	2.11	2.07
16	4.49	3.63	3.24	3.01	2.85	2.74	2.66	2.59	2.54	2.49	2.42	2.35	2.28	2.24	2.19	2.15	2.11	2.06	2.01
17	4.45	3.59	3.20	2.96	2.81	2.70	2.61	2.55	2.49	2.45	2.38	2.31	2.23	2.19	2.15	2.10	2.06	2.01	1.96
18	4.41	3.55	3.16	2.93	2.77	2.66	2.58	2.51	2.46	2.41	2.34	2.27	2.19	2.15	2.11	2.06	2.02	1.97	1.92
19	4.38	3.52	3.13	2.90	2.74	2.63	2.54	2.48	2.42	2.38	2.31	2.23	2.16	2.11	2.07	2.03	1.98	1.93	1.88
20	4.35	3.49	3.10	2.87	2.71	2.60	2.51	2.45	2.39	2.35	2.28	2.20	2.12	2.08	2.04	1.99	1.95	1.90	1.84
21	4.32	3.47	3.07	2.84	2.68	2.57	2.49	2.42	2.37	2.32	2.25	2.18	2.10	2.05	2.01	1.96	1.92	1.87	1.81
22	4.30	3.44	3.05	2.82	2.66	2.55	2.46	2.40	2.34	2.30	2.2	2.15	2.07	2.03	1.98	1.94	1.89	1.84	1.78
23	4.28	3.42	3.03	2.80	2.64	2.53	2.44	2.37	2.32	2.27	2.20	2.13	2.05	2.01	1.96	1.91	1.86	1.81	1.76
24	4.26	3.40	3.01	2.78	2.62	2.51	2.42	2.36	2.30	2.25	2.18	2.11	2.03	1.98	1.94	1.89	1.84	1.79	1.73
25	4.24	3.39	2.99	2.76	2.60	2.49	2.40	2.34	2.28	2.24	2.16	2.09	2.01	1.96	1.92	1.87	1.82	1.77	1.71
26	4.23	3.37	2.98	2.74	2.59	2.47	2.39	2.32	2.27	2.22	2.15	2.08	1.99	1.95	1.90	1.85	1.80	1.75	1.69
27	4.21	3.35	2.96	2.73	2.17	2.46	2.37	2.31	2.25	2.20	2.13	2.06	1.97	1.93	1.88	1.84	1.79	1.73	1.67
28	4.20	3.34	2.95	2.71	2.56	2.45	2.36	2.29	2.24	2.19	2.12	2.04	1.96	1.91	1.87	1.82	1.77	1.71	1.65
29	4.18	3.33	2.93	2.70	2.55	2.43	2.35	2.28	2.22	2.18	2.10	2.03	1.94	1.90	1.85	1.81	1.75	1.70	1.64
30	4.17	3.32	2.92	2.69	2.53	2.42	2.33	2.27	2.21	2.16	2.09	2.01	1.93	1.89	1.84	1.79	1.74	1.68	1.62
40	4.08	3.23	2.84	2.61	2.45	2.34	2.25	2.18	2.12	2.08	2.00	1.92	1.84	1.79	1.74	1.69	1.64	1.58	1.51
60	4.00	3.15	2.76	2.53	2.37	2.25	2.17	2.10	2.04	1.99	1.92	1.84	1.75	1.70	1.65	1.59	1.53	1.47	1.39
120	3.92	3.07	2.68	2.45	2.29	2.17	2.09	2.02	1.96	1.91	1.83	1.75	1.66	1.61	1.55	1.50	1.43	1.35	1.25
∞	3.84	3.00	2.60	2.37	2.21	2.10	2.01	1.94	1.88	1.83	1.75	1.67	1.57	1.52	1.46	1.39	1.32	1.22	1.00